HONG KONG PRIVATE INTERNATIONAL LAW

This book is a one-stop reference to Hong Kong private international law.

It provides clear expositions on questions of jurisdiction, choice of law, recognition and enforcement, transnational arbitration, and inter-regional and international harmonisation of Hong Kong conflict of laws. It covers a range of areas, including the law of obligations at common law and in equity, the law of real and personal property, intellectual property law, family law, company law, insolvency and bankruptcy law, competition law, and admiralty law. It includes discussions of cross-border dispute resolution, jurisdiction and choice of law clauses.

The book focuses on practical issues, emphasising the rapidly developing local jurisprudence of recent years. It also offers theoretical insights and suggestions for law reform when appropriate. Moreover, it systematically analyses conflict of laws issues arising out of inter-regional cases between Hong Kong on the one hand and Mainland China, Taiwan, and Macao on the other.

The book will be indispensable to judges, practitioners, scholars and students in Hong Kong, Greater China, Asia, and worldwide.

Volume 12 in the series Studies in Private International Law – Asia

Studies in Private International Law – Asia

Editor: Anselmo Reyes
Advisory Editor: Paul Beaumont
Assistant Editors: Kazuaki Nishioka and Wilson Lui

Much has been written about private international law in the EU and the US. Less is known about the conflict of laws in Asia. Thus, little attention has been paid so far to the modernisation of private international law codes and rules that has been taking place over the last decade all over Asia. That trend continues. Now is the time to take stock of those reforms that have already taken place and suggest further improvements for the future.

Published under the celebrated series *Studies in Private International Law*, this monograph sub-series provides a forum for discussion and analysis of private international law in Asia. The series is not solely a survey of jurisdictions for practitioners. Comprising both in-depth thematic and country-specific studies, each volume considers the private international law of Asian countries from a variety of perspectives. An underlying assumption is that private international law in different jurisdictions follows broadly discernible patterns. Each volume in this sub-series highlights those patterns and discusses how rules in different Asian jurisdictions are either converging with, or diverging from, the patterns identified. Such an analytical framework will assist academics, judges, lawyers and legislators to envisage ways in which laws affecting cross-border relationships can be harmonised across jurisdictions and be made more responsive to the needs of citizens in Asia and elsewhere.

Volume 1: Recognition and Enforcement of Judgments in Civil and Commercial Matters
Edited by Anselmo Reyes

Volume 2: Indonesian Private International Law
Afifah Kusumadara

Volume 3: Chinese Private International Law
Edited by Xiaohong Liu and Zhengyi Zhang

Volume 4: Direct Jurisdiction: Asian Perspectives
Edited by Anselmo Reyes and Wilson Lui

Volume 5: Japanese Private International Law
Kazuaki Nishioka and Yuko Nishitani

Volume 6: Indian Private International Law
Stellina Jolly and Saloni Khanderia

Volume 7: Treatment of Foreign Law in Asia
Edited by Kazuaki Nishioka

Volume 8: Choice of Law and Recognition in Asian Family Law
Edited by Anselmo Reyes, Wilson Lui and Kazuaki Nishioka

Volume 9: Private International Law in East Asia: From Imitation to Innovation and Exportation
Edited by Olivier Gaillard and Krista Nadakavukaren Schefer

Volume 10: Overriding Mandatory Rules in International Commercial Disputes: Korean and Comparative Law
Min Kyung KIM

Volume 11: Privacy and Personal Data Protection Law in Asia
Edited by Adrian Mak, Ching Him Ho and Anselmo Reyes

Volume 12: Hong Kong Private International Law
Wilson Lui and Anselmo Reyes

Hong Kong Private International Law

Wilson Lui
and
Anselmo Reyes

•HART•
OXFORD • LONDON • NEW YORK • NEW DELHI • SYDNEY

HART PUBLISHING

Bloomsbury Publishing Plc

Kemp House, Chawley Park, Cumnor Hill, Oxford, OX2 9PH, UK

1385 Broadway, New York, NY 10018, USA

Bloomsbury Publishing Ireland Limited, 29 Earlsfort Terrace, Dublin 2, D02 AY28, Ireland

HART PUBLISHING, the Hart/Stag logo, BLOOMSBURY and the Diana logo are trademarks of Bloomsbury Publishing Plc

First published in Great Britain 2025

1

A catalogue record for this book is available from the British Library.

A catalogue record for this book is available from the Library of Congress.

Library of Congress Control Number: 2024949977

ISBN: HB: 978-1-50995-647-0
ePDF: 978-1-50995-649-4
ePub: 978-1-50995-648-7

Typeset by Compuscript Ltd, Shannon
Printed and bound in Great Britain.

MIX
Paper | Supporting responsible forestry
FSC® C013604

For product safety related questions contact productsafety@bloomsbury.com

To find out more about our authors and books visit www.hartpublishing.co.uk. Here you will find extracts, author information, details of forthcoming events and the option to sign up for our newsletters.

SERIES EDITORS' PREFACE

In broad terms, the common law's approach to private international law is pragmatic, eschewing rules, but seeking instead empirically to apply the law most closely connected with a matter, taking account of all circumstances case-by-case. By contrast, again speaking generally, the civil law's approach is to formulate a priori general and special rules covering conflict of laws issues, while taking care to have 'provisos' or 'escape clauses' to cater for unusual situations in which the strict application of a rule might lead to blatant injustice. The common law approach might be thought to be 'just' since it caters for the individual features of a case. But the common law approach is conducive to uncertainty, so that time and money are often spent at the start of a dispute, arguing whether a jurisdiction is *forum conveniens* or what the proper law should be in respect of some aspect of the dispute. The civil law approach, in contrast, puts a premium on certainty, but at the cost of overlooking potentially important subtle differences between one set of facts and another. Hong Kong is indisputably a common law jurisdiction, so this book unabashedly adheres to the common law way. That means that this book is first and foremost practical in its outlook and emphasis.

Second, this book is about the private international law as practised in *Hong Kong* today. There is a natural tendency in works on the conflict of laws of a common law jurisdiction (especially a small one) to rely heavily on the abundance of English case law built up over the centuries. But Hong Kong is not England. It is firmly rooted in Asia and for nearly 30 years now has not been under British sovereignty. Further, between the UK joining the EU in 1973 and Brexit in 2020, English conflict of laws increasingly reflected EU legislation, which did not apply to Hong Kong. As a result, over nearly 50 years, English law became an uncertain guide on how Hong Kong private international law should develop. A key feature of this book is therefore the deliberate attempt to cite recent Hong Kong case law in preference to English precedents as much as possible. Despite its small area, as an international financial and trading hub and as the only common law jurisdiction within the PRC, the Hong Kong court has since 1997 been producing significant case law on disputes involving cross-border issues. This book considers such cases to take stock of where Hong Kong is now and how it might move on.

By the foregoing, the book does not mean to imply that Hong Kong should ignore developments in the civil law system. The House of Lords has itself at least twice affirmed the value of academic writing in deciding cross-border cases.[1] Unlike other branches of the law, private international law relies heavily on theoretical scholarship. This is especially the case where, under the civil law approach, codes are supposed to enact rules that most rationally apply to given situations involving transnational elements. In that spirit, this book urges

[1] *Hesperides Hotels Ltd v Muftizade* [1979] AC 508, 536; *Spiliada Maritime Corp v Cansulex Ltd* [1987] AC 460, 488.

Hong Kong judges to be bolder than they have been and proactively consider private international law developments in civil law jurisdictions. A third feature of this book is that it does not shrink from looking to the civil law for guidance. Just as sometimes the citation of a seminal English conflicts case is inevitable, so is taking account of what has or will become the private international law norm in most civil law jurisdictions.

This is the fifth volume in Hart's *Studies in Private International Law – Asia* series to focus on private international law as practised in a specific Asian jurisdiction (the other books having covered Indonesia, China, Japan and India). This book's structure mirrors that of the current four volumes in the series. It is hoped that this similarity will facilitate readers' attempts at comparing the laws of relevant jurisdictions. Such perspectives can only assist when considering reform and harmonisation initiatives within Asia.

Finally, a word about the composition of this work. The book was initially drafted by Wilson Lui from beginning to end. Thereafter, Anselmo Reyes went through the draft manuscript, extensively revising and commenting on each chapter. A finalised version (involving further dialogue between the two authors) was then produced. Consequently, although both authors accept full responsibility for its contents, this volume should be regarded as the conception and brainchild of the lead author Wilson Lui.

The Editors
Kyoto and Melbourne
1 October 2024

ACKNOWLEDGEMENTS

Wilson Lui would like to thank his parents, family and friends for their support, as well as his students in private international law at the University of Hong Kong for providing him with constant motivation and inspiration.

Several students have assisted at various junctures of the book. We do not name them individually, but simply express our deep gratitude to them.

Critical assistance has been received from Kenneth Tsui, Nathan Tsang and Jonathan Ho.

The law is stated as we believe it to have been on 1 January 2025.

Wilson Lui and Anselmo Reyes

1 January 2025

CONTENTS

PART II
JURISDICTION

PART III
CHOICE OF LAW

PART IV
RECOGNITION AND ENFORCEMENT

PART V
ARBITRATION

PART VI
HARMONISATION

LIST OF ABBREVIATIONS

ADR	alternative dispute resolution
AO	Adoption Ordinance (Cap 290)
AO	Arbitration Ordinance (Cap 609)
BO	Bankruptcy Ordinance (Cap 6)
BVI	British Virgin Islands
CA	Court of Appeal
CACO	Child Abduction and Custody Ordinance (Cap 512)
CEPA	Closer Economic Partnership Arrangement
CFA	Court of Final Appeal
CFI	Court of First Instance
CISG	United Nations Convention for the International Sale of Goods
CJ	Chief Judge of the Court of Final Appeal
CJHC	Chief Judge of the High Court
CO	Companies Ordinance (Cap 622)
CO	Competition Ordinance (Cap 619)
COMI	centre of main interests
CTR	Competition Tribunal Rules (Cap 619D)
CWUMPO	Companies (Winding Up and Miscellaneous Provisions) Ordinance (Cap 32)
CWUR	Companies (Winding-up) Rules (Cap 32H)
DC	District Court
DHCJ	Deputy Judge of the Court of First Instance of the High Court
DO	Domicile Ordinance (Cap 596)
DRC	Democratic Republic of the Congo
e-APP	electronic Apostille Programme
EO	Evidence Ordinance (Cap 8)

EU	European Union
FJREO	Foreign Judgments (Reciprocal Enforcement) Ordinance (Cap 319)
FJRREO	Foreign Judgments (Restriction on Recognition and Enforcement) Ordinance (Cap 46)
GMO	Guardianship of Minors Ordinance (Cap 13)
HCCH	Hague Conference on Private International Law
HCO	High Court Ordinance (Cap 4)
HK	Hong Kong
HKC	*Hong Kong Cases*
HKCFAR	*Hong Kong Court of Final Appeal Reports*
HKIAC	Hong Kong International Arbitration Centre
HKLII	Hong Kong Legal Information Institute
HKLRD	*Hong Kong Law Reports and Digest*
HRTO	Human Reproductive Technology Ordinance (Cap 561)
IP	intellectual property
IPR	intellectual property right
ISDS	investor-state dispute settlement
J	Judge of the Court of First Instance of the High Court
JA	Justice of Appeal of the Court of Appeal of the High Court
JFEO	Judgments (Facilities for Enforcement) Ordinance (Cap 9)
MCO	Matrimonial Causes Ordinance (Cap 179)
MJCCMREO	Mainland Judgments in Civil and Commercial Matters (Reciprocal Enforcement) Ordinance (Cap 645)
MJMFCO	Mainland Judgments in Matrimonial and Family Cases (Reciprocal Recognition and Enforcement) Ordinance (Cap 639)
MJREO	Mainland Judgments (Reciprocal Enforcement) Ordinance (Cap 597)
MO	Marriage Ordinance (Cap 181)
MOREO	Maintenance Orders (Reciprocal Enforcement) Ordinance (Cap 188)
MPPO	Matrimonial Proceedings and Property Ordinance (Cap 192)
MRO	Marriage Reform Ordinance (Cap 178)
NPCSC	Standing Committee of the National People's Congress

NPJ	Non-Permanent Judge of the Court of Final Appeal
NSL	National Security Law
PCO	Parent and Child Ordinance (Cap 429)
PJ	Permanent Judge of the Court of Final Appeal
PRC	People's Republic of China
RHC	Rules of the High Court (Cap 4A)
ROAP	Regional Office for Asia and the Pacific
ROLAC	Regional Office for Latin America and the Caribbean
RTO	Recognition of Trusts Ordinance (Cap 76)
SAR	Special Administrative Region
SC	senior counsel
SICC	Singapore International Commercial Court
SOE	state-owned enterprise
UK	United Kingdom
UNCITRAL	United Nations Commission on International Trade Law
UNCTAD	United Nations Conference on Trade and Development
UNIDROIT	International Institute for the Unification of Private Law
USA	United States of America
VP	Vice-President of the Court of Appeal of the High Court
WTO	World Trade Organisation

LIST OF CASES

Australia

Canada

Cayman Islands

China

Dubai International Financial Centre Courts

European Union

France

Germany

Hong Kong

Jersey

International Court of Justice

Ireland

Malaysia

New Zealand

Singapore

United Kingdom

United States

LIST OF LEGISLATION

Australia

British Virgin Islands

China

Hong Kong

New Zealand

Organisation of Eastern Caribbean States

Scotland

Singapore

South Korea

Switzerland

Taiwan

United Kingdom

United States

LIST OF BILATERAL AND INTERNATIONAL INSTRUMENTS

Bilateral Instruments

Hong Kong SAR–Mainland China

China–UK

International Instruments

European Union

Hague Conference on Private International Law (HCCH)

International Conventions

International Soft Law Instruments

PART I

Introduction

1

The Subject Matter of Private International Law

The subject of private international law can be described as complex and technical. But ask any practitioner in Hong Kong and they will say the subject is essential and practical. It must be confronted head-on in Hong Kong.

Private international law, also known as the conflict of laws,[1] refers to the branch of law which deals with cases having a foreign element.[2] The subject is at work when a case involves foreign legal systems or laws other than the local domestic legal system or law. Any non-local or 'international' element may have to be resolved via the principles of private international law. If an action is a purely domestic one, for example, an action in a Hong Kong court between two Hong Kong parties concerning an obligation to be performed in Hong Kong, then Hong Kong law will apply. But once a non-local element becomes involved, private international law principles may have to be applied to decide whether the Hong Kong court can or should decide the dispute and (if so) whether Hong Kong or foreign law should apply to the dispute.

Following the definition above, for the purposes of private international law in Hong Kong, a foreign element or foreign country means a non-Hong Kong element or a non-Hong Kong jurisdiction. From the view of private international law, Hong Kong (as a Special Administrative Region of the People's Republic of China) is a jurisdiction, just as Mainland China, the Macao Special Administrative Region and Taiwan constitute jurisdictions within the People's Republic of China. Civil and commercial relations among these jurisdictions are dealt with under private international law principles.[3]

[1] For the reasons we explain in this chapter, we use the label 'private international law' as we see an international dimension in this branch of law, which encompasses more than conflict of laws. But the terms are used interchangeably in this book, as 'both titles are used throughout the world and as nobody has found a better one, it hardly seems worthwhile to devote further thought to this merely terminological issue': Lord Collins of Mapesbury and Jonathan Harris (gen eds), *Dicey, Morris and Collins on the Conflict of Laws*, 16th edn (Sweet & Maxwell, 2022) para 1-003.

[2] The definition of a 'foreign element' should have a broad scope. The question of whether a case has a foreign element is decided by the law of the forum (*lex fori*). In Mainland China, the definition of a 'foreign-related civil relationship' is contained in the Interpretation of the Supreme People's Court on Several Issues Concerning Application of the Law of the People's Republic of China on Choice of Law for Foreign-related Civil Relationships (I) (2020 Amendment), Fa Shi [2020] No 18, Art 1; Interpretation of the Supreme People's Court on the Application of the Civil Procedure Law, Fa Shi [2022] No 11, Art 520.

[3] Interpretation on Choice of Law for Foreign-related Civil Relationships (I) (n 2), Art 17; Interpretation on the Application of the Civil Procedure Law (n 2), Art 549. The interactions among these jurisdictions are sometimes studied as 'inter-regional private international law'. See ch 25.

The subject of private international law traditionally answers three questions:[4]

1. Jurisdiction: what are the conditions under which a domestic court will accept jurisdiction to deal with matters that involve cross-border or foreign elements? The parties may have conferred jurisdiction on a domestic court by agreement, or there may be matters in which a court will decline jurisdiction.
2. Applicable law: what system or systems of law will be applied to resolve a dispute involving cross-border or foreign elements? It is possible that parties have agreed that a specified law is to be applied, or there may be situations in which a court will apply its own local laws or a foreign law, regardless of the parties' choice.
3. Recognition and enforcement: in what circumstances will foreign judgments (and arbitral awards) that purport to determine issues between parties or grant remedies be recognised and enforced?

However, within the modern discipline of private international law, we are of the view that a fourth question should be added to the foregoing trilogy of questions.[5] That fourth question centres on the harmonisation of private international law rules. To what extent is it possible, desirable or worthwhile to harmonise the various private international law rules of different jurisdictions? That issue of harmonisation is the ultimate objective of the Hague Conference on Private International Law (HCCH), which states in Article 1 of the statute by which it was formally constituted in 1955 that the HCCH is to 'work for the progressive unification of the rules of private international law'. As a result, the question of harmonisation emphasises what is 'international' about 'private international law'.

The label of 'private international law' may cause certain confusion and lead to some dissenting voices. One might say that the subject of private international law is not 'international', as the subject merely concerns how domestic courts deal with cross-border or 'international' cases. Almost every 'rule' in private international law is a domestic rule, with nothing elevating the same to an international level. It is therefore strange (for some) to see private international law compared with public international law, which consists of supranational rules created to regulate relationships between states (as opposed to private entities) and support a global system of law, for example, the Rome Statute governing the International Criminal Court and the Statute of the International Court of Justice. However, increasingly today, scholars see interactions between public and private international law.[6] These include the continuous influence of public international law ideas in private international law, for example, the interpretation and application of concepts of sovereignty and immunities in contexts of jurisdiction and enforcement of judgments. As such, one view is to take public international law (regulating international political relations), private international law (regulating international civil and commercial relations) and international economic law (regulating international economic relations) as

[4] This is the structure of private international law as adopted in most common law jurisdictions.

[5] See, eg Wilson Lui and Anselmo Reyes, 'Introduction' in Anselmo Reyes and Wilson Lui (eds), *Direct Jurisdiction: Asian Perspectives* (Hart Publishing, 2021) 1.

[6] See, eg Alex Mills, *The Confluence of Public and Private International Law: Justice, Pluralism and Subsidiarity in the International Constitutional Ordering of Private Law* (Cambridge University Press, 2009); Poomintr Sooksripaisarnkit and Dharmita Prasad (eds), *Blurry Boundaries of Public and Private International Law: Towards Convergence or Divergent Still?* (Springer, 2022).

complementary and mutually influential in the development of international relations generally.[7]

Bearing in mind that the principles of private international law are domestic in nature, there are significant divergences among different jurisdictions (even within common law jurisdictions) in their approaches and methodologies in private international law. A strategic lawyer will likely seek to manoeuvre these differences to their client's advantage. But a scholar, with the goal of harmonisation in mind, may see it as more appropriate to develop a 'global private international law' by taking a global and comparative approach to various elements of the modern development of private international law.[8] A recent study has fitted the 'strength' of each aspect of global private international law into one of the following six categories: (1) strong; (2) developing strongly; (3) has great potential; (4) weak but could be revived; (5) non-existent but could be created; and (6) not advised to be created in the near future.[9] The ultimate aim, it seems, is to see private international law as a worldwide phenomenon, eventually harmonising or progressively unifying the rules of private international law globally.

However, when dealing with the subject at a philosophical level, one can perceive difficulties in understanding private international law as a subject that is capable of 'progressive unification' as suggested by the HCCH. Private international law rules exist to resolve conflicts across substantive domestic laws of jurisdictions.[10] The rules attempt (without at this stage evaluating whether they succeed) to allocate jurisdiction to the 'most appropriate' court, to apply the 'proper' choice of law and to enforce 'properly obtained' judgments and arbitral awards. However, as mentioned above, private international law rules vary across jurisdictions. Therefore, conflicts re-emerge at a higher level, namely, as conflicts across the private international law rules of jurisdictions. The fourth question of harmonisation attempts to resolve this higher-level conflict by proposing 'the solution of solutions' or 'the norm of norms'. So far, many such proposals have not met with much popularity or success.

Does that mean the search in private international law is necessarily a futile exercise? It is suggested that what private international law provides are relations and interactions between different legal systems ('worlds'). It is a space that generates pragmatic responses, while keeping the respective laws ('worldviews') intact.[11] The goal is to create an order for international civil and commercial relations which is based on equality, freedom and mutual benefit.

That is even more true in the development of Asian private international law.[12] There is an impressive plurality and diversity in Asian laws, in terms of their traditions,

[7] Shuangyuan Li and Fuyong Ou (gen eds), *Guoji Sifa* [*Private International Law*], 6th edn (Peking University Press, 2022) 1.

[8] See, eg Paul Beaumont and Jayne Holliday (eds), *A Guide to Global Private International Law* (Hart Publishing, 2023).

[9] ibid, ch 41.

[10] Another way to resolve conflict of laws is by formulating and applying an international uniform substantive law. But that has inevitable limitations in its scope and applicability.

[11] Ralf Michaels, 'Private International Law and the Legal Pluriverse' in Roxana Banu, Michael S Green and Ralf Michaels (eds), *Philosophical Foundations of Private International Law* (Oxford University Press, 2024) 258–77.

[12] See, eg Wilson Lui, 'Researching and Teaching Asian and Hong Kong Private International Law' (2023) 20(2) *Indonesian Journal of International Law* 173; Wilson Lui, 'Asian Private International Law and Hong Kong' (2024) 12 *Korean Journal of International and Comparative Law* 73.

governance structures, languages, cultures, economic developments, laws and legal systems.[13] Convergence and divergence within and between laws and legal systems has therefore become a feature of Asian laws. This leads to unique trajectories in the development of Asian private international laws. Moving forward, Asian law should not merely be seen as a projection of Western ideas, devoid of an internal homogeneity and identity of its own. The West should not be seen as providing a universal standard, with Asia as a (deficient) mirroring image. There should be less focus on comparison with the West and more on comparison within Asia. As Professor Ralf Michaels aptly put, 'Asia is no longer object or subject but method, no longer one but many parts that are in dialogue with each other, no longer recipient or opponent of Western law and instead co-producer of modernity and of modern law'.[14] Hong Kong could not be more apt as an illustration of such co-production. Through developing the subject matter of Asian and Hong Kong private international law, we are indeed looking into foundational philosophical issues that ground our study of laws and their conflicts.

[13] Ralf Michaels, 'How Asian Should Asian Law Be?' in Gary Low (ed), *Convergence and Divergence of Private Law in Asia* (Cambridge University Press, 2022) 228.
[14] ibid 232.

2

History and Sources of Private International Law in Hong Kong

Hong Kong has developed a relatively comprehensive set of private international law rules, although they are scattered across various sources, such as statutes (ordinances), cases and international instruments (as incorporated into domestic legislation). Hong Kong's rich history under British administration, coupled now with China's active international participation, makes for an interesting amalgam. This chapter traces the history and sources of private international law in Hong Kong. The present and future development of private international law in Hong Kong is inextricably linked to that history.

I. Introduction

Hong Kong projects itself internationally as a sophisticated, cosmopolitan and bilingual common law jurisdiction and a hub for regional and international dispute resolution. This is reinforced by the metropolis's constitutional status as a Special Administrative Region of the PRC and the various sources that comprise Hong Kong private international law. A few legal doctrines have originated locally, but what has been more influential are doctrines from outside the jurisdiction which have been directly adopted or adapted into local contexts. This amalgamation of sources began with the British administration of Hong Kong Island in 1842 and continues to this day following the PRC's exercise of sovereignty since 1 July 1997. In light of Hong Kong's rich legal history, a range of cross-border issues can only be resolved by the skilful combination of legal sources, including:

1. Common law and statutory rules prior to 1 July 1997. Article 8 of the Hong Kong Basic Law preserves the laws previously in force in Hong Kong, including common law, rules of equity, ordinances, subordinate legislation and customary law. Other laws in force in Hong Kong include national laws listed in Annex III to the Basic Law and laws enacted by the legislature of Hong Kong before 1 July 1997.
2. Cases decided by Hong Kong courts since 1 July 1997.
3. Statutes or statutory amendments passed by Hong Kong's legislature that have come into effect since 1 July 1997. Within this category, there is a distinction between (i) statutes which originate from regional and international conventions or instruments subsequently incorporated into domestic law and (ii) those created to codify or amend pre-existing domestic rules.

II. Historical Background

A. 1842 and the Transplantation of Common Law

The founding of the British colony of Hong Kong began with the 1842 Treaty of Nanking, the 1860 Convention of Peking and the 1898 Convention for the Extension of Hong Kong Territory, laying down the boundaries of Hong Kong that remain in force today. The Hong Kong Letters Patent established the framework for the colonial government. The Legislative Council was established as a deliberative body whose advice and consent were necessary for the Governor to 'make laws for the peace, order, and good government of the Colony'.[1] The Legislative Council enacted ordinances to adopt and adapt English law to Hong Kong. The Supreme Court Ordinance in 1844 stated that the law of England shall be in full force in Hong Kong.[2] This was later qualified by the Supreme Court Ordinance in 1873, section 5 of which stated:[3]

> [T]he laws of England as existed … on the 5th day of April, 1843, shall be in force … except so far as the said laws are inapplicable to the local circumstances of the Colony or of its inhabitants, and except so far as they have been modified by laws passed by the said legislature.

This spawned the adaptation and application of common law rules in Hong Kong.

With regard to the colonial judiciary, sections 7 and 8 of the Supreme Court Ordinance in 1844 established the Supreme Court of Hong Kong with analogous authority within Hong Kong to the jurisdictions of the then English Courts of King's Bench, Common Pleas and Exchequer, as well as the Court of Chancery. This meant that the courts of Hong Kong applied both common law and equity since 1844, well before their English counterparts were allowed to do so after their reorganisation by the Supreme Court of Judicature Acts 1873 and 1875.[4]

The ability of the Hong Kong legislature and judiciary to resolve disputes and prevailing social problems independently from Westminster contributed to the self-standing development of Hong Kong's legal system into the twentieth century. As the colonial legislature could adapt statutes to local needs, no Legislative Council ordinance has been vetoed by the British exercising their supervisory power since 1913. Following World War II and the Japanese occupation, Hong Kong's industrial and commercial growth meant that the colonial government was sufficiently autonomous to implement changes to Hong Kong's legal sources. The Application of English Law Ordinance (Cap 88) was enacted in 1966 to identify 70 pieces of British legislation that would continue to have effect in Hong Kong and to disapply a majority of pre-existing Acts. The Official Languages Ordinance (Cap 5) enacted in 1974 afforded equal official status to English and Chinese and was later amended in 1995 to extend such status to court proceedings.[5] These developments positioned Hong Kong to become a leading international financial and dispute resolution centre from the late 1970s.

[1] Letters Patent, Art IX. For the full text, see https://oelawhk.lib.hku.hk/items/show/1021.

[2] Supreme Court Ordinance (No 15 of 1844), s 3.

[3] Supreme Court Ordinance (No 3 of 1873), s 5. For the full text, see https://oelawhk.lib.hku.hk/items/show/19. See also *Re Estate of Chak Chiu Hang* (1925) 20 HKLR 1, 5–9. For the dual prospective system of Chinese and English law applicable during the first few decades after 1841, see *Ho Tsz Tsun v Ho Au Shi* (1915) 10 HKLR 69, 79.

[4] 36 & 37 Vict c 66; 38 & 39 Vict c 77.

[5] Official Languages Ordinance (Cap 5), ss 3 and 5.

B. 1997 and the Theme of Continuity

Mainland China entered the 'Reform and Opening Up' era in 1978. In 1982, Beijing announced its intention to resume the exercise of sovereignty over Hong Kong when the 1898 Convention for the Extension of Hong Kong Territory would lapse on 1 July 1997. Multiple subsequent meetings between Chinese and British leaders culminated in the Sino-British Joint Declaration in 1984, outlining a constitutional solution to the question of sovereignty post-1997. Paragraph 3 of the Joint Declaration outlined the establishment of a Special Administrative Region under Article 31 of the Constitution of the People's Republic of China with a high degree of autonomy, independent judicial power and the power of final adjudication. The Declaration crucially proclaimed that the laws then in force in Hong Kong would 'remain basically unchanged', and that the judicial system would be maintained except for changes enacted by the Hong Kong courts.[6] Other principles of continuity important to the development of Hong Kong after 1997 were also included: the preservation of the socio-economic system, the retention of private property, enterprise and foreign investment rights, and the protection of Hong Kong's status as a free port, foreign exchange centre and international financial centre.[7]

The Basic Law of the Hong Kong Special Administrative Region was adopted and promulgated by the PRC's Standing Committee of the National People's Congress (NPCSC) on 4 April 1990.[8] This document constitutes the foundation for the continuation of the common law system beyond 1 July 1997. It provides several aspects of the development of private international law in Hong Kong. Under the 'One Country, Two Systems' principle,[9] Hong Kong shall enjoy 'a high degree of autonomy',[10] and be vested with legislative power,[11] independent judicial power and the power of final adjudication.[12] Hong Kong courts are to have jurisdiction over all cases in the Region, subject to restrictions on jurisdiction previously in force;[13] further, the Hong Kong courts have no jurisdiction over acts of state, such as defence and foreign affairs.[14] Articles 80–96 of the Basic Law stipulate the various bodies, powers and functions of the Hong Kong judiciary. Hallmarks of the common law tradition and the rule of law are also preserved: an independent court system,[15] trial by jury,[16] the

[6] Joint Declaration, Annex I, s III.

[7] ibid para 3.

[8] The power to interpret the Basic Law is vested in the NPCSC: Basic Law, Art 158. The power to amend the Basic Law is vested in the National People's Congress: Basic Law, Art 159.

[9] Basic Law, Preamble.

[10] ibid Art 2.

[11] ibid Art 17(1). See also ibid Art 17(3), which states that laws enacted by Hong Kong deemed by the NPCSC as not in conformity with the Basic Law regarding affairs within the responsibility of the Central Authorities or regarding the relationship between the Central Authorities and Hong Kong could be invalidated.

[12] Basic Law, Arts 11, 19(1).

[13] ibid Art 19(2).

[14] ibid Art 19(3). The decision whether cases involve 'acts of state such as defence and foreign affairs' is determined by the Central People's Government of the PRC, through a certificate obtained by the Chief Executive. See also ch 8, s IV.

[15] Basic Law, Art 81(2), except for the establishment of the Court of Final Appeal, which succeeds the Judicial Committee of the Privy Council in exercising the power of final adjudication under Art 82. See also Arts 85 (independent judiciary free from interference), 88 (establishment and composition of the Judicial Officers Recommendation Commission) and 89–93 (appointment and removal procedures for judicial officers, judges from overseas common law jurisdictions, etc).

[16] Basic Law, Art 86.

rights previously enjoyed by parties to civil and criminal proceedings, including the right to a fair trial without delay and the presumption of innocence.[17] Importantly, Hong Kong can retain pre-existing provisions for admitting local and overseas lawyers to practise in Hong Kong,[18] maintain juridical relations and render assistance between the Hong Kong judiciary and its overseas counterparts,[19] and engage in reciprocal judicial assistance (such as recognition and enforcement of judgments) between Hong Kong and foreign states.[20]

III. Sources of Law

Like other common law jurisdictions, Hong Kong operates the doctrines of precedent and *stare decisis*. As described in section I above, the Basic Law provides that the common law, the rules of equity and customary law[21] previously in force in Hong Kong are preserved.[22] While only pre-1997 decisions on appeals from Hong Kong to the Judicial Committee of the Privy Council are strictly binding on Hong Kong courts, the common law and rules of equity laid down prior to 1997 are preserved as Hong Kong law according to the Basic Law. After 1997, decisions of the Privy Council, the House of Lords and the UK Supreme Court remain highly persuasive.[23] Moreover, Article 84 of the Basic Law expressly provides that the Hong Kong courts may refer to precedents of other common law jurisdictions. Therefore, judgments of common law jurisdictions, such as England and Wales, Singapore, Australia, New Zealand and Canada, are persuasive authorities in Hong Kong.

The precedents in Hong Kong are further complemented by cases decided by the local courts. Within the Hong Kong local court hierarchy, the Court of Final Appeal issues decisions which are binding on the Court of Appeal and lower courts, and it may depart from its previous decisions 'with great circumspection'.[24] The Court of Appeal is bound by its previous decisions, but it may depart from a previous decision where it is satisfied that it is 'plainly wrong'.[25]

Apart from case law principles, statutes (ordinances and subordinate legislation) previously in effect in Hong Kong[26] as supplemented by local enactments by the Legislative

[17] ibid Art 87.
[18] ibid Art 94.
[19] ibid Art 95.
[20] ibid Art 96.
[21] This includes T'sing customary law applying to indigenous residents of the New Territories. These traditional Chinese customs and laws still govern various matters in land, family and probate: see, eg Basic Law, Art 40; New Territories Ordinance (Cap 97), s 13; Marriage Reform Ordinance (Cap 178); *Suen Toi Lee v Yau Yee Ping* (2001) 4 HKCFAR 474 [28]–[34]; *Kwok Cheuk Kin v Director of Lands* (2021) 24 HKCFAR 349, [2021] HKCFA 38.
[22] Basic Law, Art 8. These are subject to invalidation for laws which contravene Basic Law provisions, and amendments by the Legislative Council.
[23] *A Solicitor v The Law Society of Hong Kong* (2008) 11 HKCFAR 117 [6]–[17]. See also *Monat Investment Ltd v All Person(s) in Occupation of Part of the Remaining Portion of Lot No 591 in Mui Wo DD 4, No 16 Ma Po Tsuen, Mui Wo, Lantau Island* [2023] 2 HKLRD 1311, [2023] HKCA 479 [52.1]–[52.5].
[24] *A Solicitor* (n 23) [18]–[20].
[25] ibid [21]–[52].
[26] Basic Law, Art 18(1). This is qualified by a short list of pre-existing statutes (application of English law, foreign marriage, nationality, provisions for elections, etc) which are disapplied by the NPCSC under Basic Law, Art 160: Decision of the NPCSC Concerning the Handling of the Laws Previously in Force in Hong Kong (Instrument A206) (23 February 1997).

Council since 1997 remain a source of codified law. While national laws of the PRC are generally not to be applied in Hong Kong,[27] national laws listed in Annex III of the Basic Law apply to Hong Kong either through local legislation or by direct application.[28]

Some enactments have codified, consolidated and refined legal rules relating to various substantive and procedural matters. A notable example is the amendments implementing the Civil Justice Reform, which came into effect on 2 April 2009 and led to a change of culture in the conduct of the court proceedings and dispute resolution on the part of the judiciary, the legal profession and the public.

Meanwhile, some other statutes enacted by the legislature have codified and incorporated provisions from international or inter-regional instruments. The provisions of the International Covenant on Civil and Political Rights, the International Covenant on Economic, Social and Cultural Rights and international labour conventions remain in force, and are implemented in Hong Kong through various ordinances,[29] such as the Hong Kong Bill of Rights Ordinance (Cap 383), the Disability Discrimination Ordinance (Cap 487) and the Sex Discrimination Ordinance (Cap 480). Other examples include the UNCITRAL Model Law on International Commercial Arbitration, which was adopted and adapted by the Arbitration Ordinance (Cap 341) in 1990 and later as the Arbitration Ordinance (Cap 609) in 2011, and the 1970 HCCH Convention on the Taking of Evidence Abroad in Civil or Commercial Matters, which has been implemented by section 75 of the Evidence Ordinance (Cap 8) and Order 70 of the Rules of the High Court (Cap 4A). Bilateral conventions and arrangements are usually incorporated through domestic legislation in Hong Kong, the most recent example being the Mainland Judgments in Civil and Commercial Matters (Reciprocal Enforcement) Ordinance (Cap 645), which came into operation on 29 January 2024.

Hong Kong law is easily accessible. Both statutes and cases of Hong Kong law are available through official means, while some unofficial means are also available.

Hong Kong legislation is organised by chapter number in the Laws of Hong Kong, available online through the Hong Kong e-Legislation database,[30] with its official status accorded by statute.[31] A copy of a database instrument that is published on or printed directly from an approved website and bears an official verification mark is a verified copy of the instrument. Such a verified copy is presumed, unless the contrary is proved, to contain the official text of a statute or other instrument as at the date specified in the copy.[32] All legislation in available in both official languages, which are equally authentic.[33] When there are differences in meaning which the rules of statutory interpretation ordinarily cannot resolve, the meaning which best reconciles the two texts, having regard to the object and purposes of the particular legislation, is to be adopted.[34]

[27] Basic Law, Art 18(2).

[28] ibid Arts 18(3) and 18(4). See www.basiclaw.gov.hk/en/basiclaw/national-laws.html.

[29] Basic Law, Art 39.

[30] www.elegislation.gov.hk. For a chronological index of all legislative enactments in Hong Kong, see www.elegislation.gov.hk/index/chronologicaltable.

[31] Legislation Publication Ordinance (Cap 614), s 3.

[32] ibid s 5.

[33] Official Languages Ordinance (Cap 5), s 4.

[34] Interpretation and General Clauses Ordinance (Cap 1), s 10B. Needless to say, the attempt to reconcile bilingual legal discrepancies is a difficult task: see, eg *T v Commissioner of Police* (2014) 17 HKCFAR 593.

Most judgments in Hong Kong are available through the Legal Reference System operated by the judiciary.[35] Judgments are delivered in the language in which the case is heard (English or Chinese). A translated version might be available in a limited number of cases, but the translation has no legal status as a judgment. In addition, there are various law reports published by commercial publishers. The most frequently used law reports in Hong Kong include the *Hong Kong Court of Final Appeal Reports* (HKCFAR), the *Hong Kong Law Reports and Digest* (HKLRD) and *Hong Kong Cases* (HKC). Neutral citations of local cases are also assigned to every judgment from 1 January 2018 onwards.[36] Unreported judgments can be downloaded from the Legal Reference System, in which the original Word format is preferred over the online format.[37]

Some judgments are accompanied by press or case summaries in both Chinese and English. These usually include all cases from the Court of Final Appeal, as well as cases at other court levels which have generated significant public attention.[38] However, these are not part of the judgments and therefore have no official status. The Department of Justice also prepares summaries of 'notable judgments' for selected cases which involve important or significant legal principles or issues, issues that attract strong media or public interest, or issues that have an educational purpose.[39] Again, these summaries have no legal effect and are not intended to be cited as authorities of any kind.

Another notable unofficial means of access to Hong Kong law is the Hong Kong Legal Information Institute (HKLII).[40] HKLII is a free legal information system developed and jointly operated by the Department of Computer Science and the Faculty of Law of the University of Hong Kong. The website has been accessed more than 17 million times since its establishment on 11 November 2011.

IV. Developments in Private International Law

This section provides a brief historical account of private international law globally and its trends as applied in Hong Kong. Flowing from the sources of law in this jurisdiction, the historical advance of private international law in Hong Kong is influenced not only by the territory's commercial development, but also by developments in private international law in the UK and common law jurisdictions worldwide.

A. International Developments

Rules governing cross-border cases have their roots in Roman law. In addition to the office of urban praetor administering the *ius civile* or the civil law of Rome between Roman citizens,

[35] https://legalref.judiciary.hk/lrs/common/ju/judgment.jsp.
[36] Practice Direction 5.5, para 5.
[37] Practice Direction 5.5, para 6.
[38] https://legalref.judiciary.hk/lrs/common/ju/ps.jsp?L1=FA.
[39] www.doj.gov.hk/en/notable_judgments.
[40] www.hklii.hk.

the office of peregrine praetor was created in 242 BC to handle disputes in Rome involving a foreigner, with a distinct body of law known as the *ius gentium* or the law of nations, based on an amalgam of Roman and foreign (particularly Greek) legal institutions.[41] The distinction eventually collapsed due to the gradual reception of the *ius gentium* into the urban praetor's jurisdiction and the subsequent extension of Roman citizenship to all inhabitants of the Roman Empire by the Edict of Caracalla in 212 AD.[42] For a few centuries during the Early Middle Ages subsequent to the fall of the Roman Empire in 476 AD, a person was regulated only by the laws of their respective race regardless of the territory they live in. In contrast, during the High Middle Ages, with the establishment of various kingdoms, a person was regulated only by the laws of that territory regardless of their race. As such, any conflict of laws during these periods simply did not arise.

Private international law found its modern roots in the development of *statuta* or municipal laws in Italy city-states in the twelfth century, as this gave rise to conflicts of *statuta* in cases between residents of different cities.[43] Since then, various early scholarships regarding the theory of statutes were developed.[44]

In continental Europe, building upon Hugo Grotius' (1583–1645) characterisation of conflict of laws as the product of voluntary state interaction and state sovereignty,[45] Dutch jurists Paul Voet (1619–67) and John Voet (1647–1713) drew on natural law and positivist theory to explain that the application of foreign laws by a state was a consequence of its voluntary act and international comity.[46] Ulrik Huber (1636–94) adopted an even more positivist approach. Summarising the role of territorial sovereignty in conflict of laws, he posited that states will so act by way of comity to recognise rights acquired within the limits of a foreign government so long as the state's own power, law or citizenry are not prejudiced.[47] The account of conflict of laws articulated by Georg Hegel (1770–1831) and Pasquale Mancini (1817–88) recognised the same commitment to state sovereignty.[48] But they saw sovereignty as only one of the principles governing mutual relations between states. Both Hegel and Mancini argued that nationality should be the pointer to the applicable law in a cross-border civil dispute. Mancini believed that a nation was founded on personal connections among its people, their history and culture, all expressions of statehood, rather than territorial power.[49] Recognising the existence of other sovereign nations thus meant recognising and effectuating foreign laws as a constitutive principle of the society of states.[50]

[41] Reid Mortensen, Richard Garnett and Mary Keyes, *Private International Law in Australia*, 5th edn (LexisNexis, 2023) 8. For an account of early modern private international law grounded in legal positivism, see Alex Mills, *The Confluence of Public and Private International Law: Justice, Pluralism and Subsidiarity in the International Constitutional Ordering of Private Law* (Cambridge University Press, 2009) 27–44.

[42] Mortensen et al (n 41) 8.

[43] ibid.

[44] See Nikitas E Hatzimihail, *Preclassical Conflict of Laws* (Cambridge University Press, 2021).

[45] Mills (n 41) 42.

[46] ibid 45–46.

[47] ibid 46–47. See also Ernest G Lorenzen, 'Huber's De Conflictu Legum' (1919) 13 *Illinois Law Review* 199.

[48] Mills (n 41) 62. See also Georg Wilhelm Fredrich Hegel, *Elements of the Philosophy of Right* (1821) (trans HB Nisbet, Cambridge University Press, 1991) 366–68.

[49] Mills (n 41) 63–64.

[50] ibid 64.

In the USA, Joseph Story (1779–1845) considered that there was a single international system in which the objective of conflict of laws was to develop a system of jurisprudence which 'shall elevate the policy, subserve the interests and promote the common convenience of all nations'.[51] This approach thus straddled positivism as well, since Story emphasised territorial sovereignty as the foundation of conflict of laws, and the force and obligations of foreign laws as dependent solely on a country's consent.[52] However, he stressed the 'comity of nations' as equally important: the application of foreign laws in a state was *ex comitate*, and the courts would presume the tacit adoption of foreign law unless there were any positive rules stating otherwise, or that the foreign laws were repugnant to public policy or local interests.[53]

In Germany, Friedrich Karl von Savigny (1779–1861) took a different route from the positivist approach. He accepted the influence of territorial sovereignty and comity.[54] But his core suggestion was the seat theory (*Sitztheorie*): in every legal relationship or dispute, a 'seat' can be located methodically as the centre of 'gravity', by looking at the legal relationship of the parties and the connections between the parties and the case.[55] The ideal was that, regardless of where the case was heard, the law of the same country (the 'seat') would be consistently identified and applied to resolve the dispute.[56] The concepts of characterisation and 'seat' have been influential in the modern development of the subject.

In the UK, conflict of laws was regularly debated in the late 1700s. This was due to the conflict of laws between England and Scotland, and later, in the 1800s, between Britain, continental Europe and British overseas territories.[57] Under the influence of natural law, scholars such as William Blackstone (1723–80) and Henry Wheaton (1785–1848) regarded international law as governing trans-boundary and private relationships. 'Universal law' was a 'system of rules, deducible by natural reason, and established … in order to decide all disputes … frequently [occurring] between … independent states, and the individuals belonging to each'.[58] Wheaton analysed conflict of laws as originating 'only from considerations of utility and the mutual convenience of States'.[59] John Westlake (1828–1913) considered conflict of laws to be a body of rules identifying what a sovereign state 'commands' to be the right in a matter, before applying the European concept of international comity to determine whether such right should be upheld.[60]

[51] Mills (n 41) 48. See also Joseph Story, *Commentaries on the Conflict of Laws* (Hilliard, Gray & Co, 1834).
[52] Story (n 51) 24–25.
[53] ibid 37.
[54] Friedrich Carl von Savigny, *Private International Law: A Treatise on the Conflict of Laws and the Limits of their Operation in Respect of Place and Time*, 2nd edn (trans William Guthrie, Stevens & Sons, 1880) 147.
[55] ibid 35.
[56] ibid 69–70. This was later known as the idea of 'decisional harmony'.
[57] Lord Collins of Mapesbury and Jonathan Harris (gen eds), *Dicey, Morris and Collins on the Conflict of Laws*, 16th edn (Sweet & Maxwell, 2022) para 1-009.
[58] Mills (n 41) 55. See also William Blackstone, *Commentaries on the Laws of England: Book IV: Of Public Wrongs* (Oxford University Press, 2016) ch 5.
[59] Henry Wheaton, *Elements of International Law*, 8th edn (Little, Brown & Co, 1866) 112.
[60] Mills (n 41) 51–52. See also John Westlake, *A Treatise on Private International Law or The Conflict of Laws with Principal Reference to its Practice in the English and Other Cognate Systems of Jurisprudence* (W Maxwell, 1858) 130–32 and 154.

The nineteenth-century positivist tradition was summed up by Albert Venn Dicey (1835–1922), who saw conflict of laws as part of the law of a state, and not belonging to an international order.[61] Focusing solely on English case law, Dicey echoed Westlake's emphasis on sovereign command as the foundation of conflict of laws, but departed from the concept of international comity. His theory of vested rights suggested that 'the Courts … of England never in strictness enforce foreign law; when they are said to do so, they enforce not foreign laws, but rights acquired under foreign laws'.[62] The enforcement therefore relied not on foreign law but on domestic law, and the reason to enforce these rights lay not in the comity between nations, but the potential inconvenience and injustice to litigants who acquired legal rights and obligations in the foreign country.[63] Despite the theory of vested rights being subject to criticisms, many of Dicey's views – through his work of restating conflict of laws principles as developed in English case law – have become so embedded in English conflict of laws that they are themselves 'tantamount to being a source of law'.[64]

The idea of vested rights was likewise stressed in the USA by Joseph Beale (1861–1943). He advocated that the doctrine of vested rights would dictate any legal relationship or right to 'vest' on the last event that could create that relationship or right by the law of the place where the events occur. As such, the governing law of the tort would be the law of the place where the contract was made, and the governing law for tort would be the law of the place where the tort occurred. Accordingly, a state's law would govern all torts occurring, contracts made and property located within its territory, which was consistent with the nature of law to exclusively apply to everything within its jurisdiction.[65] Subsequent objections to such rigidity led to the 'American conflicts revolution', with Brainerd Currie (1912–65) proposing the theory of interest analysis by giving effect and priority to the interests and legislative policies of the forum.[66] The current US approach requires the consideration of multiple factors in choosing the applicable law in default of statutory directives.[67]

In short, themes of sovereignty, territoriality and international comity have run through the history and development of private international law, with greater or lesser emphasis being placed on one or other of the concepts by different theorists.

The end of the nineteenth century saw the first generation of countries worldwide codifying choice of law rules in national civil codes.[68] Against the then prevailing view that the question of choice of law was not susceptible to codification, states nevertheless began

[61] Mills (n 41) 52. See also Albert Venn Dicey, *A Digest of the Law of England with Reference to the Conflict of Laws* (Stevens & Sons, 1896).

[62] Dicey (n 61) 10.

[63] ibid.

[64] Mills (n 41) 53.

[65] Symeon C Symeonides, *Codifying Choice of Law Around the World: An International Comparative Analysis* (Oxford University Press, 2014) 41. See also Joseph H Beale, *A Treatise on the Conflict of Laws* (Baker, Voorhis & Co, 1935).

[66] See Brainerd Currie, *Selected Essays on the Conflict of Laws* (Duke University Press, 1963).

[67] Restatement (Second) of Conflict of Laws (1971), s 6.

[68] Symeonides (n 65) 2.

to implement codified choice of law rules.[69] In the UK, codification in the first half of the twentieth century was 'haphazard, sporadic, slight and unimportant'.[70] This was due to a substantial body of case law providing effective regulation, while codification was reflected in isolated areas of the law, such as probate and family law.[71] There was also some codification of reciprocal enforcement arrangements among states.[72] Notably, rules for resolving conflict of laws relating to bills of exchange were codified.[73]

Two major influences in the twentieth century, constitutionalism and globalisation, changed this pattern.[74] The mass movement of populations in the aftermath of World War II, technological advances in transportation and communication, and transformations in social and commercial life led to modernisation of legal rules.[75] This encouraged a more universalist approach, based on international law rather than state sovereignty.[76] These transformations culminated in a constitutionalist process which allocated rule-making power between different international and intra-national authorities.[77] This process generated international treaties and instruments dealing with numerous concerns in private international law.[78] The second half of the twentieth century and the early part of the twenty-first century witnessed a spurt of codifications and recodifications worldwide, mostly in civil law jurisdictions.[79] It was a striking feature of the modern developments in private international law that statutes have been the primary engine of change.[80]

This trend has also radically altered the development in private international law in the UK since the 1950s.[81] Numerous enactments were passed to effect ratifications to international conventions, including the various instruments concluded by international organisations such as the Hague Conference on Private International Law (HCCH),[82] the United Nations and the EU.[83] These enactments included statutes implementing international conventions

[69] ibid 2–3.

[70] *Dicey, Morris and Collins* (n 57) para 1-010.

[71] Wills of Personalty by British Subjects Act 1861 (wills made by British subjects at any place, including overseas, enforceable across countries of the UK); Matrimonial Causes Act 1937, s 13; Law Reform (Miscellaneous Provisions) Act 1949, s 1; Family Allowances and National Insurance Act 1956, s 3 (all of which have since been consolidated in enactments of their respective areas of law).

[72] Judgments Extension Act 1868 (repealed by Civil Jurisdiction and Judgments Act 1982); Maintenance Orders (Facilities for Enforcement) Act 1920; Administration of Justice Act 1920, Pt II; Foreign Judgments (Reciprocal Enforcement) Act 1933; Maintenance Orders Act 1950.

[73] Bills of Exchange Act 1882, s 72.

[74] Mills (n 41) 72. For a multi-layered, modern critique of the positivist view of private international law, see Mills (n 41) 75–81.

[75] *Dicey, Morris and Collins* (n 57) para 1-009.

[76] Mills (n 41) 81–83.

[77] ibid 99–101.

[78] ibid 101.

[79] Symeonides (n 65) 14–15. For a statistical summary of choice of law codifications between 1962 and 2012, see ibid 4–26 and 35–36.

[80] Peter North, 'Private International Law: Change or Decay?' (2001) 50(3) *ICLQ* 477, 496; Symeonides (n 65) 3, 34.

[81] *Dicey, Morris and Collins* (n 57) paras 1-010 and 1-011.

[82] See the various HCCH Conventions at www.hcch.net/en/instruments/conventions. See also Thomas John, Rishi Gulati and Ben Köhler (eds), *The Elgar Companion to the Hague Conference on Private International Law* (Edward Elgar, 2020). In this book, the HCCH Conventions are referred to as the 'Hague' Conventions interchangeably.

[83] For international conventions relating to choice of law, see Symeonides (n 65) 30–34. For European Union Conventions and Regulations, see ibid 26–30.

relating to the Admiralty jurisdiction, civil procedure and enforcement, international sale of goods, probate, recognition of family judgments, arbitration proceedings, diplomatic arrangements, logistics and carriage, and child abduction.[84] In the late twentieth century, the UK saw private international law reforms initiated by its own Law Commission relating to torts, marriages and limitation periods.[85] As the UK withdrew from the EU in early 2020, a variety of private international legal issues flowing from its decades of membership in the latter emerged. Many EU regulations, and judgments relating to those regulations, ceased to be applicable in the UK,[86] with only a few exceptions.[87]

B. Local Developments

The history of private international law in Hong Kong began with the adoption of English rules in resolving issues of choice of law, jurisdiction and enforcement in the nineteenth and twentieth centuries. These rules included statutory instruments regulating conflict of laws, and international conventions and treaties into which the UK had entered before 1997. Following the theme of adoption and adaptation, these codifications have been introduced in Hong Kong with appropriate amendments, and a majority of these provisions have subsisted until today. For example, section 72 of the Bills of Exchange Ordinance (Cap 19) is a near-identical provision to section 72 of the English Bills of Exchange Act 1882. This section stipulates rules on the validity and interpretation of bills of exchange, the duties of a bill-holder, and payments under bills of exchange, including those drawn from or payable in different jurisdictions.

Since the 1950s, Hong Kong has also aligned its private international law rules with those worldwide by implementing conventions adopted by the HCCH and other international organisations. A summary of international conventions on private international law matters which have been implemented in the UK, and usually extended to Hong Kong, is given in Table 1.[88]

[84] See Table 1.

[85] See, eg Matrimonial Proceedings (Polygamous Marriages) Act 1972, amended by Matrimonial Causes Act 1973, s 47; Domicile and Matrimonial Proceedings Act 1973; Matrimonial and Family Proceedings Act 1984, Pt III; Foreign Limitation Periods Act 1984; Family Law Act 1986, Pt I; Family Law Reform Act 1987; Private International Law (Miscellaneous Provisions) Act 1995. See also Peter North, 'Problems of Codification in a Common Law System' (1982) 46 *The Rabel Journal of Comparative and International Private Law* 490, 500–01.

[86] eg Regulation (EU) 1215/2012 of the European Parliament and of the Council of 12 December 2012 on jurisdiction and the recognition and enforcement of judgments in civil and commercial matters, [2012] OJ L351/1 (Brussels I (Recast) Regulation); Civil Jurisdiction and Judgments (Amendment) (EU Exit) Regulations 2019; Jurisdiction and Judgments (Family) (Amendment etc) (EU Exit) Regulations 2019. See *Dicey, Morris and Collins* (n 57) paras 1-011–1-016.

[87] eg Regulation (EC) 593/2008 of the European Parliament and of the Council of 17 June 2008 on the law applicable to contractual obligations, [2008] OJ L177/6 (Rome I Regulation); Regulation (EC) 864/2007 of the European Parliament and of the Council of 11 July 2007 on the law applicable to non-contractual obligations, [2008] OJ L199/40 (Rome II Regulation); Law Applicable to Contractual Obligations and Non-Contractual Obligations (Amendment etc) (EU Exit) Regulations 2019; Civil, Criminal and Family Justice (Amendment) (EU Exit) Regulations 2020.

[88] For a list of multilateral agreements in force in Hong Kong, see www.doj.gov.hk/en/external/treaties.html.

Table 1 Implementation of Selected International Conventions on Private International Law in the UK and Hong Kong

International convention(s)	Respective English act(s)	Comparable Hong Kong ordinance(s)
Convention for the Unification of Certain Rules Relating to Bills of Lading (Hague, 1924), as amended by its Protocols (Brussels, 1968 and Brussels, 1979) (Hague–Visby Rules)	Carriage of Goods by Sea Act 1971	Carriage of Goods by Sea Ordinance (Cap 462)
Convention for the Unification of Certain Rules Relating to the Immunity of State-owned Vessels (Brussels, 1926)	State Immunity Act 1978, section 10	State Immunity Act 1978 as extended to Hong Kong by State Immunity (Overseas Territories) Order 1979, ceased to have effect on 1 July 1997
Convention for the Unification of Certain Rules Relating to International Carriage by Air (Warsaw, 1929), as amended by its Protocol (Hague, 1955) Convention, Supplementary to the Warsaw Convention, for the Unification of Certain Rules Relating to International Carriage by Air Performed by a Person Other than the Contracting Carrier (Guadalajara, 1961) Convention for the Unification of Certain Rules for International Carriage by Air (Montreal, 1999)	Carriage by Air Act 1961 Carriage by Air (Supplementary Provisions) Act 1962 Carriage by Air and Road Act 1979	Carriage by Air Ordinance (Cap 500), sections 2A, 3 and 10
Convention on International Civil Aviation (Chicago, 1944) Convention on Offences and Certain Other Acts Committed on board Aircraft (Tokyo, 1963)	Civil Aviation Act 1949, section 8 Tokyo Convention Act 1967 See also Civil Aviation Act 1982	Civil Aviation Ordinance (Cap 448), section 2A Aviation Security Ordinance (Cap 494), section 4
Convention on Certain Rules Concerning Civil Jurisdiction in Matters of Collision (Brussels, 1952) Convention Relating to the Arrest of Seagoing Ships (Brussels, 1952)	Administration of Justice Act 1956, sections 3 and 4 Senior Courts Act 1981, sections 20–24	High Court Ordinance (Cap 4), sections 12A–12E
Convention on the Recovery Abroad of Maintenance (New York, 1956)	Maintenance Orders (Reciprocal Enforcement) Act 1972, Part II	Maintenance Orders (Reciprocal Enforcement) Ordinance (Cap 188)

(continued)

Table 1 ***(Continued)***

International convention(s)	Respective English act(s)	Comparable Hong Kong ordinance(s)
Convention on the Contract for the International Carriage of Goods by Road (Geneva, 1956) Convention Concerning International Carriage by Rail (Bern, 1980), as amended by its Protocol (Vilnius, 1999)	Carriage of Goods by Road Act 1965 International Transport Conventions Act 1983 See also Carriage by Railway Act 1972, Carriage by Air and Road Act 1979	Not adopted
Convention on the Recognition and Enforcement of Foreign Arbitral Awards (New York, 1958)	Arbitration Act 1975 Arbitration Act 1996, sections 100–04	Arbitration Ordinance (Cap 609), sections 87–91
Vienna Convention on Diplomatic Relations (Vienna, 1961) Vienna Convention on Consular Relations (Vienna, 1963)	Diplomatic Privileges Act 1964 Consular Relations Act 1968 See also International Organisations Act 1968, Diplomatic and Other Privileges Act 1971	Consular Relations Ordinance (Cap 557) See also International Organizations and Diplomatic Privileges Ordinance (Cap 190), Administration of Estates by Consular Officers Ordinance (Cap 191), Consular Conventions Ordinance (Cap 267), International Organizations (Privileges and Immunities) Ordinance (Cap 558)
Convention on the Conflicts of Laws Relating to the Form of Testamentary Dispositions (HCCH/Hague, 1961)	Wills Act 1963	Wills Ordinance (Cap 30), sections 24–29
Convention Relating to a Uniform Law on the International Sale of Goods (Hague, 1964) Convention Relating to a Uniform Law on the Formation of Contracts for the International Sale of Goods (Hague, 1964)	Uniform Laws on International Sales Act 1967	Not adopted
Convention on the Service Abroad of Judicial and Extrajudicial Documents in Civil or Commercial Matters (HCCH/Hague, 1965)	Civil Procedure Rules 1998, rules 6.31 and 6.42–6.43	Rules of the High Court (Cap 4A), Orders 11 and 69

(continued)

Table 1 ***(Continued)***

International convention(s)	**Respective English act(s)**	**Comparable Hong Kong ordinance(s)**
International Convention on Civil Liability for Oil Pollution Damage (Brussels, 1969), as superseded by its Protocol (London, 1992) International Convention on the Establishment of an International Fund for Compensation for Oil Pollution Damage (Brussels, 1971), as superseded by its Protocol (London, 1992)	Merchant Shipping (Oil Pollution) Act 1971 Merchant Shipping Act 1979 Merchant Shipping Act 1995, Part VI, chapters III and IV	Merchant Shipping (Liability and Compensation for Oil Pollution) Ordinance (Cap 414)
Convention on the Recognition of Divorces and Legal Separations (HCCH/Hague, 1970)	Recognition of Divorces and Legal Separations Act 1971	Matrimonial Causes Ordinance (Chapter 179), Part IX
Convention on the Taking of Evidence Abroad in Civil or Commercial Matters (HCCH/Hague, 1970)	Evidence (Proceedings in Other Jurisdictions) Act 1975	Evidence Ordinance (Cap 8), Part VIII Rules of the High Court (Cap 4A), Orders 38, 39 and 70
Convention Providing a Uniform Law on the Form of an International Will (Washington, 1973)	Administration of Justice Act 1982, sections 27 and 28 (not yet in operation)	Wills Ordinance (Cap 30), sections 23D and 23E (never came into operation, repealed)
Convention on the Limitation Period in the International Sale of Goods (New York, 1974)	Non-party; reforms implemented in Foreign Limitation Periods Act 1984	Not adopted; no relevant reforms
Convention Relating to the Carriage of Passengers and their Luggage by Sea (Athens, 1974), as amended by its Protocol (London, 1976)	Merchant Shipping Act 1979 Merchant Shipping Act 1995, section 183	Merchant Shipping (Limitation of Shipowners Liability) Ordinance (Cap 434), section 3
Convention on Limitation of Liability for Maritime Claims (London, 1976)	Merchant Shipping Act 1979 Merchant Shipping Act 1995, section 185	Merchant Shipping (Limitation of Shipowners Liability) Ordinance (Cap 434), section 12
Convention on Contracts for the International Sale of Goods (Vienna, 1980)	Non-party	Sale of Goods (United Nations Convention) Ordinance (Cap 641)
Convention on the Civil Aspects of International Child Abduction (HCCH/Hague, 1980)	Child Abduction and Custody Act 1985	Child Abduction and Custody Ordinance (Cap 512)

(continued)

Table 1 ***(Continued)***

International convention(s)	Respective English act(s)	Comparable Hong Kong ordinance(s)
Convention on the Law Applicable to Trusts and on their Recognition (HCCH/Hague, 1985)	Recognition of Trusts Act 1987	Recognition of Trusts Ordinance (Cap 76)
International Convention on Salvage (London, 1989)	Merchant Shipping (Salvage and Pollution) Act 1994, section 1	Merchant Shipping (Collision Damage Liability and Salvage) Ordinance (Cap 508), section 9
Convention on the Protection of Children and Cooperation in Respect of Intercountry Adoption (HCCH/Hague, 1993)	Adoption (Intercountry Aspects) Act 1999 Adoption and Children Act 2002, Part 1, chapters 4, 6	Adoption Ordinance (Cap 290), Part 5
Convention on Jurisdiction, Applicable Law, Recognition, Enforcement and Co-operation in respect of Parental Responsibility and Measures for the Protection of Children (HCCH/Hague, 1996)	Private International Law (Implementation of Agreements) Act 2020	Not adopted
Convention on Choice of Court Agreements (HCCH/Hague, 2005)		
Convention on the International Recovery of Child Support and Other Forms of Family Maintenance (HCCH/Hague, 2007)		

Divergence between Hong Kong and English rules began in the 1980s, when English reforms and EU directives stopped being implemented in Hong Kong.[89] Since the 1980s, Hong Kong's rules governing private cross-border disputes have been predominantly affected by (i) Hong Kong's context as a leading international finance and trade centre and (ii) its geographical proximity to commercial and trading partners in the Asia-Pacific. While some of these major trading partners are common law jurisdictions (eg Singapore, Australia and New Zealand), many others are civil law jurisdictions, such as Mainland China, the majority of ASEAN states, South Korea and Japan.[90] These practical considerations form the basis on

[89] See, eg choice of law in contract and tort (Contracts (Applicable Law) Act 1990 and Private International Law (Miscellaneous Provisions) Act 1995, implementing the Rome I and Rome II Regulations respectively); limitation periods of foreign claims (Foreign Limitation Periods Act 1984); jurisdiction relating to torts to foreign immovable property (Civil Jurisdiction and Judgments Act 1982, s 30).

[90] www.tid.gov.hk/english/aboutus/publications/factsheet/factsheet_maincontent.html.

which the local legislature and judiciary have created, adapted and adopted private international law doctrines into the Hong Kong setting. The complexity of cross-border dealings in Hong Kong has culminated in the demand for a less mechanical private international law regime. This pragmatic preference for flexibility in Hong Kong, together with the necessary legislative intervention by the EU in light of the UK's membership, resulted in Hong Kong's divergence from the UK's substantial reform in their private international law rules to incorporate codified EU rules.

The advance of modern private international law rules in Hong Kong has been two-pronged. On the one hand, it has relied on judges to decide cases with reference to developments in other common law jurisdictions in relation to jurisdiction and choice of law rules[91] in lieu of the wholesale reform and codification seen in the UK. On the other hand, there have been occasional statutory reforms to consolidate and codify Hong Kong's private international law rules, which began slowly near the end of the twentieth century. Key areas that have seen codification are domicile and the 'closest connection' principle,[92] interim relief in support of existing or prospective foreign proceedings,[93] reciprocal recognition and enforcement of judgments from Mainland China,[94] and support on international arbitration.[95]

[91] See, eg ch 7 (evidence), ch 9 (service out of jurisdiction), ch 20 (cross-border insolvency) and ch 23 (recognition and enforcement of foreign judgments in common law).

[92] See ch 4.

[93] See ch 9, s V.

[94] See ch 23.

[95] See ch 24.

3

Preliminary Matters

This chapter discusses various preliminary matters in private international law. These include characterisation, *renvoi*, the incidental question, *depeçage* and the time factor. As will be seen in this chapter, Hong Kong courts do not seem to have a problem with any of these issues. They take a practical approach with little discussion on these preliminary matters. This chapter is, thus, necessarily limited to introducing these concepts and pointing out potential theoretical difficulties.

I. Characterisation

The question of characterisation is traditionally seen as a fundamental problem in the conflict of laws whereby applicable rules can be chosen with reference to juridical concepts or categories and localising elements or connecting factors. For example, a rule which states 'succession to immovables is governed by the law of the *situs*' will have categorised 'succession to immovables' as a category and *situs* as a connecting factor. It is, therefore, necessary to undertake a measure of characterisation to determine which juridical concept or category is applicable in any given case. The matching of categories with connecting factors underlies the system of private international law in many jurisdictions, including Hong Kong, the UK and Singapore. Characterisation is therefore important, as it requires categorising the facts appropriately so as to answer questions about the law or laws applicable to such facts. In other words, characterisation of an issue 'requires a parallel exercise in classification of the relevant rule of law'.[1]

There is voluminous literature on characterisation. Yet, the theoretical debate has had almost no influence on the practice of the courts.[2] A prominent debate is on the choice of law of the characterisation itself. What system of law determines how characterisation should be conducted? The main schools of thought espouse the application of the law of the forum (*lex fori*) or the law of the cause of action (*lex causae*). It is now settled under English law (and Hong Kong law) that characterisation or classification is governed by the *lex fori*.[3]

The modern approach requires characterising the issue, not the rule, as characterising between (say) substantive and procedural rules will lead to problems of gap (no law applies to the dispute) and of culmination (multiple laws apply to the dispute).[4] The proper approach is to look beyond the formulation of a claim and to identify, according to the *lex fori*, the

[1] *Macmillan Inc v Bishopsgate Investment Trust plc (No 3)* [1996] 1 WLR 387, 407.
[2] ibid 392.
[3] See, eg *Altimo Holdings and Investment Ltd v Kyrgyz Mobil Tel Ltd* [2011] UKPC 7, [2012] 1 WLR 1804 [108].
[4] A classical illustration is *Re Cohn* [1945] Ch 5. See also ch 5.

true issue or issues thrown up by the claim and defence. Accordingly, 'the rules of conflict of laws should be directed at the particular issue of law which is in dispute, rather than the cause of action which is relied upon'.[5] Staughton LJ proposed a three-stage approach:[6]

> First, it is necessary to characterise the issue that is before the court. Is it for example about the formal validity of a marriage? Or intestate succession to moveable property? Or interpretation of a contract?
>
> The second stage is to select the rule of conflict of laws which lays down a connecting factor for the issue in question. Thus the formal validity of a marriage is to be determined, for the most part, by the law of the place where it is celebrated; intestate succession to movables, by the law of the place where the deceased was domiciled when he died; and the interpretation of a contract, by what is described as its proper law.
>
> Thirdly, it is necessary to identify the system of law which is tied by the connecting factor found in stage two to the issue characterised in stage one. Sometimes this will present little difficulty, though I suppose that even a marriage may now be celebrated on an international video link. The choice of the proper law of a contract, on the other hand, may be controversial.

This approach has been endorsed in later cases, subject to the qualifications that: (i) the three-stage process cannot be pursued by taking each step in turn and in isolation;[7] and (ii) it is a methodology which must not be carried out mechanistically, but with regard to the objective of identifying the most appropriate law to govern the issue, in a spirit of comity.[8] In *Raiffeisen Zentralbank Österreich AG v Five Star General Trading LLC*, it was said when dealing with the characterisation of issues that:[9]

> The overall aim is to identify the most appropriate law to govern a particular issue. The classes or categories of issue which the law recognises at the first stage [ie for characterisation] are man-made, not natural. They have no inherent value, beyond their purpose in assisting to select the most appropriate law. A mechanistic application, without regard to the consequences, would conflict with the purpose for which they were conceived. They may require redefinition or modification, or new categories may have to be recognised …

Seen in this light, the characterisation of issues is for the courts to seek common-sense solutions based on practical considerations.[10] It is submitted that courts should not over-complicate matters, but should as much as possible favour intuitively obvious and straightforward characterisations of issues.

II. *Renvoi*

When one states that 'the law of a jurisdiction' is applied, that 'law' may refer to (i) the narrower (and more usual) sense of the substantive domestic law of that jurisdiction or

[5] *Relevant Employees Whose Shares in China Shanshui Investment Co Ltd Were Held by Zhang Caikui on Trust v Zhang Caikui* (unreported, HCA 1661/2014, 13 May 2015) [78], citing *Macmillan Inc* (n 1) 399C, 407B and 418A–B.

[6] *Macmillan Inc* (n 1) 391, approved in *First Laser Ltd v Fujian Enterprises (Holdings) Co Ltd* [2011] 2 HKLRD 45 [49].

[7] *Raiffeisen Zentralbank Österreich AG v Five Star General Trading LLC* [2001] EWCA Civ 68, [2001] QB 825 [25]–[27].

[8] *Investec Trust (Guernsey) Ltd v Glenalla Properties Ltd* [2018] UKPC 7, [2019] AC 271 [66].

[9] *Raiffeisen Zentralbank Österreich AG* (n 7) [27].

[10] *Konamaneni v Rolls Royce Industrial Power (India) Ltd* [2002] 1 WLR 1269 [45]–[50].

(ii) the wider sense of the substantive domestic law of that jurisdiction and its rules of the private international law.[11] The ambiguity in the meaning of the foreign 'law' and the possibility of understanding the reference in a wider sense gives rise to the question of *renvoi*.

Renvoi originated as a device for mitigating the rigidity of the English conflict rule for the formal validity of wills.[12] Today, however, *renvoi* refers to the legal reasoning which looks at what happens when the court of jurisdiction A refers an issue to the foreign law of jurisdiction B and where, under that jurisdiction B's rules of private international law, the issue is remitted back to the law of jurisdiction A or referred (transmitted) to the law of a third jurisdiction C.[13]

Three techniques are usually deployed to get around *renvoi*.

First, one can reject *renvoi*. This is the 'internal law' solution. Under this solution, the court of jurisdiction A might apply the substantive domestic law of foreign jurisdiction B, ignoring the fact that the courts of jurisdiction B will apply foreign law pursuant to the private international law rules of jurisdiction B. This solution merely requires proof of the substantive domestic law of foreign jurisdiction B. Such a solution has commonly been rejected in the past.[14] Nevertheless, the approach is one typically employed by international instruments. See, for instance, Article 8 of the 2015 HCCH Principles on Choice of Law in International Commercial Contracts and Article 28(1) of the UNCITRAL Model Law on International Commercial Arbitration, the latter of which is incorporated by section 64 of the Arbitration Ordinance (Cap 609).

Second, there can be partial or single *renvoi*. Under this solution, if the private international law rules of jurisdiction B refer back to the law of jurisdiction A, the court in jurisdiction A can accept the remission and apply its own substantive law. On the other hand, if the law of jurisdiction B refers to the law of jurisdiction C, the court of jurisdiction A can accept the transmission and apply the substantive domestic law of jurisdiction C. This solution requires proof of the private international law rules of the foreign jurisdiction B.

Third, there can be total or double *renvoi*. Under this solution, the court of jurisdiction A should decide the case in the same way that it would be decided by the court of jurisdiction B. It requires proof not just of jurisdiction B's private international law rules, but also evidence as to how the court of jurisdiction B will deal with *renvoi*. It appears that the current position in the UK is the third solution of double *renvoi*.[15] If the foreign law refers to English law and rejects *renvoi* altogether, the result will be that English domestic law is applicable. If the foreign law refers to English law and adopts the doctrine of single *renvoi*, the result is that the law of jurisdiction B will apply.

What about the situation where the foreign court also adopts the doctrine of total or double *renvoi* as well? In this situation, logically, there is no possible solution unless either court abandons its theory. A perpetual vicious cycle would be constituted. This question has

[11] It was suggested that such a distinction may not be easy to draw in the first place: *Neilson v Overseas Projects Corp of Victoria Ltd* (2005) 223 CLR 331.

[12] See Lord Collins of Mapesbury and Jonathan Harris (gen eds), *Dicey, Morris and Collins on the Conflict of Laws*, 16th edn (Sweet & Maxwell, 2022) paras 2-105–2-115.

[13] *Dallah Real Estate and Tourism Holding Co v Ministry of Religious Affairs, Government of Pakistan* [2010] UKSC 46, [2011] 1 AC 763 [123]–[125].

[14] *Re Ross* [1930] 1 Ch 377, 402.

[15] *Dicey, Morris and Collins* (n 12) paras 2-114–2-115, citing *Re Annesley* [1926] Ch 692 and *Re Askew* [1930] 2 Ch 359.

only appeared in theory, but it is not inconceivable. It is suggested that the most rational solution to break the inextricable circle would be for the original court to apply its own domestic law once the issue is remitted back to it.[16]

It has more recently been advocated that there need not be a single or uniform approach to the doctrine of *renvoi*. In the High Court of Australia,[17] it was suggested that the correct question for the court seised is the interpretation and application of the source and content of the choice of law rules of the forum, having regard to the specific legal context governing the rights and obligations of parties. The court should not be confined by a single rigid doctrine of *renvoi*. The doctrine of *renvoi* should instead be resorted to when it is appropriate to support the goals of the choice of law rules.[18] Such a flexible approach might be preferable as in some situations the doctrine of *renvoi* is convenient and promotes justice, whereas in other situations the doctrine is cumbersome and ought to be rejected. Choosing one theory of *renvoi* as applicable to all cases where a choice of law must be made would ignore differences among cases, and dogmatism must yield to pragmatism.[19]

The choice under *renvoi* is also subject to public policy. In the Nova Scotia case of *Vladi v Vladi*,[20] the Nova Scotia conflict-of-law rule provided that the governing law was 'the law' of the place where the spouses had their last common habitual residence, which was Germany. The German conflict-of-law rule, however, referred to the law of Iran, the country of which the spouses were nationals. The Nova Scotia court was prepared in principle to apply *renvoi* and follow the transmission to Iranian law. However, it considered that the application of Iranian matrimonial property law would be contrary to substantial justice (public policy) because it was unfair to women. The Nova Scotia court thus had to decide between applying the internal law of Germany or the *lex fori* (which is normally applicable when the relevant provision of foreign law is contrary to public policy). It chose German law on the ground that the rejection of Iranian law did not justify disregarding the original reference to German law.

Renvoi has not posed problems in Hong Kong legal practice. There have been many cases in which the domestic rules of foreign law have been applied without reference to the foreign state's private international law rules, and parties were not concerned to argue that the reference to foreign law included the foreign state's rules on the private international law.[21] Judicial pragmatism in Hong Kong is likely to provide a solution to problems of *renvoi*. Similar pragmatism is seen in Australia and Singapore.[22] In some jurisdictions such as China and some international instruments, *renvoi* is expressly excluded.[23]

[16] *Casdagli v Casdagli* [1918] P 89, 111, approved in *Casdagli v Casdagli* [1919] AC 145, applied in *Kotia v Nahas* [1941] AC 403.

[17] *Neilson* (n 11).

[18] This is suggested also to be the case for the question of characterisation: *Raiffeisen Zentralbank* (n 7) [26]–[29].

[19] *Neilson* (n 11) [97]–[99].

[20] *Vladi v Vladi* (1987) 38 DLR (4th) 563 (NS).

[21] *Dicey, Morris and Collins* (n 12) para 2-117. See also *Macmillan Inc* (n 1), where a case involving competing claims to shares in a New York company, the argument for *renvoi* was 'mercifully (or sadly, as the case may be)' abandoned: *Macmillan Inc* (n 1) 405.

[22] *Neilson* (n 11); *Ong Ghee Soon Kevin v Ho Yong Chong* [2017] 3 SLR 711 [103]–[106].

[23] See, eg Law of the People's Republic of China on Choice of Law for Foreign-related Civil Relationships, Art 9; 1985 HCCH Convention on the Law Applicable to Trusts and on their Recognition, Art 17; HCCH Principles on Choice of Law in International Commercial Contracts (2015), Art 8.

In any event, the role played by *renvoi* is controversial and can be complex. It would be dependent on the 'doubtful and conflicting evidence of foreign experts',[24] which is a question of fact that typically has to be proved by evidence in each case. If the evidence is misleading or inadequate, the result may be unreal and unjust.[25]

III. The Incidental Question

The incidental question concerns the situation where a court is to decide a main question involving foreign elements but, to decide that main question, the court has first to consider a subsidiary (incidental) question which also involves foreign elements. Logically, such a situation of incidental question will occur only if three conditions are satisfied: first, the main question must, by the Hong Kong conflict-of-law rule, be governed by the law of some foreign country; second, there must be a subsidiary question involving foreign elements which is subject to determination by a different conflict-of-law rule; and third, the Hong Kong conflict rule for the determination of the subsidiary question must lead to a different result from the corresponding conflict rule governing the main question.

Thus, for instance, where it is alleged that a defendant has breached a contract governed by the law of country X, there may be an incidental question as to whether the defendant (a national of country Y) had the capacity to execute the relevant contract. Suppose that, by Hong Kong private international law rules, the incidental question is governed by the law of country Y. Should the Hong Kong court decide the question of the defendant's capacity by reference to the law of country Y, or should the defendant's capacity be governed by the law of country X which applies to the main question?

An argument in favour of the law of country Y is to ensure internal consistency within the private international law rules of the forum (Hong Kong), reaching the same outcome regardless of the context in which the question arises. An argument in favour of the law of country X is to ensure international harmony in the uniformity of outcome, avoiding different answers between the main and incidental questions and thus different results.[26]

It is neither possible nor desirable to find a one-size-fits-all solution which would apply in every case. Rather, each situation should be looked at separately to arrive at a solution that produces the best result, in the sense of producing a fair and practical outcome. Instead of trying to solve the problem based on general theory, one should consider the practical consequences of applying different laws to the related situations. There should be a flexible approach that takes policy considerations into account. Hong Kong courts have not discussed in any depth how incidental questions should be handled.[27]

[24] *Re Askew* (n 15) 278.

[25] See, eg *Re O'Keefe* [1940] Ch 124.

[26] Tiong Min Yeo, *Commercial Conflict of Laws* (Academy Publishing, 2023) para 11.064.

[27] For an illustration of cases from other jurisdictions, see *Dicey, Morris and Collins* (n 12) paras 2-048–2-062, citing, among other cases, *Haque v Haque* (1962) 108 CLR 230 (Australia) and *Schwebel v Ungar* [1965] SCR 148 (Canada). In Mainland China, see Interpretation of the Supreme People's Court on Several Issues Concerning Application of the Law of the People's Republic of China on Choice of Law for Foreign-related Civil Relationships (I) (2020 Amendment), Fa Shi [2020] No 18, Art 10.

IV. *Dépeçage*

The concept of *dépeçage* can be understood in two ways.[28] The first is the idea that not all aspects of a contractual relation will necessarily be governed by the same foreign law, so that different foreign laws may govern different aspects of a contractual obligation. For instance, the question whether a defendant has breached a contractual obligation governed by the law of country X may depend on whether it was illegal to perform the obligation in country Y, where the parties intended the contract to be carried out. The second is the notion that different laws may apply to different parts of a contract. Thus, an obligation under a contract may be governed by the law of one state, while another obligation under the same contract might be governed by the law of another state. Taking their cue from English decisions, Hong Kong courts may recognise that different obligations under the same contract can be governed by different laws.[29]

Despite there being no theoretical objection, in practice, it is inconvenient and infrequent to have different laws apply to different aspects of a contract or contractual relation. In principle, there is a presumption that a party's 'general obligation' under a contract is governed by a single law. Accordingly, aspects of that 'general obligation' (for example, the issue of whether the contract is discharged by frustration) should be governed by the same law. Unless there is a clear indication to the contrary, the Hong Kong court 'will not split the contract readily or without good reason'.[30] If the choice of a single law will lead to logical inconsistencies or contradictions, then the court may also refuse to respect the choice.[31]

Turning to the possibility of *dépeçage* in trusts, the 1985 HCCH Convention on the Law Applicable to Trusts and on their Recognition (the Hague Trusts Convention) as implemented by the Recognition of Trusts Ordinance (Cap 76) explicitly allows for this possibility. Article 9 of the Hague Trusts Convention provides that 'a severable aspect of the trust, particularly matters of administration, may be governed by a different law'. The court will therefore respect a choice by the settlor of multiple laws to govern different issues or different types of property under the trust, or to choose some other law for the administration of a trust.[32] Similarly, however, in the absence of a clear indication by the settlor, it will be rare for the court to conclude that different laws apply to a trust. It is desirable that, as much as possible, a trust should be treated as a whole, with trusts of all the property comprised therein governed by a single law. The fact that some trust property is movable and some immovable should not defeat this general policy.[33] It is likely that the validity, interpretation and effect of a trust, on the one hand, and the administration of a trust, on the other hand, are governed by the same law.[34]

[28] *Dicey, Morris and Collins* (n 12) para 32-041.

[29] See, eg *Enka Insaat ve Sanayi AS v OOO Insurance Co Chubb* [2020] UKSC 38, [2020] 1 WLR 4117 [38]–[42]. In the EU, this possibility was recognised by Art 3(1) of the Rome I Regulation, which contemplates that different parts of the same contract may be governed by different laws.

[30] ibid [39]. This is followed in *China Railway (Hong Kong) Holdings Ltd v Chung Kin Holdings Co Ltd* [2023] HKCFI 132 [35(d)].

[31] *Avonwick Holdings Ltd v Azitio Holdings Ltd* [2020] EWHC 1844 (Comm) [498].

[32] If there is a dispute as to the word 'administration', the law applicable to the construction of the trust should be applied: *Crociani v Crociani* [2014] UKPC 40, [2015] WTLR 975 [23]–[24].

[33] *Re Fitzgerald* [1904] 1 Ch 573.

[34] *Chellaram v Chellaram* [1985] Ch 409.

V. The Time Factor

As with other branches of law, problems of time should be considered in private international law. The time factor usually involves three different aspects:[35]

(i) when there is a change in the content of the private international law rule of the forum;
(ii) when there is a change in the content of a connecting factor (eg a change in domicile); and
(iii) when there is a change in the content of the *lex causae*.

In the first situation, the problem is usually resolved by a clear indication in the language of the relevant statute as to when a new rule comes into force and to what extent it operates retrospectively. As a matter of legal policy, except in relation to procedural matters, changes in the law should not take effect retrospectively. Thus, unless the contrary intention appears, a statute is presumed not to be intended to have a retrospective operation.[36] In this regard, general rules of statutory interpretation are applicable to determine how the time factor should be resolved. There may be difficulties if a new statutory rule does not expressly refer to or abolish an earlier common law rule, leaving it open for a litigant to argue that the common law rule continues in effect. But no such situation has so far been encountered in Hong Kong.[37]

In the second situation, some connecting factors may change over time, and it may, therefore, be necessary to 'stabilise' or 'crystallise' the connecting factor. For example, a forum's choice of law rule stating that succession to movables is governed by the law of the deceased's domicile is a variable connecting factor. the deceased may have had several domiciles in his or her lifetime, but adding the words 'at the time of the deceased's death' will define which of the deceased's various domiciles is relevant. No general principles can be formulated for dealing with this problem. Similarly, there can be no general answer to the question of whether it is possible to take account of facts and circumstances which occur subsequent to the time when a connecting factor is ascertained. In many situations, a later change may not make a difference. But the overarching consideration remains whether the result of applying a connecting factor as at a particular time enables the most convenient and just outcome.

In the third situation, changes in the *lex causae* may pose some conundrums. In particular, under the declaratory theory at common law, a change of law due to a court decision holding that a previous understanding of a cause of action was erroneous is supposed to have retrospective effect.[38] That is because the court does not legislate, but is supposed to declare the law as it always has been. The prevailing practice seems to be to apply the *lex causae* in its entirety, as it exists from time to time, taking account of retrospective changes if necessary. But this is likely subject to qualification and exception in the interests of public policy and fairness. However, there is a dearth of authorities on this question.

[35] *Dicey, Morris and Collins* (n 12) para 2-065.
[36] Diggory Bailey and Luke Norbury, *Bennion, Bailey and Norbury on Statutory Interpretation*, 8th edn (LexisNexis, 2022) paras 7.13–7.18.
[37] For a curious situation in the UK, see *Dicey, Morris and Collins* (n 12) paras 2-068–2-069.
[38] See ibid paras 2-076–2-094.

4

Connecting Factors

This chapter introduces several concepts in relation to connecting factors. Connecting factors establish a legal relationship between a natural or legal person and a territory having a distinctive legal system. That legal system may then be regarded as the personal law of the party concerned.

I. Nationality

For the purposes of conflict of laws in Hong Kong, nationality generally has no direct relevance.[1] However, it may have indirect relevance as, inter alia, a factor relevant to the determination of matters such as domicile and 'closest and most real connection'. Hong Kong has no standalone law on nationality; the eligibility as residents of Hong Kong is stated in Article 24 of the Basic Law and the Immigration Ordinance (Cap 115). Whether a person possesses a foreign nationality is determined by the foreign law.[2]

II. Domicile

Domicile is a difficult concept to understand. Previous cases have understood it to mean a 'permanent home'.[3] Hong Kong rules for determining a person's domicile on or after 1 March 2009 have departed from the previous common law position, and are now contained in the Domicile Ordinance (Cap 596) (DO).[4] However, if it is necessary to decide a person's domicile before 1 March 2009, the common law position remains applicable.[5] When the domicile of an individual is an issue before any court in Hong Kong, it should be determined according to Hong Kong law.[6] For the purposes of the DO, the facts indicating a party's domicile need to be proved on the balance of probability.[7]

[1] This may be contrasted with private international law rules in other jurisdictions, particularly civil law jurisdictions. In Mainland China, see Law of the People's Republic of China on Choice of Law for Foreign-related Civil Relationships, Art 19.

[2] *Oppenheimer v Cattermole* [1976] AC 249.

[3] *Whicker v Hume* (1858) 7 HL Cas 124, 160, 11 ER 50, 64; *Winans v A-G* [1904] AC 287.

[4] DO, ss 13 and 14. See also *W v C* [2013] 2 HKLRD 602; *ZC v CN* [2014] 5 HKLRD 43 [7.1]–[7.6]; *LCYP v JEK* [2015] 4 HKLRD 798 [33]–[35].

[5] DO, s 13.

[6] ibid s 3(3).

[7] ibid s 12; *Re Ip Pui Man Nina* [2011] 3 HKLRD 299 [32].

As the common law rules are now largely obsolete, the following paragraphs focus on the modern rules under the DO.

The DO deals with the domicile of children and of adults,[8] and also with the rules for acquiring a domicile in Hong Kong[9] and in another country or territory.[10] All individuals must have one, and only one, domicile for a given purpose at a given time.[11] An individual's domicile continues until another domicile is acquired.[12]

A. Children

A child is domiciled in the country or territory in which he or she is for the time being most closely connected.[13] Two presumptions assist with ascertaining the domicile of children. First, where the child's parents are domiciled in the same country or territory and the child has his or her home with either or both of them, it is presumed that the child is most closely connected with that country or territory.[14] Second, where the child's parents are not domiciled in the same country or territory and the child has his or her home with one of them but not with the other, it is presumed that the child is most closely connected with the country or territory in which the parent with whom he or she lives is domiciled.[15] No presumption will apply, however, if the two parents are domiciled in different countries or territories but the child lives with both.

B. Adults

The DO distinguishes between adults of full capacity and adults with an incapacity.[16] An adult of full capacity retains the domicile that he or she had immediately before becoming an adult. Otherwise, an adult of full capacity acquires a new domicile in a country or territory if he or she is present there and intends to make a home there for an indefinite period.[17] There must be intention when the individual is physically present in the place alleged to be his or her new domicile. In determining whether an adult intends to make a home in a particular place, a Hong Kong court will have regard to:[18]

(i) length of residence;
(ii) conditions of residence (that is, whether the individual has purchased or leased property, whether they have furnished lodgings or whether they are staying at a hotel);

[8] DO, ss 4 and 5.
[9] ibid s 6.
[10] ibid s 7.
[11] ibid ss 3(1) and 3(2).
[12] ibid s 9.
[13] ibid s 4(1).
[14] ibid s 4(2).
[15] ibid s 4(3).
[16] ibid s 5(1).
[17] ibid s 5(2).
[18] *W v C* [2013] 2 HKLRD 602 [20], citing *Y v W* (unreported, FCMC 1847/2011, 11 August 2011). The factors themselves originated from Lawrence Collins (gen ed), *Dicey, Morris and Collins on the Conflict of Laws*, 14th edn (Sweet & Maxwell, 2006) para 6-049.

(iii) marriage with a local partner;
(iv) whereabouts of the individual's family;
(v) business interests;
(vi) whereabouts of personal belongings;
(vii) whereabouts of the individual's property and investments;
(viii) the fact of naturalisation;
(ix) decisions made as to the nationality of children (if any);
(x) education of children (if any);
(xi) memberships of clubs or religious associations;
(xii) place of work; and
(xiii) relationship between the individual and his or her family.

Whether the individual's presence in a country or territory is lawful by the law of that country or territory will also be considered by a Hong Kong court.[19] However, unlawful presence does not preclude a determination that the individual has acquired a domicile in a country or territory.[20] An exception to this is if the domicile in question is Hong Kong. In such a case, an adult must be lawfully present to acquire domicile in Hong Kong,[21] unless strict adherence to the requirement of lawful presence would result in injustice.[22] There is a presumption in favour of lawful presence.[23]

An adult who lacks the capacity to form the intention necessary for acquiring a domicile is domiciled in the country or territory with which he or she is for the time being most closely connected.[24] Whether an adult lacks such a capacity is a question of fact.[25] If capacity is restored, the adult retains the domicile that he or she had immediately before the capacity was restored.[26]

It is possible to change one's domicile. There are cases deciding whether a person has acquired PRC domicile[27] and Singapore domicile.[28]

C. Corporations

A corporation is domiciled in the jurisdiction under whose law it is incorporated. The place of incorporation is therefore sometimes described as the place of the corporation's 'domicile'. A corporation's domicile is independent of (and separate from) the domicile of its members, who may have their domiciles elsewhere.[29] A corporation incorporated in one jurisdiction cannot have more than one domicile if it is reincorporated elsewhere. If there were such a case in Hong Kong, two distinct corporations would be created.[30]

[19] DO, s 7(a).
[20] ibid s 7(b).
[21] ibid s 6(1).
[22] ibid s 6(3).
[23] ibid s 6(2).
[24] ibid s 8(1).
[25] ibid s 8(2).
[26] ibid s 8(3).
[27] *Re Ku Chu Keung* [2007] 2 HKLRD 292; *Re Cheung Shing Sheung* (unreported, HCB 6679/2015, 16 May 2017) [22].
[28] *Re Ip Pui Man Nina* (n 7).
[29] *Princess of Reuss v Bos* (1871–72) LR 5 HL 176.
[30] Graeme Johnston and Paul Harris, *The Conflict of Laws in Hong Kong*, 3rd edn (Sweet & Maxwell, 2017) para 7.018.

III. Residence

In private international law, the concept of residence on its own has limited relevance.[31] Rather, the laws will usually employ the notion of ordinary residence or habitual residence as a connecting factor. There seems to be a conceptual difference between these two notions, but the practical difference is, if anything, minimal.[32] While one can only have one domicile, one may have more than one habitual or ordinary residence.[33]

A. Ordinary Residence

Ordinary residence has significant relevance in a diverse range of fields. For instance, it is widely encountered in regulatory and taxation statutes. It operates as an aspect of one criterion of long-arm jurisdiction;[34] a basis of bankruptcy jurisdiction;[35] a relevant factor in the protection of well-known trade marks;[36] and a condition for the exercise of some of the court's powers.[37]

The concept of 'ordinary residence' is not defined in the statutes of Hong Kong. Ordinary residence is judicially defined as being 'habitually and normally resident here apart from temporary or occasional absences of long or short duration'.[38] 'Habitual' residence means that it must be 'adopted voluntarily and for settled purposes'.[39] More specifically, ordinary residence usually

> refers to a [person's] abode in a particular place or country which he [or she] has adopted voluntarily and for settled purposes as part of the regular order of his [or her] life for the time being, whether or short or long duration.[40]

This will be the case unless the statutory framework or legal context in which the words are used indicate a different meaning. In addition, ordinary residence is a 'much less exacting notion' than domicile.[41] Indeed, it has been held that 'the requirement of "settled purposes" is far less rigorous than the subjective element in the definition of domicile'.[42]

Cases have held that, in determining whether a person is 'ordinarily resident' in Hong Kong, the following guidelines are helpful:[43]

(i) whether a person is ordinarily resident in Hong Kong is a question of fact and degree, and must be determined in all circumstances;

[31] Residence is only found as a basis for matrimonial jurisdiction and with the statutory regime for enforcement of foreign judgments. By itself, residence requires more than a fleeting presence, but is less than domicile, ordinary residence and habitual residence: *de Lasala v de Lasala* (unreported, CACV 6/1976, 17 December 1976).

[32] *Vallejos v Commissioner of Registration* (2013) 16 HKCFAR 45 [32].

[33] *Ikimi v Ikimi* [2001] EWCA Civ 873, [2002] Fam 72.

[34] Rules of the High Court (Cap 4A), Ord 11, r 1(1)(a).

[35] Bankruptcy Ordinance (Cap 6), s 4(3)(a).

[36] Trade Marks Ordinance (Cap 559), s 4(1)(a).

[37] See Johnston and Harris (n 30) para 7.019.

[38] *R v Barnet London Borough Council, ex p Shah* [1983] 2 AC 309, approved in eg *Re Kok Hiu Pan, ex p Wing Lung Bank Ltd* [2002] 3 HKLRD 20. See also *Vallejos* (n 32).

[39] *IRC v Lysaght* [1928] AC 234. See also s III.B below.

[40] *Lau San Ching v Apollonia Liu* (1995) 5 HKPLR 23, 28; *Re Cheung Shing Sheung* (n 27) [23].

[41] Johnston and Harris (n 30) para 7.004.

[42] *R v Barnet London Borough Council* (n 38) 344.

[43] *Lau San Ching* (n 40) 28; *Re Cheung Shing Sheung* (n 27) [23].

(ii) a person can have ordinary residence in two (or possibly more) countries at the same time;
(iii) the residence must be voluntary and cannot be forced against the person's free will;
(iv) involuntariness may negate ordinary residence; and
(v) temporary or occasional absences of long or short duration do not negate ordinary residence; and
(vi) unlawful residence does not constitute ordinary residence.

For children, ordinary residence will usually follow that of the parent with whom they reside.[44]

B. Habitual Residence

'Habitual residence' is a concept which has long been associated with the Hague Conference on Private International Law (HCCH).[45] As such, issues regulated by HCCH Conventions as implemented in Hong Kong by domestic legislation refer to this phrase, such as the formal validity of wills, intercountry adoptions and international child abduction.[46] Other occurrences of the concept in Hong Kong include jurisdictional issues in shipping collision, contractual choice of law clauses and various matrimonial, paternity and legitimacy issues.[47]

The concept of 'habitual residence' has deliberately not been defined in HCCH Conventions or by statute. The rationale for this was to render it less technical than the concept of domicile and to leave it for each country adopting a relevant convention to define what 'habitual residence' entails. It was suggested that the concept 'should not be treated as a term of art with some special meaning'.[48] Nevertheless, the courts have held that when the expression is used in the context of married parents living together, it refers to

> their abode in a particular place or country which they have adopted voluntarily and for settled purposes as part of the regular order of their life for the time being, whether of short or of long duration. All that the law requires for a 'settled purpose' is that the parents' shared intentions in living where they do should have a sufficient degree of continuity about them to be properly described as settled.[49]

The following principles have also been found helpful:[50]

(i) the question of whether a person is habitually resident in a particular country is a question of fact;

[44] Johnston and Harris (n 30) para 7.020.
[45] Lord Collins of Mapesbury and Jonathan Harris (gen eds), *Dicey, Morris and Collins on the Conflict of Laws*, 16th edn (Sweet & Maxwell, 2022) para 6-137.
[46] Wills Ordinance (Cap 30), s 24; Adoption Ordinance (Cap 290), s 20B and Sch 3; Child Abduction and Custody Ordinance (Cap 512). See also ch 26.
[47] High Court Ordinance (Cap 4), ss 12B and 12C; Control of Exemption Clauses Ordinance (Cap 71), s 17; Unconscionable Contracts Ordinance (Cap 458), s 7; Parent and Child Ordinance (Cap 429), ss 6 and 12; Matrimonial Causes Ordinance (Cap 179), ss 3, 4, 6, 56 and 58.
[48] *B v B* (unreported, HCMP 1874/1999, 20 April 1999), citing *In re J (a minor)* [1990] 2 AC 562.
[49] *BLW v BWL* [2007] 2 HKLRD 193 [31]; *ZC v CN* [2014] 5 HKLRD 43 [8.1].
[50] *BLW v BWL* (n 49) [31].

(ii) although it is not necessary for an individual to remain continuously present in a particular country to retain habitual residence there, it is not possible to acquire habitual residence in one country while remaining throughout physically present in another;
(iii) where both parents have joint parental responsibility, neither of them can unilaterally change the habitual residence of the child by removing the child wrongfully and in breach of the other parent's rights;
(iv) the habitual residence of young children of parents who are living together is the same as the habitual residence of the parents; and
(v) while habitual residence can be lost in a single day, the assumption of habitual residence requires an appreciable period of time and a settled intention to reside in a particular place.

5

Substance and Procedure

This chapter discusses the distinction between substance and procedure, which is an important distinction in private international law.[1] However, there are some practical difficulties in understanding and applying that distinction.

I. Introduction

It is a well-accepted principle that matters of procedure in legal proceedings are governed by the domestic law of the courts of the jurisdiction seised. Such domestic law is also known as the *lex fori*, the law of the forum.[2] This may be contrasted with matters of substance, which are governed by the law to which the court is directed by its choice of law rules. This law is also known as the *lex causae*, the law of the cause, and is ascertained through the choice of law process.

While the distinction is evident, it is not always easy to apply in practice. In this context, 'procedure' has a specialised meaning. Traditionally, a wider meaning was given to 'procedure' to exclude the application of foreign law. The rationale was to limit the complexity of choice of law issues and to minimise the inconvenience in the forum's administration of justice. However, this approach implied that a different result might be reached if a matter were litigated in the court of the *lex causae* and thus promoted forum shopping. In *First Laser Ltd v Fujian Enterprises (Holdings) Co Ltd*, the Court of Final Appeal held:[3]

> In the past there has been a tendency to classify rules as procedural for the purposes of the conflict of laws if those rules are classified as procedural in cases without an international element. But the more modern, and preferable approach is to say that matters which affect the existence, extent or enforceability of the rights or duties of the parties to an action are matters that are concerned with issues of substance, not with issues of procedure: *John Pfeiffer Pty Ltd v Rogerson* (2000) 203 CLR 503 at 543.

Contemporary courts have therefore limited the ambit of 'procedure'. Matters which are clearly procedural in nature include

> the mode of commencing and pursing proceedings; rules as to the discovery, production, admissibility and assessment of documentary evidence; rules as to the form of witness evidence

[1] See also Richard Garnett, *Substance and Procedure in Private International Law* (Oxford University Press, 2012).

[2] Lord Collins of Mapesbury and Jonathan Harris (gen eds), *Dicey, Morris and Collins on the Conflict of Laws*, 16th edn (Sweet & Maxwell, 2022) para 4R-001.

[3] *First Laser Ltd v Fujian Enterprises (Holdings) Co Ltd* (2012) 15 HKCFAR 569 [95].

> (including such matters as depositions, witness statements and cross-examination); the mode of trial, other hearings and written procedures; the availability of costs orders; and the enforcement of judgments.[4]

But uncertainties remain as to the proper limits of the notion of 'procedure' in other areas.

II. Illustrations

A. Limitation Periods

Limitation periods are generally considered at common law to be a question of procedural law and not substantive law,[5] but in Hong Kong, this must also depend on whether the statute of limitation merely bars a remedy or extinguishes a right. Difficulties may arise in making this distinction, and special rules may apply in particular circumstances.[6] In *China Agri-Products Exchange Ltd v Wang Xiu Qun*, the Court of First Instance discussed this distinction in obiter:[7]

> 516. Under the conflict of laws rules, matter of procedure is governed by *lex fori* and matter of substance is governed by *lex causae*. As to the question on limitation, a distinction is drawn under the common law between two kinds of statutes of limitation: those which merely bar a remedy and those which extinguish a right. Statutes of the former kind are procedural, while statutes of the latter kind are substantive. This distinction remains applicable in Hong Kong where there is no equivalent of the Foreign Limitation Periods Act 1984 in the United Kingdom.
>
> 517. In considering foreign rules as to limitation, the English courts traditionally applied their own classification based on the distinction between barring a right and extinguishing a remedy. In other words, the classification is to be determined by reference to the *lex fori* and not the foreign law.
>
> 518. Difficulties can occur in deciding whether the true nature of the foreign rule is to bar a remedy or extinguish a right. Mr Ho suggests that in cases where a right of the relevant nature may in principle (i.e. not necessarily on the facts of the particular case) still be asserted defensively after expiry of the relevant period, for example by way of set-off, or to resist dispossession, then the foreign rule is clearly of a procedural nature, whereas if a right of that nature may in no circumstances be asserted, then it has in substance been extinguished and the relevant rule should be regarded as substantive: [citing *Johnston and Harris*, para 2.038].
>
> 519. In the Mainland limitation statutes cited by the Defendants, the limitation rule is formulated by reference to seeking relief from the people's court for protection of civil rights (向人民法院请求保护民事权利的诉讼时效期间). Adopting the same differentiating principle, the limitation statutes fall within the category of statutes barring a remedy, as opposed to extinguishing a right. As a result, the question of limitation period is a matter of procedure and should be governed by the *lex fori*, i.e. Hong Kong law.

[4] Graeme Johnston and Paul Harris, *The Conflict of Laws in Hong Kong*, 3rd edn (Sweet & Maxwell, 2017) para 2.013.

[5] *Peregrine Fixed Income Ltd v JP Morgan Chase Bank* [2005] 3 HKLRD 1 [31]; *Patrick James Joseph O'Mara v Chin Shau Tong* [2023] 1 HKC 387, [2022] HKCFI 3457 [11]–[14].

[6] In respect of debts of the estate of a deceased, the law of the administration applies: *BP Exploration Co (Libya) Ltd v Hunt (No 2)* [1982] 1 All ER 925. See also Johnston and Harris (n 4) para 2.038.

[7] *China Agri-Products Exchange Ltd v Wang Xiu Qun* [2021] HKCFI 137 [516]–[521].

> 520. It is trite that any defence of limitation under Hong Kong law must be expressly pleaded: [citing the Rules of the High Court (Cap 4A), Order 18, rule 8(1)]. In the absence of any plea of limitation periods under the Limitation Ordinance (Cap 347), the Defendants are not entitled to rely on any limitation defence.
>
> 521. Even if the limitation period is a matter of substantive law, the time limit for bringing a civil claim in the Mainland court can be extended in special circumstances, and so the Plaintiff's claim may not have been time-barred under Mainland law.

The distinction attempts to characterise the rules of limitation as substantive and procedural, and may therefore run into the problems of gap and culmination.[8] Moreover, if both laws apply (the foreign rule being substantive and the local rule being procedural), the claim will be defeated by the shorter of the two limitation periods. Statutory or judicial interventions in other common law jurisdictions abandoned the approach and directed the courts to apply the limitation period of the substantive claim.[9] That reform is yet to come in Hong Kong.[10]

B. Capacity and Bars to be Sued

Whether a party can be sued in the Hong Kong courts is a procedural matter for the Hong Kong courts, and hence Hong Kong law applies as the *lex fori*.[11] Where a foreign law prevents particular persons from commencing an action against each other, the matter should be regarded as substantive in nature. This is distinguished from bars on actions against foreign states and their agents, which are matters for the *lex fori*.[12]

C. Evidence

Matters of evidence are generally regarded as procedural in nature. Admissibility of evidence to prove facts is therefore usually a matter for the *lex fori*. However, there are exceptions, particularly where an evidential rule is 'not … to further the establishment of the legally relevant facts but, rather, to define the facts which are deemed to be legally relevant to a particular matter'.[13] For instance, rules relating to the admissibility of evidence that is intended to assist in the interpretation of a written contract or other instrument are substantive. Such rules define legally relevant facts. Issues of admissibility are most likely to arise where there are issues of 'implied terms, collateral contracts, estoppel by convention or rectification'.[14]

[8] See ch 3, s I.

[9] See, eg Foreign Limitation Periods Act 1984 (UK); Foreign Limitation Periods Act 2012 (Singapore); *Tolofsen v Jensen* [1994] 3 SCR 1022 (Canada); *John Pfeiffer Pty Ltd v Rogerson* (2000) 203 CLR 503 (Australia).

[10] See also Alan Gibb and King Fung Tsang, 'Conflicting Limitation Periods: A Comparison Between Hong Kong and Mainland China' (2021) 5(1) *Cardozo International and Comparative Law Review* 1.

[11] *ING Bank NV v Industrial and Commercial Bank of China Ltd* [2024] HKCFI 2220 [67].

[12] Johnston and Harris (n 4) para 2.044.

[13] ibid para 2.016.

[14] ibid para 2.017.

Additionally, burdens of proof, as well as irrebuttable[15] and rebuttable[16] presumptions, are likely to be substantive in nature. Such rules have an impact on the outcome of cases and cannot be applied in isolation from the substantive rules with which they interact. However, this should be distinguished from the standard of proof, which was suggested to be a procedural matter as it is 'simply an aspect of the machinery by which a court determines facts already deemed legally relevant'.[17]

Most species of estoppel (proprietary estoppel, promissory estoppel and estoppel by convention) are matters of substance, despite some commentators labelling estoppel as a 'rule of evidence'. Indeed, estoppels will generally relate to a wider body of substantive law.[18] For example, promissory estoppel may be pleaded in connection with a contractual issue. Thus, the law of the main issue to which an estoppel relates should govern the matter.[19] Notably, though, issue estoppels based on foreign judgments are procedural matters governed by the *lex fori*.[20]

D. Remedies

The availability of non-monetary remedies, such as injunctions and declarations, is procedural in nature. As such, remedies may raise issues of personal freedom and security of property; a Hong Kong court's remedial discretion should remain unfettered by foreign law. However, the basic principle is that any remedies sought in the forum court must 'harmonise with the right according to its nature and extent as fixed by the foreign law'.[21]

The issue is less clear in relation to damages. Issues such as heads of damages, causation, remoteness, mitigation and contributory negligence tend to be substantive,[22] whereas the quantification of damages is usually procedural.[23] It was suggested that the award of exemplary damages should generally be regarded as a procedural matter for the *lex fori*.[24] It is likely that caps on liability are substantive, departing from the earlier position that they are procedural.[25]

As for equitable remedies, given that equity jurisprudence has rapidly developed into a body of substantive law from a system of remedies, it may now be regarded as substantive matters. However, some cases may still present difficulties, such as equitable tracing.[26]

As for matters concerning interest, the right to claim interest is generally substantive, while the power to award interest is procedural.[27]

[15] *Re Cohn* [1945] Ch 5.

[16] See, eg *Bank of Africa Ltd v Cohen* [1909] 2 Ch 129 (presumption of undue influence); *Damberg v Damberg* (2001) 52 NSWLR 492 (presumption of resulting trust and presumption of advancement of property).

[17] Johnston and Harris (n 4) para 2.020.

[18] See eg *First Laser Ltd* (n 3) [90]–[106].

[19] Johnston and Harris (n 4) para 2.022.

[20] ibid. See also ch 23, s I.

[21] *Phrantzes v Argenti* [1960] 2 QB 19, 35.

[22] See *Livesley v Horst Co* [1924] SCR 605; *Boys v Chaplin* [1971] AC 356.

[23] But see *John Pfeiffer Pty Ltd* (n 9) [102]–[103]; *Goh Suan Hee v Teo Cher Teck* [2010] 1 SLR 367 [16]–[22].

[24] Johnston and Harris (n 4) para 2.027.

[25] See, eg *John Pfeiffer Pty Ltd* (n 9); *Harding v Wealands* [2004] EWCA Civ 1735, [2005] 1 WLR 1539.

[26] *Rappo, Tania v Accent Delight International Ltd* [2017] 2 SLR 265 [107]–[108]; contra *Byers v Saudi National Bank* [2023] UKSC 51, [2024] AC 1191 [68].

[27] *Maher v Groupama Grand Est* [2009] EWCA Civ 1191, [2010] 1 WLR 1564.

E. Set-offs

Where a set-off is an absolute defence to a plaintiff's claim, it should be classified as substantive.[28] An example is where a set-off is pleaded as defence against a claim such that the court refuses to make an order for summary judgment.

However, if a set-off is a counterclaim that the defendant has against a plaintiff and which the court may or may not allow the defendant to raise in the same proceedings as the plaintiff's claim, it is procedural in nature. Examples include the set-off of a liquidated amount due to the defendant from the plaintiff[29] or the set-off of an unliquidated amount said to be due to the defendant in a matter which may be related or unrelated to the plaintiff's claim.[30]

F. Priorities between Creditors

Where an issue of priority arises between creditors *inter se*, the matter will be governed by the *lex fori* regardless of the specific laws which may govern the creditors' individual respective claims, save to the extent of establishing the existence of the debt.[31]

[28] *Macfarlane v Norris* (1862) 2 B&S 783; *Meridien BIAO Bank GmbH v Bank of New York* [1997] 1 Lloyd's Rep 437.

[29] Sometimes referred to as a 'legal set-off'.

[30] Sometimes referred to as an 'equitable set-off'.

[31] *Cook v Gregson* (1854) 2 Drew 286, 61 ER 729 (insolvent estates); *Ex p Melbourn* (1870–71) LR 6 Ch App 64 (bankruptcy).

6

Foreign Law*

Pleading and proving foreign law is a fundamental and important issue in legal disputes and proceedings, particularly cross-border commercial cases.[1] At times, establishing foreign law directly establishes the parties' legal rights and duties.[2] Approaches towards the proof of foreign law may affect the parties' choice of forum, their readiness to settle, the cost and duration of proceedings, and the way in which a case is argued. There may be a higher litigation risk for parties if proof of foreign law in a jurisdiction involves considerable uncertainty.[3]

I. Introduction

Hong Kong courts frequently hear disputes which may not be closely connected with Hong Kong and which may be governed by foreign law. At common law, a judge may be called upon to apply foreign law.[4] Matters of procedure are governed by domestic law (*lex fori*). This would be Hong Kong law. In contrast, matters of substance are governed by the law to which the court is directed by its choice of law rules (*lex causae*). This may or may not be Hong Kong law.[5]

Most choice of law rules in Hong Kong originated from the common law. The application of choice of law rules may lead to the application of foreign law in certain circumstances. Unless there are overriding mandatory provisions, the Hong Kong court does not have a

* Part of this chapter is derived from Wilson Lui, 'Hong Kong' in Kazuaki Nishioka (ed), *Treatment of Foreign Law in Asia* (Hart Publishing, 2023) 25–50.

[1] Pleading and proving foreign law is also important for non-commercial cases. For example, in Hong Kong, where a surrogacy arrangement and/or birth takes place outside Hong Kong, expert evidence should be adduced to show, at least, whether or not surrogacy is permitted in that foreign jurisdiction, and how the law defines the legal relationship amongst the surrogate mother, her husband, the child and the commissioning parents; this would assist the court on the issue of whether there has been abuse of public policy: see *Re A and B* [2019] 5 HKLRD 366, [2019] HKCFI 1749. In cases involving the Law of the People's Republic of China on Safeguarding National Security in the Hong Kong Special Administrative Region (the National Security Law, NSL), it was thought that the relevant substantial law of Mainland China may inform the construction of the NSL or a particular NSL provision: *HKSAR v Lui Sai Yu* [2023] 1 HKLRD 751, [2022] HKCA 1780 [87]–[89]. This submission was rejected by the Court of Final Appeal: *HKSAR v Lui Sai Yu* (2023) 26 HKCFAR 332, [2023] HKCFA 26 [43]–[48].

[2] Richard Fentiman, 'Laws, Foreign Laws, and Facts' (2006) 59(1) *Current Legal Problems* 391, 404.

[3] Adopting the risk analysis in Richard Fentiman, *International Commercial Litigation*, 2nd edn (Oxford University Press, 2015).

[4] Alex Mills, 'Arbitral Jurisdiction and the Mischievous Presumption of Identity of Foreign Law' (2008) 67(1) *CLJ* 25, 25; Adrian Briggs, *Private International Law in English Courts*, 2nd edn (Oxford University Press, 2023) 26.

[5] The distinction between substance and procedure is not always easy to make. See ch 5.

preference as to whether it will apply foreign law or not.[6] In Hong Kong, questions of foreign law are treated as questions of fact (albeit described as special questions of fact), which a party is at liberty to raise or not. Any foreign law pleaded by the parties is usually proved by expert evidence. A Hong Kong court is generally not allowed to introduce or apply foreign law on its own motion.[7]

Hong Kong law regards Mainland (PRC) law,[8] Macao law[9] and Taiwan law[10] as foreign law. Chinese customary law may be directly applied to Chinese persons domiciled in Hong Kong as it is incorporated into Hong Kong domestic law through Article 8 of the Basic Law.[11] But a Hong Kong court can (and usually will) rely on expert evidence when parties plead and prove Chinese customary law.[12] Nonetheless, it is not always necessary to adduce expert evidence to determine questions of fact pertaining to Chinese customary law.[13]

II. Foreign Law in Courts

A. Nature of Foreign Law

As stated by the Hong Kong Court of Final Appeal, 'expert evidence of foreign law, although a matter of fact, will be treated differently to other, ordinary, findings of fact'.[14] Thus, foreign law is treated by the courts of Hong Kong as a question of fact to be ascertained by a process of pleading and proof involving expert witnesses. The latter are usually examined and cross-examined at trial.[15]

[6] See ch 8, s I.

[7] For an interesting historical account on how English courts 'ascertain' foreign law as law (not as fact), by consultation or certification (not by sworn expert evidence), see JH Baker, 'Ascertainment of Foreign Law: Certification to and by English Courts Prior to 1861' (1979) 28(1) *ICLQ* 141.

[8] *Ding Shu Ju v Chu Sai Keung* [2021] HKCA 626 [42.1] ('This is because the PRC and Hong Kong have different legal systems, and as such, PRC law is regarded as foreign law which has to be proved by expert evidence.'). There had been some confusion in an early post-handover case: *Nan Tung Bank Ltd, Zhu Hai v Wangfoong Transportation Ltd* [1999] 2 HKC 606 [13] ('In fact, Mainland law can no longer be strictly said to be foreign law after the resumption of the exercise of sovereignty over Hong Kong'). In a similar vein, a Mainland judgment is considered a foreign judgment and will be enforced or recognised in Hong Kong only if it fulfils the conditions under the Mainland Judgments (Reciprocal Enforcement) Ordinance (Cap 597), the Mainland Judgments in Civil and Commercial Matters (Reciprocal Enforcement) Ordinance (Cap 645) or common law. For a detailed analysis of recognition and enforcement of foreign judgments in Hong Kong, see ch 23.

[9] See, eg *MGM Grand Paradise Ltd v Wong Sing Wa* (unreported, HCA 2140/2011, 21 May 2012) [17]; *MGM Grand Paradise Ltd v Chiu Tak Wah* (unreported, HCA 259/2012, 8 October 2012) [57]–[59]; *Venetian Macau Ltd v Chen Mei Huan* (unreported, HCA 1440/2012, 27 January 2014) [50].

[10] See, eg *Robin Hargreaves v Taian Insurance Co Ltd* [2006] 3 HKLRD 70.

[11] Art 8 reads: 'The laws previously in force in Hong Kong, that is, the common law, rules of equity, ordinances, subordinate legislation and customary law shall be maintained, except for any that contravene this Law, and subject to any amendment by the legislature of the Hong Kong Special Administrative Region.'

[12] *Suen Toi Lee v Yau Yee Ping* (2001) 4 HKCFAR 474 [28]–[38]; *Tang Tak Sum v Tang Kai Fong* [2015] 1 HKLRD 286 [24]–[27]. See ch 19.

[13] *Wong Zhong Lan Xiang v Wong Frank* [2003] 4 HKC 609 [41]–[43]; *Fung Ying Cheung v Yip Woon Yung* [2019] HKCFI 1818 [20]–[28].

[14] *Zhang Hong Li v DBS Bank (Hong Kong) Ltd* (2019) 22 HKCFAR 392, [2019] HKCFA 45 [97(c)].

[15] ibid [95], citing Graeme Johnston and Paul Harris, *The Conflict of Laws in Hong Kong*, 3rd edn (Sweet & Maxwell, 2017) para 2.060. See also, eg *Szeto Wing Hong v Maintown Industries Ltd* [2021] HKCFI 179 [63].

The question of foreign law is addressed only if a party pleads it. The burden of proving foreign law lies on the party who bases a claim or defence upon it.[16] The party must show that it has a good claim or defence under that foreign law.[17] If a party opts not to adduce foreign law evidence on a matter, the court will proceed on the basis that there is no difference between foreign law and Hong Kong law on that matter.[18]

This does not mean that whenever a claim is governed by foreign law it is necessary for the claimant to plead and prove the material content of that law (or indeed, as a logically prior matter, to plead a case as to governing law at all).[19] If no foreign law is pleaded, then a case with foreign elements will be decided as though it were a purely domestic case, through applying the 'default rule'. This is different from the situation where the parties have pleaded but failed to prove foreign law, where a 'presumption' of similarity between the foreign law and the *lex fori* will apply. The distinction between failing to plead foreign law at all, and pleading but not proving foreign law, is discussed in more detail in section II.C below.

B. Ascertainment of Foreign Law

(i) How can the Court Ascertain Foreign Law?

A court is generally not qualified to decide an issue of foreign law without the assistance of a foreign law expert.[20] There is no principle of *iura novit curia* (the court knows the law) in Hong Kong. Therefore, Hong Kong courts cannot take judicial notice of foreign law, even if that law is notorious.[21] A court also cannot introduce issues of foreign law on its own motion.[22] It is considered wrong for the court to conduct its own research into issues of foreign law, regardless of whether such issues have or have not been raised by the parties.[23] As Hong Kong courts are not at liberty to introduce foreign law, there is currently no mechanism for them to ascertain foreign law through making enquiries of domestic or foreign institutions, whether judicial or non-judicial, or through direct communication with foreign judges. Moreover, it is not possible, and indeed is incorrect, for parties to fill the evidentiary vacuum of foreign law by way of counsel submissions in Hong Kong.[24] Whether

[16] *Wang Qian Wei v 郭文雨* [2019] 1 HKC 413, [2018] HKCFI 2253 [35].

[17] *Brownlie v FS Cairo (Nile Plaza) LLC* [2021] UKSC 45, [2022] AC 995 [116].

[18] *Madison Communications Private Ltd v Le Ecosystem Technology India Private Ltd* [2017] 5 HKLRD 284 [64].

[19] *Iranian Offshore Engineering and Construction Co v Dean Investment Holdings SA* [2018] EWHC 2759 (Comm), [2019] 1 WLR 82 [3].

[20] *Kaefer AG v Winfield Marine Services Co Ltd* [2021] HKDC 656 [93].

[21] *Lazard Brothers & Co v Midland Bank Ltd* [1933] AC 289, 297–98, approved in *Hong Jing Co Ltd v Zhuhai Kwok Yuen Investment Co Ltd* [2013] 1 HKLRD 441 [73]. But see *Saxby v Fulton* [1909] 2 KB 208, 211 ('it is notorious that at Monte Carlo roulette is not an unlawful game'). The English courts seem to welcome the idea of taking judicial notice of decisions of foreign courts (and perhaps academic writings) in deciding what the relevant foreign law is: *Morgan Grenfell & Co Ltd v SACE – Istituto per I Servizi Assicurativi del Commercio* [2001] EWCA Civ 1932 [53]; HM Courts & Tribunals Service, *The Commercial Court Guide*, revised 11th edn (2023) para H.3.3(d), www.judiciary.uk/wp-content/uploads/2023/06/14.341_JO_Commercial_Court_Guide_FINAL.pdf.

[22] *Caspian Resources Development Pte Ltd v Fortune Oil plc* [2015] 5 HKLRD 836 [31]. As for the rationale behind such a policy, Johnston and Harris (n 15) para 2.061 noted that: 'There is simply no established machinery for the ascertainment of points of foreign law which the parties have not raised, and it seems most unjust for the court to raise a point which it has (or thinks it has) identified and demand that the parties address it.'

[23] *Bumper Development Corp v Commissioner of Police of the Metropolis* [1991] 1 WLR 1362, 1371.

[24] *Lim Yi Shenn v Wong Yuen Yee* [2012] 3 HKLRD 505 [60].

there is a future possibility for Hong Kong to depart from these practices is discussed in section IV below.

Lord Leggatt recently suggested in the UK Supreme Court case of *Brownlie v FS Cairo (Nile Plaza) LLC* (*Brownlie (No 2)*, but simply known as *Brownlie* in this chapter) that there should be more flexibility in the nature of procedures available to ascertain the content of foreign law:[25]

> The old notion that foreign legal materials can only ever be brought before the court as part of the evidence of an expert witness is outdated. Whether the court will require evidence from an expert witness should depend on the nature of the issue and of the relevant foreign law. In an age when so much information is readily available through the internet, there may be no need to consult a foreign lawyer in order to find the text of a relevant foreign law. On some occasions the text may require skilled exegesis of a kind which only a lawyer expert in the foreign system of law can provide. But in other cases it may be sufficient to know what the text says.

Whether this approach will be adopted in Hong Kong is untested, not least because, at the time of writing, no Hong Kong case has addressed this aspect of *Brownlie*. However, the English courts have enthusiastically embraced Lord Leggatt's suggestion. For instance, the Privy Council approved the Cayman Court of Appeal's approach to consider the text of the foreign legislation and case law directly in discerning the content of the applicable foreign law.[26] The English Court of Appeal even suggested that the examples given in *Brownlie* – foreign legal texts and online translations of foreign legal materials – are not 'exhaustive of the sources of evidence on which a court might draw' in working out the content of the applicable foreign law.[27] The latest edition of the *Commercial Court Guide* edited by the judges of the Commercial Court of England and Wales provides detailed guidance on their current approach towards expert evidence on foreign law, which has been influenced by *Brownlie*.[28]

There is much to be said in favour of Lord Leggatt's approach.[29] After all, the Hong Kong courts recognise that they are 'entitled, indeed bound, to contribute [their] own legal skill and experience in reaching [their] conclusions on foreign law'.[30] With the ease by which foreign legal materials can be accessed in light of technological advances, there is no reason to impose an absolute bar on judges consulting such materials in the absence of expert evidence. This is even more so if the foreign legal issues concerned are of a nature familiar to Hong Kong courts, such as those of other common law systems. In *Perry v Lopag Trust Reg (No 2)*, the Privy Council suggested a 'spectrum approach' which may find applicability in Hong Kong.[31] At one end of the spectrum are cases 'in which the foreign law is a common law system which applies the same or analogous principles and means of legal analysis' as Hong Kong law. In these cases, there will be considerable scope for the trial judge to use his or her legal skills and experience in domestic law in determining and applying the foreign

[25] *Brownlie* (n 17) [148], applied in eg *Suppipat v Narongdej* [2022] EWHC 1806 (Comm).

[26] *Gol Linhas Aereas SA v MatlinPatterson Global Opportunities Partners (Cayman) II LP* [2022] UKPC 21, [2022] 2 All ER (Comm) 841 [46]–[47].

[27] *Soriano v Forensic News LLC* [2021] EWCA Civ 1952, [2022] QB 533 [64].

[28] *Commercial Court Guide* (n 21). See also s IV below.

[29] Contrast the scepticism expressed in Briggs (n 4) 38–39.

[30] *MCC Proceeds Inc v Bishopgate Investment Trust plc* [1999] CLC 417 [13]; *Shenzhen Development Bank Co Ltd v New Century International (Holdings) Ltd* (unreported, HCA 2976/2001, 31 July 2002) [25]–[27]; *Hong Jing Co Ltd* (n 21) [110].

[31] *Perry v Lopag Trust Reg (No 2)* [2023] UKPC 16, [2023] 1 WLR 3494.

law. At the other end of spectrum are cases of disputed foreign law 'in which the skill and experience of the judge in domestic law has a minimal role to play in the ascertainment and application of foreign law', dependent on the evidence of expert witnesses. In these cases, the trial judge's findings on the content and application of foreign law 'have a close kinship' to other findings of fact. The 'spectrum approach' also has impact on appeals against findings of foreign law, discussed in section II.D below.

(ii) Expert Evidence

With the assistance of expert evidence, the courts of Hong Kong are in a position to apply foreign law.[32] The approach which the Hong Kong courts adopt in assessing expert evidence of foreign law is essentially the same as with other types of expert evidence. The adducing of such evidence is subject to civil procedure rules, as well as cross-examination. In particular, experts owe an overriding duty to the court.[33] They should not be biased or act as 'hired guns'. Moreover, as long as foreign law evidence is submitted in good time ahead of a trial so that the parties have had ample opportunity to respond to the same, there cannot be any complaint of unfairness.[34]

In interlocutory applications, foreign law may have to be determined without pleading.[35] For interlocutory matters, evidence of foreign law can be given by affidavit. This is because

> [i]n practice, the Hong Kong courts are more relaxed because of the interlocutory nature and urgency. The courts often rely for interlocutory purposes upon unsworn letters or opinions exhibited to an affidavit of the adducing party's solicitor. However, evidence in that form may, in the court's discretion, be given somewhat lesser weight in cases of doubt.[36]

As such evidence is not subject to cross-examination, judges have encountered difficulties in resolving issues of foreign law in interlocutory hearings.[37] Failure to plead foreign law in the statement of claim when it is plain and obvious that foreign law should apply constitutes a material non-disclosure and may sometimes justify a discharge of *ex parte* leave to serve a writ abroad.[38]

Moreover, for cases that involve foreign law, the procedure in Order 14A of the Rules of the High Court (Cap 4A) (RHC) is not appropriate. Order 14A concerns the court's power to dispose summarily of an action by determining a point of law without a full trial of the action. But the court cannot rely on an expert opinion on foreign law, which is a question of fact, to decide a point of law. It would simply be impossible for the court to determine foreign law issues summarily.[39] When the plaintiff disputes the applicability or thrust of foreign law, the court cannot simply determine the application on assumed facts and would

[32] *Mehta v Mehta* [2007] 2 HKLRD 520 [39], applied in *China Shanshui Cement Group Ltd v Tianrui (International) Holding Co Ltd* [2020] HKCFI 3043 [65(d)].

[33] Rules of the High Court (Cap 4A), Ord 38, r 35A.

[34] *China NPL Holdings Pte Ltd v Mo Haidan* [2021] 1 HKLRD 344, [2020] HKCA 1014 [96].

[35] ibid [96]. For the English practice, see, eg *Commercial Court Guide* (n 21) para F.8.10.

[36] *Agritrade Resources Ltd v Ashok Kumar Sahoo* [2021] HKCFI 685 [26].

[37] See, eg *The Polessk* [1996] 2 Lloyd's Rep 40; *The Spirit of Independence* [1999] 1 Lloyd's Rep 43.

[38] *Tremendous Success Holdings Ltd v Sinosoft Technology Group* (unreported, HCA 2345/2013, 11 July 2016) [19]–[47].

[39] *Nativivat v Nativivat* [2012] 3 HKLRD 747 [27]–[28]; *Nagravision SA v Zhuhai Gotech Intelligent Technology Co Ltd* [2020] HKCFI 1422 [20]–[21].

need to resolve the conflicts in the expert evidence.[40] It would be counterproductive if, in the course of the Order 14A procedure, the court finds that it has to hear oral evidence to determine questions of fact or foreign law. The court cannot ignore such potential risks and it would be safer for the court to conduct the trial in the conventional manner.[41]

Under Hong Kong law, there are no specific requirements on the formal qualifications of an expert. Section 59(1) of the Evidence Ordinance (Cap 8) (EO) provides:

> A person who is suitably qualified to do so on account of his knowledge or experience is competent to give, in civil proceedings, expert evidence as to the law of any country or territory outside Hong Kong, irrespective of whether he has acted or is entitled to act as a legal practitioner there.

The burden is on the party adducing that person's evidence to establish that the person is 'suitably qualified to do so on account of his knowledge or experience'.[42] Thus, despite the broad formulation of section 59(1), parties will usually appoint experts who are sufficiently competent and credible to give evidence on foreign law, considering their qualifications and achievements. Such persons will usually be a lawyer, a retired judge, an academic or a person *peritus virtute officii* (the holder of an official position which requires and therefore implies legal knowledge). Moreover, evidence on foreign law must be given in the capacity as an expert. In the context of criminal law, the Court of Appeal held that whether gambling was unlawful in Myanmar is a question of foreign law, which must be proved by expert evidence. The second prosecution witness, a police officer, was not tendered or regarded as an expert, and his opinion on the illegality under Myanmar law therefore could not support the conviction.[43]

In trials, when there is a dispute over foreign law, a party has to seek expert evidence to prove or dispute the contested points. In Hong Kong, it is common to appoint separate experts for matters of foreign law. But, after the Civil Justice Reform, the courts have encouraged the use of a single joint expert as 'the growing trend' and 'the mainstream in modern litigation'.[44] The task of a foreign law expert is to provide assistance on matters of foreign law. The functions of the expert are:[45]

(i) to inform the court of the relevant contents of the foreign law, identifying statutes or other legislation and explaining, where necessary, the foreign court's approach to their construction;
(ii) to identify judgments or other authorities, explaining what status they have as sources of the foreign law; and
(iii) where there is no authority directly on point, to assist the judge in making a finding as to what the foreign court's ruling would be if the issue were to arise for decision there.

[40] *G H Property Holdings Ltd v Able Profit Investment Ltd* [2018] HKCFI 2480 [26].
[41] *Nagravision SA* (n 39) [28].
[42] *TJB v DMT* [2022] HKCA 1223 [15.2].
[43] Criminal Procedure Ordinance (Cap 221), s 65DA; *HKSAR v Tam Hung* (unreported, CACC 127/2010, 27 July 2011) [19]–[28].
[44] *Peace Mark (Holdings) Ltd (in liq) v Chau Cham Wong Patrick* (unreported, HCA 2371/2009, 2 November 2017) [35]–[64]. See also *ING Bank NV v Industrial and Commercial Bank of China Ltd* [2024] HKCFI 2220 [79]–[81].
[45] *MCC Proceeds Inc* (n 30) [23]–[24]. See also *Guangzhou Green-Enhan Bio-Engineering Co Ltd v Green Power Health Products International Co Ltd* [2004] 3 HKLRD 223 [2(a)]; *Hung Fung Enterprises Holdings Ltd v Agricultural Bank of China* [2012] 3 HKLRD 679 [58].

It is the third function that gives scope for opinion evidence, which is the basic role of the expert witness. The purpose for which this evidence is given is to predict the likely decision of a foreign court, rather than to press upon the judge the expert witness's personal views as to what the foreign law might be. In fact, where there is authority directly in point, there is little room for experts to give evidence to determine the likely outcome of the foreign court applying the foreign law, 'unless … there are conflicting decisions in the foreign court or where it is clear that a piece of relevant legislation had not been considered'.[46]

Foreign law experts are obliged to set out not only their conclusion, but also the source materials, legal principles and process of reasoning leading to that conclusion.[47] Opinions on foreign law simply consisting of assertions for which no basis is established on the face of the opinion are unlikely to carry serious weight.[48] No weight is given to suggestions that the opinion is correct through inquiring and confirming with some unspecified person.[49]

There is a difference in the expert's role in relation to foreign legislation and an instrument or document governed by foreign law. While an expert is entitled to give an opinion on foreign legislation, it is the court which applies the foreign legislation and determines the interpretation, effect or validity of the instrument or document, based on submissions from the parties. The expert's role is simply to give an opinion as to the relevant foreign rules governing the dispute.[50]

In addition to expert reports, the court is entitled to draw on its knowledge of the common law and of the rules of statutory construction insofar as the latter may have a bearing on the resolution of a dispute.[51]

Moreover, as a common law jurisdiction and as stated in Article 84 of the Basic Law, Hong Kong courts are at liberty to refer to other common law cases as persuasive authorities when deciding matters of Hong Kong law. In such references, no expert evidence is required to 'prove' foreign law. Counsel can directly cite these authorities, preferably in an official reported format, to support their propositions. What weight (if any) is to be given to these authorities is a matter for the court.

If foreign law is pleaded by one party and admitted by the other party, this constitutes an admission. No further evidence will be admissible on the question of foreign law.

If all parties agree, and the trial court does not consider it inappropriate, then the court may apply foreign statutes directly without any expert evidence, or directly refer to law reports and even textbooks.[52] In these 'consent' cases, it is more difficult for an appellate court to interfere with the findings on foreign law.

[46] *National Bank of Egypt International Ltd v Oman Housing Bank SAOC* [2002] EWHC 1760, cited in *Guangzhou Green-Enhan Bio-Engineering Co Ltd* (n 45) [2(b)], [3].

[47] *Newmark Capital Corp Ltd v Coffee Partners Ltd* [2007] 1 HKLRD 718 [47].

[48] *GM Commercial Consultants Corp v Euro-Asia Zhong Ji (HK) Ltd* [2021] HKCFI 1378 [64]–[65]. See also Johnston and Harris (n 15) para 2.067.

[49] *The Adhiguna Meranti* [1986] HKLR 487 [72]–[73], where the expert claimed to have 'made inquiries at the Supreme Court of the Republic of Indonesia and have been advised that my opinion on this issue, is correct'.

[50] ibid [31].

[51] See n 30 above. For example, in *Re Lee Yang, Shiu Chuen Joyce* [2021] 4 HKLRD 252, [2021] HKCFI 2468 [20], after the party failed to adduce evidence of British Virgin Islands (BVI) law, the judge referred to s 220(1) of the Business Companies Act 2004 (BVI) to establish the principle that the Attorney-General of the BVI should be joined as the respondent and that the failure to do so is a procedural irregularity. See also the deduction process in *Lim Yi Shenn* (n 24) [61]–[69].

[52] *Celltech Chiroscience Ltd v Medimmune Inc* [2002] EWHC 2167 (Patents) [8]; Johnston and Harris (n 15) para 2.070, citing *Jabbour v Custodian of Israeli Absentee Property* [1954] 1 WLR 139.

(iii) The Effect of Expert Evidence on Judicial Authorities

The court is not bound to accept all expert evidence adduced on foreign law. The general approach is set out in the Court of Final Appeal case of *Traffic Steam Infrastructure Co Ltd v Full Wisdom Holding Ltd*.[53] Thus, even if the expert evidence on foreign law is uncontradicted, 'the court will examine the content … and will reject it as unsatisfactory if the circumstances so warrant'.[54] In assessing the validity of an opinion on foreign law, the court will not simply accept any conclusions of foreign law as correct. The court is entitled to evaluate the legal reasoning to determine what weight should be attached to the opinion and, if necessary, to examine the foreign sources to form its own conclusion as to their effect.[55]

(iv) Foreign Law Based on a Court Decision

In addition to expert evidence, a finding of foreign law based on a court decision can also be evidence of foreign law. However, a decision by a Hong Kong or English court as to foreign law is not binding as a precedent in the face of a later decision of the Hong Kong court. This is because questions of foreign law are questions of fact which can be disputed in each case.[56] There can also be changes in the foreign law over time. However, if the Hong Kong court has determined a question of foreign law under specified proceedings, that determination is admissible as evidence in a later case to establish foreign law, unless the contrary is proved. In Hong Kong, section 59 of the EO provides that:

> (2) Where any question as to the law of any country or territory outside Hong Kong with respect to any matter has been determined (whether before or after the commencement of this Part) in any such proceedings as are mentioned in subsection (4), then in any civil proceedings (not being proceedings before a court which can take judicial notice of the law of that country or territory with respect to that matter) –
>
> (a) any finding made or decision given on that question in the first-mentioned proceedings shall, if reported or recorded in citable form, be admissible in evidence for the purpose of proving the law of that country or territory with respect to that matter; and
>
> (b) if that finding or decision, as so reported or recorded, is adduced for that purpose, the law of that country or territory with respect to that matter shall be taken to be in accordance with that finding or decision unless the contrary is proved:
>
> Provided that paragraph (b) shall not apply in the case of a finding or decision which conflicts with another finding or decision on the same question adduced by virtue of this subsection in the same proceedings.
>
> (3) Except with the leave of the court, a party to any civil proceedings shall not be permitted to adduce any such finding or decision as is mentioned in subsection (2) by virtue of that subsection

[53] *Traffic Stream Infrastructure Co Ltd v Full Wisdom Holdings Ltd* (2004) 7 HKCFAR 442 [21]–[22]; *Zhang Hong Li* (n 14) [96].

[54] *Zhang Hong Li* (n 14) [97(d)].

[55] See, eg *Full Wisdom Holdings Ltd v Traffic Stream Infrastructure Co Ltd* [2004] 2 HKLRD 1016 [23]; *Traffic Stream Infrastructure Co Ltd* (n 53) [21]; *Newmark Capital Corp Ltd* (n 47) [49]; *Employees for Whom Zhang Caikui is Holding Shares in China Shanshui Investment Co Ltd v Zhang Caikui* [2017] 5 HKLRD 240 [40]–[41]; *Zhang Hong Li* (n 14) [96]; *GM Commercial Consultants Corp* (n 48) [64].

[56] *Seridom Servicios Integrados Idom SAU v Heng Wen Trade Co Ltd* [2019] HKCFI 85 [116], citing Johnston and Harris (n 15) para 2.060.

unless he has in accordance with rules given to every other party to the proceedings notice that he intends to do so.

(4) The proceedings referred to in subsection (2) are the following, whether civil or criminal, namely –

(a) proceedings at first instance in the High Court or in the Supreme Court of England as constituted by section 1 of the Courts Act 1971 (1971 c. 23 U.K.);
(b) appeals arising out of proceedings as are mentioned in paragraph (a);
(c) proceedings before the Court of Final Appeal.

(5) For the purposes of this section a finding or decision on any such question as is mentioned in subsection (2) shall be taken to be reported or recorded in citable form if, but only if, it is reported or recorded in writing in a report, transcript or other document which, if that question had been a question as to the law of Hong Kong, could be cited as an authority in legal proceedings in Hong Kong.

Order 38, rule 7 of the RHC provides that:[57]

7. Evidence of finding on foreign law (O. 38, r. 7)

(1) A party to any cause or matter who intends to adduce in evidence a finding or decision on a question of foreign law by virtue of section 59 of the Evidence Ordinance (Cap. 8) shall –

(a) in the case of an action to which Order 25, rule 1, applies within 28 days after the pleadings in the action are deemed to be closed, and
(b) in the case of any other cause or matter, within 21 days after the date on which an appointment for the first hearing of the cause or matter is obtained,

or in either case, within such other period as the Court may specify, serve notice of his intention on every other party to the proceedings.

(2) The notice shall specify the question on which the finding or decision was given or made and specify the document in which it is reported or recorded in citable form.

(3) In any cause or matter in which evidence may be given by affidavit, an affidavit specifying the matters contained in paragraph (2) shall constitute notice under paragraph (1) if served within the period mentioned in that paragraph.

The failure of a party to give notice of its intention to rely on foreign case law as required by section 59(3) of the EO and Order 38, rule 7 of the RHC may be fatal.[58] An extension of time may be granted upon application, although a late application is usually disallowed, particularly in light of the Civil Justice Reform and the unfairness it would inflict on the other party.

The section 59 mechanism provides an effective and economical way of proving foreign law in a case where there is or can be no substantial dispute as to foreign law. However, where there is a real dispute as to foreign law, expert evidence is usually employed, and this provision is seldom relied upon.

[57] The Rules of the District Court (Cap 336H), Ord 38, r 7 contains an identical provision.

[58] See, eg *Lesnina H DOO v Wave Shipping Trade Co Ltd* [2022] 2 HKLRD 727, [2022] HKCFI 1070, where one of the four Hong Kong decisions was excluded because the notice of intention was filed only a week before the hearing. That line of decisions (notably *DBS Bank (Hong Kong) Ltd v Pan Jing* [2020] 4 HKC 395, [2020] HKCFI 268 and *TTI Global Resources Hong Kong Ltd v Hongkong Myphone Technology Co Ltd* [2021] HKCFI 306) is frequently adduced by s 59 of the EO, which concerns 'underground banking' or 'underground money exchange transaction' in breach of Art 45 of the PRC's Administrative Regulations on Foreign Exchange and Arts 30 and 39 of the PRC's Foreign Exchanges Measures for Individuals.

C. Failure to Establish Foreign Law

On matters of fact generally, a party has the burden of adducing evidence to substantiate what it asserts. To plead but to not adduce evidence of what has been pleaded leaves a gap. In these cases, the court will proceed on the basis that the fact has not been established.

However, on matters of foreign law, the court cannot proceed if there is a gap, and an action cannot be dismissed simply because the contents of the foreign law and the elements of the cause of action are not established.[59]

'Any principle of foreign law or foreign legislative provision upon which a party's case is based must be clearly identified and the basis of its application explained.'[60] However, the parties are entitled to raise or not raise foreign law as they see fit. There can be situations where, even though a claim is theoretically governed by foreign law, a party opts not to plead foreign law.[61] If foreign law is not pleaded, that is, there is no allegation of foreign law, then Hong Kong law applies. A case with foreign elements will be decided as if it were a purely domestic case.

If a party pleads foreign law as a basis for the claim or defence, the burden of proving foreign law lies on that party. If foreign law is pleaded but not proved, that is, no evidence is adduced as to the content of the foreign law, there is a presumption[62] that the relevant foreign law is the same as Hong Kong law. In other words, in the absence of proof of foreign law despite pleading it, the Hong Kong courts will apply Hong Kong law *in place of* the foreign law.

The distinction between the default rule and the presumption of similarity was endorsed by the UK Supreme Court in *Brownlie v FS Cairo (Nile Plaza) LLC*, where Lord Leggatt summarised the position as follows:[63]

> [It is] preferable in the interests of clarity not to treat the terms 'presumption' and 'default rule' as interchangeable and to recognise that there are two different rules which are conceptually quite distinct. So too are their respective rationales. The presumption of similarity is a rule of evidence concerned with what the content of foreign law should be taken to be. By contrast, the 'default rule' … is not concerned with establishing the content of foreign law but treats English law as applicable in its own right where foreign law is not pleaded.

While Hong Kong has constantly applied the substance of the two rules,[64] it is suggested that a clear distinction must be made in Hong Kong between the default rule and the presumption of similarity as in *Brownlie*, to avoid the conflation between pleading and proving

[59] *Iranian Offshore Engineering and Construction Co* (n 19) [11].

[60] *Commercial Court Guide* (n 21) para C.1.3(f). See also *Iranian Offshore Engineering and Construction Co* (n 19) [11].

[61] *Iranian Offshore Engineering and Construction Co* (n 19) [20].

[62] It may be more appropriate to characterise this presumption as an evidential assumption to reflect its nature.

[63] *Brownlie* (n 17) [112]. Before *Brownlie* was decided, the default rule and the presumption of similarity were subsumed under a single rule in Lord Collins of Mapesbury (gen ed), *Dicey, Morris and Collins on the Conflict of Laws*, 15th edn (Sweet & Maxwell, 2012) para 9R-001. The rule is updated after *Brownlie*: Lord Collins of Mapesbury and Jonathan Harris (gen eds), *Dicey, Morris and Collins on the Conflict of Laws*, 16th edn (Sweet & Maxwell, 2022) para 3R-001. See also William Day, 'Pleading and Proving Foreign Law' (2022) 81(1) *CLJ* 24, 25.

[64] See, eg *Sera Ltd v Excelling Profit Investments Ltd* [1992] 2 HKC 262, 268H; *Li Yuen Ling v Tang Kwong Wai Thomas* [2010] 1 HKLRD 522 [26]; *China Metal Recycling (Holdings) Ltd (in compulsory liq) v Chun Chi Wai* [2021] HKCFI 378 [71]; *Ding Shu Ju* (n 8) [42.1].

foreign law.[65] The two rules act in mutual exclusiveness of each other. When a party does not plead foreign law, the default rule applies and there is no scope for the presumption of similarity to operate. On the other hand, the presumption of similarity only applies unless and until foreign law is pleaded but not proved.[66]

There are a few more observations on the application of the presumption of similarity. First, the presumption of similarity can be applied in most general cases, although it is subject to exceptions.[67] It may not be applicable where: (i) it is not in the interests of justice to apply the same; (ii) the foreign law is not based on the common law; (iii) the domestic law alters the common law; (iv) it is inherently improbable that foreign law is the same; and (v) fairness requires it.[68] Lord Leggatt in *Brownlie* reiterated that the application of the presumption is fact-specific, but proceeded to make a few observations: (i) the presumption is more likely to be appropriate where the applicable foreign law stems from a common law system rather than one based upon the civil law; (ii) the presumption is less likely to be appropriate where the relevant domestic law is contained in a statute; (iii) the procedural context should also be considered, with more scope for reliance at an early stage of proceedings versus at trial; and (iv) whether the presumption can be relied on may often be uncertain, but this is not problematic given that the reliance is always a matter of choice by the parties.[69]

Second, where a foreign statute is involved and there is a Hong Kong equivalent to that instrument, there has to be 'some degree of universality' between the foreign law statute and the *lex fori* statute.[70] Essentially, they have to be 'materially similar'.[71] For example, foreign company law is considered to be different across jurisdictions. In *Shaker*, the English Court of Appeal held that accounting provisions in the English Companies Act were not applicable to a Pennsylvanian company because: (i) the Companies Act only applied to companies incorporated under it; and (ii) it could not be expected that the Pennsylvanian company would comply with the accounting provisions under that Act.[72] Another example is foreign taxation law, where there is great reluctance to apply the presumption of similarity.[73] This is because revenue laws are more likely to vary significantly across different legal systems with different local economic, financial and societal conditions. The Hong Kong courts refused to assume that Taiwanese[74] and Russian tax laws[75] are similar to Hong Kong tax laws.

Third, it is suggested that it would be unjust to apply the presumption of similarity against a party whose liability depends on the foreign law which was pleaded but not proved

[65] For example, in *Caspian Resources Development Pte Ltd* (n 22) [30], 'the default rule concerns proof of foreign law and only applies when foreign law has been pleaded but not proved'. This should now be known as the 'presumption of similarity'. Johnston and Harris (n 15) para 2.075 also referred to the 'presumption of similarity' (in the *Brownlie* sense) as the 'default rule'.

[66] *Caspian Resources Development Pte Ltd* (n 22) [30].

[67] *Belhaj v Straw* [2014] EWCA Civ 1394, [2015] 2 WLR 1105 [157].

[68] *Balmoral Group Ltd v Borealis UK Ltd* [2006] EWHC 1900 (Comm) [428], [2006] 2 CLC 220, 347E–F, citing *Damberg v Damberg* (2001) 52 NSWLR 492.

[69] *Brownlie* (n 17) [144]–[147]. See also Day (n 63).

[70] *Capsian Resources Development Pte Ltd* (n 22) [30]–[37], citing *Shaker v Al-Bedrawi* [2002] EWCA Civ 1452, [2003] Ch 350. It seems that the notion of 'universality' is unduly uncertain and imprecise.

[71] *Brownlie* (n 17) [126].

[72] *Capsian Resources Development Pte Ltd* (n 22); *Shaker* (n 70) [67]–[68].

[73] *Damberg* (n 68) [162].

[74] *Igal Dafni v CMA CGM SA* [2013] 2 HKLRD 73 [42]–[48].

[75] *Autonomous Non-Commercial Organization 'Organizing Committee etc of 2014 Sochi Winter Olympics' v Pico Projects (International) Ltd* [2021] 2 HKLRD 246, [2021] HKCFI 606 [18].

by the other party,[76] or where fairness requires a claimant to establish its case positively, for example regarding allegations of fraud.[77]

Some criticisms have been made against the presumption of similarity, on the ground that it unfairly reverses the burden of proof.[78] For example, Fentiman has argued that the presumption is

> unacceptable … [allowing] a party to seek the application of foreign law and at the same time, with luminous inconsistency, to invite the court to apply [Hong Kong] law by declining to offer evidence of any other. It is also potentially unfair that one party should (in effect) be made to prove (or disprove) a matter which another has introduced.[79]

D. Appeal

The appellate court may interfere with findings of foreign law by the lower court. This is despite foreign law being treated as a fact by the courts of Hong Kong. The reasoning is that issues of foreign law are treated as facts 'of a peculiar kind'.[80] The UK Supreme Court noted

> the notion that the resolution of a dispute as to foreign law involves a factual finding rather than a legal conclusion is somewhat artificial, and in any event, the Judge did not hear any oral evidence from the expert foreign law witnesses. We are therefore in as good a position as he was to analyse the effect of the evidence as to foreign law.[81]

In *Perry*, the 'spectrum approach' was applied to determine the approach of the first appellate court against findings of foreign law.[82] For findings of foreign law in common law systems which apply the same or analogous principles and means of legal analysis, the first appellate court can also bring in their own skills and experience in domestic law. Otherwise, findings of foreign law which are highly dependent on the evidence of expert witnesses with a minimal role from the trial judge are considered concurrent findings of fact, and the first appellate court will be slow to intervene in the judge's assessment.

In Hong Kong, the general view is that appellate courts should be slow to interfere with a trial judge's finding on foreign law, although it is appropriate to adopt a more nuanced view:[83]

> The Court of Appeal should in appropriate cases be more ready to question the judge's conclusions on an issue of foreign law than it is on other questions of fact. But it should be extremely reluctant to substitute its own views where questions of credibility are concerned, since the judge has had the benefit of seeing and hearing the witnesses.

[76] *D'Oz International Pte Ltd v PSB Corp Pte Ltd* [2010] 3 SLR 267 [25].

[77] *Österreichische Länderbank v S'Elite Ltd* [1981] 1 QB 565.

[78] Anthony Gray, 'Choice of Law: The Presumption in the Proof of Foreign Law' (2008) 31(1) *UNSW Law Journal* 136.

[79] Richard Fentiman, *Foreign Law in English Courts* (Oxford University Press, 1998) 152–53.

[80] *Parkasho v Singh* [1968] P 233, 250, 254; *Bumper Development Corp* (n 23) 1370.

[81] *Actavis UK Ltd v Eli Lilly & Co* [2017] UKSC 48, [2018] 1 All ER 171 [93].

[82] *Perry* (n 31) [15].

[83] *Waddington Ltd v Chan Chun Hoo Thomas* [2016] HKCA 200 [139], citing *Grupo Torras SA v Sheik Fahad Mohammed Al Sabah* [1995] CLC 1025, 1037. See also *Mok Hing Chung v Wong Kwong Yiu* [2019] HKCA 452 [53].

In fact, the appellate court in Hong Kong has shown a readiness to question judges' conclusions on foreign law.[84] For example, the Court of Final Appeal in *Zhang Hong Li* held that it was not precluded from reaching conclusions contrary to the courts below on the issue of whether trustees owed certain equitable duties under Jersey law.[85]

It is submitted that there is no universal proposition that appellate courts should be slow to interfere with findings on foreign law. Given the nature of foreign law as 'quasi-legal' findings of fact, judges should be able to

> use [their] legal training where it has a bearing in determining such [issues], especially where the concepts are not very different from Hong Kong law, and where appropriate may form his own view as to the meaning of the statutes of another jurisdiction.[86]

III. Foreign Law in Arbitrations

It might be thought that foreign law in arbitral proceedings must be proved as fact through adducing expert evidence, just as in common law court proceedings. However, this is not a pragmatic and efficient approach in international arbitration. Instead,

> in almost all international arbitrations, 'law' is treated as 'law'. The relevant provisions of that law are then identified and substantiated either in written submissions by counsel (or by a lawyer experienced in that law acting as co-counsel), or by way of expert testimony in the form of an expert opinion by legal experts on the law in issue, with the possibility that those experts may be called as witnesses to explain their reasoning and conclusions.[87]

Similar observations have been made in Hong Kong, where 'it is common in arbitrations for some parties to seek to submit expert evidence of foreign law, while others assert that foreign law may be the subject of legal submissions by a party's advocate'.[88] Section 47(3) of the Arbitration Ordinance (Cap 609) provides arbitral tribunals with great flexibility in receiving evidence:

> When conducting arbitral proceedings, an arbitral tribunal is not bound by the rules of evidence and may receive any evidence that it considers relevant to the arbitral proceedings, but it must give the weight that it considers appropriate to the evidence adduced in the arbitral proceedings.

In practice, arbitral proceedings seated in Hong Kong will 'increasingly allow the parties to determine for themselves whether [the proof of foreign law] should be done through oral and written legal submissions from counsel, or via expert legal witnesses'.[89] This approach is consistent with the Arbitration Ordinance, which was enacted to facilitate 'the fair and

[84] See, eg *Nomura Funds Ireland plc v The Collector of Stamp Revenue* [2021] 3 HKLRD 744, [2021] HKCA 1040 [32]–[45]. See also *Li Xiao Yun v China Gas Holdings Ltd* [2015] 5 HKLRD 845 [9.1]–[9.2].

[85] *Zhang Hong Li* (n 14) [91]–[101]. See also *Perry* (n 31) [22]–[23].

[86] *Relevant Employees Whose Shares in China Shanshui Investment Co Ltd Were Held by Zhang Caikui on Trust v Zhang Caikui* [2018] HKCFI 195 [51].

[87] Nigel Blackaby and Constantine Partasides, *Redfern and Hunter on International Arbitration*, 7th edn (Oxford University Press, 2022) para 6.152.

[88] Geoffrey Ma and Denis Brock (gen eds), *Arbitration in Hong Kong: A Practical Guide*, 5th edn (Sweet & Maxwell, 2021) para 8.152.

[89] ibid para 21.062.

speedy resolution of disputes by arbitration without unnecessary expense'.[90] It also accords with the position of Hong Kong as a leading centre for international legal and dispute resolution services.

IV. Reform and Future Directions

Hong Kong generally has an effective and efficient framework to facilitate the adducing of foreign law in Hong Kong proceedings. Nevertheless, it may be advisable for Hong Kong to codify its rules in relation to proof of foreign law. This can be done on various fronts.

In relation to the more welcoming attitude (as reflected in *Brownlie*) towards different kinds of legal materials that can be adduced as evidence of foreign law, reference may be made to section 144 of the New Zealand Evidence Act 2006. The New Zealand framework provides for a wider range of legal materials that can be adduced as evidence of foreign law, including reports of judgments or any publications that describe or explain the law of a country.[91] As provided in section 144(5) of the New Zealand Act, the weight to be given to such evidence is a matter for the judge to decide. In addition to these provisions, codification would be welcome in relation to how the court should fill the gap in foreign law, by expressly distinguishing between the default rule and the presumption of similarity.

In contrast, the issue of whether courts can receive submissions on foreign law directly may be more controversial in Hong Kong, as this goes against current practice. However, some common law courts can decide foreign law issues by way of counsel submissions.[92] The Singapore International Commercial Court (SICC) has explicit provisions allowing questions of foreign law to be determined on the basis of submissions instead of expert evidence.[93] The Dubai International Financial Court has also adopted an 'international approach' which allows counsel to make legal submissions on foreign law.[94]

There may also be potential in Hong Kong for direct court-to-court cooperation or interaction regarding proof of foreign law. Such arrangements to ascertain foreign law by reference 'may not always be more cost effective than proof by expert evidence … [but a] reference will always … provide a more accurate answer, indeed, an authoritative answer, than expert evidence'.[95] If Hong Kong adopts direct court-to-court communication, this might be contrary to the traditional common law position that there is no principle of

[90] Arbitration Ordinance (Cap 609), s 3(1).

[91] Evidence Act 2006 (New Zealand), s 144. See also an attempt to apply the framework to the customary law of *tikanga* in Māori: *Ngāti Whātua Ōrākei Trust v A-G (No 4)* [2022] 3 NZLR 601 [380]–[390].

[92] *Celltech Chiroscience Ltd* (n 52) [8]; Ian Fletcher, 'Foreign Law in English Courts: Pleading, Proof and Choice of Law' (1999) 115 *LQR* 518, 520, citing *Robinson v Bland* (1760) 96 ER 129, 141; Justin Hogan-Doran and Dominique Hogan-Doran, 'New and Alternative Approaches to Proof of Foreign Law: A Practitioners' Perspective' in Michael Douglas et al (eds), *Commercial Issues in Private International Law: A Common Law Perspective* (Hart Publishing, 2019) 243–44 on examples from the USA to grant foreign lawyers a right of appearance *pro hac vice* to make submissions as to foreign law, and to be available for questions from and arguments before the bench; *Commercial Court Guide* (n 21) para H.3.5: '[In the England and Wales Commercial Court, the] parties will often have retained foreign lawyers … It will not always be necessary to instruct a separate foreign law expert to provide the expert evidence.'

[93] SICC Rules 2021, Ord 16, r 8. They are mutually exclusive: *DKB v DKC* [2024] SGHC(I) 31 [30].

[94] *Fidel v Felecia* [2015] DIFC CA 002 [48]–[76].

[95] JJ Spigelman, 'Proof of Foreign Law by Reference to the Foreign Court' (2011) 127 *LQR* 208, 213.

iura novit curia. However, improvements may also take the form of facilitating access of foreign law in inter-regional cases. For example, under cooperation or mutual assistance arrangements, parties may be able to prove foreign law by ascertaining its contents through a competent authority of the other jurisdiction. Currently, in Mainland China, the Supreme People's Court has established a procedure known as the 'ascertainment of foreign law process',[96] and the China International Commercial Court also permits various methods to be used to answer foreign legal questions.[97] However, if Hong Kong is to adopt such arrangements, which entity should be made the competent authority for Hong Kong remains to be determined.

Arrangements to facilitate access to foreign law have also been seen in other jurisdictions. For example, the SICC has explicit provisions for referring issues of foreign law to courts in New South Wales, Dubai and Bermuda or for requesting opinions on foreign law from China.[98] But it is important to note the potential disadvantages of these processes. For instance, despite the British Law Ascertainment Act 1859 allowing an English court to remit contested questions of foreign law to the courts of other Commonwealth countries, the process has seldom been employed because of the delay, increased cost and unpredictability involved.[99] Similar criticisms have been made against the 1968 European Convention on Information on Foreign Law.[100] More time is required to see how similar arrangements might work out for Hong Kong.

More generally, there may be room for courts to be given a broad, discretionary power to determine the procedure by which foreign law issues will best be resolved. Academics have suggested that any procedure may be adopted, subject only to 'proper notice … given by the party raising the matter to the court and other parties'.[101] Some relaxation from the traditional strictures in favour of a more malleable framework is not only normatively compelling, but also practically sensible.[102] There is also potential to explore inter-regional approaches within the Greater Bay Area or Greater China in relation to foreign law.

[96] Law of the People's Republic of China on Choice of Law for Foreign-related Civil Relationships, Art 10; Interpretation of the Supreme People's Court on Several Issues Concerning Application of the Law of the People's Republic of China on Choice of Law for Foreign-related Civil Relationships (II), Fa Shi [2023] No 12.

[97] Provisions of the Supreme People's Court on Several Issues Regarding the Establishment of the International Commercial Court, Fa Shi [2018] No 11, Art 8. Nevertheless, it was observed that 'although protocols have been introduced in the Mainland to facilitate Mainland courts determining issues of foreign law, courts generally have little experience of doing so': *Citicorp International Ltd v Tsinghua Unigroup Co Ltd* [2022] 2 HKLRD 1225, [2022] HKCFI 1558 [10].

[98] SICC Rules 2021, Ords 15 and 15A.

[99] Fentiman (n 79) 238–39. See also *International Energy Group Ltd v Zurich Insurance plc* [2013] EWCA Civ 39; *Dicey, Morris and Collins* (2022) (n 63) para 3-022.

[100] Hogan-Doran and Hogan-Doran (n 92) 251.

[101] ibid 254.

[102] See also *Suppipat* (n 25); *Commercial Court Guide* (n 21) paras H.3.3–H.3.4.

7

Evidence

Obtaining evidence is a crucial part of the litigation process. Such process may become complex when more than one jurisdiction is involved. Section I discusses taking evidence abroad for use in Hong Kong proceedings and section II discusses taking evidence in Hong Kong for use in foreign proceedings. The Evidence Ordinance (Cap 8) (EO) and the Rules of the High Court (Cap 4A) (RHC) specify the requirements governing these processes. Section III discusses the application of the 1970 HCCH Convention on the Taking of Evidence Abroad in Civil or Commercial Matters (the Hague Evidence Convention) in Hong Kong, pursuant to section 75 of the EO and Order 70 of the RHC.

I. Taking Evidence Abroad for Use in Hong Kong Proceedings

A. Procedural Requirements in the Rules of the High Court

Order 39, rules 1–3A of the RHC set out the procedure for the High Court to issue letters of request to seek assistance from courts outside Hong Kong in obtaining evidence. Letters will not be issued by the Hong Kong courts unless the evidence is directly material to an issue in the case and necessary in the interests of justice. Letters are not a means to obtain discovery.[1] The Hong Kong courts will only exercise the discretion to issue letters if there is an obligation on the recipient judicial authority to execute the letter under the Hague Evidence Convention, a bilateral agreement, or local laws in the recipient jurisdiction providing for execution or at least an established practice of executing letters.[2]

(i) Taking Examination of Witnesses

Unless otherwise directed, the examination of a witness proceeds as set out in Order 39, rules 5–10 and 11(1)–11(3) of the RHC.[3] Any order for the examination-in-chief of a witness shall permit the cross-examination of the witness (i) by a person who has the chief examiner's approval to do so and is affected by the examination or (ii) by that person's legal representative. The persons tasked with examining witnesses are usually those who are

[1] *Ehrmann v Ehrmann* [1896] 2 Ch 611; *Lee Samuel Tak v Hong Kong Chinese Christian Churches Union* (unreported, HCAL 27/2008, 25 September 2009).

[2] *Re Kwan Kai Ming* [2002] 2 HKC 69; *Kwan Chui Kwok Ying v Tao Wai Chun* (unreported, CACV 194/2002, 13 December 2022).

[3] RHC, Ord 70, r 4(2). See also Joseph Fok and others (gen eds), *Hong Kong Civil Procedure 2025* (Sweet & Maxwell, 2024) paras 39/1–39/11.

familiar with the Hong Kong laws of procedure, who may be foreign lawyers or consular officers.[4]

(ii) Dealing with Depositions

Unless otherwise directed, the examiner before whom the examination is taken must send the deposition of that witness to the Registrar. The Registrar will provide a certificate, bearing the court seal for use out of Hong Kong and identifying annexed documents (that is, the request, the court order for examination and the deposition taken under the order), and send the certificate with its annexes to the Chief Secretary for Administration of Hong Kong.[5]

B. Procedural Requirements Relating to Criminal Procedures in Hong Kong

Part VIIIA of the EO governs the taking of evidence abroad for use in Hong Kong criminal proceedings. There are no specific provisions for this process. The Court of First Instance may issue a Letter of Request[6] to a court or tribunal exercising jurisdiction outside Hong Kong. The letter will request the overseas forum to assist in obtaining evidence for Hong Kong criminal proceedings.

The key condition for the order is whether it appears to the Court of First Instance that criminal proceedings have been (or are likely to be) instituted in Hong Kong for which the evidence to be obtained from abroad is material.[7] Pursuant to a letter of request issued by the Registrar under section 77E of the EO, depositions obtained abroad, together with any annexed document or exhibit, shall on production be admitted in criminal proceedings as prima facie evidence of any fact stated there, if it is agreed by the prosecution and every defendant that such material may be tendered in evidence.[8]

II. Taking Evidence in Hong Kong for Use in Foreign Proceedings

Part VIII of the EO governs the taking of evidence pursuant to a foreign request. In dealing with such request, the Hong Kong court has to decide (i) whether it has jurisdiction to give effect to the request and, if so, (ii) whether as a matter of discretion it should make the order.[9] These powers may be exercised by the Court of First Instance or the Registrar.[10]

[4] RHC, Ord 70, r 4(3). See also *Hong Kong Civil Procedure 2025* (n 3) para 70/4/3.
[5] RHC, Ord 70, r 5.
[6] For the development of Letters of Request, see *Panayiotou v Sony Music Entertainment UK Ltd* [1994] Ch 142.
[7] EO, s 77E(1).
[8] ibid s 77F(1).
[9] *Angela Chen v Vivien Chen* (unreported, HCMP 1478/2011, 7 December 2011) [22]. See also *Hong Kong Civil Procedure 2025* (n 3) para 70/1/6.
[10] RHC, Ord 70, r 1.

A. Conditions for Recognising Foreign Letters of Request

Hong Kong courts have jurisdiction to give effect to applications for assistance in obtaining evidence[11] if the conditions in section 75 of the EO are met.[12] There must be an application to the Court of First Instance to recognise a letter of request issued by a court or tribunal outside Hong Kong.[13]

Section 75 of the EO stipulates that such an application may be for civil or criminal proceedings in the requesting forum. For criminal proceedings, the relevant proceedings must have been instituted or their institution would be likely if the evidence is obtained.[14] However, the Hong Kong courts have no jurisdiction to recognise letters if, upon consideration of (i) the accused's behaviour,[15] (ii) the parties' motivation[16] and (iii) all surrounding circumstances, the overseas criminal proceedings involve matters of a political nature.[17] The court may decide whether or not this is the case based on a reading of the letter of request and supporting documents.[18]

For civil or commercial proceedings, the evidence to be obtained must be for the purposes of civil proceedings which have been instituted or which are contemplated. 'Substantial and cogent' grounds are required to justify an application when proceedings are merely contemplated. This last requirement is to be satisfied on a case-by-case basis.[19]

Proceedings must be regarded as 'civil' both under the law of the requesting state and as a matter of Hong Kong law.[20] The term 'civil proceedings' is broadly construed, covering all kinds of suits, summonses, applications, etc of which courts are competent to take cognisance,[21] as well as 'letters rogatory', consisting of orders or processes issued under the powers of the requesting court.[22] Revenue law proceedings also fall broadly within 'civil proceedings', as long as the assistance does not involve the direct or indirect enforcement of foreign revenue law in Hong Kong.[23]

When facing a blurred boundary between assisting the obtaining of evidence for foreign proceedings and the outright enforcement of foreign law, the courts are willing to apply a 'blue-pencil' approach to strike out any orders sought by the foreign court which are deemed to be outside the courts' powers.[24]

[11] EO, s 76.

[12] *Rio Tinto Zinc Co v Westinghouse Electric Co* [1978] AC 547, 633C–E; *Atlantica Holdings Inc v Sovereign Wealth Fund S-K JSC* [2019] EWHC 319 (QB), [2019] 4 WLR 62 [58].

[13] EO, s 75.

[14] ibid s 77B(1)(a).

[15] Case law suggests that circumstances pertinent to the consideration of a 'political offence' under s 5(1) of the Fugitive Offenders Ordinance (Cap 503) are admissible to the consideration in EO, s 77B(3): *Re Troielli* [1995] 2 HKC 785, 797C. See also *Schtraks v Government of Israel* [1964] AC 556, 582–84; *Re Extradition Act 1870, ex p Treasury Solicitor* [1969] 1 WLR 12.

[16] *Crown Solicitor v Datuk Dr Jeffrey Kitingan* [1994] 1 HKC 516, 534F; *Re Troielli* (n 15) 797A–C.

[17] EO, s 77B(3).

[18] *Re Moreno* [1987] 3 HKC 279, 287A.

[19] EO, ss 74 and 75(b). For deciding whether proceedings were 'contemplated, imminent or impending', see *Rio Tinto Zinc Co* (n 12) 633; *Camaro Trading Co Ltd v Nissei Sangyo America Ltd* [1993] 3 HKC 94, 97, 99.

[20] *Re State of Norway's Application* [1990] 1 AC 723, 806F–G.

[21] *Re Extradition Act 1870* (n 15); *Re a Civil Matter Now Pending in the United States District Court (Letter of Request)* [2020] 5 HKLRD 30, [2020] HKCA 766.

[22] *Rio Tinto Zinc Co* (n 12) 611G–612B.

[23] *Re State of Norway's Application* (n 20) 800C–803F.

[24] ibid 808D. See below for the court's 'blue-penning' discretionary powers.

Crucially, the jurisdiction is invoked only when a letter is issued by a 'court or tribunal' under the law of the requesting state and Hong Kong law.[25] A state or federal court[26] will likely satisfy this third requirement. However, in *AB v X*,[27] the letter of request was issued by an administrative law judge of the Board of Governors of the US Federal Reserve. Although the judge considered herself to be a 'court', the judge was held to be incapable of issuing letters of request under US and Hong Kong law, and the requirement was therefore not met.[28]

It is rare for letters of request to be entirely refused.[29] The Hong Kong court has the power and discretion to apply a 'blue-pencil' approach, that is, to follow the request so far as possible, while deleting from the foreign request any parts that are excessive as regards oral or documentary evidence.[30] The court may not substitute a different category of documents or recast the request in different terms,[31] the basis for resort to 'blue-pencilling' being restrictions on the court's jurisdiction under Hong Kong law and not the parties' consent.[32]

Additionally, the Hong Kong court must be satisfied that it is appropriate to give effect to the request. The Hong Kong court will thus consider whether the application is 'frivolous, vexatious or an abuse of the process of the court'.[33]

Hong Kong courts will not, however, accept requests that are merely fishing expeditions. The documents sought by a request have to be particularised, so that descriptions of documents may be struck down for failing clearly to identify documents with precision.[34] It is essentially for the requesting court to decide whether the evidence requested is relevant and admissible. Given a statement in the letter of request that a person is a necessary witness, the Hong Kong court will likely take the same at face value and will not closely examine the issues in the action and the circumstances of the case to assess relevance and admissibility.[35] The court may find that the letter of request amounts to an abuse of process if the evidence sought is inadmissible in the foreign proceedings, regardless of relevance.[36]

B. Scope of Taking Evidence

The Order 70 process under the RHC to obtain evidence following a foreign request should be distinguished from *Norwich Pharmacal* relief.[37] The latter is investigatory in nature.

[25] EO, s 75(a); *Re Troielli* (n 15) 793H–794A.

[26] eg a judge of a US state's Superior Court: *Angela Chen* (n 9), or a US District Court: *Re United States District Court for the Central District of California* [2008] 1 HKLRD 581 [18]–[23].

[27] *AB v X* [2022] HKCFI 132.

[28] ibid [66]–[71] and [81]–[85].

[29] *Re Moreno* (n 18) 285.

[30] *Primarius Capital LLC v Jayhawk Capital Management LLC* [2009] 4 HKLRD 58 [33]; *Angela Chen* (n 9).

[31] *Mid Pacific Services Inc v Crown Solicitor* [1992] 1 HKLR 367, 372–73; *Re Q Ltd* [1997] 4 HKC 439, 444B; *Prediwave Co v New World TMT Ltd* [2007] 4 HKC 207 [49].

[32] *Mid Pacific Services Inc* (n 31) 371–72; *Champion Concord Ltd v Lau Koon Foo (No 2)* (2011) 14 HKCFAR 837 [3]–[4].

[33] *Seyfang v GD Searle* [1973] QB 148; *Rio Tinto Zinc Co* (n 12) 640D; *Society of Lloyd's v Clementson (No 2)* [1996] CLC 1205.

[34] *Prediwave Co* (n 31) [26]–[28]; *Primarius Capital LLC* (n 30) [35] and [47]–[48]; *Re a Civil Matter Now Pending in the United States District Court* (n 21).

[35] *Rio Tinto Zinc Co* (n 12) 654; *Prediwave Co* (n 31) [37]–[39]; *Primarius Capital LLC* (n 30) [41]–[44(1)].

[36] *Crown Solicitor* (n 16) 537–38.

[37] *Norwich Pharmacal Co v Customs and Excise Commissioners* [1974] AC 133.

Applications for *Norwich Pharmacal* orders will typically be mounted in support of potential foreign proceedings and aimed at ascertaining the identities of possible defendants to such proceedings.[38]

Subject to the court's blue-pencil power, upon an application under Order 70, rule 2 of the RHC,[39] the Hong Kong courts may direct:[40]

(i) the examination of witnesses by any means, including by way of a live television link;
(ii) the production of documents;
(iii) the inspection, photographing, preservation, custody or detention of any property;
(iv) the taking of samples of any property and the carrying out of any experiments on or with any property; and
(v) the medical examination of any person.

Where an applicant in foreign proceedings lacks an agent or legal representative in Hong Kong to make an application under Order 70, rule 2 of the RHC, the letter of request can be sent through the Chief Secretary for Administration to the Registrar. The latter will allow the Law Officer (International Law) of the Department of Justice to make and effect an application for obtaining evidence.[41]

However, the court has no power to make orders which go beyond what it can usually direct for the obtaining of evidence in civil proceedings.[42] A court shall not require a person (i) to state what relevant documents are or have been in his possession, custody or power, or (ii) to produce specified documents that are not (or are unlikely to be) in his or her possession, custody or power.[43] Moreover, a person shall not be compelled to give evidence which he could not be compelled to give in civil proceedings in Hong Kong or (subject to certain requirements) in civil proceedings in the requesting court, or any evidence which would be prejudicial to national security or the security of Hong Kong.[44]

An interested person may apply to a Court of First Instance judge in chambers to set aside an order made under section 76 of the EO or Order 70 of the RHC. The usual principles that govern applications for setting aside an *ex parte* order (found in Orders 2, 29 and 32 of the RHC) apply.[45] While the courts have yet to articulate the principles applicable to an appeal of the Order 70 process to the Court of Appeal, the latter is likely to adopt a conservative approach and to be slow to interfere with the first instance judge's exercise of discretion, unless there is an error of law or principle, or the first instance decision was plainly wrong.[46]

[38] *Smith Kline and French Laboratories Ltd v Global Pharmaceutics Ltd* [1986] RPC 394; *Manufacturer's Life Insurance Co v Harvest Hero International Ltd* [2002] 1 HKLRD 828; *Evergreen International Storage & Transportation Co v Hong Kong and Shanghai Banking Co Ltd* [2008] 5 HKLRD 49.

[39] Preferably made *ex parte* to a Master on notice, and supported with an affidavit exhibiting the letter of request. An English translation of the letter should also be exhibited if the original letter is in another language: RHC, Ord 70, r 2. For documents to be included in the affidavit, see *Hong Kong Civil Procedure 2025* (n 3) para 70/2/2.

[40] EO, s 76(2).

[41] RHC, Ord 70, r 3. For the examination of witnesses by the Law Officer (International Law), see also *Hong Kong Civil Procedure 2025* (n 3) para 70/3/4.

[42] EO, s 76(3).

[43] ibid s 76(4).

[44] ibid s 77.

[45] *Hong Kong Civil Procedure 2025* (n 3) paras 70/2/3–70/2/4.

[46] *Law Wai Duen Nina v Chan Shiu Chick* (unreported, CACV 85/2004, 15 October 2004) [9] and [13]. See also High Court Ordinance (Cap 4), s 14AA(4).

III. The Hague Evidence Convention

The Hague Evidence Convention was concluded on 18 March 1970 and came into effect on 7 October 1972. Prior to Hong Kong's return to PRC sovereignty in July 1997, the Convention was ratified by the UK on Hong Kong's behalf and was applied in Hong Kong. The Convention remains in effect in Hong Kong, and the PRC became a party to the same on 8 December 1997. The Hague Evidence Convention has not been specifically enacted into Hong Kong domestic law, but its provisions are reflected in Hong Kong legislation.

Hong Kong courts have held that letters of request can be recognised separately under the Hague Evidence Convention, as distinct from the Order 70 process[47] and the arrangements under civil procedure conventions to which Hong Kong is a party.[48] It is likely to be an abuse of process to apply to the court for an order for production of evidence from abroad, when the evidence ought to have been pursued by way of letters of request under the Convention.[49]

The aims of the Hague Evidence Convention are to facilitate the transmission and execution of letters of request and improve mutual judicial cooperation in civil or commercial matters.[50] These goals (in particular, international comity) inform how Convention articles should be interpreted. Guided by these aims, the Convention generally cover three different processes of taking evidence, namely:

(i) the procedure whereby a judicial authority of a contracting state requests the central authority of another contracting state to obtain evidence;
(ii) the procedure whereby a diplomatic officer or consular agent of a contracting state may take evidence in another contracting state in which he or she exercises functions; and
(iii) the procedure whereby a person appointed as a commissioner takes evidence in a contracting state.

A. Procedural Requirements in the Hague Evidence Convention

(i) Evidence Taking Upon Request by a Judicial Authority of a Contracting State

Chapter I of the Hague Evidence Convention deals with the letter of request needed for this method of taking evidence. Orders by the Hong Kong court to issue letters of request are valid as long as the recipient is a contracting state.[51]

After a central authority designated by a contracting state receives a letter of request from the judicial authority of another contracting state, it should transmit them to the authority competent directly to execute them.[52] This would either be the Chief Secretary of

[47] *Hong Kong Civil Procedure 2025* (n 3) paras 70/1/10–70/1/13.
[48] *Rio Tinto Zinc Co* (n 12) 632–33.
[49] *MacKinnon v Donaldson Lufkin & Jenrette Securities Corp* [1986] Ch 482.
[50] Hague Evidence Convention, Art 1.
[51] *Kwan Chui Kwok Ying v Tao Wai Chun* (unreported, CACV 194/2002, 13 December 2022) [24]–[31].
[52] Hague Evidence Convention, Art 2; *Re Kwan Kai Ming* (n 2) [23]–[24].

Administration or the Registrar[53] for the receipt of foreign letters. A letter of request shall specify:[54]

(i) the authority requesting its execution and the authority requested to execute it, if known to the requesting authority;
(ii) the names and addresses of the parties to the proceedings and their representatives;
(iii) the nature of the proceedings for which the evidence is required; and
(iv) the evidence to be obtained.

A letter of request must be in the language of the authority being requested to execute the letter or be accompanied by a translation into that language.[55]

The judicial authority which executes a letter of request shall apply its own laws as to the methods and procedures to be followed when taking evidence. This will generally follow the procedures of the Order 70 process described above.[56] However, the requesting authority may ask that a special procedure be followed, unless this is incompatible with the internal laws of the state of execution, is impossible or is impractical. A letter of request should be executed expeditiously.[57] Execution of a letter of request may be refused if: (i) execution of the letter does not fall within the functions of the judiciary to which the request is directed; or (ii) the requested state considers that its sovereignty or security will be prejudiced.[58] Upon refusal, the requesting authority is to be informed immediately and advised of the reasons.[59]

(ii) Evidence Taking by a Diplomatic Officer

A diplomatic officer or consular agent in a contracting state may take evidence without compulsion in aid of court proceedings in the state which he or she represents.[60] Where a diplomatic officer or consular agent is authorised to take evidence, the latter may take such evidence as is compatible with the law of the state where the evidence is taken. The evidence may be taken in the manner provided by the law applicable in the court where the action is pending, provided that such manner is not forbidden by the law of the state where evidence is being taken.[61]

(iii) Evidence Taking by a Commissioner

In a civil or commercial matter, a person appointed as a commissioner may take evidence in aid of proceedings in the courts of a contracting state if (i) a competent authority designated by the state where the evidence is to be taken has given permission and (ii) the commissioner complies with the conditions specified in the permission given by the competent

[53] RHC, Ord 70, r 3.
[54] Hague Evidence Convention, Art 3.
[55] ibid Art 4.
[56] *Hong Kong Civil Procedure 2025* (n 3) para 70/1/11.
[57] Hague Evidence Convention, Art 9.
[58] ibid Art 12.
[59] ibid Art 13.
[60] ibid Art 16.
[61] ibid Art 21.

authority.[62] The scope and manner of taking evidence is similar in the case of a diplomatic officer or consular agent.[63]

B. Scope of Application of the Hague Evidence Convention in Hong Kong

As mentioned above, the Hague Evidence Convention has continued to apply in Hong Kong after 1997. However, China has stipulated reservations in the way that the Convention applies in Hong Kong.[64] First, in respect of Article 16 of the Convention, a diplomatic officer or consular agent in Hong Kong is not permitted to take evidence from nationals of a third state. Second, concerning Article 23 of the Convention, Hong Kong will not execute letters of request issued for the purpose of obtaining pre-trial discovery of documents. Third, in accordance with Articles 4 and 33 of the Convention, Hong Kong will not accept a letter of request in French.

The procedure for obtaining evidence with foreign assistance under the Hague Evidence Convention should also be distinguished from *Norwich Pharmacal* relief. Once potential defendants have been identified and proceedings initiated, the Convention procedures can only be used to obtain evidence for the use in support of those proceedings.[65]

[62] ibid Art 17.

[63] ibid Art 21.

[64] See www.hcch.net/en/instruments/conventions/status-table/notifications/?csid=493.

[65] *Guangdong Shirong Zhaoye Co v The Hongkong and Shanghai Banking Co Ltd* [2022] 4 HKLRD 536, [2022] HKCFI 2594 [9]–[10].

8

Mandatory Rules, Public Policy, Public Laws, Acts of State and the Evasion of Law

This chapter discusses various issues in the jurisdiction and choice of law contexts, including the potential application of Hong Kong and foreign mandatory rules, public policy, foreign public laws, foreign acts of state and the evasion of law.

I. Hong Kong Mandatory Rules and Public Policy

Ordinary choice of law principles may be overridden by the mandatory rules and public policy of Hong Kong. The rationale is that such mandatory rules embody some fundamental value, interest or policy of the forum. In such circumstances, the Hong Kong court may apply a domestic law that would not otherwise be applicable under normal choice of law principles. Alternatively, the court may refuse to apply a law that would otherwise be applicable.

A. Mandatory Rules

The Hong Kong legislature may expressly provide for a substantive law of Hong Kong to apply regardless of ordinary choice of law principles. It is clear that a substantive law is mandatory where it is expressly stated to be. An example is section 17 of the Control of Exemption Clauses Ordinance (Cap 71):

> (1) Where the proper law of a contract is the law of Hong Kong only by choice of the parties (and apart from that choice would be the law of a jurisdiction other than Hong Kong), sections 7 to 12 do not operate as part of the proper law.
>
> (2) This Ordinance has effect notwithstanding any contract term which applies or purports to apply the law of a jurisdiction other than Hong Kong, where (either or both) –
>
> (a) the term appears to the court or arbitrator to have been imposed wholly or mainly for the purpose of enabling the party imposing it to evade the operation of this Ordinance; or
>
> (b) in the making of the contract one dealt as consumer, and he was then habitually resident in Hong Kong, and the essential steps necessary for the making of the contract were taken there, whether by him or by others on his behalf.

Section 17(1) provides that sections 7–12 of the Ordinance (relating to certain exclusions and restrictions of liability) do not have effect.[1] In *Chimbusco Pan Nation Petro Chemical Co Ltd v Arkstar Ship Management Pte Ltd*,[2] the Court of First Instance applied section 17(1) and disapplied the restrictions on exemption clauses under the Ordinance, deciding (under Hong Kong law) that the contract would be governed by Singapore law if there was no express choice of law. Section 17(2) is a mandatory rule which expressly states that the Ordinance still has effect if a party is dealing as a consumer, is habitually resident in Hong Kong and the essential steps for the contract took place in Hong Kong. This protects local consumers who might otherwise be taken advantage of due to a lack of bargaining power when negotiating with a business for the choice of law clause in a contract.

Difficulties arise when determining whether the Hong Kong legislature impliedly provided for a law to be mandatory. In these situations, the particular statutory provision, its framework and context must be examined to ascertain its nature. An example is section 70 of the Employment Ordinance (Cap 57). Section 70 provides: 'Any term of a contract of employment which purports to extinguish or reduce any right, benefit or protection conferred upon the employee by this Ordinance shall be void.' In *Cantor Fitzgerald Europe v Boyer*,[3] the court held that the employment contract, although governed by English law, was subject to section 70 of the Employment Ordinance as an overriding provision. The court held:[4]

> 90. … Given EO s.70, then EO ss.6 and 7 must be treated as over-riding provisions. EO ss.6 and 7 form part of the 'mandatory employment laws of Hong Kong' binding on [the plaintiff]. One cannot attempt to get around the protection afforded by the EO to employees working here through the expedient of choosing a foreign law. Such attempt will be struck down by EO s.70.
>
> 91. Support for my conclusion is to be found … from EO s.4. EO s.4(1) provides for the application of the EO to every employee engaged here under a contract of employment, to an employer of such employee, and to a contract of employment between such employer and employee. EO s.4(2) then carves out an exception to the wide ambit of s.4(1). Under that exception, the EO is not to apply to 'a person who is serving … on board a ship which is not registered in Hong Kong'. Crew on board a ship which is not registered in Hong Kong are unlikely to be employed under contracts governed by Hong Kong law. The deliberate carving out of their contracts as an exception to s.4(1) suggests that EO was intended to apply to all employments in Hong Kong, including employments governed by some law other than Hong Kong law.

This may be contrasted to the decision in *HSBC Bank plc v Wallace*,[5] where the court (in drawing a preliminary conclusion in the course of an application for an interlocutory injunction) held that there was a bona fide express choice of English law as the governing law of the employment contract. This meant that the employee was not entitled to salary in lieu of the required notice of termination of the employment agreement under sections 7(1A) and 7(2) of the Employment Ordinance, a right not available under English law. In that case, the court considered the facts that the employer and the employee were British, and that the employee was recruited in London and seconded to Hong Kong.

[1] See also Control of Exemption Clauses Ordinance (Cap 71), s 16, which exempts certain international sales contracts from its application.

[2] *Chimbusco Pan Nation Petro Chemical Co Ltd v Arkstar Ship Management Pte Ltd* [2019] HKCFI 57.

[3] *Cantor Fitzgerald Europe v Boyer* (unreported, HCA 1160/2011 and HCA 44/2012, 29 February 2012).

[4] ibid [90]–[91].

[5] *HSBC Bank plc v Wallace* [2008] 1 HKLRD 613.

Other statutory provisions providing for the mandatory application of Hong Kong law include:

(i) section 8 of the Supply of Services (Implied Terms) Ordinance (Cap 457), which prohibits the contracting out of liability under the Ordinance against a consumer;
(ii) section 7 of the Unconscionable Contracts Ordinance (Cap 458), which has the same wording as section 17 of the Control of Exemption Clauses Ordinance discussed above;
(iii) provisions in the Sex Discrimination Ordinance (Cap 480), the Family Status Discrimination Ordinance (Cap 527), the Disability Discrimination Ordinance (Cap 487) and the Race Discrimination Ordinance (Cap 602), which prohibit the contracting out of the four anti-discrimination ordinances in Hong Kong;[6] and
(iv) section 31(1) of the Employees' Compensation Ordinance (Cap 282), which provides that

> any such contract or agreement to relinquish an employees' right to compensation from an employer for personal injury by accident arising out of and in the course of his employment shall be null and void in so far as it purports to remove or reduce the liability of any person to pay compensation under the provisions of this Ordinance.

B. Public Policy

The concept of 'public policy' finds its place in various issues of private international law. In certain narrow circumstances, a Hong Kong court may decline to apply ordinary choice of law principles. Instead, the court may deny the effect that would otherwise be given to an applicable law, on the basis that giving effect to the applicable law would be contrary to the 'public policy' of Hong Kong. This is also reflected in rules such as the non-enforcement of foreign and Mainland judgments, as well as arbitral awards which are contrary to public policy.[7]

The definition of 'public policy' in Hong Kong is found in *Hebei Import & Export Corp v Polytek Engineering Co Ltd*.[8] Although that case was decided in the context of arbitration, it provides useful guidance for applications of the concept of public policy. The Hong Kong courts have not deviated from such a definition in the private international law context.[9] In the *Hebei* case, Bokhary PJ held that 'the award must be so fundamentally offensive to that jurisdiction's notions of justice that, despite its being party to the Convention, it cannot reasonably be expected to overlook the objection'.[10] Sir Anthony Mason NPJ gave a narrower construction, saying that 'it has been generally accepted that the expression "contrary to the public policy of that country" in [Article V(2)(b) of the

[6] Sex Discrimination Ordinance (Cap 480), s 87(3); Family Status Discrimination Ordinance (Cap 527), s 65; Disability Discrimination Ordinance (Cap 487), s 83(3); Race Discrimination Ordinance (Cap 602), s 81(3).

[7] Foreign Judgments (Reciprocal Enforcement) Ordinance (Cap 319), s 6(1)(a)(v); Mainland Judgments (Reciprocal Enforcement) Ordinance (Cap 597), s 18(1)(j); Mainland Judgments in Civil and Commercial Matters (Reciprocal Enforcement) Ordinance (Cap 645), s 22(1)(j); Arbitration Ordinance (Cap 609), ss 86(2)(b), 89(3)(b), 95(3)(b) and 98D(3)(b).

[8] *Hebei Import & Export Corp v Polytek Engineering Co Ltd* (1999) 2 HKCFAR 111. See also *Chen Li Hung v Ting Lei Miao* (2000) 3 HKCFAR 9 [33]–[36].

[9] See, eg *Pusan Newport Co Ltd v Milano Bridge (Owners)* [2022] 1 HKLRD 1151, [2022] HKCA 157.

[10] *Hebei Import & Export Corp* (n 8) [31].

New York Convention] means "contrary to the fundamental conceptions of morality and justice" of that forum'.[11]

Whatever the precise scope given to the application of public policy, the doctrine should be kept within proper limits and 'only be invoked in clear cases in which the harm to the public is substantially incontestable'.[12] The same narrow and cautious approach should be adopted for any potential application of mandatory rules, which can be seen as an expression of public policy,[13] so that the basis of the choice of law system is not frustrated.

II. Foreign Mandatory Rules and Public Policy

A Hong Kong court will not take into account a foreign mandatory rule unless that rule (i) forms part of the applicable law according to ordinary choice of law principles[14] or (ii) renders the performance of the contract illegal in the intended place of performance.[15] There is also no place for foreign public policy to apply in Hong Kong, as the Hong Kong court has to apply its own standards and law when deciding whether a matter would be contrary to the public policy of Hong Kong.[16] As such, a violation of 'fundamental conceptions of morality and justice' might be sufficient for the Hong Kong court to deny the effect of a foreign law which offend against basic human rights or established rules of international law.[17]

International custom or usages, or 'general principles' of any law, have generally no application in private international law in Hong Kong unless expressly agreed by parties.

III. Foreign Public Laws

It is a universal principle that the courts of one country will not enforce the penal and revenue laws of another country.[18] In *Government of India v Taylor*,[19] the enforcement of

[11] ibid [99].

[12] *Fender v St John-Mildmay* [1938] AC 1, 12.

[13] See, eg the wording used in Mainland China: Interpretation of the Supreme People's Court on Several Issues Concerning Application of the Law of the People's Republic of China on Choice of Law for Foreign-related Civil Relationships (I) (2020 Amendment), Fa Shi [2020] No 18, Art 8.

[14] *Dow MBF Ltd v Detrick Ltd* [1988] 1 HKLR 344, 351H–352G; *Bank of Credit and Commerce International (Overseas) Ltd (in liq) v Bank of Credit and Commerce International (Overseas) Ltd – Macau Branch (in liq)* [1997] HKLRD 304; *Shenzhen Development Bank Co Ltd v New Century International (Holdings) Ltd* (unreported, HCA 2976/2001, 31 July 2002). See also *Kleinwort, Sons & Co v Ungarische Baumwolle Industrie AG* [1939] 2 KB 678.

[15] *Ryder Industries Ltd v Chan Shui Woo* (2015) 18 HKCFAR 544 [39]. This is consistent with the approach in Art 9(3) of the Rome I Regulation. Academic commentaries, however, diverged as to whether this approach is justified. See, eg Adeline Chong, 'The Public Policy and Mandatory Rules of Third Countries in International Contracts' (2006) 2(1) *Journal of Private International Law* 27; Andrew Dickinson, 'Third-Country Mandatory Rules in the Law Applicable to Contractual Obligations: So Long, Farewell, Auf Wiedersehen, Adieu?' (2007) 3(1) *Journal of Private International Law* 53.

[16] See, eg *Song Lihua v Lee Chee Hon (No 2)* [2023] 5 HKLRD 488, [2023] HKCFI 2540 [53].

[17] See, eg *Oppenheimer v Cattermole* [1976] AC 249; *Kuwait Airways Corp v Iraqi Airways Co (Nos 4 and 5)* [2002] UKHL 19, [2002] 2 AC 883; *Belhaj v Straw* [2017] UKSC 3, [2017] AC 964 [250]–[257].

[18] See, eg *Sydney Municipal Council v Bull* [1909] 1 KB 7; *Re Visser, Queen of Holland v Drucker* [1928] Ch 877; *Government of India, Ministry of Finance (Revenue Division) v Taylor* [1955] AC 491; *Williams & Humbert Ltd v W&H Trade Marks (Jersey) Ltd* [1986] AC 368, 428. In Hong Kong, see, eg *Nanus Asia Co Inc v Standard Chartered Bank* [1990] 1 HKLR 396; *Re Anson Garment Ltd* (unreported, HCAL 187/2002 and HCAL 11/2003, 3 June 2003).

[19] *Government of India* (n 18) 511.

such claims was regarded as an extension of the foreign sovereign power which imposed the taxes. It was 'an assertion of sovereign authority by one State within the territory of another, as distinct from a patrimonial claim by a foreign sovereign', and thus 'contrary to all concepts of independent sovereignties'. Hong Kong civil courts should not become 'a general enforcement arm of foreign governments'.[20]

A 'penal' law is defined as a law which imposes a punishment for 'crimes, including in that term all breaches of public law punishable by pecuniary mulct [fine] or otherwise, at the instance of the [foreign] Government, or of someone representing the public'.[21] A penal law is thus effectively a law that 'punishes or prevents an offence'.[22] However, the law does not have to form part of the criminal code of a country to fall within the ambit of this principle.[23]

The principle encompasses direct and indirect enforcement of penal or revenue laws. It prohibits foreign states from seeking to obtain money, property or other relief in reliance on the foreign rule in question. The limits of the prohibition are unclear. However, the prohibition has restricted courts from: (i) enforcing foreign judgments based on penal or revenue laws;[24] (ii) allowing creditors to sue for debts arising under a contract designed to ensure the debtor's compliance with foreign criminal laws;[25] and (iii) enabling a bank in Hong Kong to freeze a customer's account at the request of a foreign tax authority.[26] Whether a foreign law or a claim under foreign law is to be characterised as penal or revenue law depends on the *lex fori*.[27]

In *Her Majesty's Revenue & Customs v Shahdadpuri*,[28] the Hong Kong Court of Appeal granted a *Mareva* injunction to support a UK Revenue & Customs claim for unpaid value-added tax. It was argued that this amounted to an indirect enforcement of foreign revenue law. But the Court of Appeal reasoned:[29]

> A robber would be subject to extradition. I find it difficult to accept that enforcement of a judgment to recover the loot should fail on the ground that it amounts to an indirect enforcement of foreign revenue law. I do not believe that *Government of India* compels such a conclusion. If, it does, I am respectfully of the view that our courts may wish to consider whether *Government of India* should be followed.

This was consistent with a more recent Court of Appeal authority which suggested that a claim to enforce a Russian judgment in unjust enrichment does not amount to indirect enforcement of Russian revenue laws, as the foreign revenue laws were enforceable in the

[20] Graeme Johnston and Paul Harris, *The Conflict of Laws in Hong Kong*, 3rd edn (Sweet & Maxwell, 2017) para 4.008.

[21] *Huntington v Attrill* [1893] AC 150, 156. See also *Regazzoni v KC Sethia (1944) Ltd* [1958] AC 301; *Hung Fung Enterprises Holdings Ltd v Agricultural Bank of China* [2012] 3 HKLRD 679.

[22] Lord Collins of Mapesbury and Jonathan Harris (gen eds), *Dicey, Morris and Collins on the Conflict of Laws*, 16th edn (Sweet & Maxwell, 2022) para 8-008.

[23] See, eg *A-G of New Zealand v Ortiz* [1984] AC 1, 34–35.

[24] *Rossano v Manufacturers Life Insurance Co* [1963] 2 QB 352; *US v Inkley* [1989] 1 QB 255.

[25] *US* (n 24).

[26] *Cido Car Carrier Service Ltd v Woori Bank* [2011] 4 HKC 430.

[27] See, eg *Islamic Republic of Iran v Barakat Galleries Ltd* [2007] EWCA Civ 1374, [2009] QB 22; *Autonomous Non-Commercial Organization 'Organizing Committee etc of 2014 Sochi Winter Olympics' v Pico Projects (International) Ltd* [2021] 5 HKLRD 754, [2021] HKCA 1798 [29].

[28] *Her Majesty's Revenue & Customs v Shahdadpuri* [2012] 1 HKLRD 223.

[29] ibid [47].

foreign jurisdiction at the point of payment and had already been enforced in that foreign jurisdiction, leaving no tax due and nothing to enforce in Hong Kong.[30]

However, there are circumstances in which the Hong Kong courts should have regard to a foreign penal or revenue law. These circumstances fall into three categories. The first two categories may be raised as defences to a contractual claim. First, where a governing foreign law renders a contract illegal, the Hong Kong court will refuse to enforce the same as that would be contrary to the public policy of Hong Kong.[31] It is necessary, though, to ensure that the territorial scope of the foreign law is ascertained. Such a law should not be applied extraterritorially contrary to the intention of the foreign legislature. Nor must it be excessively extraterritorial.[32] Second, where performance of a contract would be illegal in the place where it is agreed or mutually intended to be performed, a Hong Kong court will refuse to enforce the contract. A court may refuse enforcement even where there are alternative modes or places of performing the contract legally. Identifying the place at which the parties intend performance to occur may involve an objective evaluation of the factual context at the time of contracting. Third, the court may consider a foreign penal or revenue law where it is relevant to the background of a private liability.

Applying these principles, an order by a foreign criminal court to compensate a victim for loss suffered as a result of a crime is enforceable as a civil judgment.[33] Equally, a judgment obtained by a public body for compensation or restitution for suffering by a victim as a result of a defendant's wrongful activity is also enforceable for similar reason.[34] A foreign statute that imposes criminal sanctions and civil liability for the same conduct would be enforceable by Hong Kong courts provided that the civil liability is compensatory or restitutionary (as opposed to penal) in nature and enforcement would not be contrary to Hong Kong public policy.[35]

A foreign civil court judgment that imposes a penalty for non-compliance with a prior judgment will likely not be enforced. Recognition of the penalty would effectively make foreign injunctions directly enforceable against persons in Hong Kong.[36] Moreover, a remedy in civil disputes which is punitive, rather than compensatory, is also likely not enforceable. For example, in *Hung Fung Enterprises Holdings Ltd v Agricultural Bank of China*,[37] a double interest granted by the Mainland Chinese court under (currently Article 264 of) the Civil Procedure Law in China was not enforced in Hong Kong. The Court of Appeal stated:[38]

> 90. Mr Tong sought to support the judge's decision on a different ground namely that the double interest was in the nature of a penalty. He submitted that the purpose of article 229 of the Civil [Procedure] Law is to punish or sanction those who have breached a court order. The double interest bears no relation to any loss suffered by the defendant, nor was there any inquiry as to the loss. And as the defendant was already ordered by the PRC courts to pay interest according to the contractual terms and the interest rates set by the People's Bank of China until the judgment debts

[30] *Pico Projects (International) Ltd* (n 27). See also *Skatteforvaltningen v Solo Capital Partners LLP* [2023] UKSC 40, [2024] AC 539.

[31] Johnston and Harris (n 20) para 4.012.

[32] ibid.

[33] *Raulin v Fisher* [1911] 2 KB 93.

[34] Johnston and Harris (n 20) para 4.024.

[35] ibid para 4.028.

[36] ibid para 4.029.

[37] *Hung Fung Enterprises Holdings Ltd* (n 21).

[38] ibid [90]–[92].

> have been fully discharged, the imposition of double interest cannot be protective, remedial or compensatory as far as the defendant is concerned.
>
> 91. The judge did recognise that the double interest was to penalise the plaintiffs for not complying with the orders of the PRC courts to pay the judgment sums within ten days of the judgments coming into effect. Where he has gone wrong is to attach undue significance to the fact that double interest is recoverable at the instance of the judgment creditor in a civil litigation, and not by the state under a penal law or other public law. That the sum is not payable to the state is not a determinative factor. If the court is satisfied that the purpose of the amount ordered was not to compensate for the loss suffered but to punish the defendant and deter others from acting in the same way, this could properly be regarded as a penalty. The award of punitive damages which the court in *Schnabel v Lui* declined to enforce is an example of this.
>
> 92. I agree with Mr Tong that the double interest imposed by the PRC courts is a penalty and the judge is correct in not enforcing it, albeit for the wrong reason.

In addition to penal and revenue laws, the Hong Kong courts will not enforce foreign 'public laws' as a wider general category of which penal and revenue laws are merely specific examples. However, it is difficult to define what 'public laws' means. The expression 'public laws' might refer to laws which do not affect private rights and interests. 'Public laws' do not concern 'liabilities which arise out of, or are reasonably calculated directly to vindicate or protect, the plaintiff's own private rights or interests'.[39] Instead, 'public laws' are 'imposed for some other purpose, for example to protect the public interest by punishment, deterrence or regulation'.[40]

IV. Foreign Acts of State

Despite the very interesting line of recent cases and discussion in the UK,[41] the position in Hong Kong regarding foreign acts of state is significantly different. Prior to the handover in 1997, the theoretical answer was likely that the Hong Kong courts would have no jurisdiction to entertain an action founded upon an act of state. A court could not enquire into a sovereign act done within the territory of a foreign state, subject to certain exceptions. However, after the handover in 1997, Hong Kong has become part of the People's Republic of China (PRC) as a Special Administrative Region. Article 19(3) of the Basic Law specifically provides that:

> The courts of the Hong Kong Special Administrative Region shall have no jurisdiction over acts of state such as defence and foreign affairs. The courts of the Region shall obtain a certificate from the Chief Executive on questions of fact concerning acts of state such as defence and foreign affairs whenever such questions arise in the adjudication of cases. This certificate shall be binding on the courts. Before issuing such a certificate, the Chief Executive shall obtain a certifying document from the Central People's Government.

[39] Johnston and Harris (n 20) para 4.020.

[40] ibid.

[41] See, eg *Dicey, Morris and Collins* (n 22) paras 8-030–8-059; *Belhaj v Straw* [2017] UKSC 3, [2017] AC 964; *Deutsche Bank AG London Branch v Receivers Appointed by the Court* [2021] UKSC 57, [2023] AC 156 (better known as *Maduro Board v Guaidó Board*).

The words 'act of state' in this Article are given a wide interpretation in the Hong Kong context. In *Democratic Republic of the Congo v FG Hemisphere Associates LLC*, the Standing Committee of the National People's Congress issued an interpretation (as sought by the Court of Final Appeal) to the effect that state immunity was within the realm of 'acts of state' in Article 19(3), and the Hong Kong courts must apply the same approach of state immunity in alignment with the PRC's rules and policies.[42]

It is therefore submitted that on the face of Article 19(3) of the Basic Law, the Hong Kong courts will simply have no jurisdiction at all over 'acts of state' (including acts of China and of foreign states). It may be necessary to refer the matter under Article 19(3) of the Basic Law to the Chief Executive and the Central People's Government if such a case arises in the future.[43] Nevertheless, in light of the continuous application of the common law in Hong Kong, it is also submitted that the common law principles will mandate a Hong Kong court to refuse recognising jurisdiction over acts of state, subject to various limitations and exceptions.[44]

V. Evasion of Law

There is no doctrine of evasion of law in Hong Kong.[45] It has not been discussed or applied in Hong Kong. But it could be said that Hong Kong's overriding mandatory rules discussed in section I.A above, such as section 17(2) of the Control of Exemption Clauses Ordinance (which expressly uses 'to evade the operation of this Ordinance') and section 70 of the Employment Ordinance, are there to prevent evasion of law.

[42] *Democratic Republic of the Congo v FG Hemisphere Associates LLC* (2011) 14 HKCFAR 95; *Democratic Republic of the Congo v FG Hemisphere Associates LLC (No 2)* (2011) 14 HKCFAR 395. See also ch 12, s I.

[43] However, such reference must be based on (i) there is a question of fact concerning an act of state, and (ii) the resolution of this question of fact which may concern the act of state is necessary for the adjudication of the dispute: *Democratic Republic of the Congo* (2011) 14 HKCFAR 95 (n 42) [360] and [362]; *Bank A v Bank B* [2024] 5 HKLRD 250, [2024] HKCFI 2529 [40]–[68].

[44] These are summarised in *Deutsche Bank AG London Branch* (n 41) [136].

[45] In Mainland China, see Interpretation on Choice of Law for Foreign-related Civil Relationships (I) (n 13), Art 9.

PART II

Jurisdiction

9

Jurisdiction *in personam*

This chapter considers the principles on jurisdiction *in personam* in Hong Kong. Sections I and II discuss two general ways by which the court has jurisdiction over a person: (i) service and (ii) submission. Jurisdiction conferred by parties' agreement is discussed in chapter thirteen. Section III considers ways in which the defendant may challenge jurisdiction. This includes: (i) arguing that the court lacks jurisdiction and (ii) admitting the court's jurisdiction but inviting the court to stay the proceedings on the ground of *forum non conveniens*. Section IV discusses the doctrine of *forum non conveniens*, which may lead to a stay of local proceedings in favour of a clearly or distinctly more appropriate forum. Section V considers the range of interim relief that the court may order. Section VI deals with a particular relief known as anti-suit injunctions, which may restrain a person from commencing or continuing with foreign proceedings. Sections VII and VIII look at service of process from Hong Kong to abroad, and from abroad to Hong Kong respectively.

I. Establishing Jurisdiction by Service

The Hong Kong court has personal jurisdiction over a defendant when process has been, or is deemed to have been, served on him, whether in Hong Kong or abroad. In other words, the rules on service determine jurisdiction.

The court can assert judicial power over anyone validly served within the territory.[1] Service within the jurisdiction is 'as of right'. This means that, in general, a claimant does need not the leave of the court before serving a defendant in Hong Kong. This reflects the notion that the courts can exercise judicial power over all those present in the territory.

By contrast, if a defendant cannot be served in Hong Kong, a claimant is required to obtain the court's leave before serving a claim on a defendant outside of Hong Kong. Several requirements will then have to be satisfied before the court will exercise extraterritorial jurisdiction.

A. Service within Hong Kong

A claimant can serve a defendant within Hong Kong 'as of right'. Physical presence within Hong Kong is sufficient to found jurisdiction, no matter how transient a defendant's presence in Hong Kong may be.[2] Service would be valid even if the defendant refuses to accept

[1] Adrian Briggs, *The Conflict of Laws*, 5th edn (Oxford University Press, 2024) 44.
[2] *Maharanee of Baroda v Wildenstein* [1972] 2 QB 283.

the writ of summons. It is enough if the process server leaves the writ with the defendant and tells the latter that it is a legal document which requires attention.[3] There is an exception if the defendant was induced by fraud to enter into the jurisdiction for the concealed purpose of making service.[4]

The general rules for service of process within jurisdiction is contained in the Rules of the High Court (Cap 4A) (RHC), Order 10.[5] If a defendant has an address in Hong Kong, service can be effected by sending the originating process to the defendant's usual or last known address,[6] or by insertion through the letterbox of that address in a sealed envelope addressed to the defendant.[7] For service to be effective, the defendant's actual knowledge of the service is necessary. The defendant need not be physically present within Hong Kong when the originating process is sent or placed through the letterbox. Service will take effect when the defendant's presence and actual knowledge coincide.[8]

Other common methods of service include service by an agreed method, for example on an agent.[9] Service can also be made on the defendant's solicitor who has instructions to accept service on the defendant's behalf.[10] This would be effective even if the defendant were outside the jurisdiction.[11] If ordinary service methods are impractical for any reason,[12] a claimant can apply to the court for substituted service, such as by advertisement in a newspaper.

Service on a foreign firm or partnership depends on whether it has partners or a place of business in Hong Kong. Service can be effected: (i) on any partner; (ii) at the principal place of business of the partnership in Hong Kong, on any person having control or management of the partnership business at the time of service; or (iii) by sending a copy of the originating process by registered post to the partnership at its principal place of business in Hong Kong.[13] Thus, a claimant was able to serve on a New York-registered defendant firm by serving on its resident partners in Hong Kong, as the New York firm carried on business in Hong Kong for many years.[14] If a foreign firm cannot be served in Hong Kong, the claimant will need to apply for leave to serve out of the jurisdiction.[15]

Service on companies is governed by the Companies Ordinance (Cap 622). Service on a Hong Kong company can be made by leaving a judicial or other document at its registered office, or by posting the same to that office.[16]

[3] *Dynasty Line Ltd v Sukamto Sia* [2009] 4 HKLRD 454 [20]–[26].

[4] *Watkins v North American Land and Timber Co Ltd* (1904) 20 TLR 534; *Colt Industries Inc v Sarlie* [1966] 1 WLR 440, 443–44.

[5] There are nearly identical provisions in Rules of the District Court (Cap 336H), Ord 10. The provisions in the RHC introduced in this book are likely to have equivalent provisions in the Rules of the District Court. The High Court is a court of unlimited civil and criminal jurisdiction: High Court Ordinance (Cap 4), s 3. The District Court only has civil and criminal jurisdiction conferred specifically by the District Court Ordinance (Cap 336) and other enactments.

[6] RHC, Ord 10, r 1(2)(a).

[7] ibid Ord 10, r 1(2)(b).

[8] *Barclays Bank of Swaziland v Hahn* [1989] 1 WLR 506.

[9] RHC, Ord 10, r 3.

[10] ibid Ord 10, r 1(4).

[11] *Manta Line Inc v Seraphim Sofianites* [1984] 1 Lloyd's Rep 14.

[12] RHC, Ord 65, r 4.

[13] ibid Ord 81, r 3(1).

[14] *China Medical Technologies Inc (in liq) v Paul, Weiss, Rifkind, Wharton & Garrison LLP (a firm)* [2019] HKCFI 2631 [33]–[36], [103]–[106].

[15] *Excelsior Capital Asia (HK) Ltd v Zhang Hengshun* [2018] HKCFI 181 [2]–[3].

[16] Companies Ordinance (Cap 622), s 827.

A foreign company which is registered in Hong Kong[17] can be served through its authorised representative, by leaving the relevant document at (or posting it to) the latter's last known address in Hong Kong.[18] If no details of the authorised representative are shown on the Companies Register, or every one of the company's authorised representatives refuses to accept service, service can be effected by leaving the document at (or posting it to) any place of business of the company in Hong Kong.[19] If the company no longer has a place of business in Hong Kong, the document can be served by registered post to the company's registered office and principal place of business in the company's place of incorporation as shown on the Companies Register. Where no such addresses are on the Companies Register, service can be effected by leaving the relevant document at (or posting it to) any place in Hong Kong at which the company has had a place of business within the previous 12 months.[20]

An unregistered foreign company can be served by leaving the document at (or sending it by post to) the company's place of business in Hong Kong. If it established (but no longer has) a place of business in Hong Kong, service can be made by registered post to the company's registered office and principal place of business in the company's place of incorporation. If the address of that registered office or principal place of business cannot be ascertained but the company had a place of business in Hong Kong within the previous 12 months, service can be effected by leaving the document at (or posting it to) that former Hong Kong address.[21]

Other bodies corporate to which no provisions are made by any written law may be effected by serving on 'the chairman or president of the body, or the clerk, secretary, treasurer or other similar officer' within the territory.[22]

The foregoing methods constitute service within the territory as of right. Service on foreign companies outside of Hong Kong follows the principles in section I.B below.

B. Service Outside Hong Kong

If a defendant cannot be served in Hong Kong, the claimant will need to serve out of the jurisdiction. Service out of jurisdiction is regulated under Order 11 of the RHC.

The vast majority of cases fall under Order 11, rule 1(1) of the RHC, which requires leave of the court to serve out of jurisdiction. An affidavit exhibiting the material documents supporting the claim is required.[23] In practice, this is accompanied by a draft statement of claim and a draft order for service abroad. A court master will determine the application on paper without a hearing. However, the master may make written requisitions to the claimant. If leave is granted, the claimant can serve the defendant out of the jurisdiction in accordance with the court order.

[17] Under ibid Pt 16.
[18] ibid s 803(1).
[19] ibid ss 803(2) and 803(3).
[20] ibid s 803(4).
[21] ibid s 803(5). See also *CMF Global Quantitative Multi-Asset SPC-CMF Chaos China Growth SP v Blossom International Investment Holdings Ltd* [2024] HKCFI 1453.
[22] RHC, Ord 65, r 3(1). Owing to the extensive statutory framework described above, this provision has limited application.
[23] RHC, Ord 11, r 4(1).

A minority of cases fall under Order 11, rule 1(2) of the RHC, which does not require leave of the court. These cases cover claims which, by virtue of any written law, the court has power to hear and determine, notwithstanding that the person against whom the claim is made is not within the jurisdiction of the court, or that the wrongful act, neglect or default giving rise to the claim did not take place within its jurisdiction. Examples of these claims include sections 213 and 274 of the Securities and Futures Ordinance (Cap 571) involving false trading.[24] It was held that Order 11, rule 1(2) of the RHC should be

> limited to cases where the written law in question clearly contemplates proceedings being brought against persons who are not within the jurisdiction of the court or where the wrongful act, etc, giving rise to the claim did not take place within the jurisdiction. It is not enough that the written law is of general application and may be invoked against persons who may happen to be within as well as out of the jurisdiction.[25]

Order 11 applications are made on an *ex parte* basis, that is, without notice to the defendant. Consequently, there is a duty on the plaintiff to make full and frank disclosure of all material facts and legal principles in an application for service abroad.[26] Failure on the part of the plaintiff to fulfil this duty (that is, where there is material non-disclosure) may lead to the discharge of the order for service abroad, although it does not bar a re-grant.[27]

In the past, a strict approach was adopted in Order 11 applications due to the exorbitant nature of the courts' jurisdiction.[28] This approach appears to have been based on an assumption that service abroad is an 'interference with the sovereignty' of the foreign state.[29] However, the Court of Appeal stated in *Deutsche Bank AG v Zhang Hong Li*:[30]

> [Given that] Hong Kong has always adopted the doctrine of *forum non conveniens* … it is correct to say that in the great majority of cases where service on a person in [a foreign jurisdiction] is authorised, there will have been either a contractual submission to the jurisdiction of the Hong Kong court or else a substantial connection between the dispute and Hong Kong. Similarly, litigation between the residents of [foreign jurisdictions] and Hong Kong has become a routine incident of our commercial life … [S]ervice on a person in [a foreign jurisdiction] should be regarded as a pragmatic decision in the interests of the efficient conduct of litigation in an appropriate forum.

As the previous view might remain influential,[31] it would be prudent for parties to mount Order 11 applications with care.[32]

[24] *David Subotic v Securities and Futures Commission* (2023) 26 HKCFAR 488, [2023] HKCFA 32. Other examples include the Protection of Trading Interests Ordinance (Cap 471), s 8(5) and RHC, Ord 73, r 10(5) regarding service out of an *ex parte* order giving leave to enforce an arbitral award under statute. Enforcement of an arbitral award under common law requires leave under RHC, Ord 11, r 1(1)(m).

[25] *David Subotic* (n 24) [29].

[26] *Dong Shing F&T Co Ltd v Hanmec Co Ltd* [2010] 5 HKLRD 261 [27], applied in eg *Chen Hongqing v Persons Whose Names are Set Out in the Second Column of the Schedule to the Re-Amended Writ of Summons Filed on 26 March 2018* [2019] HKCFI 2121 [57].

[27] *Dong Shing F&T Co Ltd* (n 26) [38]–[39]; *Tecnomar & Associates Pte Ltd v SBM Offshore NV* [2021] SGCA 36.

[28] See, eg *Kayden Ltd v Securities and Futures Commission* (2010) 13 HKCFAR 696 [36]–[37].

[29] *Cecil v Bayat* [2011] EWCA Civ 135, [2011] 1 WLR 3086 [65].

[30] *Deutsche Bank AG, Hong Kong Branch v Zhang Hong Li* [2016] 3 HKLRD 303 [74], approving *Abela v Baadarani* [2013] UKSC 44, [2013] 1 WLR 2043 [53].

[31] See, eg *Liao Chen Toh v Loyal International Enterprises Co Ltd* [2021] 4 HKLRD 202 [21]. See also *MAN Diesel & Turbo SE v IM SKaugen SE* [2020] 1 SLR 327 [112].

[32] *Chen Hongqing* (n 26) [58]–[60].

(i) Substantive Requirements for Service Out

To obtain leave to serve a defendant abroad under Order 11, rule 1 of the RHC, a plaintiff must satisfy three requirements.[33] The onus is on the plaintiff to establish the existence of each requirement.[34] The court must eventually be satisfied that the case is a proper one for service out of the jurisdiction.[35]

The first requirement is that there must be a good arguable case that the claim comes within one or more of the gateways listed in Order 11, rule 1 of the RHC. This means that the plaintiff needs to show 'something more than a prima facie case or being merely sufficient to raise an issue, but less than proof on the balance of probabilities'. Observing that 'being able to show a good arguable case generally means that the party has the "better of the argument"',[36] the Court of First Instance in *China Medical Technologies* held that:[37]

> What is meant [by showing a good arguable case] is (i) that the claimant must supply a plausible evidential basis for the application of a relevant jurisdictional gateway; (ii) that if there is an issue of fact about it, or some other reason for doubting whether it applies, the Court must take a view on the material available if it can reliably do so; but (iii) the nature of the issue and the limitations of the material available at the interlocutory stage may be such that no reliable assessment can be made, in which case there is a good arguable case for the application of the gateway if there is a plausible (albeit contested) evidential basis for it.

The second requirement is that there must be a serious issue to be tried on the merits of the case. It must be shown that there is 'a substantial question of fact or law, or both'.[38] This is the same test as that applied for summary judgment, namely, 'whether there is a real (as opposed to a fanciful) prospect of success'.[39]

The third requirement is that Hong Kong has to be the appropriate forum for the trial of the action under the principles governing *forum conveniens*. These principles on *forum (non) conveniens* will be examined in detail in section IV below.

(ii) Jurisdictional Gateways

There are 19 gateways for service out of jurisdiction under Order 11, rule 1(1) of the RHC. These are:

> **1. Principal cases in which service of writ out of jurisdiction is permissible (O. 11, r. 1)**
>
> (1) Provided that the writ is not a writ to which paragraph (2) of this rule applies, service of a writ out of the jurisdiction is permissible with the leave of the Court if in the action begun by the writ –

[33] *Dynasty Line Ltd* (n 3) [29]; *Relevant Employees Whose Shares in China Shanshui Investment Co Ltd Were Held by Zhang Caikui on Trust v Zhang Caikui* (unreported, HCA 1661/2014, 13 May 2015) [47]; *Securities and Futures Commission v Isidor Subotic* [2023] 1 HKLRD 983, [2022] HKCA 1909 [19.3]. See also *Seaconsar Ltd v Bank Markazi* [1994] 1 AC 438; *Altimo Holdings and Investment Ltd v Kyrgyz Mobil Tel Ltd* [2011] UKPC 7, [2012] 1 WLR 1804 [71].

[34] *Chen Hongqing* (n 26) [56].

[35] RHC, Ord 11, r 4(2).

[36] *China Medical Technologies Inc* (n 14) [50]. See also *Chen Hongqing* (n 26) [63].

[37] *China Medical Technologies Inc* (n 14), citing with approval *Brownlie v Four Seasons Holdings Inc* [2017] UKSC 80, [2018] 1 WLR 192 and *Goldman Sachs International v Novo Banco SA* [2018] UKSC 34, [2018] 1 WLR 3683.

[38] *Altimo Holdings and Investment Ltd* (n 33) [71].

[39] ibid.

(a) relief is sought against a person domiciled or ordinarily resident within the jurisdiction;
(b) an injunction is sought ordering the defendant to do or refrain from doing anything within the jurisdiction (whether or not damages are also claimed in respect of a failure to do or the doing of that thing);
(c) the claim is brought against a person duly served within or out of the jurisdiction and a person out of the jurisdiction is a necessary or proper party thereto;
(d) the claim is brought to enforce, rescind, dissolve, annul or otherwise affect a contract, or to recover damages or obtain other relief in respect of the breach of a contract, being (in either case) a contract which –
  (i) was made within the jurisdiction, or
  (ii) was made by or through an agent trading or residing within the jurisdiction on behalf of a principal trading or residing out of the jurisdiction, or
  (iii) is by its terms, or by implication, governed by Hong Kong law, or
  (iv) contains a term to the effect that the Court of First Instance shall have jurisdiction to hear and determine any action in respect of the contract;
(e) the claim is brought in respect of a breach committed within the jurisdiction of a contract made within or out of the jurisdiction, and irrespective of the fact, if such be the case, that the breach was preceded or accompanied by a breach committed out of the jurisdiction that rendered impossible the performance of so much of the contract as ought to have been performed within the jurisdiction;
(f) the claim is founded on a tort and the damage was sustained, or resulted from an act committed, within the jurisdiction;
(g) the whole subject-matter of the action is land situate within the jurisdiction (with or without rents or profits) or the perpetuation of testimony relating to land so situate;
(h) the claim is brought to construe, rectify, set aside or enforce an act, deed, will, contract, obligation or liability affecting land situate within the jurisdiction;
(i) the claim is made for a debt secured on immovable property or is made to assert, declare or determine proprietary or possessory rights, or rights of security, in or over movable property, or to obtain authority to dispose of movable property, situate within the jurisdiction;
(j) the claim is brought to execute the trusts of a written instrument being trusts that ought to be executed according to Hong Kong law and of which the person to be served with the writ is a trustee, or for any relief or remedy which might be obtained in any such action;
(k) the claim is made for the administration of the estate of a person who died domiciled within the jurisdiction or for any relief or remedy which might be obtained in any such action;
(l) the claim is brought in a probate action within the meaning of Order 76;
(m) the claim is brought to enforce any judgment or arbitral award;
(n) the claim is brought under the Carriage by Air Ordinance (Cap. 500);
(o) [Repealed]
(oa) the claim is made under the Mutual Legal Assistance in Criminal Matters Ordinance (Cap. 525);
(ob) the claim is for an order for the costs of and incidental to a dispute under section 52B(2) of the Ordinance;
(oc) the claim is for interim relief or appointment of a receiver under section 21M(1) of the Ordinance;
(od) the claim is for a costs order under section 52A(2) of the Ordinance against a person who is not a party to the relevant proceedings;
(p) the claim is brought for money had and received or for an account or other relief against the defendant as constructive trustee, and the defendant's alleged liability arises out of acts committed, whether by him or otherwise, within the jurisdiction.

The Order 11 gateways are exhaustive. They define an entire code of claims for which the court may grant leave to the plaintiff to serve the defendant out of the jurisdiction. A plaintiff may choose to rely on one or more of the gateways for each claim. However, they may only proceed with claims that fall within a gateway. There is no residual power on the court's part to grant leave for a claim which does not fall within any of the gateways in Order 11.[40] The applications of these gateways are discussed in more detail in chapter ten.

In *Fong Chak Kwan v Ascentic Ltd*, Lord Collins NPJ held:[41]

> The purpose of the [Order 11] gateways is to set out a list of the situations in which the legislator considers that there may be a sufficient link with Hong Kong to justify a defendant in another country or law district being sued in Hong Kong. In some cases the link may be tenuous … [Put differently,] O 11, r 1(1) does not reveal a legislative purpose that every gateway must be construed to require a real connection with Hong Kong.

Hence, 'when the court construes the gateways, it should not superimpose an additional requirement of a "real" or "substantial" connection between the foreign defendant and Hong Kong'.[42] A case must fall within the spirit, and not just the letter, of a gateway.[43] The Court of Final Appeal held that such wider and principled view should be adopted:[44] 'it would certainly contravene the spirit and … the letter of the rule if jurisdiction were assumed on the strength of some relatively minor or insignificant act having been committed here, perhaps fortuitously'.

II. Establishing Jurisdiction by Submission

The court may also establish jurisdiction *in personam* by a person's consent or voluntary submission to the court's jurisdiction. If there is submission, then there is no need for service out of jurisdiction. If a defendant does not challenge jurisdiction based on Order 12, rule 8 of the RHC (discussed in section III below), then the acknowledgement by a defendant of service of a writ should be treated as a submission by the defendant to the jurisdiction of the court in the proceedings.[45] A party may also be taken to have submitted to jurisdiction by voluntarily taking a step in the proceedings that amounts to an unequivocal acknowledgement of the court's jurisdiction in respect of the claim, as such conduct is inconsistent with the challenge of jurisdiction.

[40] *Re Sunni International Ltd* [2014] 5 HKLRD 558 [63]–[64]. The regime of exhaustive grounds is abolished in Singapore: see Rules of Court 2021 (S 914/2021) (SG), Ord 8, r 1; Supreme Court Practice Directions 2021 (SG), Pt 8, para 63.

[41] *Fong Chak Kwan v Ascentic Ltd* (2022) 25 HKCFAR 136, [2022] HKCFA 12 [105], [109].

[42] *Isidor Subotic* (n 33) [19.3].

[43] *Fong Chak Kwan* (n 41) [117].

[44] ibid, citing with approval *Metall und Rohstoff AG v Donaldson, Lufkin & Jenrette Inc* [1990] 1 QB 391. For a case where the court considered RHC, Ord 11, r 4(2) and approved the principle that a case must fall within both the letter and the spirit of the jurisdictional gateways in RHC, Ord 11, see *Haller AG v Vestey International Group Ltd* [2023] 1 HKLRD 39, [2022] HKCA 1743 [33].

[45] RHC, Ord 12, r 8(7). The defendant is required to make an Ord 12 application 'within the time limited for service of a defence'. An extension may be made by issuing a summons for time to file a defence, which has the effect of extending the time for challenging jurisdiction: *Lawson v Midland Travellers Ltd* [1993] 1 WLR 735.

The principles on submission have been summarised by DHCJ Reyes SC in *Hwoo Huang Linda v Fu Being San* as follows:[46]

> (1) A party may be treated as having submitted to the jurisdiction if he files a pleading setting out his case on the substantive merits of an action.
>
> (2) A party may be treated as having submitted to the jurisdiction if he invokes the Court's jurisdiction to obtain an interlocutory or final order requiring the opposite party to perform some act (for example, disclose documents, provide further and better particulars, or answer interrogatories).
>
> (3) A party does not submit to the jurisdiction if he merely acts to preserve the status quo pending the mounting and resolution of an application to challenge forum.
>
> (4) A party does not submit to the jurisdiction if he merely takes defensive action in interlocutory injunction proceedings brought by the other side.
>
> (5) A party may be able to preserve an option to challenge forum, despite having engaged in conduct which might be regarded as submission to the jurisdiction, if before or at the time of such conduct he makes it clear that his action is without prejudice to the bringing of a challenge to forum.
>
> (6) The Court should adopt a common sense approach. It must not be overly subtle or astute to find that a party has submitted to the jurisdiction. Otherwise the question of submission could easily become a technicality trap for the unwary. The real question is whether a party's conduct is so inconsistent with maintaining an option to challenge forum that the party should be assumed to have waived such option. In the case of any doubt, the party proposing to challenge forum should probably be given the benefit of that doubt.

III. Challenging Jurisdiction

There are three courses of action which a defendant can take in response to a service of proceedings. First, one can accept service and contest the claim. Second, if one thinks the court lacks jurisdiction or should not exercise it, one can dispute the court's jurisdiction. To do so, the defendant is required to acknowledge service and lodge a jurisdictional challenge under Order 12, rule 8 of the RHC. This is the focus of this section. Third, one can take no action. The obvious risk with this last option is that a judgment which is enforceable against one's assets will be made at some point. This is not to mention the interim measures which the Hong Kong court may grant against a defendant. Thus, a defendant, especially one with assets in Hong Kong, will usually elect one of the first two options.

There are two types of jurisdictional dispute. The first type challenges the court's jurisdiction, arguing that the court does not have the competence to deal with the case in the first place. In this category, the defendant will typically contend that service was invalid, that leave for service abroad should be set aside or that the court lacks subject matter jurisdiction. If the court so finds on any of these points, the proceedings will be terminated and cannot be revived. The second type accepts that the court has jurisdiction, but asks the court

[46] *Hwoo Huang Linda v Fu Being San* [2013] 1 HKLRD 259 [26]. It was a decision handed down in 2002, although it was only reported in 2013. See also *Zoom Communications Ltd v Broadcast Solutions Pte Ltd* [2014] 4 SLR 500; *Balram Chainrai v Kushnir Family (Holdings) Ltd* [2019] HKCFI 234 [39]–[40]; *Shanghai Turbo Enterprises Ltd v Liu Ming* [2019] 1 SLR 779; *Allenger, Shiona v Pelletier, Olga* [2022] 3 SLR 353.

not to exercise it. If the court finds in favour of the defendant, it will stay the proceedings. A stay is temporary in nature and may be granted upon terms.[47] Thus, the stay may be lifted by the court and the proceedings resumed in the future.

This distinction is clear from the separate provisions in Order 12, rule 8(1) (which deals with the first type) and rule 8(2) (which deals with the second type) of the RHC. Order 12, rule 8 provides:

> **8. Dispute as to jurisdiction (O. 12, r. 8)**
>
> (1) A defendant who wishes to dispute the jurisdiction of the court in the proceedings by reason of any such irregularity as is mentioned in rule 7 or on any other ground shall give notice of intention to defend the proceedings and shall, within the time limited for service of a defence, apply to the Court for –
>
> (a) an order setting aside the writ or service of the writ on him, or
> (b) an order declaring that the writ has not been duly served on him, or
> (c) the discharge of any order giving leave to serve the writ on him out of the jurisdiction, or
> (d) the discharge of any order extending the validity of the writ for the purpose of service, or
> (e) the protection or release of any property of the defendant seized or threatened with seizure in the proceedings, or
> (f) the discharge of any order made to prevent any dealing with any property of the defendant, or
> (g) a declaration that in the circumstances of the case the court has no jurisdiction over the defendant in respect of the subject-matter of the claim or the relief or remedy sought in the action, or
> (ga) an order staying the proceedings, or
> (h) such other relief as may be appropriate.
>
> (2) A defendant who wishes to argue that the Court should not exercise its jurisdiction in the proceedings on one or more of the grounds specified in paragraph (2A) or on any other ground shall also give notice of intention to defend the proceedings and shall, within the time limited for service of a defence, apply to the Court for –
>
> (a) a declaration that in the circumstances of the case the Court should not exercise any jurisdiction it may have, or
> (b) an order staying the proceedings, or
> (c) such other relief as may be appropriate, including the relief specified in paragraph (1)(e) or (f).
>
> (2A) The grounds specified for the purposes of paragraph (2) are that –
>
> (a) considering the best interests and convenience of the parties to the proceedings and the witnesses in the proceedings, the proceedings should be conducted in another court,
> (b) the defendant is entitled to rely on an agreement to which the plaintiff is a party, excluding the jurisdiction of the Court, and
> (c) in respect of the same cause of action to which the proceedings relate, there are other proceedings pending between the defendant and the plaintiff in another court.
>
> (3) An application under paragraph (1) or (2) must be made by summons and the summons must state the grounds of the application.
>
> (4) An application under paragraph (1) or (2) must be supported by an affidavit verifying the facts on which the application is based and a copy of the affidavit must be served with the summons by which the application is made.

[47] As in *China Construction Bank (Asia) Corp Ltd v Shanghai Pudong Development Bank Co Ltd* (unreported, CACV 14/2016, 3 February 2017) [9.2].

> (5) Upon hearing an application under paragraph (1) or (2), the Court, if it does not dispose of the matter in dispute, may give such directions for its disposal as may be appropriate, including directions for the trial thereof as a preliminary issue.
>
> (6) A defendant who makes an application under paragraph (1) or (2) shall not be treated as having submitted to the jurisdiction of the court by reason of his having given notice of intention to defend the action; but if the Court makes no order on the application or dismisses it, the notice shall stand unless otherwise directed by the Court and the defendant shall be treated as having given notice of intention to defend the action.
>
> (6A) If the Court makes no order on an application under paragraph (1) or (2) or dismisses it, it may give such directions as may be appropriate for service of a defence and the further conduct of the proceedings.
>
> (7) Except where the defendant makes an application in accordance with paragraph (1) or (2), the acknowledgment by a defendant of service of a writ shall, unless the acknowledgment is withdrawn by leave of the Court under Order 21, rule 1, be treated as a submission by the defendant to the jurisdiction of the Court in the proceedings.

It is now accepted that any disputes as to jurisdiction are based on Order 12, rule 8 of the RHC, regardless of whether the plaintiff establishes jurisdiction (1) 'as of right' (for example, by the presence of defendant within jurisdiction) or (2) by applying for leave to serve out under Order 11, rule 1 of the RHC.[48] In type (1) cases, the court will apply the full *forum non conveniens* exercise (see section IV below).[49] However, in type (2) cases, the court will first apply *forum conveniens* as part of the requirements for service out stated in section I.B above, as the court will only grant leave to serve out if the plaintiff satisfies the court that Hong Kong is the most appropriate forum to try the action. The plaintiff bears this burden at both the *ex parte* and *inter partes* stages. The burden is not on the defendant to demonstrate that there is an alternative forum which ought to entertain the action; rather, it remains on the plaintiff throughout to persuade the court to grant an order to serve out and that Hong Kong is clearly the appropriate forum for the trial of the action.[50] After this is shown, the court then engages in the remaining parts of the *forum non conveniens* doctrine.

Before launching any jurisdictional challenge, a defendant must not have submitted to the court's jurisdiction. Submission will preclude a defendant from disputing the court's jurisdiction, thereby confirming the court's jurisdiction. As to what constitutes submission, see section II above.

There are two major grounds for a stay application: (1) the existence of an alternative and more appropriate foreign forum to which the court should defer (including the existence of *lis alibi pendens*); and (2) the existence of a jurisdiction agreement. Ground 1 is the doctrine of *forum non conveniens*, discussed in section IV.A below. Ground 2 is covered in chapter thirteen. These two grounds correspond with the statutory language in Order 12, rule 8(2A) of the RHC, but rule 8(2) is clear: the rule 8(2A) grounds are not exhaustive.[51]

[48] *Noble Power Investments Ltd v Nissei Stomach Tokyo Co Ltd* [2008] 5 HKLRD 631 [22(1)].

[49] ibid.

[50] ibid [22(2)], citing *Spiliada Maritime Corp v Cansulex Ltd* [1987] AC 460, 481E.

[51] *Deltatre SpA v Hong Kong Sports Industrial Development Ltd* [2018] 4 HKLRD 478, [2018] HKCFI 1942 [35]. The ground of *lis alibi pendens* (existing parallel proceedings) in Order 12, rule 8(2A)(c) is subsumed under the ground of *forum non conveniens*, as it was held that *lis alibi pendens* is only one of the relevant factors in the *forum non conveniens* enquiry: see *Bright Shipping Ltd v Changhong Group (HK) Ltd* [2020] HKCFA 24 [10]; s IV.A below. Contrast this with the position in Mainland China, where three individual grounds are provided: Civil Procedure Law (effective from 1 January 2024) (China), Arts 280 (exclusive jurisdiction agreement), 281 (*lis alibi pendens*) and 282 (*forum non conveniens*).

It is possible to stay an action by the existence of an arbitration agreement under section 20 of the Arbitration Ordinance (Cap 609). However, that power of stay is not subject to the regime in Order 12, rule 8 of the RHC.[52] That ground is covered in chapter twenty-four, section II. Moreover, the court is likely to have case management powers or inherent jurisdiction to stay proceedings by or against third parties in favour of anticipated or ongoing arbitration proceedings in appropriate circumstances.[53]

The grant or refusal of stay involves the judge conducting an evaluative exercise and is a matter of discretion. An appellate court should only interfere when there is a clear error in principle.[54]

IV. *Forum non conveniens* and *lis alibi pendens*

The *forum non conveniens* doctrine is frequently invoked by defendants in stay applications. It provides that a court has the power to order a stay of proceedings if the defendant shows there to be another court with competent jurisdiction which is clearly or distinctly more appropriate than Hong Kong for the trial of the action, unless the claimant can show that it is unjust for it to be deprived of the right to trial in Hong Kong. The doctrine, which originated in the landmark English case of *Spiliada Maritime Corp v Cansulex Ltd*,[55] has authoritatively been restated by the Court of Final Appeal in *SPH v SA* as follows:[56]

> 1. The single question to be decided is whether there is some other available forum, having competent jurisdiction, which is the appropriate forum for the trial of an action ie in which the action may be tried more suitably for the interests of all the parties and the ends of justice?
>
> 2. In order to answer this question, the applicant for the stay has to establish that first, Hong Kong is not the natural or appropriate forum ('appropriate' in this context means the forum has the most real and substantial connection with the action) and second, there is another available forum which is clearly or distinctly more appropriate than Hong Kong. Failure by the applicant to establish these two matters at this stage is fatal.
>
> 3. If the applicant is able to establish both of these two matters, then the plaintiff in the Hong Kong proceedings has to show that he will be deprived of a legitimate personal or juridical advantage if the action is tried in a forum other than Hong Kong.
>
> 4. If the plaintiff is able to establish this, the court will have to balance the advantages of the alternative forum with the disadvantages that the plaintiff may suffer. Deprivation of one or more personal advantages will not necessarily be fatal to the applicant for the stay if he is able to establish to the court's satisfaction that substantial justice will be done in the available appropriate forum.

Five observations may be added to this summary.

[52] *Yip Chi Wan v The Incorporated Owners of Merry Court, Kowloon* [2022] 5 HKLRD 530, [2022] HKDC 1264 [14]–[21].

[53] See, eg *Danone Asia Pacific Holdings Pte Ltd v Fonterra Co-operative Group Ltd* [2014] NZHC 1681; *Tomolugen Holdings Ltd v Silica Investors Ltd* [2016] 1 SLR 373.

[54] See, eg *SPH v SA* (2014) 17 HKCFAR 364 [65]; *Bright Shipping Ltd v Changhong Group (HK) Ltd (No 2)* [2019] 5 HKLRD 30, [2019] HKCA 1062 [5]–[11].

[55] *Spiliada Maritime Corp* (n 50). The *Spiliada* test was first adopted in Hong Kong by the Court of Appeal in *The Adhiguna Meranti* [1987] HKLR 904. It was further approved by the Court of Appeal in *DGC v SLC (née C)* [2005] 3 HKC 293 and later by the Court of Final Appeal in *SPH v SA* (n 54).

[56] *SPH v SA* (n 54) [51].

First, regarding point 2 (being 'Stage 1' of the *Spiliada* test), although the Court of Final Appeal suggested that the first stage consists of two parts, practically speaking, the court will assess all relevant factors in the round to decide which is the more appropriate forum. The relevance of the connecting factors should be look at with the trial of the action in mind and would involve identifying the likely issues to be canvassed at the trial.[57] Where a party relies on a particular fact or matter as a ground for a stay, it is to establish a 'good arguable case' in that respect.[58] The usual connecting factors to be balanced include the location and availability of evidence and witnesses,[59] the governing law, the domicile or place of incorporation of the parties and any existing or pending foreign proceedings.[60]

Second, it was once thought that the existence of parallel foreign court proceedings (*lis alibi pendens*) constituted an independent ground of stay. However, this view no longer holds true following the determination of the Appeal Committee of Court of Final Appeal in *Bright Shipping Ltd v Changhong Group (HK) Ltd*.[61] There, Fok PJ emphasised that *lis alibi pendens* is only 'one of the relevant factors that a court will take into account when addressing the Stage 1 question of whether an applicant for a stay has demonstrated that another jurisdiction is clearly or distinctly more appropriate than Hong Kong'.[62] Multiplicity of proceedings is not of itself a material factor when considering *forum non conveniens*, unless it will cause unusual hardship to a defendant.[63]

Third, the failure of a defendant to raise or identify a defence to the plaintiff's claim in an application for a stay on the *forum non conveniens* ground is fatal.[64] But the fact that a party is seeking a negative declaration (declaring that it is not liable) does not count against that party for the purposes of *forum conveniens*, provided that there is utility for the relief sought.[65]

Fourth, regarding point 3 (being 'Stage 2' of the *Spiliada* test), the claimed personal or juridical advantage must be established objectively by evidence on a balance of probabilities. Examples of personal or juridical advantages include: the entire non-availability of substantive claims and defences in the foreign jurisdiction;[66] the plaintiff's claim being time-barred in the appropriate forum despite not acting unreasonably in failing to commence proceedings;[67] the damages available being higher in Hong Kong and lower elsewhere;[68] or the enforceability of a judgment.[69] Credible threats, intimidation or physical harm to the

[57] *Rambas Marketing Co LLC v Chow Kam Fai David* [2001] 3 HKC 250 [7]–[8]; *Dynasty Line Ltd* (n 3) [57]–[61].

[58] *ING Bank NV v Industrial and Commercial Bank of China Ltd* [2024] HKCFI 2220 [37].

[59] Although the location of witnesses and the mere practical inconvenience for potential witnesses to attend trial at the forum are relatively unimportant and not sufficient for a stay: *PT Krakatau Steel (Persero) v Mount Kerinci LLC* [2009] 1 HKLRD 264 [80]. Witnesses may be permitted by the Hong Kong court to give evidence via video conferencing facilities.

[60] *Spiliada Maritime Corp* (n 50) 478; *Pusan Newport Co Ltd v Milano Bridge (Owners)* [2021] 2 HKLRD 994, [2021] HKCFI 1283 [39]. A Hong Kong choice of law clause is only one relevant factor.

[61] *Bright Shipping Ltd* (n 51).

[62] ibid [10]. The remarks in *The Abidin Daver* [1984] AC 398, 411–12 should now be read as relevant to 'Stage 2' of the *Spiliada* test.

[63] *Bright Shipping Ltd v Changhong Group (HK) Ltd* [2018] HKCFI 2474 [45].

[64] See, eg *四川順利昌隆科技有限公司 v Sze Ming Yee* [2021] HKCFI 2289.

[65] *Ho Siu Pui v Yue Sheng Finance Ltd* [2003] 1 HKC 621; *Anna Dorothea Erna Lungershausen v Thomas Joseph Dillon Jr* [2004] 1 HKLRD 881.

[66] See, eg *Melvin Waxman v Li Fei Yu* [2013] 3 HKLRD 711; *China Medical Technologies Inc* (n 14) [211].

[67] See, eg *Spiliada Maritime Corp* (n 50); *The Kappa Sea* [2018] HKCA 77.

[68] See, eg *The Kapitan Shvetsov* [1997] HKLRD 374; *Bright Shipping Ltd* (n 63); *Pusan Newport Co Ltd* (n 60).

[69] See, eg *Sharab v HRH Prince Al-Waleed Bin Talal Bin Abdal-Aziz Al-Saud* [2009] EWCA Civ 353, [2009] All ER (D) 232 [63]; *Vedanta Resources plc v Lungowe* [2019] UKSC 20, [2020] AC 1045 [85(ix)].

plaintiff if they travel to the alternative jurisdiction is sufficient to constitute personal disadvantage, as staying the Hong Kong proceedings would amount to denial of justice.[70] As for an allegation that substantial justice cannot be obtained in some forum, the court would be extremely cautious and a party would have to demonstrate with 'cogent evidence' that there was a real risk that substantial justice could not be obtained:[71] for example, a fair hearing simply cannot be obtained in the foreign court, or that the circumstances will plainly be unjust. Mere prejudice or disadvantage is not sufficient.

If such personal or juridical advantage is successfully established, then the court undertakes the balancing exercise in point 4 (being 'Stage 3' of the *Spiliada* test).

Fifth, it will not be sufficient for an applicant to point to the potential applicability of foreign law in support of an application for a stay on the *forum non conveniens* ground. As a popular forum for international litigation, the Hong Kong court commonly receives, and is accustomed to dealing with and applying, evidence of foreign law from experts.[72] There is little risk of injustice in resolving issues of foreign law before the Hong Kong with the assistance of experts, and the need to ascertain foreign law will therefore rarely be a decisive factor in favour of a stay of proceedings.[73] A defendant must identify and articulate what the disputed issues of foreign law are, and show that they are so 'substantial or difficult' that the Hong Kong court 'will not feel itself confident to deal' with them,[74] or that there is an 'appreciable' risk that justice will not be done as the court might reach a wrong conclusion.[75] The novelty of a point of foreign law is a factor to be taken into account, but the existence of a novel point of foreign law does not in itself call for a stay.[76] Even where the novel point involves foreign public policy, the party has to identify some specific public policy (as distinguished from general notions of public policy), and the court has to consider the nature of that public policy and assess whether the Hong Kong court would feel confident to deal with it at trial.[77]

V. Interim Relief

A. General Principles

The jurisdiction for Hong Kong courts to grant interlocutory or interim relief is provided by section 21L(1) of the High Court Ordinance (Cap 4) (HCO).[78] It states:

[70] *Ho Yuen Ki Winnie v Ho Hung Sun Stanley* [2008] 4 HKC 544.

[71] *DP World Djibouti Fzco v China Merchants Port Holdings Co Ltd* [2020] 1 HKC 224, [2019] HKCFI 3104 [107], [112], upheld on appeal: *DP World Djibouti Fzco v China Merchants Port Holdings Co Ltd* [2022] 2 HKC 267, [2022] HKCA 84. See also, eg *Cherney v Deripaska* [2009] EWCA Civ 849, [2010] 2 All ER (Comm) 456; *Altimo Holdings and Investment Ltd* (n 33).

[72] In particular, the Hong Kong court is well placed and experienced in dealing with cases involving PRC law and evidence in Chinese: *Bright Shipping Ltd* (n 63) [38].

[73] See, eg *Rambas Marketing Co LLC* (n 57) 266–67; *China International Fund Ltd v West China Cement Ltd* [2020] HKCFI 2976 [47].

[74] *Rambas Marketing Co LLC* (n 57) 266–67; *DP World Djibouti Fzco* (CA) (n 71) [58]–[69].

[75] *DP World Djibouti Fzco* (CFI) (n 71) [85].

[76] *DP World Djibouti Fzco* (CA) (n 71) [26].

[77] *DP World Djibouti Fzco v China Merchants Port Holdings Co Ltd* [2022] HKCA 1330 [27].

[78] See, eg *Lai Hoi Ping v Persons Occupying Portions of Nathan Road near to and between Argyle Street and Dundas Street to Prevent or Obstruct Normal Vehicular Traffic from Passing and Trespassing the Occupied Areas* (unreported, HCMP 2975/2014 and HCMP 2976/2014, 15 November 2014).

> The Court of First Instance may by order (whether interlocutory or final) grant an injunction or appoint a receiver in all cases in which it appears to the Court of First Instance to be just or convenient to do so.

An intended plaintiff can apply for interim relief against a foreign defendant. In such applications, leave to serve on the defendant out of jurisdiction should be sought pursuant to Order 11, rule 1(1)(b).[79] Failure to apply for and obtain leave to serve out (in addition to applying for the relief itself) may risk the interlocutory order being set aside in future.[80]

Common examples of such reliefs include interlocutory injunctions, *Mareva* injunctions,[81] disclosure orders, *Anton Piller* orders,[82] and the appointment of receivers.[83] An application can be made before[84] or after the commencement of proceedings, with or without notice to the defendant,[85] depending on the circumstances of a case. It is also possible to apply for 'interim-interim' injunctions as a practicable stop gap measure pending a full hearing of the interim injunction.[86]

The principles to grant an interlocutory injunction have been set out in *American Cyanamid v Ethicon Ltd*[87] and are generally applied by the courts in Hong Kong.[88] Under the *American Cyanamid* principles, the court is required to determine: (i) if there is a serious question to be tried; (ii) whether damages are an adequate remedy; and (iii) where the balance of convenience lies.[89] There should be no undue delay in applying for an interlocutory injunction.[90] However, there will be flexibility to meet the needs of a particular case. Delay *per se* would not necessarily bar relief, although it might be a factor against its grant.[91]

[79] For applications for service out, see s I.B above.

[80] *China Shanshui Cement Group Ltd v Mi Jingtian* [2018] HKCFI 1553 [182]–[191].

[81] Named after *Mareva Compania Naviera SA v International Bulkcarriers SA* [1980] 1 All ER 213, a Mareva injunction is a freezing order which prohibits a defendant within or outside Hong Kong from disposing of his assets, with the object of facilitating the enforcement of a potential future judgment against him. The template in Practice Direction 11.2 includes terms known as the *Banabaft* proviso to limit the effect of *Mareva* injunctions on foreign third parties: *Babanaft International Co SA v Bassatne* [1990] Ch 13; *Derby & Co Ltd v Weldon (No 2)* [1990] Ch 65. It has yet to include a further *Baltic Shipping* proviso now commonplace in England: *Baltic Shipping v Translink Shipping Ltd* [1995] 1 Lloyd's Rep 673; *Bank of China v NBM LLC* [2001] EWCA Civ 1933, [2002] 1 WLR 844; *Illustrious Assets Ltd v Lu Chung Chun* [2008] 3 HKLRD 432.

[82] Named after *Anton Piller KG v Manufacturing Processes Ltd* [1976] Ch 55, an *Anton Piller* order is an order for the inspection, detention, custody or preservation of any property or evidence which is the subject matter of the cause or matter.

[83] See, eg *Chen Hongqing v Mi Jingtian* (unreported, HCMP 962/2017, 27 June 2017); *Co A v Co D* [2018] HKCFI 2240.

[84] RHC, Ord 29, r 1. An action before action is usually confined to a 'case of urgency': RHC, Ord 29, r 1(2). See also Practice Directions 11.1 and 11.2.

[85] The applicant should carefully consider the timing of his application and whether to notify the respondent. If he inappropriately invokes an urgent procedure or unreasonably fails to notify the other party, the application may be refused: see, eg *Goliath Far East Ltd v Teng Fei Run Trade Ltd* [2019] 4 HKLRD 282, in which a disclosure order application was initially refused when notice was not given to the respondent bank.

[86] See, eg *China Shanshui Cement Group Ltd v Zhang Caikui* [2018] HKCA 409.

[87] *American Cyanamid v Ethicon Ltd* [1975] AC 396.

[88] See, eg *Wah Nam Holdings Co Ltd v Excel Noble Development Ltd* [2000] 3 HKC 118; *Tsit Wing (Hong Kong) Co Ltd v TWG Tea Co Pte Ltd* [2013] 2 HKLRD 505. Different considerations (based on abuse of process) apply for the grant of an injunction to prevent the presentation of a winding up or bankruptcy petition: see, eg *Hua She Asset Management (Shanghai) Co Ltd v Gao Yan* [2023] 4 HKLRD 575, [2023] HKCFI 2229.

[89] It is not possible to exhaust all cases in relation to the grant of interlocutory injunctions. See the commentaries for Order 29 in Joseph Fok and others (gen eds), *Hong Kong Civil Procedure 2025* (Sweet & Maxwell, 2024).

[90] *King Fung Vacuum Ltd v Toto Toys Ltd* [2006] 2 HKLRD 785.

[91] *Convoy Collateral Ltd v Cho Kwai Chee* [2020] 6 HKC 81, [2020] HKCA 537 [78].

Under the Crown Proceedings Ordinance (Cap 300), it is not possible to grant relief by way of an injunction or specific performance against the HKSAR Government.[92] No order may be granted against an officer of the HKSAR Government if the effect will be to grant relief that is not available against the government.[93] An interlocutory or final injunction, therefore, may not be granted against the HKSAR Government or its officials if the effect would be to prevent the government from doing an act.

B. 'Free-standing' Interim Relief

Under section 21M of the HCO, the court has jurisdiction to grant interim relief in aid of proceedings outside Hong Kong which have been or are to be commenced, and are capable of giving rise to a judgment which may be enforced in Hong Kong under any ordinance or at common law.[94] This is known as 'free-standing' interim relief as it does not require a substantive cause of action in Hong Kong. For example, a plaintiff may apply for a *Mareva* injunction to support existing or prospective foreign proceedings. There is also no requirement for the interim relief to be identical to the substantive proceedings commenced in Hong Kong.[95] As stated in section 21N(1) of the HCO, the section 21M power is ancillary to proceedings that have been or are to be commenced in a place outside Hong Kong, and for the purpose of facilitating the process of a court outside Hong Kong that has primary jurisdiction over such proceedings. Where the defendant cannot be served in Hong Kong, the plaintiff should additionally apply for leave of service out under Order 11, rule 1(1)(oc) of the RHC.

Section 21M of the HCO provides an avenue for such interim relief to be sought independently in aid of foreign proceedings. This was traditionally impossible under section 21L, and section 21M reverses the effect of a line of cases in common law[96] which requires an applicant to show an existing cause of action justiciable within the jurisdiction before interim relief can be granted.[97] That common law requirement was successfully challenged as held by a majority of the Privy Council in *Convoy Collateral Ltd v Broad Idea International Ltd*.[98] However, given the operation of section 21M in Hong Kong, it is not necessary for the Hong Kong courts to extend the construction of section 21L in the same manner.

A two-stage test is adopted for determining the grant of interim relief under section 21M of the HCO:[99]

(i) whether the facts of the case warrant the grant of interim relief if substantive proceedings were brought in Hong Kong; and

[92] Crown Proceedings Ordinance (Cap 300), s 16(1)(a).

[93] ibid s 16(2).

[94] High Court Ordinance, s 21M(1); *Top Gains Minerals Macao Commercial Offshore Ltd v TL Resources Pte Ltd* [2016] 3 HKC 44 [22]; *Compania Sud Americana de Vapores SA v Hin-Pro International Logistics Ltd* (2016) 19 HKCFAR 586 [47], [53].

[95] *Top Gains Minerals Macao Commercial Offshore Ltd* (n 94) [22].

[96] *The Siskina* [1979] AC 210, 256; *Mercedes-Benz v Leiduck* [1996] AC 284.

[97] HCO, s 21M(3)(a); *Compania Sud Americana de Vapores SA* (n 94) [44].

[98] *Convoy Collateral Ltd v Broad Idea International Ltd* [2021] UKPC 24, [2023] AC 389. That case held by a majority that the BVI High Court has the power at common law and under the Eastern Caribbean Supreme Court Act, s 24(1) (*in pari materia* with High Court Ordinance, s 21L) to grant freezing orders, despite the absence of substantive proceedings before it.

[99] *Top Gains Minerals Macao Commercial Offshore Ltd* (n 94) [23].

(ii) under section 21M(4) of the HCO, whether it is unjust or inconvenient to grant the interim relief.

At the first stage, the court follows and applies the general principles governing the grant of interim relief in local proceedings.[100] The plaintiff has to show that:[101]

(i) there is a good arguable case against the defendant in respect of the claim;
(ii) the defendant has no assets or insufficient assets within the jurisdiction to satisfy the claim; and
(iii) the refusal or the relief sought would involve a real risk of dissipation of the defendant's asset in such a way that a judgment in favour of the plaintiff would go unsatisfied.

At the second stage, the court considers whether it would be unjust or inconvenient to grant the interim relief. Five factors could be taken into account:[102]

(i) whether the making of the order will interfere with the management of the case in the primary court;
(ii) whether it is the policy in the primary jurisdiction not to make worldwide freezing orders;
(iii) whether there is a danger that the orders made will give rise to disharmony or confusion and/or the risk of conflicting, inconsistent or overlapping orders in other jurisdictions, in particular the courts of the state where the person enjoined resides or where the assets affected are located;
(iv) whether at the time the order is sought there is likely to be a potential conflict as to jurisdiction rendering it inappropriate and inexpedient to make a worldwide order; and
(v) whether, in a case where jurisdiction is resisted and disobedience to be expected, the court will be making an order which it cannot enforce.

VI. Anti-suit Injunctions[103]

The statutory basis for Hong Kong courts to grant anti-suit injunctions is in section 21L of the HCO. An anti-suit injunction does not purport to interfere with any foreign court, but may act personally upon a defendant by restraining him from commencing or continuing proceedings in a foreign court where the ends of justice require.[104] As a party has generally no right not to be sued in a particular forum,[105] and that an anti-suit injunction may

[100] ibid [26].

[101] *Akai Holdings Ltd (in compulsory liq) v Ho Wing On, Christopher* (unreported, HCCL 37/2005, 9 February 2009) [35]–[36]; *Compania Sud Americana de Vapores SA* (n 94) [49]–[53]. See also *Gatecoin Ltd v BD Multimedia HK Ltd* [2019] HKCFI 2025 [42]–[45].

[102] *Top Gains Minerals Macao Commercial Offshore Ltd* (n 94) [27]; *Compania Sud Americana de Vapores SA* (n 94) [54].

[103] See also Thomas Raphael, *The Anti-Suit Injunction*, 2nd edn (Oxford University Press, 2019); Steven Gee, *Commercial Injunctions*, 7th edn (Sweet & Maxwell, 2021) ch 14.

[104] *Stichting Shell Pensioenfonds v Krys* [2014] UKPC 41, [2015] AC 616 [17].

[105] *Turner v Grovit* [2001] UKHL 65, [2002] 1 WLR 107 [25]; *Liaoyang Shunfeng Iron and Steel Co Ltd v Yeung Tsz Wang* (unreported, HCA 1415/2010, 13 July 2011) [30]; *Liaoyang Shunfeng Iron and Steel Co Ltd v Yeung Tsz Wang*

indirectly interfere with the foreign court's jurisdiction, such injunctions are only granted when properly justified. The fact that the local forum is the natural forum and that foreign proceedings have been commenced at an inappropriate forum is not sufficient in itself for an anti-suit injunction.[106]

Several general principles may be distilled regarding the grant of anti-suit injunctions:

1. An injunction is to be granted where the 'ends of justice' require.[107] There must be wrongful or unconscionable conduct amounting to vexation to oppression on the party to be restrained to warrant a grant of anti-suit injunction.[108] In assessing and balancing the ends of justice, the court should take into account both the injustice to the applicant if the injunction is not granted, and the injustice to the party to be restrained if the injunction is granted.[109]
2. As an order indirectly affects the jurisdiction of the foreign court, the jurisdiction to order an anti-suit injunction is one to be exercised with caution.[110] The forum granting an anti-suit injunction should have a sufficient interest in, or connection with, the issue in dispute.[111] It is necessary to show that Hong Kong is the natural forum for the trial of the dispute, and that justice does not require the action to proceed in the foreign court,[112] but it is not enough to justify an anti-suit injunction simply by showing these matters.[113]
3. Before granting an anti-suit injunction, there must be a strong or convincing prima facie case established by the applicant.[114]
4. A failed jurisdictional challenge in the overseas court is not fatal to an application of anti-suit injunction.[115] While delay in applying for anti-suit relief is not fatal, it leads to a stronger argument that the injunction would amount to a breach of comity and would be tantamount to overturning previous judgments.[116]
5. If the court decides to grant an injunction to restrain foreign proceedings, its order is directed against the parties of the proceedings or those who threaten to proceed, but

(unreported, CACV 234/2011, 14 June 2012) [84]; *Suen Kwai Kam v Central China Dragon Select Growth Fund* [2020] HKCFI 69 [25(1)].

[106] *Plain Sail Holdings Ltd v Lau Wing Yan* [2020] HKCFI 653 [43]–[44].

[107] *Société Nationale Industrielle Aérospatiale v Lee Kui Jak* [1987] AC 871, 892; *Airbus Industrie GIE v Patel* [1999] 1 AC 119, 133; *Liaoyang Shunfeng Iron and Steel Co Ltd* (CFI) (n 105) [31]; *Liaoyang Shunfeng Iron and Steel Co Ltd* (CA) (n 105) [85]; *Suen Kwai Kam* (n 105) [25(2)].

[108] *Lee Kui Jak* (n 107) 896; *Airbus Industrie GIE* (n 107) 133; *Turner* (n 105) [27]; *Liaoyang Shunfeng Iron and Steel Co Ltd* (CFI) (n 105) [32]–[33].

[109] *Lee Kui Jak* (n 107) 892, 895, 896; *Liaoyang Shunfeng Iron and Steel Co Ltd* (CFI) (n 105) [35]; *Suen Kwai Kam* (n 105) [25(5)].

[110] See also *The Angelic Grace* [1994] 1 Lloyd's Rep 87.

[111] *Compania Sud Americana de Vapores SA v Hin-Pro International Logistics Ltd* [2015] 2 HKLRD 458 (CA) [45]; *Airbus Industrie GIE* (n 107) 138; *Liaoyang Shunfeng Iron and Steel Co Ltd* (CFI) (n 105) [31].

[112] *Airbus Industrie GIE* (n 107) 138; *Liaoyang Shunfeng Iron and Steel Co Ltd* (CFI) (n 105) [34].

[113] *First Laser Ltd v Fujian Enterprises (Holdings) Co Ltd* (unreported, HCA 4414/2001, 12 December 2002) [70]; *Suen Kwai Kam* (n 105) [25(4)].

[114] *Liaoyang Shunfeng Iron and Steel Co Ltd* (CA) (n 105) [110]; *Suen Kwai Kam* (n 105) [25(3)].

[115] *AES Ust-Kamenogorsk Hydro Power Plant LLP v Ust-Kamenogorsk Hydropower Plant JSC* [2013] UKSC 35, [2013] 1 WLR 889 [61]; *Ecobank Transnational Incorp v Tanoh* [2015] EWCA Civ 1309 [133]; *Sea Powerful II Special Maritime Enterprises (ENE) v Bank of China Ltd* [2016] 3 HKLRD 352; *Dickson Valora Group (Holdings) Co Ltd v Fan Ji Qian* [2019] 2 HKLRD 173, [2019] HKCFI 482; *Linde GmbH v Ruschemalliance plc* [2024] 1 HKC 62, [2023] HKCFI 2409 [29].

[116] *Sea Powerful II Special Maritime Enterprises (ENE)* (n 115) [17]–[27]; *Plain Sail Holdings Ltd* (n 106) [92]–[99].

> not at the foreign court.[117] In other words, it operates *in personam*. An injunction will only be issued to restrain a party who is amenable to the jurisdiction of the court, and against whom an injunction will be an effective remedy.[118]

The following subsections illustrate the application of anti-suit injunctions in various situations. A distinction is to be drawn between applications for an anti-suit injunction founded upon a contractual right and applications not founded on such, in which it is necessary to show that the foreign proceedings are vexatious or oppressive, such as foreign proceedings commenced in bad faith for the purpose of frustrating proceedings in Hong Kong.[119]

A. Anti-suit Injunctions in Favour of Exclusive Jurisdiction Agreements

Anti-suit injunctions are granted routinely in cases of exclusive jurisdiction agreements. The presence of an exclusive jurisdiction agreement, by itself, suggests that there is a contractually agreed appropriate forum and a legitimate interest to enforce that contractual right against the other party.[120] Parties should be held to their bargain to have the dispute resolved in a designated forum or via an agreed method,[121] and an anti-suit injunction is justified 'on the clear and simple ground that the defendant has promised not to bring [foreign proceedings]'.[122] Breach of an exclusive jurisdiction agreement suggests that there is a clearly unconscionable conduct on the part of the party sought to be restrained.[123]

An anti-suit injunction in this context is not regarded as a breach of comity as it merely requires the parties (A and B) to honour the contractual agreement between themselves, namely the exclusive jurisdiction clause.[124] However, when third parties (C) are involved, both the relationship of privity between A and B, and the interests of C must be considered. Generally, an anti-suit injunction may only be granted if the foreign action has been brought against C for ulterior reasons to bypass or avoid the jurisdiction or arbitration agreement, making the foreign proceedings vexatious or oppressive between A and B, or (if successfully shown) between B and C.[125]

B. Anti-suit Injunctions in Favour of Arbitration Agreements

The principles regarding exclusive jurisdiction agreements extend to the context of arbitration agreements. The rule is stated clearly in *Ever Judger Holding Co Ltd v Kroman Celik Sanayii Anonim Sirketi*.[126] The Hong Kong court will

[117] *Lee Kui Jak* (n 107) 892; *Compania Sud Americana de Vapores SA* (n 94) [56].
[118] *Lee Kui Jak* (n 107) 892. See also *China Light & Power Co Ltd v Wong To Sau Heung* [1993] 2 HKC 238.
[119] *Suen Kwai Kam* (n 105) [25(6)].
[120] *Turner* (n 105) [24] and [27]; *Suen Kwai Kam* (n 105) [25(8)].
[121] *The Angelic Grace* (n 110), approved in *Compania Sud Americana de Vapores SA* (n 94) [56].
[122] *The Angelic Grace* (n 110).
[123] *Turner* (n 105) [24]–[25]. See also *Spiliada Maritime Corp* (n 50); *The Angelic Grace* (n 110).
[124] *Deutsche Bank AG v Highland Crusader Offshore Partners LP* [2009] EWCA Civ 725, [2010] 1 WLR 1023 [51].
[125] *Donohue v Armco Inc* [2001] UKHL 64, [2002] 1 All ER 749; *Asiana Airlines Inc v Gate Gourmet Korea Co Ltd* [2024] SGCA(I) 8 [61]–[88].
[126] *Ever Judger Holding Co Ltd v Kroman Celik Sanayii Anonim Sirketi* [2015] 2 HKLRD 866. See also *The Angelic Grace* (n 110) 96; *Giorgio Armani SpA v Elan Clothes Co Ltd* [2019] 2 HKLRD 313, [2019] HKCFI 530 [23]–[25];

ordinary grant an injunction to restrain the pursuit of foreign proceedings brought in breach of an agreement for Hong Kong arbitration, at any rate where the injunction has been sought without delay and the foreign proceedings are not too far advanced, unless the defendant can demonstrate strong reason to the contrary.[127]

C. Anti-suit Injunctions in Favour of Non-exclusive and Asymmetric Jurisdiction Agreements

A non-exclusive jurisdiction agreement is not breached by the bringing of proceedings in a forum other than the named forum.[128] Parties to a non-exclusive jurisdiction agreement are taken to have anticipated and accepted the possibility of some parallel proceedings. As a result, only foreign proceedings which are vexatious and oppressive for some reason independent of the mere presence of the non-exclusive agreement will be restrained by injunction.[129]

As for asymmetric jurisdiction agreements, the exclusively bound party is treated to have entered into an exclusive jurisdiction agreement and may be subject to an anti-suit injunction.[130]

D. Anti-suit Injunctions in Cases of Wrongful or Unconscionable Conduct

Anti-suit injunctions may also be granted not in reliance on a contractual or legal right. In these cases, the legitimate interest to protect is the existence of proceedings in Hong Kong as the *forum conveniens*.[131] Thus, it has to be shown that the continuation of the foreign proceedings is vexatious, oppressive or otherwise unconscionable.[132] This is determined in the eyes of the court asked to grant the anti-suit injunction.[133]

The concept of 'vexatious and oppressive' proceedings should not be strictly defined.[134] In general, there are two types of vexatious and oppressive proceedings: (i) pure vexation, involving plainly unmeritorious proceedings which are patently absurd and cannot possibly succeed;[135] and (ii) an alternative form of vexation when the

GM1 v KC [2020] 1 HKLRD 132, [2019] HKCFI 2793 [12]–[14]; *Giorgio Armani SpA v Elan Clothes Co Ltd (No 2)* [2020] 1 HKLRD 354, [2019] HKCFI 2983 [22]–[25]; *X v ZPRC* [2020] HKCFI 631 [26]–[37]; *Linde GmbH* (n 115).

127 *Ever Judger Holding Co Ltd* (n 126) [45]. A prima facie valid arbitration agreement is sufficient: *Asiana Airlines Inc* (n 125) [92]–[96]; *Friendship Shipping and Trading SA v IVL Dhunseri Polyester Co SAE* [2024] HKCFI 3180.

128 *Deutsche Bank AG* (n 124) [120].

129 ibid [105]–[115], [120]; *Suen Kwai Kam* (n 105) [25(9)]. See also *Sabah Shipyard (Pakistan) Ltd v Islamic Republic of Pakistan* [2002] EWCA Civ 1643, [2003] 2 Lloyd's Rep 571 [37]–[38], [44]–[45].

130 *Industrial and Commercial Bank of China (Asia) Ltd v Wisdom Top International Ltd* [2020] 5 HKC 537, [2020] HKCFI 322 [17], [55].

131 *Liaoyang Shunfeng Iron and Steel Co Ltd* (CFI) (n 105) [25(7)].

132 *Lee Kui Jak* (n 107) 893. In the matrimonial context, interim anti-suit injunctions of a limited duration (known as *Hemain* injunctions) can be granted under this basis to maintain the status quo pending the jurisdictional challenge: *Hemain v Hemain* [1988] 2 FLR 388; *R v R* [2005] 1 FLR 386.

133 *CSR Ltd v Cigna Insurance Australia Ltd* (1997) 189 CLR 345, 393–94.

134 *McHenry v Lewis* (1882) 22 Ch D 397, 407–08; *Asiana Airlines Inc* (n 125) [89]–[90].

135 *Lee Kui Jak* (n 107) 893; *Shell International Petroleum Co Ltd v Coral Oil Co Ltd* [1999] 2 Lloyd's Rep 606, 609.

plaintiff sues the defendant in multiple courts at the same time with no benefit to the plaintiff.[136]

For example, an anti-suit injunction may be granted where the plaintiff has commenced proceedings against another party in respect of the same issue before the Hong Kong court and a foreign court. The defendant might request the Hong Kong court to compel the plaintiff to elect in which jurisdiction the case is to proceed, as there is nothing to be gained over and above what might be gained in local proceedings.[137] Another example is when parties have commenced proceedings with some motive other than a bona fide desire to determine disputes,[138] or even *mala fides* in the institution of foreign proceedings.[139] In *Liaoyang Shunfeng and Steel Co Ltd v Yeung Tsz Wang*, an anti-suit injunction was granted as the defendant used the same evidence inconsistently across various proceedings in different jurisdictions. The purpose of using that evidence contradictorily was found to be entirely tactical, with the intention to frustrate or subvert the Hong Kong proceedings commenced by the plaintiff in Hong Kong, and therefore must be vexatious and oppressive.[140] An anti-suit injunction may also be granted if a defendant in foreign proceedings has difficulty in bringing, or is unable to bring, all cross-claims for contribution or indemnity in the proceedings which attempts to establish liability.[141]

E. Anti-anti-suit Injunctions and Anti-anti-anti-suit Injunctions

An anti-anti-suit injunction would order a party not to seek anti-suit injunctive relief in another forum regarding proceedings in the issuing forum. An anti-anti-anti-suit injunction would attempt to restrain the possibility of a party seeking anti-anti-suit relief. In principle, an anti-anti-suit injunction or an anti-anti-anti-suit injunction could possibly be granted by the Hong Kong court.[142] However, the grant of such injunctions could threaten comity as counter actions, and retaliatory injunctions by foreign courts could spiral and damage international judicial harmony.

F. Anti-arbitration Injunctions

In Hong Kong, it is possible to grant anti-arbitration injunctions to restrain a person from commencing or continuing arbitration, based either on a contractual right to have a matter litigated or it being unconscionable for other reasons.[143]

[136] *Peruvian Guano Co v Bockwoldt* (1883) 23 Ch D 225, 230; *Asiana Airlines Inc* (n 125) [89].
[137] *Bank of Tokyo Ltd v Karoon* [1987] AC 45. This proposition was criticised as 'surprisingly absolute' in the context of the equitable jurisdiction of anti-suit injunctions, as (among other reasons) the fact that there is something to be gained in the foreign proceedings does not prevent equity's intervention: Martin Davies et al, *Nygh's Conflict of Laws in Australia*, 10th edn (LexisNexis, 2020) para 9.27.
[138] *McHenry* (n 134) 414.
[139] *Turner v Grovit* [2000] QB 345, 362.
[140] *Liaoyang Shunfeng Iron and Steel Co Ltd* (CA) (n 105) [106]–[107].
[141] *Lee Kui Jak* (n 107).
[142] *China Light & Power Co Ltd* (n 118); *Ecom Agroindustrial Corp Ltd v Mosharaf Composite Textile Mill Ltd* [2013] EWHC 1276 (Comm), [2013] 2 All ER (Comm) 983.
[143] *SA v KB* [2016] 2 HKLRD 1249; *Xiamen Xinjingdi Group Co Ltd v Eton Properties Ltd* [2023] 4 HKC 573, [2023] HKCFI 1327. See also *Sabbagh v Khoury* [2019] EWCA Civ 1219, [2019] 2 Lloyd's Rep 178; *Sodzawiczny v Smith* [2024] EWHC 231 (Comm), [2024] 1 Lloyd's Rep 466.

VII. Service of Process Outside Hong Kong

The methods of effecting service out of jurisdiction are set out in Order 11, rules 5–7A of the RHC.[144] These methods include personal service,[145] service on the defendant's solicitors,[146] substituted service, service in accordance with contractual terms,[147] service according to the laws of the country in which the defendant is to be served,[148] service pursuant to the 1965 HCCH Convention on the Service Abroad of Judicial and Extrajudicial Documents in Civil or Commercial Matters (the Hague Service Convention) or other civil procedure convention relating to service or in accordance with any agreement between the Hong Kong Government and other jurisdictions. Order 11, rule 7A of the RHC provides special rules for service on a foreign state under the Carriage by Air Ordinance (Cap 500).

In cases involving service to be effected at places where there is a relevant bilateral agreement or international convention governing service, Hong Kong courts must have regard to the provisions in the relevant instrument.[149]

Under the Hague Service Convention, each contracting state designates a competent authority to receive requests for service coming from other contracting states.[150] For service to be effected from Hong Kong to a country which is a party to the Hague Service Convention, Order 11, rule 6(2A) of the RHC provides that:

> (2A) Where in accordance with these rules, a writ is to be served on a defendant in any country which is a party to the Hague Convention, the writ may be served: –
>
> (a) through the authority designated under the Convention in respect of that country; or
>
> (b) if the law of that country permits –
>
> (i) through the judicial authorities of that country, or
>
> (ii) through a British consular authority in that country.

The word 'may' in Order 11, rule 6(2A) indicates that the methods provided in that sub-rule are not exclusive. Service may also be effected by private means provided that nothing is done in the country where service is to be effected which is contrary to the law of that country as prohibited under Order 11, rule 5(2).[151] This is consistent with Article 19 of the Hague Service Convention, which provides that:

> To the extent that the internal law of a Contracting State permits methods of transmission, other than those provided for in the preceding Articles, of documents coming from abroad, for service within its territory, the present Convention shall not affect such provisions.

For service to be effected from Hong Kong to Mainland China and Macao, the Arrangements for Mutual Service of Judicial Documents in Civil and Commercial Matters, which entered

[144] RHC, Ord 11, rr 8 and 8A provide that the person making the request must undertake to pay expenses incurred in respect of the service requested. RHC, Ord 11, r 9 provides that the service out of the jurisdiction of a writ is equally applicable to the service of an originating summons, notice of motion or petition.

[145] RHC, Ord 11, r 5(1), applying RHC, Ord 10, r 1(1).

[146] RHC, Ord 11, r 5(1), applying RHC, Ord 10, r 1(4).

[147] RHC, Ord 10, rr 3(1)(b) and 3(2).

[148] ibid Ord 11, r 5(3)(a).

[149] *AXA China Region Insurance v Leong Fong Cheng* [2016] 6 HKC 220, [2016] HKCA 639 [26].

[150] For a list of these authorities in each contracting state, see www.hcch.net/en/instruments/conventions/authorities1/?cid=17.

[151] *Union Bank of India v Glory Universal Group Inc* [2021] 1 HKLRD 381, [2020] HKCFI 3057 [51].

into force in 1999 and 2020 respectively, should be followed. Order 11, rule 5A of the RHC gives effect to those Arrangements by providing that the writ must be served through the judicial authorities of the Mainland or Macao, as the case may be, and sets out the relevant requirements. It is also possible to order substituted service on a defendant residing on the Mainland.[152] It is currently illegal for a foreign authority or individual to serve process (or take evidence) without permission from the competent authorities on the Mainland.[153]

For service to other countries, the relevant decision whether to order service to these countries would involve pragmatic considerations of whether such litigation is in the interests of efficiency and in an appropriate forum, and whether it could be ensured that the party to be served receives communication of the document.[154] This pragmatic approach was taken in Hong Kong by making orders for substituted service.[155]

The validity of the service of a document under Hong Kong law should primarily be determined by reference to Hong Kong law irrespective of the law of the place of service. However, the law of the place of service can be relevant because, as a matter of Hong Kong law, if the serving of documents is illegal per se at the place of service, that mode of service would not be valid.[156]

Defective service of proceedings – however gross the defect, and even a total failure to serve – is an irregularity which can be cured by the court through the exercise of the discretion in Order 2, rule 1 of the RHC, as long as the existence of the proceedings is nevertheless known to the defendant.[157] Such a discretion was exercised in *Union Bank of India v Glory Universal Group Inc*.[158] There, leave for service out had been properly obtained, and the method of service used (private means) was not positively illegal or unlawful, although it was contrary to the mode of service provided by Indian law, which requires writs to be sent to the court in India. The defendants were nevertheless fully aware of the proceedings and had not been prejudiced by the irregularity.

VIII. Service of Foreign Proceedings in Hong Kong

There are two modes for serving foreign proceedings in Hong Kong.

The first is private service. A foreign party intending to serve a document will engage a Hong Kong process server to effect service, according to requirements under the laws of the foreign jurisdiction and any terms in the foreign court order.

The second is service through the court under Order 69 of the RHC, which covers service of judicial documents from parties to the Hague Service Convention,[159] Mainland

[152] *Deutsche Bank AG* (n 30).

[153] Civil Procedure Law (effective from 1 January 2024) (China), Art 294; *Deutsche Bank AG* (n 30) fn 13; *AXA China Region Insurance* (n 149) [26].

[154] *Abela* (n 30) [37] and [53]; *AXA China Region Insurance* (n 149) [20]–[21] (service to Thailand).

[155] *Deutsche Bank AG* (n 30) (service to Mainland China); *AXA China Region Insurance* (n 149) (service to Thailand).

[156] *AXA China Region Insurance* (n 149) [25].

[157] *Union Bank of India* (n 151) [67].

[158] ibid [68].

[159] Those include a foreign country in relation to which there subsists a civil procedure convention providing for service in that country of process of the Court of First Instance of the High Court, which includes a country that is a party to the Hague Service Convention: RHC, Ord 69, r 1.

China and certain other countries. A request should be made to the Registrar of the High Court by: (i) the Chief Secretary for Administration, with a recommendation by him that service should be effected; (ii) the court or tribunal in a convention country, or a consular or other authority of that country; or (iii) the judicial authorities in Mainland China.[160] Upon such request, the Registrar will arrange service by the Chief Bailiff of the High Court.[161] The foreign process may be served by personal service or insertion through a letterbox,[162] by substituted service[163] or in accordance with other enactments. If the documents are in a language other than English or Chinese, they should be accompanied by a translation into either of the latter two languages, unless the court or tribunal of the foreign country certifies that the person to be served understands the language of the process.[164]

[160] RHC, Ord 69, r 2.
[161] ibid Ord 69, r 4.
[162] ibid Ord 69, rr 3(2) and 3(3).
[163] ibid Ord 69, r 3(5).
[164] ibid Ord 69, r 3(1).

10

Special Rules for Jurisdiction *in personam*

This chapter analyses special rules for jurisdiction *in personam*, including jurisdictional gateways in Order 11, rule 1(1) of the Rules of the High Court (Cap 4A) (RHC)[1] and other statutes. For rules on jurisdiction *in personam* generally, including the principles of *forum non conveniens* and anti-suit injunctions, see chapter nine.

I. Law of Obligations

A. Specific Contracts

Gateway (d) provides that there can be leave to serve out if:

> the claim is brought to enforce, rescind, dissolve, annul or otherwise affect a contract, or to recover damages or obtain other relief in respect of the breach of a contract, being (in either case) a contract which:
>
> (i) was made within the jurisdiction, or
>
> (ii) was made by or through an agent trading or residing within the jurisdiction on behalf of a principal trading or residing out of the jurisdiction, or
>
> (iii) is by its terms, or by implication, governed by Hong Kong law, or
>
> (iv) contains a term to the effect that the Court of First Instance shall have jurisdiction to hear and determine any action in respect of the contract …

Gateway (d)(i) refers to contracts made within the jurisdiction. In this regard, the proper law or the putative proper law of the contract (not the *lex fori*) will determine where and when a contract was made.[2] Section 19 of the Electronic Transactions Ordinance (Cap 553) is relevant in determining the time and place of the sending and receiving of electronic 'records', such as text messages, including the acceptances of offers. Gateway (d)(ii) applies whenever the contract comes into existence through the 'mediation' of an agent.[3] The gateway only applies when the defendant (not the plaintiff) is the agent's principal.[4]

[1] Unless otherwise indicated, a 'gateway' in this chapter refers to a gateway in Ord 11, r 1(1) of the RHC. The gateways in the RHC, except gateways (l), (m), (oa) and (oc), can also be found in the Rules of the District Court (Cap 336H), Ord 11, r 1(1).

[2] See, eg *Ferromin Ltd v Nittetsu Shoji Co Ltd* (unreported, HCCL 41/1998, 29 January 1999). See also ch 15, s I.B.

[3] *Gill and Duffus Ltd v London Export Corp GmbH* [1982] 2 Lloyd's Rep 627.

[4] *Transamerica Occidental Life Insurance Co Ltd v King Sound Industry Co Ltd* [2005] 1 HKLRD 125; *Robin Hargreaves v Taian Insurance Co Ltd* [2006] 3 HKLRD 70.

Gateway (d)(iii) applies not only when there is an express or implied choice that the contract be governed by Hong Kong law, but also when Hong Kong law is found to be the proper law of the contract as the law with the 'closest and most real connection'.[5] Gateway (d)(iv) applies to an express or implied choice of Hong Kong jurisdiction. See chapter thirteen for a discussion on jurisdiction agreements.

Gateway (e) provides that there can be leave to serve out if:

> the claim is brought in respect of a breach committed within the jurisdiction of a contract made within or out of the jurisdiction, and irrespective of the fact, if such be the case, that the breach was preceded or accompanied by a breach committed out of the jurisdiction that rendered impossible the performance of so much of the contract as ought to have been performed within the jurisdiction ...

Gateway (e) requires that there must be a contract between the plaintiff and defendant, that there was a breach of the contract and that the breach was committed in Hong Kong. The breach can be a positive act committed in Hong Kong, irrespective of whether the contract was to be performed in Hong Kong,[6] or a negative act. An example of the latter is a failure to perform an obligation while a defendant was in Hong Kong. As there is a need to show a good arguable case on breach of the contract, this gateway is more difficult than gateway (d). The latter phrase in gateway (e) ('irrespective of the fact ... ought to have been performed within the jurisdiction') reverses the House of Lords decision in *Johnson v Taylor*, which would have unduly restricted the jurisdiction under this head.[7]

Related gateways include gateways (h) and (i), which provide that there can be leave to serve out if:

> (h) the claim is brought to construe, rectify, set aside or enforce an act, deed, will, contract, obligation or liability affecting land situate[d] within the jurisdiction;
> (i) the claim is made for a debt secured on immovable property or is made to assert, declare or determine proprietary or possessory rights, or rights of security, in or over movable property, or to obtain authority to dispose of movable property, situate[d] within the jurisdiction ...

Gateway (h) includes declarations of trust that are concerned with land,[8] as well as claims for rent, for possession and breach of covenant to repair,[9] and to enforce a charging order.[10]

B. Specific Torts

Gateway (f) provides that there can be leave to serve out where: 'the claim is founded on a tort and the damage was sustained, or resulted from an act committed, within the

[5] *Amin Rasheed Shipping Corp v Kuwait Insurance Co* [1984] AC 50, 69; *Continental Mark Ltd v Verkhers-Club de Schweiz* [2001] 4 HKC 469 [28]–[30].

[6] For ascertaining whether there is a good arguable case that the place of performance is Hong Kong, see *Komala Deccof & Co SA v Perusahaan Pertambangan Minyik Dan Gas Bumi Negara (Pertamina)* [1982] 1 HKLR 158, 162–63.

[7] *Johnson v Taylor* [1920] AC 144.

[8] See, eg *A-G v Drapers Co* [1894] 1 IR 185; *Official Solicitor v Stype Investments (Jersey) Ltd* [1983] 1 WLR 214.

[9] *Tassell v Hallen* [1892] 1 QB 321.

[10] *Mority v Stephan* (1888) 58 LT 850.

jurisdiction'. The plaintiff must show that there was a claim founded on a tort[11] and that either the damage was sustained in Hong Kong or the damage resulted from an act done in Hong Kong. The tort can occur in Hong Kong while the damage is sustained elsewhere, and vice versa. If the tort and damage took place entirely abroad, gateway (f) is not engaged. Whether a tort claim fits within the gateway is determined by the governing law of the tort.[12] This means that the plaintiff must normally satisfy the double actionability rule. For this, the plaintiff has to show that the elements of the alleged wrong constitute a tort in Hong Kong and would be actionable as a civil wrong in the place abroad. See chapter fifteen, section III for a detailed discussion of the double actionability rule and its exception.

The gateway was discussed in *Fong Chak Kwan v Ascentic Ltd*.[13] The case concluded that it is enough that significant damage has been sustained in the relevant jurisdiction. It need not be direct damage, but there should be significant detriment suffered by the plaintiff because of the defendant's alleged tortious conduct. When there is indirect damage in more than one jurisdiction, it is enough if the indirect damage in Hong Kong is of some significance.[14] However, it is not possible to create jurisdiction under gateway (f) by simply travelling to the jurisdiction and seeking medical treatment there for ongoing injuries.[15] The doctrine of *forum non conveniens* would then operate to forestall an abuse of gateway (f) where there is merely a casual or tenuous link between a claim and a forum.[16] In defamation cases under gateway (f), damage will have occurred in the place where the alleged defamatory material is viewed or downloaded, rather than where it is posted or uploaded on a server. Nevertheless, the plaintiff must have a reputation capable of being damaged in such jurisdiction.[17]

C. Unjust Enrichment

Gateway (p) provides that there can be leave for service outside the jurisdiction if:

> the claim is brought for money had and received or for an account or other relief against the defendant as constructive trustee, and the defendant's alleged liability arises out of acts committed, whether by him or otherwise, within the jurisdiction.

Gateway (p) conflates three types of claim: (i) unjust enrichment or restitution; (ii) liability to account; and (iii) constructive trusteeship. From the wording of gateway (p), it appears that actions in unjust enrichment not involving claims for money had and received may be excluded from gateway (p). Claims for the imposition of constructive trusts and actions based on an alleged proprietary interest are typically brought under gateways (a), (c), (g) and (p).

[11] As to what causes of action may constitute or not constitute 'founded on a tort' under Hong Kong law, see Joseph Fok and others (gen eds), *Hong Kong Civil Procedure 2025* (Sweet & Maxwell, 2024) para 11/1/331.

[12] *Tugushev v Orlov* [2019] EWHC 645 (Comm) [195]–[197].

[13] *Fong Chak Kwan v Ascentic Ltd* [2020] HKCFI 679 [211]–[260]; *Fong Chak Kwan v Ascentic Ltd* [2021] 6 HKC 401, [2021] HKCA 1138; *Fong Chak Kwan v Ascentic Ltd* (2022) 25 HKCFAR 135, [2022] HKCFA 12.

[14] *Fong Chak Kwan* (CFA) (n 13) [68].

[15] ibid [118].

[16] ibid [95].

[17] *Dr Yeung Sau Shing Albert v Google Inc* [2014] 4 HKRLD 493 [37]; *Oriental Press Group Ltd v Google LLC* [2018] 1 HKLRD 1042, [2018] HKCA 69 [3.1], [3.7], [3.35].

Other jurisdictions have reformed gateway (p). For example, paragraph 3.1(16) of Practice Direction 6B in the UK is more generous, allowing service abroad if:

> a claim is made for restitution where –
>
> (a) the defendant's alleged liability arises out of acts committed within the jurisdiction; or
> (b) the enrichment is obtained within the jurisdiction; or
> (c) the claim is governed by the law of England and Wales.

D. Trusts and Charitable Foundations

Gateway (j) provides that there can be leave for service outside the jurisdiction where:

> the claim is brought to execute the trusts of a written instrument being trusts that ought to be executed according to Hong Kong law and of which the person to be served with the writ is a trustee, or for any relief or remedy which might be obtained in any such action …

Gateway (j) is also available where a claim is brought against an express trustee or relief is sought against a person who has aided and abetted a breach by such trustee.[18]

II. Law of Property

A. Immovable Property

Gateway (g) provides for service abroad if 'the whole subject-matter of the action is land situate within the jurisdiction (with or without rents or profits) or the perpetuation of testimony relating to land so situate'. The rationale for the rule needs little explanation, given that the land is situated in Hong Kong.

Gateways (h) and (i) cover liabilities affecting land within Hong Kong and debts secured on immovable jurisdiction in Hong Kong. These are discussed in section I.A above. However, reference should be made to the common law principle known as the *Moçambique* rule. That principle posits that the court has no jurisdiction to hear disputes involving title to (or rights of possession in) foreign immovable property.[19] Care must be taken in any application of the rule.[20] For example, consider an action in Hong Kong that raises issues of title to land abroad as an incidental question with the court's determination on the issue of title to that land only intended to bind the parties to the dispute.[21] The court's finding on title is simply meant to facilitate the resolution of the main question being litigated by the parties before it. The fact that property is situated abroad should not deprive the Hong Kong

[18] *Clark Quantum Kent v Hai Tin Ltd* [2019] HKCFI 2758 [41].

[19] *British South Africa Co v Companhia de Moçambique* [1893] AC 602. See also *Hesperides Hotels Ltd v Muftizade* [1979] AC 508, with part of its effect reversed by the Civil Jurisdiction and Judgments Act 1982 (UK), s 30(1).

[20] See *DX v LN* (unreported, FCMC 7870/2014, 30 November 2015) [24]–[60] and [68]. It is suggested that the *forum conveniens* exercise should apply without an automatic blanket exclusionary rule.

[21] See, eg *British South Africa Co* (n 19) 625; *Re Duke of Wellington* [1948] Ch 118. See also *St Pierre v South American Stores Ltd* [1936] 1 KB 382; *The Tolten* [1946] P 135; *Ng Teck Sim Colin v Hat Holdings Pte Ltd* [2010] 4 SLR 840.

court of jurisdiction. Likewise, where claims are solely made to enforce personal rights or equities under a contract,[22] lease[23] or trust,[24] the actions may proceed before the court. Consequently, for example, a defendant may be ordered to transfer foreign land under a contract held enforceable in the forum, or to return foreign land purchased under a contract vitiated by some factor.[25] The court is merely acting on personal obligations owed by the defendant to the plaintiff, even though such obligations may arise in connection with foreign land. The *Moçambique* rule is also inapplicable: (i) when the court administers a trust or estate that includes both local property and foreign immovable property;[26] and (ii) in an *in rem* action to enforce a maritime lien for damage tortiously done by the ship to foreign immovable property.[27]

B. Movable Property

Gateway (i) provides for service abroad in relation to movable property if:

> the claim is made for a debt secured on immovable property or is made to assert, declare or determine proprietary or possessory rights, or rights of security, in or over movable property, or to obtain authority to dispose of movable property, situate within the jurisdiction …

What constitutes movable property may give rise to questions. It is debatable, for instance, whether confidential information constitutes property.[28] Shares in Hong Kong companies are treated as situated in Hong Kong for the purposes of the gateway.[29] Cryptoassets are property, at least as seen by the courts.[30]

C. Succession to Property

Hong Kong law distinguishes between probate (if there is a valid will) and the administration of an estate (in other situations).[31] The court is given jurisdiction in all matters relating to probate and administration of deceased's estates, with power to grant probates of wills and letters of administration to the estates of deceased persons and to alter or revoke

[22] See, eg *Penn v Lord Baltimore* (1750) 1 Ves Sen 444, 27 ER 1132.

[23] See, eg *Pepin v Bruyere* [1900] 2 Ch 504.

[24] See, eg *Deschamps v Miller* [1908] 1 Ch 856; *Dawson v Perpetual Trustee Co Ltd* (1953) 89 CLR 138; *Webb v Webb* [1994] 1 QB 696.

[25] See, eg *Cranstown v Johnston* (1796) 3 Ves 170, 30 ER 952; *Richard West & Partners (Inverness) Ltd v Dick* [1969] 2 Ch 424.

[26] *Re Duke of Wellington* (n 21).

[27] *The Tolten* (n 21).

[28] *Ashton Investments Ltd v OJSC Russian Aluminium* [2006] EWHC 2545 (Comm), [2007] 1 Lloyd's Rep 311 [65]; *China Celgard LLC v Shenzhen Senior Technology Material Co Ltd* [2020] EWCA Civ 1293 [58].

[29] *Relevant Employees Whose Shares in China Shanshui Investment Co Ltd Were Held by Zhang Caikui on Trust v Zhang Caikui* (unreported, HCA 1661/2014, 13 May 2015) [68].

[30] *Re Gatecoin Ltd (in liq)* [2023] 2 HKLRD 1079, [2023] HKCFI 914. See also *AA v Persons Unknown* [2019] EWHC 3556 (Comm), [2020] 4 WLR 35 [59], following *B2C2 Ltd v Quoine Pte Ltd* [2019] 4 SLR 17 [142]; ch 17, s IV.

[31] See, eg Probate and Administration Ordinance (Cap 10); Intestates' Estates Ordinance (Cap 73); Non-contentious Probate Rules (Cap 10A); RHC, Ords 76 and 85; Practice Directions 20.1 and 20.2.

such grants.[32] The traditional common law rule is that grants of probate and administration are made only when there is presence of property in Hong Kong.[33] However, statute has extended such jurisdiction to cover cases where there is no property in Hong Kong.[34] Thus, gateway (l) stipulates that leave for service abroad may be granted where 'the claim is brought in a probate action within the meaning of Order 76'. In contrast, gateway (k) provides that there can be leave to serve out if 'the claim is made for the administration of the estate of a person who died domiciled within the jurisdiction or for any relief or remedy which might be obtained in any such action'.

In the situation where the deceased was domiciled outside Hong Kong, rule 29 of the Non-contentious Probate Rules (Cap 10A) provides that a grant may be issued to the personal representative entrusted by the court of the deceased's *lex domicilii* (thus following the foreign grant) or a person entitled to administer the estate under the *lex domicilii*.[35] Gateways (l) and (k) remain available in such situation.

A foreign grant from a 'designated country or place' can be resealed in Hong Kong.[36] Grants from other jurisdictions will require a new grant from the Hong Kong court.

III. Other Jurisdictional Gateways

Gateway (a) provides that there can be leave to serve out if 'relief is sought against a person domiciled or ordinarily resident within the jurisdiction'. For a consideration of the terms 'domicile' and 'ordinary residence', see chapter four.

Gateway (b) provides that there can be leave to serve out if 'an injunction is sought ordering the defendant to do or refrain from doing anything within the jurisdiction (whether or not damages are also claimed in respect of a failure to do or the doing of that thing)'. This gateway deals with injunctions against conduct within the jurisdiction.[37] A good arguable case has to be established for the injunction itself.[38] It is not possible to 'piggyback' other claims on the injunction claim.[39]

Gateway (c) provides that there can be leave to serve out where 'the claim is brought against a person duly served within or out of the jurisdiction and a person out of the jurisdiction is a necessary or proper party thereto'. This is one of the three gateways (together with gateways (m) and (oc)) which do not require any territorial connection between the claim or the intended defendant and Hong Kong. This gateway, which concerns subject matter jurisdiction, is one that has routinely been invoked in service out applications.

[32] Probate and Administration Ordinance, s 3(1).
[33] *In the Goods of Tucker* (1864) 3 Sw & Tr 585.
[34] Probate and Administration Ordinance, s 3(2).
[35] See also *Adrienne Marsh Lefkowitz v The Bank of New York* (unreported, HCMP 1638/1992, 20 December 1995); *Adrienne Marsh Lefkowitz v The Bank of New York* [1996] 3 HKC 591.
[36] Probate and Administration Ordinance, ss 3(3) and 49, Sch 2. These jurisdictions include the Australian states of Tasmania, Victoria and South Australia, the Northern Territory of Australia, New Zealand, Singapore, Sri Lanka and the UK.
[37] *Securities and Futures Commission v Isidor Subotic* [2021] 3 HKLRD 777, [2021] HKCFI 2172.
[38] *Chen Hongqing v Persons Whose Names are Set Out in the Second Column of the Schedule to the Re-Amended Writ of Summons Filed on 26 March 2018* [2019] HKCFI 2121 [80]–[81], [108].
[39] *Securities and Futures Commission v Isidor Subotic* [2021] HKCFI 3350 [25].

It is not a fatal objection to the use of this gateway that an anchor defendant be sued in Hong Kong for the sole purpose of obtaining leave to serve a party outside; however, it must be shown that there is a serious issue to be tried against the Hong Kong defendant.[40] Care is therefore exercised under this gateway to avoid abuse.[41] Under this gateway, a three-stage enquiry is required as follows:[42]

Stage I: Establishing that proceedings have been properly commenced in Hong Kong against an anchor defendant (who may or may not be in the jurisdiction) for the determination of a real issue.

Stage II: Establishing that the proposed defendant is a necessary or proper party to the foregoing proceedings.

Stage III: Establishing that it is appropriate for the claim against the proposed defendant to proceed in Hong Kong as the *forum conveniens*, bearing in mind that an action is already pending in Hong Kong.

Gateway (m) provides for leave to serve out if 'the claim is brought to enforce any judgment or arbitral award'. This is because (apart from land) the presence of a person's assets within the jurisdiction would not by itself give the court jurisdiction over that person.[43] It includes any relevant modes of claim, including writ actions to enforce judgments or awards at common law,[44] and applications to register judgments under the Foreign Judgments (Reciprocal Enforcement) Ordinance (Cap 319).[45] Statutory enforcement regimes under the Arbitration Ordinance (Cap 609) follow Order 73, rules 7 and 10 of the RHC, and gateway (m) is therefore inapplicable. Considerations of *forum conveniens* are not relevant under this gateway; the foreign judgment or award in itself is sufficient for the grant of leave.[46] However, the plaintiff must show a real prospect of a legitimate benefit (which may be indirect or prospective) from the local proceedings.[47]

Gateway (oc) deals with claims for interim relief or the appointment of a receiver under sections 21M and 21N of the High Court Ordinance (Cap 4). The gateway mirrors section 25 of the Civil Jurisdiction and Judgments Act 1982 in the UK. The application for relief is made under Order 29, rule 8A of the RHC. This power is discussed in chapter nine, section V.B.

IV. Intellectual Property Law

Intellectual property rights (IPRs) are generally strictly territorial in nature. The registration and validity of IPRs follow domestic law. It might therefore be thought that claims for

[40] *Fong Chak Kwan* (CA) (n 13) [54], citing *Nilon Ltd v Royal Westminster Investments SA* [2015] UKPC 2, [2015] BCC 521.

[41] See, eg *Haller AG v Vestey International Group Ltd* [2023] 1 HKLRD 39, [2022] HKCA 1743 [24]–[33].

[42] See ibid [30]; *Hong Kong Civil Procedure 2025* (n 11) para 11/1/268.

[43] *The Siskina* [1979] AC 210; *Mercedes Benz v Leiduck* [1996] AC 284.

[44] For the enforcement of awards under common law, see *Xiamen Xinjingdi Group Co Ltd v Eton Properties Ltd* (2020) 23 HKCFAR 348, [2020] HKCFA 32. See also ch 24, s VI.

[45] For the recognition and enforcement of judgments under common law and statute, see ch 23. See also *Xu Hongbiao v Oasis Investment Group Ltd* [2023] HKCFI 860.

[46] *Fonu v Demirel* [2007] EWCA Civ 799.

[47] See, eg *Zhang Rui Kang v Tunghsu Group Co Ltd* [2024] HKCA 361.

the infringement of IPRs are most conveniently determined by the domestic court whose IPR law is alleged to have been infringed. On this argument, there can be no service out of Hong Kong in respect of the infringement of IPRs by conduct abroad.[48] But the modern view is that it is possible to sue defendants over whom a court has *in personam* jurisdiction for the infringement of a foreign IPR. This was held by the UK Supreme Court in *Lucasfilm v Ainsworth*, which concluded that it was permissible to sue in the English courts for the infringement of foreign copyright law.[49] Further, in *Actavis Group HF v Eli Lilly & Co*,[50] the English court found that infringement actions based on foreign patents were equally justiciable before the English courts.

There has been no direct judicial approval or application of these UK cases in Hong Kong. In *Great Genius Industrial Ltd v LG Corp Ltd*,[51] it was held obiter that a suit based on foreign patents would not be justiciable in Hong Kong. That conclusion was apparently reached without consideration of *Lucasfilm* and *Actavis*. In *Nagravision SA v Zhuhai Gotech Intelligent Technology Co Ltd*,[52] the court considered *Lucasfilm* to be a 'novel legal proposition' but did not decide on its validity for Hong Kong. It is suggested that the difficulty in accepting the English authorities is attributable to the double actionability rule, which remains in effect in Hong Kong but has been abolished in the UK. The double actionability rule would regard the infringement of a foreign IPR as not actionable in Hong Kong because IPRs are territorial and cannot be infringed in more than one jurisdiction.

In *Lucasfilm*, the UK Supreme Court reasoned that it is possible to bring an action in relation to foreign IPRs despite the double actionability rule. Thus, one can apply the exception to the double actionability rule in *Red Sea Insurance*.[53] The UK Supreme Court stated:[54]

> But the [double actionability] rule in *Phillips v Eyre* was first eroded by case-law and then abolished by statute. Following the lead of Lord Wilberforce and Lord Hodson in *Boys v Chaplin* [1971] AC 356, in *Red Sea Insurance Co Ltd v Bouygues SA* [1995] 1 AC 190 the Privy Council decided that the first limb of the rule in *Phillips v Eyre* could be displaced so that an issue might be governed by the law of the country which with respect to that issue had the most significant relationship with the occurrence and with the parties. That exception was applied in *Pearce v Ove Arup Partnership Ltd* [2000] Ch 403, in which the Court of Appeal held that a claim in England for infringement of a Dutch copyright was not defeated by the first limb of the rule in *Phillips v Eyre*, because the issues had the most significant relationship with the Netherlands. Accordingly, the court held that Dutch law was the applicable law and not the combination of English law and Dutch law required by *Phillips v Eyre*. In *KK Sony Computer Entertainment v Van Veen* (2006) 71 IPR 179 (High Court of New Zealand), MacKenzie J held (in reasoning which is not entirely clear) that, in a claim for infringement of United Kingdom and Hong Kong copyrights, the first limb of the rule in *Phillips v Eyre* was satisfied.

[48] See, eg *Shanghai Reeferco Container Co Ltd v Waggonbau Elze GmbH & Co Besitz KG* [2005] 2 HKLRD 711; *Mary Kay Inc v Zhejiang Tmall Network Co Ltd* [2021] 5 HKC 30, [2021] HKCFI 1403.

[49] *Lucasfilm v Ainsworth* [2011] UKSC 39, [2012] 1 AC 208 [106].

[50] *Actavis Group HF v Eli Lilly & Co* [2012] EWHC 3316 (Pat).

[51] *Great Genius Industrial Ltd v LG Corp Ltd* [2020] HKCFI 2890 [13].

[52] *Nagravision SA v Zhuhai Gotech Intelligent Technology Co Ltd* [2020] HKCFI 1422.

[53] For a detailed discussion on the double actionability rule, see ch 15, s III.

[54] *Lucasfilm* (n 49) [80].

The analysis coincides with the outcome in *Esquel Enterprises Ltd v Tal Apparel Ltd*,[55] a case involving defamation in relation to allegations of infringement of Japanese and American IPRs. The Court of Appeal concluded that the *Moçambique* rule does not require the English court to refuse a claim for the infringement of Dutch copyright and that the same approach might be taken with foreign patents.[56] However, where the case involves the infringement of a foreign patent, there may still be issues of *forum non conveniens* to surmount.[57]

In intellectual property disputes, the plaintiff is often concerned to restrain by injunction the future infringement of its IPRs.[58] In cross-border passing off cases, the court has jurisdiction to restrain passing off abroad.[59] However, injunctions obtained in one country, as a non-monetary remedy, are unlikely to be enforced in other countries. Therefore, it is common for IPR litigation to be brought in multiple jurisdictions, with much unnecessary duplication in time and cost.

In cases involving foreign defendants, the infringement of IPRs is a tort for the purposes of gateway (f).[60] However, service of originating process in IP proceedings on a registered proprietor of an IPR outside the jurisdiction is not required in actions relating to IPRs (patents, trademarks and registered designs) registered in Hong Kong. The registered proprietor of a Hong Kong IPR may be served directly at the latter's address for service in Hong Kong.[61] It is unclear, however, whether such address can be used to serve proceedings that do not relate to the validity of the IPR registration.

Moreover, for actions relating solely to a claim for infringement of a patent, trademark or registered design, it is arguable that a plaintiff can rely on Order 11, rule 1(2) of the RHC for service out of the jurisdiction without leave as 'by virtue of written law, the Court of First Instance has the power to hear and determine' such claims. The Patents Ordinance (Cap 514), Trade Marks Ordinance (Cap 559) and Registered Designs Ordinance (Cap 522) do not specifically state that the court has jurisdiction to deal with a claim if the defendant is not in the jurisdiction. They do, though, all provide that the Court of First Instance has sole jurisdiction to determine infringements of Hong Kong IPRs.[62] It was held obiter that service of revocation proceedings can be effected out of the jurisdiction without leave under Order 11, rule 1(2) of the RHC.[63] However, this view may have to be revisited in light of the Court of Final Appeal's decision in *David Subotic v Securities and Futures Commission*, which held that Order 11, rule 1(2) of the RHC should be limited to cases where the written law in question clearly contemplates proceedings being brought against persons who are not within the jurisdiction of the court or where the wrongful act, etc, giving rise to the claim did not take place within the jurisdiction.[64]

[55] *Esquel Enterprises Ltd v Tal Apparel Ltd* [2006] 2 HKLRD 363.

[56] Citing *Pearce v Ove Arup Partnership Ltd* [2000] Ch 403 as support for the proposition.

[57] *Esquel Enterprises Ltd* (n 55) [38].

[58] *Spectravest Inc v Apernit Ltd* [1988] FSR 161, 174–75.

[59] See, eg *Pei Zheng Middle School v China Pui Ching Education Foundation Ltd* (unreported, CACV 262/2005, 21 February 2006).

[60] *Anheuser-Busch Inc v Budejovicky Budvar, Narodni Podnik* (unreported, HCA 11095/1999, 4 October 2000) [23]–[31].

[61] *Re Yoshida & Co Ltd* [2004] 2 HKC 577; *Re Yoshida & Co Ltd* (2004) 7 HKCFAR 625.

[62] Trade Marks Ordinance (Cap 559), s 2; Patents Ordinance (Cap 514), ss 2 and 80; Registered Designs Ordinance (Cap 522), ss 2 and 48.

[63] *Yoshida & Co Ltd* (CFA) (n 61).

[64] *David Subotic v Securities and Futures Commission* (2023) 26 HKCFAR 488, [2023] HKCFA 32 [29].

As for parallel proceedings, it has been held that multi-jurisdictional copyright and patent litigations should be allowed to proceed. In the English case of *Philips Domestic Appliances and Personal Care BV v Salton Europe Ltd*, the defendant made an application for English proceedings be stayed in favour of parallel Hong Kong litigation. The court nevertheless allowed the multi-jurisdictional copyright litigation to proceed.[65] It was up to the claimant to 'decide who he sues, where and when, and the court should be reluctant to interfere with that choice'. A court should only interfere in 'compelling' situations where it is plain that some other sequence of bringing suit is to be preferred. In Hong Kong, a stay of Hong Kong patent proceedings in favour of parallel proceedings in the English Patents Court was refused.[66] The court acknowledged that a decision by the English court in respect of the disputed patent would inevitably 'have a profound effect on the Hong Kong action'. Any decision by the latter would mean that the parties in the Hong Kong action 'will have to re-assess their position on the claims and the defences' and 'there may even be questions of issue estoppel'. However, the court did not think that such reality justified a stay because, whichever way the English decision goes, 'this does not mean that a trial in Hong Kong can be avoided in the absence of a settlement'.

In Hong Kong, intellectual property cases are governed by Order 72 of the RHC and Practice Direction 22.1. When seeking interlocutory injunctions in intellectual property cases,[67] it is necessary to be precise. It is essential to state clearly if an order is intended to have extraterritorial effect to restrain acts in one or more foreign jurisdictions. Orders that do not provide a geographical limitation or extension will be presumed to be limited to Hong Kong.[68]

The foregoing principles are largely in alignment with the International Law Association's *Guidelines on Intellectual Property and Private International Law* (2021) (the Kyoto Guidelines). Guideline 3 provides that the courts where the defendant has habitual residence should have territorially unlimited jurisdiction, and Guidelines 4–8 provide for alternative fora in appropriate circumstances. Notably, Guideline 5 provides that a person may be sued for infringement in any courts where the alleged infringer has acted to initiate or further the alleged infringement. Guideline 11 provides that the validity of registered IP rights shall be exclusively determined by the courts of the state of registration, unless the question arises incidentally. Guideline 9 respects parties' choice of court. Guidelines 17 and 18 consider parallel proceedings. Guidelines 13 and 14 deal with provisional and protective measures. Guidelines 12 and 15 permit declaratory actions and counterclaims. Guidelines 10 and 16 deal with submission and grounds of indirect jurisdiction.

V. Family Law

Hong Kong courts hear and determine family law matters under three broad categories: (i) matrimonial causes and proceedings; (ii) family proceedings; and (iii) child-related

[65] *Philips Domestic Appliances and Personal Care BV v Salton Europe Ltd* [2004] EWHC 2092 (Ch).
[66] *Intel Corp v Via Technologies Inc* [2002] 3 HKC 650.
[67] See, eg *Guccio Gucci SpA v Cosimo Ludolf Gucci* [2009] 4 HKLRD 28.
[68] See, eg *Wah Nam Holdings Co Ltd v Excel Noble Development Ltd* [2000] 3 HKC 118.

proceedings, including child protection, child abduction and wardship proceedings.[69] Most family proceedings are initiated in the District Court, where there is a separate family jurisdiction, conducted by the Family Court. The Court of First Instance (the High Court) hears wardship proceedings, proceedings under the 1980 HCCH Convention on the Civil Aspects of International Child Abduction and the 1993 HCCH Convention on the Protection of Children and Co-operation in Respect of Intercountry Adoption, and cases transferred from the District Court. The Court of Appeal and the Court of Final Appeal exercise appellate jurisdiction.

The Family Procedure Ordinance (Cap 646) was gazetted on 30 June 2023 and will come into full operation in the near future. The Ordinance amends and consolidates the law relating to the courts' jurisdiction, powers, practice and procedure in family matters, and establishes the Family Procedure Rules Committee for implementing a consolidated set of family procedure rules. These rules will give effect to procedural reforms drawing on recommendations put forward in the judiciary's 'Final Report on the Review of Family Procedure Rules' published in May 2015. The Ordinance will introduce a consolidated regime of procedural rules in family law to enhance the efficiency, certainty, user-friendliness and cost-effectiveness of the family justice system.

A. Marriage

The Marriage Reform Ordinance (Cap 178) (MRO), the Matrimonial Causes Ordinance (Cap 179) (MCO) and the Marriage Ordinance (Cap 181) (MO) provide how various forms of marriages are celebrated or recognised in Hong Kong. For a detailed discussion on the essential and formal validity of marriages, see chapter nineteen, section I. For the recognition of foreign marriages, see chapter twenty-three, section VI.A.

B. Divorce, Nullity and Separation

The court's jurisdiction in proceedings for divorce, nullity of marriage, judicial separation and presumption of death is covered in the MCO.[70] Section 3 of the MCO specifies three bases for the court's jurisdiction in divorce proceedings: (i) domicile; (ii) habitual residence for three years; and (iii) 'substantial connection' with Hong Kong at the date of a petition or application. Whether a person has a 'substantial connection' with Hong Kong is a question of fact, and the connection must be of sufficient significance or worth to justify the courts of Hong Kong assuming jurisdiction.[71]

Hong Kong does not recognise, and therefore the court has no jurisdiction over, foreign same-sex or polygamous marriages, as marriage under the MCO is limited to monogamous relationships 'involving the voluntary union for life of one man and one woman to the

[69] Practice Direction 15.12, paras 2, 4 and 5. For a definition of 'family proceeding', see also Family Procedure Ordinance (Cap 646), s 3.

[70] MCO, ss 3–6. The Matrimonial Causes Rules (Cap 179A) provides specific rules on service of process in these cases.

[71] *ZC v CN* [2014] 5 HKLRD 43 [9.1]–[9.9]; *ZJW v SY* (unreported, CACV 10/2017, 1 December 2017); *CW v CC* [2024] HKFC 92.

exclusion of all others'.[72] In *Sham Tsz Kit v Secretary for Justice*,[73] the Court of Final Appeal held that (i) the exclusion of same-sex couples from the institution of marriage and (ii) the refusal to recognise foreign same-sex marriages did not violate the right of equality and were constitutional. However, the court held by a majority (Ribeiro and Fok PJJ and Keane NPJ, with Cheung CJ and Lam PJ dissenting) that the failure of the law to provide alternative means for the recognition of same-sex partnerships (such as civil unions) violated the right to privacy and private life under Article 14 of the Hong Kong Bill of Rights and was therefore unconstitutional. It remains to be seen what the legislature will do to comply with the court's judgment. More generally, the recognition of same-sex marriages, civil unions and registered partnerships, as well as their ancillary rights, is currently developing in a piecemeal manner. A more comprehensive statutory framework setting out the status, rights and obligations of these persons will be of value to the Hong Kong community. Ideally, that framework should set out jurisdiction, choice of law and recognition issues in respect of such relationships.

Hong Kong courts will only exercise jurisdiction over a marriage if a specific statute so authorises. For example, the Separation and Maintenance Orders Ordinance (Cap 16) extends to 'a marriage celebrated or contracted outside Hong Kong in accordance with the law in force at the time and in the place where the marriage was performed' (section 2). This would include foreign same-sex and polygamous marriages. The Domestic and Cohabitation Relationships Violence Ordinance (Cap 189) extends to any 'cohabitation relationship', defined as 'a relationship between two persons (whether of the same sex or of the opposite sex) who live together as a couple in an intimate relationship' (section 2). Under the Inheritance (Provision for Family and Dependants) Ordinance (Cap 481), a cohabitant may claim for reasonable financial provision under section 3(1)(ix) as 'any person who immediately before the death of the deceased was being maintained, either wholly or substantially, by the deceased'.

Turning to the other types of family proceedings, section 4 of the MCO identifies five bases of jurisdiction for nullity proceedings:

(a) either of the parties to the marriage was domiciled in or had a substantial connexion with Hong Kong at the date of the petition;
(b) either of the parties to the marriage was habitually resident in Hong Kong throughout the period of 3 years immediately preceding the date of the petition;
(c) both parties to the marriage were resident in Hong Kong at the date of the petition;
(d) the respondent in the proceedings was resident in Hong Kong at the date of the petition; or
(e) the marriage was celebrated in Hong Kong.

Section 5 of the MCO specifies three bases of jurisdiction for judicial separation proceedings:[74]

(a) either of the parties to the marriage was domiciled in Hong Kong at the date of the petition;

[72] MCO, ss 2 and 9. The origin of the rule is from common law: *Hyde v Hyde* (1865–69) LR 1 P&D 130. However, it is likely that homosexuality, as a sexual orientation, is recognised as a 'status' for the purposes of the Hong Kong Bill of Rights, Arts 1 and 22. The Hong Kong Bill of Rights is contained in the Hong Kong Bill of Rights Ordinance (Cap 383), s 8, which is adapted from the International Covenant on Civil and Political Rights.

[73] *Sham Tsz Kit v Secretary for Justice* (2023) 26 HKCFAR 385, [2023] HKCFA 28. The lower courts have rejected all three challenges: *Sham Tsz Kit v Secretary for Justice* [2020] 4 HKLRD 930, [2020] HKCFI 2411; *Sham Tsz Kit v Secretary for Justice* [2022] 4 HKLRD 368, [2022] HKCA 1247.

[74] MCO, s 5(c) has been repealed.

(b) both parties to the marriage were resident in Hong Kong at the date of the petition; or …
(d) either of the parties to the marriage had a substantial connexion with Hong Kong at the date of the petition.

Section 6 of the MCO gives two bases of jurisdiction for presumption of death proceedings:

(a) the petitioner was domiciled in or had a substantial connexion with Hong Kong at the date of the petition; or
(b) the petitioner was habitually resident in Hong Kong throughout the period of 3 years immediately preceding the date of the petition.

For choice of law issues in matrimonial causes, see chapter nineteen, section II. For the recognition of foreign decrees of divorce, nullity and separation, see chapter twenty-three, section VI.B.

C. Matters Relating to the Well-being of the Child

Jurisdiction in matters relating to the well-being of the child is scattered in various statutes, such as the Guardianship of Minors Ordinance (Cap 13), the Legitimacy Ordinance (Cap 184), the Adoption Ordinance (Cap 290), the Parent and Child Ordinance (Cap 429) and the Child Abduction and Custody Ordinance (Cap 512). The proposed Children Proceedings (Parental Responsibility) Bill will place Hong Kong's child protection regime in line with other developed common law jurisdictions. The statute, when enacted, will substantially change the current law relating to the responsibilities and rights of parents for children, by abolishing the current custody and access orders and replacing them with a new range of orders. For a detailed discussion of these statutes, see chapter nineteen, section III. For the recognition of foreign orders and judgments on matters relating to the child, see chapter twenty-three, sections VI.C and VI.D.

VI. Law of Corporations and Insolvency

The main legislation in Hong Kong regarding companies includes the Companies Ordinance (Cap 622) (CO) and the Companies (Winding Up and Miscellaneous Provisions) Ordinance (Cap 32) (CWUMPO). See chapter nine, section I.A and chapter twenty, section II for detailed discussions of rules of jurisdiction and service in the company law context.

The avoidance powers in sections 265A–266D of the CWUMPO (including the reversal of transactions at an undervalue and unfair preferences) extend to transactions occurring outside Hong Kong or involving property outside Hong Kong.[75]

[75] *The Joint and Several Liquidators of B+B Construction Co Ltd v Ulrich Weinmann* (unreported, HCCW 114/2001, 8 June 2004) [63]–[66].

VII. Law of Bankruptcy

A. Presentation of Bankruptcy Petition

Section 4 of the Bankruptcy Ordinance (Cap 6) (BO) provides that a bankruptcy petition shall not be presented to the court unless the debtor:

(1) is domiciled in Hong Kong;
(2) is personally present in Hong Kong on the day on which the petition is presented; or
(3) at any time in the period of 3 years ending with that day:
    (a) has been ordinarily resident in Hong Kong;
    (b) has had a place of residence in Hong Kong; or
    (c) has carried on business in Hong Kong.

It is also possible to serve a petition on a person outside Hong Kong by one of the extraterritorial gateways outlined above. It is possible to bankrupt a deceased estate.[76]

The gateway of domicile in section 4(1) should now be seen in light of the Domicile Ordinance (Cap 596), which sets out rules to determine a person's domicile on or after 1 March 2009.[77] When a debtor challenges the jurisdiction of the Hong Kong court on the basis of domicile elsewhere than in Hong Kong, the court may order the debtor to attend for cross-examination. In such situation, the usual order on default of appearance would be that the debtor's affidavit in the bankruptcy proceedings cannot be used.[78]

The gateway of personal presence in section 4(2) allows a petition to be served on a person who might have only a tenuous connection to Hong Kong.[79] The fact that this was the only jurisdictional criterion met on the day when the petition was presented will not be sufficient on its own to dismiss the petition.[80] It is not a requirement that the debtor has to be present in Hong Kong when service of a statutory demand is effected.[81] However, under section 5(3) of the BO, the Hong Kong court has the discretion to dismiss a bankruptcy petition or to stay proceedings on such terms and conditions as it thinks fit.

The gateway of ordinary residence in section 4(3)(a) refers to the debtor having lived in Hong Kong as part of his or her settled order of life. In other words, the debtor has been 'habitually and normally resident [in Hong Kong] apart from temporary or occasional absences of long or short duration'.[82] It is a question of fact and degree if the debtor has been ordinarily resident in Hong Kong within the relevant period.[83] It is not enough if there is only a mere transient presence, or if the duration of the residence is not substantial.[84] In contrast, it is possible for a person to have ordinary residence in Hong Kong and a main

[76] BO, s 112.
[77] See ch 4, s II.
[78] RHC, Ord 38, r 2(3); *Re Chow Kam Fai* [2004] 2 HKLRD 260.
[79] *Re Damnerncharnwanit* [2000] 1 HKC 579.
[80] *Re Dai Guoliang* [2019] 2 HKLRD 332, [2019] HKCFI 597.
[81] *Re Ho Kai Wa Francis* [2015] 1 HKLRD 277.
[82] *R v Barnet London Borough Council, ex p Shah* [1983] 2 AC 309. See also ch 4, s III.
[83] *Re Kok Hiu Pan, ex p Wing Lung Bank Ltd* [2002] 3 HKLRD 20, 28.
[84] ibid 29.

residence abroad.[85] In *Re Aiyer Vembu Subramaniam*, the facts that the debtor had a Hong Kong identity card and Hong Kong bank accounts were hardly determinative.[86]

The gateway of place of residence in section 4(3)(b) requires an intention to occupy that place. It is not necessary to occupy the place of residence for the entirety of the three years stipulated in the BO so long as the debtor had a place of residence there over that period.[87]

The business gateway in section 4(3)(c) includes the carrying on of business (i) through a firm or partnership and (ii) by an agent or a manager on behalf of an individual or firm.[88] Carrying on business includes a trade or profession. A shareholder in a trading company is not carrying on business,[89] even if that person is in complete control or a director of the company.[90] It is necessary to look at all relevant circumstances. Thus, it is possible to show by appropriate evidence that the debtor has carried on business personally, independently of any company owned and controlled by the debtor.[91] While the signing of a company's annual returns over several years and similar activities by a debtor have previously been held to be indicative of carrying on a business,[92] this line of authority has not been adhered to in recent cases.[93]

It must be noted that section 4 of the BO does not include the presence of assets in Hong Kong. This was a deliberate policy choice by Hong Kong's Law Reform Commission. It was suggested that this is an unfortunate omission in the jurisdictional framework for cross-border bankruptcies in Hong Kong.[94]

B. Grounds of Creditor's Petition

According to section 6(2) of the BO, a creditor's petition may be presented to the court in respect of a debt or debts if at the time the petition is presented:[95]

(a) the amount of the debt, or the aggregate amount of the debts, is equal to or exceeds $10,000 or a prescribed amount;
(b) the debt, or each of the debts, is for a liquidated sum payable to the petitioning creditor, or one or more of the petitioning creditors, either immediately or at some certain, future time, and is unsecured;
(c) the debt, or each of the debts, is a debt which the debtor appears either to be unable to pay or to have no reasonable prospect of being able to pay; and
(d) there is no outstanding application to set aside a statutory demand served under section 6A in respect of the debt or any of the debts.

A statutory demand is a ground for a creditor's petition under the BO. Section 6A deems that a debtor is unable to pay a debt if the creditor has served a demand for payment and

[85] *Re Bright* (1903) 19 TLR 203.
[86] *Re Aiyer Vembu Subramaniam* [2014] 5 HKC 203. See also *Re Wong Lei Kwan Joanne* [2009] 3 HKLRD 173; *Re Ip Pui Man Nina* [2011] 3 HKLRD 299; *Re Lela Tong* (unreported, HCB 14214/2009, 15 June 2011).
[87] *Re Brauch, ex p Britanic Securities & Investments Ltd* [1978] Ch 316.
[88] BO, s 4(2).
[89] *Salomon v Salomon & Co* [1897] AC 22.
[90] *Re Cheung Shing Sheung* (unreported, HCB 6679/2015, 16 May 2017) [27]–[29].
[91] *Re Brauch* (n 87).
[92] *Re Ku Chu Keung* [2007] 2 HKLRD 292.
[93] See, eg *Re Cai Sui Xin* [2019] 6 HKC 329, [2019] HKCFI 330.
[94] See, eg Charles D Booth, 'Living in Uncertain Times: The Need to Strengthen Hong Kong Transnational Insolvency Law' (1996) 34 *Columbia Journal of Transnational Law* 389.
[95] This is subject to BO, ss 6A–6C.

three weeks have elapsed without payment. Since a statutory demand is not a court document, leave to effect service on a debtor outside the jurisdiction is not required. A creditor can, however, adopt the procedure in RHC, Order 11, rule 6 to serve a demand outside the jurisdiction.[96]

Rule 44 of the Bankruptcy (Forms) Rules (Cap 6B) prescribes forms of statutory demands. The debtor has only 21 days from service to pay the amount demanded before the creditor may present a bankruptcy petition. The debtor can apply to the court within 18 days of the demand to set aside the statutory demand.[97] However, if a statutory demand is to be served outside Hong Kong, the respective time limits of 21 and 18 days are each extended by 21 days.[98]

Rule 46(2) of the Bankruptcy Rules (Cap 6A) requires a creditor to do everything reasonable to bring a statutory demand to the debtor's attention, including effecting practical service if that is possible. According to paragraph 2.1 of Practice Direction 3.1, there are three methods which will normally be regarded as complying with rule 46(2):

(a) If the debtor is represented by a solicitor, personal service may be attempted through such solicitor. Rule 49(4) of the Bankruptcy Rules enables a solicitor to accept service of a statutory demand on behalf of a client.
(b) If the debtor has agreed with the creditor to use electronic means (emails, WhatsApp, WeChat etc) to receive communications relating to the debt or the debtor has used such electronic means to communicate with the creditor within the preceding 12 months, the creditor may send the statutory demand through the relevant electronic means.
(c) Substituted service of the petition may be employed.

Advertisement can only be used as a means of substituted service of a statutory demand without first attempting personal service if the demand is based on a judgment or order of any court and the requirements of Rule 46(3) of the Bankruptcy Rules are met. The advertisement should be in a language which the debtor is expected to understand. As there is no statutory form of advertisement, the court will normally accept an advertisement in the form set out in paragraph 2.4 of Practice Direction 3.1.

Rules 47 and 48 of the Bankruptcy Rules state that a debtor may apply to the court to set aside a statutory demand within 18 days from service of the statutory demand (unless an extension of time is applied). The debtor must produce a supporting affidavit stating the grounds for setting aside, and bears the burden to satisfy the court that sufficient cause is shown for the demand to be set aside.

C. Bankruptcy Order

The making of a bankruptcy order is a matter of discretion. Once the jurisdictional criteria have been met, the court will decide whether to order the relief. Under section 9(3) of the BO:

> If the court is not satisfied with the proof of the petitioning creditor's debt or of the service of the petition, or is satisfied by the debtor that he is able to pay his debts or has a reasonable prospect of

[96] Practice Direction 3.1, para 2.2.
[97] Bankruptcy (Forms) Rules (Cap 6B), r 44.
[98] Practice Direction 3.1, para 2.3.

> being able to pay them, or considers that for other sufficient cause no order ought to be made, the court may dismiss the petition.

It is possible to refuse relief if there is clearly a more appropriate forum for the proceeding. This ground would constitute 'other sufficient cause'. The court may also adjourn or stay bankruptcy proceedings.[99] For choice of law issues on the effect of bankruptcy, see chapter twenty-one.

D. Avoidance Powers

The avoidance powers in sections 49–51B of the BO (including the reversal of transactions at an undervalue and unfair preferences) extend to transactions occurring outside Hong Kong or involving property outside Hong Kong. For example, in *Chan Pui Sze and Mak Hau Yin v Wang Jue*, section 49 of the BO, on the avoidance of transactions at an undervalue, applied to real property overseas.[100] This is in line with English jurisprudence.[101] It is submitted that this is a reasonable outcome, as Hong Kong trustees-in-bankruptcy have to be empowered with extraterritorial avoidance powers to 'reach assets that have been transferred out of Hong Kong in anticipation of the filing of a bankruptcy petition'.[102] However, there is no rule in the Bankruptcy Rules that provides for the service of process on a person outside the jurisdiction.[103] There is consequently no mechanism for serving process relating to avoidance powers on persons outside Hong Kong.[104]

VIII. Competition Law

The Competition Tribunal was established under section 134 of the Competition Ordinance (Cap 619) as a superior court of record, with the jurisdiction to hear and determine the following matters as specified in section 142(1) of the Competition Ordinance:

> (a) applications made by the Commission with regard to alleged contraventions, or alleged involvements in contraventions, of the competition rules;
> (b) applications for the review of reviewable determinations;
> (c) private actions in respect of contraventions, or involvements in contraventions, of the conduct rules;
> (d) allegations of contraventions, or involvements in contraventions, of the conduct rules raised as a defence;
> (e) applications for the disposal of property;

[99] BO, ss 100 and 104.
[100] *Chan Pui Sze and Mak Hau Yin v Wang Jue* [2019] HKCFI 2515.
[101] See, eg *Re Paramount Airways Ltd* [1993] Ch 223 (undervalue transaction); *Barclays Bank plc v Homan* [1993] BCLC 680 (unfair preference).
[102] Charles D Booth et al, *Hong Kong Personal Insolvency Manual*, 3rd edn (LexisNexis, 2024) para 14-66.
[103] This may be contrasted with the Insolvency Rules 1986 (UK), r 12.12(3).
[104] See also Charles D Booth and Philip St J Smart, 'The New Avoidance Powers under Hong Kong Insolvency Law: A Move from Territoriality to Extraterritoriality' (2000) 34 *International Lawyer* 255.

(f) applications for the enforcement of commitments; and
(g) any matter related to a matter referred to in paragraph (a), (b), (c), (d), (e) or (f) if the matters arise out of the same or substantially the same facts.

The Tribunal has the same jurisdiction to grant remedies and reliefs, equitable or legal, as the Court of First Instance,[105] and has the powers set out in section 143 of the Competition Ordinance. The constitution, jurisdiction and powers, and practice and procedure of the Tribunal are further set out in Part 10 of the Competition Ordinance. The Tribunal has published the Competition Tribunal Rules (Cap 619D) and Practice Directions CT PD 1 and CT PD 2 on its practice and procedures. Where no provisions are made for a matter, the RHC will apply as appropriate. A more detailed discussion of the competition law in Hong Kong is provided in chapter twenty-two.

[105] Competition Ordinance (Cap 619), s 142(2).

11

Jurisdiction in Shipping Claims

Questions as to which forum should have jurisdiction to determine a case have been a perennial question in maritime law. Both wet shipping (eg collision) and dry shipping (eg carriage of goods) disputes typically involve parties from different countries, hence they often touch upon systems of law other than Hong Kong law.

This chapter summarises jurisdiction and choice of law relating to shipping claims. Section I introduces the Admiralty jurisdiction in Hong Kong, in particular the extent to which it covers foreign vessels or shipping claims involving foreign element. Section II discusses methods to establishing jurisdiction in the Hong Kong courts. There are four methods, namely: (i) service within the jurisdiction; (ii) service out of jurisdiction; (iii) submission by conduct; and (iv) submission by jurisdiction agreement. The first three methods have been set out in chapter nine. Submission by jurisdiction clause will be elaborated here due to a series of cases peculiar to shipping. Section III discusses challenging jurisdiction before the Hong Kong courts, focusing on connecting factors unique to shipping claims, in addition to the general rules in chapter nine. Section IV deals with ship arrest in Hong Kong, a key method for enforcing a shipping claim and obtaining security for the same. Section V deals with the enforcement of an action *in rem* after obtaining judgment *in personam*.

I. Admiralty Jurisdiction

The Admiralty jurisdiction in Hong Kong is statutory, being conferred by sections 12A–12E of the High Court Ordinance (Cap 4) (HCO) and Order 75 of the Rules of the High Court (Cap 4A) (RHC).

The Admiralty court has jurisdiction to entertain a suit in respect of foreign vessel. The case of *The Jupiter (No 2)*[1] concerns the English counterpart of section 12A(2)(a) of the HCO.[2] The vessel was owned by a Russian company. Following the Russian Revolution, private property in shipping was abolished by a Russian government decree in 1918. An English company acted as agents for the Soviet government to sell the vessel to an Italian buyer. The Russian company brought proceedings in an English court to claim possession of the vessel. The Italian buyer challenged against the jurisdiction. The English Court of Appeal held that the Admiralty court had jurisdiction to deal with the claim even though the parties were foreign.[3]

[1] *The Jupiter (No 2)* [1925] P 69.
[2] HCO, s 12A(2)(a) concerns the claim to the possession or ownership of a vessel.
[3] *The Jupiter (No 2)* (n 1) 74–75.

Under section 12A(2)(e) of the HCO, the Admiralty court has jurisdiction to hear claims for damage done by a ship.[4] The jurisdiction can cover damage sustained outside Hong Kong.[5] For damage to goods carried in a ship,[6] the court has discretion to allow proceedings in Hong Kong despite the contract stipulating for disputes to be judged elsewhere.[7] The court can hear claims based on wage disputes, regardless of where the claim originated, the nationality or registration of the ship, or the owner's domicile.[8] However, the court has the discretion to refuse to hear a wage claim brought by the master or a crew member of a foreign ship.[9]

Common law prevented foreign states from being sued in Hong Kong courts against their will. In practice, the court is generally unable to consider claims pertaining to foreign state-owned vessels.[10] Foreign sovereigns are prima facie immune from suits *in rem*.[11] The immunity does not cover vessels owned by foreign sovereign but operated as an ordinary merchant ship.[12]

II. Establishing Jurisdiction – Jurisdiction Agreements in the Shipping Context

A. Effect of an Express Jurisdiction Agreement

The effect of express jurisdiction agreements are covered in detail in chapter thirteen. An agreement to submit to a jurisdiction can be exclusive or non-exclusive.[13] Typically, an action commenced in Hong Kong in breach of an agreement to submit to a foreign jurisdiction will be stayed.[14] However, the existence of a jurisdiction agreement does not prevent a party from applying for a stay of proceedings and arguing that the case should be heard elsewhere, if strong cause can be shown.

The Pioneer Container illustrates the high threshold of what constitutes strong cause in the shipping context.[15] In that case, a container ship was carrying goods from Taiwan to Hong Kong. It sank due to heavy fog. The plaintiff cargo owners arrested the vessel's sister ship. The bill of lading contained an exclusive jurisdiction clause for Taiwan courts and a Chinese governing law clause.[16] The defendant shipowner applied for a stay of proceedings in Hong Kong. The trial judge refused the stay and allowed the Hong Kong actions to proceed, finding that the plaintiffs had not acted unreasonably in allowing the time bar to elapse in Taiwan, as the plaintiffs would have been required to put up (i) advance costs and

[4] HCO, s 12A(2)(e). See also HCO, s 12B(3).
[5] *The Tolten* [1946] P 135. See also *The Chr Knudsen* [1932] P 153.
[6] HCO, s 12A(2)(g).
[7] *The Fehmarn* [1958] 1 WLR 159.
[8] HCO, s 12A(2)(n).
[9] HCO, s 12E(2).
[10] *The Parlement Belge* (1880) 5 PD 197; *The Porto Alexandre* [1920] P 30.
[11] *Young v The Scotia* [1903] AC 501.
[12] *The Philippine Admiral* [1977] AC 373 (PC, on appeal from Hong Kong).
[13] *Noble Power Investments Ltd v Nissei Stomach Tokyo Co Ltd* [2008] 5 HKLRD 631 [24]–[45]. See ch 13.
[14] *The Eleftheria* [1970] P 94.
[15] *The Pioneer Container* [1994] 2 AC 324 (PC, on appeal from Hong Kong).
[16] ibid 332–33.

(ii) counter security in the event of a ship arrest in Taiwan.[17] This conclusion was overturned by the Court of Appeal, which did not regard the two matters as sufficient justification for 'strong cause' to depart from the exclusive jurisdiction clause, and held that the plaintiffs had deliberately and advisedly allowed the time limit to expire in Taiwan. The Privy Council upheld the Court of Appeal's order to stay the actions.[18]

Guidance on general principles can be found in the earlier case of *The El Amria*.[19] In that case, the bill of lading included clauses stating that the jurisdiction and applicable law were to be those of the country of the carrier's principal place of business.[20] The owners applied for a stay of English proceedings, as having been brought in breach of the jurisdiction agreement. Brandon LJ stressed that, given the jurisdiction clause, the court should only allow proceedings elsewhere if there is compelling reason. The following non-exhaustive factors should be considered:[21]

(i) the place where evidence is more readily available;
(ii) whether foreign law is applicable and substantially differs from the law of the forum seised;
(iii) the forum with which the parties are most closely connected;
(iv) whether a party is merely seeking procedural or tactical advantages afforded by a given forum; and
(v) whether a party will be seriously prejudiced by proceedings in a given forum.

B. Validity of an Express Jurisdiction Agreement

Jurisdiction clauses may remain effective despite the main contract (such as a contract of carriage) being void. In *Mackender v Feldia AG*,[22] despite the non-disclosure of a practice of smuggling would render the insurance contract void from the moment of avoidance, and the illegality would render it unenforceable, the Belgian exclusive jurisdiction clause remained effective and should be respected.[23] Similarly, arbitration clauses are severable from the main contract. However, it was held that express reference is required to incorporate an arbitration clause in a charterparty into a bill of lading.[24]

A jurisdiction agreement is of no effect if its enforcement would be against the Hague–Visby Rules, which has the force of law in Hong Kong under the Carriage of Goods by Sea Ordinance (Cap 462).[25]

In *The Iran Vojdan*,[26] the bill of lading contained a floating jurisdiction and choice of law clause which gave the carrier an option to elect between: (i) English law and the exclusive

[17] ibid 348.
[18] ibid 349.
[19] *The El Amira* [1981] 2 Lloyd's Rep 119.
[20] ibid 121.
[21] ibid 123–24.
[22] *MacKender v Feldia AG* [1967] 2 QB 590.
[23] ibid 598–99.
[24] Arbitration Ordinance (Cap 609), s 34; *OCBC Wing Hang Bank Ltd v Kai Sen Shipping Co Ltd* [2020] 1 HKLRD 1217, [2020] HKCFI 375.
[25] *The Hollandia* [1983] 1 AC 565.
[26] *The Iran Vojdan* [1984] 2 Lloyd's Rep 380.

jurisdiction of the courts in London; (ii) Iranian law and the exclusive jurisdiction of the courts in Tehran; or (iii) German law and the exclusive jurisdiction of the courts in Hamburg. The carrier opted for German law and the courts in Hamburg. The counterparty objected. Bingham J began his analysis on the assumption that German or Iranian law applied. If German law was applicable, the jurisdiction clause would be invalid. If Iranian law was applicable, in the absence of evidence to the contrary, it would be presumed that Iranian law was the same as English law. In this case, Bingham J held that the jurisdiction clause was ineffective under both English and Iranian law, as the jurisdiction clause depended on a floating choice of law agreement, which was too uncertain to be enforceable.[27] Thus, the contract did not confer exclusive jurisdiction.

III. Challenging Jurisdiction

The majority of the operative principles have been covered in chapter nine, section IV. While the principles in chapter nine primarily concern claims *in personam*, the *forum non conveniens* principles are equally applicable to shipping claims.[28] This section therefore only draws attention to the connecting factors specific to shipping claims which are to be taken into account in a *forum non conveniens* analysis.

Following *The Adhiguna Meranti*, the court has to be satisfied overall that the justice of a case points to a stay on the basis of *forum non conveniens*. The court will therefore consider a wider set of circumstances which go beyond those taken into account when considering connecting factors to the alternative jurisdiction.[29] There is no exhaustive list of factors to be considered.[30] The court is entitled to examine a broad range of connecting factors, but it is not a mechanical exercise of totting up the number of factors connecting the claim with a particular jurisdiction and those against. The burden of proof is on the party challenging the jurisdiction and is not lightly discharged.[31]

In maritime disputes, tonnage limitation is an important factor to be taken into account as it may substantively affect overall fairness.[32] *Bright Shipping Ltd v Changhong Group (HK) Ltd* held that limitations of liability and ceilings on liability were manifestations of international public policy.[33] Thus, the deprivation of a limitation advantage may lead to injustice. In the second stage of the *forum non conveniens* analysis, significant weight is attached to

[27] See ch 14, s IV.

[28] See, eg *New Link Consultants Ltd v Air China* [2005] 2 HKC 260; *The Peng Yan* [2009] 1 HKLRD 144; *Bright Shipping Ltd v Changhong Group (HK) Ltd (No 2)* [2019] 5 HKLRD 30, [2019] HKCA 1062; *Bright Shipping Ltd v Changhong Group (HK) Ltd* [2020] HKCFA 24; *Pusan Newport Co Ltd v Milano Bridge (Owners)* [2021] 2 HKLRD 994, [2021] HKCFI 1283; *Pusan Newport Co Ltd v Milano Bridge (Owners)* [2022] 1 HKLRD 1151, [2022] HKCA 157.

[29] *Spiliada Maritime Corp v Cansulex Ltd* [1987] AC 460, 478.

[30] *Pusan Newport Co Ltd* (CFI) (n 28) [38]–[44].

[31] ibid [42]–[44]. See also *Spiliada Maritime Corp* (n 29); *Rambas Marketing Co LLC v Chow Kam Fai David* [2001] 3 HKC 250.

[32] *Pusan Newport Co Ltd* (CA) (n 28) [28] and [31]; *The Andhika Samyra* (unreported, HCAJ 14/1998, 28 September 1988) [31].

[33] *Bright Shipping Ltd* (CA) (n 28) [68]–[72].

tonnage limitation.[34] Nonetheless, the deprivation of a higher tonnage limit favouring a plaintiff does not mean that a stay of proceedings will invariably be refused.[35]

A court may grant a stay on conditions. In *The Ocean Friend*,[36] the holder of the bill of lading commenced an action *in rem* against the defendant for the non-delivery of goods. An English jurisdiction clause was incorporated in the bill of lading. The plaintiff argued that the Hong Kong court should not stay the proceedings because: (i) the plaintiff would lose its security for the action; (ii) the right of action in England was time barred; (iii) the defendant did not genuinely wish for a trial in England; (iv) the parties had stronger connections with Hong Kong than England; (v) the evidence could more conveniently be heard in Hong Kong; and (vi) the defendant's counterclaim would in any event be heard in Hong Kong. Except from the arguments on security and time bar, the court did not accept the other arguments as good enough reasons to refuse a stay. The court stayed proceedings on the conditions that: (i) the defendant had to provide acceptable security to satisfy any judgment that the plaintiff might obtain in England; and (ii) the defendant had to undertake not to rely on the time bar in English proceedings.

In the context of an arrest claim in Hong Kong giving rise to jurisdiction, the *res* (ie vessel) provides security for the plaintiff. Since the plaintiff has arrested the vessel and founded jurisdiction in Hong Kong as of right, the defendant applying for a stay on *forum non conveniens* grounds bears the burden of establishing that some other jurisdiction is more appropriate. Possible ways to discharge this burden include showing that: (i) the plaintiff has brought the Hong Kong action in breach of a foreign jurisdiction clause or arbitration agreement; and (2) alternative security is available in the alternative forum.[37]

IV. Ship Arrest in Hong Kong

Arresting a ship is an important method for obtaining security for and enforcing a shipping claim. The ability to arrest a ship depends on whether the plaintiff can establish Admiralty jurisdiction and commence an action *in rem* against a ship.

A. Statutory Framework

The Hong Kong Admiralty jurisdiction can be traced back to the Colonial Courts of Admiralty Act 1890 in the UK, which came into force in Hong Kong on 1 July 1891. The Admiralty enforcement powers have historically developed in line with the law in England. In particular, the Administration of Justice Act 1956 in the UK was extended to Hong Kong by the Admiralty Jurisdiction (Hong Kong) Order in Council (No 1547 of 1962). By partially adopting the 1952 Convention Relating to the Arrest of Seagoing Ships (the Arrest Convention), the Administration of Justice Act 1956 expanded the enforcement powers

[34] See also *Pusan Newport Co Ltd* (CA) (n 28) [28], [31], [38] and [46].
[35] ibid [44] and [61].
[36] *The Ocean Friend* [1981] 1 HKLR 253.
[37] ibid.

of the English and Hong Kong Admiralty courts. The UK re-enacted the Administration of Justice Act 1956 in essentially the same terms in sections 20–24 of the Senior Courts Act 1981, which was also extended to Hong Kong as sections 12A–12E of the HCO.

Section 12B of the HCO provides that (i) an action *in rem* may be brought in the High Court against the ship or property in connection with which a claim arises and (ii) an action *in personam* may be brought in the High Court in all cases within the Admiralty jurisdiction of the court. Section 12C of the HCO defines the High Court's *in personam* jurisdiction in collision cases. Moreover, for certain maritime claims, an action *in rem* can be brought not just against the ship in which a claim arises, but also against a sister ship. More specifically, under section 12B(4) of the HCO, if:

> (1) the claim arises in connection with a ship [Ship A]; and
> (2) the person who would be liable on the claim in an action *in* personam (the relevant person) was, when the cause of action arose, the owner or charterer of, or in possession or in control of, the ship,

then an action *in rem* may be brought against:

(i) Ship A, if at the time when the action is brought the relevant person is either the beneficial owner of all shares[38] in Ship A or the demise charterer of Ship A, or
(ii) any other ship (sister ship) of which, at the time when the action is brought, the relevant person is the beneficial owner of all shares in it.

A person is the 'beneficial owner as respects all the shares' in a ship in two main scenarios. One situation is where the vessel's registered owner is the full owner (ie the registered owner holds full legal and equitable title in the ship). The other situation is where the registered owner is a nominee for the true beneficial owner of the vessel and merely holds legal title to the ship's shares on trust. The insertion of the adjective 'beneficial' was intended to cater for the possibility of a trust and to tackle the mischief that would otherwise exist if the true beneficial owner were able to operate its ship under the cloak of a trust. Ultimately, the question is whether a person holds the entire proprietary interest in a ship so that a plaintiff can enforce a claim against it.[39]

The Decurion (No 2) held that each claim in an action *in rem* must fall within the court's Admiralty jurisdiction.[40] The plaintiff must assess (i) whether each claim falls within the ambit of section 12A of the HCO and (ii) whether the Admiralty jurisdiction may be exercised by the court under section 12B of the HCO with respect to each claim. If either of the two requirements was not fulfilled, the plaintiff would have to 'piggyback' speculative claims onto claims within the Admiralty jurisdiction and seek to invoke the exercise of jurisdiction in respect of the claim in large.[41]

The distinction between actions *in rem* and *in personam* is important. The former action enables a plaintiff to arrest a vessel and hold it as security for its claim. The latter action is (as its name implies) an unsecured personal action.

[38] Traditionally, a ship is divided into 64 equal shares. This can be traced back to the Registering of British Vessels Act 1845 (8 & 9 Vict c 89), s 32.

[39] *The Convenience Container* [2007] 3 HKLRD 575 [47]. See also Anselmo Reyes, 'Cross-border Insolvency and Shipping Companies' [2016] *Lloyd's Maritime and Commercial Law Quarterly* 517.

[40] *The Decurion (No 2)* [2013] 2 HKLRD 930.

[41] ibid [35]. See also *The Oriental Dragon* [2014] 1 HKLRD 649; *The Ruby Star* [2015] 1 HKLRD 543.

B. Arresting *in rem*

(i) Arresting in rem *under a Maritime Lien*

Maritime liens enjoy high priority, and remain enforceable regardless of the transfer of ownership in a ship. This is because such liens are specific to a ship and can only be enforced against the ship to which they are attached.[42] A maritime lien will only be extinguished if the vessel wholly ceases to exist[43] or if there is a judicial sale.[44] Maritime liens attach only to claims for salvage, damage done by a ship, seaman's wages, master's wages, master's disbursements, bottomry and respondentia. Under section 12B(3) of the HCO, an action *in rem* may be brought against a ship, aircraft or property which can be arrested. The expression 'maritime lien' only refers to maritime liens under English law; foreign maritime liens that have no equivalent in English law are not recognised.[45]

(ii) Arresting in rem *under a Statutory Lien*

Statutory liens cover a wider range of claims against ships than maritime liens. Arrests based on the statutory liens listed in sections 12A(2)(a), 12A(2)(b), 12A(2)(c) or 12A(2)(r) of the HCO can be enforced against the ship in connection with which a claim arises. A claim under this head can be brought upon issue of the writ *in* rem by the plaintiff.[46] Arrests based on the statutory liens in sections 12A(2)(e)–12A(2)(q) of the HCO can be enforced *in rem* (i) against the ship in question or (ii) against a sister ship. The requirements are set out in section 12B(4) of the HCO.[47]

(iii) Stay of Proceedings and Arrest of a Vessel

The Admiralty court has jurisdiction to maintain the arrest of a vessel even when there has been a stay of proceedings. In *The Britannia*, Waung J had no doubt that the law did not prohibit arrest despite stay of proceedings.[48] The case involved a stay in favour of arbitration. But there is nothing prohibiting the same to be applied in the context of jurisdiction agreement.[49]

To maintain an arrest, the arrest application will have to show that an arbitration award in one's favour is unlikely to be satisfied by the defendant. The applicant will have to adduce evidence of the defendant's inability to satisfy an adverse arbitration award or foreign

[42] HCO, s 12B(3).
[43] *The Madonna D'Idra* (1811) 165 ER 1224, 1225.
[44] *On Demand Information plc v Michael Gerson (Finance) plc* [2002] UKHL 13, [2003] 1 AC 368 [7]. See also the 2022 United Nations Convention on the International Effects of Judicial Sales of Ships, to which China is a signatory.
[45] *The Halcyon Isle* [1981] AC 221.
[46] High Court Ordinance, s 12B(2).
[47] For cases, see, eg *The Convenience Container* (n 39); *The Decurion (No 2)* (n 40); *The Almojil 61* [2014] 4 HKLRD 313; *The Bo Shi Ji 393* [2015] 3 HKLRD 242.
[48] *The Britannia* [1998] 1 HKC 221.
[49] In *The Ocean Friend* (n 36), the court ruled that it is possible to grant a stay of proceedings on condition that the defendant has to pay security.

judgment. For instance, the fact that a defendant has no known financial assets and has not paid hire, wages or legal fees may justify maintenance of an arrest despite a stay.[50]

V. Enforcement via an Action *in rem* after Obtaining an *in personam* Judgment

A cause of action *in rem* does not merge in a judgment *in personam*.[51] The cause of action *in rem* is not superseded by a judgment *in personam*. The cause of action remains available as long as the judgment remained unsatisfied. This principle applies equally to arbitral awards, so that an unsatisfied arbitral award is no bar in Hong Kong to a cause of an action *in rem*;[52] this has been adopted in Hong Kong, where the existence of an arbitral award does not bar a cause of action *in rem*.[53]

[50] See, eg *The Britannia* (n 48).
[51] *The Alas* [2014] 4 HKLRD 160 [13]–[21].
[52] *The Cella* (1888) 13 PD 82, 85; *The Rena K* [1979] 1 QB 377, 405.
[53] *The Alas* (n 51) [8]–[25].

12

Immunities from Jurisdiction

In certain situations, a foreign state, state entity or state representative may enjoy immunity from jurisdiction. Those immunities are discussed in this chapter.

I. State Immunity

Based on the sovereign equality of states in international law and relations, state immunity dictates the maxim *par in parem non habet imperium* ('equals have no authority over one another'),[1] and requires that 'the courts of a country will not implead a foreign sovereign'.[2] Generally, the following subjects may be concluded as 'state' for the purpose of state immunity:

(i) the state and its various organs of the government;[3]
(ii) public property of any state destined for public use and any property of the ambassador;[4]
(iii) the person of any sovereign,[5] ambassadors or representatives of any other state acting in that capacity;[6]
(iv) units of a federal state or political subdivisions of the state, which are entitled to perform acts in the exercise of sovereign authority and are acting in that capacity;[7] and
(v) agencies or instrumentalities of the state or other entities, to the extent that they are entitled to perform and are performing acts in the exercise of the sovereign authority of the state.[8]

There are two approaches to the concept and rule of state immunity. The first approach is absolute immunity, where foreign states and sovereigns are accorded immunity for all activities, whether acting in a governmental or commercial capacity. The second approach is restrictive immunity, where acts of government (*acta jure imperii*) and acts of a commercial nature (*acta jure gestionis*) are distinguished. While acts of government are protected by immunity, commercial acts are excluded from immunity.

[1] See generally James Crawford, *Brownlie's Principles of Public International Law*, 9th edn (Oxford University Press, 2019) ch 22.
[2] *The Cristina* [1938] AC 485, 490.
[3] 2004 United Nations Convention on Jurisdictional Immunities of States and Their Property, Art 2(b)(i).
[4] *The Parlement Belge* (1880) 5 PD 197, 214.
[5] ibid.
[6] 2004 United Nations Convention on Jurisdictional Immunities of States and Their Property, Art 2(b)(iv).
[7] ibid Art 2(b)(ii).
[8] ibid Art 2(b)(iii).

Prior to the return of Hong Kong's sovereignty to the People's Republic of China (PRC), Hong Kong had followed the English legislation, the State Immunity Act 1978. The Act adopted restrictive immunity, whereby the court can establish jurisdiction over states' non-sovereign activities; and recognised certain exceptions in relation to commercial transactions[9] and certain contractual obligations.[10] Before the State Immunity Act 1978 when there was a gradual transition from absolute immunity towards restrictive immunity, it was held in *Philippine Admiral*,[11] a case appealed from Hong Kong to the Privy Council, that sovereign immunity from suit should not be granted in proceedings *in rem* against a trading ship of which a foreign sovereign state was the registered owner.[12]

After the PRC's resumption of sovereignty over Hong Kong in 1997, as China had been (until the end of 2023) adhering to the approach of absolute immunity rather than restrictive immunity, questions about which approach to adopt in the Hong Kong courts had remained uncertain until *Democratic Republic of the Congo v FG Hemisphere Associates LLC*. In that case, the Democratic Republic of the Congo (DRC) entered into credit agreements with a Yugoslavian company (Y) relating to electricity projects which Y had agreed to construct in the DRC. The DRC defaulted on its repayment obligations, and two arbitral awards from the International Chamber of Commerce (the Awards) were made in France and Switzerland in favour of Y. The plaintiff, FG Hemisphere Associates LLC, was assigned with the benefit of the Awards and obtained leave in Hong Kong to enforce them against fees said to be payable to the DRC by a consortium of Chinese state-owned enterprises (the Chinese Party) along with injunctions to prevent their payment to the DRC. The Chinese Party had entered into a joint venture agreement with the DRC to develop the DRC's infrastructure in consideration for the right to exploit the DRC's mineral reserves, and the fees were entry fees payable under the joint venture agreement. The DRC asserted state immunity. This raised an important question of law on the extent of the state immunity from suit (and execution) available in the courts of Hong Kong. Is it absolute immunity or restrictive immunity? Following decisions at the Court of First Instance[13] and a 2–1 divided Court of Appeal,[14] the case reached the Court of Final Appeal. In a 3–2 divided judgment, the majority (Chan and Ribeiro PJJ, Sir Anthony Mason NPJ) held that Hong Kong has to adhere to the position of the PRC on absolute immunity, instead of restrictive immunity under the common law or the State Immunity Act 1978 in the UK (which is no longer applicable after the handover). Two reasons supported the majority of the court's finding for the adoption of absolute immunity:

1. Under common law, the practice or doctrine of state immunity adopted in a unitary state should apply uniformly to the whole state. A 'one voice principle' should be adhered to, and divergencies between decisions taken by national courts and the views of the government of the state on matters affecting international relations should

[9] State Immunity Act 1978 (UK), s 3(1)(a).
[10] ibid s 3(1)(b).
[11] *The Philippine Admiral* [1977] AC 373.
[12] ibid 403.
[13] *Democratic Republic of the Congo v FG Hemisphere Associates LLC* [2009] 1 HKLRD 410 (CFI) (Reyes J).
[14] *Democratic Republic of the Congo v FG Hemisphere Associates LLC* [2010] 2 HKLRD 66 (CA) (Stock VP and Yuen JA, Yeung JA dissenting). In dissent, Yeung JA considered that restrictive immunity has not yet become part of customary international law.

be avoided.[15] Further, there is nothing in the common law jurisprudence to suggest that a region or municipality forming part of a unitary state can establish its own state immunity practice at variance with that of the state to which it belongs.[16]

2. Under the Basic Law, all laws previously in force in Hong Kong shall be construed with such modifications, adaptations, limitations and exceptions as may be necessary so as not to contravene the Basic Law and to bring them into conformity with the status of Hong Kong as a Special Administrative Region of the PRC.[17] The Basic Law has reserved the responsibility of dealing with foreign affairs to the Central People's Government,[18] and the state immunity policy concerns relations between states, falling within the meaning of 'foreign affairs'. Accordingly, the maintenance of restrictive immunity would conflict with the exclusion of foreign affairs from the sphere of autonomy of the HKSAR[19] and, thus, the Basic Law. A modification or adaptation of the restrictive immunity is warranted.

Moreover, the majority sought an interpretation of the relevant Basic Law provisions from the Standing Committee of the National People's Congress (NPCSC) under Article 158 of the Basic Law as the issue of state immunity, as a matter of foreign affairs, is the responsibility of the Central People's Government, and the interpretation will affect the judgment in question. The minority (Bokhary PJ and Mortimer NPJ) delivered separate judgments to the effect that the courts of Hong Kong are to apply the common law, including the law of restrictive immunity, and did not find a reference to the NPCSC necessary.

The NPCSC Interpretation issued on 26 August 2011 confirmed that the absolute immunity approach applies in Hong Kong. The approach of state immunity to be applied in Hong Kong must not depart from or be inconsistent with the rules and policies determined by the Central People's Government.[20]

Thus, the conclusion in *Congo* was that Hong Kong

> cannot as a matter of legal and constitutional principle adhere to a doctrine of state immunity which differs from that adopted by the Central People's Government[,] and that the doctrine of state immunity practised in the HKSAR … is accordingly a doctrine of absolute immunity.[21]

The only exception is the waiver of immunity upon unequivocal or explicit submission[22] to the jurisdiction of the forum state, for example, by instituting the proceedings[23] or taking

[15] *Democratic Republic of the Congo v FG Hemisphere Associates LLC* (2011) 14 HKCFAR 95 [269]–[270] (Chan and Ribeiro PJJ, Sir Anthony Mason NPJ).

[16] ibid [267]–[268].

[17] Interpretation and General Clauses Ordinance (Cap 1), s 2A.

[18] Basic Law, Art 13.

[19] *Democratic Republic of the Congo* (n 15) [324]–[325].

[20] Interpretation by the Standing Committee of the National People's Congress Regarding the First Paragraph of Article 13 and Article 19 of the Basic Law of the Hong Kong Special Administrative Region of the People's Republic of China (Instrument A114) (26 August 2011).

[21] ibid [336]–[337]; *Democratic Republic of the Congo v FG Hemisphere Associates LLC (No 2)* (2011) 14 HKCFAR 395 [1] (Chan and Ribeiro PJJ, Sir Anthony Mason NPJ).

[22] Legislation on implied waiver can be found in the UK, Australia or the USA, where a submission to an arbitration can be an implied waiver for proceedings related to the enforcement of the arbitration, but Hong Kong has no such legislation, following the common law rules and being chary about implying any waiver. See *Democratic Republic of the Congo* (n 15) [386]–[387].

[23] Lord Collins of Mapesbury and Jonathan Harris (gen eds), *Dicey, Morris and Collins on the Conflict of Laws*, 16th edn (Sweet & Maxwell, 2022) para 9-033.

active steps defending the merits in the proceedings[24] at the time when the forum state's jurisdiction is invoked against the impleaded state.[25] This is further discussed in section IV below.

The Law of the People's Republic of China on Foreign State Immunity adopted the restrictive immunity approach and took effect on 1 January 2024. There are no provisions in that law as to its effect in Hong Kong (or Macao). Under Article 18(2) of the Basic Law:

> National laws shall not be applied in the Hong Kong Special Administrative Region except for those listed in Annex III to this Law. The laws listed therein shall be applied locally by way of promulgation or legislation by the Region.

As the Foreign State Immunity Law is currently not included under Annex III of the Basic Law, it has no direct effect in Hong Kong. But in light of the *Congo* case and the NPCSC Interpretation, it is likely that Hong Kong will have to apply the change to restrictive immunity as effected by the Law. According to the answer to question 4 in the NPCSC Interpretation, the pre-1997 common law position in Hong Kong on state immunity is to be applied, 'subject to such modifications, adaptions, limitations or exceptions as are necessary as to be consistent with the rules or policies on state immunity that the Central People's Government has determined'.[26] It is therefore unclear as to: (i) whether the change to the restrictive immunity approach is automatic on 1 January 2024; (ii) whether parties are entitled to rely on the provisions of the Foreign State Immunity Law; and (iii) to what extent and how the common law position on restrictive immunity should be modified, adapted, limited or excluded as necessary to be consistent with Mainland China's rules and policies.

It was suggested that, under common law, immunity may be refused for states or parties which are engaged in fundamental abuses or violations of international law, such as international crimes of aggression and modern slavery.[27] However, in light of the wide interpretation of Article 19(3) regarding the words 'acts of state such as defence and foreign affairs', it is likely that the Hong Kong courts will have to defer to the views and policies of the Central People's Government when faced with such claims.

II. Crown Immunity and State-Owned Entities

Unlike state or sovereign immunity, crown immunity is based on the inequality in positions of those ruling and those ruled.[28] It reflects the notion that 'the Crown can do no wrong', under which the Crown enjoys immunity from being sued in its own courts unless there is waiver by submission.

[24] ibid.

[25] *Democratic Republic of the Congo* (n 15) [386]–[387].

[26] NPCSC Interpretation (n 20) para 4.

[27] See, eg *Basfar v Wong* [2022] UKSC 20, [2023] AC 33; *Ghanem Al-Masarir v Kingdom of Saudi Arabia* [2022] EWHC 2199 (QB). But see, eg *Zhang v Zemin* [2010] NSWCA 255; *Jurisdictional Immunities of the State (Germany v Italy: Greece intervening)* [2012] ICJ Rep 99 [82]; *Belhaj v Straw* [2017] UKSC 3, [2017] AC 964 [14]; *Young v A-G* [2018] 3 NZLR 827.

[28] *The Hua Tian Long (No 2)* [2010] 3 HKLRD 611 [45]–[46].

In Hong Kong, before 1 July 1997, a statutory regime conferred the ability to sue the Government of the Colony in circumstances to which the British Crown was not subject.[29] After 1 July 1997, the issue arose as to how the expression 'Crown' should be construed. This was discussed in *The Hua Tian Long (No 2)*, where the court reasoned that the Central People's Government should be placed in the same position as the British Crown prior to 1997.[30] This is also consistent with the reading under paragraph 1 of Schedule 8 of the Interpretation and General Clauses Ordinance (Cap 1). Thus, the PRC is immune from being sued in Hong Kong courts.

China's state-owned enterprises (SOEs) do not enjoy crown immunity. This is apparent from the comments of Li Fei, the then vice-chairman of the National People's Congress Standing Committee Legislative Affairs Commission, that 'immunity laws did not apply to Chinese state-owned enterprises as they have assumed the legal status of a company', and that 'immunity will not be taken advantage of by China's State-owned enterprises to evade debts in Hong Kong, as it only applies to foreign entities'.[31] This presumption is consistent with English law, as found in *La Générale des Carrières et des Mines v FG Hemisphere Associates LLC*:[32]

> Especially where a separate juridical entity is formed by the state for what are on the face of it commercial or industrial purposes, with its own management and budget, the strong presumption is that its separate corporate status should be respected, and that it and the state forming it should not have to bear each other's liabilities.[33]

Under some circumstances, the presumption that SOEs are not immune from jurisdiction or execution may be displaced when the state and enterprise are so closely bound with each other that the enterprise cannot be regarded as distinct. The assessment may involve factors such as constitutional arrangements, the state's control over the enterprise, and the enterprises activities and functions.[34]

In *The Hua Tian Long (No 2)*, the Hong Kong court suggested the 'control' test for defining whether an entity should be deemed part of 'the Crown', taking account of 'the control which the Crown has over that corporation', asking 'whether the corporation in question is able to exercise independent powers of its own', as well as 'the objects and function of that corporation', although the latter is not that crucial.[35]

In *TNB Fuel Services Sdn Bhd v China National Coal Group Corp*,[36] the Hong Kong court concluded that crown immunity should be decided by reference to the law of the place of incorporation and the control test.[37] In applying the control test, the court

[29] Such right was first provided for by the Code of Civil Procedure Ordinance (No 13 of 1873), and later the Crown Proceedings Ordinance (Cap 300). See ibid [55]–[59].

[30] *The Hua Tian Long (No 2)* (n 28) [88]: 'as a concept imported from customary international law [crown immunity] continued to exist at common law unaffected by the [Crown Proceedings Ordinance] until the handover to the new sovereign power, the PRC, which in turn must enjoy the like crown immunity hitherto accorded to the British Crown'.

[31] 'Beijing Brings HK into Line on State Immunity' (South China Morning Post, 27 August 2011), www.scmp.com/article/977252/beijing-brings-hk-line-state-immunity.

[32] *La Générale des Carrières et des Mines v FG Hemisphere Associates LLC* [2012] UKPC 27, [2013] 1 All ER 409.

[33] ibid [29]–[30].

[34] ibid.

[35] *The Hua Tian Long (No 2)* (n 28) [52]–[53]. On the facts, the Guangzhou Salvage Bureau was entitled to assert crown immunity.

[36] *TNB Fuel Services Sdn Bhd v China National Coal Group Corp* [2017] 3 HKC 588.

[37] ibid [25]–[26].

found the following factors to be relevant: (i) the independent discretion enjoyed by the entity; (ii) the control exercised by the state as investor; (iii) the enterprise's separate legal personality; (iv) the state's power to appoint or remove the enterprise's senior officers; and (v) the enterprise's financial autonomy.[38]

III. Other Immunities

A. Diplomatic and Consular Immunities

Due to the exclusion of foreign affairs from Hong Kong's autonomy, sources of law to solve issues related to diplomatic and consular immunity in Hong Kong are relatively broad, covering those relevant from the perspective of both Mainland China and Hong Kong.

In general, interpretations of public international law by the Central People's Government shall be respected in Hong Kong.[39] The PRC's Regulations Concerning Diplomatic Privileges and Immunities[40] and the Regulations Concerning Consular Privileges and Immunities[41] were implemented in Hong Kong through promulgation. Moreover, the Consular Relations Ordinance (Cap 577) and the International Organizations and Diplomatic Privileges Ordinance (Cap 190), as domestic legislation, are also applicable.

Under these instruments, a diplomatic agent enjoys personal immunity from civil jurisdiction unless:

(i) the case is an action relating to succession in which the agent is involved as a private person;[42] or
(ii) the case is an action relating to any professional or commercial activity conducted by the agent outside official functions.[43]

Immunity enjoyed by consular officers and members of the administrative or technical staff of the consular post only covers acts performed in the exercise of their functions, and is subject to the following exceptions:

(i) an action arising out of a contract not concluded expressly as an agent of the sending state;[44]
(ii) an action relating to private immovable property situated in the territory of China, unless they hold it as an agent of the sending state for the purposes of the consular post;[45]

[38] ibid [29]–[30]. On the facts, the China National Coal Group Corporation was not entitled to assert crown immunity.
[39] Graeme Johnston and Paul Harris, *The Conflict of Laws in Hong Kong*, 3rd edn (Sweet & Maxwell, 2017) para 4.082.
[40] Promulgation of National Laws 1997 (LN 379 of 1997), Sch 5.
[41] Promulgation of National Laws (No 2) 1997 (LN 386 of 1997), Sch 3.
[42] Regulations of The People's Republic of China Concerning Diplomatic Privileges and Immunities, Art 14(1).
[43] ibid Art 14(2).
[44] Regulations of The People's Republic of China Concerning Consular Privileges and Immunities, Art 14(1).
[45] ibid Art 14(2).

(iii) an action to succession in which the officer or member is involved as a private person;[46] and
(iv) an action for damages arising from an accident in China caused by a vehicle, vessel or aircraft.[47]

However, it should be noted that the scope of consular immunity may be enlarged to cover acts outside the exercise of their functions through bilateral treaties or agreements between China and other countries on the principle of reciprocity.[48]

B. Immunity of the Red Cross and International Organisations

The Privileges and Immunities (International Committee of the Red Cross) Ordinance (Cap 402) provides that the International Committee of the Red Cross[49] and its delegates[50] are immune from suit and legal process for things done or omitted to be done during the performance of official duties unless its delegates are involved in a case of civil action by a third party for damages arising from a traffic accident in Hong Kong.[51]

Other international organisations also enjoy immunity from suit and legal process in Hong Kong under the International Organizations and Diplomatic Privileges Ordinance (Cap 190)[52] if the organisation is one of which the governments of 'one or more sovereign powers are members and of which the Government of Hong Kong or of the People's Republic of China is a member or an associate member'.[53] The representatives, members of committees, high officers and persons on missions from these international organisations enjoy similar immunity as is accorded in the PRC to an envoy of a foreign sovereign power accredited to the Central People's Government.[54]

The International Organizations (Privileges and Immunities) Ordinance (Cap 558) empowers the Hong Kong Chief Executive in Council to declare that the provisions of

> an international agreement relating to the status, privileges and immunities of an international organisation and of persons connected with such an organisation [or] an arrangement in writing that is entered into between the Ministry of Foreign Affairs and the Government of the Hong Kong Special Administrative Region relating to the status, privileges and immunities of a body concerned in the establishment of an international organisation and of persons connected with such a body

have the force of law in Hong Kong.[55] This Ordinance does not require the international organisation to meet the definition in the International Organizations and Diplomatic Privileges Ordinance (Cap 190) stated above.

[46] ibid Art 14(3).
[47] ibid Art 14(4).
[48] ibid Art 14.
[49] Privileges and Immunities (International Committee of the Red Cross) Ordinance (Cap 402), Sch 1.
[50] ibid Sch 2, para 1(1).
[51] ibid Sch 2, para 1(2).
[52] International Organizations and Diplomatic Privileges Ordinance (Cap 190), Sch 1, Pt I, para 1.
[53] ibid Sch 2, Pt I. A list of these international organisations may be found via the subsidiary legislation to the International Organizations and Diplomatic Privileges Ordinance (Cap 190).
[54] ibid Sch 1, Pt II, para 1.
[55] International Organizations (Privileges and Immunities) Ordinance (Cap 558), s 3.

C. Immunity of Central Banks

The PRC Law on Judicial Immunity from Compulsory Measures Concerning the Property of Foreign Central Banks, having been added in the Annex III to the Basic Law ('National Laws to be Applied in HKSAR'), accords judicial immunity from compulsory measures of property preservation and execution[56] to the central bank of a foreign country, a regional economic integration organisation or a financial administration institution exercising the functions of a central bank in Hong Kong.[57]

D. Immunity of the Hong Kong Garrison

The Hong Kong courts may exercise jurisdiction over any member, organ or unit of the military forces stationed by the Central People's Government in Hong Kong, ie the Hong Kong Garrison, in civil actions where the civil rights of any Hong Kong resident or other person not of the Hong Kong Garrison are infringed.[58] The only exception is that cases of tort arising from acts committed by members of the Hong Kong Garrison when performing their official duties fall within the jurisdiction of the Supreme People's Court of the PRC, while compensation for the loss or injury incurred is governed by Hong Kong law.[59] Article 19(1) of the Garrison Law provides that: 'Any member of the Hong Kong Garrison who contravenes any national law or law of the Hong Kong Special Administrative Region shall be investigated for legal responsibility according to law.'

Articles 23 and 24 of the Garrison Law cover civil disputes and contractual disputes respectively. However, Article 26 of the Garrison Law provides that acts of state, such as defence affairs, shall not be subject to the jurisdiction of the Hong Kong courts.

IV. Waiver of Immunities

Questions of waiver only arise when the relevant entity qualifies for immunities; otherwise, there is nothing to waive. It was held by the majority in *FG Hemisphere* that states may choose to waive any immunity they have and submit themselves to the jurisdiction of the courts of the forum state.[60] The following points distilled from *FG Hemisphere* show what will constitute waiver of immunity as recognised by the Hong Kong courts:

1. 'The common law rule as to waiver is consonant with elementary good sense by requiring an unequivocal submission to the jurisdiction of the forum State at the time when the forum State's jurisdiction is invoked against the impleaded State.

[56] Law of the People's Republic of China on Judicial Immunity from Compulsory Measures Concerning the Property of Foreign Central Banks, Art 1.

[57] ibid Art 2.

[58] Garrison Law of the Hong Kong Special Administrative Region of the People's Republic of China, Art 23.

[59] ibid.

[60] *Democratic Republic of the Congo* (n 15) [229] and [374], approving *Duff Development Co Ltd v Government of Kelantan* [1924] AC 797, 822.

Courts would be ill-advised to attempt to deem an impleaded State to have submitted to their jurisdiction when it has not done so explicitly by its words or conduct and where its objection to such jurisdiction is made clear in the recognition proceedings.'[61] As such, a voluntary submission to the Hong Kong courts by invoking the Hong Kong court's jurisdiction (most usually as a plaintiff) or by appearing as a defendant without any jurisdictional objections will constitute waiver.

2. 'When a State enters into an arbitration agreement with a private individual or company, that act does not constitute a submission to any other State's jurisdiction. It involves merely the assumption of contractual obligations *vis-à-vis* the other party to the agreement. So if a State fails to honour a promise made in the arbitration agreement to carry out the award and waive its immunity, it may put itself in breach of its contract but it will have done nothing to submit to the jurisdiction of any forum State.'[62] A waiver of immunity contained in the arbitration agreement (in *Congo*, through the incorporation of the ICC Paris rules) is insufficient to constitute waiver.
3. '... by taking part in an arbitration, a State is obviously agreeing to submit to the contractual jurisdiction of the arbitrators. But that is obviously not the same thing as submitting to the jurisdiction of another State's courts. Such conduct may however constitute an implicit submission to the jurisdiction of the courts ... exercising a supervisory jurisdiction over the conduct of the arbitration.'[63] As such, a Hong Kong arbitration agreement will be understood to imply an acceptance of the supervisory jurisdiction of the Hong Kong courts.
4. However, 'a party seeking to enforce an arbitration award (or a judgment) against a foreign State on the basis of a waiver of state immunity must establish a waiver at two distinct stages. The impleaded State must have waived both its jurisdictional immunity from suit in the forum State and the immunity of its property from execution by the forum State's process.'[64] 'Even where the recognition proceedings are successful, when the applicant subsequently seeks to execute the award (now treated like a judgment of the court), the impleaded State has a further right to object to execution against the targeted property on the ground of state immunity.'[65]

The discussion in *FG Hemisphere* is limited to waiver of state immunity, although it is submitted that these principles will also apply to other types of immunities. In *The Hua Tian Long (No 2)*, it was not in dispute that the same principles governing the waiver of sovereign immunity should govern the question of waiver of crown immunity.[66] It was further held in the same case that the Chinese state-owned enterprise defendant had effectively waived its immunity by actively participating in the proceedings, going as far as filing a counterclaim before raising its claim to immunity.[67]

[61] *Democratic Republic of the Congo* (n 15) [392].
[62] ibid [377].
[63] ibid [378].
[64] ibid [379], citing *The Cristina* (n 2) 490–91.
[65] ibid [383].
[66] *The Hua Tian Long (No 2)* (n 28) [128].
[67] ibid [151].

13

Jurisdiction and Dispute Resolution Agreements

This chapter introduces different aspects of jurisdiction and dispute resolution agreements, and explains their effect under Hong Kong law. For principles on anti-suit injunctions in breach of jurisdiction agreements, see chapter nine, section VI. For choice of law agreements, see chapter fourteen. For arbitration agreements, see chapter twenty-four, sections II and III. For the relationships and interactions between jurisdiction and arbitration agreements and insolvency and bankruptcy petitions, see chapter twenty, section IV.

I. General Principles

By jurisdiction and dispute resolution agreements, parties submit to the jurisdiction of a particular court or mode of dispute resolution. Such choices are often based on commercial considerations, including political risk and cultural considerations.[1] It is generally advisable to include such clauses in transaction agreements so that there will be certainty, if a dispute eventually arises, about how the dispute is to be resolved. It is also advisable to negotiate such agreements at the time of contracting, rather than trying to agree only after a dispute arises.

There is a strong public policy in favour of upholding contractual bargains, including jurisdictional agreements.[2] Such agreements are, moreover, likely to be treated as separate or severable from the main agreement for the purposes of determining their validity. In other words, a jurisdiction and dispute resolution clause may be treated as valid even if the main agreement in which the clause is embedded is invalid, unenforceable, illegal or otherwise incapable of taking effect.[3] This aligns with the way that arbitration clauses are treated.[4]

A jurisdiction (or choice of law) agreement may be incorporated into an agreement. For example, an express reference in a contract X to a jurisdiction, arbitration or foreign law clause in some other document will typically be sufficient for those clauses to be

[1] *Deltatre SpA v Hong Kong Sports Industrial Development Ltd* [2018] 4 HKLRD 478, [2018] HKCFI 1942 [87].

[2] ibid. See also *Hyundai Engineering Construction Co Ltd v UBAF (Hong Kong) Ltd* (unreported, HCA 175/2012, 25 September 2013) [23], approving *Euromark v Smash Enterprises Pty Ltd* [2013] EWHC 1627 (QB) [13].

[3] See, eg *Deutsche Bank AG v Asia Pacific Broadband Wireless Communications Inc* [2008] EWCA Civ 1091 [24]; *China National Geological & Mining (HK) Ltd v Tianjin Hopetone Co Ltd* [2020] HKCFI 1338 [50]–[52].

[4] The separability of arbitration agreements is expressly stated under Arbitration Ordinance (Cap 609), s 34, incorporating Art 16 of the UNCITRAL Model Law on International Commercial Arbitration.

incorporated into contract X.[5] However, with bills of lading, specific words of incorporation are necessary to incorporate 'collateral' or 'ancillary' clauses, such as jurisdiction or arbitration clauses. General words of incorporation in a bill of lading will not normally be sufficient to incorporate an arbitration clause in a charterparty.[6]

The interpretation of jurisdiction agreements follows the same approach as the interpretation of contracts, namely that they should be construed according to the words used, as understood in the factual context and applying business common sense.[7]

II. Exclusive Jurisdiction Agreements

An exclusive jurisdiction clause contains words to the effect that the courts of a particular jurisdiction are to have exclusive jurisdiction to determine any disputes arising out of in connection with an agreement.[8] Hong Kong cases suggest that the differences between the phrases 'under', 'arising out of', 'in relation to' or 'in connection with' used in these clauses are minimal.[9] Any of those phrases signify an intention that all disputes relating to a contract (even matters not directly concerned with the breach of a contractual obligation) should be resolved in a particular forum. The scope of disputes covered by the clause is to be construed broadly and may include non-contractual claims, such as a claim for damages for fraudulent misrepresentation.[10]

In contrast, some exclusive jurisdiction agreements may stipulate that the courts of a particular jurisdiction have an exclusive jurisdiction to grant such interim, provisional or protective measures as may be available in those courts. It is suggested that these clauses will not preclude a party to apply to other courts for such measures. This is because the overriding consideration must be whether it is just and convenient to apply to a particular court for an interim measure.[11] Thus, a jurisdiction clause may confer authority on a Hong Kong-seated arbitral tribunal to determine a dispute, including the grant of interim measures. However, if a party wishes to enforce an interim measure in Mainland China, there may be little option other than for the party to apply to the court of Mainland China for that measure.[12] Currently, PRC law only allows PRC courts to grant interim measures that will be enforceable in Mainland China.

Whether a jurisdiction clause is exclusive depends on the construction of its scope, validity and effect. The context or purpose of the agreement should be considered, and the

[5] *The Rena K* [1979] 1 QB 377, 390F–391C; *The Delos* [2001] 1 Lloyd's Rep 703, 705–06; *Sea Powerful II Special Maritime Enterprises (ENE) v Bank of China Ltd* [2016] 1 HKLRD 1032 [22].

[6] *Thomas & Co Ltd v Portsea Co Ltd* [1912] AC 1; *OCBC Wing Hang Bank Ltd v Kai Sen Shipping Co Ltd* [2020] 1 HKLRD 1217, [2020] HKCFI 375.

[7] See, eg *Investors Compensation Scheme Ltd v West Bromwich Building Society* [1998] 1 WLR 896; Kim Lewison, *The Interpretation of Contracts*, 8th edn (Sweet & Maxwell, 2023).

[8] *Noble Power Investments Ltd v Nissei Stomach Tokyo Co Ltd* [2008] 5 HKLRD 631 [25].

[9] See, eg *The Incorporated Owners of Hamden Court v Mega Miles Construction Co Ltd* [2015] 5 HKC 179; *Houtai Investment Holdings Ltd v Leung Yat Tung* [2021] HKCFI 1504. This is in line with the *Fiona Trust* presumption, discussed at s VII below.

[10] *Donohue v Armco Inc* [2001] UKHL 64, [2002] 1 All ER 749 [60].

[11] High Court Ordinance (Cap 4), s 21L.

[12] A party might potentially be benefited from the Arrangement Concerning Mutual Assistance in Court-ordered Interim Measures in Aid of Arbitral Proceedings by the Courts of the Mainland and Hong Kong: see ch 25, s I.H.

court is required to consider whether a clause which does not use the adjective 'exclusive' is in substance an exclusive jurisdiction clause.[13] In *Bank of China Ltd v Yang Fan*, the court held that:[14]

> the key question is to construe its meaning as it would convey to a reasonable person having all the background knowledge which would reasonably have been available to the parties in the situation in which they were at the time of the contract, and having regard to the ordinary meaning of the language used. The absence of the words 'exclusive', 'must', 'shall', '應' or '須' in Chinese, is not fatal or conclusive. The test is whether the agreement obliged the Plaintiff to litigate in the chosen jurisdiction.

A clause may be considered exclusive even if it uses permissive words (such as 'can' or '可以').[15] For example, for the purposes of section 3(1) of the Mainland Judgments (Reciprocal Enforcement) Ordinance (Cap 597), the failure to use the word 'exclusive' in a jurisdiction clause is not fatal under section 3(1) of the Ordinance.[16] By similar token, a clause may be considered permissive even if it uses the word 'shall'.[17]

The effects of exclusive and non-exclusive jurisdiction agreements are extensively considered in *Noble Power Investments Ltd v Nissei Stomach Tokyo Co Ltd*.[18] The approach of Hong Kong law to exclusive jurisdiction agreements is clear:[19]

> If a party agrees to submit to the jurisdiction of the courts of a state, it does not easily lie in its mouth to complain that it is inconvenient to conduct its litigation there (ie to assert that the agreed forum is a *forum non conveniens*).

The courts will usually hold parties to their contractual bargain. The fact that the parties have expressly agreed to submit to a jurisdiction indicates that they regard that jurisdiction as an appropriate forum for the resolution of their disputes. That contractual expression of intent must be given due weight.[20] The court will enforce an exclusive jurisdiction clause without engaging in a *forum non conveniens* analysis, unless it can be demonstrated that there are strong reasons for not doing so.[21] These reasons should only stem from factors not contemplated by the parties when contracting and would not include foreseeable factors going to convenience, save for exceptional circumstances involving the administration of justice.[22]

[13] *Industrial and Commercial Bank of China (Asia) Ltd v Wisdom Top International Ltd* [2020] 5 HKC 537, [2020] HKCFI 322 [51], citing *Export-Import Bank of China v Taifeng Textile Group Co Ltd* [2018] HKCFI 1840 [63], [66]–[67].

[14] *Bank of China Ltd v Yang Fan* [2016] 3 HKLRD 7 [28].

[15] *黃书建 v 代威* [2020] 1 HKC 309, [2019] HKCFI 1386 ('本協議在履行過程中若發生爭議，應友好協商解決。協商不成的，各方均可向本合同簽訂地北京市朝陽區有管轄權的法院起訴。' [translation: 'If there is dispute in the course of the performance of this agreement, the parties should try to resolve their dispute through mutual consultation. If it is not successful, any party can, in the Beijing Chaoyang district which is the place for the signing and the making of this agreement, institute legal proceedings']).

[16] The operation of the Ordinance is discussed in ch 23, s IV.C.

[17] *Hwoo Huang Linda v Fu Being San* [2013] 1 HKLRD 259 [44]–[45].

[18] *Noble Power Investments Ltd* (n 8). The reasoning of that case was unsuccessfully challenged later in *Chinachem Financial Services Ltd v Century Venture Holdings Ltd* (unreported, HCA 410/2013, 21 April 2015).

[19] *Ace Insurance SA-NV v Zurich Insurance Co* [2001] EWCA Civ 173, [2001] 1 All ER (Comm) 802, 820A, cited in *Noble Power Investments Ltd* (n 8) [40].

[20] *Noble Power Investments Ltd* (n 8) [64].

[21] *Donohue* (n 10) [24]; *Noble Power Investments Ltd* (n 8) [37]–[40].

[22] *Noble Power Investments Ltd* (n 8) [71], citing *Antec International Ltd v Biosafety* [2006] EWHC 47 (Comm) [7(iii)]; *Li Lian International Ltd v Herport Hong Kong Ltd* [2019] HKCFI 826; *Re Lam Kwok Hung Guy, ex p Tor Asia Credit Master Fund LP* [2022] 4 HKLRD 793, [2022] HKCA 1297 [28]; *A v B* [2022] HKCFI 1031 [25].

Examples of strong reasons include: (i) obvious risks of inconsistent findings in cases with multiple defendants, only some of whom are covered by an exclusive jurisdiction clause, (ii) no effective remedies available to a party in the foreign forum; and (iii) public policy considerations that a party's statutory right is fettered.[23] The strength of the parties' cases are irrelevant. However, a stay of proceedings may be refused even though an exclusive jurisdiction clause was breached if the applicant is acting abusively in applying for the stay or where granting a stay may amount to a denial of justice.[24]

When the court is asked to stay an action that has been brought in Hong Kong despite an exclusive jurisdiction clause in favour of a foreign court, the court has discretion to order a stay. But that discretion should be exercised by granting a stay unless strong cause for not doing so is shown.[25] In *The El Amria*, Brandon LJ summarised the principles as follows:

> (1) Where plaintiffs sue in England in breach of an agreement to refer disputes to a foreign Court, and the defendants apply for a stay, the English Court, assuming the claim to be otherwise within its jurisdiction, is not bound to grant a stay but has a discretion whether to do so or not.
> (2) The discretion should be exercised by granting a stay unless strong cause for not doing so is shown.
> (3) The burden of proving such strong cause is on the plaintiffs.
> (4) In exercising its discretion the Court should take into account all the circumstances of the particular case.
> (5) In particular, but without prejudice to (4), the following matters, where they arise, may properly be regarded:
>   (a) In what country the evidence on the issues of fact is situated, or more readily available, and the effect of that on the relative convenience and expense of trial as between the English and foreign Courts.
>   (b) Whether the law of the foreign Court applies and if so, whether it differs from English law in any material respects.
>   (c) With what country either party is connected, and how closely.
>   (d) Whether the defendants genuinely desire trial in the foreign country, or are only seeking procedural advantages.
>   (e) Whether the plaintiffs would be prejudiced by having to sue in the foreign Court because they would: (i) be deprived of security for their claim; (ii) be unable to enforce any judgment obtained; (iii) be faced with a time bar not applicable in England; or (iv) for political, racial, religious or other reasons be unlikely to get a fair trial.

Upon granting a stay, indemnity costs may be awarded against the party who has acted in breach of the jurisdiction clause, but in Hong Kong this is not a general rule or presumption.[26]

[23] *Joseph Ghossoub v Team Y&R Holdings Hong Kong Ltd* [2016] 3 HKLRD 778; *Quaestus Capital Pte Ltd v Everton Associates Ltd* [2021] 4 HKC 605, [2021] HKCFI 1367.

[24] *Vinmar Overseas (Singapore) Pte Ltd v PTT International Trading Pte Ltd* [2018] 2 SLR 1271; *Deltatre SpA* (n 1); *Re Lam Kwok Hung Guy* (n 22) [29]–[41], citing *Euromark Ltd* (n 2). See also *Lo Ka Lee Kelly t/a Leader Packing (HK) Co v Spiriant Asia Pacific Ltd* [2021] 3 HKLRD 461, [2021] HKDC 787 [39].

[25] *The Eleftheria* [1970] P 94; *The El Amria* [1981] 2 Lloyd's Rep 119, 123–24; *The Pioneer Container* [1994] 2 AC 324, 347E–G; *Noble Power Investments Ltd* (n 8) [37]; *Joseph Ghossoub* (n 23) [105]; *Joseph Ghossoub v Team Y&R Holdings Hong Kong Ltd* (unreported, CACV 6/2017, 21 July 2017) [42]–[44]; *Re Lam Kwok Hung Guy* (n 22) [28].

[26] *A v B (Costs)* [2007] EWHC 54 (Comm), [2007] 1 All ER (Comm) 633; *Deltatre SpA* (n 1) [125]–[126]; *Re Lam Kwok Hung Guy, ex p Tor Asia Credit Master Fund LP (No 2)* [2023] 5 HKLRD 463, [2023] HKCA 1099.

A party might also be able to claim for damages against the party in breach of the jurisdiction clause for loss suffered as a result (such as any additional expense incurred in having to litigate in another forum).[27] Moreover, anti-suit injunctions can be granted in cases involving breach of exclusive jurisdiction clauses.[28]

III. Non-exclusive Jurisdiction Agreements

Non-exclusive jurisdiction agreements have the following characteristics: (i) the clause will designate a forum (usually the court of a given place) to which the parties may submit their disputes; but (ii) the parties nevertheless enjoy a liberty to institute proceedings in other jurisdictions (which may be unidentified).[29] Each party has thus agreed to *submit* to a named jurisdiction if an action is brought against them. Each party therefore implicitly acknowledges that the designated forum is appropriate for the trial of any action arising out of their contract.[30] In this regard, exclusive and non-exclusive jurisdiction clauses have the same effect, in the sense that the parties have agreed that, if sued in the named forum, they will have to submit to that forum.[31] It follows from this that

> where proceedings are instituted in the named forum (to which the parties have agreed to submit), the party who seeks a stay or otherwise to contest the jurisdiction or appropriateness of that forum, has a very heavy burden to discharge, since that party has by definition agreed contractually to submit to the jurisdiction. In other words, he is seeking to avoid a forum to which he has, by contract, agreed to submit.[32]

Accordingly, 'strong or overwhelming reasons or exceptional circumstances must be shown, such as the existence of factors not contemplated by the parties at the time the relevant agreement was made'.[33] It is not a matter simply of searching for and weighing up connecting factors (or the lack thereof) (for example, the location of relevant witnesses, the residence of the parties, etc) as though the court were faced with a stay application based on *forum non conveniens*.[34] The existence or non-existence of connecting factors will be irrelevant, unless it can somehow be shown that these constitute a strong reason why the non-exclusive jurisdiction clause should not be enforced.[35]

When a party institutes proceedings in Hong Kong despite it not being a forum explicitly identified in a non-exclusive jurisdiction clause,[36] the Hong Kong court resorts

[27] *Quaestus Capital Pte Ltd* (n 23) [61], citing *Donohue* (n 10) [36], [48], [75]; Adrian Briggs, *Agreements on Jurisdiction and Choice of Law* (Oxford University Press, 2008) para 6.68.

[28] See ch 9, s VI.A.

[29] *Noble Power Investments Ltd* (n 8) [24].

[30] ibid [28], citing *Mercury Communications Ltd v Communication Telesystems International* [1999] 2 All ER (Comm) 33, 40G–J.

[31] *Noble Power Investments Ltd* (n 8) [29]–[30], [33(1)], citing *JP Morgan Securities Asia Private Ltd v Malaysian Newsprint Industries Sdn Bhd* [2001] 2 Lloyd's Rep 41 and *Import Export Metro Ltd v Compania Sud Americana De Vapores SA* [2003] EWHC 11 (Comm), [2003] 1 All ER (Comm) 703.

[32] *Noble Power Investments Ltd* (n 8) [31].

[33] ibid [36].

[34] ibid [39]–[40].

[35] ibid [40].

[36] ibid [33(3)].

to *forum non conveniens* principles to resolve the matter.[37] This entails identifying the most appropriate jurisdiction where a case may be tried in the interests of all the parties and for the ends of justice.[38] The non-exclusive jurisdiction clause carries far less weight and is simply a factor in the discretionary exercise.[39] In contrast, a non-exclusive jurisdiction designating a named forum coupled with an express choice of the law of that forum as governing a contract would constitute significant connecting factors in favour of the named forum as the appropriate one for the resolution of the parties' dispute.[40]

The risk of parallel proceedings is contemplated with a non-exclusive jurisdiction clause.[41] Hence, when there is a breach of a non-exclusive jurisdiction clause, the strength of the case to grant an anti-suit injunction is not as strong as an exclusive jurisdiction clause.[42]

IV. Asymmetric Jurisdiction Agreements

Asymmetric or unilateral jurisdiction clauses are a long-established and practical feature of international financial documentation.[43] Such a clause

> ensures that a creditor can always litigate in a debtor's home court whilst preserving its right to bring proceedings where the debtor's assets may be located at the time a dispute arises. This increases the prospect of a creditor successfully recovering a debt owed to it, which in turn contributes to the readiness of the creditor to provide finance and reduces the costs of borrowing, by minimizing the risk that a debtor's obligations will be unenforceable.[44]

However, an asymmetric jurisdiction clause should not be construed as a submission to the jurisdiction of every court in the world, however exorbitant.[45] In an asymmetric jurisdiction clause:[46]

> Y is limited to jurisdiction A, but X may proceed in that jurisdiction or in other courts which have competent jurisdiction. X can sue anywhere under such a clause but only if and to the extent that a court other than in A has jurisdiction. Moreover, if Y sues in A, X is not able to challenge the court's jurisdiction since it has agreed to it. In this situation, X may not be able to sue elsewhere.

[37] Unless the wording of the clause is that the other forum is one to which the parties have also agreed to submit in the event of their being sued: ibid [32] and [33(2)]. This situation would be 'unusual' as admitted in the case.

[38] ibid [27], [38], [44] and [64]; *Rich Village Ltd v Grand Pride Holdings Ltd* [2012] 5 HKLRD 124.

[39] *T & K Electronics v Tai Ping Insurance Co Ltd* [1998] 1 HKLRD 172, 177G–I; *Noble Power Investments Ltd* (n 8) [32] and [42].

[40] *Peregrine Fixed Income Ltd v JP Morgan Chase Bank* [2005] 3 HKLRD 1 [50]–[54].

[41] *Chinachem Financial Services Ltd v Century Venture Holdings Ltd* (unreported, HCA 410/2013, 8 January 2015) (stay refused in favour of Mainland proceedings in light of non-exclusive jurisdiction clause in favour of Hong Kong).

[42] See ch 9, s III.

[43] See also Brooke Marshall, *Asymmetric Jurisdiction Clauses* (Oxford University Press, 2023).

[44] *Etihad Airways PJSC v Prof Dr Lucas Flöther* [2019] EWHC 3107 (Comm) [162], cited in *Industrial and Commercial Bank of China (Asia) Ltd* (n 13) [17].

[45] *Allahabad Bank v UD Trading Group Holding Pte Ltd* [2020] HKCFI 3030 [19], citing *Mauritius Commercial Bank Ltd v Hestia Holdings Ltd* [2013] EWHC 1328 (Comm), [2013] 2 All ER (Comm) 899 [38].

[46] *Commerzbank Aktiengesellschaft v Liquimar Tankers Management Inc* [2017] EWHC 161 (Comm), [2017] 1 WLR 3497 [40]–[41], cited in *Industrial and Commercial Bank of China (Asia) Ltd* (n 13) [16]. See also *Mauritius Commercial Bank Ltd* (n 45).

There is difficulty with recognising asymmetric jurisdiction agreements because the rights conferred are not equal. Asymmetric jurisdiction clauses are not 'exclusive choice of court agreements' within the meaning of Article 3(a) of the 2005 HCCH Convention on Choice of Court Agreements (the Hague Choice of Court Convention).[47]

However, in Hong Kong, asymmetric jurisdiction agreements are usually recognised as valid and effective. In *Industrial and Commercial Bank of China (Asia) Ltd v Wisdom Top International Ltd*, the court held that the asymmetric jurisdiction clause in that case was an exclusive choice of court agreement if the debtor was the party instituting the action but not if the action was commenced by the creditor.[48] It was therefore an exclusive jurisdiction clause for the purposes of the Mainland Judgments (Reciprocal Enforcement) Ordinance (Cap 597), even though that Ordinance follows the definition of 'choice of court agreement' under the framework of the Hague Choice of Court Convention. The effect of asymmetric jurisdiction clauses in conferring complete freedom on a creditor to bring proceedings in any country which would have jurisdiction has also been recognised in *Union Bank of India v Glory Universal Group Inc*.[49]

V. Innominate Jurisdiction Agreements

Innominate jurisdiction agreements do not expressly state whether they are exclusive or non-exclusive. Such clauses give rise to questions of construction: are they exclusive or non-exclusive? Under Hong Kong law, this is a matter of construction in each case; there is no presumption of exclusivity. The question is whether on its true construction the clause obliges the parties to resort to the relevant jurisdiction, irrespective of whether the word 'exclusive' is used. While the matrix background or surrounding circumstances can be considered, the negotiations or the subjective intention of the parties in construing a contract should not be considered.[50]

Whether a jurisdiction clause provides for an exclusive or non-exclusive forum is to be determined by the governing law of the contract.[51] The Hong Kong court considered the position in *China Railway (Hong Kong) Holdings Ltd v Chung Kin Holdings Co Ltd*.[52] The case held that, in construing a contract to discover the parties' intention, a choice of law clause in the main contract should generally be treated as also applying to a jurisdiction clause.[53] This promotes certainty, consistency and coherence, and reduces complexities and artificiality. The court's task is to discover the governing law of the jurisdiction clause by

[47] Explanatory Report of the 2005 HCCH Convention [106]; *Industrial and Commercial Bank of China (Asia) Ltd* (n 13) [29].

[48] *Industrial and Commercial Bank of China (Asia) Ltd* (n 13).

[49] *Union Bank of India v Glory Universal Group Inc* [2021] 1 HKLRD 381, [2020] HKCFI 3057.

[50] *Yu Lap Man v Good First Investment Ltd* [1999] 1 HKC 622, 624C–E, approving *Sohio Supply Co v Gatoil (USA) Inc* [1989] 1 Lloyd's Rep 588; *Hwoo Huang Linda* (n 17) [39]–[47]; *Rich Village Ltd* (n 38) [17].

[51] *Hong Ziyun v Chan Kwan Ming* [2019] 4 HKLRD 405, [2019] HKCFI 2125. See also *Luso International Banking Ltd v Summi (Group) Holdings Ltd* [2021] 4 HKC 272, [2021] HKCFI 906. For determining the proper governing law of the contract, see *First Laser Ltd v Fujian Enterprises (Holdings) Co Ltd* (2012) 15 HKCFAR 569; ch 15, s I.

[52] *China Railway (Hong Kong) Holdings Ltd v Chung Kin Holdings Co Ltd* [2023] HKCFI 132.

[53] ibid [27]–[31], approving *Enka Insaat ve Sanayi AS v OOO Insurance Co Chubb* [2020] UKSC 38, [2020] 1 WLR 4117 [54]. For the application of *Enka* in the arbitration context, see ch 24, s III.

objectively discerning what law the parties intended to the clause. It is only if that intention cannot readily be ascertained that the court will resort to the closest connection test. Thus, in construing the parties' intention, an express choice of law clause applicable to the main contract will often be regarded as applying equally to a jurisdiction clause in the same contract.[54]

It is theoretically possible to have 'floating' jurisdiction and dispute resolution agreements, which provide for various possibilities of dispute resolution mechanisms based on certain events in the future. While such 'floating' agreements are not inherently objectionable, it is submitted that such agreements, like 'floating' choice of law agreements, add uncertainties and complexities, and are not consistent with business efficacy and certainty.[55]

VI. Hybrid and Multi-tiered Dispute Resolution Agreements

Hybrid dispute resolution clauses provide for arbitration as an alternative to civil litigation in a named court, often at the option of one party. In some jurisdictions, these provisions may encounter the same difficulties as asymmetric clauses. Under Hong Kong law, these clauses are generally valid and effective. An example is an agreement stating that parties 'can' ('可') refer the disputes to arbitration, and an express subclause stating that the parties confirmed and agreed that arbitration is only one of the ways to resolve the dispute and difference.[56]

Multi-tiered dispute resolution clauses provide for an informal conciliatory dispute resolution process in the first instance, with litigation in a specified jurisdiction as a final resort if the informal process fails. Given that such provisions are intended to promote informality in the resolution of disputes, they often specify those modes of alternative dispute resolution (ADR), such as negotiation, conciliation, mediation, neutral evaluation or adjudication, that should be attempted in the first instance. Under Hong Kong law, these agreements are generally valid and effective, as confirmed by the Court of Final Appeal in *C v D*.[57]

C v D involved an application to set aside an arbitral award, and the issue was whether a failure to fulfil pre-arbitral procedural conditions or requirements should affect the arbitral tribunal's jurisdiction or should only affect the admissibility of the claim before the tribunal. The Court of First Instance[58] refused to set aside the award because it held that the failure to comply with preconditions to arbitrate or escalation mechanisms (in that case, negotiations before arbitration) goes to the admissibility of the claim instead of the arbitral tribunal's jurisdiction, unless the parties have expressly agreed that non-compliance with preconditions would exclude the arbitral tribunal's jurisdiction. In other words, if there is

[54] ibid [35(b)].

[55] *HBZ Finance Ltd v Nippon Yusen Kaisha* (unreported, CACV 3185/2001, 12 June 2002). For floating choice of law agreements, see ch 14, s IV.

[56] *The Incorporated Owners of Wing Fai Building, Shui Wo Street v Golden Rise (HK) Project Co Ltd* (unreported, DCCJ 225/2016, 23 June 2016).

[57] *C v D* (2023) 26 HKCFAR 216, [2023] HKCFA 16 [43].

[58] *C v D* [2021] 3 HKLRD 1, [2021] HKCFI 1474 [53], approved in *Kinli Civil Engineering Ltd v Geotech Engineering Ltd* [2021] 6 HKC 524, [2021] HKCFI 2503 [8].

an agreed procedure for dispute resolution, the appropriate forum to determine whether the procedure has been duly followed or whether the reference to arbitration is premature is the tribunal itself. Both questions of admissibility and of jurisdiction in relation to arbitral disputes are matters for the tribunal. That view was unanimously upheld on appeal to the Court of Appeal.[59]

In the Court of Final Appeal, all five judges (Cheung CJ, Ribeiro, Fok and Lam PJJ and Gummow NPJ) agreed that the appeal should be dismissed, holding that an arbitral tribunal's determination on the fulfilment of a pre-arbitration condition (that the parties should first attempt to resolve their dispute by a specified mechanism) was not subject to recourse to the Court under Article 34(2)(a)(iii) of the UNCITRAL Model Law on International Commercial Arbitration. However, the Court (in obiter) differed as to whether the conceptual distinction between a challenge to an arbitral tribunal's 'jurisdiction' and a challenge to the 'admissibility' of a particular claim should be adopted to resolve the case. The majority (Ribeiro PJ, with Cheung CJ, Fok PJ and Lam PJ concurring) adopted the distinction and considered that the objection to the compliance with pre-arbitration conditions goes to the admissibility of the claim.[60] The minority (Gummow NPJ) did not adopt the distinction but reached the same conclusion even if the distinction was disregarded by construing the arbitration agreement.[61] In his Lordship's view, the inquiry is not whether an issue is classified as one of 'jurisdiction' or 'admissibility', and the refusal of recourse to a court is based on the grounds laid down in Article 34 of the Model Law.

VII. Conflicting Dispute Resolution Agreements

Generally, the courts will strive to reconcile apparently conflicting dispute resolution clauses. In *AAA v DDD*, the Court of First Instance identified three broad paradigms in which conflicting dispute resolution clauses might feature: a basic paradigm, an intermediate paradigm and a generalised paradigm.[62] The Court then explained each of these paradigms:[63]

> A basic paradigm is the situation where there is a single contract with two or more conflicting dispute resolution clauses. An intermediate paradigm is the situation where there are multiple related contracts, but only one of the contracts contains a dispute resolution clause, while the others do not. Thus, the conflict in the intermediate paradigm is not so much between two or more contrary clauses, as opposed to whether (say) an arbitration clause in a single contract should be treated as governing disputes arising out a related contract which has no dispute resolution clause, or whether the latter disputes must be litigated before the court. A generalised paradigm is where there are multiple related contracts with conflicting dispute resolution clauses in two or more (but not necessarily all) of the contracts.

[59] *C v D* [2022] 3 HKLRD 116, [2022] HKCA 729.

[60] In *C v D* (CFA) (n 57) [90], Ribeiro PJ expressly approved *C v D* (CFI) (n 58), which also employed the distinction.

[61] In *C v D* (CFA) (n 57) [134], Gummow NPJ expressly approved *C v D* (CA) (n 59) [61], which reached the same conclusion even if the distinction was disregarded.

[62] *AAA v DDD* [2024] 1 HKLRD 1358, [2024] HKCFI 513 [46]. The paradigms are not meant to be exhaustive of every permutation that can occur.

[63] ibid [47].

The term 'multiple related contract' referred to

> agreements that appear to form a package aimed at achieving some objective. Typically, the related contracts will have been executed at about the same time and the parties to the contracts will be the same or nearly the same. If the parties to a set of contracts are not the same, there may be evidence that a company signing a given contract with a dispute resolution clause, was acting on behalf of itself and as the agent of affiliated companies. In civil law jurisdictions, it may be possible to link multiple contracts to affiliated companies by characterising the companies as a single economic entity. But the doctrine of a single economic entity has yet to gain traction in the common law world.[64]

However, regardless of whether a case involved the basic, intermediate or generalised paradigm,

> the authorities are unanimous that determining the scopes of conflicting dispute resolution clauses is essentially an exercise in objectively construing the clauses to ascertain the parties' likely intentions. Absent contrary indications, one may employ certain common-sense presumptions or assumptions as an aid to construction. But one must be careful not to use the presumptions or assumptions in a manner that runs roughshod over the parties' intentions as manifested in the dispute resolution clauses agreed among them.[65]

For the basic paradigm (singleton contracts with apparently conflicting internal dispute resolution clauses), the 'one-stop presumption' in the *Fiona Trust & Holding Corp v Privalov* would be applicable,[66] which is approved in Hong Kong cases such as *Houtai Investment Holdings Ltd v Leung Yat Tung*.[67] That 'presumption' states:[68]

> [T]he construction of an arbitration clause should start from the assumption that the parties, as rational businessmen, are likely to have intended any dispute arising out of the relationship into which they have entered or purported to enter to be decided by the same tribunal. The clause should be construed in accordance with this presumption unless the language makes it clear that certain questions were intended to be excluded from the arbitrator's jurisdiction.

For the intermediate paradigm situation (multiple related contracts with dispute resolution clauses in only some contracts), an 'extended *Fiona Trust* presumption' was suggested in *Terre Neuve SARL v Yewdale Ltd*[69] and seemingly accepted in *AAA v DDD*.[70] On this approach, 'a jurisdiction agreement contained in one contract may, on its proper construction, extend to a claim that is made under another contract'. This approach would work where the parties to the various contracts involved are the same and the contracts 'have been concluded at the same time as part of a single package or transaction or (if concluded at different times) dealt with the same subject-matter'. In this situation, there would be scope for a presumption that, absent evidence to the contrary, the parties intended all disputes arising out of their commercial package to be resolved by reference to the dispute resolution clause in the one contract.

[64] ibid [48].
[65] ibid [50].
[66] *Fiona Trust & Holding Corp v Privalov* [2007] UKHL 40, [2007] 4 All ER 951.
[67] *Houtai Investment Holdings Ltd* (n 9).
[68] *Fiona Trust & Holding Corp* (n 66) [13].
[69] *Terre Neuve SARL v Yewdale Ltd* [2020] EWHC 772 (Comm).
[70] *AAA v DDD* (n 62) [54]. However, it was not applicable on the facts of the case.

For the generalised paradigm (multiple contracts with different dispute resolution clauses), after reviewing authorities, including *Trust Risk Group SpA v AmTrust Europe Ltd*,[71] the Court of First Instance espoused a centre of gravity approach:[72]

> 62. … [T]here can be no initial presumption that the parties intended all their disputes to be resolved in a single forum, if there are several contracts with different dispute resolution clauses. … Instead of applying a presumption, one must construe each contract in the package to map out what disputes must have been intended to be covered by the dispute resolution clause of a given contract.
>
> 63. The mapping may not be a straightforward or neat exercise. The contractual arrangements here being inter-related, disputes among the parties may involve intertwined issues which might reasonably be regarded as falling within the ambit of two or more dispute resolution clauses. If so, in deciding whether a particular forum has jurisdiction to deal with an intertwined issue or dispute between the parties, one must locate the 'centre of gravity' of that issue or dispute as best one can, assessing which resolution clause is 'closer' to the issue or dispute.
>
> 64. I accept that expressions such as 'centre of gravity' and 'closer to an issue or dispute' can be nebulous concepts. Inevitably, the determination of an issue's 'centre of gravity' or 'closeness' to a dispute resolution clause cannot be rocket science. For this reason, in making an assessment, one should adopt a liberal and generous (as opposed to a pedantic) attitude.
>
> 65. … [A] possible test for determining whether an intertwined or overlapping issue falls within or outside of a tribunal's jurisdiction, might be to look at the ultimate relief sought in connection with that issue. If granting the ultimate relief being sought falls within the scope of the arbitration agreement under which a tribunal was appointed, the issue could be regarded as coming within the tribunal's jurisdiction or 'centre of gravity'. The issue would be a question which reasonably needs to be answered by the tribunal as a stepping stone to deciding whether the relief sought should be granted. This would be the position, even though the issue may also be relevant to the resolution of some other dispute within the 'centre of gravity' of a jurisdictional clause in another contract.

[71] *Trust Risk Group SpA v AmTrust Europe Ltd* [2015] EWCA Civ 437, [2016] 1 All ER (Comm) 325.
[72] *AAA v DDD* (n 62) [62]–[65].

PART III

Choice of Law

14

Choice of Law Agreements

This chapter deals with express agreements between parties as to the choice of governing law for their contract. For jurisdiction and dispute resolution agreements, see chapter thirteen. For choice of law in arbitration agreements, see chapter twenty-four, section III.

I. General Requirements

A choice of law agreement specifies which jurisdiction's laws will govern the interpretation and enforcement of the contract. Choice of law is an important question in private international law. This is due to increasing complexity of cross-border disputes. Whether parties have made a choice of law is a question determined by the law of the forum.[1] The freedom to choose the governing law of an agreement has long been established in the English courts[2] and is widely accepted in Hong Kong.[3] The parties' autonomy to choose the law governing a commercial contract has been recognised in the 2015 HCCH Principles on Choice of Law in International Commercial Contracts (the Hague Choice of Law Principles).[4]

Subject only to narrow statutory exceptions for certain types of contracts, it is established that the parties' choice of a law will be respected by the court. Nevertheless, there are some requirements to be fulfilled.

First, choice of law clauses have to be certain. Second, an absence of connection between the designated law and the subject matter of a contract will not by itself be evidence of a lack of bona fides.[5] *Vita Food Products Inc v Unus Shipping Co Ltd* held that it is not necessary for the choice of law to have real connection with the subject matter of a contract;[6] the only requirement is that the choice be made in good faith and should not contravene public policy.[7] However, the fact that there is no link between the choice of law and the subject of a contract may be evidence of a lack of good faith.[8] Third, the chosen law must be one of a

[1] *Enka Insaat ve Sanayi AS v OOO Insurance Co Chubb* [2020] UKSC 38, [2020] 1 WLR 4117 [31]–[33].

[2] *Amin Rasheed Shipping Corp v Kuwait Insurance Co* [1984] AC 50.

[3] *First Laser Ltd v Fujian Enterprises (Holdings) Co Ltd* (2012) 15 HKCFAR 569 [53].

[4] Hague Choice of Law Principles, Art 2.

[5] *Shenzhen Development Bank Co Ltd v New Century International (Holdings) Ltd* (unreported, HCA 2976/2001, 31 July 2002) [21]–[24].

[6] *Vita Food Products Inc v Unus Shipping Co Ltd* [1939] AC 277.

[7] ibid 290. For a case where the choice is purely a sham, see *Snook v London & West Riding Investments Ltd* [1967] 2 QB 786. It is difficult to envisage circumstances where a choice of law can be said to violate Hong Kong's public policy: see, eg *Dynamit AG v Rio Tinto Co Ltd* [1918] AC 292; *The Hollandia* [1983] 1 AC 565. See also Hague Choice of Law Principles, Art 11.

[8] *Credit Agricole Indosuez v Shanghai Erfangji Co Ltd* (unreported, HCA 14569/1999, 12 June 2002) [30].

'civilised and organised society'.[9] As for the choice of non-state law, including internationally recognised principles of law, soft law instruments or international practice, the choice cannot be denied effect merely on the ground that a non-state law has been chosen.[10] It may be that while arbitral tribunals will give effect to non-state laws, the Hong Kong court may not. But the rationale for this distinction in treatment of non-state law, depending on the mode of dispute resolution, is unclear.[11]

II. Uncertain Choice of Law Agreements

The Hong Kong courts only demand that choice of law agreements have to be substantially clear. The rule does not require the language to be exact. For instance, *The Thor Scan* held that it was possible to have a governing law defined by reference to facts extrinsic to a contract.[12] Simply put, if an agreement as to governing law can be inferred from particular facts, such agreement will be effective. In *Amin Rasheed Shipping Corp*, it was stated that the court should examine the contract in order to see whether the parties have, by its express terms or by necessary implication from the language used, evinced a common intention as to the system of law by reference to which their mutual rights and obligations under it are to be ascertained.[13]

In *York Air Conditioning & Refrigeration Inc v Lam Kwai Hung*,[14] the court held that, in the absence of an express choice, the court should first examine, from the terms and nature of the contract and the general circumstances of the case, whether there is any indication of the parties' intention. Only if there is no such indication will the court consider the system of law with which the contract has its closest and most real connection. That approach was adopted in *S Megga Telecommunications Ltd v Etowaru Co Ltd*.[15]

III. Closest and Most Real Connection

In the absence of a designated law, a contract's proper law is that system of law to which the contract has its closest and most real connection.[16] The approach is for the court to put itself in the place of the reasonable man, to see what ordinary, reasonable, sensible businessmen in the circumstances would likely decide had their minds been directed to the question.[17] The application of the test requires an assessment of factors such as: (i) the location of the

[9] *Carl Zeiss Stiftung v Rayner & Keeler Ltd (No 2)* [1967] 1 AC 853.

[10] Hague Choice of Law Principles, Art 3. In the EU, this possibility was recognised by Preamble 13 of the Rome I Regulation.

[11] See, eg *Musawi v RE International (UK) Ltd* [2007] EWHC 2981 (Ch), [2008] 1 All ER (Comm) 607, in which the parties agreed that 'Sharia Law' would apply to their contract. Richards J thought that such choice of law, while possibly valid in arbitrations, was invalid as far as a court was concerned.

[12] *The Thor Scan* [1999] 2 HKLRD 136.

[13] *Amin Rasheed Shipping Corp* (n 2) [61].

[14] *York Air Conditioning & Refrigeration Inc v Lam Kwai Hung* [1995] 2 HKLR 256 [18]–[20].

[15] *S Megga Telecommunications Ltd v Etowaru Co Ltd* [1995] 2 HKC 761.

[16] *Whitworth Street Estates (Manchester) Ltd v James Miller & Partners Ltd* [1970] AC 583, 604.

[17] *First Laser Ltd v Fujian Enterprises (Holdings) Co Ltd* [2011] 2 HKLRD 45 [58.3].

subject matter of the contract; (ii) the place of intended performance; (iii) the validity and effectiveness of the contract; (iv) the place where the contract was made or negotiated; (v) the parties' domicile; (vi) the use of certain legal terminology; (vii) the language of the contract; (viii) the existence of a dispute resolution clause; (ix) the currency of the contract; and (x) related transactions (if any).[18] Each of these factors is discussed in turn below, and not all of them are attached significant weight in their modern application. These factors are merely indicative, and reasonable judgments may often differ in practice as to the conclusion to be reached in a particular case.[19]

A. Location of the Subject Matter of the Contract

A contract which involves land as the subject matter is very likely to be governed by the law of the location where the land is located. A contract that involves chattels may apply the law of the specific location where the chattels are present at the time of contracting, yet the relevant importance will not be as pivotal as that in cases of land, and other factors will be more important.[20] If the asset is intangible or if a tangible asset only represents a minor, non-dominant aspect of the transaction, it is less significant.

B. Place of Intended Performance

The place of intended performance is generally considered to be an important factor in determining the system with which the contract has the closest and most genuine connection.[21] However, this does not mean that this factor 'is not to be weighed against the other factors'.[22] In *First National Bank of Chicago v Carroway Enterprises Ltd*,[23]

> there is a tendency to regard the fact that payment under a contract is to be made in a particular place as a strong indication that the legal system of that place is the one with which the contract has the closest and most real connection.

In *The Cavalry*, the place of the lender's business and the place where the money was lent and was repayable were together considered to be 'crucial' factors in determination of proper law.[24]

C. Validity and Effectiveness of the Contract

The validation principle provides that, as a matter of contractual interpretation, an interpretation which upholds the validity of a transaction or a clause is to be preferred to one

[18] *Waxman v Li Fei Yu* [2013] 3 HKLRD 711 [22].
[19] *Choi Hon Cheung v Chan Chong Man* [2024] HKCFI 538 [71].
[20] *Cammell v Sewell* (1860) 5 H&N 617, 157 ER 615; *Cammell v Sewell* (1860) 5 H&N 728, 157 ER 1371; *Inglis v Robertson* [1898] AC 616.
[21] *First Laser Ltd* (n 3) [55]–[56].
[22] *Bank of India v Gobindram Naraindas Sadhwani* [1988] 2 HKLR 262, 268.
[23] *First National Bank of Chicago v Carroway Enterprises Ltd* [1990] 2 HKLR 10, 14.
[24] *The Calvary* [1987] HKLR 287.

which would render it invalid or ineffective.[25] In the choice of law context, between two possible proper laws, the court will favour the proper law that would uphold the validity of an agreement rather than one that would invalidate it.[26] Thus, in the context of arbitration agreements, commercial parties are generally unlikely to have intended a choice of governing law for the contract to apply to an arbitration agreement if there is 'at least a serious risk' that a choice of that law would 'significantly undermine' that agreement.[27]

D. Place of Making or Negotiating the Contract

The location of the contract's execution is relevant, but is now of much less significance due to the advancement of technology and changes in negotiation methods. It was stated in *Bank of India* that the courts frequently take into account where the negotiations took place before the contract was signed.[28] However, recent cases have shown that it is now of much diminished significance as a pointer to a contract's closest and most real connection.[29]

E. Domicile of Parties

In *The Calvary*, the place of the lender's business was said to be one of 'the factors crucial to any objective determination of the proper law'.[30] In *Bank of India*, two of the four guarantors lived in Japan, including the guarantor who played an active part and took the decisions for the four. The court considered this when ruling Japanese law to have the strongest and most direct relationship to the contract.[31] However, it is inappropriate to give too much weight to domicile unless the domicile or residence of both parties of the contract is identical.[32]

F. Use of Certain Legal Terminology

If a contract uses terminology of a specific legal system, the court might infer that this is the system's correct law. This has been evidenced in *Amin Rasheed Shipping Corp* and *S Megga Telecommunications*.[33] In *Amin Rasheed Shipping Corp*, the contract was more closely connected with Kuwait than England, but the contract was replete with English law terminology, suggesting a more substantial connection with English law.[34] In *Mayer Holdings*

[25] See, eg *Enka Insaat ve Sanayi AS* (n 1) [95].
[26] ibid [198].
[27] *Sulamérica Cia Nacional de Seguros SA v Enesa Engenharia SA* [2012] EWCA Civ 638, [2013] 1 WLR 102 [31]; *Enka Insaat ve Sanayi AS* (n 1) [109].
[28] *Bank of India* (n 22) 268.
[29] *First Laser Ltd* (n 3) [56]; *Choi Hon Cheung* (n 19) [72].
[30] *The Calvary* (n 24) 297.
[31] *Bank of India* (n 22) 269.
[32] Graeme Johnston and Paul Harris, *The Conflict of Laws in Hong Kong*, 3rd edn (Sweet & Maxwell, 2017) para 5.009.
[33] *S Megga Telecommunications Ltd* (n 15) 767B–C.
[34] *Amin Rasheed Shipping Corp* (n 2).

Ltd v Xu Lidi,[35] the court scrutinised the letter of undertaking, which was made in respect of three capacities of the plaintiff, as director and the 'legal representative' of two companies, referring to both Hong Kong law and PRC law, even though the letter of undertaking specifically mentioned various Hong Kong laws and regulations. As such, the exercise is not a purely quantitative one.[36]

G. Language of the Contract

The language of a contract is a rather unimportant factor, but could occasionally be relevant. In situations where the interpretation of documents in one language is crucial and the courts involved have different working languages, it is considered fair for the courts with the same working language as the documents, rather than the other courts, to decide on the true meaning. This is deemed to be in the interest of the parties involved and justice as a whole.[37]

H. Existence of a Dispute Resolution Clause

The parties may designate a court or a place of arbitration for the resolution of any dispute arising out of their contract, but they may omit to specify a governing law. Can it be presumed that they have chosen the law of the location where the designated court is situated or the arbitration seated? It appears that there is no strong presumption to that effect.[38] Yet the dispute resolution clause remains an important factor. It may be decisive in many cases, unless there is a strong indication from other circumstances that some other system of law should be treated as the proper law of the contract. The choice of seat of arbitration may be of less weight for this analysis than the selection of a court.

I. Currency of the Contract

According to *Bank of India*, the use of a specific currency in a contract suggests that the law of the country using that currency is considered the chosen law by the parties involved, rather than the law of the place with the closest and strongest connection.[39] But the weight of this factor is doubtful. 'Currency relates to the implied choice of law of the parties rather than the place of closest and most real connection and it is recognised there are clearly limits to the relevance of this factor.'[40]

[35] *Mayer Holdings Ltd v Xu Lidi* [2022] 2 HKC 620, [2022] HKCFI 275.
[36] ibid [21].
[37] *Hady v Bazar* [2012] 3 HKLRD 29.
[38] *Compagnie d'Armement Maritime SA v Compagnie Tunisienne de Navigation SA* [1971] AC 572, 593. In the arbitration agreement context, see ch 24, s III.
[39] *Bank of India* (n 22) 268.
[40] *Choi Hon Cheung* (n 19) [73].

J. Related Transactions

Courts frequently assume that contracts that are related to each other are meant to be governed by the same law.[41] For instance, it is more likely than not that a guarantee and the primary obligation will be subject to the same law,[42] while the governing law of the original contract is not important when making a claim under a bill of exchange.[43]

IV. Floating Choice of Law Agreements

A floating choice of law clause allows a party to choose the governing law that will apply to their agreement at some point in the future, often when a dispute arises. The choice of law provision 'floats' because it does not specify a particular jurisdiction's law at the time of the contract's formation, but instead crystallises on the occurrence of specified contingencies in the future. An example of such clause would be the following:

> This contract is to be governed by the law of party A's habitual residence if party B commences an action against party B and by the law of party B's habitual residence if party A commences an action against party B.

Floating choice of law agreements can provide flexibility. However, these agreements can also raise uncertainty and make it difficult to predict the governing law that will apply to a dispute.

In *The Armar*, the court held that the proper law of a contract had to be ascertainable at the time of the making of the contract.[44] The same view has been expressed in *The Iran Vojdan*.[45] Similarly, in *Chan Chi Keung v Delmas Hong Kong Ltd*, the judge cited *The Armar* and *Chitty on Contracts*, and concluded that 'there cannot be a proper law which "floats" ie not identified when the contract is made but which is left to be determined later by the unilateral act of one of the parties'.[46] It seems, then, that Hong Kong law would strike down floating law clauses. The reference to a choice to be 'made or modified at any time' in Article 2(3) of the Hague Choice of Law Principles does not validate a floating choice of law clause; there must be a choice of proper law when the contract is made.

Nevertheless, it is possible for a choice of law to be changed by what happens at a later time. In *Astro Venturoso Compania Naviera v Hellenic Shipyards SA*,[47] the bill of lading contained a clause which stated:

> Any claim and/or dispute arising under this Bill of Lading shall be referred to arbitration in London pursuant to English Arbitration Law … but if for any reason it is ruled by a competent

[41] *Dow MBF Ltd v Detrick Ltd* [1988] 1 HKLR 344.
[42] *First National Bank of Chicago* (n 23) [20].
[43] *York Air Conditioning & Refrigeration Inc* (n 14) [59].
[44] *The Armar* [1981] 1 WLR 207, 215.
[45] *The Iran Vojdan* [1984] 2 Lloyd's Rep 380.
[46] *Chan Chi Keung v Delmas Hong Kong Ltd* [2004] 4 HKC 28 [31]–[33]. See also *Shanghai Turbo Enterprises Ltd v Liu Ming* [2018] SGHC 172 [31]; *Shanghai Turbo Enterprises Ltd v Liu Ming* [2019] 1 SLR 779.
[47] *The Mariannina* [1983] 1 Lloyd's Rep 12.

> authority that the … arbitration provision is unenforceable then any claim and/or dispute … shall be governed by Greek Law and solely decided by the competent Greek Courts …

Such a clause does not pose any problem. If parties can choose the governing law at the outset, they should also be able to change it at a later time. This type of clause does not create a logical issue as it does not leave a void. It simply provides for a change in the applicable law from the one initially chosen in the contract when an identifiable event occurs. This aligns with the requirement of certainty.

15

Law of Obligations

This chapter discusses choice of law rules in relation to the law of obligations, namely obligations in contract, tort and restitution.

For choice of law rules in trusts and equitable obligations, see chapter sixteen.

I. Contracts

There are several potential candidates for the 'proper' governing law of a contract. These include the *lex loci contractus*, that is, the law of the place where the contract was made, and the *lex loci solutionis*, that is, the law of the place in which the contract is to be performed. However, neither of these will have considered the holistic context and circumstances of the contract. It is now accepted that there is a 'proper law' of the contract, meaning the express or implied choice of law by the parties, or, failing such a choice, the law of the place where the contract has its 'closest and most real connection'.[1] This 'proper law' will govern the effect, interpretation and discharge of a contract, as well as the issues of causation and damages in the event of a breach of contract.

A. Governing Law of Contracts

The approach to determine the governing law of a contract in Hong Kong is well settled after the Court of Final Appeal's decision in *First Laser Ltd v Fujian Enterprises (Holdings) Co Ltd*:[2]

> The common law rule is that the law applicable to a contract is the system of law by which the parties intended the contract to be governed, or, where their intention is neither expressed nor to be inferred from the circumstances, the system of law with which the transaction has its closest and most real connection.

This is, in theory, a three-stage approach, but as the Court of Final Appeal pointed out in the same paragraph:

> The line between the search for the inferred intention and the search for the system of law with which the contract has its closest and most real connection is a fine one which is frequently blurred. In theory, in the absence of an express choice as the first test, the court should consider as a second test whether there are any other indications of the parties' intention, and only if there is no such indication to go on to consider the third stage, namely with what system of

[1] *Bonython v Commonwealth of Australia* [1951] AC 201.

[2] *First Laser Ltd v Fujian Enterprises (Holdings) Co Ltd* (2012) 15 HKCFAR 569 [53].

law the contract has its closest and most real connection. But in practice the same result can be reached by the application of the second or third tests, and frequently the courts move straight from the first stage to the third stage. This is largely because the tests of inferred intention and close connection merged into each other, and because before the objective close connection test became fully established the test of inferred intention was in truth an objective test designed not to elicit actual intention but to impute an intention which had not been formed: *Dicey*, para 32-006.

To ascertain the governing law of a contract, the first step is to find what is the express intention of the parties. These are also known as choice of law agreements. These are discussed in chapter fourteen.

Failing an express intention as to the governing law, the court will attempt to ascertain the implied intention of the parties. This is inferred through the terms and nature of the contract, and from the general circumstances of the case. For a case where this was done, see *T v A*.[3]

If there is no express or implied choice of governing law that can be ascertained, then the court should search for the 'system of law with which the transaction has its closest and most real connection'.[4] The factors in which the court may consider are discussed in chapter fourteen, section III. Some of those may be of particular importance, others less so; but they are all merely indicative, and conclusions are reached based on all the facts and circumstances of the case.

B. Putative Proper Law

If the existence and validity of a contract is accepted, then the determination of the governing law of the contract follows the approach set out immediately above. However, there are circumstances in which the existence or validity of a contract is disputed. In this situation, courts have employed the concept of the 'putative proper law'.

Putative proper law refers to the law which would be the proper law of the contract if there was a valid contract. In the English case of *Albeko Schuhmaschinen AG v Kamborian Shoe Machine Co Ltd*,[5] E in England offered to appoint S in Switzerland as agent. S claimed that the offer was accepted by post, but the acceptance was in fact lost in the post. If English law (*lex fori*) governed the validity of the contract, the postal rule would have applied and there would have been an acceptance of an offer at the time of posting. However, if Swiss law governed the validity of the contract, the acceptance letter had to be received before a contract would be formed, thus there would have been no concluded agency agreement. The English court held that there was no contract, because it had not been proved that the letter of acceptance had been posted. The view expressed was that if the letter had been posted, Swiss law would govern and there would still be no contract. This was because if a contract had been concluded, Swiss law would have been its governing law. There was no reason why the intended agent in Switzerland would have been familiar with English law so as to expect that an agency was concluded at the time of posting.

[3] *T v A* [2018] 3 HKLRD 730, [2018] HKCFI 1756 [29]–[32].
[4] *First Laser Ltd* (n 2) [53]. See also *S Megga Telecommunications Ltd v Etowaru Co Ltd* [1995] 2 HKC 761.
[5] *Albeko Schuhmaschinen AG v Kamborian Shoe Machine Co Ltd* (1961) 111 LJ 519.

As seen from the above scenario, there may be problems with the 'putative proper law' being the law which would be the proper law of the contract if there was a valid contract. There may be injustice to one of the parties in the application of putative proper law, and it is suggested that a party should simply be able to rely on the law of his or her place of business or residence.[6] The *lex fori* may have a role to play in these situations. In *MacKender v Feldia AG*,[7] the English underwriters sought to avoid a policy, which was expressed to be governed by Belgian law and subject to the exclusive jurisdiction of the Belgian courts, on the ground that the insured had failed to disclose material facts. The English court distinguished between the effect of misrepresentation and mistake. It held that the non-disclosure only rendered the contract void from the moment when the underwriters avoided the same. But the court suggested obiter that the position might have been different if the allegation had been that there never had been a contract at all, because of a plea of *non est factum* or fraud. Only Diplock LJ dealt with the question as to what law might govern such questions. He thought that the concept of putative objective governing law was 'confusing'. He thought that if

> the question is whether there was any real consensus *ad idem*, it may well be that this question has to be determined by English law and not by the law which would have been agreed by them as the proper law of the contract if they had reached an agreement.[8]

It was also suggested, in *Royal Boskalis Westminster NV v Mountain*,[9] that public policy can override the putative proper law. The circumstances involved an extreme case of duress, and the *lex fori* (English law) was held to override the putative proper law (Iraqi law).

Despite the foregoing, the modern position seems to be that the formation of a contract is governed by the law which would have been the governing law had the contract been validly concluded, not by the *lex fori*. In *Dimskal Shipping Co SA v International Transport Workers Federation*,[10] the House of Lords held that whether a contract was voidable on the ground of economic duress depended on English law as the putative governing law of the contract, not Swedish law as law of the place where the duress allegedly occurred. That was also the position in Hong Kong in *Chen Hongqing*.[11] When deciding whether choice of law and arbitration clauses have been incorporated into a contract, Hong Kong courts will generally regard the designated law as the putative applicable law. See, for example, *Sea Powerful II Special Maritime Enterprises (ENE)*.[12] The court further stated:[13]

> As a general rule, issues on the 'material validity' of a contract or of any term of a contract, such as formation of the agreement or incorporation of terms, are determined by the putative applicable law of the contract, viz the law which would govern the contract if the contract or term were valid.

[6] Lord Collins of Mapesbury and Jonathan Harris (gen eds), *Dicey, Morris and Collins on the Conflict of Laws*, 16th edn (Sweet & Maxwell, 2022) para 32-141.

[7] *MacKender v Feldia AG* [1967] 2 QB 590.

[8] ibid 603.

[9] *Royal Boskalis Westminster NV v Mountain* [1999] QB 674.

[10] *Dimskal Shipping Co SA v International Transport Workers Federation* [1992] 2 AC 152.

[11] *Chen Hongqing v Persons Whose Names are Set Out in the Second Column of the Schedule to the Re-Amended Writ of Summons Filed on 26 March 2018* [2019] HKCFI 2121 [130].

[12] *Sea Powerful II Special Maritime Enterprises (ENE) v Bank of China Ltd* [2016] 1 HKLRD 1032. In Singapore, the formation of the contract is governed by the law that would meet the reasonable expectations of the parties: *Solomon Lew v Kaikhushru Shiavax Nargolwala* [2021] 2 SLR 1.

[13] *Sea Powerful II Special Maritime Enterprises (ENE)* (n 12) [19], citing *Tung Ho Wah v Star Cruises (HK) Ltd* [2006] 3 HKLRD 254 [21].

C. Capacity

Capacity refers to whether a person has substantive legal power to enter into contracts generally or into particular types of contract. The capacity of a natural person to enter into a contract may be validated by either the objective proper law or the law of the domicile and residence. The capacity of a legal person (corporation) to enter into a contract is determined by its constitution and, in turn, by the law of the place of its incorporation, and in appropriate circumstances the proper law of the contract. For example, a company may not be allowed under either or both laws to acquire or hold land; its capacity is accordingly limited.[14] The putative proper law of the contract may be relevant when deciding whether a purported company director has apparent or implied authority to bind the company to a contract.[15]

D. Formal Validity

The *Giuliano-Lagarde Report* defines 'formal validity' as 'every external manifestation required on the part of a person expressing the will to be legally bound and in the absence of which such expression of will would not be regarded as fully effective'.[16] Formal validity thus refers to the 'formalities' or 'formal requirements' with which a contract must comply to be valid. More specifically, formal validity is concerned with requirements such as that a contract be made in writing, under seal, before witnesses, and so on. Several formal requirements are still found in English or Hong Kong law, for example, in relation to contracts for the sale of land, certain types of consumer contracts and guarantees. It was suggested that formal validity is satisfied and a contract will be upheld if it complies with the formal requirements of the place where it was made or with those of the putative proper law.[17]

E. Material Validity

Material validity, also known as 'essential validity', refers to everything apart from formal validity that makes a contract enforceable. It is concerned with the existence and validity of the contract. It therefore encompasses matters such as the formation of a contract (including the effect of silence), the absence of consideration, misrepresentation, duress, mistake and the legality of a contract. Material validity is governed by the proper law of the contract or (if the existence or validity of the contract is disputed) by the putative proper law of the contract. This is discussed in section I.B above.

[14] *Great West Saddlery Co v R* [1921] 2 AC 91; *Haugesund Kommune v Depfa ACS Bank* [2010] EWCA Civ 579, [2011] 1 All ER 190.

[15] *Noble Power Investments Ltd v Nissei Stomach Tokyo Co Ltd* [2008] 1 HKLRD 134 [40].

[16] Report on the Convention on the Law Applicable to Contractual Obligations by Mario Giuliano, Professor, University of Milan, and Paul Lagarde, Professor, University of Paris I [1980] OJ C282/30.

[17] Graeme Johnston and Paul Harris, *The Conflict of Laws in Hong Kong*, 3rd edn (Sweet & Maxwell, 2017) para 5.010.

F. Mandatory Rules

Hong Kong mandatory rules may override the parties' choice of law in a contract. Examples of mandatory rules are section 17(2) of the Control of Exemption Clauses Ordinance (Cap 71), section 70 of the Employment Ordinance (Cap 57) and the four Hong Kong anti-discrimination ordinances. These are discussed in chapter eight, section I.A.

G. Foreign Illegality

The effect of foreign illegality in Hong Kong was reviewed in *Ryder Industries Ltd v Chan Shui Woo*.[18] The Court of Final Appeal endorsed the following principles on illegality:[19]

> First, if the contract is unenforceable under its proper law (whether chosen by the parties or otherwise), then it will not be enforced by the Hong Kong court. The importance of this principle is that it applies to limit the enforceability of the contract regardless of the place of required, intended or actual performance. Moreover, it is irrelevant whether the bar on enforcement is a foreign penal law of the sort which will not be directly enforced by a Hong Kong court.
>
> Secondly, if the performance of the contract requires or necessarily involves conduct which is illegal under the laws of the place where it is required to be performed, then it will not be given effect regardless of its proper law.
>
> Thirdly, the contract will not be given effect regardless of its proper law 'if the real object and intention of the parties [at the time of concluding the contract] necessitates them joining in an endeavour to perform in a foreign and friendly country some act which is illegal by the law of such country notwithstanding the fact that there may be, in a certain event, alternative modes or places of performing which permit the contract to be performed legally' [citing *Foster v Driscoll* [1929] 1 KB 470, 521, per Sankey LJ].
>
> Fourthly, violation of foreign laws in the actual performance of a contract may, even though not required or initially intended, lead to the unenforceability of the contract before a Hong Kong court, regardless of its proper law. It has recently been stated in England at first instance that a contract will not be enforced if it has been 'performed in such a way that one party (or both parties) commits a legal wrong'. It is, however, respectfully suggested that this is to state the principle too rigidly, and that a more flexible approach having regard to the seriousness of the foreign illegality is required to determine whether public policy and comity really require enforcement of the contract to be denied in such a case.
>
> Fifthly, the above four principles apply irrespective of whether the illegality under foreign law existed at the time of contracting or arose subsequently.

The rationale for this rule is the desire to uphold international comity and Hong Kong public policy. The latter is the policy that the courts 'should not … assist or sanction the breach of the laws of other independent States'.[20] However, the Court of Final Appeal believed that 'a more flexible approach having regard to the seriousness of the foreign illegality is

[18] *Ryder Industries Ltd v Chan Shui Woo* (2015) 18 HKCFAR 544.

[19] ibid [39], citing Graeme Johnston, *The Conflict of Laws in Hong Kong*, 2nd edn (Sweet & Maxwell, 2012) para 5.012.

[20] *Ralli Bros v Compania Naviera Sota y Aznar* [1920] 2 KB 287, 304; Johnston and Harris (n 17) para 5.012.

required to determine whether public policy and comity really require enforcement of the contract to be denied'.[21] Consistently with this reasoning, not every breach of foreign laws will lead to unenforceability.[22] A defence of illegality will only succeed if the alleged criminality is significant and not trivial.[23] See, for instance, *Ryder Industries Ltd v Chan Shui Woo*,[24] where the Court of Final Appeal refused relief because there was no evidence that the performance complained of constituted a serious illegality in Mainland China. Moreover, a Hong Kong court may not recognise a foreign law that would render performance of a contract illegal, if the law is contrary to the public policy of Hong Kong.[25] However, this would be rare in practice as a matter of comity. It was also noted that 'a contract may be enforced by a foreigner through the Hong Kong courts even though he [or she] thereby commits an offence under the laws of his [or her] own country'.[26]

II. Specific Contracts

A. Agency

The relationship and duties between principal and agent (also known as the 'internal' aspect of the law of agency) can arise by contract or otherwise (for example, an agent may be liable in tort for unlawful interference or in equity for fiduciary duties; in those situations, the relevant choice of law rules discussed elsewhere will apply). At common law, a contract of agency is governed by its proper law, which in general is the law of the place where the relationship of principal and agent was created.[27] If this place cannot be determined, the court will attempt to discern objectively what law the parties have intended to govern their agency relationship.[28] Possible candidates would be the law of the place where the principal's business is carried on,[29] the law of the place where the agent is supposed to act[30] and the law of the place which has the closest and most real connection with the contract.[31] The governing law will be applicable to the construction of the contract, including the terms of the agency, the limits of the agent's authority, the rights and obligations of the parties, and the consequences of breach of either party's respective contractual obligations.

For the relationship between principal and third party (also known as the 'external' aspect of the law of agency), the issue of whether the agent can bind the principal to a

[21] *Ryder Industries Ltd* (n 18) [39].
[22] ibid [56]. See also *Re O'Connor's Bill of Costs* [1993] 1 Qd R 423.
[23] *Lesnina H DOO v Wave Shipping Trade Co Ltd* [2022] 2 HKLRD 727, [2022] HKCFI 1070 [54], citing Andrew Burrows, *A Restatement of the English Law of Unjust Enrichment* (Oxford University Press, 2012) 121.
[24] *Ryder Industries Ltd* (n 18).
[25] ibid [57]. See also *Foster v Driscoll* [1929] 1 KB 470; *Regazzoni v KC Sethia (1944) Ltd* [1958] AC 301.
[26] *Ryder Industries Ltd* (n 18) [57], citing *Kahler v Midland Bank* [1950] AC 24. See also *Rossano v Manufacturers Life Insurance Co* [1963] 2 QB 352.
[27] *Arnott v Redfern* (1825) 2 C&P 88; *Re Anglo-Austrian Bank* [1920] 1 Ch 69.
[28] *Albeko Schuhmaschinen AG* (n 5); *Mauroux v Pereira* [1972] 1 WLR 962; *Wahbe Tamari & Sons Co v Bernhard Rothfos* [1980] 2 Lloyd's Rep 553. In these cases, the parties showed intentions to have the contract being governed by different systems of law.
[29] *Arnott* (n 27); *Re Anglo-Austrian Bank* (n 27).
[30] *Albeko Schuhmaschinen AG* (n 5); *Mauroux* (n 28).
[31] *Wahbe Tamari & Sons Co* (n 28).

contract with a third party and the terms of contract is governed by the putative governing law if the agent's authority were established.[32]

B. Bailment

The relationship between bailor and bailee is treated as similar to a contractual relationship for the purposes of choice of law. The governing law is determined at the time when the bailment is created. The relationship is not affected by the *situs* of the goods bailed or the residence of the parties.[33] It is submitted that, in the absence of an express choice of law, the law with the closest and most real connection is likely to be the *lex loci solutionis*, that is, the law of the place in which the goods bailed are to be held.[34]

C. Carriage of Goods by Sea, Air or Land

The ordinary principles for governing law of contracts will apply. Nonetheless, some statutory provisions in Hong Kong override the common law in various contexts.

The Carriage by Air Ordinance (Cap 500) provides that the 1929 Warsaw Convention for the Unification of Certain Rules Relating to International Carriage of Air (as amended by the 1955 Hague Protocol) has the force of law in Hong Kong, irrespective of the nationality of the aircraft performing the carriage. The Ordinance also provides that certain provisions of the 1961 Guadalajara Convention, insofar as they relate to the rights and liabilities of carriers, carriers' servants and agents, passengers, consignors, consignees and other persons, have the force of law in Hong Kong in respect of a carriage of air to which the Convention applies. Moreover, the 1999 Montreal Convention for the Unification of Certain Rules for International Carriage by Air was implemented by the Ordinance in 2005.

The Carriage of Goods by Sea Ordinance (Cap 462) provides that the 1924 Hague Rules (Convention for the Unification of Certain Rules Relating to Bills of Lading), as amended by the 1968 and 1979 Brussels Protocols (Hague–Visby Rules) has the force of law in Hong Kong. Moreover, the Merchant Shipping (Limitation of Shipowners' Liability) Ordinance (Cap 434), which applies to domestic and international shipping cases, implements the 1974 Athens Convention Relating to the Carriage of Passengers and their Luggage by Sea and the 1976 London Protocol. The Ordinance originally only concerned 'international carriage', but was amended in 2005 to extend to the carriage of passengers and their luggage by sea between Hong Kong and Macao or between Hong Kong and Mainland China. It has no application to carriage within Hong Kong or transport by sea within a foreign country.

Regarding other types of maritime civil liability, the Merchant Shipping (Collision Damage Liability and Salvage) Ordinance (Cap 508) implemented the 1952 Convention

[32] See, eg *Merrill Lynch Capital Services Inc v Municipality of Piraeus* [1997] CLC 1214; *Marubeni Hong Kong and South China Ltd v Mongolian Government* [2004] EWHC 472 (Comm), [2004] 2 Lloyd's Rep 198.
[33] See, eg *Kahler* (n 26); *Zivnostenska Banka National Corp v Frankman* [1950] AC 57.
[34] *Kahler* (n 26).

on Certain Rules Concerning Civil Jurisdiction in Matters of Collision and the 1989 International Convention on Salvage. The Merchant Shipping (Limitation of Shipowners' Liability) Ordinance (Cap 434) implemented the 1976 Convention on Limitation of Liability for Maritime Claims. The Merchant Shipping (Liability and Compensation for Oil Pollution) Ordinance (Cap 414) implemented (i) the 1969 International Convention on Civil Liability for Oil Pollution Damage (as amended by the 1992 Protocol) and (ii) the 1971 International Convention on the Establishment of an International Fund for Compensation for Oil Pollution Damage (as amended by the 1992 Protocol and further modified in 2000). The Bunker Oil Pollution (Liability and Compensation) Ordinance (Cap 605) implemented the 2001 International Convention on Civil Liability for Bunker Oil Pollution Damage.

For carriage by land, rail and road, there is no specific Hong Kong legislation for the cross-border carriage of goods or passengers. However, section 6 of the Guangzhou–Shenzhen–Hong Kong Express Rail Link (Co-location) Ordinance (Cap 632) provides that part of the West Kowloon station in Hong Kong is to apply Mainland laws and the Mainland courts have jurisdiction.

D. Credit and Security

Contracts of credit and security follow the principles outlined above. In determining the law with the closest and most real connection, 'the place of the lender's business and the place where the money is lent and repayable are crucial factors'.[35] In relation to the potential application of the Money Lenders Ordinance (Cap 163) (which concerns persons carrying on the business of a money lender in Hong Kong only), the court has held that it should first be determined whether the proper law of the contract is Hong Kong law. It held:[36]

> If the proper law of the contract by objective standards, ie by asking 'what is the system of law with which the transaction has its closest and most real connection' so ascertained is foreign, MLO has no application. If it is domestic, then the court has a base from which to judge the validity of the challenge to the bona fides of any choice of law provision in the agreement. The advantage of this approach is to avoid the rigidity of the location test which makes location a decisive weight; supply the best test of bona fides; and the best answer to avoidance.

In *Re Han, Catherine*, the court held that the governing law of guarantees should generally be the same as the principal contract (usually a loan agreement), on the ground that the same law should govern both the principal and the secondary obligations.[37]

E. Consumer Contracts

The Sale of Goods Ordinance (Cap 26) applies to contracts of which the proper law is Hong Kong law. The Control of Exemption Clauses Ordinance (Cap 71) applies subject to the exemptions in sections 16 and 17(1), but provides for a mandatory rule to apply the

[35] *The Calvary* [1987] HKLR 287, 298A–D; *Central Southwood Ltd v Ma Wai Kin* [2019] HKDC 457 [66(vi)].
[36] The *Calvary* (n 35) 296E–I; *Central Southwood Ltd* (n 35) [66(iii)].
[37] *Re Han, Catherine* [2019] HKCFI 2274 [29].

Ordinance in section 17(2) if a party is dealing as a consumer, is habitually resident in Hong Kong and the essential steps for the contract took place in Hong Kong. The Unconscionable Contracts Ordinance (Cap 458) also has effect subject to the exemption in section 7(1) and the mandatory rule in section 7(2). The specific provisions of the latter two Ordinances are discussed in chapter eight, section I.A. Additionally, section 15 of the Control of Exemption Clauses Ordinance provides that an arbitration agreement cannot be enforced against a person dealing as a consumer, and section 8 of the Supply of Services (Implied Terms) Ordinance (Cap 457) provides that liability under the Ordinance cannot be excluded or restricted against a consumer by reference to any contract term.

F. Employment Contracts

The Employment Ordinance (Cap 57) applies to every employee engaged under a contract of employment, to the employer of that employee and to the contract of employment between the employer and employee.[38] It is reasonable to assume that there can be an express choice of law agreement applying the Employment Ordinance to an employment contract.[39] Contracts of employment entered into in Hong Kong between an employer not in Hong Kong and an employee for the performance, whether wholly or partially, of primarily manual work outside Hong Kong are regulated by the Contracts for Employment Outside Hong Kong Ordinance (Cap 78).

The four anti-discrimination ordinances in Hong Kong – the Sex Discrimination Ordinance (Cap 480), the Family Status Discrimination Ordinance (Cap 527), the Disability Discrimination Ordinance (Cap 487) and the Race Discrimination Ordinance (Cap 602) – protect employees and job applicants who are in actual or prospective employment at an 'establishment in Hong Kong', regardless of the governing law of the employment contract.[40] An employment in an 'establishment in Hong Kong' is defined negatively to mean all employment 'unless the employee does … work wholly or mainly outside Hong Kong', subject to certain minor exceptions.[41] It is not possible to contract out of the anti-discrimination ordinances.[42] Moreover, the Rehabilitation of Offenders Ordinance (Cap 297) does not extend to foreign convictions, and foreign rehabilitative legislation is not recognised by Hong Kong courts.[43] Job applicants may therefore be asked to disclose minor foreign convictions, regardless of whether their conviction has been spent under foreign law.

The Employees' Compensation Ordinance (Cap 282) applies to most contracts of service with an employer.[44] That includes contracts with seafarers employed as crew of a Hong

[38] Employment Ordinance (Cap 57), s 4(1). The limited number of exceptions are set out in s 4(2).

[39] No express statutory provision like s 17(1) of the Control of Exemption Clauses Ordinance is present in the Employment Ordinance.

[40] Sex Discrimination Ordinance (Cap 480) (SDO), s 11; Family Status Discrimination Ordinance (Cap 527) (FSDO), s 8; Disability Discrimination Ordinance (Cap 487) (DDO), s 11; Race Discrimination Ordinance (Cap 602) (RDO), s 10.

[41] Defined in SDO, s 14; FSDO, s 10; DDO, s 14; RDO, s 16.

[42] SDO, s 87(3); FSDO, s 65; DDO, s 83(3); RDO, s 81(3).

[43] Rehabilitation of Offenders Ordinance (Cap 297), s 2.

[44] Employees' Compensation Ordinance (Cap 282), s 2(1).

Kong ship.[45] The Ordinance can apply in certain instances to seafarers, including seafarers recruited in Hong Kong to serve on a non-Hong Kong ship who suffer personal injury abroad.[46]

It is not possible to contract out from the Employees' Compensation Ordinance. According to section 31(1) of the Employees' Compensation Ordinance, any such contract or agreement to relinquish an employee's right to compensation from an employer for personal injury by accident arising out of and in the course of his employment shall be null and void insofar as it purports to remove or reduce the liability of any person to pay compensation under the provisions of this Ordinance. As to whether section 70 of the Employment Ordinance, which provides that any term of a contract of employment 'which purports to extinguish or reduce any right, benefit or protection conferred upon the employee by this Ordinance shall be void' is a mandatory provision, see chapter eight, section I.A.

G. Gaming and Wagering Contracts

The principal legislation in Hong Kong on statutory prohibitions on gambling is the Gambling Ordinance (Cap 148). The statute does not expressly deal with gaming and wagering contracts, but stipulates that gambling activities are 'unlawful' and imposes criminal liability in most of such activities. The Ordinance can therefore have an effect on the validity of gambling contracts governed by Hong Kong law. The statute does not, however, strike down gambling contracts governed by foreign law. It seems that there is no public policy objection to the enforcement of foreign gambling contracts in Hong Kong, even though the contract would have been illegal and unenforceable if the relevant acts were carried out in Hong Kong. Consequently, a gambling contract that is valid by its governing law will be enforceable in Hong Kong.[47] An action on a loan for gambling will succeed if the loan is valid by its governing law.[48]

H. Insurance Contracts

Ordinary principles will apply, although some authorities suggested that, in the absence of express choice, the law of the insurer's head office will apply.[49] However, it is submitted that this approach should be discarded. Instead, the law of closest and most real connection should be ascertained on a case-by-case basis following the general principles.

I. Negotiable Instruments (Including Bills of Exchange)

The 'closest and most real connection' test has no application in negotiable instruments, due to a resultant lack of predictability. Section 72 of the Bills of Exchange Ordinance (Cap 19) sets out five rules for determining applicable law:

[45] ibid s 29.
[46] ibid s 30B.
[47] *Wong Hon v Sheraton Desert Inn Corp* [1995] 3 HKC 331 [8]–[9].
[48] ibid [21].
[49] *Shanti Ramesh Ramchandani v Commissioner of Estate Duty* [1981] HKLR 85.

72. Rules where laws conflict

Where a bill drawn in one country is negotiated, accepted, or payable in another, the rights, duties, and liabilities of the parties thereto are determined as follows –

(a) the validity of a bill, as regards requisites in form, is determined by the law of the place of issue, and the validity, as regards requisites in form, of the supervening contracts, such as acceptance or indorsement or acceptance suprà protest, is determined by the law of the place where such contract was made:

Provided that –

(i) where a bill is issued out of Hong Kong, it is not invalid by reason only that it is not stamped in accordance with the law of the place of issue;

(ii) where a bill issued out of Hong Kong conforms, as regards requisites in form, to the law of Hong Kong, it may, for the purpose of enforcing payment thereof, be treated as valid as between all persons who negotiate, hold, or become parties to it in Hong Kong;

(b) subject to the provisions of this Ordinance, the interpretation of the drawing, indorsement, acceptance, or acceptance suprà protest of a bill is determined by the law of the place where such contract is made:

Provided that where an inland bill is indorsed in a place outside Hong Kong, the indorsement shall, as regards the payer, be interpreted according to the law of Hong Kong;

(c) the duties of the holder with respect to presentment for acceptance or payment and the necessity for or sufficiency of a protest or notice of dishonour, or otherwise, are determined by the law of the place where the act is done or the bill is dishonoured;

(d) where a bill is drawn out of but payable in Hong Kong and the sum payable is not expressed in the currency of Hong Kong, the amount, if the bill is paid in Hong Kong and in the currency of Hong Kong, shall, in the absence of any express stipulation, be calculated according to the rate of exchange for sight drafts in Hong Kong on the day on which the bill is actually paid; and

(e) where a bill is drawn in one country and is payable in another, the due date thereof is determined according to the law of the place where it is payable.

The foregoing statutory rules apply with necessary modifications to promissory notes.[50]

J. Contracts for the Sale of Goods and Movable Property

Ordinary principles will apply. However, for the international sale of goods, in the absence of express choice or exclusion, the 1980 United Nations Convention for the International Sale of Goods (CISG) would apply and prevail other laws by virtue of the Sale of Goods (United Nations Convention) Ordinance (Cap 641). Article 1(1) of the CISG states that the Convention applies to contracts of sale of goods between parties whose places of business are in different states: (i) when the states are contracting parties; or (ii) when the rules of private international law lead to the application of the law of a contracting state. In default of parties' agreement, the CISG will apply to a contract for the sale of goods that falls within Article 1(1) and does not fall within the exceptions in Articles 2–5.[51] Article 6 permits the

[50] Bills of Exchange Ordinance (Cap 19), s 95.

[51] For instance, Art 2 of the Convention provides that it does not apply to sales: (a) of goods bought for personal, family or household use, unless the seller, at any time before or at the conclusion of the contract, neither knew nor ought to have known that the goods were bought for any such use; (b) by auction; (c) on execution or otherwise by

parties to exclude the application of the CISG or to derogate from or vary the effect of any of its provisions. Article 7(1) provides that the interpretation of the CISG 'must have regard to its international character and to the need to promote uniformity in its application and the observance of good faith in international trade'. Article 7(2) further provides that questions not governed by the CISG are to be settled 'in conformity with the general principles on which it is based or, in the absence of such principles, in conformity with the law applicable by virtue of the rules of private international law'. A detailed commentary of the CISG can be found elsewhere.[52]

The discussion in section II.E above regarding the Sale of Goods Ordinance, the Control of Exemption Clauses Ordinance and the Unconscionable Contracts Ordinance also applies.

K. Contracts for the Sale of Immovable Property

Ordinary principles will apply. The *situs* of the immovable property will be a significant (if not the decisive) factor in determining the law with the closest and most real connection.

L. Contracts Involving the Transfer of Foreign Currency

When a contractual obligation is expressed in foreign currency, there is a distinction between the amount or currency that the debtor pays (the money of account) and the amount or currency that the debtor makes the payment (the money of payment).[53] The general principle is nominalism, where the debtor's duty is to pay the nominal amount, ie the face value, of the designated money of account, regardless of any changes in the internal or external value of the specified currency.[54]

In principle, the courts will not enforce a contract which is contrary to exchange controls under the governing law.[55] But the previous position that 'all kinds of illegality (save for *de minimis* ones) would preclude reliance on the change of position defence and the bona fide purchaser for value without notice defence' was overly rigid and involved conflicting legal authorities.[56] In Hong Kong, there is a line of cases dealing with 'underground banking' or 'underground money exchange transaction' where the allegation was that certain foreign exchange transactions were in breach of Article 45 of the PRC's Administrative Regulations on Foreign Exchange and Articles 30 and 39 of the PRC's Foreign Exchanges Measures for Individuals.[57]

authority of law; (d) of stocks, shares, investment securities, negotiable instruments or money; (e) of ships, vessels, hovercraft or aircraft; (f) of electricity.

[52] See, eg Ingeborg Schwenzer and Ulrich G Schroeter, *Schlechtriem & Schwenzer: Commentary on the UN Convention on the International Sale of Goods (CISG)*, 5th edn (Oxford University Press, 2022).

[53] See, eg *Woodhouse AC Israel Cocoa Ltd SA v Nigerian Produce Marketing Co Ltd* [1971] 2 QB 23, 54.

[54] *Gilbert v Brett* (1604) Davis 18. For a general discussion of foreign money obligations, see, eg *Dicey, Morris and Collins* (n 6) ch 37; Roy Goode and Ewan McKendrick, *Goode and McKendrick on Commercial Law*, 6th edn (LexisNexis, 2020) paras 37.104–37.110; Charles Proctor, *Mann and Proctor on the Law of Money*, 8th edn (Oxford University Press, 2023). For foreign currency judgments, see Practice Direction 16.2.

[55] *DBS Bank (Hong Kong) Ltd v Pan Jing* [2020] 4 HKC 395, [2020] HKCFI 268 [56].

[56] See the discussion in *Lesnina H DOO* (n 23) [51]–[59].

[57] See, eg *DBS Bank (Hong Kong) Ltd* (n 55); *Lesnina H DOO* (n 23).

III. Torts

Tort in Hong Kong domestic law has been described as

> a convenient classification of different types of liability with certain common characteristics, rather than a strict legal category with particular legal consequences. In the international choice of law context, it is suggested that, in principle and as a general rule, a 'tort' should be regarded as a non-contractual civil cause of action in respect of harm suffered by the claimant as a result of the actions or causal omissions of the defendant. It ought not to matter whether, as a matter of Hong Kong domestic law or foreign law, the claim is considered to arise in law or in equity; or whether it is based on case law or statute.[58]

A. Governing Law of Torts

There are several potential candidates for the 'proper' governing law of a tort. There is the *lex fori*, the *lex loci delicti* and the law of the place of the tort. It might also be possible to choose the law of some other country based on overall connections. The difference between a Hong Kong tort and a foreign tort lies in the *locus delicti*, the place of tort.

For a Hong Kong tort, it is clear that the *lex fori* applies. If the tort is committed was the damage suffered in Hong Kong, the proper governing law for the determination of disputes is Hong Kong law as the *lex loci delicti*. The double actionability rule has no application.[59] The suggestion that an exception, akin to the *Boys v Chaplin* or *Red Sea* exception, may be applied for a *local* tort (a tort committed in Hong Kong), such that Hong Kong law will be displaced by some other law as the law applicable to the tort, has been rejected.[60]

In a situation where some of the elements of the tort took place in Hong Kong and some in a foreign jurisdiction ('double locality cases'), the court should first consider whether, by reference exclusively to Hong Kong law, a tort has been committed within the jurisdiction of Hong Kong courts. In doing so, the substance test is applied. The test was described as follows:[61] 'The right approach is, when the tort is complete, to look back over the series of events constituting it and ask the question, where in substance did this cause of action arise?'

This test has been approved by the Hong Kong courts.[62] A choice of law clause in a related contract will not be relevant in determining the place of the tort.[63]

[58] *Securities and Futures Commission v Isidor Subotic* [2021] 3 HKLRD 777, [2021] HKCFI 2172 [54]. See also the principles distilled at [65].

[59] ibid; *GDH Ltd v Creditor Co Ltd* [2008] 5 HKLRD 895. See the paragraphs below for the operation of the double actionability rule.

[60] *China Medical Technologies Inc (in liq) v Paul, Weiss, Rifkind, Wharton & Garrison LLP (a firm)* [2020] HKCFI 567 [6]. See the paragraphs below for the operation of the exception.

[61] *Distillers Co (Biochemicals) Ltd v Laura Ann Thompson* [1971] AC 458, 468E; *Metall und Rohstoff AG v Donaldson, Lufkin & Jenrette Inc* [1990] 1 QB 391, 446D.

[62] *Shanghai Reeferco Container Co Ltd v Waggonbau Elze GmbH & Co Besitz KG* [2005] 2 HKLRD 711 [41]; *Hong Kong Exchanges and Clearing Ltd v Shi Huaifang* [2019] HKCFI 1212 [67]; *China Medical Technologies Inc (in liq) v Paul, Weiss, Rifkind, Wharton & Garrison LLP (a firm)* [2019] HKCFI 2631 [127]. The appeal failed: *China Medical Technologies Inc* (n 60) [4].

[63] *China Medical Technologies Inc* (n 60) [130], approving *Morin v Bonhams & Brooks Ltd* [2003] EWHC 467 (Comm) [31] and declining to follow *Trafigura Beheer BV v Kookmin Bank* [2006] EWHC 1450 (Comm) as it was

In the situation of a foreign tort, Hong Kong applies the double actionability rule.[64] The rule was summarised thus in Hong Kong:[65]

> 47. To recap, the double actionability rule states, as a general rule, that an act done in Country A is a tort and actionable as such in Country B, only if it is both
>
> (a) actionable as a tort according to the law of Country B (*lex fori*), or in other words is an act which, if done in Country B, would be a tort; and
>
> (b) actionable according to the law of Country A where it was done (*lex loci delicti*).
>
> In the *Red Sea* case, the central issue arising on the appeal was whether the defendant could rely on Saudi Arabian law (*lex loci delicti*), to establish direct liability in tort when Hong Kong law (*lex fori*) does not recognise such liability. In summary, the Privy Council addressed the question in this way. The first requirement of the double actionability rule, that is, the act must be actionable as tort according to the *lex fori*, is not a test of jurisdiction. It is a rule of choice of law to decide which law should be chosen to determine the relevant issue or issues. That is not an invariable rule. English law (so does Hong Kong law for that purpose) recognises that a particular issue between the parties to litigation may be governed by the law of the country which, with respect to that issue, has the most significant relationship with the occurrence and with the parties. In an appropriate case, a plaintiff could rely exclusively on the *lex loci delicti* even if under the *lex fori* his claim would not be actionable. This is the exception to the double actionability rule.

In other words, the double actionability rule provides that, for acts or omissions on the part of defendant(s) to give rise to tortious liability, the matter must be actionable under the *lex fori* and the *lex loci delicti*.[66] If both limbs are satisfied, the *lex fori* will apply as the substantive law to determine the rights and liabilities of the parties,[67] subject to the *Red Sea Insurance* exception discussed below.

The first limb means that there can be no liability for a foreign civil wrong unless the elements of the foreign wrong would constitute a tort in Hong Kong.[68] Generally, any substantive defences under the *lex fori* may be relied upon as defence. For example, in *Anderson v Eric Anderson Radio & TV Pty Ltd*, the claim failed because contributory negligence was a complete defence under the *lex fori*, even though it was only a ground of apportionment under the *lex loci delicti*.[69]

The second limb requires that the plaintiff show that the defendant has committed a civil wrong under the foreign law. Generally, any substantive defences in the *lex loci delicti* may

decided by reference to ss 10–12 of the Private International Law (Miscellaneous Provisions) Act 1995 (UK) and did not reflect the common law of Hong Kong. Even under the context of that statute, it was held in *VTB Capital plc v Nutritek International Corp* [2013] UKSC 5, [2013] 2 AC 337 that the substance of the tort has to be considered. In that case, it was held that English law governs the tort because, although the misrepresentations originated in Russia, they reached the claimant in London and were relied upon by the claimant there; the claimant sustained its loss by disposing of money in and from London.

[64] *Phillips v Eyre* (1870–71) LR 6 QB 1; *Boys v Chaplin* [1971] AC 356; *Red Sea Insurance Co Ltd v Bouygues SA* [1995] 1 AC 190 (PC, appeal from Hong Kong).

[65] *Shanghai Reeferco Container Co Ltd* (n 62) [47], with some formatting changes for clarity.

[66] *Xiamen Xinjingdi Group Co Ltd v Eton Properties Ltd* [2016] 2 HKLRD 1106 [215].

[67] *Fong Chak Kwan v Ascentic Ltd* [2020] HKCFI 679 [165], [172].

[68] See, eg *The Halley* (1867–69) LR 2 PC 193; *Boys* (n 64); *Red Sea Insurance Co Ltd* (n 64).

[69] *Anderson v Eric Anderson Radio & TV Pty Ltd* (1965) 144 CLR 20 (HCA). In Hong Kong, it was a ground of apportionment, with the plaintiff's claim limited to the amount recoverable after apportionment due to contributory negligence: Law Amendment and Reform (Consolidation) Ordinance (Cap 23), s 21(1).

be relied upon to escape liability. For example, in *Boys v Chaplin*, the plaintiff and defendant were English soldiers temporarily stationed in Malta. Their motor vehicles collided, causing injury to the plaintiff. The defendant admitted liability, but the quantum was in dispute. Under English law, the plaintiff could recover more than £2000 for pain and suffering, but this head of damages was not recognised under Maltese law. Maltese law would have capped the plaintiff's damages at £53. Before applying the exception, that cap could be relied on to limit liability under the double actionability rule.

However, in *Boys v Chaplin*, the majority of the House of Lords held that the Maltese law on damages should be displaced, because the plaintiff and defendant were both English soldiers temporarily stationed in Malta. They held:[70]

> No purely mechanical rule can properly do justice to the great variety of cases where persons come together in a foreign jurisdiction for different purposes with different pre-existing relationships, from the background of different legal systems. It will not be invoked in every case or even, probably, in many cases. The general rule must apply unless clear and satisfying grounds are shown why it should be departed from and what solution, derived from what other rule, should be preferred.

This exception was refined in *Red Sea Insurance Co Ltd v Bouygues SA*.[71] As a result, the exception may be restated thus: if a country X has the most significant relationship with the parties and the alleged wrong, or if there are issues between the parties which ought to be governed by the law of country X, then the substantive law of country X should be applied.

How should the exception be applied? Some cases favour an interest analysis. This analysis asks whether the foreign state has an interest in having its law applied to the matter.[72] *Red Sea Insurance* considered the following factors before holding in favour of the *lex loci delicti* (Saudi Arabian law):[73]

> [T]he policy of insurance was subject to Saudi Arabian law, the project was to be carried out in Saudi Arabia and the property was owned by the government. The main contract, the supply contract and the HOK+4 consortium's service contract are all subject to the law of Saudi Arabia and were to be performed there. The breaches and the alleged damage occurred in Saudi Arabia. The expense of repairing alleged damage occurred in Saudi Arabia. The defendant, though incorporated in Hong Kong, had its head office in Saudi Arabia.

Red Sea Insurance confirmed the following two points. First, in applying the exception in *Red Sea Insurance*, the *lex fori* (Hong Kong law) can be displaced in favour of the *lex loci delicti* (Saudi Arabian law). It was said that:[74]

> There is obviously a difference between a court being able to apply its own law exclusively and it being required to apply exclusively another legal system. This, however, is not necessarily fatal to the contention that only the *lex loci delicti* be applied since the foreign law can be proved and it is clear that in appropriate cases the *lex loci delicti* can be applied to give a just result when the *lex fori* might not do so … To limit the rule so as to enable an English court only to apply English

[70] *Boys* (n 64) 391G–H.
[71] *Red Sea Insurance Co Ltd* (n 64) 206C.
[72] See, eg *Johnson v Coventry Churchill International Ltd* [1992] 3 All ER 14; *Sophocleous v Secretary of State for Foreign and Commonwealth Affairs* [2018] EWCA Civ 2167, [2019] QB 949 (claim time-barred under Cypriot law).
[73] *Red Sea Insurance Co Ltd* (n 64) 207D–E.
[74] ibid 206F–H.

> law would be in conflict with the degree of flexibility envisaged by Lord Wilberforce, though the fact that the forum is being required to apply a foreign law in a situation where its own law would give no remedy will be a factor to be taken into account when the court decides whether to apply the exception.

Second, the application of the exception is not limited to a specific issue, but may also apply to the entire claim:[75]

> Although the cases may be rare where the exception should be applied to the whole case, their Lordships do not consider that to apply the exception to the whole case is in principle necessarily excluded. In their Lordships' view the exception is not limited to specific isolated issues but may apply to the whole claim, for example where all or virtually all of the significant factors are in favour of the *lex loci delicti*.

Hong Kong is one of the few common law jurisdictions retaining the double actionability rule. As of the time of writing, only Hong Kong and Singapore still adopt the double actionability rule. The rule was abolished in the UK by the Private International Law (Miscellaneous Provisions) Act 1995, which entered into force on 1 May 1996 (with one exception on defamation, in section 13). Double actionability has also been abolished in Canada, Australia and New Zealand.[76] The Singapore Law Reform Committee proposed abolition in 2003.[77] It does not seem that Hong Kong has any intention of reforming the double actionability rule in the near future.

IV. Specific Torts

The place of commission of the tort is important for the purposes of choice of law under *Metall und Rohstoff AG*, discussed above.

A. Negligence

In determining where the tort occurred, the courts have in negligent misstatements or negligent advice claims consistently looked at where advice was, or should have been, received and relied upon. The courts have preferred the place of receipt and reliance over the place where the advice was prepared or from which it was sent (if elsewhere).[78] For a claim on negligent advice to be actionable, not only must the negligent advice be communicated, it must also be acted upon by the plaintiff and result in damage. Damage is the gist of the cause of action of negligent misstatement.[79] Damage is sustained at the place where the advice was received and acted upon.[80]

[75] ibid 207A–B.

[76] *Tolofsen v Jensen* [1994] 3 SCR 1022 (SC Canada); *Regie Nationale des Usines Renault SA v Zhang* (2002) 210 CLR 491 (HCA); Private International Law (Choice of Law in Tort) Act 2017 (New Zealand).

[77] Law Reform Committee of the Singapore Academy of Law, 'Reform of the Choice of Law Rule Relating to Tort' (31 March 2003).

[78] *China Medical Technologies Inc* (n 62) [134].

[79] ibid [140].

[80] ibid.

B. Conspiracy and Inducement of Breach of Contract

The factors to consider as to where the tort of conspiracy occurred are

> the identity, importance and location of the conspirators, the locations where any agreements or combinations took place, the nature and places of the concerted acts or means, the location of the plaintiff and the places where the plaintiff suffered losses.[81]

In particular, the place of agreement is likely to be where the tort took place, and the law of that place is likely govern the tort.[82] Conspiracy is not a cause of action under Mainland law,[83] and even though there may be other causes of action under Mainland law (such as breach of confidence and unfair competition), they are different from the tort of conspiracy to injure and may not assist in establishing the double actionability rule.[84]

The factors to consider as to where the tort of inducement of breach of contract occurred are the locations of the acts of inducement, the induced breaches of contract, the parties and the losses suffered.[85]

C. Defamation

The *locus deliciti* of the tort of defamation is not a straightforward issue. The following paragraph in *Dicey, Morris and Collins* was approved in Hong Kong:[86]

> Very difficult questions could arise in trying to determine the place of commission of the torts of libel or slander, slander of title, slander of goods, or other malicious falsehood. However, in the context of defamation the rule appears to be have been applied is that the relevant place is the country in which the defamatory statement was published. This appears to have been accepted without argument in one case where the English court was faced with a defamation claim arising out of a publication in a foreign country. This rule creates no practical difficulty where the statement is published in only one country. Where publication occurs in several countries, each publication may, potentially, give rise to a fresh cause of action and the law of each country in which publication takes place may become relevant, it being open, presumably, to the claimant to limit the claim to one such place if he or she so wishes.

V. Concurrent Claims in Contract and Tort

The possibility of a concurrence of causes of action in contract and in tort and a plaintiff's liberty to choose between them are well recognised. Where a party can bring a claim

[81] *Securities and Futures Commission v Isidor Subotic* [2021] HKCFI 3350.
[82] *China International Fund Ltd v West China Cement Ltd* [2020] HKCFI 2976 [31].
[83] *Xiamen Xinjingdi Group Co Ltd* (n 66) [220]–[234] and [270]–[272].
[84] *TZG Partners Ltd v Peter Gang* [2021] HKCFI 3234 [78]–[84].
[85] *Metall und Rohstoff AG* (n 61).
[86] Lord Collins of Mapesbury (gen ed), *Dicey, Morris and Collins on the Conflict of Laws*, 15th edn (Sweet & Maxwell, 2012) para 35-118, cited in *Bawang International (Group) Holding Ltd v Next Magazine Publishing Ltd* (unreported, HCA 1109/2010, 23 May 2016). See also *Baturina v Times Newspapers Ltd* [2010] EWHC 696.

on alternative bases, the party can elect to proceed on the basis that is more beneficial to him.[87] In Hong Kong, the Court of Final Appeal held in *Thanakharn Kasikorn Thai Chamkat (Mahachon) v Akai Holdings Ltd (in liq)* that the plaintiff could choose between the two claims based on conversion and knowing receipt, when it came to assessing compensation.[88] There may be reasons in particular cases why a plaintiff prefers to sue on one, rather than the other, basis.[89] Examples of such reasons include: issues of limitation of actions; the absence of a right to contribution between negligent contract-breakers; rules as to remoteness of damage; and the question of leave to serve proceedings out of the jurisdiction.[90] For example, in Hong Kong, a plaintiff was permitted to sue in tort despite his cause of action in contract having become time barred.[91]

Given that one can elect between contract and tort, the plaintiff should be allowed to invoke any available advantages as a matter of private international law.[92] Accordingly, especially where there is no express governing law clause in a contract, a party should be entitled to elect whether to pursue a cause of action in contract or tort.[93] The court did not adopt the suggestion that 'where a tortious issue arises in connection with a contract, then the issue should ordinarily be regarded as determined by the law which governs the contract'.[94] A concurrent claim in tort may be affected by a contract if the latter curtails the extent of the duty of care or contains limitation clauses. To that extent, the contract would be relevant to the claim in tort. However, if the party opts to bring an action in tort, the contract's existence would not affect the ordinary application of choice of law principles in tort.[95]

VI. Restitution and Unjust Enrichment

The law of restitution is still very much developing,[96] with potentially no necessary unifying or overarching principles.[97] The choice of law rules in restitution are similarly hotly debated and controversial.[98] The scant judicial discussion in Hong Kong consists of obiter remarks

[87] *Thanakharn Kasikorn Thai Chamkat (Mahachon) v Akai Holdings Ltd (in liq)* (2010) 13 HKCFAR 479 [130], citing *Henderson v Merrett Syndicates Ltd* [1995] 2 AC 145, 193; *Kleinwort Benson Ltd v Lincoln City Council* [1999] 2 AC 349, 387; *Deutsche Morgan Grenfell Group plc v Inland Revenue Commissioners* [2006] UKHL 49, [2007] 1 AC 558 [51].

[88] *Thanakharn Kasikorn Thai Chamkat (Mahachon)* (n 87).

[89] *Midland Bank Trust Co Ltd v Hett, Stubbs and Kemp* [1979] Ch 384; *Yeung Shu v Alfred Lau & Co* [1996] 1 HKLR 119.

[90] *China Medical Technologies Inc* (n 62) [113].

[91] See, eg *Bank of East Asia Ltd v Tsien Wui Marble Factory Ltd* (1999) 2 HKCFAR 349; *Yeung Shu* (n 89).

[92] *China Medical Technologies Inc* (n 62) [116], citing, among other cases, *Base Metal Trading Ltd v Shamurin* [2004] EWCA Civ 1316, [2005] 1 WLR 1157 and *Rickshaw Investments Ltd v Nicolai Baron von Uexkull* [2007] 1 SLR(R) 377.

[93] *China Medical Technologies Inc* (n 62) [120].

[94] ibid [121], rejecting Johnston and Harris (n 17) para 5.145.

[95] *China Medical Technologies Inc* (n 62) [125].

[96] See, eg Charles Mitchell, Paul Mitchell and Stephen Watterson (eds), *Goff and Jones on Unjust Enrichment*, 10th edn (Sweet & Maxwell, 2022); Graham Virgo, *The Principles of the Law of Restitution*, 4th edn (Oxford University Press, 2024).

[97] Robert Stevens, *The Laws of Restitution* (Oxford University Press, 2023).

[98] See, eg George Panagopoulos, *Restitution in Private International Law* (Hart Publishing, 2000); Tiong Min Yeo, *Choice of Law for Equitable Doctrines* (Oxford University Press, 2004) ch 9; *Dicey, Morris and Collins* (n 6) ch 36.

in *First Laser Ltd v Fujian Enterprises (Holdings) Co Ltd*, where the Court of First Instance was dealing with *forum non conveniens*. The following remarks were made:[99]

> 38. Mr Chan submitted that the overriding issue must be whether the Plaintiff could assert any beneficial interest in respect of the FCL shares and according to the authorities cited by him, this must be governed by PRC law. I am prepared to assume, without actually deciding, that this is correct. However, this does not dispose of the action completely. There is still the alternative claim based on restitution. If the proper law of contract is Hong Kong law, the restitution claim would also be governed by Hong Kong law in accordance with Rule 200(2)(a) in Dicey & Morris.
>
> 39. Even if it were eventually resolved that the proper law of the contract is PRC law, thus the restitution claim is also governed by PRC law, it still does not mean that all the issues pertaining to the restitution claim would be governed by PRC law, see [*Macmillan Inc v Bishopsgate Investment Trust plc (No 3)* [1996] 1 WLR 387]. Assuming that the Plaintiff could establish a claim of restitution under PRC law, whether such claim could support a claim of constructive trust against the Defendants could be governed by Hong Kong law. It would depend on the examination of the nature of the obligation of the 1st Defendant owed to the Plaintiff under the law of restitution in PRC, see Chadwick J in [*Arab Monetary Fund v Hashim* (unreported, 15 June 1994, QBD)] cited and approved by Nourse LJ in [*Kuwait Oil Tanker Co SAK v Al Bader* [2000] 2 All ER (Comm) 271, 338–39]. One would also need to look into the circumstances under which funds were transferred from the 1st Defendant to the 2nd Defendant. Again, this took place in Hong Kong and is probably governed by Hong Kong law.

It was suggested that such remarks were inconclusive and that the judge was clearly not intending to resolve the matter in the interlocutory context.[100]

Choice of law rules in relation to scenarios of restitution will very much depend on a proper characterisation of relevant issues. The nature of the obligation giving rise to restitution has to be carefully analysed, and the governing law is likely the proper law of that obligation. In *Falcon Private Bank Ltd v Borry Bernard Edouard Charles Ltd*, the Court of First Instance approved the following guidelines from *Dicey, Morris and Collins*:[101]

> (1) The proper law of a restitutionary obligation arising in connection with a contract is the law applicable to the contract.
> (2) The proper law of a restitutionary obligation arising in connection with a transaction concerning an immovable property is the law of the country where the immovable is situated (*lex situs*).
> (3) The proper law of a restitutionary obligation arising in any other circumstances, its proper law is the law of the country where the enrichment occurs.

Regardless of whether the obligation is characterised as contractual, tortious, restitutionary or otherwise, the question is to locate the legal system that is most closely connected with the obligation, and the foregoing three principles can only be guidance.

[99] *First Laser Ltd v Fujian Enterprises (Holdings) Co Ltd* (unreported, HCA 4414/2001, 12 December 2002) [38]–[39].

[100] Johnston and Harris (n 17) para 5.098. For a choice-of-law proposal, see paras 5.097–5.121.

[101] *Falcon Private Bank Ltd v Borry Bernard Edouard Charles Ltd* (unreported, HCA 1934/2011, 9 July 2012) [140]. See also *Kuwait Oil Tanker Co SAK v Al Bader* [2000] 2 All ER (Comm) 271; *Barros Mattos Junior v MacDaniels Ltd* [2005] EWHC 1323 (Ch), [2005] ILPr 45; *CIMB Bank Bhd v Dresder Kleinworth Ltd* [2008] 4 SLR(R) 543.

16

Law of Trusts and Equitable Obligations

On choice of law in relation to trusts and equitable obligations, there are several issues to consider.[1] For instance, there are questions as to the law governing: (i) the formal and essentially validity of a trust; (ii) the duties of a trustee; and (iii) the proper administration of the trust. Further, in Hong Kong, the 1985 HCCH Convention on the Law Applicable to Trusts and on their Recognition (the Hague Trusts Convention) as enacted by the Recognition of Trusts Ordinance (Cap 76) (RTO) has altered some common law rules and led to complications.

Section I introduces choice of law rules for certain preliminary issues which are outside the scope of the Hague Trusts Convention. Section II introduces choice of law rules for substantive matters arising out the Hague Trusts Convention. Section III discusses the common law rules for the foregoing substantive matters, as such rules may come into play when the Hague Trusts Convention or the common law rules are more favourable in recognising trusts. Section IV discusses the rules for the administration of foreign trusts and trusts of foreign assets. Section V discusses choice of law rules for constructive trusts and resulting trusts, with references to *First Laser Ltd v Fujian Enterprises (Holdings) Co Ltd*, which has settled a number of questions as far as Hong Kong law is concerned.[2] Section VI looks at rules on choice of law in respect of constructive trusts arising from the knowing receipt of trust property or from dishonestly assisting others to act in breach of trust. Section VII discusses choice of law issues in following and tracing.

I. Choice of Law for Preliminary Issues

Article 4 of the Hague Trusts Convention states that the Convention does not apply to preliminary issues of trust, that is, the effectiveness of wills or acts transferring assets into a trust. It is therefore necessary to rely on common law rules for these preliminary issues. Examples include: (i) whether a trust is a sham; (ii) whether a will, gift or transfer of property is valid;[3] and (iii) whether a trust or the transfer of assets into the trust can be set aside. Issues on succession to property are considered in chapter seventeen, section VII. This section briefly considers the issue of *inter vivos* trusts.

[1] See also Tiong Min Yeo, *Choice of Law for Equitable Doctrines* (Oxford University Press, 2004).

[2] *First Laser Ltd v Fujian Enterprises (Holdings) Co Ltd* (2012) 15 HKCFAR 569 [66]–[72].

[3] This includes whether a resulting or constructive trust of property arises: *Relevant Employees Whose Shares in China Shanshui Investment Co Ltd Were Held by Zhang Caikui on Trust v Zhang Caikui* (unreported, HCA 1661/2014, 13 May 2015) [99]–[100].

Choice of law rules for *inter vivos* trusts are dependent on the nature of the trust assets (that is, immovables, chattels, contractual rights, equitable interests, shares, etc). The law identified by the choice of law exercise will govern the formal and substantive validity of a declaration a trust. This includes the validity of the transfer of property. But this general rule has some exceptions. For instance, where the property is immovable, the proper law governing the validity of the trust will only come into play after the immovable is confirmed to be alienable under the *lex situs*.[4] Moreover, the law of the transferee's residence governs whether the transferee's conscience is affected so as to make him or her a trustee.[5] The law of the transferor's residence governs whether the transferee holds the property as a nominee.[6]

II. Choice of Law for Substantive Questions under the Hague Trusts Convention

A. Introduction – The Hague Trusts Convention and the Recognition of Trusts Ordinance

Trusts are not generally familiar to civil law jurisdictions. However, a trust may be created, exist and be enforceable in respect of assets located in a jurisdiction even though the latter's law does not recognise trusts in any form.[7] To establish common principles between jurisdictions on trusts and enable trusts to be recognised universally, the Hague Trusts Convention was concluded on 1 July 1985. The instrument currently has 14 contracting states.[8] Note, however, that the rules of the Ordinance apply whether or not the trust is connected with a party to the Convention or not.[9] The major provisions of the Hague Trusts Convention have been incorporated into Hong Kong law through section 2(1) of the RTO.[10] The RTO covers a range of trust-related issues.[11] It stipulates mechanisms for: (i) determining the law applicable to trusts and rules for their recognition;[12] (ii) rules for identifying the governing law of a trust;[13] and (iii) the law governing the construction,

[4] *Akers v Samba Financial Group* [2014] EWCA Civ 1516, [2015] Ch 451 [38]–[54].

[5] *JF v Hexagon Investments Ltd* (2014) 18 ITELR 470.

[6] *Hamilton v Hamilton* [2016] EWHC 1132 (Ch) [176]–[177].

[7] *Akers v Samba Financial Group* [2017] UKSC 6, [2017] AC 424 [34].

[8] For the list of contracting states, see www.hcch.net/en/instruments/conventions/status-table/?cid=59.

[9] RTO, s 2(5); Hague Trusts Convention, Art 17.

[10] The majority of the provisions were enacted into Hong Kong law. Arts 13, 16(2), 16(3), 19, 20, 21, 23 and 24 of the Hague Trusts Convention were omitted from the version of the Convention in the Schedule of the RTO. Art 16 was not enacted in full due to a reservation made by the UK when it entered into the Convention. A provision similar to Art 23 of the Hague Trusts Convention (concerning territorial units of a state) has been incorporated in Hong Kong law through s 2(5) of the RTO ('the reference to a State includes a reference to any country or territory (whether or not a party to the Convention) which has its own system of law').

[11] Except preliminary issues relating to validity of wills and other acts by virtue of which assets are transferred to the trustee, see Hague Trusts Convention, Art 4. The effect of the Hague Trusts Convention is summarised in *Chu Wai Tung v Wong Ka Sek* [2017] 4 HKLRD 610 [52].

[12] Hague Trusts Convention, Art 1.

[13] ibid Arts 6 and 7.

effects and administration of a trust.[14] This section will cover the scope of application of the Hague Trusts Convention and its effects.

By way of an overview, the Hague Trusts Convention only applies to:

(i) trusts created voluntarily and evidenced in writing;
(ii) trusts of property arising under the laws of Hong Kong (Hong Kong trusts); and
(iii) trusts arising by virtue of judicial decisions in Hong Kong or elsewhere.

It does not apply:

(i) if the law which the instrument would apply does not recognise trusts or the type of trust involved;[15] or
(ii) if the law in force prior to the adoption of the Hague Trusts Convention would have been more favourable to the recognition of the trust.[16]

The effect of the RTO and the Hague Trusts Convention is that:

(i) they allow a settlor to choose the governing law of a trust and, in the absence of an express or implied choice, the governing law will be that having the closest connection to the trust; and
(ii) they provide for the law governing the construction and operation of the trust, including the appointment, rights, liabilities and obligations of trustees.

The approach to ascertaining the law applicable to some aspect of a trust should therefore be as follows:

1. Identify whether the proceedings are before the Hong Kong court.
2. If so, consider whether the RTO and the Hague Trusts Convention are applicable to determine the law governing the issue in dispute.
3. If the RTO and the Hague Trusts Convention would recognise the trust, apply the Convention.
4. If the RTO and the Hague Trusts Convention are applicable but the chosen law would not recognise the trust, apply common law rules to see whether they would lead to the recognition of the trust.
5. If the RTO and the Hague Trusts Convention do not apply, apply common law rules on choice of law.

B. Scope of the Hague Trusts Convention and the Recognition of Trusts Ordinance

(i) Definition of Trust

Article 2 of the Hague Trusts Convention defines a 'trust' as 'the legal relationship created – *inter vivos* or on death – by a person, the settlor, when assets have been placed under the

[14] ibid Art 8.
[15] ibid Art 5.
[16] ibid Art 14.

control of a trustee for the benefit of a beneficiary or for a specified purpose'. Where a trust is created, it will have the following characteristics or attributes under Article 2 of the Hague Trusts Convention:

(a) the assets constitute a separate fund and are not a part of the trustee's own estate;
(b) title to the trust assets stands in the name of the trustee or in the name of another person on behalf of the trustee;
(c) the trustee has the power and the duty, in respect of which he is accountable, to manage, employ or dispose of the assets in accordance with the terms of the trust and the special duties imposed upon him by law.

Article 2 further notes that, in creating a trust, a settlor may reserve to one's self certain rights and powers.

As characterised and defined in Article 2, the concept of 'trust' is ambiguous. The definition does not wholly resemble the notion of trusts at common law. For instance, Article 2 does not refer to: (i) the transfer of ownership by the settlor to the trustee;[17] (ii) the rights and proprietary entitlement enjoyed by the beneficiary; or (iii) the fiduciary nature of the trust.[18] The looseness of the definition enables the Hague Trusts Convention to cover concepts in civilian law that are analogous to the concept of trust at common law.[19]

Since Article 3 limits the scope of the Hague Trusts Convention's application to 'trusts created voluntarily and evidenced in writing', the Convention apparently excludes trusts created by operation of law or judicial decisions, including presumed resulting trusts, most constructive trusts and statutory trusts,[20] as exemplified in *SL v CPYD*.[21] In actuality, as far as Hong Kong is concerned, the Hague Trusts Convention is not restricted to covering trusts created voluntarily and evidenced in writing. The scope of application of the Hague Trusts Convention, as incorporated in Hong Kong, has been extended by the RTO, which is the counterpart of the Recognition of Trusts Act 1987 in the UK.[22] The statutory extension of the scope of application builds on Article 20 of the Hague Trusts

[17] Therefore, in principle, the definition laid out in Art 2 of the Hague Trusts Convention, despite being worded as 'assets have been placed under the control of a trustee', should include trusts constituted by declaration where settlors declare themselves as trustees, see Alfred E von Overbeck, 'Rapport explicatif de M Alfred E von Overbeck' in Hague Conference on Private International Law Permanent Bureau (ed), *Actes et documents de la Treizième session* (Imprimerie Nationale 1978) 328–84, para 57; *Akers* (n 7) [36]; *Schechter v RCC* [2017] UKFTT 189 (TC) [97].

[18] Jonathan Harris, *The Hague Trusts Convention: Scope, Application and Preliminary Issues* (Hart Publishing, 2002) 111.

[19] ibid; Maurizio Lupoi, 'The Shapeless Trust' (1995) 1(3) *Trusts and Trustees* 15.

[20] See David Hayton, 'Reflections on The Hague Trust Convention after 30 Years' (2016) 12 *Journal of Private International Law* 1, 8. Firstly, the wording of Art 3 of the Hague Trusts Convention seems to suggest that trusts created orally will also have to be evidenced in writing. Secondly, the wording seems to be sufficiently wide to cover: (i) resulting trusts arising where a trustee continues to hold property after exhaustion of an express trust, see Overbeck (n 17) para 51; (ii) constructive trusts that arise out of duly executed written mutual wills, see Maurizio Lupoi, *Trusts: A Comparative Study* (Cambridge University Press, 2001) 342–43; (iii) constructive trusts that arise out of a specifically enforceable written contract; and (iv) secret testamentary trusts.

[21] *SL v CPYD* [2020] HKFC 105.

[22] RTO, s 2(3) provides that the Hague Trusts Convention shall have effect not only in relation to the trusts described in Arts 2 and 3 thereof, but also in relation to any other trusts of property arising under the law of Hong Kong or by virtue of a judicial decision whether in Hong Kong or elsewhere. See also Hong Kong Hansard (25 October 1989) 41.

Convention. Section 2(3) of the RTO extends the scope of application of the Hague Trusts Convention to:

(i) trusts created voluntarily and evidenced in writing;[23]
(ii) trusts created orally and not evidenced in writing;[24]
(iii) Hong Kong trusts;[25] and
(iv) trusts arising by virtue of judicial decisions in Hong Kong or elsewhere.[26]

(ii) Trusts Arising by Virtue of Judicial Decisions

When applying the RTO and Hague Trusts Convention to ascertain the governing law of trusts arising by virtue of judicial decisions, there are two matters to note. First, the judicial decision creating the trust has to be capable of recognition as a foreign judgment.[27] Second, the precise meaning of 'trusts "arising by virtue of" judicial decision' is unclear. It is generally accepted that remedial constructive trusts will be covered. This is because remedial constructive trusts arise at the moment of judicial decision and only arise by reason of the court exercising its discretion.[28] Remedial constructive trusts therefore fall well within the scope of section 2(3) of the RTO.[29] The question is whether resulting trusts and institutional constructive trusts fall within the scope of the extension in the RTO. Unlike remedial constructive trusts, institutional constructive trusts and resulting trusts do not arise by virtue of a judicial decision.[30] Instead, they arise by operation of law from the date of the circumstances which give rise to them and the court merely declares and affirms the existence of the trust.[31] Under that premise, if one adopts a literal interpretation of section 2(3) of the RTO and emphasises the words 'arising by virtue of', institutional constructive trusts would not be covered. Section 2(3) would then only target resulting and constructive trusts that arise by virtue of a judicial decision in the way that remedial constructive trusts do.[32]

[23] Derived from Hague Trusts Convention, Arts 2 and 3.

[24] By virtue of RTO, s 2(3). See also *Berezovsky v Abramovich* [2011] EWCA Civ 153, [2011] 1 WLR 2290 [106].

[25] By virtue of RTO, s 2(3).

[26] ibid. The UK expressly declared, in accordance with Art 20 of the Hague Trusts Convention, that the Convention extends to trusts declared by judicial decisions.

[27] Note, however, the Hague Trusts Convention and the RTO exclude the use of trust device for purposes not linked to property interest, including parties being held as personally liable to account as constructive trustees: see David Hayton, 'The Hague Convention on the Law Applicable to Trusts and on their Recognition' (1987) 36 *ICLQ* 260, 264. See also *Chellaram v Chellaram* [1985] Ch 409, 462, where Scott J ruled that the Court of Equity operates *in personam*, but not *in rem*. This was accepted in *Geoffrey L Berman v SPF CDO I Ltd* [2011] HKLRD 815 [9].

[28] *Rawluk v Rawluk* (1990) 65 DLR (4th) 161, 185.

[29] Adeline Chong, 'The Common Law Choice of Law Rules for Resulting and Constructive Trusts' (2005) 54(4) *ICLQ* 855, 859.

[30] See, eg *Ip Man Shan Henry v Ching Hing Construction (No 2)* [2003] 1 HKC 256, 286; *Cheung Hon Hung v Siu Wai Chun* (unreported, DCCJ 874/2012, 29 August 2014) [76]. *cf* Hui Jing, 'The Remedial Constructive Trust Approach in the Hong Kong Law of Proprietary Estoppel' (2023) *Conveyancer and Property Lawyer* 30, where it is argued that the Court of Final Appeal has shown a slightly different attitude towards remedial constructive trusts in the case of *Cheung Lai Mui v Cheung Wai Shing* (2021) 24 HKCFAR 116, [2021] HKCFA 19.

[31] *Westdeutsche Landesbank Girozentrale v Islington London Borough Council* [1996] AC 669, 716.

[32] Harris (n 18) 145–47.

To give full effect to the Hague Trusts Convention and due respect to the public policy of Hong Kong, it is submitted that section 2(3) of the RTO should be read as enabling a general recognition of resulting and constructive trusts, thereby stressing the proprietary consequences of judicial decisions giving rise to trusts and adherence to the principle of enforcing foreign judgments *in rem*.[33]

In any event, when applying the RTO, the fact that a foreign law does not have a concept of trusts should not bar the recognition in Hong Kong of institutions having a similar effect to trusts under that foreign law. The appropriate analysis, as stated by the Hong Kong Court of Final Appeal in *First Laser Ltd v Fujian Enterprises (Holdings) Co Ltd*, is to ask

> whether, under the *lex causae*, the defendants owe obligations which would impose on the defendant under the law a liability to disgorge benefits. If the answer is positive, the court may hold the defendant liable as constructive trustee when giving remedial effect to the substantive right arising under the *lex causae*.[34]

C. Identifying the Governing Law

It is submitted that the common law choice of law rules applicable to contract should be extended to trusts.[35] The Hague Trusts Convention is compatible with the application of common law rules. The approach would first look for an express choice. If no choice has been made, one would ascertain an implied choice based on circumstances. If there is neither an express nor implied choice of law, one would resort to the law of closest connection to the trust.

(i) Express Choice

Under Article 6 of the Hague Trusts Convention, a trust is governed by the law chosen by the settlor, expressly or impliedly in the instrument creating the trust or in written evidence of the trust. If necessary, the choice of law can be determined in light of the circumstances of the case. Thus, if the trust is created orally, the governing law will be determined by reference to the words used when creating the trust.[36]

Article 6 allows the settlor to choose the governing law.[37] The freedom is threefold. First, the settlor enjoys the freedom to choose the governing law of trusts not just of movable

[33] See Lord Collins of Mapesbury and Jonathan Harris (gen eds), *Dicey, Morris and Collins on the Conflict of Laws*, 16th edn (Sweet & Maxwell, 2022) para 29-007; Lynton Tucker et al (eds), *Lewin on Trusts*, 20th edn (Sweet & Maxwell, 2020) paras 12-075–12-076. Nonetheless, it is observed that the authentic French text of the Hague Trusts Convention was 'créés par', which means 'created by'. Therefore, it is more likely that the 'trust arising by virtue of judicial decision' will only cover remedial constructive trust, which is generally not recognised in Hong Kong. *cf* Chong (n 29).

[34] *First Laser Ltd* (n 2) [66]–[72].

[35] *Augustus v Permanent Trustee Co (Canberra) Ltd* (1971) 124 CLR 245.

[36] *Berezovsky v Abramovich* [2010] EWHC 647 (Comm) [117].

[37] This is the same as the common law position that the settlor is free to select the governing law of trust: *Re Hernando* (1884) 27 Ch D 284, 292–93; *Re Fitzgerald* [1904] 1 Ch 573, 587. There is no Hong Kong authority on this point.

property, but also of immovable property.[38] This modifies the common law rule that the governing law of immovable property is *lex situs*.[39] Second, a settlor or testator domiciled in a foreign jurisdiction may choose Hong Kong law as the governing law of a trust, and a settlor or testator domiciled in Hong Kong is free to choose a foreign law as the governing law.[40] Third, the governing law will not be struck down even if it is objectively not connected with the trust[41] and the trust has closer connection from an objective standpoint with a place which does not recognise the trust.[42] The only requirements are that the choice of law must be of a recognised legal system and, if the state is comprised of several territorial units, the choice must refer to a specific territorial unit.[43] If the settlor's choice is the law of a state which does not recognise trusts, the situation will be treated as one of an absence of choice.[44]

(ii) Implied Choice

Where there is no express choice, the court examines whether the settlor has made an implied choice.[45] Case precedents on whether choice of law can be implied in contracts may be applied by analogy.[46] The instrument creating the trust or written evidence of the trust may supply clues as to whether a governing law can be implied.[47] For this purpose, a trust instrument should be construed in light of all circumstances[48] with a view to ascertaining the settlor's intention when the trust was created.[49] The court will thus look at all relevant factors to discern the settlor's intention.[50]

Depending on the type of trust involved, the factors for discerning intention can differ. With an *inter vivos* trust, a jurisdiction clause will be compelling evidence of the settlor's intention.[51] With a trust created by a will, the law of the testator's last domicile will normally be treated as governing the trust and succession to movables devised under the will.[52] For trusts created or declared by a judicial decision, the law of the forum will usually be the governing law.[53] At common law, other factors may also be considered. The factors

[38] See *Lewin on Trusts* (n 33) para 12-090.

[39] The common law position is well established in *Re Piercy* [1895] 1 Ch 83. See also ch 17.

[40] *A-G v Campbell* (1871–72) LR 5 HL 524; *Chellaram* (n 27) 431–32.

[41] Harris (n 18) 179. This is different from the common law position in *Augustus* (n 35).

[42] Despite being rarely exercised, Art 13 of the Hague Trusts Convention endows the court with the discretion not to recognise a trust has its greatest objective connection to a non-trust state.

[43] Hague Trusts Convention, Art 23.

[44] Hague Trusts Convention, Art 6(2).

[45] Hague Trusts Convention, Art 6(2). This is similar to the common law rule laid down in *Bonython v Commonwealth of Australia* [1951] AC 201, 221, where it was held that if the governing law choice has not been expressed, it shall be ascertained as a 'matter of implication to be derived from all circumstances of the transaction'. See also *Augustus* (n 35); *Rickshaw Investments Ltd v Nicolai Baron von Uexkull* [2007] 1 SLR(R) 377.

[46] See ch 15, s I.

[47] Overbeck (n 17) para 69.

[48] ibid paras 64 and 69.

[49] See *Dicey, Morris and Collins* (n 33) para 29-020.

[50] *Berezovsky* (n 36) [108]; *李明寶 v Ace Lead Profits Ltd* [2022] HKCFI 3342 [81].

[51] *A-G v Jewish Colonization Association* [1901] 1 KB 123.

[52] *Campbell* (n 40); *Saliba v Falzon* (unreported, 1 July 1998) (NSWSC).

[53] *Chellaram* (n 27) 428; *Chellaram v Chellaram (No 2)* [2002] EWHC 532 (Ch), [2002] 3 All ER 17 [46]. See also *A and B v C* [2020] HKCFI 2628.

examined may overlap with connecting factors pointing to the place of closest connection.[54] The *situs* of trust assets will be given weight when ascertaining intention, especially if immovable property is involved.[55] A place of administration specified in the trust instrument may be treated as a strong pointer.[56] The use of certain legal terminology may be indicative of a settlor's or testator's intention.[57] A trust scheme involving declarations of trust with express governing law is an indication that the same law governs the trust scheme.[58] The place where the trust instrument was executed, formed or prepared may be fortuitous and therefore will be of less significance.[59] Personal connecting factors to the settlor, the beneficiary or the trustee are of less significance.[60]

(iii) Default of Choice

Article 7 of the Hague Trusts Convention primarily provides that, in default of choice, a trust will be governed by the law of the place with which it is most closely connected.[61] The Convention indicates four major factors in ascertaining the place of close connection:[62]

(i) the place of administration of the trust designated by the settlor;
(ii) the *situs* of the trust assets;
(iii) the place of business or residence of the trustees; and
(iv) the objects of the trust and the places where those objects are to be fulfilled.

The foregoing factors are, however, neither conclusive nor exhaustive.[63] The time by reference to which any close connection is to be assessed has not been specified in Article 7. It is suggested that the factors should be assessed at the time when the trust was created or when the will was made.[64] It is conceivable that the relevant factors point to the closest connection being a jurisdiction that does not recognise trusts.[65] If so, the Hague Trusts Convention is inapplicable and a trust would simply not be recognised.[66]

[54] The list of connecting factors to be considered in the rule of closest connection test is stated in Art 7 of the Hague Trusts Convention. See s II.C(iii) below.

[55] *Campbell* (n 40); *Lindsay v Miller* [1949] VLR 13; *Iveagh v IRC* [1954] Ch 364.

[56] *Chellaram* (n 27); *Lindsay* (n 55).

[57] *Peillon v Brooking* (1858) 25 Beav 218, 53 ER 620; *Lindsay* (n 55); *Re Lord Cable* [1977] 1 WLR 7.

[58] *李明實* (n 50) [81]–[88].

[59] *Duke of Marlborough v A-G (No 1)* [1945] Ch 78; *Harris Investment Ltd v Smith* [1934] 1 DLR 748; *Lindsay* (n 55); *Iveagh* (n 55); *cf Chellaram (No 2)* (n 53).

[60] *Jewish Colonization Association* (n 51); *Iveagh* (n 55); *Revenue Commissioners v Pelly* [1940] IR 122; *Chellaram* (n 27).

[61] This is similar to the common law approach. However, the line between implied choice and the applicable law in the absence of choice under the common law approach is fine and hard to be drawn clearly. One difference might be that the closest connection test allows a wider range of objective factors to be considered, whereas the test to ascertain the implied choice of law is closed to certain factors that would be adopted to discern the settlor's intention. See Harris (n 18) 215.

[62] Overbeck (n 17) paras 72–77; *Tod v Barton* [2002] EWHC 264 (Ch), [2002] WTLR 469; *Re Carapiet's Trusts* [2002] EWHC 1304 (Ch), [2002] WTLR 989; *Schechter* (n 17) [117]–[119]; *JSC VTB Bank v Skurikhin* [2019] EWHC 1407 (Comm) [203]; Harris (n 18) 215.

[63] Harris (n 18) 178.

[64] *Re Constantinou* [2013] 2 Qd R 219 [44]; *Lewin on Trusts* (n 33), paras 12-087–12-088.

[65] *Akers* (n 7).

[66] Hague Trusts Convention, Art 5.

(iv) Situs *of Property*

The *situs* of property plays a role in ascertaining the governing law. However, in the Hague Trusts Convention, the word 'property' does not specifically refer to movable or immovable property.[67] Typically, the law governing immovable property and trusts of immovable property is the *lex situs*.[68] This has been modified, as a settlor is free to choose under Article 6 of the Hague Trusts Convention.[69] In default of choice, the *situs* of property might be of heavier weight if the trust assets consist largely of immovable property.[70]

The *situs* of trust property may trigger the application of the *Moçambique* rule, that is, the rule that a court has no jurisdiction to deal with the title or interest in foreign immovable property.[71] In *Chang Wing Ka John v Chang Wing Dee*, DHCJ To ruled that the Moçambique rule was not applicable if the trust or estate involves movable and immovable property in Hong Kong and immovable property in a foreign jurisdiction.[72]

(v) Change in Governing Law

Once a trust is created, its proper law governs its validity and cannot be changed by changes in the place of investment of the trust property,[73] the residence of the trustees[74] or the domicile of the beneficiaries.[75] The governing law can only be changed if the trustee has such power under the trust instrument, there is power reserved in the trust instrument to enable a change,[76] the beneficiaries agree to change the governing law[77] or an application to change the governing law is made under the Variation of Trusts Ordinance (Cap 253).[78] A change in governing law will only be accepted if it is in the interest of the beneficiaries.[79] Article 10 of the Hague Trusts Convention states that the original governing law will be applied to determine whether the law may be replaced by the law of another state. It is unclear whether a change of governing law constitutes a variation of the existing trust or should be treated as the creation of a new trust.[80]

[67] This was deliberately left open: Overbeck (n 17) para 76.

[68] *Lewin on Trusts* (n 33) para 12-143.

[69] Subject to the limitation of Hague Trusts Convention, Arts 15, 16 and 18, as incorporated by the RTO.

[70] *Chellaram* (n 27). See also *Chang Wing Ka John v Chang Wing Dee* [2021] HKCFI 47 [226]–[229].

[71] *British South Africa Co v Companhia de Moçambique* [1893] AC 602; *Wong Yuen Wai v Hark Chung Wong* (unreported, HCA 469/2013, 4 July 2017) [32]; *DX v LN* (unreported, FCMC 7870/2014, 30 November 2015). For the operation of the *Moçambique* rule, see ch 10, s II.A.

[72] *Chang Wing Ka John* (n 70), approved in *Chang Wing Ka John v Chang Wing Dee* [2023] HKCA 876.

[73] *Re Fitzgerald* (n 37) 588; *Duke of Marlborough* (n 59) 85.

[74] *Re Hewitt's Settlement* [1915] 1 Ch 228, 233–34; *Duke of Marlborough* (n 59) 85.

[75] *Re Hewitt's Settlement* (n 74) 233–34.

[76] It was held in *Chellaram (No 2)* (n 53) that provisions reserving the power to change the governing law might be valid.

[77] *Duke of Marlborough* (n 59).

[78] See *Re Seale's Marriage Settlement* [1961] Ch 574; *Re Windeatt* [1969] 1 WLR 692; *Hong Kong Bank Trustee Ltd v Ho Shai Lai* [1985] 2 HKC 704; *HSBC Trustee (Hong Kong) Ltd v Wilhelmina Wu* [1997] 2 HKC 576.

[79] *HSBC Trustee (Hong Kong) Ltd* (n 78) [12]–[14]; *Oakley v Osiris Trustees Ltd* [2008] UKPC 2, [2009] WTLR 461 [44].

[80] In *Wilmington Trust Co v Wilmington Trust Co* 24 A 2d 309, 26 Del Ch 397 (1942), the Delaware court accepted that the change will be treated as a creation of new trust: Paul Matthews, *Trusts: Migration and Change of Proper Law* (Key Haven Publications, 1997) 67. Alternatively, it could be argued that a law can only be changed because the original governing law so allows.

D. Effect of the Hague Trusts Convention and the Recognition of Trusts Ordinance

Article 8 of the Hague Trusts Convention states:[81] 'The law specified by Articles 6 or 7 shall govern the validity of the trust, its construction, its effects and the administration of the trust.' This is similar to the common law position in Hong Kong before the enactment of the RTO.[82]

(i) Validity

Article 8 is qualified by Article 4, which provides that the Hague Trusts Convention does not govern the validity of wills or other acts by which assets are transferred to a trustee.[83] Further, the Hague Trusts Convention does not preclude a trust from having to adhere to formal requirements other than those prescribed by its governing law.[84] Whether a resulting or constructive trust of property arises is considered to be a preliminary question, falling outside the scope of the Hague Trusts Convention.[85]

(ii) Construction

Construction of a trust will be governed by its proper law. Construction often involves reference to extrinsic evidence. A court's ability to accept such material would be a matter of procedure and therefore governed by the *lex fori*.

E. Severability of Trusts

Article 9 of the Hague Trusts Convention provides that different aspects of a trust may be governed by a different law. This allows the settlor to designate a different law to govern administration of a trust, while the rest of the trust is governed by some other law. Unless there is an express or implied choice of distinctive laws for different aspects of a trust, the court should proceed on the basis that one law was intended to apply to all aspects of a trust.[86]

F. Recognition of Foreign Trusts

The primary rule is that a trust created in accordance with the law specified under the Hague Trusts Convention's choice of law rules should be recognised.[87] This is subject to the

[81] It is noted that the list is not intended to be exhaustive, see Overbeck (n 17) para 81.

[82] See, eg *Re Fitzgerald* (n 37); *Lindsay* (n 55); *Trustees Executors and Agency Co Ltd v Margottini* [1960] VR 417; *Perpetual Executors and Trustees Association of Australia Ltd v Roberts* [1970] VR 732; *Augustus* (n 35).

[83] These matters will be governed by the common law rules stated in the previous section.

[84] Overbeck (n 17) paras 82–83. For an example, see, eg *Schechter* (n 17) [123], where despite a trust of English land being governed by foreign law, the formalities in s 53(1)(b) of the Law of Property Act 1925 (UK) must still be complied with.

[85] *Zhang Caikui* (n 3) [99]–[100].

[86] *Chellaram* (n 27); *In re Pollak's Estate* [1937] TPD 91.

[87] Hague Trusts Convention, Art 11.

limitations in Articles 15 (the Mandatory Rule), 16 (the Overriding Rule) and 18 (the Public Policy Rule) of the Convention. The Hong Kong courts are also allowed to allow common law rules in force before the enactment of the RTO if such rules are more favourable to the recognition of a trust.[88]

(i) Mandatory and Overriding Rules

Article 15 of the Hague Trusts Convention reads:

> The Convention does not prevent the application of provisions of the law designated by the conflicts rules of the forum, in so far as those provisions cannot be derogated from by voluntary act, relating in particular to the following matters:
>
> (a) the protection of minors and incapable parties;
> (b) the personal and proprietary effects of marriage;
> (c) succession rights, testate and intestate, especially the indefeasible shares of spouses and relatives;
> (d) the transfer of title to property and security interests in property;
> (e) the protection of creditors in matters of insolvency;
> (f) the protection, in other respects, of third parties acting in good faith.
>
> If recognition of a trust is prevented by application of the preceding paragraph, the court shall try to give effect to the objects of the trust by other means.

Although the Hague Trusts Convention has conferred a wide degree of freedom on the settlor, it does not allow the creation of a trust to override mandatory rules that may be applicable on the basis of Hong Kong choice of law rules. Thus, the law designated by a settlor and the law relating to the matters listed in Article 15 may not coincide. To the extent that the listed matters are subject to overriding mandatory rules which are applicable pursuant to Hong Kong choice of law principles, the settlor cannot avoid or circumvent such overriding mandatory rules by designating some other law.

Article 16 provides that the Convention does not prevent the application of those provisions of the law of the forum which must be applied even to international situations, irrespective of rules of conflict of laws. Article 16(2) of the Hague Trusts Convention (on the application of overriding rules of another state which has a sufficiently close connection with a case) does not apply to Hong Kong due to the reservation made under Article 16(3) when the UK entered into the Convention.

Section 2(4) of the RTO provides that

> where Articles 15 and 16 do not prevent the application of any provision of law, that provision of law shall, to the extent specified in Articles 15 and 16, apply notwithstanding anything to the contrary in any other Article of the Convention.

(ii) Public Policy

Article 18 of the Hague Trusts Convention states: 'The provisions of the Convention may be disregarded when their application would be manifestly incompatible with public policy.'

[88] ibid Art 14.

Article 18 preserves Hong Kong public policy and excuses the Hong Kong courts from applying foreign law in cases when the application of that law would lead to an outcome which is contrary to Hong Kong public policy.[89]

(iii) Effect of Recognition

The result of recognition on the nature of trust and the role of trustee will be that: (i) the trust property constitutes a separate fund; (ii) the trustee may sue and be sued as a trustee; and (iii) the trustee may appear as a trustee before a notary or other official.[90] The effect on trust assets will be that: (i) the trustee's personal creditors have no recourse against the trust assets; (ii) trust assets do not form part of the trustee's estate upon insolvency; (iii) trust assets do not form part of the trustee's estate or matrimonial property; and (iv) the trust assets may be recovered if in breach of trust they become mixed with a trustee's property or are given away by the trustee. But the rights and obligations of any third party who comes to hold the trust assets shall remain subject to the law determined by the forum's choice of law rules.[91] As far as registration of trust assets as belonging to a trust is concerned, the trustee will be able to do so in accordance with the law of the state recognising the trust.[92]

Most of the foregoing rules are akin to Hong Kong and English common law. The exception is Article 11(3)(d) of the Hague Trusts Convention to the effect that the forum's choice of law rules will be applied to ascertain the law concerning third party holders of trust assets disposed of in breach of trust. This essentially concerns the tracing and recovery of trust assets. Where a Hong Kong court is the forum, it will employ its choice of law rules to determine the applicable law in such situations.[93]

III. Choice of Law for Substantive Questions under the Common Law

It is necessary to examine the common law rules as they continue to apply if they are more favourable to recognition than those of the Hague Trusts Convention.[94] It is also relevant for acts done or omitted before the enactment of the RTO on 30 March 1990.[95] This section therefore discusses the common law choice of law rules to be applied in respect of the validity, interpretation and administration of trusts, both testamentary and *inter vivos*.

[89] Public policy concerns include serious infringement of human rights, see *Oppenheimer v Cattermole* [1976] AC 249. See also *Kuwait Airways Corp v Iraqi Airways Co* [2002] UKHL 19, [2002] 2 AC 883; *First Laser Ltd v Fujian Enterprises (Holdings) Co Ltd* (unreported, HCA 4414/2001, 5 February 2008) [113]–[114]. Foreign exchange control law that is an instrument of oppression would be disregarded: *Re Helbert Wagg & Co* [1956] Ch 323, 351; *The Playa Larga* [1983] 2 Lloyd's Rep 171, 190.

[90] Hague Trusts Convention, Art 11(2).

[91] ibid Art 11(3).

[92] ibid Art 12.

[93] Overbeck (n 17) para 113. These rules will be discussed in s VII below.

[94] Hague Trusts Convention, Art 14.

[95] RTO, s 2(6); Hague Trusts Convention, Art 22.

The main principle is that a trust should be treated as a single unit and be governed by one law, although there is the possibility of *dépeçage*.[96]

A. Testamentary Trust

In Hong Kong, the law governing the validity of a will, and hence of any trust created thereby, is determined by reference to the rules in the Wills Ordinance (Cap 30).[97] The law governing the construction of a will is the law intended by the testator. Absent a choice, the presumption is that the law of the testator's domicile at the time of the will applies.[98] The governing law will not be altered by a change in testator's domicile after the execution of the will.[99]

Where a trust involves foreign elements, the application of Hong Kong law will not necessarily be excluded. In *Secretary for Justice v Wong Tak Wai*, multiple factors pointed towards Hong Kong law being the governing law of the charitable trust created under a will. These factors included: (i) the will being executed in Hong Kong; (ii) the testatrix being domiciled in Hong Kong when the will was executed and at her death; (iii) the majority of the assets being in Hong Kong; (iv) the assets being largely managed and administered in Hong Kong; and (v) the will being construed in accordance with Hong Kong law. The fact that part of the operation and the administration of the trust, namely, (i) the setting up of a Chinese prize intended to be a prestigious award of worldwide significance and (ii) the appointment of the Premier of the People's Republic of China and the Secretary-General of the United Nations as the monitoring organisation, did not exclude the application of Hong Kong law to the trust overall.[100]

B. *Inter vivos* Trust

If an *inter vivos* trust consists of movable property, it will be governed by the settlor's express or implied choice of proper law or that system of law with which the trust has its closest and most real connection.[101] If the *inter vivos* trust comprises immovable property in a single country, it will be governed by *lex situs*. If the trust property comprises immovables in different countries or a mixture of immovables and movables, it is submitted that the trust should be treated as a unit and that the trust should be governed by a single law. This is likely to be the proper law of the trust.[102]

[96] See ch 3, s IV.

[97] Wills Ordinance (Cap 30), ss 24 and 25. See ch 17, s VII.

[98] *Ewing v Orr-Ewing* (1883) 9 App Cas 34, 43; *Re Fergusson's Will* [1902] 1 Ch 483; *Re Cunnington* [1924] 1 Ch 68; *Philipson-Stow v IRC* [1961] AC 727, 761.

[99] Wills Ordinance, s 27.

[100] *Secretary for Justice v Wong Tak Wai* [2022] HKCFI 3255 [133]–[139].

[101] *Campbell* (n 40); *Duke of Marlborough* (n 59); *Iveagh* (n 55); *Chellaram* (n 27).

[102] There is a dearth of cases in this regard. The proposition was proposed in Lawrence Collins (gen ed), *Dicey and Morris on the Conflict of Laws*, 11th edn (Stevens & Sons, 1987) Rule 157. See also *Re Fitzgerald* (n 37).

C. Jurisdiction Agreements in a Trust Instrument

A settlor might incorporate a choice of court agreement into the trust instrument to confer jurisdiction to the specified forum. The validity and effect of the jurisdiction agreement is uncertain as the relevant judicial authorities and academic discussion on the subject are relatively sparse when compared to the contractual context.

It is attractive in theory to apply normal rules on jurisdiction clauses in contracts in the context of trusts by analogy.[103] This means that under an exclusive jurisdiction clause in a trust instrument, a claimant is generally not allowed to sue outside the chosen forum unless 'strong reasons' are shown, and third parties and strangers to the trust (as opposed to beneficiaries) are generally unlikely to be bound by the exclusive jurisdiction clause.[104] In *Crociani v Crociani*, the Privy Council held in obiter that the weight to be given to an exclusive jurisdiction clause in a trust instrument is less than a contractual exclusive jurisdiction clause, and a beneficiary should have a lighter burden of 'good reasons' to overcome the jurisdiction clause in a trust instrument, as the beneficiaries were not involved in the bargaining of the jurisdiction clause, and the court has an inherent jurisdiction to supervise the administration of the trust to protect the interests of the beneficiaries.[105] This lower threshold of 'good reasons' was accepted in Hong Kong in *A v B*. In that case, there was an exclusive jurisdiction clause designated the Bahamas court in a deed of settlement setting up a trust, with a Bahamas company acting as the trustee. The court found that the lower threshold applied as neither party to the proceedings was a party to the trust deed, but on the facts, there were no sufficiently good reasons not to enforce the exclusive jurisdiction clause.[106]

IV. Administering Foreign Trusts

The Hong Kong courts have jurisdiction to administer a foreign trust involving foreign trust property. In *Ewing v Orr-Ewing*, a trust was created by the will of a testator domiciled in Scotland and the subject matter of the trust was personal property in Scotland. The House of Lords ruled that the English courts had jurisdiction to administer the trust as equity operated *in personam*, not *in rem*.[107] This principle was adopted by the Hong Kong court in *Chang Wing Ka John v Chang Wing Dee*.[108] The case confirmed that: (i) the Hong Kong court has inherent jurisdiction to administer a trust, including the removal and appointment of trustees;[109] (ii) enforcement of a trust was a procedural matter governed by the

[103] See, eg *Bank of New York Mellon v GV Films* [2009] EWHC 2338 (Comm); *Okada v Okada* [2018] HKCFI 2310; *A v B* [2022] HKCFI 1031.

[104] *Zhang Caikui* (n 3) [104]–[105]; *A v B* (n 103).

[105] *Crociani v Crociani* [2014] UKPC 40, [2015] WTLR 975 [36]–[37]. See also *EMM Capricorn Trustees Ltd v Compass Trustees Ltd* [2001] WTLR 997; Ardavan Arzandeh, 'Exclusive Jurisdiction Clauses in International Trust Deeds' (2021) 41(4) *Legal Studies* 527; Richard Garnett and Ying Khai Liew, 'Trusts Jurisdiction Clauses: An Analysis' *LQR* (forthcoming).

[106] *A v B* (n 103) [22]–[58]. However, in *Ivanishvili v Credit Suisse AG* [2020] 2 SLR 638, the Singapore Court of Appeal assumed the 'strong cause' test applied without argument.

[107] *Ewing* (n 98) 40–41 and 45–46. See also *Chellaram* (n 27).

[108] *Chang Wing Ka John* (n 70) [218]–[234].

[109] ibid [220]–[221], [225] and [234].

law of the court which has assumed jurisdiction;[110] and (iii) the administration of a trust of foreign property did not violate the Moçambique rule as long as part of the immovable trust property was situated in Hong Kong.[111] The court illustrated the exercise of the inherent jurisdiction as follows:[112]

> In the exercise of this jurisdiction, the court will enquire what are the personal obligations binding on the trustees. If the obligations are owed in respect of foreign trust assets, the court shall make *personam* orders against the trustees requiring them to perform their obligations. It does not matter where the trust assets are situated and what is the proper law governing the trust. What is required is that the legal process has been served on the trustees and they have submitted to jurisdiction.

However, whether personal representatives can obtain foreign property for a trust is a different question, which is governed by the law where the property is situated. This is because the grant of probate or letters of administration in (say) Hong Kong cannot give personal representatives authority to collect foreign assets, or compel the delivery of foreign trust property to them. Whether they are entitled to obtain possession of the foreign trust property must depend on the law of the foreign country in which the trust assets are situated.[113] Further, although part of the administration of the trust involves a foreign element, it is still possible, if there are an overwhelming number of factors connecting the trust to Hong Kong, for the overall trust scheme to be governed by Hong Kong law.[114]

V. Resulting and Constructive Trusts

It remains controversial whether the choice of law rules in the Hague Trusts Convention, as implemented in Hong Kong by the RTO, are sufficiently defined to cover all resulting and constructive trusts. On the basis that they do not cover these trusts, common law rules will be significant. However, there are only a few common law precedents on conflict of law rules for constructive trusts.[115] This section accordingly sets out tentative propositions on the proper choice of law rules for resulting and constructive trusts.

The first proposition is to adopt the Hague Trusts Convention rules as common law choice of law rules for resulting and constructive trusts. In other words, such trusts should be governed by the law to which they are most closely connected.[116] This is for two main reasons: first, there is the merit of convenience; and second, the flexibility enables the court to take into account different factors depending on the circumstances.[117] However, there will inevitably be a measure of uncertainty.

[110] But the nature and the extent of the beneficiaries' right is determined by the law applicable to the trust: ibid [224].
[111] ibid [227]–[228].
[112] ibid [225].
[113] *Ng Kit v Wu Tsun Hua* [2021] HKCFI 877 [70]–[73].
[114] See *Wong Tak Wai* (n 100) [133]–[139].
[115] Chong (n 29) 855.
[116] ibid 863.
[117] For example, if the resulting trusts arise from a failed contract, the connecting factor might well be the contract; if the constructive trusts arise out of a stolen property, the connecting factor might be the *situs* of property.

The second proposition is to characterise resulting and constructive trusts as equitable obligations. This is founded on a line of cases which have ruled that equitable rights over foreign property are to be determined by the *lex fori*.[118] The court's jurisdiction over equitable rights in a foreign land could be justified on the basis of *in personam* jurisdiction over the defendant and will reflect the analogous principle upheld by the court in *Chang Wing Ka John v Chang Wing Dee*.[119] However, scholars have argued against this principle as the cases were developed by the Court of Chancery, where the forum hearing the case and the defendant necessarily shared some connection.[120]

The third proposition is to characterise constructive trusts as restitutionary obligations governed by the choice of law rules for restitution or unjust enrichment. As a matter of principle, the issue underlying resulting and constructive trusts is the right to restitution, and the law of unjust enrichment can be the foundation of a proprietary remedy.[121] Such classification might not be right, as trusts do not necessarily arise because of unjust enrichment.[122] In practice, as in the English case of *Westdeutsche*,[123] an institutional constructive trust might arise to prevent a defendant from being unjustly enriched.[124] But this understanding of resulting and constructive trusts may be misplaced,[125] as constructive trusts arise from the breach of fiduciary obligation, whether or not there has been enrichment, whereas resulting trusts arise only in response to unjust enrichment. A scenario in point would be a presumed resulting trust where a defendant is deemed to hold property upon trust for a claimant upon the failure of the purpose for which such property was transferred to the defendant in the first instance. The defendant will be unjustly enriched if allowed to keep the property transferred. Thus, the choice of law rules for restitution could conceivably apply.[126]

The fourth proposition is to regard resulting and constructive trusts as issues of property. This because a beneficial interest, in common law and civilian law trusts, will be proprietary in nature.[127] That would mean that the choice of law rules relating to movable and immovable property should apply. The major benefit of this classification is certainty. For instance, one would reasonably expect the transfer of title of property to be governed by the *situs* of the property.[128]

[118] *Lightning v Lightning Electrical Contractors Ltd* (unreported, 23 April 1998) (EWCA). See also *Penn v Lord Baltimore* (1750) 1 Ves Sen 444, 27 ER 1132; *National Commercial Bank v Wimborne* (unreported, 28 April 1978) (NSWSC).

[119] *Chang Wing Ka John* (n 70) [218]–[234]. See also *Lord Cranstown v Johnston* (1796) 3 Ves 170, 182; Laurette Barnard, 'Choice of Law in Equitable Wrongs: A Comparative Analysis' (1992) 51(3) *CLJ* 474, 488.

[120] Note: in the post-Judicature Act era, jurisdiction could be established by the presence of the defendant within the forum: Chong (n 29) 863; RW White, 'Equitable Obligation in Private International Law: The Choice of Law' (1986) 11 *Sydney Law Review* 92, 108.

[121] George Panagopoulos, *Restitution in Private International Law* (Hart Publishing, 2000) 66–67.

[122] It is accepted that in some jurisdictions, eg the USA and Canada, constructive trusts arise as a remedy for unjust enrichment: Chong (n 29) 871; Robert Chambers, 'Constructive Trusts in Canada (Pt 2)' (2002) 16 *Trust Law International* 2.

[123] *Westdeutsche Landesbank Girozentrale* (n 31) 714–15.

[124] See also Graham Virgo, *The Principles of the Law of Restitution*, 4th edn (Oxford University Press, 2024) 648–58.

[125] PJ Millett, 'Restitution and Constructive Trusts' (1998) 114 *LQR* 399; Barnard (n 119) 480.

[126] See ch 15, s VI.

[127] Chong (n 29) 876.

[128] ibid.

The fifth proposition relies on *First Laser Ltd v Fujian Enterprises (Holdings) Co Ltd*,[129] where a 'double accountability approach' was put forward.[130]

In that case, the parties agreed that the plaintiff was to acquire 51 per cent of the defendant's shareholding in a Mainland China project. The plaintiff paid the consideration. Instead of transferring the shares to the plaintiff, the defendant sold the agreed shareholding to another company for a profit. The plaintiff claimed against the defendant on grounds of breach, while the defendant countered that the agreement was invalid by PRC law. By that law, the plaintiff was ruled to be entitled to the restitution of the consideration that it had paid. In addition to restitution, the plaintiff submitted that the defendant held the relevant shareholding (and the profit from its sale) on trust for the plaintiff by reason of the agreement. In delivering the court's unanimous decision, Lord Collins NPJ stated:[131]

> 66. There is a paucity of authority on the applicable law in restitution cases with a foreign element. The prevailing view is the obligation to restore the benefit of an enrichment obtained at another person's expense is governed by the proper law of the obligation; and that where the obligation arises in connection with a contract the proper law is the law applicable to the contract: see Dicey, p.1863 para.34R-001; Johnston, Conflict of Laws in Hong Kong (2005) para.5.108. But that does not mean that if that law does not recognize the concept of constructive trusteeship, the plaintiff has no remedy in a court applying the common law/equity system. The appropriate analysis is to ask whether, under the *lex causae*, the defendant owes obligations which would impose on the defendant under that law a liability to disgorge a benefit. If so, the court may hold the defendant liable as constructive trustee when giving remedial effect to the substantive right arising under the *lex causae*: Dicey, p.1887 para.34-049, citing *Arab Monetary Fund v Hashim (No 9)* (unrep., QBD, 15 June 1994); *Kuwait Oil Tanker Co SAK v Al Bader*.
>
> 67. The approach in these cases has been to look at the nature of the obligation under the foreign law, for example to see whether it could be characterized as fiduciary in character, and then consider whether it was therefore capable of supporting the equitable remedies *in personam* which would be available to a claimant in an English action.

A claim for breach of equitable obligation is therefore not defeated merely because the foreign law does not recognise the concept. The analysis instead first considers whether, under the *lex causae*, the defendant owed obligations which would impose a liability to disgorge a benefit. If the answer is yes, the inquiry examines whether, if the matters complained of had taken place in Hong Kong, there would be liability under a constructive or resulting trust. If so, the defendant will be held liable as a constructive or resulting trustee under Hong Kong law to give effect to the substantive right arising under the *lex causae*. Hong Kong law will then determine the extent and enforceability of the parties' rights and the duties of the parties.[132] The approach would be to look at the available

[129] *First Laser Ltd* (n 2).

[130] The term 'double accountability approach' was used in *Shenzhen Futaihong Precision Industry Co Ltd v BYD Co Ltd* [2019] 2 HKC 175, [2018] HKCA 408 [58].

[131] *First Laser Ltd* (n 2) [66]–[67]. See also *Arab Monetary Fund v Hashim* (unreported, 15 June 1994) (QBD); *Kuwait Oil Tanker Co SAK v Al Bader* [2000] 2 All ER (Comm) 271.

[132] ibid [95]. See also *China Agri-Products Exchange Ltd v Wang Xiu Qun* [2021] HKCFI 137 [516]–[517].

remedies in the foreign jurisdiction for the wrong committed.[133] The Hong Kong court would then strive to match those foreign remedies as closely as possible with analogous remedies available under the Hong Kong law of constructive and resulting trusts.[134]

The principles just summarised are exemplified by the Court of Final Appeal's decision in *Xiamen Xinjingdi Group Co Ltd v Eton Properties Ltd.*[135]

In that case, the parties entered into an agreement governed by PRC law. Xinjingdi agreed to pay Eton for the right to develop land in Xiamen and the right to receive profits from the development. This right was held by Eton's wholly owned subsidiary S. In exchange, Eton agreed to transfer control of S to Xinjingdi along with the land. A deposit was paid but the land was never delivered. Eton later returned the deposit and suggested that the agreement could not be executed because it was contrary to PRC law. Eton underwent a restructuring whereby a company within the group (but not a subsidiary of Eton) obtained control of the land. As the group acquired control, they developed it without reference to Xinjingdi. The latter claimed against Eton, alleging that Eton had acted in breach of fiduciary obligation and held S's shares as a constructive trustee.[136]

Lord Sumption NPJ delivered the court's unanimous judgment on the issue of constructive trust:[137]

> 175. The first question for us is by what law the existence of such beneficial interest is to be determined. The existence and incidents of an interest in property is governed by the *lex situs*. In the case of shares, this is the law of the jurisdiction in which the company is incorporated: *Akers v Samba Financial Group* at [19] (Lord Mance), [84] (Lord Sumption). The position is, however, complicated where there is a contract governed by the law of some other jurisdiction. The *lex situs* determines whether an equitable proprietary interest in the shares is legally capable of existing. If it is legally capable of existing, the next question is whether it has actually been created. Where this is said to be the effect of a contract, the *lex situs* refers to the proper law of the contract to determine what it means. The question in such a case is not whether its proper law recognises constructive or indeed any trusts. The question is whether the characteristics which the proper law of the contract treats it as having, are such as the *lex situs* would regard as giving rise to a proprietary interest in equity: *Kuwait Oil Tanker Co SAK v Al-Bader (No 3)* [2000] 2 All ER (Comm) 271, at [190]-[193] (Nourse LJ); *First Laser Ltd v Fujian Enterprises (Holdings) Co Ltd* (2012) 15 HKCFAR 569 at [66]-[70] (Lord Collins of Mapesbury NPJ). As applied to the present case, the result of these principles is that the law of Hong Kong, as the situs of the shares, determines whether an equitable interest in shares of a Hong Kong company is capable of subsisting. The answer to that question is that it is, if the contract is specifically enforceable. It is then necessary to refer to the law of the PRC, as the proper law of the Agreement, to determine whether the contract has the characteristics which make it specifically enforceable in the law of Hong Kong. For this purpose, the arbitration award is a decisive source. D3 was not party to the arbitration agreement. But D3's liability as a constructive trustee depends on the position as between D1-D2 and the plaintiff, all of whom are bound by the arbitration agreement.

[133] See also *Zhang Caikui* (n 3) [96].

[134] Anselmo Reyes, 'The Application of Hong Kong Equitable Remedies to Contracts Governed by Mainland Law' (2014) 20(4) *Trusts & Trustees* 325.

[135] *Xiamen Xinjingdi Group Co Ltd v Eton Properties Ltd* (2020) 23 HKCFAR 348, [2020] HKCFA 32.

[136] The constructive trust arises out of fiduciary relationship from the executory contract for the sale of the shares: *Lysaght v Edwards* (1876) 2 Ch D 499, 506; ibid [174].

[137] *Xiamen Xinjingdi Group Co Ltd* (n 135) [175].

VI. Knowing Receipt and Dishonest Assistance

The common law choice of law rules for knowing receipt of trust property and dishonest assistance in a breach of trust are not settled.[138] It was thought that the Hong Kong courts would apply *First Laser*.[139] In the context of dishonest assistance, this is what was done in *China Agri-Products Exchange Ltd v Wang Xiu Qun*.[140] However, in *China Metal Recycling (Holdings) Ltd v Chun Chi Wai*,[141] the court held that a claim in dishonest assistance should be characterised as a tort for the purposes of choice of law rules, and the proper law should be the law of the country in which the events constituting the dishonest assistance occurred or, if they occurred in more than one country, the law of the country in which the most significant element or elements transpired. The court in *China Agri-Products Exchange Ltd* found obiter that the dishonest assistance claim as pleaded would be civilly actionable under Mainland law, and would have passed the double actionability rule.[142]

VII. Following and Tracing

In some cases, a claimant may have to prove that he or she is the owner of assets currently in the defendant's hands. This is relevant to following and tracing. The issue is whether the claimant was the original owner of the interest and continues to enjoy title to the property or whether the interest of a bona fide purchaser for value without notice has overridden the original owner's title. Following and tracing are consequently typically classified as matters of property law. On this premise, it might be thought that following and tracing should be governed by the choice of law rules for property.[143] But the distinction between the two concepts is crucial to an understanding of precisely what choice of law rule should apply to one or other institution. Following and tracing were described thus by Lord Millett in *Foskett v McKeown*:[144]

> Tracing and following … are both exercises in locating assets which are or may be taken to represent an asset belonging to the purchaser and to which they assert ownership. The processes of following and tracing are, however, distinct. Following is the process of following the same asset as it moves from hand to hand. Tracing is the process of identifying a new asset as the substitute for the old.

[138] Adeline Chong, 'Characterisation and Choice of Law for Knowing Receipt' (2023) 72(1) *ICLQ* 147, 155 and 168.

[139] *First Laser Ltd* (n 2) [66]–[67].

[140] *China Agri-Products Exchange Ltd* (n 132) [509], [516]–[522].

[141] *China Metal Recycling (Holdings) Ltd (in compulsory liq) v Chun Chi Wai* [2021] HKCFI 378 [80]–[81], approving *OJSC Oil Co Yugraneft v Abramovich* [2008] EWHC 2613 [221], [223]: 'If it was necessary, I would strongly incline to holding that a claim in dishonest assistance was, for the purposes of the [Private International Law (Miscellaneous Provisions) Act 1995] a "tort" … Dishonest assistance, a form of equitable wrongdoing, is so closely analogous to a claim in tort (as characterised for purely domestic purposes) that it should, I would have thought, be so characterised for private international law purposes.'

[142] *China Agri-Products Exchange Ltd* (n 132) [499]–[509].

[143] This is derived based on the three-stage approach laid down in *Macmillan Inc v Bishopsgate Investment Trust plc (No 3)* [1996] 1 WLR 387, 391. The crux is to identify the issue in dispute, but not the cause of action. See ch 3, s I.

[144] *Foskett v McKeown* [2001] 1 AC 102, 127.

Following merely involves locating a property. It should be characterised as an issue of property law and the choice of law rules for property will apply.[145]

Tracing is different since it encompasses changes in the original nature of a property. The commonly suggested approach is that tracing and the determination of whether a person has the ability to trace should not be governed by an independent choice of law rule but should be subject to the *lex causae*.[146] The approach of applying the *lex causae* could be justified as tracing does not in itself form a separate cause of action, but is incidental and collateral to claims already brought.[147] The general approach would be to prioritise and focus on the nature of the claim over the label of the obligations under the foreign law, where courts consider whether such an obligation is capable of supporting equitable remedies.[148]

[145] This is so irrespective of whether the claim for following is personal, proprietary, restitutionary or tortious: *Macmillan Inc* (n 143).

[146] Jonathan Harris, 'Tracing and the Conflict of Laws' (2002) 74 *British Yearbook of International Law* 65, 67–70; George Panagopoulos, 'Substance and Procedure in Private International Law' (2005) 1(1) *Journal of Private International Law* 69, 84–86; Chong (n 29) 861–62; Yeo (n 1) 127–28 and 133–34.

[147] *Zhang Caikui* (n 3) [96].

[148] *First Laser Ltd* (n 2) [67]. See also ibid.

17

Law of Property

I. Overview

In the context of private international law, there is a distinction between movable and immovable property.[1] That distinction is important in the choice of law rules for the transfer of property and succession. Note that property can also be classified into tangible and intangible property. Tangible property can further be broken down into tangible movable and tangible immovable property.

All property must have a *situs* for legal purposes.[2] The determination of the choice of law rule for property consists of three steps:

1. Apply the law of forum to identify the law of *situs*.
2. Apply the law of *situs* to distinguish the nature of the property, that is, to decide whether it is an immovable or movable property.
3. Apply the applicable choice of law rule.

II. Determination of *situs*

As *situs* is closely related to the applicable law and will be engaged in the choice of law analysis, it is important to understand how the *situs* of property is determined. Land is situated in the jurisdiction where it lies. Chattels are situated in the jurisdiction where they happen to be at a given time.[3] Choses in action are intangible property, but they are regarded as situated in the place where they are properly recoverable or can be enforced.[4] This rule, however, has only general application, as the precise determination will depend on the type of chose in action involved and may be subject to exceptions.

[1] See eg *Re Brechtold* [1923] 1 Ch 192; *Haque v Haque (No 2)* (1965) 114 CLR 98. Reference might be made to the definitions of 'immovable property' and 'movable property' in Hong Kong in the Interpretation and General Clauses Ordinance (Cap 1), s 3. The former is defined as land, any 'estate, right, interest or easement' in or over any land, and things attached to land. The latter is defined as any property not being an immovable property.

[2] *Taurus Petroleum Ltd v State Oil Marketing Co of the Ministry of Oil, Republic of Iraq* [2017] UKSC 64, [2018] AC 690 [29].

[3] The limited exceptions are ships and aircrafts which, when in or over the high seas or a *territorium nullius*, may be regarded as situated in their port or place of registration: *Air Foyle Ltd v Center Capital Ltd* [2002] EWHC 2535 (Comm), [2003] 2 Lloyd's Rep 753; *Dornoch Ltd v Westminster International BV* [2009] EWHC 889 (Admlty), [2009] 2 All ER (Comm) 399.

[4] *New York Life Insurance Co v Public Trustee* [1924] 2 Ch 101, 109; *Jabbour v Custodian of Israeli Absentee Property* [1954] 1 WLR 139, 145–46.

A debt is situated in the place where the debtor resides.[5] This is because the place of residence will be the place where the creditor can sue the debtor for payment.[6] Clauses stipulating that payment should be made in a country where the debtor is not resident will not negate the general position.[7] In cases where the debtor is in multiple jurisdictions but one of those places has been designated as the place of repayment, that jurisdiction will be where the debt is located.[8] It is different when there is no promise by the debtor to pay at a particular place of residence among his or her many residences. In that case, the place of residence where the debt would be paid in the ordinary course of business will be where the payment is situated.[9]

As for other choses in action, the rules may be summarised as follows:

1. Judgment debts are situated where the judgment was made.[10]
2. Specialty debts (debts created by deed) are situated where the deed is located.[11]
3. A mortgage is a form of specialty debt, but as it confers an interest in land, it is deemed to be situated where the land is.[12] The rule on specialty debt will apply in the context of mortgage only when it is necessary to distinguish the *situs* of the mortgagor's personal obligation to repay and the mortgagee's interest in land.[13]
4. Cheques and bills of exchange within the scope of the Bills of Exchange Ordinance (Cap 19) are governed by section 72 of that Ordinance, discussed in chapter fifteen, section II.I.
5. Other negotiable instruments (such as letters of credit) are situated where the debt created by the relevant instrument is properly recoverable.[14]
6. Bills of lading are generally deemed to be situated at the location of the document.[15] It is not settled how to determine the *situs* of cargo and property under a bill of lading. Two major contenders are the *situs* of the goods[16] and the *situs* of the documents.[17]
7. Issues of existence and priority of maritime liens are traditionally considered procedural and therefore no *situs* is required. They are governed exclusively by the *lex fori*, with recent cases recognising a limited discretion to give effect to foreign law.[18]
8. Shares in companies are situated in the place of incorporation of the company.[19]

[5] Except for judgment debts and specialty debts, discussed below.
[6] *Re Maudslay Sons & Field* [1900] 1 Ch 602; *Payne v R* [1902] AC 552. This is subject to any exclusive jurisdiction clauses in the agreement.
[7] *Re Helbert Wagg & Co Ltd* [1956] Ch 323; *Taurus Petroleum Ltd* (n 2) [30]–[41].
[8] *New York Life Insurance Co* (n 4).
[9] *Jabbour v Custodian of Israeli Absentee Property* [1954] 1 WLR 139, 146.
[10] *A-G v Bouwens* (1838) 4 M&W 171, 191.
[11] *Gurney v Rawlins* (1836) 2 M&W 87; *Commissioner of Stamps v Hope* [1891] AC 476; *Payne* (n 6); *Re Hole* [1948] 4 DLR 419.
[12] *Re Hoyles* [1911] 1 Ch 179.
[13] *Walsh v R* [1894] AC 144; *Henry v R* [1896] AC 567, 574.
[14] *Taurus Petroleum Ltd* (n 2) [30]–[31].
[15] *North Western Bank Ltd v Poynter, Son and Macdonalds* [1895] AC 56.
[16] *Inglis v Robertson* [1898] AC 616; *Hardwick Game Farm v Suffolk Agricultural Poultry Producers Association* [1969] 2 AC 31.
[17] *Hardwick Game Farm* (n 16).
[18] *The Halcyon Isle* [1981] AC 221; *Reiter Petroleum Inc v The Ship 'Sam Hawk'* (2016) 246 FCR 337.
[19] *Chen Hongqing v Persons Whose Names are Set Out in the Second Column of the Schedule Hereto* [2018] HKCFI 1170 [35]. As such, the issue of the beneficial ownership of the company shares is to be determined by the law of the place where the company was incorporated: *Tripole Trading Ltd v Prosperfield Ventures Ltd* (2006) 9 HKCFAR 1 [86]; *Hsu Ching Fang v Ng Chor Kuen* [2023] HKCFI 725 [62].

9. Unlike shares, unpaid dividends may be regarded as debts and will be governed by different rules.[20]
10. Shares in a partnership are located where the business is carried on.[21] The *situs* of a share in the partnership's land is the *situs* of the land.[22]
11. Goodwill is situated in the place where the business to which the goodwill attaches is located.[23]
12. Rights of action in tort and contract are situated where the relevant actions might be brought.[24]
13. An interest in a deceased's estate is situated in the jurisdiction where the executors or administrators can be compelled to administer the estate.[25]
14. For an interest under trust, the *situs* depends on whether, under the governing law of the trust, a person holds a beneficial interest or only a right to compel the trustees to discharge their duty. The *situs* of the trust property will determine where the former may bring a claim,[26] and the place where the trustees are to be found and may be sued will determine where rights against the trustees may be asserted.[27]

III. Immovable Property

In matters where there is a need to decide on title to land, jurisdiction generally lies with the courts of the *situs* due to the *Moçambique* rule.[28] It follows that the choice of law for rights in relation to immovable property is the *lex situs*, due to the ultimate control of the *situs* over the immovable property and respect to the policies of the *situs* regarding rights of immovable property. The *lex situs* also applies to issues of limitation periods which may give rise to titles.

The transfer of immovable property requires more careful consideration. It requires a distinction between the contract involving immovable property and the conveyance of that property. The formalities required for the conveyance of immovable property are governed by the *lex situs*. However, issues involving the formal and essential validity, and the interpretation and effect of contracts, are governed by the choice of law rules for contracts. Despite an old English authority to the contrary, the general academic consensus is that capacity to transfer is governed by the governing law of the contract.[29]

[20] *London and South American Investment Trust v British Tobacco (Australia)* [1927] 1 Ch 107, 119.

[21] *In the Goods of Ewing* (1881) 6 PD 19, 23.

[22] *Boyd v A-G of British Columbia* (1917) 54 SCR 532.

[23] *IRC v Muller & Co's Margarine Ltd* [1901] AC 217.

[24] *Sutherland v Administrator of German Property* [1934] 1 KB 423; *Lorentzen v Lydden & Co Ltd* [1942] 2 KB 202.

[25] *In the Goods of Ewing* (n 21) 23; *Minister of National Revenue v Fitzgerald* [1949] SCR 453.

[26] *Re Berchtold* (n 1); *Philipson-Stow v IRC* [1961] AC 727, 762.

[27] *Re Smyth* [1898] 1 Ch 89; *Commissioner of Stamp Duties (Queensland) v Livingston* [1965] AC 694.

[28] *British South Africa Co v Companhia de Moçambique* [1893] AC 602; *Ip Cheung Kwok v Yip Chi Keung Allen* [1994] 1 HKC 676 [11]. See ch 10, s II.A.

[29] The common law rule in *Bank of Africa Ltd v Cohen* [1909] 2 Ch 129 (that *lex situs* governs the capacity to enter into a contract of transfer of immovable property) has been widely criticised: see, eg Lord Collins of Mapesbury and Jonathan Harris (gen eds), *Dicey, Morris and Collins on the Conflict of Laws*, 16th edn (Sweet & Maxwell, 2022), paras 24-073–24-077 and 24E-087–24-088.

IV. Movable Property

The choice of law for the transfer of proprietary rights in a movable is the law of the place where the movable is situated (*lex situs*).[30] By a similar token, the acquisition and transfer of beneficial ownership in the shares of a company is determined by the *lex situs*, that is, the law of the place where the company is incorporated.[31] The *lex situs* governs issues including capacity to transfer or take transfer, how title is to pass and the effect of the transfer. It might be that transfers of proprietary rights in a movable under the *leges situs* at different time intervals are contrary to one another. Nevertheless, proprietary rights acquired under the *lex situs* at the time of the last dealing or event prevail over those under any earlier *leges situs*. So, if an overriding title to the goods is obtained under the new *lex situs* despite any defect in title of the transferor, then title is transferred.[32] The earlier *leges situs* are only relevant if the validity of the transfer under the new *lex situs* requires looking into the title of the transferor before the change in *situs*. This would, however, be subject to the exception of public policy.[33]

The validity of a transfer of property is governed by the same governing law as the method or instrument in which the transfer of property arises. The validity of an assignment of a chose in action depends on the governing law of the method or instrument by which the assignment was effected. For example, if the assignment was by contract, the validity of the assignment would depend on the proper law of the contract between the assignor and the assignee.[34]

For movable property in transit, it may be difficult to determine *situs*. In such situations, the proper law of the relevant contract or transaction will govern whether a proprietary interest in the movable is transferred. But the validity of the transfer and its effect will be governed by the law of the country in which the movable was at the time of the purported transfer of proprietary interest.[35]

For cryptoassets (assuming that they can be treated as property),[36] it is arguable that the *lex situs* is the law of the place where the person who owns the same, that is, who has the encryption key which gives access to the cryptoasset, is domiciled.[37]

[30] *Tripole Trading Ltd* (n 19) [86]; *Hsu Ching Fang v Ng Chor Kuen* [2023] HKCFI 725 [62].

[31] ibid.

[32] This may be by way of exceptions to the *nemo dat* rule, such as those contained in ss 23 (sale by person not owner), 24 (market overt), 25 (sale under voidable title) and 27 (seller or buyer in possession after sale) of the Sale of Goods Ordinance (Cap 26). For example, in *Winkworth v Christie, Manson and Woods Ltd* [1980] Ch 496, the Italian purchaser received a good title to the goods situated in Italy through a sale conducted in Italy under Italian law, where sale by a thief to a bona fide purchaser passed a good title. The preceding theft in England and the '*nemo dat quod non habet*' principle which would be applicable under English law were irrelevant.

[33] For example, the exception would apply if the buyer purchased it in bad faith, knowing that the goods were stolen, to acquire good title. In *Winkworth* (n 32), this was considered as a potential exception, but such a view was criticised in *Glencore International AG v Metro Trading Inc* [2001] 1 All ER (Comm) 1031.

[34] See, eg *Macmillan Inc v Bishopsgate Investment Trust plc (No 3)* [1996] 1 WLR 387, applied in Hong Kong in *First Laser Ltd v Fujian Enterprises (Holdings) Co Ltd* [2011] 2 HKLRD 45 [49]; *Chen Lingxia v 中國金谷國際信託有限責任公司* [2021] HKCFI 982 [69], [83].

[35] In *Dornoch* (n 3), the law of the *situs* when the goods came to rest (in Thailand) was applied, but not the law of the ship's place of registration.

[36] See, eg *AA v Persons Unknown* [2019] EWHC 3556 (Comm), [2020] 4 WLR 35 [55]–[61]; *Re Gatecoin Ltd (in liq)* [2023] 2 HKLRD 1079, [2023] HKCFI 914 [45]–[59]. See also Michael Bridge et al, *The Law of Personal Property*, 3rd edn (Sweet & Maxwell, 2022), ch 8; Law Commission, *Digital Assets: Final Report* (Law Com No 412, 2023); Robert Stevens, 'Crypto Is Not Property' (2023) 139 *LQR* 615–28; Law Commission, *Digital Assets as Personal Property: Supplemental Report and Draft Bill* (Law Com No 416, 2024).

[37] *Osbourne v Persons Unknown Category A* [2023] EWHC 39 (KB). See also Andrew Dickinson, 'Cryptocurrencies and the Conflict of Laws' in David Fox and Sarah Green (eds), *Cryptocurrencies in Public and Private Law* (Oxford

The validity of a gift (consisting of movable property) between living persons or as a *donatio mortis causa* is governed by the *lex situs* of each movable property respectively.[38]

V. Equitable Interests in Property

The choice of law rules governing equitable interests in property depend on the type of claim asserted. If the issue concerns whether the interest of property is legal or equitable, the choice of law rules for property apply.[39] If the issue is whether the defendant bears an obligation to transfer property to the claimant, the source of the obligation determines the choice of law rules to be applied.[40]

The *lex situs* might affect the enforceability of the obligation related to the property.[41] An equitable interest in property is held to be extinguished upon transfer to a person who is present in a jurisdiction which does not recognise equitable interests. For this reason, the claim for knowing receipt of trust property in the English case of *Byers v Saudi National Bank* failed.[42] As the equitable proprietary interest in the property is extinguished, it could not have been passed on to the defendant. Therefore, it fails to fulfil the requirement of 'having a continuing equitable proprietary interest in the property', which is necessary to establish a claim for knowing receipt.[43] No subsequent Hong Kong or English authorities have discussed the impact of *Byers*. However, it seems that the case will have an impact on claims for knowing receipt of trust property (as in *Byers*) and the argument and status of a bona fide purchaser for value without notice.

VI. Expropriation

Expropriations and similar exercises of state power which affect movable or immovable property are governed by *lex situs*. This *lex situs* rule extends to non-nationals' property within the expropriating state's territory at the time of a decree of expropriation.[44] For instance, a law which affects private proprietary rights in property in a foreign state will be recognised by the forum as valid if the relevant property was in the foreign state at the time when the law was passed.[45] The rule is justified as states are generally empowered to legislate

University Press, 2019) 93–137. For cryptosecurities, see Maisie Ooi, 'Choice of Law in the Shifting Sands of Securities Trading' in Andrew Dickinson et al (eds), *A Conflict of Laws Companion: Essays in Honour of Adrian Briggs* (Oxford University Press, 2021) 199–224.

[38] *Anning v Anning* (1907) 4 CLR 1049; *Re Craven's Estate (No 1)* [1937] Ch 423.

[39] *Tripole Trading Ltd* (n 19) [86]; *Xiamen Xinjingdi Group Co Ltd v Eton Properties Ltd* (2020) 23 HKCFAR 348, [2020] HKCFA 32 [175].

[40] For example, if specific performance is sought based on a contractual agreement, the source of the obligation will be one of contract. See also *Luxe Holding Ltd v Midland Resources Holdings Ltd* [2010] EWHC 1908 (Ch) [28]–[44]; *Perry, Tamar v Esculier, Bonnet Servane Michele Thais* [2022] 4 SLR 243.

[41] *Akers v Samba Financial Group* [2017] UKSC 6, [2017] AC 424 [20]–[21], [28] and [48]; *Byers v Saudi National Bank* [2023] UKSC 51, [2024] AC 1191.

[42] *Byers* (n 41).

[43] ibid. See also *Sung Chung Kwun v Addchance Holdings Ltd* [2022] HKCFI 1799 [22].

[44] *Re Helbert Wagg & Co Ltd* (n 7); *cf The Rose Mary* [1953] 1 WLR 246.

[45] *Aksionairnoye Obschestvo AM Luther v James Sagor & Co* [1921] 3 KB 532; *Princess Paley Olga v Weisz* [1929] 1 KB 718. See also *Brokaw v Seatrain UK Ltd* [1971] 2 QB 476.

in respect of property within their territory, and therefore such acts should be recognised as valid by other states.[46] Therefore, despite there being a potential public policy objection,[47] comity will severely limit its application. The recognition of expropriation is generally not seen as an indirect enforcement of foreign public law, as the expropriatory law is seen as part of the *lex situs*.[48]

In summary, the rule requires three questions to be answered:

(i) whether the property was situated in a foreign state when the latter passed its expropriatory law;
(ii) whether the expropriatory law affected properties purported to affect title to that property; and
(iii) whether the foreign state is one which the Hong Kong courts can recognise.

Questions (i) and (ii) are straightforward. Question (i) merely identifies the location of the relevant property. Question (ii) construes the scope and impact of the foreign expropriatory law.[49]

Question (iii) can be problematic. In *Chen Li Hung v Ting Lei Miao*,[50] the Court of Final Appeal recognised the rights of trustees appointed by the Taiwanese court to recover the bankrupt's assets in Hong Kong. The Court distinguished between de facto and de jure control of a government. It ruled that an order by the Taiwanese government could be recognised if: (i) the order dealt with the purely private rights and acts of everyday occurrence or merely perfunctory acts of administration; (ii) recognition of the Taiwanese order was in the interest of justice and not against Hong Kong's public policy; and (iii) recognising and giving effect would not be inimical to the PRC's interest.

The distinction between de facto and de jure control can lead to competing claims by rival governments. In *Luther v Sagor*,[51] two governments claimed to be the Russian government, one de jure and the other de facto. The English Court of Appeal found that each had competence only within the territory under their respective control. This finding would consequently affect whether the Hong Kong court will recognise one or other government's legislative acts. When determining whether a government is recognised for the purpose of expropriation in private international law, the court will consider: (i) whether the government was the constitutionally appointed government; (ii) the degree, nature and stability of its administrative control over the relevant territory; (iii) whether the Hong Kong government has had dealings with that foreign government and nature thereof; and (iv) the extent of the government's recognition internationally.[52]

[46] *Re Helbert Wagg & Co Ltd* (n 7) 344–45.
[47] *Williams & Humbert Ltd v W&H Trade Marks (Jersey) Ltd* [1986] AC 368, 428.
[48] ibid.
[49] This involves an interpretation of the policy or law, and the common law courts tend not to construe it in a manner which gives the policy or law an extraterritorial effect, see *Lecouturier v Rey* [1910] AC 262; *The Jupiter (No 3)* [1927] P 122, 145; *Re Russian Bank for Foreign Trade* [1933] Ch 745, 767. See also *A-G of New Zealand v Ortiz* [1984] AC 1; *Kuwait Airways Corp v Iraqi Airways Co (Nos 4 and 5)* [2002] UKHL 19, [2002] 2 AC 883.
[50] *Chen Li Hung v Ting Lei Miao* (2000) 3 HKCFAR 9.
[51] *Aksionairnoye Obschestvo AM Luther* (n 45).
[52] *Republic of Somalia v Woodhouse Drake and Carey (Suisse) SA* [1993] QB 54.

As an exception to the *lex situs* rule, it seems that whether a discharge of a debt by garnishment or seizure should be recognised by the forum should be governed by the proper law of the debt but not the *lex situs*.[53]

When intangibles[54] are expropriated or confiscated under the *lex situs*, the Hong Kong courts will likely: (i) recognise the compulsory acquisition legislation of the foreign state without reference to the merits of that law; and (ii) acknowledge the change of title to property under the control of the foreign state and the consequences of that change in title.[55]

VII. Succession to Property

A. Wills

Sections 24–29 of the Wills Ordinance (Cap 30) provide a statutory regime in relation to the choice of law in relation to wills. The provisions implemented the 1961 HCCH Convention on the Conflicts of Laws Relating to the Form of Testamentary Dispositions (the Hague Form of Wills Convention). Section 24 stipulates the key principle as to the formal validity of a will:

> **24. General rule as to formal validity**
>
> A will shall be treated as properly executed if its execution conformed to the internal law in force in the territory where it was executed, or in the territory where, at the time of its execution or of the testator's death, he was domiciled or had his habitual residence, or in a state of which, at either of those times, he was a national.

Sections 25 contains additional rules on wills executed on board a vessel or aircraft, wills that dispose of immovable property (for which compliance with the *lex situs* will suffice),[56] wills which revoke earlier wills, and wills which exercise powers of appointment.

The essential validity and personal capacity to execute wills is governed:

(i) in the case of movable property, by the law of the testator's domicile;[57] and
(ii) in the case of immovable property, by the *lex situs*.

A will is construed by the law chosen by the testator[58] or, absent such choice, according to the law of the testator's domicile at the time of execution.[59] This applies both to movable and

[53] *Société Eram Shipping Co Ltd v Hong Kong and Shanghai Banking Corp Ltd* [2003] UKHL 30, [2004] 1 AC 260; *WestLB AG v Philippine National Bank* [2012] 4 SLR 894 [96]–[101]; *The Republic of the Philippines v Maler Foundation* [2014] 1 SLR 1389 [90]–[92].

[54] For instance, shares of a company with a *situs* in the place of the company's incorporation. See n 19 above.

[55] *Williams & Humbert Ltd* (n 47).

[56] See also *Vidhya Nativitat v Vitoon Nativivat* [2013] 4 HKLRD 340 [7].

[57] It was suggested that, in consistency with the traditional leaning in common law in favour of testamentary validity, a testator has capacity and a will is valid under the law of the testator's domicile either at the time of execution or at the time of death: Martin Davies et al, *Nygh's Conflict of Laws in Australia*, 10th edn (LexisNexis, 2020) para 38.09. That is also consistent with the approach in Wills Ordinance (Cap 30), s 24 regarding formal validity.

[58] The fact that the testator made a will in the form and language appropriate to another country is not sufficient as a choice: *Re Cunnington* [1924] 1 Ch 68.

[59] *Re Lungley* [1965] SASR 313; *Re Blyth* [1997] 2 Qd R 567.

immovable property, but the latter is subject to the overriding requirement that it must in no way conflict with the law of the country in which the immovable property is situated.[60] The relevant timing ('at the time of execution') is consistent with section 27 of the Wills Ordinance, which states that the construction of a will 'shall not be altered by reason of any change in the testator's domicile after the execution of the will'. Therefore, the effectiveness of a revocation of a will by marriage, divorce or otherwise,[61] is likely to be governed by the law of the testator's domicile at the time of revocation.[62] Revocation of a will by a subsequent will depends on the validity of that subsequent will.

The 1973 Washington Convention Providing a Uniform Law on the Form of an International Will was enacted into Hong Kong law in 1995 by sections 23D and 23E of the Wills Ordinance, but has never come into effect. The insertion was subsequently repealed by the Statute Law (Miscellaneous Provisions) Ordinance 2024.

The rules governing the formal and essential validity of a will also govern the validity of gifts in a will.[63]

B. Intestacy

Intestate succession is governed:

(i) in the case of movable property, by the law of the deceased's domicile at death;[64] and
(ii) in the case of immovable property, by the *lex situs*.[65]

Section 8A of the Intestates' Estates Ordinance (Cap 73) takes into account the value of any beneficial interests in the intestate's estate acquired by the intestate's husband or wife under any foreign law of intestacy or of partial intestacy, and accordingly diminishes the value of interests obtained under the Ordinance.

C. Financial Provision

The Inheritance (Provision for Family and Dependants) Ordinance (Cap 481) provides that if the deceased died either domiciled in Hong Kong or having been ordinarily resident in Hong Kong at any time in the three years immediately preceding his death, the court may grant an order to make reasonable financial provision for certain family members or 'any person … who immediately before the death of the deceased was being maintained, either wholly or substantially, by the deceased'.[66] This application is based solely under Hong Kong law, and may be exercised regardless of whether the deceased died testate or (partially) intestate.

[60] *Philipson-Stow* (n 26) 761.
[61] For the position in Hong Kong, see Wills Ordinance (Cap 30), s 14.
[62] *Re Traversi's Estate* 64 NYS 2d 453 (1946).
[63] See, eg *Whicker v Hume* (1858) 7 HL Cas 124, 11 ER 50; *Municipality of Canterbury v Wyburn* [1895] AC 89; *Philipson-Stow* (n 26); *Re Blyth* (n 59).
[64] *Pipon v Pipon* (1744) Amb 25, 27 ER 14; *Bremer v Freeman* (1857) 10 Moo PC 306, 358, 14 ER 508, 527.
[65] *Re Ralston* [1906] VLR 689; *Re Collens* [1986] Ch 505.
[66] Inheritance (Provision for Family and Dependants) Ordinance (Cap 481), s 3.

D. Administration of Estates

Under Hong Kong law, personal representatives of deceased persons are of two types: executors and administrators. An executor is appointed by will and gains title as soon as the testator dies. An executor has full ownership of the estate's property without distinction between legal and equitable interests, holding it for the purpose of carrying out the functions and duties of administration.[67] In contrast, an administrator acquires title only when granted letters of administration, and can only institute an action after a grant is obtained.[68]

A personal representative's powers and duties are governed by the law from which the personal representative derives his or her office and authority, but not by the law of the deceased person's domicile.[69] As such, an executor is entitled to bring proceedings in Hong Kong at once after the deceased's death by virtue of being named as executrix, subject to the production of probate by the time the matter reaches trial; it does not matter that the position was different under foreign law.[70] Other than that situation, a personal representative appointed under foreign law is not entitled to sue in that capacity in a Hong Kong court without first obtaining a Hong Kong grant of probate or letters of administration. The foreign personal representative may take advantage of rule 29 of the Non-contentious Probate Rules (Cap 10A) to apply for a Hong Kong grant.[71]

In the administration of the Hong Kong estate of a deceased domiciled abroad, foreign creditors are entitled to dividends *pari passu* with local creditors.[72]

[67] *Livingston* (n 27).
[68] *Chetty v Chetty* [1916] 1 AC 603; *Jogie v Sealy* [2022] UKPC 32.
[69] *Re Lorillard* [1922] 2 Ch 638, 645–46; *Viegas v Cutrale* [2024] EWCA Civ 1122 [100]–[114].
[70] *Chetty* (n 68); *Jennison v Jennison* [2022] EWCA Civ 1682, [2023] Ch 225.
[71] See also ch 10, s II.C.
[72] See, eg *Re Kloebe, Kannreuther v Geiselbrecht* (1884) 28 Ch D 175.

18

Intellectual Property Law

This chapter focuses on private international law issues that may arise from disputes over intellectual property rights (IPRs).[1] Readers are invited to consult other texts for the intellectual property law and practice in Hong Kong.[2] For jurisdictional issues in intellectual property law, see chapter ten, section IV.

I. Introduction

Intellectual property (IP) refers to creations of the mind, such as inventions, literary and artistic work, designs, symbols, names and images used in commerce.[3] IP is often divided into two categories: (i) industrial property; and (ii) copyright and related rights. Industrial property includes patents for inventions, industrial designs, trademarks and geographical indications. Copyright includes literary, artistic and scientific works, and related rights include the right to reproduce, distribute and perform such works.

IPRs ensure that those who have created products out of their intellect have a mechanism to protect those products. The protection of IPRs through international law dates back to the promulgation of the 1883 Paris Convention for the Protection of Industrial Property and the 1886 Berne Convention for the Protection of Literary and Artistic Works.

The orthodox position is that IPRs are generally strictly territorial in nature. As such, while the breach or infringement of a Hong Kong IPR will certainly give rise to an actionable claim in the Hong Kong court, the breach or infringement of a foreign IPR may give rise to jurisdiction and choice of law problems in Hong Kong. However, it is also observed that the traditional principle of territoriality has been challenged by technological developments, the greater mobility of goods and services, and an increased integration of markets. That has become particularly apparent in the jurisdiction context since the shifting away from the Moçambique rule in relation to foreign IPRs.[4] For the purposes of choice of law, IPRs are movable property, situated in the jurisdiction of its creation.

Parties will need to determine which law is to be applied to questions of registration, validity and infringement of IPRs, as well as the applicable law to any associated contracts.

[1] See also Paul LC Torremans, *Intellectual Property and Private International Law*, 3rd edn (Oxford University Press, 2024).

[2] See, eg Kenny Wong and Alice Lee, *Intellectual Property Law and Practice in Hong Kong*, 2nd edn (Sweet & Maxwell, 2017); Douglas Clark, *Intellectual Property in Hong Kong*, 3rd edn (LexisNexis, 2024).

[3] WIPO, 'About IP', www.wipo.int/about-ip/en/.

[4] See ch 10, s IV.

If an IPR is invalid, it cannot be infringed. As IPRs are territorial, their registration and validity are typically determined by the domestic court. Possible applicable laws would be:

(i) the *lex fori*;
(ii) the *lex loci protectionis*, that is, the law of the place in which the protection is claimed; and
(iii) the *lex originis*, that is, the law of the place where the IPR originated.

As there are very few Hong Kong cases on choice of law in cross-border IP matters, it is suggested that the International Law Association's *Guidelines on Intellectual Property and Private International Law* (2021) (the Kyoto Guidelines) may be used as a framework on issues of jurisdiction and applicable law in international IP matters, principally copyright, trademarks, patents, registered designs and trade secrets.[5] The Kyoto Guidelines are model provisions to promote a more efficient resolution of cross-border IP disputes and provide a blueprint for legislative initiatives. Guideline 19 suggests that, generally, the *lex loci protectionis* should be applied.

Sections II–VII provides a brief overview of various IPRs and how they are protected in Hong Kong. Section VIII then explains the current approach of referring to the *lex loci protectionis* and proposes a framework under which choice of law can be conducted.

II. Copyright

In Hong Kong, the main legislation on copyright is the Copyright Ordinance (Cap 528).[6] Copyright subsists in original literary, dramatic, musical or artistic works,[7] sound recordings, films, broadcasts or cable programmes[8] and the typographical arrangement of published editions.[9] The work must be recorded, in writing or otherwise,[10] and must fall within a specific description of work under sections 4–10 of the Ordinance. The duration of copyright varies slightly under sections 17–21 of the Ordinance among different descriptions of work. Copyright cannot be registered in Hong Kong and is considered as transmissible personal or movable property.[11]

Copyright in Hong Kong comprises both economic rights and moral rights. Economic rights include the rights to control the reproduction and distribution of the work, which are set out in Part II, Division II of the Ordinance, and the exceptions are set out in Part II, Division III of the Ordinance. Moral rights include the rights to be acknowledged as the author of a work and to prevent the work from being altered in a way that might damage the creator's reputation, which are set in Part II, Division IV of the Ordinance.

[5] ILA Committee on Intellectual Property and Private International Law, 'International Law Association's Guidelines on Intellectual Property and Private International Law' (2021) 12(1) *Journal of Intellectual Property, Information Technology and E-Commerce Law* 1.
[6] See also the Prevention of Copyright Piracy Ordinance (Cap 544).
[7] Copyright Ordinance (Cap 528), s 2(1)(a).
[8] ibid s 2(1)(b).
[9] ibid s 2(1)(c).
[10] ibid s 4(2).
[11] ibid s 101(1).

Copyright (whether present or future) may be transmissible by assignment, by testamentary disposition or by operation of law, as personal or moveable property, as long as the assignment is in writing and signed by or on behalf of the assignor.[12] The assignment may be partial, in terms of both its scope and its duration.[13] A copyright owner may also grant a licence to authorise a licensee to exercise a right which would otherwise be exercisable exclusively by the copyright owner. A licence is binding on every successor in title to his interest in the copyright, except a purchaser in good faith for valuable consideration and without notice (actual or constructive) of the licence or a person deriving title from such a purchaser.[14] Moral rights are not assignable,[15] and are only transmitted upon the person's death.[16]

III. Trademarks

In Hong Kong, the main legislation on trademarks is the Trade Marks Ordinance (Cap 559).[17] Trademarks is most commonly protected by registration in Hong Kong under the Ordinance. A registered trademark is a property right obtained by the registration of the trademark under the Ordinance, and the owner of a registered trademark has the rights and is entitled to the remedies provided by the Ordinance.[18]

A trademark is any sign capable of distinguishing the goods or services of one undertaking from those of another and of being represented graphically.[19] A trademark may consist of words (including personal names), indications, designs, letters, characters, numerals, figurative elements, colours, sounds, smells, the shape of goods or their packaging, or any combination of such signs.[20] A trademark must also have some distinctive character to be registered.[21] The other absolute and relative grounds for refusal of registration are set out in sections 11 and 12 of the Ordinance. The duration of registration in Hong Kong is 10 years.[22] Registration can be renewed subject to payment of the prescribed renewal fee.[23] Therefore, a trademark can be protected indefinitely in practice.

A registered trademark is infringed by acts specified in section 18 (infringement of registered trademark) of the Ordinance, but are subject to the exceptions specified in sections 19 (exceptions to infringement), 20 (exhaustion of rights conferred by registered trademark) and 21 (use in advertising, etc) of the Ordinance. An infringement of a registered trademark is actionable by the owner of the trademark via infringement proceedings under Part III of the Ordinance.

[12] ibid ss 101(1), 101(3) and 102(1).
[13] ibid s 101(2).
[14] ibid ss 101(4) and 102(3).
[15] ibid s 105.
[16] ibid s 106.
[17] See also the Trade Descriptions Ordinance (Cap 362).
[18] Trade Marks Ordinance (Cap 559), s 10.
[19] ibid s 3(1).
[20] ibid s 3(2).
[21] ibid s 11(1)(b).
[22] ibid s 49.
[23] ibid s 50.

Generally, trademarks registered in a state are independent of those registered in other states.[24] The Madrid System for the International Registration of Trademarks (consisting of the Madrid Agreement Concerning the International Registration of Marks and the Madrid Protocol) administered by the World Intellectual Property Organization (WIPO) provides for international registration and protection of trademarks for each of the designated contracting parties. The implementation of the Madrid Protocol is facilitated by Part XA of the Ordinance, and full implementation is expected in the near future.

Alternatively, a trademark may be protected in common law by the tort of passing off in the Hong Kong courts. To succeed, a party must prove

> (1) a misrepresentation (2) made by a trader in the course of trade, (3) to prospective customers of his or ultimate consumers of goods or services supplied by him, (4) which is calculated to injure the business or goodwill of another trader (in the sense that this is a reasonably foreseeable consequence) and (5) which causes actual damage to a business or goodwill of the trader by whom the action is brought or (in a *quia timet* action) will probably do so.[25]

IV. Patents

In Hong Kong, the main legislation on patents is the Patents Ordinance (Cap 514). An invention is patentable if it is new, involves an inventive step and is susceptible of industrial application.[26] An invention does not include: (i) a discovery, scientific theory or mathematical method; (ii) an aesthetic creation; (iii) a scheme, rule or method for performing a mental act, playing a game or doing business, or a program for a computer; or (iv) a presentation of information.[27] Moreover, a plant or animal variety, or an essentially biological process for the production of plants or animals (other than a microbiological process or its products), is not patentable.[28] A right to a patent generally belongs to the inventor or the inventor's successor in title.[29]

The Hong Kong patent regime provides for three kinds of patent application:

1. A Standard Patents by Re-registration (Standard Patent (R)) application. The registration is effective for a 20-year period from the deemed date of filing of the application. It is based on the pre-existing registration of a patent by the China National Intellectual Property Administration, the European Patent Office or the UK Intellectual Property Office.[30] Only a formality examination is required for the application.[31]
2. A Standard Patents by Original Grant (Standard Patent (O)) application. The registration is effective for a 20-year period from the deemed date of filing of the application. The application is by direct filing locally. The application is subject to a formality examination[32] and a substantive examination by the Registrar.[33]

[24] 1883 Paris Convention for the Protection of Industrial Property, Art 6.
[25] *Erven Warnink Besloten Vennootschap v J Townend & Sons (Hull) Ltd* [1979] AC 731, 742.
[26] Patents Ordinance (Cap 514), s 9A(1). See also ss 9B, 9C and 9D.
[27] ibid s 9A(2).
[28] ibid s 9A(6).
[29] ibid s 9E.
[30] These patent offices are designated by the Chief Executive in Council: ibid s 8.
[31] ibid s 11.
[32] ibid Pt 2.
[33] ibid Pt 3.

3. A short-term patent application. The registration is effective for an eight-year period from the deemed date of filing of the application. The application can be done locally. Although the application will only go through a formality examination, a substantive examination must be made before a registration is enforced.[34]

A patent proprietor may prevent the direct or indirect use of the invention.[35] Civil proceedings may be brought in respect of such acts of infringement.[36] Any patent or application for a patent is personal property (without being a thing in action), and any patent or any such application and rights in or under it may be transferred, created or granted.[37]

Many countries have developed regional patent systems to reduce the costs of dealing with different national legal systems. An example is the African Regional Intellectual Property Organization. Under most of these systems, applicants may request protection for an invention in one or more countries in the group. Each country decides whether to offer patent protection within its borders after an application has been submitted. WIPO administers the Patent Cooperation Treaty System, an international system that allows applicants to request protection under the Patent Cooperation Treaty in as many signatory states as they wish through a single application.

V. Registered Industrial Designs

In Hong Kong, the main legislation on registered industrial designs is the Registered Designs Ordinance (Cap 522). A design which is new may be registered when applied by the person claiming to be the owner.[38] 'Design' refers to features of the shape, configuration, pattern or ornamentation of an article produced by an industrial process; in a finished product, these features appeal to (and are judged by) the eye.[39] However, a method or principle of construction, and features of shape or configuration of an article which are dictated solely by the function of an article or are dependent upon the appearance of an another product of which the article is an integral part, would not be considered 'design'.[40]

Grounds for refusal of registration would include the following:

1. The design is not novel, but is similar to a previously registered or published design, save only for immaterial details.[41]
2. The article's appearance is immaterial, if (for instance) aesthetic considerations are not normally taken into account by persons acquiring articles of that description.[42]
3. The design contravenes public order or morality.[43]

[34] ibid s 115.
[35] ibid ss 73, 74 and 75.
[36] ibid Pt 11.
[37] ibid s 50.
[38] Registered Designs Ordinance (Cap 522), s 5.
[39] ibid s 2(1).
[40] ibid.
[41] ibid s 5(2).
[42] ibid s 6.
[43] ibid s 7.

4. The registration is for computer programs, layout designs and some designs for articles of a primarily literary or artistic character.[44]
5. The design consists of or contains the national or a regional flag or emblem.[45]

In Hong Kong, the initial registration protects a design for five years. The period may be extended by another five years at a time, subject to a renewal fee. Protection will not exceed a total of 25 years from the filing date of the application for registration.[46] WIPO administers the Hague System (under the Hague Agreement Concerning the International Registration of Industrial Designs), where applicants can file a single application for the registration of up to 100 designs in as many signatory states as they choose.

As summarised above, trademarks, patents and design rights are conferred by registration, which is a near-universal global practice. As registration inevitably involves the engagement of public authorities, it is submitted that when foreign elements are involved, comity should be respected in the absence of a good reason to the contrary.

VI. Trade Secrets

A party who has received information in confidence should not take unfair advantage of the information or profit from its wrongful use or publication. Therefore, if a defendant is proved to have used confidential information, directly or indirectly obtained from a plaintiff without his consent, express or implied, the defendant will be guilty of an infringement of the plaintiff's rights.[47]

In Hong Kong, there is no statutory regime for the protection of confidential information or trade secrets.[48] Trade secrets may be protected under common law by a breach of confidence in tort or (if appropriate) a breach in contract.[49] The three elements in an action of breach of confidence are:[50]

(i) the information itself must have the necessary quality of confidence about it;
(ii) that information must have been imparted in circumstances importing an obligation of confidence; and
(iii) there must be an unauthorised use of that information to the detriment of the party communicating it.

VII. Other Intellectual Property Rights in Hong Kong

Other forms of IPRs protected in Hong Kong concern integrated circuits and plant varieties, as set out in the Layout-design (Topography) of Integrated Circuits Ordinance (Cap 445)

[44] ibid s 8.
[45] ibid s 8A.
[46] ibid s 28.
[47] *Fraser v Thames Television Ltd* [1984] 1 QB 44, 48.
[48] See the definition in *Thomas Marshall (Exports) Ltd v Guinle* [1979] Ch 227, 248.
[49] In the context of a contract of employment, see, eg *Faccenda Chicken Ltd v Fowler* [1987] Ch 117.
[50] *Coco v AN Clark (Engineers) Ltd* [1969] RPC 41, 47.

and the Plant Varieties Protection Ordinance (Cap 490) respectively. There is no formal protection in Hong Kong for geographical indications.

VIII. Choice of Law

Actions relating to IPRs can be categorised as contractual, proprietary or tortious in nature. In contractual actions relating to trademarks, patents and designs, the choice of law rules applicable to contracts as set out in chapter fifteen, section I will govern the contract generally. In tortious actions, the choice of law rules discussed in chapter fifteen, section III will apply, namely the double actionability rule. However, since IPRs are generally strictly territorial in nature, a foreign infringement of an IPR can never satisfy the first limb of the double actionability rule, namely that the foreign infringement is actionable as a tort under the *lex fori*. It is therefore necessary to engage with the flexible exception of the double actionability rule in *Red Sea Insurance Co Ltd v Bouygues SA*,[51] namely that the law of the place which has a strong connection with the infringement may be applied. When the harm caused by an infringement occurs in several jurisdictions, the court might consider whether some other law should be applied. For instance, the law of the parties' habitual residence or principal place of business, or of the place where substantial activities were carried out in furtherance of the infringement, might be considered.[52] It seems that this displacement will be relatively easy to succeed as the court will have little difficulty in concluding that the infringement is not connected with the *lex fori* and hence allow the party to rely exclusively on the *lex loci delicti*.[53]

On proprietary issues, as IPRs in respect of foreign trademarks, patents and designs typically arise by registration in foreign states, it is a question of choice of law in property, and they are likely to be subject to the law of the place where the right is created and protected. Such proprietary issues (including the validity of foreign IPRs) may therefore not be justiciable in Hong Kong. However, IPRs not protected by way of registration are not subject to the territorial restriction and such difficulties generally do not arise.[54] In relation to the ownership and transferability of the copyright, the law of the creator's 'principal home' or the proper law of the contract where the copyrighted work was created under a contractual arrangement can be applied.[55] For issues related to the use of IPR as a security right, the UNCITRAL Model Law on Secured Transactions (2016) proposes the application of the *lex loci protectionis* to govern the creation, effectiveness against the third party and priority of a security right in IP.[56]

[51] *Red Sea Insurance Co Ltd v Bouygues SA* [1995] 1 AC 190.

[52] ILA Committee on Intellectual Property and Private International Law (n 5) 58–59.

[53] *Pearce v Ove Arup Partnership Ltd* [2000] Ch 403, 442–44. The double actionability rule and the exception were applied in *Pearce* despite the abolition of the rule in the UK by the Private International Law (Miscellaneous Provisions) Act 1995 (UK), s 10, as the plaintiff's claim concerned events occurring before 1996.

[54] However, this is still subject to proof of any elements which may be territorial in nature. For example, in the tort of passing off, goodwill is territorial in nature; the claimant has no claim under the *lex fori* if it has no goodwill in the forum: *Starbucks (HK) Ltd v British Sky Broadcasting Group plc* [2015] UKSC 31, [2015] 1 WLR 2628.

[55] Annabelle Bennett and Sam Granata, *When Private International Law Meets Intellectual Property Law: A Guide for Judges* (WIPO, 2019) 53–54.

[56] UNCITRAL Model Law on Secured Transactions, Art 99(1).

The Kyoto Guidelines recommend certain choice of law rules for each of the three categories of claim just canvassed. It is submitted that these rules are sensible and should be applicable to a future cross-border IP dispute litigated in Hong Kong.

Guideline 19 suggests that the law of the state in which protection is sought should apply to questions of the existence, validity, registration, duration, transferability and scope of an IPR. Guideline 20 deals with the initial ownership and allocation of IPRs. In respect of contractual claims, Guideline 21 recognises that 'parties may choose the law governing their contractual relationship'. Guideline 22 considers the general situation where no law is chosen in an IP-related contract. Guideline 23 focuses on employment contracts. Guideline 24 provides for the formal validity of IP-related contracts. Guideline 25 deals with tortious claims for the infringement of an IPR. Guideline 26 specifies the law applicable to ubiquitous or multi-state infringements. Guideline 27 stipulates rules on collective rights management in the field of copyright. Guideline 28 suggests that 'the application of the law determined under these Guidelines may be refused only to the extent that its effects would be manifestly contrary to the public policy of the forum'. Guideline 29 provides that 'nothing in these Guidelines shall restrict the application of the overriding mandatory provisions of the law of the forum'. Guideline 30 excludes *renvoi*, while Guideline 31 deals with the arbitrability of IPR disputes.

19

Family Law*

This chapter focuses on the current state and future development of international family law in Hong Kong, with the increasing number of family law cases in Hong Kong with an international element.[1] Readers are invited to consult other texts for family law and practice in Hong Kong.[2] Cross-border family law issues have been and will remain highly contested in Hong Kong for the foreseeable future, and there is much potential for the courts to develop a set of workable and consistent principles for these cases. For jurisdictional issues in family law, see chapter ten, section V. For recognition and enforcement issues in family law, including the recognition of decrees of marriage and matrimonial causes and other related orders and judgments, see chapter twenty-three, section VI.

I. Marriages

The validity of a marriage in the eyes of a Hong Kong court depends on demonstrating both the formal and the essential validity of the marriage. The governing law when determining formal validity and essential validity will not necessarily be Hong Kong law. As provided by section 20A(1) of the Matrimonial Causes Ordinance (Cap 179) (MCO), in accordance with the rules of private international law in Hong Kong, if any matter affecting the validity of a marriage falls to be determined by reference to the law of a place outside Hong Kong, then that foreign law shall determine the matter. It follows that a marriage might be declared invalid on foreign grounds of nullity unknown to Hong Kong law, subject to public policy concerns.[3] However, Hong Kong can only apply substantive foreign law, not the procedural laws of foreign jurisdictions.[4] The forum applies its own laws for procedural issues.

* Part of this chapter is derived from Wilson Lui, 'Hong Kong' in Anselmo Reyes, Wilson Lui and Kazuaki Nishioka (eds), *Choice of Law and Recognition in Asian Family Law* (Hart Publishing, 2023) 51–80.

[1] The term 'international family law' is not an official term, but is used here to refer to the law regulating families in Hong Kong which has an international element. The globalisation and international dimensions of family law are similarly observed in the groundbreaking text in Singapore by Debbie Ong, Judge of the Appellate Division and concurrently Presiding Judge of the Family Justice Courts in Singapore: Debbie Ong, *International Issues in Family Law in Singapore* (Academy Publishing, 2015).

[2] See, eg Philippa Hewitt and others (eds), *Family Law and Practice in Hong Kong* 3rd edn (Sweet & Maxwell, 2018); Keith Hotten and Dennis Ho, *Hotten and Ho: Family Law Practice and Procedure in Hong Kong* 4th edn (LexisNexis, 2021); Azan Marwah et al (eds), *Hong Kong Family Court Tables 2024–2025* (Authors, 2024).

[3] An example where public policy may intervene with the contended invalidity is if a foreign bar on marriage amounts to an infringement of human rights, such as grounds based on discrimination or criminal conviction.

[4] See, eg *Ogden v Ogden* [1908] P 64.

'Formal validity' refers to the formalities required to contract a marriage. They are matters regarded as necessary and sufficient conditions for a marriage to be considered valid according to the law of the place where the marriage was performed or entered into (the *lex loci celebrationis*).[5] The failure to follow the formalities of the *lex loci celebrationis* will render the marriage null, unless it can be characterised as a 'common law marriage'. Hong Kong recognises, to a limited extent, foreign 'common law marriages' which are entered into without a formal ceremony.[6]

The *lex loci celebrationis* determines whether the marriage is monogamous or polygamous.[7] A polygamous marriage permits the husband to take more than one wife during the subsistence of that marriage. Capacity to enter into a polygamous marriage is determined by the *lex domicilii* of each party.

'Essential validity' involves the parties' capacity to marry. Capacity to marry may depend on factors such as: the age of the spouses; consanguinity between spouses; the ability of the spouses to enter into a polygamous marriage; the ability of the spouses to enter into a same-sex relationship; and the spouses' consent to marriage.

The orthodox position in Hong Kong law on the choice of law for essential validity is that both parties must have the capacity to marry under their respective antenuptial domiciles (the *lex domicilii*). This dual domicile test has been accepted by the Hong Kong Court of Final Appeal.[8] Once domicile is determined under Hong Kong law by reference to the common law or (on or after 1 March 2009) the Domicile Ordinance (Cap 596),[9] the applicable law of that domicile must be applied. Alternatively, some cases have suggested that capacity should be determined by the law having the most real and substantial connection with the marriage.[10] While this might introduce vagueness and uncertainty into the law, it could also produce a more sensible result than the dual domicile test in certain cases. Whenever appropriate, the courts will seek to uphold the concept of marriage as a matter of public policy by adopting alternative ways to recognise particular marriages.[11] This chapter proceeds on the basis that the dual domicile test will apply in Hong Kong in determining the essential validity of marriage.

An exception to the dual domicile test is the rule in *Sottomayor v De Barros (No 2)*.[12] Under this exception, the validity of a marriage celebrated in Hong Kong between parties, one of whom has a Hong Kong domicile and the other a foreign domicile, is not affected by an incapacity which does not exist under the law of Hong Kong, even though the incapacity exists under the law of the foreign domicile. This exception has limited practical significance, as it will not apply if the marriage takes place outside Hong Kong or if both parties are domiciled in Hong Kong or both are domiciled outside Hong Kong. No Hong Kong case has applied the exception.

[5] See, eg ibid; *Berthiaume v Dastous* [1930] AC 79.
[6] See ch 23, s V.A.
[7] See, eg *Hussain v Hussain* [1983] Fam 26.
[8] ibid [40].
[9] See ch 4, s II.
[10] *Vervaeke v Smith* [1983] 1 AC 145; *Lawrence v Lawrence* [1985] Fam 106.
[11] *KC v City of Westminster Social and Community Services Dept* [2008] EWCA Civ 198, [2009] Fam 11 [74]. One other alternative would be the law of the place of the intended matrimonial home: see, eg *Radwan v Radwan (No 2)* [1972] 3 All ER 1026.
[12] *Sottomayor v De Barros (No 2)* [1874–80] All ER Rep 97.

One important problem in the choice of law regarding capacity to marry is age. The minimum age of marriage in Hong Kong is 16.[13] Other places may have different requirements. Applying the dual domicile test, it is possible for an underage marriage to be recognised in Hong Kong. For example, a marriage involving a girl aged 13 was recognised in the UK as her antenuptial domicile (Nigeria) permitted such a marriage.[14] The courts would be reluctant to declare such marriages void on grounds of public policy.[15] However, it is likely that Hong Kong has an overriding public policy which requires a marriage to be entered into with 'the free and full consent of the intending spouses'.[16] If a person is held to be too young to give informed consent to the marriage, the court may not recognise the marriage. The threshold to refuse recognition of a foreign proper marriage requires that the court, after '[exercising] common sense, good manners and a reasonable tolerance', finds the marriage to be 'so offensive to the conscience of the [Hong Kong] court'.[17] The public policy exception will thus be invoked only sparingly.

The dual domicile test applies to other requirements of capacity. For example, marriages within prohibited degrees of relationship are void on grounds of consanguinity as long as either party's antenuptial domicile treats such marriage as void.[18] As Hong Kong does not recognise polygamous marriages, concubinage or same-sex relationships, persons domiciled in Hong Kong cannot contract a valid marriage of these types.

Consent presents another problem. Under Hong Kong law, the court may declare a marriage voidable due to a lack of consent by reason of mistake, duress or unsoundness of mind.[19] It was suggested that the dual domicile test will apply in respect of a foreign marriage involving different domiciliary laws on consent.[20] However, if parties have different domiciles, the modern view suggests that the dual domicile rule would not apply. Instead, the applicable law should be that of the domicile of the party alleged to lack consent. A party who has fully consented under the law of that party's domicile should not evade a marriage by simply establishing the lack of consent by the other party under the law of that person's domicile.[21] The question should be whether the law of the other party's domicile will recognise the marriage as valid, despite a lack of consent by the other party.

We now turn to identify and define the various kinds of marriages available in Hong Kong. All marriages entered into in Hong Kong from 7 October 1971 – the appointed date of the Marriage Reform Ordinance (Cap 178) (MRO) – must be monogamous marriages contracted in accordance with the Marriage Ordinance (Cap 181) (MO).[22] However, other marriages celebrated in Hong Kong before the appointed day can be recognised in Hong Kong, including for the purposes of divorce.

[13] Marriage Ordinance (Cap 181), s 13. This is calculated by the Gregorian and not the traditional Chinese lunar calendar: Interpretation and General Clauses Ordinance (Cap 1), s 3.

[14] *Mohamed v Knott* [1969] 1 QB 1.

[15] ibid; *Cheni v Cheni* [1965] P 85.

[16] Hong Kong Bill of Rights, Art 19(3).

[17] *Cheni* (n 15). See also *KC* (n 11).

[18] See, eg *Re Paine* [1940] Ch 46. For the prohibited degrees of relationship in Hong Kong, see MO, Sch 5.

[19] MCO, s 20(2)(c). See also *Lui Ming Lok v Ng Im Fong Loretta* (2024) 27 HKCFAR 406, [2024] HKCFA 21.

[20] *Szechter v Szechter* [1970] 3 All ER 905.

[21] Lord Collins of Mapesbury and Jonathan Harris (gen eds), *Dicey, Morris and Collins on the Conflict of Laws*, 16th edn (Sweet & Maxwell, 2022) para 17-115.

[22] MRO, s 4.

The formation of a lawful marriage is now solely governed by the MO. The MO takes the paradigm form of marriage to be a Christian marriage. But the MO also recognises 'the civil equivalent of a Christian marriage', that is, 'a formal ceremony recognised by the law as involving the voluntary union for life of one man and one woman to the exclusion of all others'.[23] Hong Kong currently does not recognise local or foreign same-sex marriages, civil unions or civil partnerships.

There is no further specific formulation of a valid marriage in Hong Kong, except the requirement that no marriage should involve a person under the age of 16 years.[24] Section 27 of the MO lists situations of invalid marriage: (i) marriage between persons contrary to prohibitions of affinity; (ii) marriages not celebrated by a competent authority (that is, other than by the Registrar, a competent minister in a licensed place of worship or an authorised civil celebrant); (iii) marriages celebrated under a false name; (iv) marriages celebrated without the certificate of the Registrar or the grant of a special licence; and (v) marriages in which a party is under 16 years of age.

A striking feature of Hong Kong law is that it preserves the application of traditional Chinese laws, customs and usages (known as Ts'ing or Qing customary laws, named after the dynasty which ruled China until 1911).[25] These customary laws were preserved during the colonial period and continued after the return of sovereignty to the PRC on 1 July 1997.[26] Due to the complexity and variation of these laws and customs, they are often subject to factual disputes. These Chinese customary laws have featured prominently in family law cases involving issues of marriage, concubinage, adoption, succession and land.

The application of traditional Chinese law and custom might be characterised as a direct application of Hong Kong domestic law, rather than foreign law applied through the rules of private international law.[27] But Chinese customary laws only apply when all parties are Chinese persons with a Hong Kong antenuptial domicile.[28] The validity of these traditional institutions (such as a union of concubinage) has to be determined by the dual domicile rule, just as with foreign marriages.[29] More generally, when a legal issue is governed by the law of a relevant person's domicile, the Hong Kong court will consider whether, as part of the law of the domicile, a special personal law applies to that person on the ground of membership in a particular community, such as that defined by religion or ethnicity.

[23] MO, Long Title, s 40; *W v Registrar of Marriages* (2013) 16 HKCFAR 112 [63]. In *W*, the Court of Final Appeal expanded the definitions of 'man', 'woman', 'male' and 'female' in MO, s 40 and MCO, s 20(1)(b) to include post-operative transsexual persons who have gone through full sex reassignment surgery and have been issued with certificates that their genders have been changed: [123]–[125]. See also *Q v Commissioner of Registration* (2023) 26 HKCFAR 25, [2023] HKCFA 4, where the Court of Final Appeal granted a declaration that the policy requiring transgender persons to undergo full sex reassignment surgery as a necessary condition for amending the gender markers on their HKID cards is unconstitutional. This means those who undergo less extensive treatment may qualify to amend their gender markers (but are currently not qualified to marry under their assigned gender).

[24] MO, s 13. See n 13 above.

[25] *Ho Tsz Tsun v Ho Au Shi* (1915) 10 HKLR 69; *Wong Kam Ying v Man Chi Tai* [1967] HKLR 201; *Re Wong Choi Ho* [1969] HKLR 391. MRO, s 2 defines 'Chinese law and custom' to mean 'such of the laws and customs of China as would immediately prior to 5 April 1843 have been applicable to Chinese inhabitants of Hong Kong'.

[26] Basic Law, Art 8.

[27] *Suen Toi Lee v Yau Yee Ping* (2001) 4 HKCFAR 474 [34].

[28] ibid [38].

[29] ibid [39].

This is limited by public policy considerations (such as issues of discrimination on grounds of race or sex).[30]

Chinese customary marriages celebrated before 7 October 1971 will be recognised as valid under the MRO, which has implemented a registration regime for Chinese customary marriages and validated 'modern marriages'. Chinese customary marriages were celebrated in accordance with the traditions, customs, rites and ceremonies of the parties' families, and were generally seen as an alliance of two families. The parties to a customary marriage are the husband and the principal wife (*tsai*), regardless of whether the wife is a *kit fat* or a *tin fong* wife. It does not include a concubine (*tsip*).[31] The exact practices of a customary marriage are complex and elaborate, and take various forms in different parts of China. For instance, the *Book of Rites* (*Liji*) provided for three covenants and six rites, which were later simplified. It may not be necessary to show that all six rites were performed to prove a Chinese customary marriage,[32] but there should be some evidence that a marital union was entered into. Such evidence may be wedding clothes, badges, the presence of the elders, announcements of marriage or the toasting of guests.[33] A marriage is deemed to accord with Chinese law and custom if it was celebrated before 7 October 1971 in accordance with traditional Chinese customs accepted at the time of the marriage as appropriate for the celebration of marriage (i) in the part of Hong Kong where the marriage took place or (ii) in the place recognised by the family of either party to the marriage as their family place of origin.[34]

'Modern marriages' refer to marriages 'celebrated in Hong Kong before [7 October 1971] by open ceremony as a modern marriage and in the presence of 2 or more witnesses', following a form prescribed in 1931 by the Civil Code of the Republic of China.[35] More specifically, 'modern marriages' are unions between a man and woman, both of whom were at least 16 years old and unmarried before their celebration. Their marriage will be treated as valid even if: (i) the proper personal law of one or the other spouse was Chinese law and custom; (ii) the marriage failed to comply with the requirements of Chinese law and custom; or (iii) the marriage was not in accordance with the MO.[36] The test of whether there is a valid modern marriage is whether a reasonable man would consider that a ceremony of marriage had taken place.[37]

The procedures to register a customary marriage or a validated modern marriage are in Part IV of the MRO. Sometimes, a respondent spouse may be reluctant to register the

[30] Graeme Johnston and Paul Harris, *The Conflict of Laws in Hong Kong*, 3rd edn (Sweet & Maxwell, 2017) para 7.082, citing *A-G of Ceylon v Reid* [1965] AC 720 and *Parkasho v Singh* [1968] P 233.

[31] See MRO, s 2. The *kit fat* wife was the first wife, and a *tin fong* wife was a subsequent wife. If the *kit fat* wife died or the union otherwise ended, a *tin fong* wife could be raised (*fu ching*) to the status of principal wife. A man cannot have a *kit fat* wife and a *tin fong* wife at the same time.

[32] See, eg *Chong Chui Yuk Ching v Chong Pui Cheong* [1983] HKDCLR 1; *Kwan Chui Kwok Ying v Tao Wai Chun* [1995] 1 HKC 374; *Ng Ching Man v Ng Lai Wah* [1996] 4 HKC 448.

[33] None of these were present in *Fung Sing Wai v Chow Chiu Wan* [2017] 2 HKLRD 551, and the Court of Appeal held that the formal validity of the Chinese customary marriage cannot be proved.

[34] MRO, s 7(2).

[35] MRO, s 3. For an example of a validated modern marriage, see *Ma Siu Siu Vivian v Tam Wai Mun Alice* [2020] 1 HKLRD 267, [2019] HKCFI 2886. That case also rejected the contention that the validation of a modern marriage would invalidate the subsequent valid registry marriage. See also *C v C* [2000] 3 HKLRD 27.

[36] MRO, s 8.

[37] *Lau Au Yuet Mi v Lai Ka Lam* [1981] HKC 179.

marriage as the applicant spouse will then be afforded the matrimonial remedies available under the current legislation. A customary marriage or validated marriage may be dissolved pursuant to the MCO or Part V of the MRO. The dissolution of a modern marriage before 7 October 1971 is recognised under section 14 of the MRO.

Another type of marriage in Hong Kong relates to concubinage and polygamous marriages. It was possible before 7 October 1971 to enter into unions of concubinage or contract a *kim tiu* marriage, a type of marriage where a man can formally marry more than one principal wife and maintain a household for them. These have now been prohibited under the MRO.[38] Around 40 years earlier, on 5 May 1931, concubinage ceased to be recognised under Chinese law.[39] In Hong Kong, concubinage is

> a union … entered by a male partner and a female partner before 7 October 1971, under which union the female partner has, during the lifetime of the male partner, been accepted by his wife as his concubine and recognized as such by his family generally.[40]

The validity of concubinage depends on the parties' intention. This intention must be avowed and made known by deeds, rather than a tacit undertaking between the parties.[41] A ceremony is not essential so long as there is evidence of a common intention, as well as acceptance and recognition of the relationship.[42]

Hong Kong domestic law treats both a union with a *tsai* ('wife' or 'principal wife') and a union with a *tsip* ('concubine' or 'secondary wife') as equivalent to a monogamous relationship. As such, a subsisting monogamous marriage bars the taking of a *tsip*,[43] and a subsisting *tsip* relationship bars the contracting of a marriage with a *tsai*.[44] The Court of Final Appeal made the following remarks on the status of a concubine:[45]

> Being unknown to Western legal systems, the status of a concubine is difficult to describe with any degree of accuracy in terms of those systems. But this much can be stated. A union of concubinage was a particular matrimonial relationship recognised by law. The relationship was an open one and was not adulterous. A concubine was more than a mistress and less than a second wife. Unlike a mistress, she had a recognised legal status, though it was inferior to that of the principal wife. She was entitled to be maintained by her consort while he was alive and out of his estate after his death. Her children were legitimate and regarded as full brothers and sisters of her consort's children, whether born to the principal wife or to another concubine. It is not surprising to find that she has often been described as a secondary wife, or that the courts of Hong Kong have accorded her some of the rights and subjected her to some of the disabilities of a wife. Thus she is entitled to apply for Letters of Administration to the estate of her deceased consort, subject to the prior claim of the principal wife; and she is not a competent or compellable witness in any criminal proceedings against her consort.

Although marriages outside the MO will gradually lose their relevance as time goes on, these marriages have featured (and continue to feature) in succession and other matrimonial disputes in Hong Kong.

[38] MRO, ss 5 and 6.
[39] *Chan Chiu Lam v Yau Yee Ping* [1998] 1 HKLRD 716; *Chan Chiu Lam v Yau Yee Ping* [2000] 3 HKC 167.
[40] Legitimacy Ordinance (Cap 184), s 14(2).
[41] *Ng Ying Ho v Tam Suen Yu* [1963] 4 HKLR 923; *Kwan Chui Kwok Ying* (n 32).
[42] *Re Chan Cho Chak* [2006] 1 HKC 78.
[43] *Wong Kam Ying* (n 25).
[44] *Kwan Chui Kwok Ying* (n 32).
[45] *Suen Toi Lee* (n 27) [60].

II. Matrimonial Causes

The MCO regulates the court's jurisdiction in proceedings for divorce, nullity of marriage, judicial separation and presumption of death.[46] Such decrees may only be made by a court if the underlying marriage was a monogamous marriage[47] or a customary marriage under section 7 of the MRO.[48] A monogamous marriage means a marriage celebrated according to the MO, a modern marriage under section 8 of the MRO or a foreign marriage

> celebrated or contracted in accordance with the law in force at the time and in the place where the marriage was performed and recognized by such law as involving the voluntary union for life of one man and one woman to the exclusion of all others.[49]

A. Divorce, Nullity and Separation

Divorce can be obtained by joint application or by the petition of a spouse.[50] The sole ground for divorce in Hong Kong is that the marriage has broken down irretrievably. A petitioner has to establish one of the following five circumstances: (i) adultery; (ii) unreasonable behaviour by their spouse; (iii) the couple's separation for one year by consent; (iv) the couple's separation for two years; or (v) desertion by their spouse.[51] Judicial separation is based on similar circumstances. In this case, however, the petitioner will not allege that the marriage has irretrievably broken down.[52] This is because judicial separation is available where a petitioner does not want divorce, but wishes to obtain ancillary relief for oneself or in respect of the children of the marriage.

The grounds for a decree of nullity are provided in section 20 of the MCO. A marriage shall be void on the grounds in section 20(1) and shall be voidable on the grounds in section 20(2).[53]

In divorce, nullity, judicial separation and presumption of death proceedings, the issues are determined in accordance with the law which would apply if both parties were domiciled in Hong Kong at the time of the proceedings.[54] In other words, foreign parties do not

[46] MCO, ss 3–6. See ch 10, s V.

[47] MCO, s 9.

[48] Previously, the dissolution of a Chinese customary marriage was a private act and was not subject to the court's jurisdiction. It can be dissolved in three main ways: (i) the husband writing and serving a letter of divorce (*xiu shu*) to the wife, in the form of a letter or a formal document executed under the husband's hand and seal; (ii) a state-mandated annulment of marriage, applicable when one spouse committed a serious crime against the other or his or her clan; (iii) the husband unilaterally declaring a divorce, based on one of the seven following reasons ('seven ousts'): (a) disobedience (or lack of filial piety) to parents-in-law; (b) bearing no son; (c) lascivious conduct; (d) jealousy; (e) malignant disease; (f) loquacity; and (g) theft. Such unilateral divorce is subject to three clearly defined exceptions ('three non-ousts'): (i) the wife had no family to return to; (ii) the wife had observed a full three-year period of mourning for a parent-in-law; and (iii) the husband was poor when they married and was now rich.

[49] MCO, s 2.

[50] MCO, ss 11B and 12.

[51] MCO, ss 11 and 11A.

[52] MCO, s 24.

[53] See, eg *L v L* [2006] 1 HKFLR 121; *L v C* [2007] 3 HKLRD 819; *Fung Sing Wai* (n 33); *WN v XJX* [2018] 2 HKLRD 627, [2018] HKFC 39; *Lui Ming Lok* (n 19).

[54] MCO, s 8.

receive different treatment. If the Hong Kong court assumes jurisdiction over the MCO proceedings, Hong Kong law will apply to the parties, including foreign parties.

A court may apply foreign law in some cases, for example, where the parties have agreed that foreign law is to apply to their dispute. But Hong Kong law will usually be applied in respect of applications for ancillary relief. In *SPH v SA*, involving a foreign prenuptial agreement and a foreign separation agreement, the Court of Final Appeal held that nuptial agreements are not final and binding: there is always the possibility of resorting to the principles for ancillary relief of the *lex fori*.[55] Nor is there reason to distinguish between prenuptial and separation agreements. In respect of both, the possibility that foreign law may be applied is not a strong factor by itself for the Hong Kong court to decline jurisdiction.[56] A prenuptial agreement is simply a factor to consider on the question of appropriate forum.

B. Presumption of Death

A married person who has reasonable grounds to suppose that their spouse is dead can petition the court to declare that the latter has passed away. The marriage is dissolved as a result.[57] To obtain a decree, a petitioner must show that their spouse has been absent for at least seven years and, in the absence of contrary proof, the petitioner has no reason to believe that their spouse is still living.[58] The onus lies with the petitioner. Determining whether there is reason to believe the other spouse is alive is an objective exercise, depending on what a reasonable person would conclude.[59] There are only a handful of Hong Kong cases that have involved petitions for a decree of presumption of death.[60]

C. Financial Relief

In matrimonial and family proceedings, the court has the power to grant short- and long-term financial remedies (known as 'ancillary relief') to the parties to a marriage and in respect of their children. In Hong Kong, issues of financial relief are regulated by the Matrimonial Proceedings and Property Ordinance (Cap 192) (MPPO). The statute covers ancillary financial relief consequent on a decree of divorce, nullity or judicial separation.[61]

[55] *SPH v SA* (2014) 17 HKCFAR 364, following *Radmacher v Granatino* [2010] UKSC 42, [2011] 1 AC 354.

[56] *Rambas Marketing Co LLC v Chow Kam Fai David* [2001] 3 HKC 250.

[57] MCO, s 26. The jurisdiction requirement is in MCO, s 6.

[58] MCO, s 26(2). This is also known in common law as the legal presumption of death, which is an evidential presumption of law: *Bullock v Bullock* [1960] 1 WLR 975.

[59] *Thompson v Thompson* [1956] P 414.

[60] *Re Estate of Yu Leung Fong* [1991] 1 HKC 494; *Wang Din Shin v Nina Kung* [1999] 4 HKC 263; *Liu Yun Hop v Fung Kai Public School* [2017] 1 HKLRD 1009; *Wong Yuk Chun Kitty v Wong Yuk King* [2019] 5 HKC 574, [2019] HKDC 1323.

[61] MPPO, ss 4, 5, 6 and 6A. Other financial reliefs include periodical payments by way of maintenance pending suit and maintenance where there has been wilful neglect to maintain: MPPO, ss 3 and 8. Together with the Separation and Maintenance Orders Ordinance (Cap 16), s 5, these form the common law liability of a husband to provide reasonable maintenance for his wife and children before the dissolution of a marriage, having regard to the standard of living that he had previously maintained: *Scott v Scott* [1951] P 245; *Ridley v Ridley* [1953] P 150.

The court can order periodical and lump-sum payments from one spouse to the other, the transfer of property, and variation of settlements and transfers of property.

When exercising its powers, the court must have regard to the conduct of the parties and all circumstances, including the factors explicitly stated in section 7(1) of the MPPO in relation to a party to the marriage:

(a) the income, earning capacity, property and other financial resources which each of the parties to the marriage has or is likely to have in the foreseeable future;
(b) the financial needs, obligations and responsibilities which each of the parties to the marriage has or is likely to have in the foreseeable future;
(c) the standard of living enjoyed by the family before the breakdown of the marriage;
(d) the age of each party to the marriage and the duration of the marriage;
(e) any physical or mental disability of either of the parties to the marriage;
(f) the contributions made by each of the parties to the welfare of the family, including any contribution made by looking after the home or caring for the family;
(g) in the case of proceedings for divorce or nullity of marriage, the value to either of the parties to the marriage of any benefit (for example, a pension) which, by reason of the dissolution or annulment of the marriage, that party will lose the chance of acquiring.

The proper approach in making financial relief was considered by the Court of Final Appeal in *LKW v DD*,[62] which adopted the principles in *White v White*.[63] This chapter is not the place to discuss the starting point of equal division, the caveats and the court's very wide discretion to divide the matrimonial property 'fairly'.[64]

In terms of choice of law, Hong Kong law will apply to applications for ancillary relief. In a case involving foreign elements, it might be necessary to consider any relevant foreign law at the court's discretion.[65] Where property or financial arrangements have been agreed between the spouses and there is an express choice of law agreement, the court will usually hold the parties to their bargain[66] and respect their choice of law.[67] If there is no express choice of law, the court will consider if there is an implied choice of law. Failing this, the court will apply the law of the place with which the marriage has its closest connection (sometimes referred to the 'matrimonial domicile').

In the case of customary marriages and validated modern marriages, financial relief may be granted under section 7A of the MCO upon dissolution (whether by the MRO or the MCO). Payment of maintenance may also be granted under section 5 of the Separation and Maintenance Orders Ordinance (Cap 16) to a party of a marriage.[68] Cohabitees and same-sex couples in Hong Kong do not fall within the current statutory regime of financial relief unless their relationships are recognised as legal marriages under their respective foreign

[62] *LKW v DD* (2010) 13 HKCFAR 537.
[63] *White v White* [2001] 1 AC 596.
[64] See, eg Hewitt (n 2) ch 4; Hotten and Ho (n 2) ch 4.
[65] Johnston and Harris (n 30) para 7.121, citing *C v C* [2004] Fam 141 [26].
[66] In *L v C* (n 53), the Court of Appeal confirmed that when parties that are legally competent to manage their own affairs freely enter into a bargain for the division of matrimonial assets, the courts will hold the parties to their bargain, unless there are either: (i) unfair or unconscionable circumstances surrounding the conclusion of the agreement; or (ii) material and drastic unforeseen circumstances arising thereafter, which could cause manifest prejudice to one of the parties.
[67] *LKW v DD* (n 62).
[68] For the definition of 'marriage' in this context, see Separation and Maintenance Orders Ordinance (Cap 16), s 2.

domiciles. Cohabitees will typically dispute the division of property pursuant to a common intention constructive trust.[69]

Previously, the Hong Kong court had no jurisdiction to grant financial relief for marriages dissolved outside Hong Kong. Under the pre-2011 MPPO, the court's powers were conditional upon the grant of a decree of divorce by a Hong Kong court. If a party obtained a divorce abroad and then applied in Hong Kong for the recognition of the divorce, the Hong Kong court could not itself grant a divorce, the marriage having been dissolved abroad. The party could not then apply for financial relief. This caused hardship. In *ML v YJ*,[70] the wife obtained a divorce order in Shenzhen and therefore could not seek financial relief in respect of assets in Hong Kong. The wife raised various arguments to support her case, including an argument that the denial of financial relief rendered the recognition of the Shenzhen divorce order manifestly contrary to public policy. The wife lost before the Court of Final Appeal. But the court criticised the previous regime. To address the problem, the Matrimonial Proceedings and Property (Amendment) Ordinance 2010 was enacted and came into operation on 1 March 2011. It added Part IIA to the MPPO, taking for a model Part III of the Matrimonial and Family Proceedings Act 1984 in the UK. Coincidentally, the Part III in the UK Act was also enacted following judicial calls for remedial legislation after a decision to recognise a foreign divorce decree left the wife without a right to claim ancillary relief.[71]

Under Part IIA of the MPPO, either spouse may apply for financial relief if: (i) a marriage has been ended by judicial or other proceedings outside Hong Kong; and (ii) the termination of the marriage is recognised in Hong Kong.[72] As section 29AB(1) of the MPPO refers to a 'marriage' as defined in the MO, same-sex couples married in foreign jurisdictions are unlikely to be entitled to financial relief in Hong Kong upon divorce.[73]

The basis for the court to consider ancillary relief applications is similar to its jurisdiction in divorce proceedings, namely, that either of the parties to the marriage was domiciled or habitually resident in Hong Kong, or had a substantial connection with Hong Kong, on the date on which the foreign divorce, annulment or legal separation took effect.[74] However, if a party remarries outside Hong Kong after a marriage has ended, the latter is not entitled to make an application in relation to that marriage.[75]

The court will only grant financial relief if the court considers that there are substantial grounds for the application, and the relief may be subject to any conditions the court thinks fit.[76] The court must consider whether, in all the circumstances and the factors in

[69] See, eg *Stack v Dowden* [2007] UKHL 17, [2007] 2 AC 432; *Jones v Kernott* [2011] UKSC 53, [2012] 1 AC 776. In Hong Kong, see, eg *Chen Tek Yee v Chan Moon Shing* (unreported, HCA 954/2010, 7 May 2015). See also *Chan Chui Mee v Mak Chi Choi Nelson* [2009] 1 HKLRD 343; *Mo Ying v Brillex Development Ltd* [2014] 2 HKLRD 224 (CFI); *Mo Ying v Brillex Development Ltd* [2015] 2 HKLRD 985 (CA).

[70] *ML v YJ* (2010) 13 HKCFAR 794 (Ribeiro PJ, Litton and Sir Anthony Mason NPJJ; Chan and Bokhary PJJ dissenting).

[71] *Quazi v Quazi* [1980] AC 744.

[72] MPPO, s 29AB(1).

[73] Hotten and Ho (n 2) 245, para 4-5, fn 25 suggested that there has not been a definitive ruling on this, and it is unclear whether a restrictive interpretation of 'marriage' can survive the reasoning of the Court of Final Appeal in *W* (n 23).

[74] MPPO, s 29AE.

[75] MPPO, s 29AB(2).

[76] MPPO, ss 29AC(1), 29AC(2) and 29AC(4).

the MPPO, an order would be appropriate.[77] The court can grant any of the orders that it could make under section 4, 5 or 6 of the MPPO as if a divorce, nullity or judicial separation had been granted in Hong Kong.[78] Interim orders for maintenance are possible if the applicant or a child is in immediate need of financial assistance.[79] There are anti-avoidance provisions to deal with any dispositions or transactions that are intended to defeat applications for financial relief or interfere with their enforcement.[80] The court may grant leave despite an order having been made by a competent authority outside Hong Kong requiring the other party to the marriage to make a payment or transfer property to the applicant or child.[81] Such orders are without prejudice to the court's usual power to grant injunctions.[82] The regime in Part IIA of the MPPO and its application have been considered in detail in *C v H*.[83]

III. Children

The word 'child' encompasses the biological child of two persons and any other child who has been treated by the latter as a child of their family.[84] The word includes an illegitimate or adopted child.[85] In Hong Kong, a person becomes an 'adult' and attains 'full age' or their 'majority' at the age of 18 years.[86] Those who have not attained the age of 18 are 'infants' or 'minors'.[87] The High Court has an inherent jurisdiction to protect children, and this jurisdiction provides extensive discretionary powers to protect the child, extending far beyond what a natural parent can do.[88] The court has inherent jurisdiction to make an order or determine an issue in respect of a child to ensure that the child is properly taken care of. The jurisdiction is exercisable to the extent that it would be just and equitable to do so, unless restricted by an enactment or case law. Moreover, under the Guardianship of Minors Ordinance (Cap 13) (GMO), the Hong Kong court has jurisdiction to make orders giving or withdrawing custody of, access to, guardianship of and maintenance of a child.[89] Such jurisdiction is 'notwithstanding that any party to the proceedings is not domiciled in Hong Kong',[90] and the court has the power to dispense with rules of service. The GMO does not impose cross-border limitations on the court's jurisdiction. This is in line with the general principle in section 3 of the GMO to treat the welfare of the child as paramount.

[77] MPPO, s 29AF.
[78] MPPO, ss 29AG and 29AH.
[79] MPPO, s 29AD.
[80] MPPO, ss 29AJ and 29AK.
[81] MPPO, s 29AC(3).
[82] MPPO, s 29AL. More specifically, the High Court may grant an interlocutory injunction under s 21L or 21M of the High Court Ordinance (Cap 4). See ch 9, s V.
[83] *C v H* [2012] HKFLR 199.
[84] MPPO, s 2. See also *W(RJ) v W(SJ)* [1972] Fam 152; *A v A* [1974] Fam 6; *F v F* [2003] 1 HKLRD 836.
[85] MPPO, s 2.
[86] Age of Majority (Related Provisions) Ordinance (Cap 410).
[87] Interpretation and General Clauses Ordinance (Cap 1), s 3.
[88] See, eg *Tameside Metropolitan Borough Council v AM* [2021] EWHC 2472 (Fam), approved in *Re YL (a minor)* [2022] 3 HKLRD 699, [2022] HKCFI 2001; *Z v Y* [2023] 2 HKLRD 772, [2022] HKCFI 3695.
[89] GMO, ss 10, 11 and 12.
[90] GMO, s 26.

A. Wardship

Wardship proceedings may be instituted by a parent or interested party without the need for divorce or judicial separation proceedings. Upon institution of wardship proceedings in the High Court, the child immediately becomes a ward of the court. The court has the custody of the child and every major decision regarding that child's welfare must be referred to the court. The court has wide powers to make any order to protect the welfare and interest of the child as its ward. These powers may also be seen as the court exercising its inherent *parens patriae* (parental) jurisdiction in the best interests of the child, whether or not the child is a ward of the court.[91] Even for cases where the 1980 HCCH Convention on the Civil Aspects of International Child Abduction (the Hague Child Abduction Convention) and the Child Abduction and Custody Ordinance (Cap 512) are not applicable (for example, Taiwan), wardship can still be used, applying the general principles of the Hague Child Abduction Convention with some modifications.[92]

Wardship has been used in innovative ways by the Hong Kong courts to resolve gaps in the protection of children. In *S v J*, two children were born of respective surrogate mothers under a surrogacy arrangement in India, before the family relocated to Hong Kong. The parents commenced divorce proceedings two years later.[93] As Hong Kong law did not recognise the commissioning parents as the legal parents of the children, a parental order under section 12 of the Parent and Child Ordinance (Cap 429) (PCO) had to be sought for recognition of the children's status.[94] The commissioning mother did not consent to the parental order, or an order under section 6 of the PCO. Without any of these orders, the divorce proceedings could not confer jurisdiction on the court to deal with the children. The guardianship regime of Hong Kong is based on recognised parental rights and therefore could not be utilised either.[95] Nor was an application for adoption made. The court eventually resorted to wardship, making the children wards of the court, under the court's inherent jurisdiction 'to fill the lacuna of the law until better arrangements are made as to their legal identities and status'.[96] However, in *NF v R*, the court in obiter warned against applying *parens patriae* jurisdiction to rescue a child in danger or to bridge a legislative gap, and refused to exercise the inherent *parens patriae* jurisdiction as the circumstances in that case did not so warrant.[97]

B. Parental Responsibility, Guardianship and Custody

The court can make any order for the 'custody and education' of a minor.[98] The court can make orders regarding the custody of and right of access to the minor by either parent.[99]

[91] *In re P (GE) (an infant)* [1965] Ch 568; *QMY v GSS* (2017) 20 HKCFAR 303 [10]–[16].
[92] *C v N* [2016] 2 HKLRD 765. For the operation of the Hague Child Abduction Convention in Hong Kong, see s III.G below.
[93] *S v J* [2017] 5 HKLRD 129.
[94] See s III.F below.
[95] GMO, s 8D(2)(b).
[96] *S v J* (n 93) [30].
[97] *NF v R* [2023] 5 HKLRD 58, [2023] HKCFI 2233 [148]–[159].
[98] MPPO, s 19.
[99] GMO, s 10.

There is no presumption that a child should be living with either parent.[100] The normal options for custody include sole custody, joint custody and split custody (custody with one parent and daily care and control with the other).[101] The modern approach in Hong Kong is to encourage joint custody unless there are good reasons to depart from this.[102] This approach emphasises joint parental responsibility, rather than the parents' individual rights.

The paramount consideration in any application (regardless of any foreign element) is the best interests of the child.[103] This is the welfare principle. The principle subordinates all conflicting interests.[104] It encompasses not only monetary or material needs and physical well-being, but also touches on medical, moral, religious and emotional considerations.[105] This is stated in Article 3(1) of the United Nations Convention on the Rights of the Child and is an implied obligation of the government under Article 24 of the International Covenant on Civil and Political Rights (Article 20 of the Hong Kong Bill of Rights). The welfare principle has legal effect through section 3(1) of the GMO and through the MPPO generally. When applying the welfare principle, Hong Kong judges consistently adopt (but are not bound by) the matters specified in section 1(3) of the Children Act 1989 in the UK, known as the 'welfare checklist'.[106] The checklist is mentioned in paragraph 6 of Hong Kong's Practice Direction SL6 and is set out in clause 3 of the proposed Children Proceedings (Parental Responsibility) Bill.

Therefore, although Hong Kong does not currently recognise foreign same-sex marriages and civil partnerships, it is possible for Hong Kong courts to grant parental rights over a child to a non-biological spouse, including custody, care and control, and guardianship, in accordance with the welfare principle. In *AA v BB*, involving a same-sex couple who ended a cohabitation relationship of 17 years and reached a co-parenting agreement, the Court of First Instance granted joint custody, care and control of the children to the birth mother and the foster mother, appointed the foster mother as guardian and ordered that the children cease to be wards of the court.[107]

C. Maintenance

When a marriage has been dissolved or annulled by the Hong Kong court under the MCO or when judicial separation is pronounced, the court can make maintenance orders for a child of the family under Part II of the MPPO. When a divorce, annulment or judicial separation has been ordered outside Hong Kong, the regime in Part IIA of the MPPO (introduced in section II.C above) applies. Possible maintenance orders include orders for periodical or lump-sum payment and for the transfer of property.[108] In exercising its powers, the court

[100] *Re W (a minor)* [1992] 2 FLR 332.

[101] For definition of terms such as 'custody' and 'care and control', see, eg *SEB v ZX* [2007] HKFLR 165; *PD v KWW* [2010] 4 HKLRD 191; *SKP v YITT* [2012] HKFLR 422. For split custody, see, eg *Dipper v Dipper* [1980] 3 WLR 626. Hong Kong courts are reluctant to make such an order except in exceptional circumstances: *YLS v TL* [2009] HKFLR 19 [33].

[102] *PD v KWW* (n 101).

[103] The two terms are synonymous: *H v N* [2012] 5 HKLRD 498 [22]. See also *F v F* (n 84).

[104] *J v C* [1970] AC 668.

[105] *H v N* (n 103).

[106] See, eg *SMM v TWM* (unreported, CACV 209/2009, 9 June 2010); *H v N* (n 103) [27]–[31].

[107] *AA v BB* [2021] 2 HKLRD 1225, [2021] HKCFI 1401.

[108] MPPO, ss 2, 5(2) and 6.

must have regard to all circumstances, including the factors explicitly stated in section 7(2) of the MPPO in relation to a child of the family. These include:

(a) the financial needs of the child;
(b) the income, earning capacity (if any), property and other financial resources of the child;
(c) any physical or mental disability of the child;
(d) the standard of living enjoyed by the family before the breakdown of the marriage;
(e) the manner in which he was being and in which the parties to the marriage expected him to be educated[.]

The court is to place the child, so far as is practicable and just, in the same financial position in which the child would have been if the marriage had not broken down and the parents had discharged their financial obligations and responsibilities.

When deciding whether to exercise its powers against a spouse in favour of a child who is not the child of that spouse, the court is to have regard to the following:[109]

(a) whether that party had assumed any responsibility for the child's maintenance and, if so, to the extent to which, and the basis upon which, that party assumed such responsibility and to the length of time for which that party discharged such responsibility;
(b) whether in assuming and discharging such responsibility that party did so knowing that the child was not his or her own;
(c) the liability of any other person to maintain the child.

An application for child maintenance under section 10 of the GMO may be made for the children of married or unmarried parents.[110] It will not matter whether the child is legitimate or illegitimate.[111] Under the same section, the court can make orders in respect of a child who is neither ordinarily resident nor present in Hong Kong.[112] Therefore, the Hong Kong court has a wider jurisdiction on applications under the GMO than on applications for divorce.

Under the GMO, upon the application of a person who has custody of a minor, the court may order a parent to pay the maintenance for the child, having regard to the means of that parent.[113]

D. Legitimacy and Legitimation

When a child is born to a married couple, the child will be regarded as legitimate by the Hong Kong court. When a child is born to parents with at least one of them domiciled in a place whose laws do not distinguish between legitimacy and illegitimacy, the child will be regarded as legitimate by the Hong Kong court, even if the parties were unmarried.[114]

Section 6 of the PCO is the only way in which declarations of parentage, legitimacy, legitimation or non-legitimation can be made.[115] According to section 6(1), the child

[109] MPPO, s 7(3).
[110] GMO, s 10; *IDC v SSA* [2014] 4 HKLRD 220.
[111] GMO, ss 3 and 21; *L v C* [1994] 2 HKLR 92.
[112] *QMY v GSS* (2017) 20 HKCFAR 303.
[113] GMO, ss 10, 11, 12 and 13.
[114] Johnston and Harris (n 30) para 7.127. See also *Re Sit Yuk Cheung* (unreported, HCMP 40/1990, 24 April 1990).
[115] PCO, s 6(7). For the presumptions as to paternity and legitimacy in Hong Kong, see PCO, s 5.

(whether an infant or an adult) may apply to the court for a declaration that: (i) a person is or was the child's parent;[116] (ii) the child is legitimate; or (iii) the child has been legitimated. The jurisdictional requirements are set out in section 6(2). A declaration of legitimacy may be sought based on adoption.[117] The operation of section 6 was discussed in *OMH v MT* and *NF v R*.[118] A declaration of parentage is a confirmation as to who factually is or was in law a parent of the child, and the court must make the declaration once satisfied with the evidence, unless it is contrary to public policy.[119] In the eyes of the Hong Kong court, declarations obtained under section 6 of the PCO are binding across the world.

A negative declaration of parentage (that is, a person is not a child's parent) cannot be made under section 6 of the PCO. Instead, such a declaration comes within the court's inherent jurisdiction and can be made under Order 15, rule 16 of the Rules of the High Court (Cap 4A).[120] The court cannot declare that a person is or was illegitimate.[121] However, the issue may be determined if it arises as an incidental question in *in personam* proceedings.[122]

E. Adoption

Adoption is governed by the Adoption Ordinance (Cap 290) (AO). Under section 4 of the AO, the court can make an order authorising the adoption of an infant. An application can be made solely or jointly, and the requirements or restrictions on making adoption orders are set out in section 5 of the AO. An adoption order can be made as long as the applicant and the infant both reside in Hong Kong.[123]

Following the introduction of the AO on 1 January 1973, adoption under Chinese customary law was abolished.[124] However, any rights and status acquired by a person adopted in Hong Kong under Chinese law and custom before 1 January 1973 are unaffected.[125]

Hong Kong is a party to the 1993 HCCH Convention on Protection of Children and Cooperation in Respect of Intercountry Adoption (the Hague Adoption Convention), which entered into force on 1 May 1995. The Convention gives effect to Article 21 of the United Nations Convention on the Rights of the Child. China signed the Hague Adoption Convention on 30 November 2000 and ratified it on 16 September 2005. China further declared that the Convention applies to Hong Kong as well. It entered into force in the PRC on 1 January 2006. The Hague Adoption Convention facilitates intercountry adoption

[116] The definition of 'parent' under PCO, s 6, PCO, Pt V (birth or pregnancy resulting from medical treatment) and the common law was discussed in *NF v R* (n 97) [54]–[84]. In that case, the female same-sex couple underwent reciprocal in vitro fertilization in South Africa and gave birth to a child. It was held that the respondent (who provided the egg for the birth) could not be interpreted as the child's 'mother' or 'parent' under PCO, ss 6 and 9, and was declared a 'parent at common law'.

[117] PCO, s 4(2)(c).

[118] *OMH v MT* [2017] 3 HKLRD 323; *NF v R* (n 97).

[119] PCO, s 6(3); *NF v R* (n 97) [49], [52].

[120] *Z v Y* (n 88).

[121] PCO, s 6(8).

[122] *Skinner v Carter* [1948] Ch 387.

[123] AO, s 5(6). This is different from Convention adoption orders, which require 'habitual residence': AO, s 20C(5).

[124] AO, s 25(1). In *Liu Ying Lan v Liu Tung Yiu* [2003] 3 HKLRD 249, the Court of Appeal rejected the posthumous adoption of an adult, which was possible only under customary law but not under the AO, despite the argument that such an adoption was in substance a form of succession.

[125] AO, s 25(2).

between Hong Kong and other countries (where Hong Kong is the destination or the origin of the child), and provides substantive safeguards and procedures. As with other HCCH Conventions, the Convention provides broad principles or minimum standards, but does not serve as a uniform law of adoption. Each state (both the state of origin and the receiving state) must perform their respective functions during the adoption process and share the benefits and burdens of regulating intercountry adoption.

Section 20B of the AO provides that the Hague Adoption Convention shall have the force of law in Hong Kong,[126] subject to the provisions in Part 5 (sections 20A–20J) of the AO. The other parts of the AO also generally apply to Convention adoptions. Only the Court of First Instance has jurisdiction to hear Convention adoption proceedings.[127] Certain provisions of the AO will not apply in relation to Convention adoptions in respect of which Hong Kong acts as the receiving state.[128] Interim measures do not apply to Convention adoptions.[129]

The restriction that an adoption order cannot be made in respect of any child unless the applicant and the child reside in Hong Kong, does not apply to Convention adoptions. However, a Convention adoption order cannot be made in respect of a child unless the applicant and the child are habitual residents of the receiving and contracting state respectively (or vice versa).[130]

Applications are made by applicants to their habitual residence's central authority. The central authority in Hong Kong is the Director of Social Welfare. 'Habitual residence' refers to two features of residence: that of residence adopted (i) voluntarily and (ii) for settled purpose.[131] It refers to the quality of the residence rather than the duration, and requires an intention to reside in the relevant place. If Hong Kong is the receiving state, the court must also be satisfied that the persons who have consented to the adoption understand the nature and effect of the order.[132]

When coming to a decision in relation to adoption (whether a local adoption or a Convention adoption), Hong Kong judges have followed (but are not bound by) the matters specified in section 1(4) of the Adoption and Children Act 2002 in the UK, also known as the 'adoption checklist'.[133]

F. Child Surrogacy

The law on surrogacy and surrogacy arrangements in Hong Kong is contained in the Human Reproductive Technology Ordinance (Cap 561) (HRTO). According to section 14 of the HRTO, only the gametes of a married couple can be used in a surrogacy arrangement. Moreover, the Code of Practice on Reproductive Technology and Embryo Research

[126] AO, s 20B and Sch 3.
[127] AO, ss 2(1) and 23B.
[128] AO, s 20C(4).
[129] AO, s 20C(7).
[130] AO, s 20C(5). 'State' includes any state declared under s 20D(1): see s 20A(2). The relevant contracting states and territorial units where the Convention applies (in respect of Hong Kong) are set out in the Intercountry Adoption (Contracting States) Order (Cap 290C).
[131] See ch 4, s III.B.
[132] AO, s 20C(6).
[133] See, eg *Director of Social Welfare v YPC* [2020] 5 HKLRD 233, [2020] HKCFI 2290; *Director of Social Welfare v HJX* [2021] 1 HKLRD 519, [2020] HKCFI 3127; *Director of Social Welfare v YKK* [2021] 4 HKLRD 30, [2021] HKCFI 2078.

prepared and maintained by the Council on Human Reproductive Technology (a statutory body established under section 4 of the HRTO) stipulates that a reproductive technology procedure can only be provided to a wife who is unable to carry a pregnancy to term and for whom no other treatment option is practicable.

No person, whether in Hong Kong or elsewhere, is allowed to make or receive a payment at any stage of a surrogacy arrangement.[134] No surrogacy arrangement is enforceable by or against any person making it.[135]

Under Hong Kong law, the surrogate mother is the legal mother of the child at birth by virtue of her giving birth to the child.[136] Hong Kong courts apply this domestic law position when determining whether the parties to the proceedings are the 'parents' of a child born through surrogacy. An illustrative example is where the court rejected the commissioning parents as the legal parents of the children of two surrogate mothers under a surrogacy arrangement in India. This was despite the children having been conceived using the gametes of the commissioning parents, the children having been raised by the commissioning parents and the birth certificates issued in India bearing the names of the commissioning parents.[137]

To obtain parental rights to the child, a commissioning couple must apply to the court for a parental order in their favour, in place of the surrogate mother, under section 12 of the PCO. The application must be made by both commissioning parents.[138] The court can make a parental order providing for a child to be treated in law as the child of the parties to a marriage if the child has been carried by a woman other than the wife as a result of the placing of an embryo or sperm and eggs or artificial insemination following the use of the gametes of one or both of the spouses.[139] The commissioning couple must apply for the order within six months of the birth of the child, and must satisfy several other conditions.[140] Note that 'whether the woman was in Hong Kong or elsewhere at the time of the placing in her of the embryo or the sperm and eggs or her artificial insemination' is irrelevant.[141] When determining an application for a parental order, the best interests of the child is the paramount consideration; an order will be refused only in the clearest case of abuse of public policy.[142] Thus, a parental order was still granted even when the laws of (i) Cambodia, where the commercial surrogacy arrangement was entered, (ii) Thailand, where the surrogate gave birth and (iii) Hong Kong were breached, and the commissioning parents only found out the need to seek a parental order upon their application for divorce five years later.[143]

[134] HRTO, s 17. But expenses reasonably incurred, otherwise authorised or subsequently approved by the court might be allowed: GMO, s 12(7); *FH v WB* [2019] 5 HKC 99, [2019] HKCFI 1748. See also *Re D* [2015] 1 HKLRD 229.

[135] HRTO, s 18.

[136] PCO, s 9(1) provides: 'The woman who is carrying or has carried a child as a result of the placing in her of an embryo or of sperm and eggs, and no other woman, is to be regarded as the mother of the child.' See also PCO, s 10 for the meaning of 'father'. These provisions are technology neutral and equally applicable across all situations of assisted reproduction. See also *NF v R* (n 97) [79]–[146].

[137] *S v J* (n 93).

[138] *B v C* [2015] EWFC 17, [2015] 1 FLR 1392; *S v J* (n 93).

[139] PCO, s 12.

[140] PCO, s 12; *Re T and L* [2022] 2 HKLRD 685, [2022] HKCFI 747.

[141] PCO, s 12(8).

[142] *Re A and B* [2019] 5 HKLRD 366, [2019] HKCFI 1749; *Re T and L* (n 140).

[143] *CS v SW* [2024] HKCFI 2326. The court expressly warned against commissioning parents seeking in the future to argue that they were ignorant of the law when entering into the surrogacy arrangement: [136].

Alternatively, an adoption order is possible for the commissioning couples to adopt the child born through surrogacy. This follows the standard procedure of local adoption in the AO.

G. Wrongful Removal of Children (Child Abduction)

International child abduction occurs where a child is taken to another jurisdiction from the child's home jurisdiction by a parent, guardian or family member in breach of that person's legal obligations or the rights of another parent. The policy against child abduction is to safeguard the best interests of children, to ensure that children are not wrongfully removed to or retained in another state and to enable courts in the home jurisdiction (habitual residence) of abducted children to take decisions regarding their custody, care and access. The court is therefore provided with powers to prevent the unlawful removal of children from Hong Kong (a prohibition order), to return abducted children (a recovery order) and to assist in the return of children who have been wrongly removed.

Hong Kong (but not Mainland China) has adopted the 1980 HCCH Convention on the Civil Aspects of International Child Abduction (the Hague Child Abduction Convention). The provisions of the Convention have been implemented by the CACO, which came into force on 5 September 1997. There are two notable exceptions: Article 20 (providing that the return of a child may be refused if contrary to the fundamental principles of the requested state relating to the protection of human rights and fundamental freedoms) and Article 25 (concerning legal aid) of the Convention have not been enacted in Hong Kong. Further amendments to the CACO were made in 2016. This chapter will not go into the detailed operation of the 1980 Convention and the CACO, but a few issues relating to its implementation in Hong Kong should be noted.

First, there is a distinction between Hague abduction cases and non-Hague cases. Hague abduction cases follow the CACO procedures. The Convention cannot be applied in abduction cases involving the rest of China.[144] Common law devices such as wardship and inherent jurisdiction may be used in non-Hague abduction cases.[145] In fact, the Convention approach is not dissimilar to the approach taken in common law cases. The modern approach in common law effectively involves a presumption in favour of return, which is taken to be in the child's best interests.[146]

Second, the Convention only applies to children under 16 who were habitually resident in a contracting state immediately before any breach of custody or access rights.[147] Article 12 of the Convention provides that the court shall order the return of a wrongfully removed or retained child when the return procedure is commenced within one year of the wrongful removal or retention. A delay of several months may be interpreted as acquiescence to the wrongful removal or retention under Article 13 of the Convention. The central authority of each contracting state assists and facilitates proceedings for the return of a child. The central authority in Hong Kong is the Secretary for Justice.[148]

[144] See *K v K* [2006] HKFLR 445, where an application could not be made to bring a child to Hong Kong (as a proxy for Taiwan or the Mainland) who was wrongfully retained in another Convention jurisdiction.

[145] See, eg *N v O* [1998] 4 HKC 574, where the Court of First Instance made the child a ward of court after dismissing an application for summary return of the child under the Convention.

[146] See, eg *Re F (a minor)* [1991] Fam 25; *C v N* (n 92).

[147] Hague Child Abduction Convention, Art 4.

[148] CACO, s 5.

Third, exceptions may be applicable under Article 13 of the Convention. These include: (i) the non-exercise of custody rights by the left-behind parent, consent or subsequent acquiescence (Article 13(1)(a)); (ii) a grave risk of physical or psychological harm, or otherwise an intolerable situation, if the child is returned to the habitual residence (Article 13(1)(b)); and (iii) the child's objection (Article 13(2)).[149] However, the effect of establishing any of these exceptions is simply to disapply the rule of mandatory return, and the court retains a discretion to order a return.[150] The paramount consideration remains the best interests of the child.

Fourth, in line with Article 14 of the Convention, the court 'may take notice directly of the law of, and of judicial and administrative decisions, formally recognised or not in the State of habitual residence of the child'. This circumvents the common law approach of proof of foreign law. In the child abduction context, the Court of Appeal has imposed a requirement of natural justice, where Hong Kong courts must not communicate directly with foreign courts, central authorities or other stakeholders except 'in the presence and with the consent of all parties and their representatives'.[151] It was suggested that the requirement is too harsh, as speed is an important factor in these applications; there is nothing inherently unfair about unilateral communication, provided that the process is transparent and parties are given a chance to comment.[152]

Fifth, Article 15 of the Convention provides that a state may request, prior to ordering the return of the child, a decision or determination from the state of the habitual residence of the child that the removal or retention was wrongful under the Convention. Such decision is persuasive but not binding.[153]

IV. Mental Incapacity

The Hong Kong court applies domestic law, mainly the Mental Health Ordinance (Cap 136), in exercising its powers to deal with matters relating to mentally incapacitated persons.[154] Potential exceptions to this choice of law rule include:[155]

(i) where the court believes that a matter has a substantial connection with a foreign jurisdiction, it may apply the law of that jurisdiction; and

[149] See, eg *In re H* [1998] AC 72; *SC v LW* [2004] 1 HKLRD 655; *EW v LP* [2013] HKFLR 135; *M v E* [2015] HKFLR 337 [8.1]–[8.2]; *LA v L* (unreported, HCMP 1548/2017, 22 August 2017) [15]–[24]. The HCCH published a Guide to Good Practice specifically on the application of Art 13(1)(b) of the Convention. The current practice in Hong Kong for meeting children in matrimonial and family proceedings is set out in Practice Direction SL5.

[150] See, eg *In re M* [2007] UKHL 55, [2008] 1 AC 1288; *EW v LP* (n 149) [113]–[118].

[151] *D v G* [2002] 1 HKLRD 62. Facilitated by the development of the International Hague Network of Judges, the current practice in Hong Kong for direct judicial communications in international family disputes affecting children is set out in Practice Direction SL7.

[152] Johnston and Harris (n 30), para 7.141.

[153] *M v E* (n 149) [6.23]–[6.27].

[154] See *Re LYO* [2005] 3 HKC 201 for a discussion of jurisdiction and choice of law rules arising out of a non-resident mentally incapacitated person.

[155] *Dicey, Morris and Collins* (n 21) para 22R-014.

(ii) where the protective measures are obtained in one jurisdiction but implemented in another, the conditions of implementation may be governed by the law of the other jurisdiction.

The application of foreign law is subject to mandatory provisions of Hong Kong law, and whether its application would be contrary to public policy. However, in the mental incapacity context, it is not clear what circumstances would lead to such a result.

The 2000 HCCH Convention on the International Protection of Adults does not apply in Hong Kong.

20

Law of Corporations and Insolvency

This chapter explains the rules of private international law in relation to corporations and insolvency. These rules have become increasingly relevant to corporate entities operating in Hong Kong, particularly when such entities become insolvent. This is due in part to the common practice of corporations operating in Hong Kong to incorporate in foreign jurisdictions such as the British Virgin Islands (BVI), Bermuda or the Cayman Islands. This practice has led to the development of a body of legal rules governing the nature and degree to which Hong Kong courts may become involved in the winding up of foreign corporations. For personal bankruptcy, see chapter twenty-one.

Section I considers choice of law rules on the operation of foreign companies in Hong Kong. Section II discusses rules in relation to corporate insolvency and winding up in Hong Kong. Section III focuses on cross-border insolvency issues. Section IV discusses the related topic of the relationships and interactions between jurisdiction and arbitration agreements and insolvency petitions (and, by extension, bankruptcy petitions).

I. Capacity and Internal Management

The main legislation in Hong Kong regarding companies include the Companies Ordinance (Cap 622) (CO) and the Companies (Winding Up and Miscellaneous Provisions) Ordinance (Cap 32) (CWUMPO). Section 776 of the CO provides that a non-Hong Kong company is required to register as a 'registered non-Hong Kong company' within one month after the establishment of the place of business in Hong Kong. This registered non-Hong Kong company will then be subject to the control of both legislation, notably Part 16 of the CO, the Companies (Non-Hong Kong Companies) Regulation (Cap 622J) and Part IVA of the CWUMPO regarding disqualification orders. Some provisions, such as Part X of the CWUMPO regarding winding up of unregistered companies (discussed in section II below) and section 360N of the CWUMPO regarding unlawful societies and prohibited organisations, apply to all non-Hong Kong companies. The jurisdiction of the courts over both registered and unregistered foreign companies and how they can be served out of jurisdiction are explained in chapter nine, section I.A. This brief section discusses the choice of law rules for questions of company law regarding non-Hong Kong companies.

Unlike some jurisdictions, such as Australia,[1] there is no legislation in Hong Kong on the rules of applicable law for foreign companies. The consistent trend under the common

[1] Foreign Corporations (Applications of Laws) Act 1989 (Cth).

law is to refer to the law of the place of incorporation of the company (*lex incorporationis*). For example, the existence of a non-Hong Kong company is determined by reference to the *lex incorporationis* and is recognised,[2] and may therefore sue or be sued in Hong Kong. The dissolution of such a company under the law of its former place of incorporation is also recognised,[3] although separate winding up proceedings may be brought in Hong Kong (see section II below) to protect creditors. The subsequent amalgamation into a new company (if any) and its succession to the rights and liabilities of its predecessors are also recognised.[4]

The capacity and powers, and indeed most matters of substantive company law, of a non-Hong Kong company are determined by the *lex incorporationis*.[5] It governs matters regarding the membership of such company and its members' rights and liabilities. It also governs issues of internal management and corporate governance, including the composition, appointment, functions and powers of the organs and officers of a company,[6] and whether the officers have the power to act on behalf of the company.[7] The statute has also extended powers of the court and members against non-Hong Kong companies, including unfair prejudice remedies, statutory derivative actions, injunctions, damages and inspection of company's records.[8]

The availability of a common law derivative action is treated in Hong Kong as a matter of substantive law, and is therefore also a matter of the *lex incorporationis*,[9] although it will be necessary to comply with the procedural requirements in Hong Kong to bring such actions.[10] For 'lifting' or 'piercing' the corporate veil,[11] the case law is unsettled as to whether the *lex incorporationis*[12] or the *lex fori*[13] should apply. It is submitted that in general, the *lex incorporationis* should govern, but where the interests of justice render it necessary, the court may decide to apply *lex fori* or some other more appropriate law.[14]

[2] See, eg *Bumper Development Corp v Commissioner of Police of the Metropolis* [1991] 1 WLR 1362.

[3] See, eg *Lazard Borthers & Co v Midland Bank Ltd* [1933] AC 289, 297.

[4] See, eg *National Bank of Greece and Athens SA v Metliss* [1958] AC 509.

[5] See, eg *Bateman v Service* (1881) 6 App Cas 386; *Banco de Bilbao v Sancha and Rey* [1938] 2 KB 176; *Joint Official Liquidators of A Co v B* [2014] 4 HKLRD 374 [4]. For foreign corporations of unrecognised states, see Foreign Corporations Ordinance (Cap 437).

[6] See, eg *Sierra Leone Telecommunications Co Ltd v Barclays Bank plc* [1998] 2 All ER 821; *Base Metal Trading Ltd v Shamurin* [2004] EWCA Civ 1316, [2005] 1 WLR 1157; *Integral Petroleum SA v SCU-Finanz AG* [2014] EWHC 702 (Comm) [59].

[7] See, eg *Carl Zeiss Stiftung v Rayner & Keeler Ltd (No 2)* [1967] 1 AC 853, 919, 939, 972; *Sierra Leone Telecommunications Co Ltd* (n 6). However, an agency relationship is regarded as contractual and is governed by its proper law: see ch 15, s II.A; *Guangzhou Zhoutouzui Development Co Ltd v Sun Zhichun* [2024] HKCFI 1940 [51]–[60].

[8] CO, s 722(1), extending powers of CO, Pt 14.

[9] *Waddington Ltd v Chan Chun Hoo Thomas* (2008) 11 HKCFAR 370 [55]; *East Asia Satellite Television (Holdings) Ltd v New Cotai LLC* [2011] 3 HKLRD 734 [32]–[37].

[10] *Base Metal Trading Ltd* (n 6) [68]; *Wong Ming Bun v Wang Ming Fan* [2014] 1 HKLRD 1108 [42].

[11] As for the distinction (if any) between the two terms, see *VTB Capital plc v Nutritek International Corp* [2013] UKSC 5, [2013] 2 AC 337 [118]–[119]; *Petrodel Resources Ltd v Prest* [2013] UKSC 34, [2013] 2 AC 415 [28].

[12] *Excalibur Ventures LLC v Texas Keystones Inc* [2013] EWHC 2767 (Comm) [1136]–[1145].

[13] *Akhmedova v Akhmedov* [2018] EWFC 23, [2018] 3 FCR 135.

[14] *Nicholas Eng Teng Cheng v Government of the City of Buenos Aires* [2024] 1 SLR 608 [37]–[42].

II. Insolvency and Winding Up in Hong Kong

A. Overview

The cross-border aspects of corporate insolvency have become increasingly prevalent in Hong Kong, due to the presence of multinational corporate groups and offshore corporate entities incorporated in foreign jurisdictions but operating within Hong Kong. When these inter-jurisdictional corporate structures become insolvent and collapse, their creditors invariably scramble to secure their debts against the company's remaining assets (often strewn across the globe), resulting in the initiation of several concurrent winding up or administration proceedings in multiple jurisdictions. As corporate insolvency is mainly covered by the statutory regime in a jurisdiction (in Hong Kong, the CO and the CWUMPO), questions of comity and practicality often arise on the extent to which the Hong Kong court should assert jurisdiction in cross-border insolvency cases. This is the consequence of differences between the winding up regimes in individual jurisdictions. A lack of coordination among different jurisdictions may lead to inconsistent findings among the courts of different countries, potentially giving rise to procedural injustice and the efficient resolution of insolvency proceedings.

Jurisdictions have historically viewed corporate insolvency in terms of the location of the company's assets, resulting in the widespread application of the *lex situs*, whereby a court's jurisdiction to make decisions and orders is limited to those assets located within that jurisdiction's territory. While this 'territorialism' did away with the cross-border concerns just identified, a drawback of this asset-focused approach was economic inefficiency. Concurrent winding up petitions would be presented in multiple jurisdictions in which a company's assets are located. Different liquidators would be appointed in different countries, increasing liquidation costs and reducing the value of assets available to the creditors. Assets would be sold piecemeal, preventing the realisation of their true value as a part of a package of assets having a much higher value when sold as a whole. However, the other end of 'universalism', where one insolvency proceeding would be administered and receive worldwide recognition and assistance, seems to be over-idealistic.

In light of this tension, a new approach known as 'modified universalism' emerged. This stresses cooperation among different jurisdictions involved in a company's insolvency. The approach culminated in the United Nations Commission on International Trade Law (UNCITRAL) Model Law on Cross-Border Insolvency (1997), which sought to harmonise insolvency proceedings among states adopting the Model Law. While Hong Kong has not adopted the Model Law, its Companies court has demonstrated a willingness to operate in line with it.[15]

This section focuses on the circumstances whereby a company may be wound up in Hong Kong and the consequences of the order. It does not discuss the interaction between the Hong Kong and foreign courts where concurrent winding up proceedings have been initiated. That topic is instead dealt with in section III below.

[15] For a detailed analysis of cross-border corporate insolvency, see s III below.

B. Winding Up of Companies Incorporated Outside Hong Kong

The Hong Kong court has the power to wind up any company, which includes companies incorporated outside of Hong Kong. The court's power to wind up a foreign incorporated company is contained in Part X of CWUMPO, which sets out the specific circumstances when such a company may be wound up.[16] For the purposes of the CWUMPO, a foreign incorporated company is treated as an 'unregistered company'[17] which may be wound up in Hong Kong, whether or not the company has in fact been registered as a foreign company operating in Hong Kong.[18] An unregistered company, and therefore a foreign incorporated company, cannot be voluntarily wound up in Hong Kong.[19]

(i) Definition of 'Unregistered Company'

The definition of an 'unregistered company' that may be wound up is found in section 326 of the CWUMPO. Unregistered companies include:

(i) any company that is not incorporated under Hong Kong law,[20] whether or not it has already been dissolved or otherwise ceased to exist as a company under the laws of its place of incorporation;[21]

(ii) a 'non-Hong Kong company',[22] namely, any company incorporated outside of Hong Kong which has established a place of business[23] in Hong Kong on or after 3 March 2014[24] or which established a place of business in Hong Kong before 3 March 2014 and continued to have a place of business in Hong Kong as from 3 March 2014;

(iii) a 'registered non-Hong Kong company', namely, a non-Hong Kong company registered in the Companies Registry in Hong Kong,[25] including non-Hong Kong companies that must be registered in the Companies Registry under section 776 of the CO;[26]

(iv) any partnership (whether limited or not) other than:

  (a) a partnership, association or company which consists of fewer than eight members and is not formed or established outside Hong Kong;[27] or

  (b) a partnership registered in Hong Kong under the Limited Partnerships Ordinance (Cap 37);[28]

[16] In general, there are three grounds under the provision: (i) if the company is dissolved, has ceased to carry on business or is carrying on business only for the purpose of winding up its affairs; (ii) if the company is unable to pay its debt; or (iii) if the court is of the opinion that it is just and equitable to have the company wound up.

[17] CWUMPO, s 326(1).

[18] ibid s 326(2).

[19] ibid s 327(2).

[20] ibid s 326(1)(a).

[21] ibid s 327A.

[22] CO, s 2(1).

[23] ibid s 776(1); CWUMPO, s 2(1).

[24] This is the commencement date of Part 16 of the CO: Companies Ordinance (Commencement) Notice 2013 (LN 163 of 2013).

[25] CWUMPO, s 2(1).

[26] CO, s 776; CWUMPO, s 2(1).

[27] CWUMPO, s 326(1)(b).

[28] ibid s 326(1)(c).

(v) any association, but not clubs[29] or any association which the legislature could not reasonably have intended to be subject to the winding up process;[30] and
(vi) any state-owned enterprise that has not been formed by an international treaty.[31]

(ii) Circumstances in which an Unregistered Company may be Wound Up

Under section 327 of the CWUMPO, an unregistered company may be wound up in the following circumstances:

(i) the company has been dissolved;[32]
(ii) the company has ceased to carry on business;[33]
(iii) the company is only carrying on business for the purpose of winding up its affairs;[34]
(iv) the company is unable to pay its debts;[35] or
(v) the court is of the opinion that it is just and equitable that the company should be wound up.[36]

For the purposes of section 327, an unregistered company is deemed to be unable to pay its debts if one of the following circumstances occurs:

(i) the company has failed within 21 days to pay a statutory demand served against it;[37]
(ii) an action or other proceeding has been instituted against a member of the company for a debt and the company has not within 10 days after being served with notice of the action:
  (a) paid, secured or compounded the debt;
  (b) caused the action to be stayed; or
  (c) indemnified the member against the action or proceeding and all costs, damages and expenses to be incurred;[38]
(iii) the company has failed to satisfy a judgment obtained and executed against it;[39] or
(iv) it is proved to the satisfaction of the court that the company is unable to pay its debts.[40]

(iii) Winding Up as an Exercise of Jurisdiction

It is now settled that while the *existence* of the court's power to wind up a foreign company is contained in section 327 of the CWUMPO, the *exercise* of that power is a matter of discretion for the court.[41] This discretionary jurisdiction has been described as an 'abnormal

[29] A club is not an 'association' in the context of winding up: *Re St James's Club* (1852) 2 De GM & G 383.
[30] *Re International Tin Council* [1989] Ch 309.
[31] *Re Zhu Kuan Group Co Ltd* (unreported, HCCW 874/2003, 2 August 2004).
[32] CWUMPO, s 327(3)(a).
[33] ibid.
[34] ibid.
[35] ibid s 327(3)(b).
[36] ibid s 327(3)(c).
[37] ibid s 327(4)(a).
[38] ibid s 327(4)(b).
[39] ibid s 327(4)(c).
[40] ibid s 327(4)(d).
[41] ibid s 327(1) provides that 'any unregistered company *may be wound up* under this Ordinance'. The discretionary nature conferred by this phrase has since been confirmed by the Court of Final Appeal in *Kam Leung*

jurisdiction', as it involves the court's assertion of jurisdiction over a body that is prima facie beyond the limits of its territory.[42] It should also be noted that the most appropriate jurisdiction for a company's winding up will usually be its place of incorporation, as it is the law of the company's domicile that govern its status as a legal entity. For this reason, the Court of Final Appeal in *Kam Leung Sui Kwan v Kam Kwan Lai* cautioned against the exercise of this 'abnormal jurisdiction' without good reason.[43]

Consequently, the Court of Final Appeal has adopted some 'necessary self-imposed constraints' by applying a three-step test when deciding whether to exercise its statutory jurisdiction to wind up a foreign company. The test is as follows:[44]

1. The company must have a sufficient connection with Hong Kong, although this does not mean that it must have assets in Hong Kong.
2. There must be a reasonable possibility that a winding up order will benefit those applying for it.
3. The court must be able to exercise jurisdiction over one or more persons in the distribution of the company's assets.

It has been held that the critical question in this three-step inquiry is the first issue of a 'sufficient connection' with Hong Kong. The other issues, of 'sufficient benefit' and 'the supervision of a distribution of assets', are necessary (but not sufficient) conditions of the first step.[45] The question of 'sufficient connection' will vary with each case, and the three-step test will apply differently depending on the circumstances.[46] The three core requirements may sometimes overlap[47] or individual steps may be dispensed with.[48] The satisfaction of one step may be sufficient.[49] Each requirement will be discussed below.

(a) 'Sufficient Connection with Hong Kong'

There is no definitive benchmark that demonstrates a 'sufficient connection' between the company sought to be wound up and Hong Kong. Nevertheless, certain factors have been considered by the court as relevant to an assessment of 'sufficient connection':

1. **Presence of assets**: While it is not a necessary precondition that a foreign company's assets be located in Hong Kong for it to be wound up, the presence of such assets in Hong Kong may demonstrate a sufficient connection.[50] This may be the case even if the assets are of negligible value.[51]

Sui Kwan v Kam Kwan Lai (2015) 18 HKCFAR 501 [19]. See also *Re Up Energy Development Group Ltd* [2022] 2 HKLRD 993, [2022] HKCFI 1329 [45].

[42] *Re Real Estate Development Co* [1991] BCLC 210, 217; *Up Energy Development Group Ltd* (n 41) [45].

[43] *Kam Leung Sui Kwan* (n 41) [19].

[44] *Re Beauty China Holdings Ltd* [2009] 6 HKC 351 [23], affirmed in *Kam Leung Sui Kwan* (n 41) [20].

[45] *Kam Leung Sui Kwan* (n 41) [24].

[46] ibid [36].

[47] ibid [22].

[48] *China Medical Technologies Inc (in liq) v Samson Tsang Tak Yung* [2018] HKCA 111 [17]–[25].

[49] The existence of substantial assets (Limb 3) is often sufficient to satisfy both the first and second requirements as well: *Kam Leung Sui Kwan* (n 41) [22].

[50] *Re Gottinghen Trading Ltd* [2012] 3 HKLRD 453.

[51] *Zhu Kuan Group Co Ltd* (n 31) [30].

2. **Carrying on of business in Hong Kong**: It is not a necessary precondition for winding up that the foreign company has had a place of business or carried on business in Hong Kong.[52] The court takes a practical approach in assessing the company's arrangements and its commercial activities within Hong Kong. The existence of a wholly owned subsidiary operating within Hong Kong may indicate a sufficient connection.[53]
3. **Hong Kong bank account**: The fact that the company has a Hong Kong bank account is not determinative. Matters such as the amount of funds in the account and the rate of transactional activity would be relevant pointers to a sufficient connection.[54]
4. **Debts or contracts arising in Hong Kong**: When taking into account the company's debt and the underlying contracts that gave rise to the debt on which a winding up is sought, the court will consider matters such as whether the relevant contract arose in Hong Kong or whether its governing law is Hong Kong law.[55]
5. **Advisers in Hong Kong**: The fact that Hong Kong solicitors have been appointed by the company to draft and negotiate the contract giving rise to the winding up debt would indicate a sufficient connection.[56] But a general appointment or retention of solicitors or other advisors (such as auditors or financial advisors) would not necessarily demonstrate a connection. Much will depend on the purpose and nature of their engagement.[57]
6. **Office-holders in Hong Kong**: If the company's only office is in Hong Kong and all its shareholders are domiciled in the jurisdiction, there will usually be a sufficient connection.[58] However, the fact that some of the company's directors or shareholders reside in Hong Kong will not demonstrate sufficient connection.[59]
7. **Listing**: It is usually sufficient to demonstrate a sufficient connection if the company is listed in Hong Kong.[60]

(b) 'Reasonable Possibility that the Winding Up Order would Benefit the Petitioner'

In *Shandong Chenming Paper Holdings Ltd v Arjowiggins HKK2 Ltd*,[61] the Hong Kong Court of Final Appeal held that a pragmatic approach should be taken to ascertain what is considered a 'reasonable' possibility that a winding up order would benefit the petitioner. Fok and Lam PJJ noted in their joint judgment that there is no doctrinal justification for confining the benefit narrowly to the distribution of assets by the liquidator in the winding up of the company. It is enough that the benefit will be enjoyed solely by the petitioners. There is also no requirement that the benefit come from the assets of the company. There have been cases where, even though there was nothing for the liquidator to administer, the court has found the second requirement to be satisfied as long as some useful purpose serving the legitimate

[52] *Kam Leung Sui Kwan* (n 41) [20].
[53] ibid [34].
[54] *Zhu Kuan Group Co Ltd* (n 31) [36].
[55] ibid [37].
[56] *Re a Company (No 003102 of 1991), ex p Nyckeln Finance Co Ltd* [1991] BCLC 539.
[57] *Beauty China Holdings Ltd* (n 44) [38].
[58] *Re Syria Ottoman Railway Co* (1904) 20 TLR 217.
[59] *Re Westminster Property Management Ltd (No 2)* [2001] BCC 305 [357].
[60] *Re Silver Base Group Holdings Ltd* [2022] HKCFI 2386.
[61] *Shandong Chenming Paper Holdings Ltd v Arjowiggins HKK2 Ltd* (2022) 25 HKCFAR 98, [2022] HKCFA 11.

interest of the petitioner can be identified. That benefit need not be monetary or tangible in nature. The fact that a similar result might be achieved by other means does not preclude reliance on a benefit as fulfilling the second requirement.[62]

In *Shandong Chenming*, the court was concerned with whether the exertion of commercial pressure through the presentation of a winding up petition could constitute a legitimate benefit for the petitioner. It was unanimously held that such commercial pressure was a legitimate benefit, as the primary consideration of the court was whether a 'reasonable possibility exists of a sufficient benefit accruing to the petitioner from being permitted to set in motion winding up procedures in Hong Kong in respect of a non-Hong Kong company'.[63] There would be a benefit if the setting in motion of winding up procedures results in the payment of an undisputed debt (as was the case on the facts).[64] The leverage generated by the presentation of a winding up petition was enough for the purposes of this second requirement.[65]

In general, a useful purpose to the petitioner will usually involve the realisation of assets to the benefit of creditors. However, as noted in *Shandong Chenming*, this is not the only beneficial situation. Any pragmatically useful purposes that a winding up petition might achieve would also be enough. The second requirement is thus a low threshold.[66]

(c) 'The Court must be Able to Exercise Jurisdiction Over One or More Persons in the Distribution of Assets'

As explained by Harris J in *Re China Medical Technologies Inc*, the third requirement asks whether

> there are persons with sufficient connection with the jurisdiction … who would become subject to the court's jurisdiction if a winding up order were … made … and sufficient economic interest in the winding up … to justify making an order which will engage the Hong Kong winding up regime.[67]

The presence of creditors who hold a material portion of the debt and who are located in Hong Kong will meet the criterion, though what a 'material' portion is will vary according to the circumstances. Additionally, the mere fact that a creditor has presented a petition is insufficient, so something more must have been done by the creditor to invoke the court's jurisdiction. Examples include being employed or resident within the jurisdiction, obtaining the benefit of a judgment debt within the jurisdiction or being registered under Part 16 of the CO with a place of business within the jurisdiction. In short, the creditor must have more than a general economic interest in the outcome of the winding up.

The absence of the court's ability to exercise jurisdiction over one or more persons in the distribution of assets is not fatal to the court's overall finding of a sufficient connection between the company and Hong Kong. This was confirmed by the Court of Appeal in

[62] ibid [54].
[63] ibid [61].
[64] ibid [63]–[67].
[65] In this case, the relevant leverage came from the possible impact that winding up proceedings would have on the company's listing status on the Hong Kong Stock Exchange: ibid [66].
[66] ibid [56].
[67] *Re China Medical Technologies Inc* [2014] 2 HKLRD 997 [48].

Re China Medical Technologies Inc, where the third condition merely served as one aspect of an overarching enquiry into the sufficiency of connection between the company and Hong Kong, and was not a necessary condition in every case.[68] So long as the connection between the company and Hong Kong is strong or there is a significant benefit to be obtained from a winding up, the third requirement may be dispensed with altogether.[69]

(iv) Winding Up of Companies Incorporated Outside Hong Kong by Shareholders' Petition

In principle, the requirement for a sufficient connection with Hong Kong applies regardless of whether winding up proceedings were brought pursuant to a creditors' or shareholders' petition. This was confirmed by the Court of Final Appeal in *Kam Leung Sui Kwan v Kam Kwan Lai*, albeit with the court noting substantive differences between the two types of petition:[70]

1. **Difference in parties**: While a company remains a necessary defendant to every winding up petition, it is a *party* against whom the dispute is raised in the context of a creditors' petition. It is more akin to the *subject* of the dispute where a shareholders' petition is concerned. This is because a shareholders' petition will usually be brought as a result of a dispute with the company's internal affairs.
2. **Difference in purpose**: A creditors' petition is usually meant to obtain repayment of a debt, while a shareholders' petition is supposed to realise the petitioners' investment in the company. The parties' dispute may then involve a lengthy and detailed examination of the management of the company's internal affairs.

While such differences do not heighten the level of sufficiency of the connection required between the company and Hong Kong, they determine the factors that a petitioner must demonstrate to establish a sufficient connection in either form of petition. In the case of a shareholders' petition, since it ultimately involves a dispute among shareholders, their presence in the jurisdiction becomes an important factor.[71] Consequently, the following key considerations identified by Harris J in *Re ACE International (BVI) Ltd* will be considered: (i) the whereabouts of the shareholders and directors; (ii) the place where the company's subsidiaries are incorporated; (iii) the place where assets (including the assets of wholly owned subsidiaries) of the corporate group are situated; (iv) the place where the company derives its income; and (v) the place where the operations of the company take place.[72]

C. Service of Documents in Winding Up Cases

Service of documents is important in litigation, including winding up. In the context of winding up, the documents to be served on an indebted company include: (i) a statutory

[68] *China Medical Technologies Inc* (n 48) [20].
[69] ibid [25].
[70] *Kam Leung Sui Kwan* (n 41) [25]–[26].
[71] ibid [30].
[72] *Re ACE International (BVI) Ltd* [2020] 2 HKLRD 508, [2020] HKCFI 498 [4].

demand; (ii) a winding up petition; (iii) an application by originating summons for winding up; and (iv) winding up orders. There are three typical scenarios: (i) documents are served on Hong Kong companies; (ii) documents are served on unregistered companies; and (iii) documents are served on companies that do not have an address in Hong Kong.

(i) Service of Statutory Demand

There are multiple grounds warranting a winding up. Section 177(1) of the CWUMPO sets out a number of grounds for a winding up application. In particular, section 177(1)(d) provides that a company may be wound up by the court if the company is unable to pay its debts as and when they become due.[73] While the creditor could prove the company's inability to pay its debts through evidence, that is often not easy to do. Section 178 of the CWUMPO deems a company to be insolvent if it fails to pay the sum stipulated in a statutory demand which has been properly served on the company. The company has 21 days in which to pay the debt, otherwise the deeming provision will take effect. Note that there must be no defence to the debt demanded. If the alleged debt is disputed by the company on arguable grounds, the statutory demand procedure cannot be used. Statutory demands therefore play an important role in winding up by providing a reason for a compulsory wind-up, and shift the evidentiary burden to the company to disprove insolvency. Service is essential as it establishes that a statutory demand was issued on a particular date and the company had notice of the demand from that date.

(a) Documents Served on Hong Kong Companies

Service of a document on Hong Kong companies is straightforward.[74] In the context of winding up under section 178(1)(a)(i) of the CWUMPO, a creditor can serve a statutory demand on a company by leaving the same at (or posting it to) the company's registered office.

(b) Documents Served on Unregistered Companies

Service of a statutory demand on an unregistered company is likewise straightforward. By section 327(4)(a) of the CWUMPO, a statutory demand may be served upon an unregistered company by leaving it at the company's principal place of business, by delivering it to an officer of the company or by other methods directed by the court.

In *Re Project Global Ltd*,[75] a BVI company left its previous office address in Hong Kong and notified the Business Registration Office of the change of place of business. The company did not, however, notify the Registrar of Companies until later. Between the change of address and the late notice to the Registrar of Companies, solicitors of the creditor had no idea of the change and served the statutory demand at the previous office. The court ruled that the 'principal place of business' in section 327 of the CWUMPO referred to the address

[73] For details of this ground, see Stefan Lo, *Company Law in Hong Kong: Insolvency 2023* (Sweet & Maxwell 2023) para 4.021.

[74] For service on companies generally, see CO, ss 803 and 827, discussed in ch 9, s I.A.

[75] *Re Project Global Ltd* [2005] 4 HKLRD 185.

as found in the Companies Registry office.[76] This enables the public to rely on the records of the Company Registry and places the burden on a company to notify the Registrar of Companies of a change of address as soon as possible.[77]

Creditors may have to seek directions from the court. In *Ironwood Capital Management Ltd v KTH Recovery Fund II Ltd*,[78] Kwan J confirmed the court's jurisdiction to give such directions. In that case, the creditor obtained an order from the court, enabling service of a statutory demand at the debtor company's last known principal place in Hong Kong and on the solicitors' firm which had previously acted for the company.[79]

(c) Companies that have no Registered Office or Principal Place of Business in Hong Kong

There is no provision or case authority as to the service of statutory demand on companies that do not have an address in Hong Kong. One might refer to Practice Direction 3.1, paragraph 2.2:

> Practitioners are reminded that a statutory demand is not a document issued by the Court. Leave to serve out of the jurisdiction and leave to effect service by way of substituted service are not, therefore, required. A creditor wishing to serve a statutory demand outside the jurisdiction in a foreign country may adopt the procedure prescribed by the Rules of the High Court in Order 11 Rule 6.

While this paragraph falls under the heading of 'Bankruptcy Proceedings', the rule still provides guidance as it points the creditors to Order 11, rule 6 of the Rules of the High Court (Cap 4A) (RHC). That rule allows litigants to serve a writ abroad through the 1970 HCCH Convention on the Service Abroad of Judicial and Extrajudicial Documents in Civil or Commercial Matters (the Hague Service Convention). The word 'may' in the provision endows the creditor with flexibility to choose whether to serve under the Hague Service Convention. If the creditor relies on the rule, it should inquire whether the destination jurisdiction is a contracting state to the Hague Service Convention.[80]

It was suggested that, not being a court document, a statutory demand may simply be notified by post to the debtor company abroad.[81] Nevertheless, a creditor should also check the legal requirements for notifying or serving a company under the relevant foreign law.

(ii) Service of Winding Up Petition

Rule 25 of the Companies (Winding-up) Rules (Cap 32H) (CWUR) states:[82]

> Every petition shall, unless presented by the company, be served upon the company at the registered office, if any, of the company, and if there is no registered office, then at the principal or last known principal place of business of the company, if any such can be found, by leaving a copy

[76] ibid [60].
[77] ibid.
[78] *Ironwood Capital Management Ltd v KTH Recovery Fund II Ltd* [2007] 2 HKLRD 288.
[79] ibid [12]–[15].
[80] See ch 9, s VII. For the contracting states, see www.hcch.net/e/conventions/menu142.html.
[81] Graeme Johnston and Paul Harris, *The Conflict of Laws in Hong Kong*, 3rd edn (Sweet & Maxwell, 2017) para 8.058.
[82] As to the manner of service, see CWUR, r 20.

with any member, officer, or servant of the company there, or in case no such member, officer, or servant can be found there, then by leaving a copy at such registered office or principal place of business, or by serving it on such member, officer, or servant of the company as the court may direct; and where the company is being wound up voluntarily, the petition shall also be served upon the liquidator (if any), appointed for the purpose of winding up the affairs of the company.

Prior to the new Practice Direction 3.1, there were no provisions on the service of a winding up petition on an unregistered company which had no Hong Kong office or place of business. In *Re Sunni International Ltd*, Godfrey Lam J observed that this situation was 'highly unsatisfactory'. The judge suggested that the solution was to construe, 'unless the court otherwise in any special case direct', rule 210 of the CWUR as empowering the court to adapt Order 11, rule 1(1) of the RHC to winding up proceedings.[83] On that footing, leave would be needed for service out of the jurisdiction on the debtor company and the court would have the discretion to grant or refuse such leave.[84] In general, the court would not grant leave to serve out of the jurisdiction unless the petitioner could demonstrate that it had a good arguable case for winding up, that there was sufficient connection between the debtor company and Hong Kong, and that the core requirements for winding up a foreign company in Hong Kong were met as a matter of first impression.[85] The conundrum has since been resolved, along similar lines, by paragraph 12.1 of the new Practice Direction 3.1. Paragraph 12.1 contains a summary as to the service of a winding up petition in different situations:

(a) In respect of a Hong Kong company, the petition shall be served at its registered office in Hong Kong.
(b) In respect of a 'registered non-Hong Kong company', the petition shall be served in Hong Kong on the authorized representative of the company or at the place of business established by the company (as the case may be) in Hong Kong in accordance with Section[s] 803(1)–(4) of the Companies Ordinance.
(c) In respect of a 'non-Hong Kong company' that has established a place of business in Hong Kong, the petition shall be served at the place of business. If the 'non-Hong Kong company' no longer has a place of business in Hong Kong, the petition shall be served in accordance with Section 803(5)(b) of the Companies Ordinance.
(d) In respect of an 'unregistered company' which has no place of business in Hong Kong and is not registered under Section 777 of the Companies Ordinance, leave to serve the petition out of the jurisdiction must be obtained from the Court under the adapted Order 11, rule 1(1) of the Rules of the High Court. The applicant has to demonstrate a good arguable case that the 3 core requirements for the Court to exercise the jurisdiction under Section 327 of the [Companies (Winding Up and Miscellaneous Provisions) Ordinance] are met and that there is a serious issue to be tried on the merits.

(iii) Service of Originating Summons

Where, in the course of winding up proceedings, either of the parties needs to serve an originating summons on a respondent outside Hong Kong, the applicant has to seek leave pursuant to Order 11 of the RHC.

[83] ibid [61]–[65].
[84] ibid [66].
[85] ibid [67]. See also *Kam Leung Sui Kwan v Kam Kwan Lai* [2014] 2 HKLRD 313 [38].

(iv) Service of Orders

Under Rule 31 of the Bankruptcy Rules (Cap 6A), if the debtor is not in Hong Kong or cannot be found, the documents arising in personal bankruptcy proceedings may be served in whatever manner the court thinks fit. In contrast, in corporate insolvency proceedings, the service of winding up orders and related documents abroad is only permissible if leave has been obtained in accordance with Order 11, rule 9 of the RHC.

D. Effect of Winding Up

When a company is wound up by a Hong Kong court, the court has the power and discretion under section 198 of the CWUMPO, on the application of the liquidator, to vest property of the company in the liquidator. The liquidator is given wide powers, as provided in section 199 and Schedule 25 of the CWUMPO. Hong Kong does not have a 'rehabilitative' corporate insolvency regime such as Chapter 11 of the United States Bankruptcy Code or the administration regime under Schedule B1 of the Insolvency Act 1986 in the UK. It was announced by the Hong Kong government in 2020 that a statutory corporate rescue procedure and insolvent trading provisions will be introduced by the Companies (Corporate Rescue) Bill for local companies and registered non-Hong Kong companies.[86] No such Bill has been introduced as of today.

III. Cross-Border Insolvency

A. Recognition and Assistance to Foreign Liquidators under Common Law

At common law, a liquidator appointed abroad who wishes to wind up a foreign company for its Hong Kong assets could commence a liquidation of the company in Hong Kong. Alternatively, the liquidator may apply to a Hong Kong court for recognition of a foreign liquidation and assistance with it.[87] A foreign liquidator may also commence civil proceedings, seek injunctive relief, seek a declaration regarding the effect of foreign insolvency proceedings, attempt to recover debts and submit a proof of debt in a Hong Kong insolvency. The foreign insolvency proceedings are not a ground for the automatic stay of actions brought by creditors in Hong Kong. However, it is possible to apply to stay the actions in Hong Kong as a means of assistance to foreign insolvency proceedings.[88]

[86] Legislative Council Panel on Financial Affairs, 'Legislative Proposals of the Companies (Corporate Rescue) Bill' (LC Paper No CB(1)48/20-21(03), 22 October 2020), www.legco.gov.hk/yr20-21/english/panels/fa/papers/fa20201102cb1-48-3-e.pdf.

[87] *Joint Official Liquidators of A Co* (n 5). See also *Rubin v Eurofinance SA* [2012] UKSC 46, [2013] 1 AC 236.

[88] See, eg *Hong Kong Institute of Education v Aoki Corp* [2004] 2 HKLRD 760 (proceedings to enforce garnishee order stayed in light of ongoing PRC bankruptcy); *CCIC Finance Ltd v Guangdong International Trust & Investment Corp* [2005] 2 HKC 589 (execution of summary judgment stayed in light of Japanese civil rehabilitation proceedings).

(i) Principles of Recognition

The prerequisite for assistance to a foreign liquidator is the recognition of the foreign insolvency proceedings and the appointment of the foreign liquidator to act on the company's behalf.[89] The Hong Kong court will consider the appropriateness of granting assistance after it has granted recognition.[90] In determining recognition, the Hong Kong courts adhere to common law principles. The common law test adopted by the Hong Kong court is two-pronged. First, the foreign insolvency proceedings will only be recognised if they constitute collective insolvency proceedings.[91] Second, the foreign insolvency proceedings must have been commenced in the debtor company's place of incorporation.[92] An order for recognition is not necessary if the foreign liquidator is merely seeking information and documents in Hong Kong.[93] However, recognition will be needed if the foreign liquidator wants to deal with the company's property in Hong Kong.[94]

(ii) Order for Assistance

An order for assistance may confer the same powers[95] on a foreign liquidator that a domestic liquidator can exercise in Hong Kong.[96] Further, the granting of assistance applies to both compulsory and voluntary winding up. That differs from the position under the English law.[97] Nonetheless, the scope does not extend to solvent winding up proceedings.[98]

The discretion to grant assistance is constrained. A foreign liquidator will only be granted assistance if he or she satisfies certain requirements:[99]

(i) the specific assistance sought has to be available under Hong Kong law and the law of the place in which the liquidator was appointed;
(ii) the grant of assistance must be consistent with the laws and policies of Hong Kong;
(iii) the assistance should not be for purposes which are more properly the subject of other schemes; and
(iv) the assistance should not be to obtain material for use in litigation.

[89] Look Chan Ho, *Cross-Border Insolvency: Principles and Practice* (Sweet & Maxwell, 2016) para 3.001.
[90] *Re Joint Liquidators of Supreme Tycoon Ltd* [2018] 1 HKLRD 1120, [2018] HKCFI 277 [12].
[91] See, eg *Re Joint Provisional Liquidators of China Lumena New Materials Corp* [2018] HKCFI 276.
[92] See, eg *Supreme Tycoon Ltd* (n 90) [12]; *Re Mr Kaoru Takamatsu* [2019] 5 HKC 505, [2019] HKCFI 802 [5]; *Re CEFC Shanghai International Group Ltd* [2020] 1 HKLRD 676, [2020] HKCFI 167 [8]. This is later extended to foreign insolvency proceedings in the jurisdiction in which the company's centre of main interests (COMI) is located. See s III.A(iii) below.
[93] *Joint Official Liquidators of A Co* (n 5).
[94] *Bay Capital Asia Fund LP (in official liq) v DBS Bank (Hong Kong) Ltd* (unreported, HCMP 3104/2015, 2 November 2016).
[95] *Supreme Tycoon Ltd* (n 90) [12]. In general, it includes powers conferred by the CWUMPO on the liquidators appointed in a Hong Kong liquidation.
[96] *Re Global Brands Group Holding Ltd (in liq)* [2022] 3 HKLRD 316, [2022] HKCFI 1789.
[97] *Supreme Tycoon Ltd* (n 90); *cf Singularis Holdings Ltd v PricewaterhouseCoopers* [2014] UKPC 36, [2015] AC 1675.
[98] *Supreme Tycoon Ltd* (n 90).
[99] *Re BJB Career Education Co Ltd* [2017] 1 HKLRD 113; *Singularis Holdings Ltd* (n 97) [18]–[19]. For the rules related to the recognition and assistance of insolvency proceedings in civil law jurisdictions, see *China Lumena New Materials Corp* (n 91); *Supreme Tycoon Ltd* (n 90); *Kaoru Takamatsu* (n 92) [9], [13]–[14].

(iii) Doctrinal Issues and Further Development

Orthodox common law recognises foreign insolvency proceedings if they are collective and have been opened in the company's country of incorporation.[100] Nonetheless, *Dicey, Morris and Collins* observes that, in some circumstances, it might be appropriate to regard jurisdictions other than the company's place of incorporation as the seat of the principal liquidation.[101] In *Re HIH Casualty and General Insurance*, Lord Hoffmann suggested obiter that there should be unitary bankruptcy proceedings in the court of the home insolvency jurisdiction. It was thought that modified universalism should apply to all an insolvent company's assets:[102]

> 6. Despite the absence of statutory provision, some degree of international co-operation in corporate insolvency had been achieved by judicial practice. This was based upon what English judges have for many years regarded as a general principle of private international law, namely that bankruptcy (whether personal or corporate) should be unitary and universal. There should be a unitary bankruptcy proceeding in the court of the bankrupt's domicile which receives worldwide recognition and it should apply universally to all the bankrupt's assets.
>
> 7. This was very much a principle rather than a rule. It is heavily qualified by exceptions on pragmatic grounds; elsewhere I have described it as an aspiration: see *Cambridge Gas Transportation Corpn v Official Committee of Unsecured Creditors of Navigator Holdings plc* [2007] 1 AC 508, 517, para 17. Professor Jay Westbrook, a distinguished American writer on international insolvency has called it a principle of 'modified universalism': see also Fletcher, *Insolvency in Private International Law*, 2nd ed (2005), pp 15–17. Full universalism can be attained only by international treaty. Nevertheless, even in its modified and pragmatic form, the principle is a potent one.
>
> …
>
> 30. … The primary rule of private international law which seems to me applicable to this case is the principle of (modified) universalism, which has been the golden thread running through English cross-border insolvency law since the 18th century. That principle requires that English courts should, so far as is consistent with justice and UK public policy, co-operate with the courts in the country of the principal liquidation to ensure that all the company's assets are distributed to its creditors under a single system of distribution. That is the purpose of the power to direct remittal.
>
> 31. In the present case I do not see that it would offend against any principle of justice for the assets to be remitted to Australia. In some cases there may be some doubt about how to determine the appropriate jurisdiction which should be regarded as the seat of the principal liquidation. I have spoken in a rather old-fashioned way of the company's domicile because that is the term used in the old cases, but I do not claim it is necessarily the best one. Usually it means the place where the company is incorporated but that may be some offshore island with which the company's business has no real connection. The Council Regulation on insolvency proceedings (Council Regulation (EC) No 1346/2000 of 29 May 2000) uses the concept of the 'centre of a debtor's main interests' as a test, with a presumption that it is the place where the registered office is situated: see article 3(1). That may be more appropriate. But in this case it does not matter because on any view, these are

[100] *Singularis Holdings Ltd* (n 97).

[101] Lord Collins of Mapesbury and Jonathan Harris (gen eds), *Dicey, Morris and Collins on the Conflict of Laws*, 16th edn (Sweet & Maxwell, 2022) para 30–146. See also *Re HIH Casualty and General Insurance* [2008] UKHL 21, [2008] 1 WLR 852 [30]–[31].

[102] *HIH Casualty and General Insurance* (n 101) [6]–[7] and [30]–[31]. See also *Cambridge Gas Transportation Corp v Official Committee of Unsecured Creditors of Navigator Holdings plc* [2006] UKPC 26, [2007] 1 AC 508.

> Australian companies. They are incorporated in Australia, their central management has been in Australia and the overwhelming majority of their assets and liabilities are situated in Australia.

Lord Hoffmann's view implies that the recognition of liquidators appointed in the place of a debtor's company incorporation can operate as a default rule. But recognition of liquidators appointed in a company's centre of main interests (COMI) can displace that rule where the place of incorporation and the COMI are different.

In *Re Global Brands Group Holding Ltd*, Harris J concurred:[103]

> 30. The position adopted in Hong Kong has historically been that a liquidator appointed in the place of incorporation is recognised. However, it would be incorrect to say that the Hong Kong recognition criteria has exclusively been tied to the debtor's country of incorporation. There are instances of the Hong Kong court granting, or being willing to grant, recognition to insolvency office-holders appointed in a foreign jurisdiction which was not the jurisdiction of incorporation. In *Re The Russo-Asiatic Bank*, the Court recognised liquidators appointed by the English court over a Russian bank. In *Bank of Credit and Commerce International (Overseas) Ltd v Bank of Credit & Commerce International (Overseas) Ltd, Macau Branch*, the Court of Appeal recognised liquidators appointed in Macau over a Cayman-incorporated bank. In *Joint Administrators of African Minerals Ltd v Madison Pacific Trust Ltd*, I took the view that there was no objection in principle to granting recognition to an English administrator over a Bermuda-incorporated company with its COMI in England.

Harris J identified four approaches to determining the COMI:[104]

> 34. … There are four established approaches. All are similar. Under the Cooperation Mechanism, COMI generally means the place of incorporation, although other factors are also relevant, including the place of the debtor's principal office, the debtor's principal place of business, and the place of the debtor's principal assets … In the context of the common law Lord Hoffmann in *HIH* regarded the following as the key COMI elements – the place of incorporation, the place of central management, and the location of assets and liabilities. In *Re Opti-Medix Ltd*, the Singapore court suggested the following common-law COMI test:
>
> The COMI will likely be the place where most dealings occur, most money is paid in and out, and most decisions are made. It is thus the place where the bulk of the business is carried out, and for that reason, provides a strong connecting factor to the courts there …
>
> I would note that on a common law adoption of the COMI test, there need not necessarily be a presumption in favour of the registered office, as there is under the Model Law or the EU Insolvency Regulation. However, such a presumption provides a sound default rule in the absence of evidence to the contrary, and provides certainty and regularity. The adoption of such a presumption would also harmonise the results on common law and statutory applications of the COMI test.

Harris J's views suggest that, going forward, the Hong Kong court will typically grant recognition and assistance to foreign liquidation in a company's COMI. For foreign insolvency proceedings in the place of incorporation, recognition and assistance is limited to 'managerial assistance' (recognising the liquidator's authority to represent a company) or those required as a matter of practicality.[105]

[103] *Re Global Brands Group Holding Ltd* (n 96) [30].

[104] ibid [34]. In addition to *Re Opti-Medix Ltd (in liq)* [2016] 4 SLR 12, the judgment also quoted *Re Investin Quay House Ltd* [2015] EWHC 2371 (Ch) [35], *Re Ocean Rig UDW Inc* 570 BR 687 (Bankr SDNY, 24 August 2017) and *Re Zetta Jet Pte Ltd* [2019] 4 SLR 1343: ibid [35]–[38].

[105] *Re Global Brands Group Holding Ltd* (n 96) [50].

(iv) Assistance Through the Z-Obee *Approach*

Domestically, the Hong Kong court is empowered to appoint provisional liquidators over a company by section 193 of the CWUMPO. The statute is silent as to the extraterritorial jurisdiction of Hong Kong liquidators. But it is clear that a Hong Kong-appointed liquidator may commence insolvency proceedings abroad in relation to companies in liquidation in Hong Kong.[106]

In *Re Legend International Resorts*, the Court of Appeal held that provisional liquidators could be appointed on the basis that the company was insolvent and that its assets were in jeopardy. The provisional liquidator can then protect and gather in the company's assets. But, according to the Court of Appeal, a provisional liquidator will not be appointed solely to facilitate a corporate rescue.[107] This implies that the Hong Kong court will not grant general stays of actions against a company and its subsidiaries merely to facilitate a global corporate restructuring.

However, the latter restriction has been circumvented by foreign liquidators applying for recognition and assistance.[108] The technique first emerged in the case of *Z-Obee*.[109] Harris J explained the rationale, operation and development of the *Z-Obee* approach as follows:[110]

> 11. … the common law power [to recognise foreign liquidators] exists to assist collective insolvency processes. If an application for recognition is made by liquidators, or their equivalent, appointed over a company that has been wound up for the purpose of collecting a company's assets and distributing them amongst its creditors, it is likely that the court will accept that it is being asked to use its common law powers for the purpose that it is intended, namely, to ensure that all a company's assets are distributed to its creditors under a single system of distribution. However, it is important to understand that many of the applications that have been made to the court since *Joint Official Liquidators of A Co v B* was decided in 2014 have not been made by liquidators for this purpose. Many have been made by provisional liquidators appointed in the place of incorporation on a soft-touch basis with a view to facilitating a restructuring of a company's debt using a scheme of arrangement introduced in both the jurisdiction of incorporation and Hong Kong. This technique is often referred to by the name of the case in which it first emerged: *Z-Obee*. It was developed to overcome difficulties created by the Court of Appeal's decision in *Legend International Resorts* Limited, which rejected the appointment of provisional liquidators as a means to restructure debt. The recognition of the foreign appointments is justified by reference to the principles of private international law discussed in *Joint Official Liquidators of A Co v B*. Assistance in the form of powers to facilitate a restructuring in Hong Kong is justified by the application of the common law principles most recently discussed in *Re Moody Technology Holdings Ltd*. …
>
> 12. However, the fact that the courts have found that the common law principles support assisting a soft-touch provisional liquidation does not mean that the courts have accepted that a foreign soft-touch provisional liquidation is for all purposes to be treated as a collective insolvency process.
>
> 13. If soft-touch provisional liquidation is properly characterised (viewed from the perspective of the Hong Kong statutory insolvency regime), as a collective insolvency process it would suggest

[106] *American Express International Banking Corp v Johnson* [1984] HKLR 372.

[107] *Re Legend International Resorts Ltd* [2006] 2 HKLRD 192, 203G–H.

[108] *Re The Joint and Several Provisional Liquidators of FDG Electric Vehicles Ltd* [2020] 5 HKLRD 701, [2020] HKCFI 2931.

[109] *Re Z-Obee Holdings Ltd* [2018] 1 HKLRD 165, [2017] HKCFI 2204.

[110] *FDG Electric Vehicles Ltd* (n 108) [11]–[13].

> that there is nothing objectionable in appointing provisional liquidators in Hong Kong with a view to them restructuring the debt of a company including restructuring through introduction of a scheme of arrangement. …

Since then, *Z-Obee* applications have become commonplace. The court has accordingly formulated a standard order for recognition and assistance. See the Appendix to *Re Centaur Litigation SPC* for the text.[111] The standard form is merely intended as guidance for practitioners, the precise language used being subject to refinement in light of different circumstances.[112] In effect, the standard order provides for a stay of proceedings against a company and its assets in Hong Kong without leave of the court. Harris J explained the intention extra-judicially: 'This is intended to broadly replicate the impact of the making of a winding up order in Hong Kong without the need for a petition and engagement of our entire insolvency regime, thereby saving time and costs.'[113]

In *Re FDG Electrical Vehicles Ltd*, however, Harris J expressed concerns over problems arising from the standard order.[114] For instance, where there are ongoing actions proceedings in Hong Kong, an application for a stay should be made in those proceedings rather than a global application before the Companies court to stay all ongoing proceedings. Harris J doubted whether it was appropriate to grant a stay *en bloc* of unidentified future proceedings. Further, where a debt is disputed, the existence of a foreign insolvency should not prevent a Hong Kong creditor from claiming a right to payment. As a matter of principle, a stay should not be granted in respect of (say) an action to establish a right to payment under a contract governed by Hong Kong law, especially if the creditor seeks a judgment in its favour for the purposes of establishing the creditor's rights in the foreign insolvency proceedings. Harris J therefore modified paragraph 4 of the standard order to read as follows:[115]

> If the Provisional Liquidators wish to apply for a stay or other directions in respect of proceedings in the High Court of any sort as a consequence of the recognition of their appointment by this order such application shall be listed before the Honourable Mr Justice Harris or such other judge as he shall direct. The Provisional Liquidators shall write to the clerk to the Honourable Mr Justice Harris seeking case management directions for the determination of any application that they wish to make pursuant to this order.

While the court did not give a conclusive view on the issue of stay and the most desirable effect of the revised paragraph 4, the latest development connotes that the court will take a more prudent approach in the future. The revision shows that the court will grant a stay on a

[111] *Re Joint Official Liquidators of Centaur Litigation SPC* (unreported, HCMP 3389/2015, 10 March 2016).

[112] *Re Rennie Produce (Aust) Pty Ltd (in liq in Australia)* (unreported, HCMP 1640/2016, 26 August 2016).

[113] Jonathan Harris, 'Understanding Cross-Border Insolvency in the Hong Kong Context' (2017) 47 *Hong Kong Law Journal* 55, 63. See also *FDG Electric Vehicles Ltd* (n 108) [7], where his Lordship explained that it 'was intended to be in the nature of a case management provision, which would ensure that action would not take place in Hong Kong without the relevant parties being aware of the impact of the foreign insolvency proceedings and, if appropriate, a stay granted'.

[114] *FDG Electric Vehicles Ltd* (n 108) [7], [8] and [15]. In particular, for the third problem, see *Antony Gibbs & Sons v La Société Industrielle et Commerciale des Métaux* (1890) 25 QBD 399, where it was ruled that a debt governed by the law of a jurisdiction cannot be discharged or compromised by a foreign insolvency proceedings; *In re OJSC International Bank of Azerbaijan* [2018] EWHC 59 (Ch), [2018] Bus LR 1270 [44]. See also s III.C below.

[115] *FDG Electric Vehicles Ltd* (n 108) [7].

case-by-case basis, instead of allowing automatic stay by way of a standard order for recognition and assistance.[116]

For a sample order for the production of documents in Hong Kong, see *Re Rennie Produce (Aust) Pty Ltd*.[117] A straightforward request for documents, such as routine banking documents, need not require additional explicit judicial assistance.[118] It is also possible for foreign liquidators to apply to examine a company director in Hong Kong.[119]

B. Recognition and Assistance between Mainland China and Hong Kong

Unlike England and Australia, whose laws provide for cross-border insolvency, Hong Kong does not have any such statutory regime. Hong Kong has not adopted the UNCITRAL Model Law on Cross-Border Insolvency. It has instead had to develop its law on cross-border insolvency through judicial precedents.[120] The only legislation providing for a cross-border assistance regime is the Mainland–Hong Kong cooperation mechanism set up in 2021.

(i) Recognition and Assistance by the Cooperation Mechanism in Shanghai, Xiamen and Shenzhen

In May 2021, the Supreme People's Court of the PRC and the Hong Kong government signed the Record of Meeting on Mutual Recognition of and Assistance to Bankruptcy (Insolvency) Proceedings. The Record of Meeting establishes a cooperative framework to deal with corporate insolvency and debt restructuring. Subsequently, the Supreme People's Court issued the 'Opinion on Taking Forward a Pilot Measure in relation to the Recognition of and Assistance to Insolvency Proceedings' (the SPC Insolvency Opinion). The SPC Insolvency Opinion promulgated rules on cooperation on insolvency matters between the Intermediate People's Courts in Shanghai, Xiamen and Shenzhen, and the Hong Kong Court of First Instance. Concurrently, Hong Kong's Department of Justice issued 'Procedures for a Mainland Administrator's Application to the Hong Kong SAR Court for Recognition and Assistance: Practical Guide' as a reference on cross-border recognition and assistance in insolvency matters. The Record of Meeting, the SPC Insolvency Opinion and the Practical Guide together constitute a cooperation mechanism between Mainland China and Hong Kong.[121]

To benefit from the cooperation mechanism, the Hong Kong liquidator must first apply by letter of request to the Hong Kong court. The application is by summons supported by an affidavit. Once the letter of request is issued, the liquidator can apply to the relevant

[116] See also Charles Z Qu, 'Cross Border Assistance as a Restructuring Device for Hong Kong: The Case for Its Retention' (2022) 18(3) *Journal of Private International Law* 468.
[117] *Rennie Produce (Aust) Pty Ltd* (n 112).
[118] *Bay Capital Asia Fund LP* (n 94).
[119] *BJB Career Education Co Ltd* (n 99).
[120] *Re Lamtex Holdings Ltd* [2021] 2 HKLRD 177, [2021] HKCFI 622 [22].
[121] These documents are available online: www.doj.gov.hk/en/mainland_and_macao/arrangements_with_the_mainland.html.

Mainland court. The application must be accompanied by the said letter of request, the Hong Kong court judgment authorising the letter and supporting documents.[122]

(a) Conditions for Letter of Request

According to *Re Trinity International Brands Ltd*, a letter of request will only be granted if the Hong Kong liquidator satisfies two conditions.[123] The first condition is that the application complies with the requirements of the cooperation mechanism. This means the following:[124]

1. The application is made by a liquidator in insolvency proceedings in Hong Kong.
2. Recognition and assistance are being sought from the People's Court in Shanghai, Xiamen or Shenzhen.
3. The order being sought is for recognition of the Hong Kong liquidator and assistance in the discharge of his or her duties.
4. Hong Kong has been the COMI for at least six months.
5. The company's principal assets are in Shanghai, Xiamen or Shenzhen, or the company has a place of business or representative office in Shanghai, Xiamen or Shenzhen.

The second condition is that the recognition and assistance being sought must be necessary to enable the liquidators to carry out their functions as liquidators of the company in Mainland China.[125] The rationale is to protect the interests of the company from unnecessary applications.[126] This limb can be satisfied if (i) the debtor company's principal or most valuable asset is situated in Mainland China and (ii) the company's acts or omissions pose a threat to its assets in Mainland China.[127] An example of this would be the failure to deal with or defend legal proceedings which would affect the assets (and harm the interests) of the company.[128]

Since the implementation of the cooperation mechanism, the Hong Kong court has evinced a willingness to accede to applications for letter of request.[129] In *Re Husk's Green Technology Holding Co Ltd*, the applicant was granted a letter of request despite not fully satisfying the requirements.[130]

[122] SPC Insolvency Opinion, Arts 6 and 7.

[123] *Re Trinity International Brands Ltd* [2023] HKCFI 1581 [12].

[124] ibid [13]. For details of how the five requirements could be satisfied, see ibid [19]; *Re Husk's Green Technology Holding Co Ltd (in liq)* [2024] 1 HKLRD 134, [2023] HKCFI 3054 [19]–[26].

[125] *Trinity International Brands Ltd* (n 123) [12].

[126] ibid.

[127] See, eg ibid [21].

[128] *Husk's Green Technology Holding Co Ltd* (n 124) [27].

[129] See, eg *Re Samson Paper Co Ltd (in liq)* [2021] 3 HKLRD 727, [2021] HKCFI 2151; *Re Zhaoheng Hydropower (Hong Kong) Ltd* [2022] HKCFI 248; *Re Ozner Water International Holding Ltd* [2022] 2 HKC 634, [2022] HKCFI 363; *Re Hong Kong Fresh Water International Group Ltd* [2022] HKCFI 924; *Trinity International Brands Ltd* (n 123); *Husk's Green Technology Holding Co Ltd* (n 124).

[130] In *Husk's Green Technology Holding Co Ltd* (n 124) [3]–[4] and [28], the applicant (ie the creditor of the debtor company) failed to meet the locus requirement as: (i) he was not the liquidator of the company and the summons was not supported with sufficient evidence; (ii) there was no evidence supporting the assertion that the winding up proceedings had been converted into one of voluntary liquidation; and (iii) there was no draft order or draft letter of request. The court deemed these failures to be unacceptable.

(b) Effects of Recognition and Available Assistance

Upon the recognition of the Hong Kong insolvency proceedings by the Mainland courts, further payments of debts to individual creditors will be invalidated.[131] Civil actions or arbitration proceedings against the debtor company will be stayed automatically until the Hong Kong liquidator takes over.[132] Executions being levied against the debtor company's property will be suspended.[133]

A wide range of assistance is available under the cooperation mechanisms. Liquidators may seek assistance by application to the Mainland courts. Assistance includes the realisation of bankruptcy property, distribution of bankruptcy property, debt restructuring arrangement, termination of bankruptcy proceedings, etc.[134] Liquidators may also seek orders conferring a wide range of powers and duties upon themselves.[135] For example, under Article 14(9) of the SPC Insolvency Opinion, the PRC court has a discretion to allow the liquidators to perform such other duties as it considers suitable. However, those duties must fall within the scope of the PRC's Enterprise Bankruptcy Law and Hong Kong law. Liquidators must seek approval from the Mainland court if creditors' interests would be impacted by a disposal of property.[136] The PRC court may appoint a Mainland China administrator to assist with the performance of the liquidators' duties in Mainland China.[137]

Under the cooperation mechanism, liquidators have to be aware of PRC rules governing the distribution of the debtor company's assets. Property in Mainland China should primarily be used to satisfy preferential claims under PRC law before being distributed in accordance with Hong Kong insolvency rules, with creditors in the same class being treated equally.[138]

Administrators appointed by the Mainland Courts in the three pilot areas of Shanghai, Xiamen and Shenzhen who seek recognition and assistance from the Hong Kong courts should adhere to the recommendations and standard forms in the Practical Guide.

(ii) Recognition and Assistance under Common Law in Other Places of Mainland China

Outside the three pilot areas, the Hong Kong court's jurisdiction to lend assistance in such cases is accordingly to be derived from the common law.[139] As recognition and assistance at common law does not require reciprocity,[140] the Hong Kong court enjoys some flexibility when deciding whether to recognise and assist liquidators appointed by Mainland courts which are not within the pilot areas. It will consider such matters on a case-by-case

[131] SPC Insolvency Opinion, Art 11.
[132] ibid Art 12.
[133] ibid Art 13.
[134] ibid Art 16.
[135] ibid Art 14.
[136] ibid.
[137] ibid Art 15.
[138] ibid Art 20.
[139] See *Singularis Holdings Ltd* (n 97).
[140] *BJB Career Education Co Ltd* (n 99) [11].

basis.[141] For example, in *Re Guangdong Overseas Construction Corp*,[142] the application was for the recognition of and the provision of assistance to an administrator appointed by the Guangzhou Intermediate People's Court. It was made under the Hong Kong court's inherent jurisdiction as common law.[143] The application was granted. The Mainland insolvency proceedings were collective insolvency proceedings. They were conducted in the jurisdiction where the COMI was located. Assistance was necessary for the administration of the Mainland winding up and the performance of the administrator's functions. The common law requirements were met, and the orders sought in the case were consistent with the substantive law and public policy of the Hong Kong court and could not be obtained under other schemes.[144] The criteria applied by the Hong Kong court in deciding the case suggests that similar applications in the future should still refer to the principles in the Practical Guide.[145] Those principles are likely to be applied by analogy in non-pilot area cases.

The Hong Kong court has also recognised and enforced keepwell deeds executed by parent companies incorporated in the PRC for bonds issued by their offshore subsidiaries, by granting declaratory and monetary judgments.[146] One of these judgments was further recognised and enforced in Mainland China.[147]

C. Schemes of Arrangement

The court is empowered to sanction a scheme of arrangement or compromise under section 673 of the CO if the statutory requirements in sections 673 and 674 of the CO are met. Cases have provided guidance as to the factors to sanction a scheme or introduce parallel schemes.[148] When sanctioning a scheme in respect of foreign companies, the court should consider (among other factors) whether there is sufficient connection between the scheme and Hong Kong, and whether the scheme is effective in other relevant jurisdictions.

The effectiveness of schemes to restructure debts governed by foreign law was discussed in *Re Rare Earth Magnesium Technology Group Holdings Ltd*. Harris J held that a scheme sanctioned by the court of a foreign jurisdiction X compromising debt governed by Hong Kong law would be treated in Hong Kong as binding on a creditor who submitted to X, with the creditor accepting that his contractual rights will be governed by the law of the foreign

[141] See the obiter in *CEFC Shanghai International Group Ltd* (n 92) [25], [33]; *Re HNA Group Co Ltd* [2021] HKCFI 2897.

[142] *Re Guangdong Overseas Construction Corp (in liq)* [2023] 3 HKLRD 262, [2023] HKCFI 1340.

[143] ibid [1].

[144] ibid [17] and [23].

[145] ibid [22].

[146] See, eg *CEFC Shanghai International Group Ltd* (n 92); *Nuoxi Capital Ltd v Peking University Founder Group Co Ltd* [2023] HKCFI 1350; *Citicorp International Ltd v Tsinghua Unigroup Co Ltd* [2023] HKCFI 1572; *Nuoxi Capital Ltd v Peking University Founder Group Co Ltd* [2024] 5 HKC 64, [2024] HKCA 445. Note that all keepwell deeds in these cases are governed by English law, with Hong Kong courts having exclusive jurisdiction.

[147] *CEFC Shanghai International Group Ltd* (2019) Hu 74 Ren Gang No 1. The Shanghai Financial Court did so on the basis of the 2006 Arrangement on Reciprocal Recognition and Enforcement of Judgments in Civil and Commercial Matters by the Courts of the Mainland and of Hong Kong Special Administrative Region Pursuant to Choice of Court Agreements between Parties Concerned, Fa Shi [2008] No 9 (see ch 25, s I.E). What approach will be taken by the Mainland Chinese courts for judgments in other jurisdictions generally under the Enterprise Bankruptcy Law and other PRC laws remains untested.

[148] See, eg *Re China Singyes Solar Technologies Holdings Ltd* [2020] HKCFI 467; *Re China Oil Gangran Energy Group Holdings Ltd* [2021] 3 HKLRD 69, [2021] HKCFI 1592.

insolvency process. The scheme would not bind a creditor who did not participate in the scheme proceedings or any associated insolvency process in jurisdiction X.[149] This is in consonance with the rule in *Gibbs*, which provided that contracts could only be discharged under the law governing the contract. A debt is treated as discharged only if it is compromised in accordance with the law of the jurisdiction which governed the instrument giving rise to the debt.[150]

However, a scheme in a foreign jurisdiction Y purporting to compromise a debt governed by the law of a third jurisdiction Z (such as New York) would not be effective in Hong Kong. In such a case, the recognition of the scheme under the law of Z (such as Chapter 15 of the United States Bankruptcy Code) does not constitute a compromise of the debt that satisfies the rule in *Gibbs*. A creditor who did not submit to Y would still be able to present a petition in the Hong Kong court to wind up the company.[151]

IV. Interactions between Jurisdiction and Arbitration Agreements and Winding Up

Hong Kong courts have been involved in a series of cases on whether there should be a stay of winding up proceedings based on a debt which is subject to an exclusive jurisdiction clause or arbitration agreement. The problem arises because winding up proceedings are intended to advance a public interest. Creditors have a statutory right to petition the court for the orderly winding up of insolvent companies which are unable to pay their debts as and when they fall due. On the other hand, exclusive jurisdiction clauses and arbitration agreements are private matters. They only bind those parties that are privy to the agreements in which such clauses are found. Winding up petitions will be dismissed if the underlying debt alleged by a petitioner is disputed by a company on genuine grounds. The issue is who should determine whether there is a genuine dispute in respect of a debt. Should the court decide the matter pursuant to public statute? Alternatively, should an arbitral tribunal or an exclusive forum do so, on the basis that the parties agreed that their disputes should be so determined? In principle, where an exclusive jurisdiction or arbitration agreement applies to a debt, any dispute over the debt (including a disagreement between the parties as to whether the debt is being genuinely disputed) has to be resolved in the manner agreed by the parties. Therefore, in deciding applications for a stay of winding up proceedings on the basis of an arbitration agreement or exclusive jurisdiction clause, the court has to balance the parties' contractual freedom against the public policy of safeguarding creditors' interests.

A. Traditional Approach

Traditionally, an arbitration clause or arbitration proceeding did not bar the court from determining the existence of a bona fide dispute in relation to the debt on which the petition

[149] *Re Rare Earth Magnesium Technology Group Holdings Ltd* [2022] 3 HKLRD 252, [2022] HKCFI 1686 [29].

[150] *Antony Gibbs & Sons* (n 114); ibid [29]. Contrast the position in Singapore in *Re Pacific Andes Resources Development Ltd* [2018] 5 SLR 125.

[151] *Re Rare Earth Magnesium Technology Group Holdings Ltd* (n 149) [32], [37]. But see the subsequent comment in *In re Modern Land (China) Co Ltd* 22-10707 (MG) (Bankr SDNY, 18 July 2022).

is premised.[152] *Hollmet AG v Meridian Success Metal Supplies Ltd*[153] held that a debtor must establish a bona fide dispute on substantial grounds regarding the debt before the court stays winding up proceedings. The court has adhered to this approach in cases subsequent to *Hollmet AG*.[154] As to what factors constituted 'a bona fide dispute on substantial grounds', it was thought that the commencement of arbitration proceedings was indicative of a bona fide dispute, as 'it may be said that there is not a debt owing'.[155] Later cases[156] suggested that neither the existence of an arbitration clause nor the existence of an arbitration proceeding was conclusive. The debtor instead had to adduce the alleged debt was genuinely disputed.

The foregoing position does not apply to every winding up proceeding. In *Re Quicksilver Glorious Sun JV Ltd*,[157] the court distinguished between winding up on insolvency and winding up on the just and equitable ground. In the former, a creditor seeks to put an insolvent company into liquidation for the benefit of all creditors. In the latter, a shareholder purports to wind up a company as a result of a dispute between the two shareholders. The question of whether the conduct of a shareholder is inconsistent with a shareholders' agreement should clearly be determined by an arbitrator.

B. The *Salford Estates/Lasmos* Approach

In *Lasmos Ltd v Southwest Pacific Bauxite (HK) Ltd*,[158] the court held that a winding up petition should be dismissed if three conditions are satisfied:[159]

1. The company disputes the debt relied on by the petitioner.
2. The contract under which the debt is alleged to arise contains an arbitration clause that covers the debt.
3. The company commences an arbitration.

This was the approach adopted by the English court in *Salford Estates (No 2) Ltd v Altomart Ltd*.[160] The first condition in *Lasmos* requires the company to dispute the debt relied on by the petitioner. It is unnecessary to prove the dispute is bona fide and on substantial grounds. It suffices that the company does not admit the debt.[161] The second condition requires the company to show that the dispute over the debt is covered by the parties' arbitration agreement. The third condition requires a Notice of Arbitration to be issued; it is not enough to send a letter stating that solicitors have been instructed to commence the process.[162]

[152] *Dayang (HK) Marine Shipping Co Ltd v Asia Master Logistics Ltd* [2020] 2 HKLRD 423, [2020] HKCFI 311 [16].

[153] *Hollmet AG v Meridian Success Metal Supplies Ltd* [1997] HKLRD 828.

[154] See, eg *Re Sky Datamann (Hong Kong) Ltd* (unreported, HCCW 487/2001, 29 January 2002); *Re Jade Union Investment Ltd* (unreported, HCCW 400/2003, 5 March 2004); *Re Southern Materials Holdings (HK) Co Ltd* (unreported, HCCW 281/2007, 13 February 2008).

[155] *Hollmet AG* (n 153) 832A–B.

[156] *Jade Union Investment Ltd* (n 154).

[157] *Re Quicksilver Glorious Sun JV Ltd* [2014] 4 HKLRD 759 [18]–[19].

[158] *Lasmos Ltd v Southwest Pacific Bauxite (HK) Ltd* [2018] 2 HKLRD 449, [2018] HKCFI 426.

[159] ibid [31].

[160] *Salford Estates (No 2) Ltd v Altomart Ltd* [2014] EWCA Civ 1575, [2015] Ch 589.

[161] *Dayang (HK) Marine Shipping Co Ltd* (n 152) [62].

[162] *But Ka Chon v Interactive Brokers LLC* [2019] 4 HKLRD 85, [2019] HKCA 873 [52].

The court rejected the traditional approach for four reasons. First, a creditor issues a petition to recover a debt due to the petitioner, rather than out of altruistic concern for the creditors of the company generally. The creditor does this in the belief that winding up proceedings are the most efficacious means of obtaining payment. Therefore, analytically, save for the public element in winding up proceedings, there is little difference between a claim for a debt pursued by writ and a claim for winding up based on the same debt.[163] Second, there is a difference between establishing that (i) the petitioner belongs to the class of the company's creditors and (ii) the class remedy of a winding up should be granted. The question whether the debt is genuinely disputed relates only to the former issue. It does not concern considerations relevant to the class generally. There is no reason why the seeking of a class remedy should be relevant to the method by which it is determined whether the petitioner is genuinely a creditor.[164] Third, if the creditor is required to arbitrate, it would merely be holding the creditor up to the contractual bargain.[165] Fourth, the fact that the agreement under which a debt is said to arise contains an arbitration clause does not preclude other creditors from invoking the collective insolvency remedy if circumstances so justify.[166]

The *Lasmos* approach struck the balance of the competing values in a stay application in favour of the court's pro-arbitration attitude. The court cited section 3 of the Arbitration Ordinance (Cap 609) (AO), stressing that the AO was intended to facilitate the fair and speedy resolution of disputes by arbitration without unnecessary expense. A court can only interfere in the arbitration of a dispute to the extent allowed by the AO.[167] The court also referred to well-known principles applied by the Hong Kong court in upholding arbitration.[168]

C. Post-*Lasmos* Reception

Although there is no appeal decision which directly decides the appropriateness of the *Lasmos* approach, later cases have expressed obiter reservations over it.[169] In *But Ka Chon v Interactive Brokers LLC*,[170] where the third condition of the *Lasmos* approach was not met,[171] the Court of Appeal observed that the approach would curtail the statutory right of a creditor to present a winding up petition, and did not cohere with the public policy underlying winding up.[172] It was acknowledged that insufficient weight had been given to the arbitration factor in pre-*Lasmos* cases.[173] But, even in pre-*Lasmos* cases, the court was not powerless to deal with tactics that may be practised by creditors to exert pressure on the

[163] *Lasmos Ltd* (n 158) [25].
[164] ibid [26]–[27].
[165] ibid [28].
[166] ibid [29].
[167] ibid [15].
[168] ibid [16], citing *KB v S* (unreported, HCCT 13/2015, 15 September 2015).
[169] *Re Golden Oasis Health Ltd* [2019] HKCFI 2173; *Sit Kwong Lam v Petrolimex Singapore Pte Ltd* [2019] 5 HKLRD 646, [2019] HKCA 1220.
[170] *But Ka Chon* (n 162).
[171] ibid [52]–[56].
[172] ibid [62]–[67].
[173] ibid [70].

debtor and bypass an arbitration agreement.[174] It is doubtful (the court thought) that a petition should be stayed in the absence of a bona fide dispute.[175] In *Sit Kwong Lam v Petrolimex Singapore Pte Ltd*,[176] the correctness of *Lasmos* similarly did not arise, as the debtor could not meet the second and third conditions of the *Lasmos* approach.[177] Nonetheless, the Court of Appeal referred to *But Ka Chon*, with a view to discouraging debtors from making opportunistic attempts to invoke the *Lasmos* approach.[178]

In *Dayang (HK) Marine Shipping Co Ltd v Asia Master Logistics Ltd*,[179] the court revisited the principles. DHCJ William Wong SC thought that the *Lasmos* approach should be rejected.[180] The deputy judge summarised what he believed should be the law:[181]

(1) First, where a debtor-company intends to dispute the existence of a debt, he must show that there is a bona fide dispute on substantial grounds. It should not suffice for the debtor-company to merely deny the debt. This test would apply in all cases whether or not the debt had arisen from a contract incorporating an arbitration clause.
(2) Secondly, the existence of an arbitration agreement should be regarded as irrelevant to the exercise of discretion.
(3) Thirdly, the fact that arbitration proceedings have commenced or would be commenced may be relevant evidence that there is a bona fide dispute. However, this alone would not be sufficient to prove the existence of a bona fide dispute on substantial grounds.
(4) Fourthly, where the creditor-petitioner petitions in circumstances where it knows there to be a bona fide dispute over the debt on substantial grounds, it runs the risk of being liable to pay the debtor-petitioner's costs on an indemnity basis. It would also be at risk of liability under the tort of malicious prosecution.

The deputy judge found that, in addition to the debt not being disputed in good faith, the third condition of the *Lasmos* approach had not been satisfied. Hence, a winding up order should be made even if the *Lasmos* approach was followed.[182]

The court criticised the *Lasmos* approach on a number of grounds. It was said that the *Lasmos* approach has two justifications: the contractual justification of party autonomy and the comparative justification to keep pace with developments in other common law jurisdictions.[183] The deputy judge thought that the contractual justification was misplaced as, upon proper interpretation, an agreement to arbitrate called only for disputes within the scope of the arbitration agreement to be determined in the prescribed forum.[184] However, the presentation of a winding up petition by the creditor would not amount to a breach of an agreement to resolve disputes by way of arbitration.[185] The court, when hearing the petition for winding up, does not decide the dispute. It would be for liquidators acting in a

[174] ibid [71].
[175] ibid [71]–[72].
[176] *Sit Kwong Lam* (n 169).
[177] ibid [25]–[26] and [40].
[178] ibid [36].
[179] *Dayang (HK) Marine Shipping Co Ltd* (n 152).
[180] ibid [50].
[181] ibid [136].
[182] ibid [51].
[183] ibid [60]–[61].
[184] ibid [66].
[185] ibid [71].

quasi-judicial capacity to resolve the dispute. The comparative justification equally lacked merit as the positions were far from settled under Singapore law or English law.[186] There was a substantial variance in Singapore as to what needed to be shown by a debtor beyond a bare denial of the debt, with different authorities referring to standards ranging from 'bona fide' to 'genuine'.[187] A judicial practice of staying or dismissing winding up proceedings on the mere say-so of a debtor-company would be a cause for concern.[188]

A series of first instance cases in 2022 have witnessed a restoration of the pre-*Lasmos* approach. In *Re Hongkong Bai Yuan International Business Co Ltd*,[189] the company submitted that the court should adopt the *Lasmos* approach. The court considered that, irrespective of whether one describes the threshold as a prima facie standard or a bona fide dispute on substantial grounds, it was incumbent on the debtor to show 'a genuine dispute on the debt which requires determination of a tribunal' despite the existence of an arbitration clause applicable to the dispute. It was pointless to require the parties to resolve their dispute through the contractually agreed forum if no genuine dispute existed. Similarly, in *DCKD v JPWL*[190] and *Re Pan Sutong*,[191] the court would only allow the parties to resolve the dispute through arbitration if there was a 'genuine dispute' or 'bona fide dispute on substantial grounds' on the debt. In all three cases, there was no such dispute on a cursory examination of the merits.

Comparatively, the *Salford Estates*/*Lasmos* approach has been followed in Singapore in *AnAn Group (Singapore) Pte Ltd v VTB Bank (Public Joint Stock Co)*.[192] The approach was also endorsed by the Malaysian High Court for some time, but was later rejected by the Malaysian Court of Appeal.[193]

D. *Re Guy Lam* Approach

The cases mentioned immediately above were considered by the Court of Appeal[194] and the Court of Final Appeal[195] in *Re Lam Kwok Hung Guy, ex p Tor Asia Credit Master Fund LP*. There, the debt was governed by an exclusive jurisdiction clause, rather than an arbitration agreement. The appellant debtor argued that the *Lasmos* approach applied to cases with exclusive jurisdiction clauses.[196] The Court of Appeal, in a majority judgment delivered by Godfrey Lam JA, held that the court should not adopt the same approach to a stay of an ordinary action based on an exclusive jurisdiction clause. Instead, the petition should be

[186] ibid [100].
[187] ibid [116].
[188] ibid [117].
[189] *Re Hongkong Bai Yuan International Business Co Ltd* [2022] HKCFI 960.
[190] *DCKD v JPWL* [2022] HKCFI 1059.
[191] *Re Pan Sutong* [2022] HKCFI 1450.
[192] *AnAn Group (Singapore) Pte Ltd v VTB Bank (Public Joint Stock Co)* [2020] 1 SLR 1158.
[193] *Awangsa Bina Sdn Bhd v Mayland Avenue Sdn Bhd* (unreported, WA-28NCC-1146-12/2018, 2 May 2019) (Malaya HC) [25]–[28]; *Swissray Asia Healthcare Co Ltd v V Medical Services M Sdn Bhd* [2024] 8 CLJ 21 (W-02(NCC)(A)-1479-08/2022, 6 June 2024) (CA) [61]–[78].
[194] *Re Lam Kwok Hung Guy, ex p Tor Asia Credit Master Fund LP* [2022] 4 HKLRD 793, [2022] HKCA 1297.
[195] *Re Lam Kwok Hung Guy, ex p Tor Asia Credit Master Fund LP* (2023) 26 HKCFAR 119, [2023] HKCFA 9.
[196] *Re Lam Kwok Hung Guy* (CA) (n 194) [24].

dismissed in the absence of 'strong reasons', pending the determination of the dispute in the agreed forum.[197] As in the case of ordinary actions, it was neither possible nor desirable to define what may constitute 'strong reasons'.[198] The majority of the Court of Appeal did not consider the correctness of the *Lasmos* approach. But the reasoning in *Re Asia Master Logistics* (to the effect that the court does not adjudicate upon the substantive rights between the parties in a bankruptcy or winding up petition and hence does not usurp an arbitration clause) was disapproved.[199] This was because a finding against that the debtor's defences did not raise any bona fide dispute on substantial grounds would itself constitute a determination of the dispute.[200]

The minority judgment of Anderson Chow JA took a different tack. The judge likewise did not rule on the correctness of *Lasmos* approach.[201] Instead, he took the view that a wholesale adoption of the *Lasmos* approach in exclusive jurisdiction clause cases was unwarranted.[202] He observed that the approach endorsed by the majority would disregard the distinction between an action on a debt and a winding up petition based on a debt, and the appeal could be disposed on a narrower basis.[203]

The Court of Final Appeal[204] endorsed the majority's approach. It held that a court has the discretion to decline jurisdiction to hear a winding up petition in an exclusive jurisdiction clause,[205] the exercise of which is decided by a 'multi-factorial' approach depending on a 'range of considerations'.[206] It believed that 'absent countervailing factors such as the risk of insolvency affecting third parties and a dispute that borders on the frivolous or abuse of process, the petitioner and the debtor ought to be held to their contract'.[207]

E. Post-*Re Guy Lam* Reception

The question posed in *Re Guy Lam* was to determine whether the dispute is 'frivolous' or amounts to an 'abuse of process'. When doing so, the courts 'should only conduct a preliminary assessment on whether it is a plain and obvious case that without attempting to undergo a mini-trial on affidavit evidence … the court is not straitjacketed by any particular policies and interests and may take into account other relevant factors in making its decision in this regard'.[208] For a case where a defence under the Money Lenders Ordinance (Cap 163) was considered frivolous or an abuse of process, see *Sun Entertainment Culture Ltd v Inversion Productions Ltd*.[209]

[197] ibid [83] and [86].
[198] ibid [86].
[199] ibid [67].
[200] ibid [68].
[201] ibid [109].
[202] ibid [110].
[203] ibid [111].
[204] *Re Lam Kwok Hung Guy* (CFA) (n 195).
[205] ibid [98]–[100] and [107].
[206] ibid [101]–[104] and [107].
[207] ibid [105].
[208] *Re Mega Gold Holdings Ltd* [2024] HKCFI 2286 [69].
[209] *Sun Entertainment Culture Ltd v Inversion Productions Ltd* [2023] HKCFI 2400, dismissed on appeal: *Sun Entertainment Culture Ltd v Inversion Productions Ltd* [2024] 4 HKLRD 991, [2024] HKCA 884.

It was thought that *Re Guy Lam* would readily extend to arbitration agreements, but there was a divergence of opinion among judges on whether it covered arbitration agreements. In *Re Simplicity & Vogue Retailing (HK) Co Ltd*,[210] Linda Chan J held that *Re Guy Lam* only concerned exclusive jurisdiction agreements and did not extend to arbitration clauses. In cases involving the latter, the court should follow the *Lasmos* approach and refer to the Court of Appeal's observations in *But Ka Chon* and *Sit Kwong Lam*.[211] The judge made the same point in a later judgment.[212] In contrast, in *Re Shandong Chenming Paper Holdings Ltd*,[213] Harris J reached the opposite conclusion. There, the debtor applied for the stay of a winding up in favour of arbitration on the basis that arbitration proceedings were ongoing, despite such proceedings have been commenced five years after the presentation of the winding up petition.[214] Harris J held that *Re Guy Lam* applied by analogy in the arbitration context.[215] He thought that *Re Simplicity* was wrong in reading *Re Guy Lam* restrictively.[216] He found that the facts fulfilled the requirement in *Re Guy Lam* and warranted a stay of the winding up.[217] The difference between Harris J's approach and that of Linda Chan J was that the latter required that a debtor seeking to stay a winding up demonstrate substantial grounds for disputing the debt grounding the winding up petition.

Both cases went to appeal. In *Re Simplicity & Vogue Retailing (HK) Co Ltd*,[218] the Court of Appeal confirmed that applicability of *Re Guy Lam* to debts covered by arbitration clauses, approving the 'multi-factorial' approach in the court's exercise of discretion while retaining flexibility.[219] In *Re Shandong Chenming Paper Holdings Ltd*,[220] the Court of Appeal further confirmed the applicability of *Re Guy Lam* to cross-claims and set-offs, that is, to situations in which the company has a genuine cross-claim against the petitioner within the ambit of the arbitration agreement which is greater than or equal to the debt owed to the petitioner.

Note, however, that the Privy Council, on appeal from the BVI, decided in *Sian Participation Corp v Halimeda International Ltd* that an exclusive jurisdiction clause or arbitration agreement should not lead to a stay or dismissal of a winding up petition unless the underlying debt is genuinely disputed on substantial grounds.[221] The Privy Council reasoned that a winding up petition or liquidation application 'does not seek to, and does not resolve or determine anything' about the debt, and the existence or amount of the debt is not a matter or issue for resolution in those proceedings.[222] The dispute is therefore 'simply' not a claim caught by the mandatory stay provisions in the arbitration context.[223] As such, the petition or application does not offend the negative obligation of the arbitration agreement (not to seek dispute resolution in court)[224] or any objectives or policies underlying the

[210] *Re Simplicity & Vogue Retailing (HK) Co Ltd* [2023] HKCFI 1443.
[211] ibid [35].
[212] *Re NT Pharma International Co Ltd* [2023] HKCFI 1623 [33].
[213] *Re Shandong Chenming Paper Holdings Ltd* [2023] 4 HKLRD 359, [2023] HKCFI 2065.
[214] ibid [1].
[215] ibid [4].
[216] ibid [4] and [18].
[217] ibid [19].
[218] *Re Simplicity & Vogue Retailing (HK) Co Ltd* [2024] 2 HKLRD 1064, [2024] HKCA 299.
[219] ibid [37]–[39], [42].
[220] *Re Shandong Chenming Paper Holdings Ltd* [2024] 2 HKLRD 1040, [2024] HKCA 352.
[221] *Sian Participation Corp (in liq) v Halimeda International Ltd* [2024] UKPC 16.
[222] ibid [88] and [94].
[223] ibid.
[224] ibid [88]–[89].

arbitration legislation.[225] Moreover, the Privy Council thought that there is nothing 'anti-arbitration' in the policy as the party who is 'likely' to be the creditor has the freedom, and is 'much more likely', to include an arbitration clause 'if it does not impede a liquidation where there is no genuine or substantial dispute'. When there is a dispute, arbitration can prevail; but requiring the creditor to go through an arbitration where there is no genuine or substantial dispute 'just adds delay, trouble and expense for no good purpose'.[226]

In so concluding, the Privy Council overruled the English Court of Appeal's decision in *Salford Estates*[227] and shared the concerns expressed by DHCJ William Wong SC in *Dayang (HK) Marine Shipping Co Ltd*.[228] It directed that its decision should apply not just to BVI law, but also to English law.[229] Nonetheless, the Privy Council qualified its direction, stating that it only applies to generally worded arbitration agreements and exclusive jurisdiction clauses.[230] Different considerations might arise if such agreements and clauses were framed in terms which specifically referred to a creditor's winding up petition.[231]

To date, the Hong Kong court has followed the reasoning in *Re Guy Lam* and *Re Simplicity & Vogue (Retailing) HK Co Ltd* as a matter of *stare decisis* and the Privy Council's approach was apparently not accepted in the Hong Kong cases.[232] In *Re Mega Gold Holdings Ltd*, in response to the Privy Council's opinion that a winding-up or bankruptcy order would not 'offend' the parties' arbitration agreement, DHCJ Richard Khaw SC observed obiter that this 'essentially turns on the basis of the underlying debt for the purpose of the petition and whether the debt and the alleged dispute fall within the scope of the arbitration agreement'.[233]

[225] ibid [90]–[92].
[226] ibid [92]–[93].
[227] ibid [88], citing *Salford Estates (No 2) Ltd* (n 160).
[228] ibid [98], citing *Dayang (HK) Marine Shipping Co Ltd* (n 152). See s IV.C above.
[229] ibid [124]–[127]. This is by giving a *Willers v Joyce* direction, named after *Willers v Joyce (No 2)* [2016] UKSC 44, [2018] AC 483, which held that the Judicial Committee of the Privy Council has jurisdiction to direct that its decision now represents the law of England and Wales.
[230] The Privy Council held that the underlying policy in relation to arbitration clauses and exclusive jurisdiction clauses is the same: *Sian Participation Corp* (n 221) [126].
[231] ibid [127].
[232] *Re Mega Gold Holdings Ltd* (n 208) [71].
[233] ibid [72].

21

Law of Bankruptcy

This chapter discusses the rules in relation to personal bankruptcy and cross-border personal bankruptcy in Hong Kong.[1] For corporate insolvency, see chapter twenty.

I. Effect of Bankruptcy on Assignments of Property

The administration of the bankrupt's property is governed by Hong Kong law. This is a matter of procedure governed by the *lex fori*.

Hong Kong takes a universal approach to property that vests in a trustee-in-bankruptcy. Section 43(1) of the Bankruptcy Ordinance (Cap 6) (BO) provides:

> (1) Subject to this section and sections 43A to 43E, a bankrupt's estate comprises –
> (a) all property belonging to or vested in the bankrupt at the commencement of the bankruptcy; and
> (b) any property which by virtue of any of the provisions of this Ordinance is comprised in that estate or is treated as falling within paragraph (a).

'Property' is defined in section 2 of the BO as including

> money, goods, things in action, land and every description of property, whether real or personal *and whether situate in Hong Kong or elsewhere*, also obligations, easements and every description of estate, interest and profit, present or future, vested or contingent, arising out of or incident to property as above defined. (emphasis added)

Upon making a bankruptcy order, the bankrupt's property, irrespective of *situs*, vests in the Official Receiver (unless the order specifies otherwise).[2]

Although the BO vests property abroad in a Hong Kong trustee, this extraterritorial reach is not binding on the court in jurisdictions where such property may be located. Whether the property is eventually passed to the Hong Kong trustee-in-bankruptcy will ultimately depend on the *lex situs*. Therefore, despite Hong Kong law treating all the bankrupt's property as vesting in the trustee, it may be difficult for the trustee to make title to foreign property effective as against a party executing against that property abroad.[3] In any event, where there is an assignment of property situated abroad, the property passes subject to any charges recognised by the *lex situs*.[4]

[1] See also, eg Charles D Booth et al, *Hong Kong Personal Insolvency Manual*, 3rd edn (LexisNexis, 2024).
[2] BO, s 58.
[3] *Kireeva v Bedzhamov* [2024] UKSC 39; Lord Collins of Mapesbury and Jonathan Harris (gen eds), *Dicey, Morris and Collins on the Conflict of Laws*, 16th edn (Sweet & Maxwell, 2022) para 31-045.
[4] ibid para 31-051.

II. Effect of Bankruptcy as a Discharge of Debts

An order of discharge in a Hong Kong bankruptcy releases the bankrupt from all the bankruptcy debts.[5] The discharge includes all debts, whether governed by Hong Kong or foreign law, and whatever their *situs* may be. However, discharge of a debt due under a contract pursuant to a foreign bankruptcy law is governed by the law applicable to the contract. Therefore, a discharge of a contractual debt under the bankruptcy law of the country whose law governs the contract is valid in Hong Kong.[6] Conversely, the discharge of a contractual debt under the bankruptcy law of any other foreign country would not be a valid discharge in Hong Kong.[7]

III. Cross-Border Bankruptcy

There are no statutory provisions in the BO on the recognition of foreign bankruptcies. There are also no provisions applicable to the granting of assistance to foreign representatives. Previously, section 122 of the Bankruptcy Act 1914 in the UK, before its repeal in 1985, provided for cooperation among bankruptcy courts throughout the Commonwealth.[8]

In the absence of statutory guidance, the common law applies. The cases suggest that that recognition may be granted if a debtor:[9]

(i) was domiciled or resident in the jurisdiction of the foreign court;
(ii) carried on a business in the jurisdiction of the foreign court;
(iii) is genuinely and substantively connected with the foreign jurisdiction; or
(iv) submits to the jurisdiction of the foreign court.

The court may refuse recognition if:[10]

(i) recognition of the foreign bankruptcy would be contrary to Hong Kong public policy;
(ii) the foreign bankruptcy decree was procured through fraud or obtained in breach of the rules of natural justice; or
(iii) the foreign bankruptcy proceedings are an attempt to enforce a foreign penal or revenue law.

The court's approach when recognising and assisting foreign bankruptcy proceedings is materially the same as foreign insolvency proceedings, adopting the 'modified universalism' doctrine.[11]

[5] BO, s 32(2). This is subject to the exceptions in the other subsections of BO, s 32; notably, debts and liabilities incurred by any fraud or fraudulent breach of trust are not discharged: BO, s 32(4).

[6] See, eg *Wight v Eckhardt Marine GmbH* [2003] UKPC 37, [2004] 1 AC 147.

[7] See, eg *Joint Administrators of Heritable Bank Plc v Winding up Board of Landsbanki Islands HF* [2013] UKSC 13, [2013] 1 WLR 725 [44]. See also *Antony Gibbs & Sons v La Société Industrielle et Commerciale des Métaux* (1890) 25 QBD 399 and the discussion in ch 20, s III.C.

[8] For Hong Kong cases that considered the repealed s 122, see *Re Estate of Aw Hoe* [1957] 2 HKLR 401; *Re Estate of Aw Hoe* [1957] 2 HKLR 539.

[9] Booth et al (n 1) para 14-28.

[10] ibid para 14-29. See also *Hong Kong Institute of Education v Aoki Corp* [2004] 2 HKLRD 760 [149]–[159].

[11] *Re Phillip James Kingston* [2024] 5 HKLRD 788, [2024] HKCFI 3311 [18]–[20]. See also ch 20, s III.

In *Chen Li Hung v Ting Lei Miao*,[12] the Taipei District Court adjudged Mr Ting Lei Miao bankrupt and appointed four Taiwanese lawyers as trustees-in-bankruptcy. The trustees brought an action in Taiwan for shares registered in the name of Madam Chen Li Hung (by whom Mr Ting had five children). The Taiwanese courts ruled in favour of the trustees, and the trustees commenced actions in Hong Kong for judgment against Madam Chen. Mr Ting later came to Hong Kong and disputed the authority of the trustees to commence the actions. In holding that the Taiwanese bankruptcy order extended to Mr Ting's assets in Hong Kong, the Court of Final Appeal held that, under Taiwanese law, the trustees had the right to sue in their own names in Hong Kong, and Taiwanese law extended to the bankrupt's assets in Hong Kong.[13]

In *Chen Li Hung*, it was argued that it was contrary to public policy to recognise the orders of the Taiwanese court, which was exercising de facto power without de jure authority. The Court of Final Appeal rejected that argument, stating:[14]

> 37. In certain circumstances our courts will give effect to the orders of non-recognized courts. By the expression 'non-recognized courts' I mean to cover courts sitting in foreign states the governments of which our sovereign does not recognize as well as courts sitting in territory under the *de jure* sovereignty of our sovereign but presently under the *de facto* albeit unlawful control of a usurper government. Our courts will give effect to the orders of non-recognized courts where:
>
> (i) the rights covered by those orders are private rights;
> (ii) giving effect to such orders accords with the interests of justice, the dictates of common sense and the needs of law and order; and
> (iii) giving them effect would not be inimical to the sovereign's interests or otherwise contrary to public policy.
>
> That is the principle; and none of it involves recognizing any unrecognised entity. It goes purely and simply to protecting private rights.
>
> 38. … the Taiwanese Bankruptcy Order is to be given effect by the Hong Kong courts. The rights thereunder are plainly private. By the general nature and particular circumstances of those rights, giving effect to them accords with the interests of justice, the dictates of common sense and the needs of law and order.
>
> 39. … there is nothing inimical to the sovereign's interests or otherwise contrary to public policy in giving effect to the Taiwanese Bankruptcy Order. The present action is not for the benefit of the usurper regime. It is for the benefit of out-of-pocket depositors. Furthermore it should be clearly understood that giving effect to the Taiwanese Bankruptcy Order does not involve recognizing the usurper regime or courts in Taiwan.

A foreign order vesting title in a foreign trustee will be effective in vesting movable property in Hong Kong, provided that the foreign law extends to property located in Hong Kong.[15] The vesting is 'consequential and instantaneous' upon the making of the foreign order, and 'no confirmation or execution by the Hong Kong court is required'.[16]

[12] *Chen Li Hung v Ting Lei Miao* (2000) 3 HKCFAR 9.
[13] ibid [20]. For this proposition, the Court of Final Appeal cited Lawrence Collins (gen ed), *Dicey and Morris on the Conflict of Laws*, 12th edn (Sweet & Maxwell, 1993) 1177.
[14] *Chen Li Hung* (n 11) [37]–[39].
[15] *Galbraith v Grimshaw* [1910] AC 508; *Re Phillip James Kingston* (n 11) [18(3)].
[16] Booth et al (n 1) para 14-36, citing Philip St J Smart, *Cross-Border Insolvency*, 2nd edn (Butterworths, 1998) 222.

Such recognition will extend to the vesting of assets acquired after the order was made, if the order intended to have that effect.[17]

A foreign order to vest immovable property is not recognised unless there is a Hong Kong court order. A foreign representative may be appointed by the court as receiver of the foreign debtor's immovable property in Hong Kong.[18] The Hong Kong court has inherent jurisdiction to assist a foreign representative. The foreign representative may commence civil proceedings, seek injunctive relief, seek a declaration on the effect of foreign insolvency proceedings, attempt to recover debts and submit a proof of debt in the Hong Kong proceedings. Alternatively, where a foreign debtor's unsecured creditors may be better protected, where it is necessary to reach the foreign debtor's immovable property or where it is necessary to obtain the benefit of a trustee's avoidance and investigatory powers, it may be possible for the foreign representative to file a bankruptcy petition. The fact that the debtor has already been adjudicated bankrupt abroad is not a bar of the Hong Kong court's jurisdiction to adjudge a debtor bankrupt in Hong Kong. There are no express provisions in the BO relating to a foreign representative commencing proceedings in Hong Kong. However, a foreign trustee should be permitted to file a bankruptcy petition in Hong Kong as a creditor of the foreign debtor, or to ask the foreign debtor's creditors or the foreign debtor itself to file a petition.[19]

[17] *Re a Debtor, ex p Viscount of Royal Court of Jersey* [1981] Ch 384.

[18] The possibility to appoint a receiver was rejected in the UK by the Supreme Court in *Kireeva* (n 3). It was thought that Insolvency Act 1986, s 426 and the Cross-Border Insolvency Regulations 2006 have already established two statutory exceptions to the immovables rule, and it would be inappropriate to further extend the common law to provide assistance. However, as Hong Kong has not established any statutory exceptions to date, it is suggested that the Hong Kong position may diverge from the UK in this regard.

[19] Booth et al (n 1) paras 14–43 and 14–44.

22

Competition Law

This chapter focuses on private international law issues that may arise under the competition law regime in Hong Kong. Readers are invited to consult other texts for competition law and practice in Hong Kong.[1]

I. Introduction

The competition law regime in Hong Kong is relatively new. The main provisions of the Competition Ordinance (Cap 619) (CO) came into operation on 14 December 2015. The only body that has jurisdiction to decide if there has been a breach of the CO is the Competition Tribunal.[2] The Tribunal has the same jurisdiction to grant remedies and reliefs, equitable or legal, as the Court of First Instance.[3] The Competition Tribunal Rules (Cap 619D) (CTR) apply to proceedings under the CO.

The CO prohibits restrictions on competition in Hong Kong through three competition rules:

(i) the first conduct rule, which prohibits anti-competitive agreements between market participants that prevent, restrict or distort competition in Hong Kong;
(ii) the second conduct rule, which prohibits undertakings having a substantial degree of market power from abusing that power to harm competition; and
(iii) the merger rule, which prohibits mergers and acquisitions that have (or are likely to have) the effect of substantially lessening competition.

Note that the merger rule has only limited application in Hong Kong to mergers of undertakings which hold (or control an undertaking that holds) a carrier licence under the Telecommunications Ordinance (Cap 106).[4]

To date, almost all cases brought under the CO have alleged the contravention of the first conduct rule. One case (*Competition Commission v Linde HKO Ltd*) complains of a contravention of the second conduct rule. One case has raised price fixing by the plaintiff as a defence to a High Court action. A list of cases brought so far is presented in Table 2.

[1] See, eg Thomas K Cheng and Kelvin Hiu Fai Kwok, *Hong Kong Competition Law: Comparative and Theoretical Perspectives* (Cambridge University Press, 2021); Daniel Beard and Catrina Lam (eds), *Competition Litigation in Hong Kong: Practice and Procedure* (Sweet & Maxwell, 2025). The Competition Commission has also published Guidelines on the First Conduct Rule, the Second Conduct Rule and the Merger Rule: see www.compcomm.hk/index.html.

[2] CO, ss 108 and 109.

[3] ibid s 142(2).

[4] ibid Sch 2 and s 7.

Table 2 List of cases brought under the Competition Ordinance (Cap 619)

Case name and summary of allegations	Judgments delivered
Competition Commission v Nutanix Hong Kong Ltd (CTEA 1/2017) (bid-rigging in response to an invitation to tender for the supply and installation of an IT server system)	[2020] HKCT 11: trial on sanctions and pecuniary penalties [2019] 3 HKC 307, [2019] HKCT 2: trial on liability under first conduct rule, whether agreement formed, attribution of conduct and knowledge, warning notice under section 82 of the CO [2018] HKCT 3: costs on application for discovery [2018] 3 HKC 173, [2018] HKCT 1: discovery of documents; rule 24 of the CTR [2017] 5 HKLRD 712: notice to attend and answer questions, self-incrimination; sections 42 and 45(2) of the CO [2017] 3 HKLRD 584: first case management conference (unreported, CTEA 1/2017, 28 March 2017): redaction in originating notice of application; rule 37 of the CTR
Competition Commission v W Hing Construction Co Ltd (CTEA 2/2017) (market sharing and price fixing in the provision of renovation services in a public housing estate)	[2022] 3 HKLRD 84, [2022] HKCA 786: appeal against trial on sanctions and pecuniary penalties [2021] 3 HKLRD 219, [2021] HKCA 877: appeal against trial on liability [2020] HKCA 930: striking out parts of notice of appeal due to abuse of process [2020] HKCT 6: leave to appeal for trial on pecuniary penalties [2020] 2 HKLRD 1229, [2020] HKCT 1: trial on sanctions and pecuniary penalties; section 93 of the CO [2019] 3 HKLRD 46, [2019] HKCT 3: trial on liability under first conduct rule, efficiency defence and sub-contractor defence [2018] 5 HKLRD 437, [2018] HKCT 6: application to amend response and file new witness statements [2018] HKCT 5: striking out parts of expert report [2018] HKCT 2: leave to substitute expert and extend time to file and serve expert report
Competition Commission v Kam Kwong Engineering Co Ltd (CTEA 1/2018) (market sharing and price fixing in the provision of renovation services in a public housing estate)	[2022] 6 HKC 95, [2022] HKCT 2: trial on pecuniary penalties for third and fifth respondents [2022] 3 HKLRD 786, [2022] HKCT 1: trial on pecuniary penalties for first, second and fourth respondents [2020] 4 HKLRD 61, [2020] HKCT 3: trial on liability under first conduct rule, disposal of proceedings by consent, *Carecraft* procedure; rule 39 of the CTR

(continued)

Table 2 ***(Continued)***

Case name and summary of allegations	Judgments delivered
Taching Petroleum Co Ltd v Meyer Aluminium Ltd (CTA 1/2018) and *Shell Hong Kong Ltd v Meyer Aluminium Ltd* (CTA 2/2018) (competition law defence of price fixing raised in High Court action)	[2022] 1 HKC 170, [2021] HKCFI 3028: disposal of High Court action [2021] HKCT 2: trial on liability under first conduct rule [2021] HKCFI 1690: pre-trial review, application for split trial on liability and quantum [2021] 3 HKC 587, [2021] HKCA 294: appeal against interlocutory decisions [2021] 1 HKLRD C2, [2020] HKCA 1005: renewed leave to appeal against interlocutory decisions [2020] 4 HKLRD 646, [2020] HKCT 7: leave to appeal against interlocutory decisions [2020] HKCT 2: leave to amend points of defence, request for better and further particulars, leave to adduce expert evidence, leave to seek unredacted documents [2019] HKCFI 515: application for stay of High Court proceedings pending Tribunal proceedings [2019] 2 HKLRD 205, [2019] HKCT 1: second case management conference, redaction and confidentiality issues [2018] HKCFI 2095: directions [2018] HKCT 4: directions, requirement to file originating notice of application and pleadings [2018] 2 HKLRD 1284, [2018] HKCFI 1074: application for summary judgment, transfer to Competition Tribunal; section 113 of the CO
Competition Commission v Fungs E&M Engineering Co Ltd (CTEA 1/2019) (market sharing and price fixing in the provision of renovation services in a public housing estate)	[2022] 3 HKLRD 84, [2022] HKCA 786: appeal against trial on sanctions and pecuniary penalties [2021] HKCT 1: trial on sanctions and pecuniary penalties [2020] HKCT 9: disqualification order against director; sections 101–103 of the CO [2020] HKCT 8: disposal by *Kam Kwong* procedure, liability under first conduct rule [2020] HKCT 5: costs against withdrawal of party's submission [2020] 5 HKLRD 1, [2020] HKCT 4: substitution, joinder and third party applications
Competition Commission v Quantr Ltd (CTEA 1/2020) (bid rigging in response to a workflow automation project)	[2020] 5 HKLRD 528, [2020] HKCT 10: disposal by *Kam Kwong* procedure, liability under first conduct rule

(continued)

Table 2 ***(Continued)***

Case name and summary of allegations	**Judgments delivered**
Competition Commission v TH Lee Book Co Ltd (CTEA 2/2020) (limiting the level of discounts to be offered in tenders for textbooks for primary and secondary schools)	[2021] 3 HKC 61, [2020] HKCT 12: simultaneous or sequential exchanges of witness statements
Competition Commission v Linde HKO Ltd (CTEA 3/2020) (abusing market power in the medical gases supply market)	[2021] 5 HKLRD 175, [2021] HKCT 3: discovery, presumption of general discovery
Competition Commission v Quadient Technologies Hong Kong Ltd (CTEA 1/2021) (arrangements between contractors not to compete in the sale of inserters for mass mailing)	[2023] HKCT 6: redacted reasons for decision and statements of fact [2023] 3 HKLRD 374, [2023] HKCT 1: disposal by *Kam Kwong* procedure, liability under first conduct rule, confidentiality orders
Competition Commission v Hong Kong Commercial Cleaning Services Ltd (CTEA 2/2021) (collusion in cleansing service contracts quotations invited by the Hong Kong Housing Authority)	
Competition Commission v Gray Line Tours of Hong Kong Ltd (CTEA 1/2022) (collusion in fixing and controlling the price of tourist attractions and transportation tickets in Hong Kong)	[2023] HKCT 7: redacted reasons for decision and statements of fact [2023] 4 HKLRD I2, [2023] HKCT 3: application for leave to be represented by solicitor without higher rights of audience; rule 30(1)(b)(ii) of the CTR [2023] HKCT 2: disposal by *Kam Kwong* procedure, liability under first conduct rule, confidentiality orders [2022] HKCT 3: case management conference
Competition Commission v ATAL Building Services Engineering Ltd (CTEA 2/2022 and CTEA 2/2023) (collusion in price fixing, market sharing and bid rigging of air-conditioning works in Hong Kong)	[2024] HKCT 1: directions for disposal by *Kam Kwong* procedure [2023] 5 HKLRD 665, [2023] HKCT 9: case management conference, decision on contentious directions [2022] 4 HKLRD 425, [2022] HKCT 4: application for redaction of confidential information, confidentiality rings

(continued)

Table 2 ***(Continued)***

Case name and summary of allegations	**Judgments delivered**
Competition Commission v The Tien Chu (Hong Kong) Co Ltd (CTEA 3/2022) (using disincentives to secure compliance with a particular minimum resale price by Tien Chu to other distributors of the goods)	
Competition Commission v Multisoft Ltd (CTEA 1/2023) (cover bidding in quotations for IT solutions in applications for a government subsidy scheme)	[2024] 4 HKLRD 37, [2024] HKCT 2: disposal by *Kam Kwong* procedure, liability under first conduct rule [2023] HKCT 8: case management conference, requirement to file verifying affirmation
Competition Commission v Midland Realty International Ltd (CTEA 3/2023) (price fixing via a minimum net commission rate for the sale of first-hand residential properties)	[2024] HKCFI 869: leave to apply for judicial review granted on the Commission's decision not to entertain the applicant's leniency application

II. Extraterritorial Application

The CO has extraterritorial applications in the sense that it covers acts performed outside Hong Kong, but only to the extent that such acts lead to a breach of the statute in Hong Kong.

Section 8 of the CO, for instance, provides for the extraterritorial application of the first conduct rule as follows:

> The first conduct rule applies to an agreement, concerted practice or decision that has the object or effect of preventing, restricting or distorting competition in Hong Kong even if –
>
> (a) the agreement or decision is made or given effect to outside Hong Kong;
> (b) the concerted practice is engaged in outside Hong Kong;
> (c) any party to the agreement or concerted practice is outside Hong Kong; or
> (d) any undertaking or association of undertakings giving effect to a decision is outside Hong Kong.

Section 23 of the CO provides for extraterritorial application of the second conduct rule as follows:

> The second conduct rule applies to conduct that has as its object or effect the prevention, restriction or distortion of competition in Hong Kong even if –
>
> (a) the undertaking engaging in the conduct is outside Hong Kong; or
> (b) the conduct is engaged in outside Hong Kong.

Section 2 of Schedule 7 of the CO concerns the extraterritorial applications of Schedule 2 of the CO to mergers.

The foregoing provisions exemplify the 'effects doctrine'. That doctrine extends the jurisdiction of a competition authority to an act, action or agreement which has effect in the jurisdiction of the competition authority.[5] Anti-competitive conduct engaged in outside Hong Kong will be caught by the CO so long as the consequences of the conduct occur in Hong Kong.

Sections 8 and 23 of the CO enable the Competition Commission to conduct investigations against persons outside of Hong Kong and agreements made elsewhere. It does not, however, authorise the Commission to act outside Hong Kong. Sections 8 and 23 are silent as to how the law can be enforced against conduct taking place abroad, or against persons having little or no connection with Hong Kong. It is also unclear how the sanctions provided for in the CO can be enforced outside Hong Kong, except that it is possible for a prohibition order to prevent a wrongdoer from leaving Hong Kong.[6] For example, if an undertaking is ordered to produce documents under section 41 of the CO and those documents are located outside of Hong Kong, it may be difficult to compel the undertaking to comply with the order if the undertaking has little or no presence in Hong Kong.

The Competition Tribunal does not have jurisdiction to deal with breaches of competition laws in other jurisdictions. The Hong Kong court can, however, decide such matters if they are relevant (for example, as incidental questions) to a main dispute over which the court has jurisdiction. For example, in a claim for breach of contract governed by foreign law, the Hong Kong court can deal with a defence that the provisions of the contract breach anti-competition legislation under that foreign law. The CO allows for defences to be raised in any actions and the Competition Tribunal has jurisdiction to determine 'allegations of contraventions, or involvements in contraventions, of the conduct rules raised as a defence'.[7]

In relation to competition law issues arising in intellectual property disputes, an arbitral tribunal can decide those issues as incidental questions necessary for the determination of the main intellectual property dispute. This is despite the CO giving exclusive jurisdiction on competition law infringement issues to the Competition Tribunal.[8]

III. Right of Private Action

In Hong Kong, there is no standalone right of private action to bring a competition law claim before the Competition Tribunal. Section 108 of the CO provides that no person may bring any proceedings independently of the CO if the cause of action is the defendant's contravention of a conduct rule.[9] If the contravention of a conduct rule is alleged as a defence in a

[5] See, eg *Commission Decision of 19 December 1984 relating to a proceeding under Article 85 of the EEC Treaty (IV/29.725 – Wood pulp)* [1985] OJ L85/1.

[6] CO, ss 151A–151C.

[7] ibid s 142(1)(d).

[8] Arbitration Ordinance (Cap 609), s 103D(4)(a); Case C-126/97 *Eco Swiss China Time Ltd v Benetton International NV* [1999] ECR I-3055.

[9] CO, s 108. See also *Loyal Profit International Development Ltd v Trade Industry Council of Hong Kong* (unreported, HCMP 256/2016, 27 April 2017) [47]; *Taching Petroleum Co Ltd v Meyer Aluminium Ltd* [2018] 2 HKLRD 1284, [2018] HKCFI 1074 [40]–[41].

High Court action, section 113 of the CO specifies that the court must transfer that part of the proceedings to the Competition Tribunal.[10] It is therefore not possible to examine the application of private international law rules in private claims involving competition law.

But ordinary citizens can bring a private follow-on action before the Competition Tribunal. The action 'follows on' in the sense that there must be a prior finding by the Competition Tribunal (or the High Court, if the case is transferred to it by the Competition Tribunal) that an undertaking has contravened a conduct rule.[11] Any follow-on claim will then be subject to Hong Kong law.

[10] CO, s 113. See also *Taching Petroleum Co Ltd* (n 9) [14]–[22].
[11] CO, ss 110(1) and 110(3).

PART IV

Recognition and Enforcement

23

Recognition and Enforcement

This chapter deals with the recognition and enforcement of foreign judgments in Hong Kong. Section I briefly introduces the distinction between recognition and enforcement and the concept of estoppel. Section II gives an overview of the regimes in the rather complex landscape of recognition and enforcement of foreign judgments in Hong Kong. Section III discusses recognition and enforcement of foreign judgments in Hong Kong under common law. Section IV discusses recognition and enforcement of foreign judgments in Hong Kong under statute, if the judgment is applicable under specific statutes. These statutes include the Foreign Judgments (Reciprocal Enforcement) Ordinance (Cap 319) (FJREO), the Mainland Judgments (Reciprocal Enforcement) Ordinance (Cap 597) (MJREO) and the Mainland Judgments in Civil and Commercial Matters (Reciprocal Enforcement) Ordinance (Cap 645) (MJCCMREO).[1] Section V focuses on restrictions on recognition and enforcement provided in the Foreign Judgments (Restriction on Recognition and Enforcement) Ordinance (Cap 46) (FJRREO). Section VI covers recognition and enforcement issues in family law, including recognition of foreign marriages, divorces and maintenance orders, as well as the Mainland Judgments in Matrimonial and Family Cases (Reciprocal Recognition and Enforcement) Ordinance (Cap 639) (MJMFCO).

For the recognition of foreign corporate insolvencies, and the principles governing the recognition of and assistance to foreign liquidators and representatives in Hong Kong, see chapter twenty, section III. For the recognition of foreign personal bankruptcies, see chapter twenty-one, section III. For the recognition and enforcement of foreign arbitral awards, see chapter twenty-four, section VI.

I. Distinction between Recognition and Enforcement

While the terms 'recognition' and 'enforcement' are frequently used in conjunction, a distinction exists between them. Regardless of whether the foreign judgment is to be enforced, a foreign judgment may be recognised by the Hong Kong court for the purpose of giving rise to a *res judicata* in Hong Kong proceedings. An example would be where recognition is sought of a foreign judgment dismissing a plaintiff's claim. If that plaintiff later commences proceedings in Hong Kong in respect of the same cause of action that was dismissed, the

[1] There may be other statutes regarding various foreign orders. For example, the Mutual Legal Assistance in Criminal Matters Ordinance (Cap 525) governs the recognition of overseas enforcement measures in criminal matters, including requests for mutual legal assistance.

defendant may apply for those proceedings to be struck out on account of *res judicata*.[2] For this purpose, the Hong Kong court would have to recognise the foreign judgment without the need to enforce it.

Res judicata consists of three conceptually distinct but interrelated principles: (i) cause of action estoppel; (ii) issue estoppel; and (iii) the 'extended doctrine' of *res judicata* (or the defence of 'abuse of process'):[3]

(i) Cause of action estoppel 'prevents a party to an action from asserting or denying, as against the other party, the existence of a particular cause of action, the non-existence or existence of which has been determined by a court of competent jurisdiction in previous litigation between the same parties'.[4]
(ii) Issue estoppel operates even when the cause of action in the earlier action and that in the later action are not identical, as long as some issue (of fact or law) which is necessarily common to both had been decided on the earlier occasion and is binding on the parties.[5]
(iii) The 'extended doctrine' of *res judicata* extends cause of action estoppel and issue estoppel to preclude a party from raising in subsequent proceedings matters which were not, but could and should have been, raised in the earlier proceedings in the absence of 'special circumstances'.[6]

Both cause of action estoppel and issue estoppel are available for foreign judgments.[7] As for the *Henderson v Henderson* extended doctrine, the limited authorities show that it is available;[8] it is suggested that the enforcement court first has to be satisfied that the same extended doctrine exists under the originating court, and then must exercise caution when determining whether it arises.[9]

Once a foreign judgment satisfies the conditions for recognition and enforcement, it is recognised as conclusive between the parties in all proceedings founded on the same cause of action, and cannot be impeached for any error either of fact or of law.[10] The court has no power to review the merits of the foreign judgment.

If a foreign judgment is to be enforced in Hong Kong, it must first be recognised by the Hong Kong court, which will then make an order for the enforcement of the foreign

[2] *Carl Zeiss Stiftung v Rayner & Keeler Ltd (No 2)* [1967] 1 AC 853, 933. See also *Virgin Atlantic Airways Ltd v Zodiac Seats UK Ltd* [2013] UKSC 46, [2014] AC 160.

[3] *China North Industries Investment Ltd v Ronald RC Chum* [2010] 5 HKLRD 1 [46]–[61]; *Turf Club Auto Emporium Pte Ltd v Yeo Boong Hua* [2017] 2 SLR 12 [82]–[85]; Patrick Keane, *Spencer Brown and Handley: Res Judicata*, 6th edn (LexisNexis, 2024).

[4] *Thoday v Thoday* [1964] P 181, 197; *Total Lubricants Hong Kong Ltd v Christophe de la Cropte de Chanterac* [2013] 2 HKLRD 838 [14]–[17].

[5] *Carl Zeiss Stiftung* (n 2) 913–17, 933–35 and 964–65; *First Laser Ltd v Fujian Enterprises (Holdings) Co Ltd* (2012) 15 HKCFAR 569 [44]–[49]. See also *Merck Sharp & Dohme Corp v Merck KGaA* [2021] 1 SLR 1102.

[6] *Henderson v Henderson* (1843) 3 Hare 100, 114–15; *Johnson v Gore Wood* [2002] 2 AC 1, 29–31; *Ko Hon Yue v Chiu Pik Yuk* (2012) 15 HKCFAR 72 [82]–[83]. See also *Ong Han Nam v Borneo Ventures Pte Ltd* [2021] 1 SLR 1248.

[7] *The Sennar (No 2)* [1985] 1 WLR 490; *Republic of India v India Steamship Co* [1993] AC 410; *First Laser Ltd* (n 5). In the arbitration context, see *The Republic of India v Deutsche Telekom AG* [2024] 1 SLR 56.

[8] *Desert Sun Loan Corp v Hill* [1996] 2 All ER 847, 854–55; *Anthony Wee Soon Kim v UBS AG Hong Kong Branch* [2006] 2 HKC 1.

[9] *Telesto Investments Ltd v UBS AG* [2013] NSWSC 503 [225]–[240].

[10] *Godard v Gray* (1870–71) LR 6 QB 139, 150.

judgment in the same way as a judgment of the Hong Kong court. An example would be where enforcement is sought of a foreign judgment ordering that the defendant pay the plaintiff a sum of money. To enforce the foreign judgment in Hong Kong, the plaintiff would have to ask the Hong Kong court to recognise the judgment and, that having been done, to convert the foreign judgment into an enforceable order of the Hong Kong court. The judgment creditor will then be able to apply for various orders (such as garnishee orders and charging orders) to recover the judgment debt.[11]

On the other hand, if recognition and enforcement was refused, that is usually the end of the matter. In very rare and exceptional circumstances involving clear unconscionability, it might be possible to grant an anti-enforcement injunction to restrain the party from relying on the foreign judgment in another jurisdiction.[12]

II. Regimes of Recognition and Enforcement in Hong Kong

The rules concerning recognition and enforcement of foreign judgments in Hong Kong derive from three sources: common law, statute and international conventions. Only the first two have direct effect. That is because Hong Kong law follows the dualist theory, whereby bilateral treaties or multilateral conventions do not become part of Hong Kong until the instruments are enacted in domestic law.

But that does not mean international conventions have no impact at all in the recognition and enforcement of foreign judgments. Quite the contrary, as will be seen in section IV below, the MJREO follows the framework of the 2005 HCCH Convention on Choice of Court Agreements (Hague Choice of Court Convention) closely, while the MJCCMREO follows the framework in the 2018 Draft of the 2019 HCCH Convention on the Recognition and Enforcement of Foreign Judgments in Civil or Commercial Matters (Hague Judgments Convention) closely. The HCCH Conventions are taken as useful guidance when preparing the local legislation. It is expected that the interpretation of the HCCH Conventions in other jurisdictions will also aid the interpretation of the MJREO and the MJCCMREO in the future.

The differences between the regimes under common law and statute are somewhat nuanced and may not be that apparent. In fact, the provisions of the FJREO (as borrowed from the Foreign Judgments (Reciprocal Enforcement) Act 1933 in the UK) were deliberately framed so as to reproduce the rules of the common law as closely as possible, although there were eventually some departures,[13] and it is considered wrong to use the statute to ascertain the common law 'by arguing backwards from the provisions of the statute'.[14] Three major differences are noted below.

[11] Details of these orders are matters of domestic civil procedure. See, eg Rules of the High Court (Cap 4A) (RHC), Ords 45–52 and the commentaries in Joseph Fok and others (gen eds), *Hong Kong Civil Procedure 2025* (Sweet & Maxwell, 2024).

[12] *Sun Travels & Tour Pvt Ltd v Hilton International Manage (Maldives) Pty Ltd* [2019] 1 SLR 732; *SAS Institute Inc v World Programming Ltd* [2020] EWCA Civ 599.

[13] *Report of the Foreign Judgments (Reciprocal Enforcement) Committee* (Cmd 4213, 1932) paras 2, 16 and 18 and Annex V, para 7.

[14] *Henry v Geoprosco International Ltd* [1976] QB 726, 751.

First, the statutory regimes provide a 'summary procedure' to register foreign judgments. Under statute, the simplified procedures of registration provide that a foreign judgment will be treated as if it were a judgment of the Hong Kong court upon registration. Under common law, a writ must be issued to claim the amount owing under the foreign judgment as a debt.

Second, in a common law action, the burden of proof lies with the judgment creditor to show that the judgment should be enforced, whereas in proceedings for the registration of a foreign judgment under statute, the burden of proof falls on the judgment debtor to show why the judgment should not be enforced.[15]

Third, there are different limitation periods under the FJREO (six years), the MJREO (two years) and the MJCCMREO (two years).[16] Under common law, the enforcement of foreign judgments is based on the implied promise to pay the judgment sum as contractual debt, and thus the six-year limitation period for simple contracts under section 4(1) of the Limitation Ordinance (Cap 347) applies. Section 4(4) of the Limitation Ordinance (which provides that 'an action shall not be brought upon any judgment after the expiration of 12 years from the date on which the judgment became enforceable') is applicable only to domestic judgments but not to foreign judgments.[17]

A judgment that falls within the FJREO, the MJREO or the MJCCMREO must be enforced under statute instead of common law.[18]

III. Recognition and Enforcement under Common Law

At common law, a foreign judgment can be recognised and enforced in Hong Kong if it satisfies the following five requirements:[19]

1. The foreign judgment is between the same parties (or their privies).[20]
2. The foreign court which rendered the judgment has international jurisdiction.
3. The foreign judgment is final and conclusive, although it may be subject to appeal.
4. The foreign judgment is for a debt or definite sum of money, which is not a sum payable in respect of taxes, fine or similar penalty.
5. The foreign judgment is not impeachable under the private international law rules in Hong Kong; for example, the enforcement of the foreign judgment would not be contrary to natural justice or public policy, or contradict a previous judgment of the Hong Kong court between the same parties on the same matter.

[15] *Beijing Renji Real Estate Development Group Co Ltd v Zhu Min* [2024] 5 HKLRD 137, [2024] HKCA 878 [42].

[16] FJREO, s 4(1); MJREO, s 7(1); MJCCMREO, s 10(1)(b)(ii).

[17] *Poh Soon Kiat v Desert Palace Inc* [2010] 1 SLR 1129 [41]–[45]; *Re Li Man Hoo* [2013] 4 HKLRD 247. *cf* Limitation Act 1980 (UK), s 24 (6 years).

[18] FJREO, s 8; MJREO, s 22(2); MJCCMREO, s 31; *Re James Chor Cheung Wong* [2018] 2 HKLRD 284, [2018] HKCFI 585 [4].

[19] Lord Collins of Mapesbury and Jonathan Harris (gen eds), *Dicey, Morris and Collins on the Conflict of Laws*, 16th edn (Sweet & Maxwell, 2022) para 14R–024; *JSC BTA Bank v Mukhtar Kabulovich* Ablyazov [2014] 5 HKC 209; *Jiang Xi An Fa Da Wine Co Ltd v Zhan King* [2019] HKCFI 2411 [52]. It is common practice to plead these requirements in the statement of claim, although theoretically the rule of pleading is simply that the defendant is indebted to the plaintiff for a fixed sum under the judgment. Reciprocity is not a requirement under the common law recognition and enforcement framework in Hong Kong.

[20] It is necessary that the defendant and the plaintiff in the forum coincide respectively with the judgment debtor and the judgment creditor in the foreign jurisdiction: *Blohn v Desser* [1962] 2 QB 116.

Note that, for the purposes of recognition and enforcement, judgments of the courts in Mainland China, Taiwan and Macao are treated as analogous to foreign judgments. In the case of a Taiwanese judgment, the Hong Kong court will recognise and enforce the same if, in addition to the foregoing criteria, the judgment concerns private rights and it would be in the common interest to recognise and enforce those rights.[21]

A foreign judgment *in rem* is capable of recognition and enforcement in Hong Kong if the subject matter of the foreign proceedings was immovable or movable property situated in that jurisdiction at the time of the proceedings.[22] However, a foreign judgment regarding the proprietary effects of immovable property (as opposed to movable property) situated outside of that foreign jurisdiction will not be enforced.[23]

A. International Jurisdiction

For a judgment to be recognised and enforced, it must be made by a court of competent jurisdiction. Whether a court is competent is assessed by reference to the law of the forum, not the law of the foreign jurisdiction.[24] As there may be different standards of jurisdiction between the originating court and the enforcement court, the concept of 'international jurisdiction' (sometimes called 'indirect jurisdiction') is introduced as the basis for the assessment. A court has 'international jurisdiction' when it assumes jurisdiction over a case having foreign elements on a ground which is widely accepted internationally as a basis on which a court can assume jurisdiction over that case.

There is no consensus on what constitute grounds of international jurisdiction. But, at a minimum, an originating court is widely accepted as exercising international jurisdiction in six situations:[25]

1. The state in which the originating court is situated is the residence of the defendant.[26]
2. The state in which the originating court is situated is the place where the defendant has a principal place of business or an establishment, branch or agency, provided that place of business, establishment, branch or agency is closely connected to the claim.[27]
3. The defendant has submitted to the originating court's jurisdiction:
   (a) by agreement;[28]

[21] *Chen Li Hung v Ting Lei Miao* (2000) 3 HKCFAR 9 [37].

[22] *Castrique v Imrie* (1869–70) LR 4 HL 414, 429.

[23] *Ip Cheung Kwok v Yip Chi Keung Allen* [1994] 1 HKC 676. See also FJREO, s 6(3)(a).

[24] See, eg *Rubin v Eurofinance SA* [2012] UKSC 46, [2013] 1 AC 236 [161].

[25] This list largely coincides with the lists of international jurisdiction provided in FJREO, s 6(2) and MJCCMREO, s 23(3), which were enacted in the context of recognising and enforcing foreign judgments and Mainland judgments in civil and commercial matters respectively. The first three situations largely coincide with *Dicey, Morris and Collins* (n 19) para 14R-058. See also *Emanuel v Symon* [1908] 1 KB 302, 309.

[26] *Schibsby v Westenholz* (1870–71) LR 6 QB 155, 161; *Emanuel* (n 25) 309. Some common law authorities suggested that mere presence is sufficient, although it is submitted that presence is an undesirable basis even for direct jurisdiction: *Maharanee of Baroda v Wildenstein* [1972] 2 QB 283. Voluntary presence not induced by compulsion, fraud or duress is necessary: *Adams v Cape Industries plc* [1990] Ch 433. See also *Rubin* (n 24) [7]–[10].

[27] *Adams* (n 26).

[28] The jurisdiction agreement can be express, implied or inferred: *Vizcaya Partners Ltd v Picard* [2016[UKPC 5, [2016] Bus LR 413. A foreign choice of law clause is not sufficient to establish international jurisdiction: *US Mortgage Finance II LLC v Dew* [2015] EWHC 3621 (Comm) [7]–[8].

(b) by defending the claim on the merits without challenging jurisdiction;[29] or
(c) by invoking the court's jurisdiction in bringing a counterclaim related to the claim.[30]

4. The plaintiff's claim relates to immovable property in the state of the originating court.[31]
5. The claim concerns a contractual obligation and the place of performance or breach was in the state of the originating court.
6. The claim concerns a non-contractual obligation and the act that gave rise to the damage (death, personal injury, damage to property) occurred in the state of the originating court.

There may be other grounds of international jurisdiction, such as: the plaintiff's nationality, residence or domicile in the state of the originating court; the defendant's presence in the territory of the court; and the fact that the defendant has assets or movable property in the territory of the originating court. But these other grounds are not as widely accepted as the six bases identified above.[32]

B. Final and Conclusive

A judgment creditor must show that the foreign court 'conclusively, finally, and forever established the existence of the debt of which it is sought to be made conclusive evidence in this country, so as to make it *res judicata* between the parties'.[33] On the foregoing definition, a judgment which is given in default of a defendant's appearance and which may potentially be set aside by the originating court if the defendant so applies at a later point in time can still be final and conclusive.[34] Nor will the possibility of an appeal against a judgment by itself mean that the judgment lacks finality.[35] In *China NPL Holdings Pte Ltd v Mo Haidan*, the Court of Appeal highlighted four scenarios:[36]

1. There is the possibility of an appeal against the foreign judgment, but no appeal had been brought.
2. The foreign judgment is subject to a pending appeal.
3. The foreign judgment has been stayed pending the determination of an appeal.

[29] Even if the foreign court might regard the defendant as having submitted to its jurisdiction, it is still open to a Hong Kong court to find that there has been no submission as a matter of Hong Kong private international law rules: *Adams* (n 26) 461; *Rubin* (n 24) [161]. See also *Akai Pty Ltd v People's Ins Co Ltd* [1998] 1 Lloyd's Rep 90.

[30] *Schibsby* (n 26); *GFH Capital Ltd v Haigh* [2020] EWHC 1269 (Comm).

[31] *The Despina GK* [1983] 1 All ER 1.

[32] Anselmo Reyes, 'Introduction: Towards a System for the Recognition and Enforcement of Judgments' in Anselmo Reyes (ed), *Recognition and Enforcement of Judgments in Civil and Commercial Matters* (Hart Publishing, 2019) 29–30; Wilson Lui and Anselmo Reyes, 'Introduction' in Anselmo Reyes and Wilson Lui (eds), *Direct Jurisdiction: Asian Perspectives* (Hart Publishing, 2021) 9–10.

[33] *Nouvion v Freeman* (1889) 15 App Cas 1, 9.

[34] *Nintendo of America Inc v Bung Enterprises* Ltd [2000] 2 HKC 629. However, if the defendant has the right to set aside that default judgment without having to show cause to do so, then the judgment is not considered final and conclusive until the defendant's right in that respect expires: *Jeannot v Furst* (1909) 25 TLR 424, 425.

[35] *Nouvion* (n 33) 13.

[36] *China NPL Holdings Pte Ltd v Mo Haidan* [2021] 1 HKLRD 344, [2020] HKCA 1014 [54]–[57].

4. The Hong Kong enforcement action was commenced before the foreign judgment was overturned on appeal.

Scenarios 1 and 2 would not preclude a foreign judgment being final and conclusive. But, in scenario 2, the Hong Kong court may grant a stay of proceedings pending the determination of the appeal.[37] In scenario 3, the Hong Kong court should consider whether the foreign court granted the stay simply to preserve the status quo pending determination of the appeal or because the foreign judgment was in error.[38] If the latter is the case, the Hong Kong court may refuse recognition or enforcement. In scenario 4, the Hong Kong court cannot consider the foreign judgment to be final and conclusive. An order of the Hong Kong court recognising the overturned foreign judgment is liable to be set aside.[39]

An issue faced by Hong Kong courts is whether a Mainland Chinese judgment can be regarded as final and conclusive if it is subject to an application for administrative review under the trial supervision system (审判监督程序) by a People's Court, the Supreme People's Court or the Supreme People's Procuratorate. In *Chiyu Banking Corp Ltd v Chan Tin Kwun*, the Hong Kong court regarded a judgment of the Fujian Intermediate People's Court as lacking in finality because it remained under administrative review.[40] This position was apparently affirmed by the Court of Appeal in *Lam Chit Man v Lam Chi To*. However, the court did not conclusively decide the matter, since neither party had adduced PRC law expert evidence on the effect of the trial supervision system on a Mainland judgment's conclusiveness.[41] Over the years, the decision in *Chiyu* has made it difficult for Hong Kong courts to recognise and enforce Mainland judgments as the latter are all potentially subject to the trial supervision system. In *Lee Yau Wing v Lee Shui Kwan*, the Court of Appeal was dealing with a challenge to a Hong Kong summary judgment predicated on a judgment by the Qingyuan People's Court. The court allowed the appeal. The court reasoned that the question whether Mainland judgments can be considered final was an issue of public importance involving complicated legal questions that could not be determined summarily.[42]

More recently, there seems to have been a sea-change in the court's view. In *Bank of China Ltd v Yang Fan*, in the course of considering an application for the continuation of a Mareva injunction, the court observed that the trial supervision system was akin to the possibility of an appeal.[43] In *Jiang Xi An Fa Da Wine Co Ltd v Zhan King*, the court found that there is no definitive authority to deprive a PRC judgment of its otherwise final and conclusive character, and the trial supervision system does not preclude finding the judgment enforceable in Hong Kong within the meaning of section 21M of the High Court Ordinance (Cap 4), which requires the foreign proceedings to be capable of giving rise to a judgment which may be enforced in Hong Kong.[44] Accordingly, given that the mere possibility of an appeal

[37] ibid [54].
[38] ibid [55]–[57].
[39] ibid [57].
[40] *Chiyu Banking Corp Ltd v Chan Tin Kwun* [1996] 2 HKLR 395, 399.
[41] *Lam Chit Man v Lam Chi To* [2001–2003] HKCLRT 133 [18]–[21].
[42] *Lee Yau Wing v Lee Shui Kwan* [2007] 2 HKLRD 749 [15]–[29], [34]–[38].
[43] *Bank of China Ltd v Yang Fan* [2016] 3 HKLRD 7 (CFI) [38]–[54]. This was followed in *Beijing Renji Real Estate Development Group Co Ltd v Zhu Min* [2022] 4 HKC 116, [2022] HKCFI 1027 [65]–[66].
[44] *Jiang Xi An Fa Da Wine Co Ltd* (n 19) [85]–[90]. See also ch 9, s V.B.

did not preclude a judgment from being final and conclusive, the mere possibility of an administrative review of a Mainland judgment did not prevent the same from being treated as final and conclusive.

C. Judgment for a Fixed Sum which is not a Penalty

At common law, only foreign monetary judgments for a fixed sum can be recognised or enforced.[45] The court in *Jiang Xi An Fa Da Wine Co Ltd v Zhan King* commented that whether non-monetary foreign judgments can be recognised at common law has never been debated. The court observed that since non-monetary judgments (such as an order for the transfer of shares) have been recognised and enforced in other common law jurisdictions, the alleged rule has to be re-examined.[46] In Canada, the Supreme Court decision of *Pro Swing Inc v Elta Golf Inc* disposed of this rule and provided three criteria for the enforcement of foreign non-monetary judgments: (i) the foreign order must be clear and specific as to the rights, duties and obligations imposed on the defendant; (ii) the foreign order must be clear about whether it was intended to apply outside the territory of the foreign country of origin; and (iii) the proceedings must have a sufficient connection with the jurisdiction of enforcement to warrant the enforcement court's intervention.[47] In Hong Kong, *Pro Swing* may be taken as too dramatic a liberalisation, and this issue remains debatable.[48]

As for the rule against enforcing penalties, the Court of Appeal in *Hung Fung Enterprises Holdings Ltd v Agricultural Bank of China* stated:[49]

> If the Court is satisfied that the purpose of the amount ordered was not to compensate for the loss suffered but to punish the defendant and deter others from acting in the same way, this could properly be regarded as a penalty.

The court then held that a double interest payment imposed by a Mainland judgment was a penalty. The judgment was unenforceable in Hong Kong as long as 'the purpose of the amount ordered was not to compensate for the loss suffered but to punish the defendant and deter others from acting in the same way'. It did not matter whether the double interest was to be paid to the plaintiff or to the government.[50] However, what constitutes a 'penalty' is not without controversy. For example, Lord Denning MR held that *résistance abusive*, a head of damages awardable under French law against a defendant who unreasonably refuses to pay a claim, was not a penalty. The sum was payable to an individual and not to the state as punishment. It was not against English public policy to enforce such a claim.[51]

[45] A judgment not for a fixed sum is not capable of enforcement: *Sadler v Robins* (1808) 1 Camp 253, 170 ER 948.
[46] *Jiang Xi An Fa Da Wine Co Ltd* (n 19) [82]–[84].
[47] *Pro Swing Inc v Eltta Golf Inc* [2006] 2 SCR 612, 629, 638–42 and 653.
[48] See also King Fung Tsang and Tsz Wai Wong, 'Enforcement of Non-monetary Judgments in Common Law Jurisdictions: Is the Time Ripe?' (2021) 45(2) *Fordham International Law Journal* 379.
[49] *Hung Fung Enterprises Holdings Ltd v Agricultural Bank of China* [2012] 3 HKLRD 679 [91]. See also *Benefit Strategies Group Inc v Prider* (2005) 91 SASR 544.
[50] *Hung Fung Enterprises Holdings Ltd* (n 49) [92].
[51] *SA Consortium General Textiles v Sun & Sand Agencies Ltd* [1978] QB 279.

D. Defences against Recognition and Enforcement

Possible common law defences against recognition and enforcement are considered below.[52]

Recognition and enforcement may be refused because the foreign judgment was obtained through fraud by the party seeking enforcement or by the originating court.[53] 'Fraud' includes 'every variety of *mala fides* and *mala praxis* whereby one of the parties misleads and deceives the judicial tribunal'.[54] An allegation of fraud is always serious, and a party applying for recognition to be refused must particularise the relevant fraud with precision and establish the same by compelling evidence[55] which is commensurate with the gravity of the allegation being levied.[56]

It is not entirely settled as to the limits of the defence of fraud. Most authorities in Canada and Australia have suggested that the ground is limited to fraud in the obtaining of the judgment, or fraud in matters that arise in evidence discovered after the foreign judgment was rendered.[57] The court is not allowed to review the merits of the original judgment.[58] For example, it does not enable the party resisting recognition to ask the Hong Kong court to review a finding by the original court that the plaintiff was not guilty of fraud in connection with the contract or other transaction giving rise to the foreign judgment.[59] Singapore adopts this approach, where the foreign judgment may only be impeached when 'fresh evidence has come to light which reasonable diligence on the part of the defendant would not have uncovered and the fresh evidence would have been likely to make a difference in the eventual result of the case'.[60] However, a long line of English authorities has not limited the defence of fraud to matters extraneous or collateral to the dispute which the foreign court determines.[61]

To date, Hong Kong has enthusiastically received the English authorities. In a common law enforcement action, the enforcing court must revisit the issue of fraud when alleged.[62] However, in an action under the FJREO, the Hong Kong court has a discretion as to whether the issue of fraud should be retried.[63] It is currently undecided which

[52] See, eg *Fabiano Hotels Ltd v Profitmax Holdings Inc* [2017] 6 HKC 414 (CFI) [18].

[53] *Price v Dewhurst* (1837) 8 Sim 279.

[54] *Jet Holdings Inc v Patel* [1990] 1 QB 355.

[55] *Hong Kong Huihuang Industrial Co Ltd v Allahabad Bank* (unreported, CACV 144/2016, 25 October 2016).

[56] ibid.

[57] *Jacobs v Beaver Silver Cobalt Mining Co* [1908] 17 OLR 496; *Keele v Findley* (1990) 21 NSWLR 444; *Quarter Investments Pty Ltd v Allardyce* (2014) 85 NSWLR 404; *Doe v Howard* [2015] VSC 75.

[58] *Duchess of Kingston's Case* [1775–1802] All ER Rep 623; *House of Spring Gardens Ltd v Waite* [1991] 1 QB 241.

[59] See, however, *Ahmed v Habib Bank* [2001] EWCA Civ 1270, where the English Court of Appeal found that fraud existed in the foreign proceedings despite the Pakistani judgment finding otherwise.

[60] *Hong Pian Tee v Les Placements Germain Gauthier Inc* [2002] 1 SLR(R) 515 [30].

[61] See, eg *Abouloff v Oppenheimer & Co* (1882) 10 QBD 295; *Jet Holdings Inc* (n 54); *Owens Bank Ltd v Bracco* [1991] 1 QB 241. See also Richard Garnett, 'Fraud and Foreign Judgments: The Defence that Refuses to Die' (2002) 2 *Journal of International Commercial Law* 161. Recent authorities further suggested that a party applying to set aside an earlier domestic judgment on the basis of fraud need not demonstrate that the evidence of fraud could not have been obtained with reasonable diligence in advance of the earlier trial: see eg *Clone Pty Ltd v Players Pty Ltd (in liq)* (2018) 264 CLR 165; *Takhar v Gracefield Developments Ltd* [2019] UKSC 13, [2020] AC 450; *Mayer Corp Development International Ltd v Alliance Financial Intelligence Ltd* [2019] 6 HKC 582, [2019] HKCA 777. It could be suggested that the same approach should apply when resisting the enforcement of foreign judgments: *Hong Pian Tee* (n 60) [33].

[62] *Tang Gang v Wong Sai Chung* [2024] 1 HKLRD 528, [2023] HKCA 1338 [38]–[39].

[63] *WFM Motors Pty Ltd v Maydwell* [1996] 1 HKC 444, 449. For the FJREO regime, see s IV.A below.

approach will apply in an action under the MJCCMREO when fraud was alleged under its section 22(1)(d).[64]

The originating court's failure to observe natural justice in the making of the foreign judgment may lead the Hong Kong court to refuse to recognise and enforce the judgment. Natural justice is usually concerned with due notice of the proceedings and a fair opportunity for both parties to present their cases. In addition, it may concern other situations where the forum's concept of substantial justice is infringed. Thus, for instance, recognition was refused where the foreign court simply accepted a claim for damages without any assessment of the same, and a party is not properly advised of the consequences of a failure to appear.[65] This ground is analogous to the Hong Kong court's discretion to refuse to recognise or enforce a foreign arbitral award due to the lack of proper notice or the arbitral tribunal's failure to afford a party with a reasonable opportunity to present its case.[66]

A foreign judgment may be refused recognition where it would be contrary to Hong Kong public policy to recognise the judgment. This ground is extremely narrow. It is not every error of law on the part of the originating court, whether in the application of its own or foreign law (including Hong Kong law), that will justify invocation of the public policy ground. This ground only applies where recognition of a foreign judgment would be repugnant to Hong Kong's fundamental legal or moral norms. This ground is analogous to the Hong Kong court's discretion to refuse recognition of a foreign arbitral award on the ground that recognition would be contrary to Hong Kong's public policy.[67] Indeed, the public policy ground and the natural justice ground discussed above may overlap. Thus, for instance, it may be that the failure to observe natural justice is so egregious that it would offend against Hong Kong's public policy.[68] A foreign judgment obtained in a manner considered as an abuse of process in Hong Kong is also contrary to public policy.[69] A judgment obtained in breach of an anti-suit injunction is considered to be against public policy, as this amounts to contempt of court.[70] The mere fact that a foreign judgment is wrong on the merits would not constitute a basis for the public policy ground.[71] However, it might amount to a contravention of public policy if the foreign judgment is 'perverse' by erroneously applying the law of the forum or failing to apply generally accepted doctrines of private international law.[72]

A foreign judgment will not be recognised if to do so would mean enforcing a foreign tax or penalty.[73]

Where a foreign judgment conflicts with a judgment of the Hong Kong court between the same parties on the same matter, the latter will have given rise to a *res judicata*. In such a case, the foreign judgment will be refused recognition and enforcement.[74] If two competing

[64] *Tang Gang* (n 62) fn 6. For the MJCCMREO regime, see s IV.D below.

[65] *Adams* (n 26).

[66] See New York Convention, Art V(1)(b), applied in AO, ss 86(1)(c), 89(2)(c), 95(2)(c) and 98D(2)(c)(ii).

[67] See New York Convention, Art V(2)(b), applied in AO, ss 86(1)(f), 89(2)(f), 95(2)(f) and 98D(2)(f).

[68] *Sang Cheol Woo v Yoo Shin Choi* [2022] HKCFI 1163 [51].

[69] *Hong Kong Huihuang Industrial Co Ltd* (n 55) [28]–[29].

[70] *Philip Alexander Securities & Futures Ltd v Bamberger* [1997] ILPr 73; *Philip Alexander Securities & Futures Ltd v Bamberger* [1997] ILPr 104; *WSG Nimbus Pte Ltd v Board of Control for Cricket in Sri Lanka* [2002] 1 SLR(R) 1088. See also s V below regarding s 3 of the FJRREO on foreign judgments obtained in breach of a jurisdiction agreement.

[71] *Hong Kong Huihuang Industrial Co Ltd* (n 55) [52].

[72] *Carl Zeiss Stiftung* (n 2) 917–18, 922. In *Merck Sharp & Dohme Corp* (n 5) [58]–[61], the question of whether the public policy defence is applicable in this situation was left open.

[73] See ch 8, s III. See also s V below regarding s 7 of the Protection of Trading Interests Ordinance (Cap 471).

[74] *Vervaeke v Smith* [1983] 1 AC 145; *Hong Kong Huihuang Industrial Co Ltd* (n 55) [30]; *Merck Sharp & Dohme Corp* (n 5) [36].

foreign judgments which both meet all common law requirements are sought to be recognised and enforced in Hong Kong, then the one earlier in time is recognised and enforced to the exclusion of the other.[75]

IV. Recognition and Enforcement under Statute

A. Foreign Judgments (Reciprocal Enforcement) Ordinance (Cap 319)

The FJREO is the primary legislation for the recognition or enforcement of foreign judgments in Hong Kong, although, as will be seen below, it only applies to a limited number of jurisdictions. A foreign judgment within the FJREO's purview must be enforced or recognised pursuant to the statute and not at common law.[76]

Section 3(1) of the FJREO empowers the Chief Executive in Council to extend the application of the FJREO to the judgments of a foreign country's superior courts if satisfied that the country will 'substantially' reciprocate by recognising the judgments of the Hong Kong court. Once extended, the courts are treated as superior courts of a foreign country covered by the FJREO.[77] The Hong Kong court has held that section 3(1) does not require actual reciprocity as opposed to an assurance that there will be reciprocity.[78] Foreign countries currently covered by the FJREO are listed in the Foreign Judgments (Reciprocal Enforcement) Order (Cap 319A). Parts of the Commonwealth subject to the FJREO are listed in the First Schedule,[79] while other foreign countries are listed in the Second Schedule.[80] There is also the Foreign Judgments (Reciprocal Enforcement) (Application to the Commonwealth) Order (Cap 319B), which applies to the judgments of superior courts of the British Commonwealth. Following Hong Kong's handover, there have been doubts whether these two orders remain in effect. Section 2A(2)(b) of the Interpretation and General Clauses Ordinance (Cap 1) stipulates:

> In any Ordinance, provisions conferring privileges on the UK or other Commonwealth countries or territories, other than provisions giving effect to reciprocal arrangements between Hong Kong and the UK or other Commonwealth countries or territories shall have no further effect.

In *Prime Credit Leasing Sdn Bhd v Tan Cho Lung*, it was suggested that both orders remain in force as long as the Chief Executive in Council remains satisfied that there continues to be substantial reciprocity between the countries and British Commonwealth nations

[75] *Showlag v Mansour* [1995] 1 AC 431; *Hong Kong Huihuang Industrial Co Ltd* (n 55) [30]; *Merck Sharp & Dohme Corp* (n 5) [36].

[76] FJREO, s 8; *James Chor Cheung Wong* (n 18).

[77] FJREO, s 3(1)(b).

[78] *Prime Credit Leasing Sdn Bhd v Tan Cho Lung* [2006] 4 HKLRD 741 [43]–[44].

[79] Foreign Judgments (Reciprocal Enforcement) Order (Cap 319A), s 2 and Sch 1. The parts of the Commonwealth listed therein are Australia and Australian External Territories, Bermuda, Brunei, India, Malaysia, New Zealand, Singapore and Sri Lanka.

[80] Foreign Judgments (Reciprocal Enforcement) Order (Cap 319A), s 3 and Sch 2. The foreign countries listed therein are Belgium, France, Federal Republic of Germany, Republic of Italy, Republic of Austria, Kingdom of the Netherlands and Israel.

listed on the one hand and Hong Kong on the other.[81] The litigant need not establish that the particular foreign jurisdiction listed in the legislation does give reciprocal enforcement in fact.

By its section 3(2), the FJREO only applies to judgments which are (i) final and conclusive[82] and (ii) for the payment of a liquidated sum which is not a tax, fine or other penalty.[83] As such, non-monetary judgments are not enforced. For example, the FJREO does not apply to a Singapore judgment requiring the sale of a property to a third party,[84] or a Mareva injunction by the High Court of New Zealand.[85] It was thought obiter that the FJREO permits the registration of foreign judgments which enforce another foreign judgment; there were subsequent criticisms to this proposition.[86]

Section 4 of the FJREO and Order 71 of the Rules of the High Court (Cap 4A) (RHC) sets out the procedure for registering judgments and the effect of registration. The judgment creditor can apply to the Court of First Instance, within six years after a final judgment, to have the same registered in Hong Kong. The judgment will not be registered if it has been wholly satisfied[87] or cannot be enforced by execution in the originating country.[88] Upon registration, the judgment will have the same force as a judgment of the Hong Kong court,[89] and interest can accrue on the judgment sum.[90] It will also be recognised as *res judicata* between the parties on the same cause of action.[91]

Under the FJREO, the Hong Kong court is not required to have jurisdiction over the judgment debtor.[92] However, by section 4(2) of the FJREO, enforcement of a registered judgment will be stayed until the judgment debtor has had an opportunity to apply to set aside the registration.

Section 6(1) of the FJREO lists the grounds for setting aside a registration. The time period under which an application to set aside a registration of foreign judgment depends upon the period stated in the order of registration.[93] The grounds are largely similar to those mentioned above for refusing recognition and enforcement at common law. A registration *shall* be set aside if:

1. The judgment is not a judgment to which the FJREO applies.[94]

[81] *Prime Credit Leasing Sdn Bhd* (n 78) [43]–[45]. See also *Koninljike Philips Electronics NV v Utran Technology Development Ltd* (unreported, HCMP 4509/2000, 26 October 2001), where a constitutional challenge against the FJREO failed.

[82] FJREO, s 3(2)(a). FJREO, s 3(3) provides that a judgment 'shall be deemed to be final and conclusive notwithstanding that an appeal is pending against it, or that it may still be subject to appeal, in the courts of the country of the original court'. See also *Biard Laboratoires SA v Rosumi Ltd* (unreported, HCMP 252/1997, 4 February 1999).

[83] FJREO, s 3(2)(b).

[84] *Cova Enterprises Ltd v Tjanaka* [2004] 1 HKLRD 199 [29].

[85] *Westpac New Zealand Ltd v Gao Hui* [2009] 4 HKC 373.

[86] *Morgan Stanley & Co International Ltd v Pilot Lead Investments Ltd* [2006] 2 HKLRD 731 [22]–[27]; *Strategic Technologies Pte Ltd v Procurement Bureau of the Republic of China Ministry of National Defence* [2020] EWCA Civ 1604, [2021] QB 999 [83]–[87].

[87] FJREO, s 4(1)(a).

[88] ibid s 4(1)(b).

[89] ibid s 4(2)(a).

[90] ibid s 4(2)(c).

[91] ibid s 10.

[92] *Hunt v BP Exploration Co (Libya) Ltd* (1980) 144 CLR 565.

[93] FJREO, s 5(1)(d); RHC, Ord 71, r 5(3).

[94] FJREO, s 6(1)(a)(i).

2. The originating court lacked international jurisdiction.[95] Sections 6(2) and 6(3) of the FJREO enumerate the situations in which originating courts are deemed or not deemed to have jurisdiction respectively.[96]
3. The judgment debtor did not receive notice of the foreign proceedings in sufficient time and did not appear.[97] The judgment debtor must have received actual notice of the foreign proceedings.[98]
4. The foreign judgment was obtained by fraud.[99]
5. Enforcement of the judgment would be contrary to Hong Kong public policy.[100]
6. The rights under the judgment were not vested in the person who applied for registration.[101]

In addition, a judgment *may* be set aside if the foreign judgment was subject to prior *res judicata* elsewhere.[102]

Since an application to register a foreign judgment is made *ex parte*, a material non-disclosure by an applicant for registration would breach the duty of full and frank disclosure and may lead to the registration being set aside as well.[103] Under section 7(1) of the FRJEO, where an appeal against the foreign judgment is pending in the originating state, the Hong Kong court may either set aside the registration (without prejudicing a further application to register the judgment when the appeal has been disposed of) or adjourn the application set aside until after the appeal is determined.

B. Judgments (Facilities for Enforcement) Ordinance (Cap 9)

The Judgments (Facilities for Enforcement) Ordinance (JFEO) provided for the registration of UK[104] and Commonwealth[105] judgments. However, it seems that the JFEO is now considered spent legislation and thus is no longer relevant. As far as the Commonwealth is concerned, the JFEO ceased to have effect. This is because section 9 of the FJREO empowered

[95] ibid s 6(1)(a)(ii).
[96] ibid ss 6(2) and 6(3). The grounds where international jurisdiction is deemed are: (i) submission by voluntary appearance (s 6(2)(a)(i)); (ii) submission by claim or counterclaim (s 6(2)(a)(ii)); (iii) prior agreement to submit to jurisdiction (s 6(2)(a)(iii)); (iv) judgment debtor as resident or with principal place of business in foreign jurisdiction (s 6(2)(a)(iv)); (v) judgment debtor with transaction effected in the foreign jurisdiction with office or place of business (s 6(2)(a)(v)); (vi) property situated in the foreign jurisdiction (s 6(2)(b)); and (vii) the jurisdiction of the original court recognised by the law of the registering court (s 6(2)(c)). The grounds where international jurisdiction is not deemed are: (i) subject matter being foreign immovable property (s 6(3)(a)) and (ii) judgment debtor entitled to immunity from jurisdiction without submission (s 6(3)(c)). In *Biard Laboratoires SA* (n 82), the defendant was found to have submitted to the foreign court under s 6(2)(a)(i) of the FJREO as it appealed against the foreign order by disputing on both jurisdiction and merits. It is perhaps more just to consider whether a party had a realistic option in the foreign court to contest jurisdiction without addressing the merits, in line with the approach in *Hwoo Huang Linda v Fu Being San* [2013] 1 HKLRD 259.
[97] ibid s 6(1)(a)(iii).
[98] *Resorts World at Sentosa Pte Ltd v Sze Siu Hung* [2018] HKCFI 1646 [32].
[99] FJREO, s 6(1)(a)(iv).
[100] ibid s 6(1)(a)(v).
[101] ibid s 6(1)(a)(vi).
[102] ibid s 6(1)(b); *Showlag* (n 75).
[103] *Resorts World at Sentosa Pte Ltd v Wong Fei Fu* [2020] HKCFI 1236.
[104] JFEO, s 3.
[105] ibid s 6.

the Governor in Council to extend provisions of the statute to the Commonwealth and, upon that happening, the JFEO would cease to have effect in respect of the Commonwealth.[106] Under the Foreign Judgments (Reciprocal Enforcement) (Application to the Commonwealth) Order (Cap 319B), the FJREO now applies to the Commonwealth, subject only to the existence of substantial reciprocity. Regarding the application of the JFEO to UK judgments, the Hong Kong court held in *Morgan Stanley & Co International Ltd v Pilot Lead Investments Ltd* that, since 1 July 1997, the UK no longer afforded reciprocity to Hong Kong judgments. Therefore, UK judgments were no longer enforceable under the JFEO and only the common law can be relied on.[107]

C. Mainland Judgments (Reciprocal Enforcement) Ordinance (Cap 597)

The MJREO was enacted to bring into effect the Arrangement on Reciprocal Recognition and Enforcement of Judgments in Civil and Commercial Matters Pursuant to Choice of Court Agreements between Parties Concerned in 2006 between the Supreme People's Court of the People's Republic of China and the Government of the Hong Kong Special Administrative Region. Following a new Arrangement on Reciprocal Recognition and Enforcement of Judgments in Civil and Commercial Matters in 2019, the MJCCMREO was enacted.[108] That statute is broader in scope than (and superseded) the MJREO. Nonetheless, the MJREO remains relevant for choice of court agreements made on or after the commencement date of the MJREO (1 August 2008) and before the commencement date of the MJCCMREO (29 January 2024). Any judgments given on the basis of such choice of court agreements remain within the scope of the MJREO.

The MJREO has a limited ambit regarding the reciprocal enforcement of Mainland judgments in Hong Kong. Mainland judgments can be registered in Hong Kong only where they arise as a result of a choice of court agreement whereby the Mainland court is granted exclusive jurisdiction over the parties' disputes.[109] The choice of a Mainland court must be expressly designated or specified, and cannot be implied or designated by the incorporation of a written term under the operation or effect of PRC law.[110] If exclusive jurisdiction is granted to a Mainland court only by implication of law, then the Mainland judgment will not be registerable under the MJREO.[111] Moreover, the choice of court agreement has to be in writing or by electronic means.[112] The ascertainment and construction of the nature and extent of the parties' agreement, including whether a clause may be interpreted as an

[106] FJREO, s 9.

[107] *Morgan Stanley & Co International Ltd* (n 86) [9].

[108] The MJCCMREO is discussed in s IV.D below. The two Arrangements (Fa Shi [2008] No 9 and Fa Shi [2024] No 2) are discussed in ch 25, ss I.E and I.G.

[109] For the definitions of 'choice of Hong Kong court agreement' and 'choice of Mainland court agreement', see MJREO, s 3.

[110] MJREO, ss 3(1) and 3(2); *Beijing Renji Real Estate Development Group Co Ltd* (CA) (n 15) [43]–[49]. However, the Court of Appeal left open the question of whether an 'implied' choice of exclusive jurisdiction based on a process of construction of the terms of a written contract (as opposed to one imposed by the legal system of the governing law of the contract) can satisfy the requirement under the MJREO.

[111] *Beijing Renji Real Estate Development Group Co Ltd* (CFI) (n 43) [42]–[43].

[112] MJREO, s 3(3).

exclusive choice of court agreement, is decided by the governing law of the agreement,[113] but whether a jurisdiction clause is a choice of court agreement under the MJREO is to be decided by reference to Hong Kong law.[114] A choice of court agreement is severable from the main contract.[115] The purpose of requiring that there be a choice of court agreement is to minimise the risk of parallel proceedings and facilitate enforcement under a summary procedure.[116] In construing the MJREO's objectives and the factual context in which it was enacted, reference may be made to extrinsic materials, such as the Explanatory Memorandum to the Bill which eventually became the MJREO and statements by responsible officials to the Legislative Council on the bill.[117]

Section 5 of the MJREO and Order 71A of the RHC set out the requirements and procedure for the registration of Mainland judgments covered by the statute. An application for registration is made to the Hong Kong Court of First Instance. The time limit for registration is stated in section 7 of the MJREO as two years from the last day by which the judgment is to be performed or otherwise from the date when the judgment takes effect. The requirements for registration are as follows:

1. The judgment must have been delivered by the Supreme People's Court, a Higher People's Court, an Intermediate People's Court or a recognised Primary People's Court.[118]
2. The judgment must have been delivered after the MJREO came into effect.[119]
3. The relevant choice of court agreement must be made on or after 1 August 2008 and before 29 January 2024.[120]
4. The judgment must be final and conclusive.[121] Section 6 of the MJREO lists the situations in which judgments are to be regarded as final and conclusive.
5. The judgment must be enforceable in Mainland China.[122]
6. The judgment must be for the payment of a liquidated amount, but not a sum payable as a tax, fine or penalty.[123] This means that the judgment

> should be clear as to a fixed, certain, quantified or at least readily quantifiable sum of money due to be paid by the judgment debtor, for which sum interest is payable from the date of registration, and against which assets of the judgment debtor may be enforced. The judgment debtor should not be in doubt or uncertain as to its liability under the judgment.[124]

[113] *Sea Powerful II Special Maritime Enterprises (ENE) v Bank of China Ltd* [2016] 1 HKLRD 1032 [19]; *Bank of China Ltd* (n 43) [30]–[34]; *Beijing Renji Real Estate Development Group Co Ltd* (CA) (n 15) [59].

[114] *Beijing Renji Real Estate Development Group Co Ltd* (CFI) (n 43) [40]; *Beijing Renji Real Estate Development Group Co Ltd* (CA) (n 15) [59].

[115] MJREO, s 4.

[116] *Industrial and Commercial Bank of China (Asia) Ltd v Wisdom Top International Ltd* [2020] 5 HKC 537, [2020] HKCFI 322 [23], [26], [50].

[117] *Export-Import Bank of China v Taifeng Textile Group Co Ltd* [2018] HKCFI 1840 [54(6)]; *Beijing Renji Real Estate Development Group Co Ltd* (CA) (n 15) [42]–[43].

[118] MJREO, Sch 1.

[119] ibid s 5(2)(a).

[120] ibid s 5(2)(b). The written exclusive jurisdiction agreement indicates the parties' prior agreement to submit to the jurisdiction rendering the judgment. Thus, the MJREO does not contain a requirement for international jurisdiction.

[121] ibid s 5(2)(c).

[122] ibid s 5(2)(d).

[123] ibid s 5(2)(e).

[124] *Foshan Nanhai Branch of Industrial and Commercial Bank of China Ltd v Foshan Ruifeng Petroleum and Chemical Fuel Co Ltd* [2019] 2 HKLRD 478, [2019] HKCFI 708 [38].

A double interest under the Civil Procedure Law in China was a penalty and therefore not registrable under the MJREO.[125]

Like other statutory regimes, the MJREO is to facilitate the recognition and enforcement of Mainland judgments by a simple and quick process of registration on the basis of a judgment already made by a competent and recognised court. Registration should be in terms of what is readily apparent on the face of the Mainland judgment, without the necessity of the Hong Kong court scrutinising or conducting the mini trial of the evidence or documents in the Mainland proceedings.[126] The effects of registration under the MJREO are specified in its sections 14 and 16. It will be given be the same force and effect as if it had been a judgment originally given in the Court of First Instance and entered on the day of registration. It will also be recognised as *res judicata* between the parties on the same cause of action.

When a court registers a Mainland judgment, it must specify a time period within which an application to set aside the registration can be made (although the period may be extended).[127] The grounds on which registration *must*[128] be set aside include the following:

1. The judgment does not meet the requirements in section 5 of the MJREO.[129]
2. The judgment has been registered in contravention of the MJREO.[130]
3. The choice of court agreement is invalid under the law of Mainland China.[131]
4. The judgment has been wholly satisfied.[132]
5. The courts in Hong Kong have exclusive jurisdiction over the case under Hong Kong law.[133]
6. The judgment debtor did not receive any or adequate notice of the Mainland proceedings.[134] This depends on what PRC law requires by way of proper or adequate notice.[135]
7. The judgment was obtained by fraud.[136]
8. A judgment on the same cause of action between the parties has been given by a court in Hong Kong or an arbitral award on the same cause of action between the parties has been made in a Hong Kong-seated arbitration.[137]
9. A judgment on the same cause of action between the parties to the judgment has been given by a foreign court or an arbitral award on the same cause of action between the parties has been made by an arbitration body seated outside Hong Kong and that judgment or award has been recognised or enforced by the Hong Kong court.[138]

[125] ibid [44]–[45], citing *Hung Fung Enterprises Holdings Ltd* (n 49).
[126] *Foshan Nanhai Branch of Industrial and Commercial Bank of China Ltd* (n 124) [39].
[127] ibid s 17.
[128] ibid s 18, which uses the word 'shall'. As seen from MJCCMREO, s 22, this is likely to be interpreted as 'must'.
[129] MJREO, s 18(1)(a).
[130] ibid s 18(1)(b).
[131] ibid s 18(1)(c).
[132] ibid s 18(1)(d).
[133] ibid s 18(1)(e).
[134] ibid s 18(1)(f).
[135] *China Citic Bank Corp Ltd (Quanzhou Branch) v Li Kwai Chun* [2019] HKCFI 2540 [41].
[136] MJREO, s 18(1)(g).
[137] ibid s 18(1)(h).
[138] ibid s 18(1)(i).

10. The enforcement of the judgment would be contrary to Hong Kong public policy.[139]
11. The judgment has been reversed or set aside pursuant to an appeal or retrial under PRC law.[140]

The burden of proof lies with the party seeking to set aside the registration on the standard of balance of probabilities.[141] Generally, when a registration has been set aside, there can be no further applications to register the same judgment.[142] When there is a pending appeal against the judgment or a retrial of the case, the court may set aside the registration (without prejudicing a further application to register the judgment) or adjourn the application until the appeal or retrial is disposed of.[143]

The recognition of Hong Kong judgments in Mainland China is a matter of PRC law. The MJREO provides a mechanism whereby Hong Kong judgments can be enforced in Mainland China. Only Hong Kong judgments that arise from choice of court agreements designating the Hong Kong court as the exclusive jurisdiction qualify under the MJREO. This choice of court agreements must be in writing, including in electronic format.[144] In these situations, the Hong Kong court has jurisdiction under section 21 of the MJREO to issue certified copies and certificates of Hong Kong judgments for the purposes of enforcing these judgments in Mainland China.

D. Mainland Judgments in Civil and Commercial Matters (Reciprocal Enforcement) Ordinance (Cap 645)

The MJCCMREO broadens the types of Mainland and Hong Kong judgments which can be recognised and enforced when compared with the MJREO. It applies to all Mainland courts. It abolishes the need for an exclusive jurisdiction clause, reflecting the approach in the 2019 Hague Judgments Convention. It instead covers judgments in all civil and commercial matters (including damages adjudged in criminal cases), excluding only judgments made in judicial reviews, bankruptcy and insolvency cases, and certain copyright and family disputes.[145] An innovation in the MJCCMREO is the abolition of the requirement that a judgment must be final prior to registration. The only requirements are that the judgment is given after the commencement date of the MJCCMREO (29 January 2024) and is effective and enforceable in the respective jurisdiction.[146]

The registration procedures and the requirements for the registration of a Mainland judgment are detailed in sections 10 and 11 of the MJCCMREO. Further guidance is provided under the Mainland Judgments in Civil and Commercial Matters (Reciprocal Enforcement) Rules (Cap 645A) and Practice Direction 38. Note that the Mainland judgment must require

139 ibid s 18(1)(j).
140 ibid s 18(1)(k).
141 *China Citic Bank Corp Ltd* (n 135) [38]–[40].
142 MJREO, s 20(1).
143 ibid ss 19 and 20(2).
144 ibid s 3.
145 For a list of excluded judgments, see MJCCMREO, s 5. A Mainland judgment is presumed (until the contrary is proved) to be in a civil or commercial matter that is effective in the Mainland if so certified by the original Mainland court: MJCCMREO, s 13(2).
146 An 'effective' judgment is defined as being enforceable and given by a specified court: ibid ss 8 (Mainland judgments) and 9 (Hong Kong judgments). There are specific provisions in s 8 regarding appeals and the trial supervision procedure in the Mainland.

the payment of a sum of money or the performance of some act, and there must have been a default of such payment or performance within two years before the application for registration.[147]

The effects of registration under the MJCCMREO are specified in its sections 26 and 28. A Mainland judgment will be recognised and enforced in Hong Kong as if it were a judgment of the Hong Kong court given on the day of registration. It will also be recognised as *res judicata* between the parties on the same cause of action.

A judgment debtor may apply to set aside the registration within the time specified in section 21 of the MJCCREO, which is typically 14 days (although that period may be extended). The grounds for setting aside registration are provided in section 22 of the MJCCMREO. Some of these grounds are similar to those in the MJREO. Situations where the court *must* set aside the registration include:

1. The judgment does not meet the requirements in the MJCCMREO.[148]
2. The jurisdictional requirements in respect of the original proceedings (that is, international jurisdiction) are not satisfied for the registered judgment.[149] A list of such jurisdictional requirements are at MJCCMREO, section 23.[150]
3. The judgment debtor was not summoned to appear in the Mainland proceedings or was otherwise not given a reasonable opportunity to present its case.[151]
4. The judgment was obtained by fraud.[152]
5. The mainland proceedings were accepted by a Mainland court after Hong Kong proceedings on the same cause of action between the same parties had started.[153]
6. There is a judgment or arbitral award on the same cause of action between the same parties by a court in Hong Kong or a Hong Kong-seated arbitration.[154]
7. There is a foreign judgment or arbitral award on the same cause of action between the same parties which has already been recognised or enforced in Hong Kong.[155]
8. The enforcement of the judgment would be manifestly incompatible with Hong Kong public policy.[156]
9. The judgment has been reversed or set aside pursuant to an appeal or retrial under PRC law.[157]

Section 22(2) of the MJCCMREO introduces a novel discretionary ground for setting aside not found in the MJREO. Under that provision, the court *may* set aside a registration 'if the applicant has proved … that the original proceedings for the judgment were contrary to a valid arbitration agreement or a valid jurisdiction agreement entered into by the same parties on the same cause of action'. But this ground is qualified by section 22(3), which

[147] ibid s 12.
[148] ibid s 22(1)(a).
[149] ibid s 22(1)(b).
[150] These grounds of international jurisdiction are similar to those under the common law: see s III.A above. Section 23 provides further details in relation to the Mainland context and specific proceedings.
[151] ibid s 22(1)(c).
[152] ibid s 22(1)(d).
[153] ibid ss 22(1)(e).
[154] ibid ss 22(1)(f) and 22(1)(h).
[155] ibid ss 22(1)(g) and 22(1)(i).
[156] ibid s 22(1)(j). The change in wording from 'contrary to' to 'manifestly incompatible with' does not alter the threshold in practice, following a similar reasoning in *Re PT Garuda Indonesia (Persero) Tbk* [2024] 3 SLR 254.
[157] ibid s 22(1)(k).

cautions that the court is not authorised to set aside a registration 'solely on the basis of a preliminary issue determined in the original proceedings for the judgment'.

In analogy with the MJREO, the burden of proof lies with the party seeking to set aside the registration on the standard of balance of probabilities.[158] Generally, when the registration has been set aside, there can be no further applications to register the same judgment.[159]

Sections 32–34 (Part 3) of the MJCCMREO deal with the requirements and procedures for recognition and enforcement of Hong Kong judgments in Mainland China, through a mechanism similar to the MJREO where the Hong Kong courts issue certified copies and certificates of Hong Kong judgments for the purposes of enforcing these judgments in Mainland China under PRC law.

V. Restrictions on Recognition and Enforcement

The FJRREO imposes restrictions on the recognition or enforcement of foreign judgments in Hong Kong. These restrictions originate from sections 32–34 of the Civil Jurisdiction and Judgments Act 1982 in the UK. The wording of FJRREO suggests that it would apply for any recognition and enforcement sought under common law or statute. However, the court thought it was reasonably arguable (without deciding) that, as far as Mainland judgments were concerned, the MJREO (and the MJCCMREO) should be the governing regime and FJRREO was not, or at least was no longer, applicable.[160]

Section 3 of the FJRREO stipulates that, save where the defendant submitted or agreed to submit to the jurisdiction of the foreign court, a foreign judgment obtained in breach of a valid choice of court agreement shall not be recognised or enforced in Hong Kong. By section 3(3), in deciding whether the choice of court agreement is valid (as opposed, for instance, to being void, inoperative, or unenforceable by reason of illegality), the Hong Kong court will not be bound by the decision of the foreign court on that question. In *Dickson Valora Group (Holdings) Co Ltd v Fan Ji Qian*, the Hong Kong court concluded that section 3(1)(a) of the FJRREO applied as long as there was an agreement under which a dispute was to be settled otherwise than in proceedings before the foreign court. It was not necessary for the plaintiff in the foreign proceedings to be a party to the choice of court agreement.[161]

Section 4 of the FJRREO lists situations in which a person is not to be treated as having submitted to the jurisdiction of the foreign court. Examples are where the person only appears to contest the foreign court's jurisdiction or asks the foreign court to stay its proceedings in favour of arbitration or litigation in the agreed forum.[162] Similarly, if a person only appears to obtain the release of property seized in the course of the foreign proceedings, one will not be held to have submitted to the foreign court.[163]

Section 5(1) of the FJRREO states:

> No proceedings may be brought by a person in Hong Kong on a cause of action in respect of which a judgment has been given in his favour in proceedings between the same parties, or their privies,

[158] *China Citic Bank Corp Ltd* (n 135) [38]–[40].
[159] ibid s 25.
[160] *Lu Yongliang v Bank of China Ltd, Dongguan Branch* [2021] 6 HKC 46, [2021] HKCA 1048 [44]–[45].
[161] *Dickson Valora Group (Holdings) Co Ltd v Fan Ji Qian* [2019] 2 HKLRD 173, [2019] HKCFI 482 [55].
[162] FJRREO, ss 4(a) and 4(b).
[163] ibid s 4(c).

in a court of an overseas country, unless that judgment is not enforceable or entitled to recognition in Hong Kong.

Section 5(1) displaces the common law rule that a foreign judgment does not extinguish the underlying cause of action on which the foreign judgment is given. Application of the common law rule would mean that fresh proceedings can be commenced in Hong Kong, despite the existence of a foreign judgment between the same parties on the same matter. As a result of section 5(1), fresh proceedings in Hong Kong cannot be brought between the same parties on the same matter unless the prior foreign judgment has been refused recognition and enforcement in Hong Kong.[164] This includes the situation where the foreign judgment was *in personam* while the fresh proceedings in Hong Kong involving the same parties and matter are brought *in rem*.[165]

In addition to the FJRREO, section 7 of the Protection of Trading Interests Ordinance (Cap 471) provides that no judgment may be registered under the FJREO or enforced under common law if it is a foreign judgment for multiple damages (by multiplying a sum assessed as compensation for the loss or damage sustained by a party).[166]

VI. Recognition and Enforcement in Family Law

A. Decrees of Marriage

The court has jurisdiction to grant a declaration that a foreign marriage is valid; this jurisdiction may be characterised as a jurisdiction for declaratory relief under Order 15, rule 16 of the RHC, as an inherent jurisdiction or as an ancillary jurisdiction to the court's statutory jurisdiction to hear divorce petitions.[167] It is suggested that foreign declarations as to status, for example, that the parties were validly married, will be recognised in Hong Kong if the Hong Kong court would (*mutatis mutandis*) have had jurisdiction to make the declaration.[168]

Hong Kong recognises 'marriages celebrated or contracted outside Hong Kong in accordance with the law in force at the time and in the place where the marriage was performed'[169] – in other words, in accordance with the *lex loci celebrationis* (the law at the place of celebration) in force at that time. For a marriage to be considered valid, it must satisfy the requirements of both essential validity and formal validity.[170] As will be seen below, the types of marriages that can be recognised in Hong Kong are more numerous than the types of marriages that can be celebrated or registered in Hong Kong.

[164] *Cova Enterprises Ltd* (n 84) [38]–[39].

[165] *The Alas* [2014] 4 HKLRD 160 [18]–[19].

[166] See, eg *Motorola Solutions Inc v Hytera Communications Corp Ltd* [2024] EWHC 2891 (Comm). In Hong Kong, this section was unsuccessfully invoked in *Re The Grande Holdings Ltd* [2013] 4 HKLRD 353. That argument failed because winding up proceedings is the exercise of a class right and does not constitute enforcement of a judgment or an arbitral award.

[167] Graeme Johnston and Paul Harris, *The Conflict of Laws in Hong Kong*, 3rd edn (Sweet & Maxwell, 2017) para 7.111.

[168] See, eg *C v C* [2019] UKPC 40, [2020] 1 WLR 1711.

[169] This formulation of 'marriage' can be seen in various statutes, including the Married Persons Status Ordinance (Cap 182), s 2(2)(a), the Intestates' Estates Ordinance (Cap 73), s 3(d), the Legitimacy Ordinance (Cap 184), s 2 and the Separation and Maintenance Orders Ordinance (Cap 16), s 2.

[170] *Suen Toi Lee v Yau Yee Ping* (2001) 4 HKCFAR 474. See ch 19, s I.

Even if the formalities or a formal ceremony of a marriage are not present, the Hong Kong court will, in principle, recognise a marriage contracted under foreign law which would have been valid if these had been satisfied; these are sometimes known as foreign 'common law marriages'. For example, in *Wong Zhong Lan Xiang v Wong Frank*, the Court of Appeal was prepared to recognise a 'common law marriage' allegedly contracted in New York in 1931 prior to the abolition of that form of marriage under New York law in 1933. A 'common law marriage' does not require any essential formal ceremony, and 'it is sufficient if the evidence establishes that legally competent parties *in praesenti* intended to become husband and wife and thereafter lived and cohabited as husband and wife'.[171] Thus, marriages celebrated by proxy (or other methods not requiring the physical presence of the parties) in a place where such proxy presence is sufficient and the marriage will have been considered valid will be recognised in Hong Kong.[172] Marriages validated retrospectively by the law of the place of celebration will also be recognised by the Hong Kong court as formally valid.[173] Section 20A(2) of the Matrimonial Causes Ordinance (Cap 179) (MCO) provides that

> in the case of a marriage which has taken place outside Hong Kong and purports to be a marriage under common law, section 20(1) [the grounds to render a marriage void] is without prejudice to any ground on which the marriages may be void by virtue of the rules governing the celebration of marriages outside Hong Kong under common law.

Polygamous marriages can no longer be celebrated in Hong Kong since 7 October 1971; any attempt to contract a second (or subsequent) marriage or concubinage in Hong Kong is void, irrespective of the parties' domicile.[174] A person domiciled in Hong Kong has no capacity to contract a polygamous marriage or a concubinage relationship anywhere in the world, in the eyes of the Hong Kong court.[175] However, if a person entered into a foreign marriage in polygamous form which is valid in that place, the Hong Kong court may treat the marriage as valid and monogamous if the person's spouse has no capacity under his or her personal law to take another spouse or concubine.[176] If both parties are not domiciled in Hong Kong, then it is possible for them to enter into a valid polygamous marriage (whether actually or potentially polygamous). Concubinage relationships contracted pursuant to a foreign law will be analysed in the same way as polygamous marriages.[177]

The effect of an allegedly polygamous marriage contracted purportedly pursuant to foreign law must depend on its characterisation under Hong Kong law. If Hong Kong law sees the marriage as a valid monogamous marriage (contrary to the allegation), then it will be treated in the same way as a normal marriage contracted in Hong Kong by parties of Hong Kong domicile. If Hong Kong law sees the marriage as a valid polygamous marriage, then the Hong Kong courts will still be able to recognise the marriage, as long as it satisfies the formal validity (under *lex loci celebrationis*) and essential validity (under both parties' antenuptial domicile) requirements above. This is in line with the policy to recognise foreign

[171] *Wong Zhong Lan Xiang v Wong Frank* [2003] 4 HKC 609.
[172] *Apt v Apt* [1948] P 83; *McCabe v McCabe* [1994] 1 FLR 410.
[173] *Starkowski v A-G* [1954] AC 155.
[174] Marriage Reform Ordinance (Cap 178) (MRO), s 4.
[175] *Suen Toi Lee* (n 170).
[176] *Hussain v Hussain* [1983] Fam 26.
[177] *Suen Toi Lee* (n 170) [79]: 'The law of Hong Kong recognises unions of concubinage validly entered into abroad just as it recognises marriages validly entered into abroad.'

valid marriages in general, subject to some strong reason or public policy to the contrary. The recognition can be used for several purposes, such as succession,[178] legitimacy[179] and the invalidity of a subsequent purported monogamous marriage. However, Hong Kong courts have no jurisdiction to grant a decree of divorce, nullity, separation or presumption of death over these foreign polygamous marriages.[180] If Hong Kong law does not even regard the marriage as valid (ie it fails to have formal validity or essential validity under the applicable laws), then naturally there can be no recognition.[181]

Same-sex marriages and civil partnerships cannot be celebrated or registered in Hong Kong,[182] and no decrees of divorce, nullity, separation or presumption of death can be granted over them.[183] However, these marriages (which are valid abroad) are likely to be recognised for the purposes of succession and legitimacy described above. This recognition is subject to the public policy exception, but it is suggested that there is no particular reason why such recognition should be denied. Moreover, there have been cases where other social, economic and other rights have been granted as ancillary to their status under the foreign marriage or civil partnership.[184] The Court of Final Appeal agreed that it would not be against public policy to allow same-sex couples to have the same benefits as heterosexual couples as it would not weaken the institution of marriage in Hong Kong.[185] The 'prevailing views of the community on marriage' is not relevant for such purposes.[186]

Religious marriages (those celebrated without a civil component) cannot be celebrated or registered in Hong Kong. Whether they can be recognised would depend on satisfying the dual domicile test.[187] The fact that foreign law allows an immediate divorce on the unilateral demand of one spouse does not seem to constitute a bar to the recognition of the validity of such marriages. However, a marriage found to be a 'sham' marriage or for a term less than life (ie merely of a temporary or casual character) will not be recognised.[188] Religious divorces cannot be recognised in Hong Kong as they fall outside the scope of jurisdiction under section 3 of the MCO.

[178] See the Intestates' Estates Ordinance (Cap 73), ss 2, 3 and 4; the Inheritance (Provision for Family and Dependants) Ordinance (Cap 481), s 2(1).

[179] The Legitimacy Ordinance (Cap 184) deploys the same notion.

[180] MCO, ss 2 and 9.

[181] In these cases, there may only be remedies under statutes which extends their protection to parties other than parties to a marriage.

[182] *MK v Government of HKSAR* [2019] 5 HKLRD 259, [2019] HKCFI 2518; *Sham Tsz Kit v Secretary for Justice* (2023) 26 HKCFAR 478, [2023] HKCFA 31. In *Sham Tsz Kit*, the New York same-sex marriage could not be recognised as Sham Tsz Kit lacked capacity under Hong Kong law, the law of his antenuptial domicile.

[183] MCO, ss 2 and 9.

[184] See, eg *W v Registrar of Marriages* (2013) 16 HKCFAR 112; *QT v Director of Immigration* (2018) 21 HKCFAR 324, [2018] HKCFA 28; *Leung Chun Kwong v Secretary for the Civil Service* (2019) 22 HKCFAR 127, [2019] HKCFA 19; *Infinger v Hong Kong Housing Authority* [2024] HKCFA 29; *Li Yik Ho v Secretary for Justice* [2024] HKCFA 30. These judgments confirmed rights of spouses in same-sex marriages in various aspects such as immigration, taxation and intestate succession.

[185] *Leung Chun Kwong* (n 184) [67].

[186] ibid [56].

[187] *Hussain* (n 176).

[188] *Khoo Hooi Leong v Khoo Cheong Yeok* [1930] AC 346; *Nachimson v Nachimson* [1930] P 217.

B. Decrees of Divorce, Nullity and Separation

The MCO has specific provisions that allow the court to recognise foreign divorces and legal separations.[189] These provisions implemented the 1970 HCCH Convention on the Recognition of Divorces and Legal Separations (the Hague Divorce Convention). Similar to foreign marriages, the general rule is that if the foreign divorce decree is obtained by proceedings in that country, where either spouse was either a habitually resident in or a national of that country, then it is generally recognised in Hong Kong.

The MCO statutory regime defines overseas divorces and legal separations as those which: (i) have been obtained by means of judicial or other proceedings in any place outside Hong Kong; and (ii) are effective under the law of that place.[190] The validity of an overseas divorce or legal separation is recognised in Hong Kong if, at the date of the institution of the proceedings (or cross-proceedings)[191] in the place in which it was obtained, either spouse was: (i) habitually resident (or domiciled) in that place; or (ii) a national of that place.[192] It is not clear whether the question of habitual residence is determined with reference to Hong Kong law or to the law of that place, although the fact that section 56(2) of the MCO refers to a special rule on domicile implies that habitual residence is a Hong Kong concept. It was suggested that satisfying either should suffice, for the policy reason of minimising the scope for technical attacks on foreign decrees.[193]

In determining whether to recognise a foreign divorce or legal separation, any express or implied finding of fact made in the foreign proceedings shall be conclusive evidence of the fact found (if both spouses appeared or took part in the proceedings), or shall be sufficient proof of that fact unless the contrary is shown (in any other case).[194] If the validity of a foreign legal separation is recognised, then the subsequently converted foreign divorce must also be recognised.[195] Where the validity of a divorce obtained in any place is entitled to recognition in Hong Kong, neither spouse shall be precluded from remarrying in Hong Kong on the ground that the validity of the divorce would not be recognised in any other place.[196]

The MCO statutory regime is the sole recognition regime in Hong Kong, but it is without prejudice to the recognition of the validity of divorces and legal separations obtained outside Hong Kong by virtue of any rule of law relating to divorces or legal separations obtained in the place of either spouse's domicile or obtained elsewhere and recognised as valid in that place, or by virtue of any other enactment.[197] Therefore, foreign divorces and legal separations may still be recognised even if they are not obtained by way of 'proceedings', or are obtained by way of 'proceedings' under a different jurisdictional basis, as long as

[189] MCO, Pt IX.
[190] ibid s 55(2).
[191] ibid s 57(1).
[192] ibid s 56. Note that the bases of indirect jurisdiction provided in this section are narrower than the bases of direct jurisdiction in s 3 of the MCO.
[193] Johnston and Harris (n 167) para 7.113.
[194] MCO, s 58.
[195] ibid s 57(2).
[196] ibid s 60.
[197] ibid s 59.

the domicile requirements are satisfied. These include a divorce or legal separation which is effective (when the spouses have a common domicile) by the law of that domicile, or (when the spouses have different domiciles) is effective in one spouse's domicile and recognised in the other's domicile, or in a place where neither spouse is domiciled but is recognised in each spouse's domicile.

The recognition of the validity of a foreign divorce or legal separation is subject to three exceptions, the first one being mandatory and the other two being discretionary.

First, recognition will be refused if it was granted or obtained at a time when, according to the law of Hong Kong (including its rules of private international law), there was no subsisting marriage between the parties.[198] Therefore, the validity of the dissolution of same-sex marriages and civil partnerships are currently not recognised in Hong Kong, as marriages entered into in Hong Kong on or after 7 October 1971 imply the voluntary union for life of one man with one woman to the exclusion of all others,[199] and Hong Kong does not recognise any marriages where 'the parties are not respectively male and female'.[200]

Second, recognition may be refused if the foreign divorce or legal separation is obtained by a spouse who, having regard to the nature of the proceedings and all the circumstances, failed to either: (i) take steps to give notice of the proceedings to the other spouse as should reasonably have been taken; or (ii) give the other spouse (for any reason other than lack of notice) such opportunity to take part in the proceedings as should reasonably have been given.[201]

Third, recognition may be refused if it would be manifestly contrary to public policy.[202] There is no specific definition of public policy, but recognition will likely be refused if fraud or substantial injustice has occurred.[203] In *ML v YJ*, the wife argued that the prohibition (under the then Matrimonial Proceedings and Property Ordinance (Cap 192) (MPPO))[204] to seek ancillary relief in respect of assets in Hong Kong after a Shenzhen divorce decree renders the recognition manifestly contrary to public policy. The Court of First Instance agreed, finding that the recognition would be fundamentally offensive to the Hong Kong courts' notions of justice, because recognising it would deprive the wife of applying for financial relief in Hong Kong, which was ancillary to the divorce suit.[205] A majority of the Court of Appeal allowed the appeal.[206] In the Court of Final Appeal, the majority held that the public policy exception is to be exercised 'sparingly', and did not apply in the present case, where the husband acted tactically (rather than fraudulently); however, the minority opined that this tactical manipulation and the harsh consequences to the wife would suffice to refuse recognition on public policy grounds.[207]

[198] ibid s 61(1).
[199] MRO, s 4. See also *W* (n 184) [63].
[200] MCO, s 20(1)(d).
[201] ibid s 61(2)(a).
[202] ibid s 61(2)(b).
[203] *Hebei Import & Export Corp v Polytek Engineering Ltd* (1999) 2 HKCFAR 111; *Chen Li Hung* (n 21). For a case of fraud, see *Kendall v Kendall* [1977] Fam 208.
[204] This problem is now addressed by the enactment of the Matrimonial Proceedings and Property (Amendment) Ordinance 2010, which came into operation on 1 March 2011, adding Part IIA to the MPPO. See ch 19, s II.C.
[205] *ML v YJ* [2008] 3 HKLRD 412 (CFI) (Lam J).
[206] *ML v YJ* [2010] 1 HKLRD 1 (CA) (Cheung JA and Sakhrani J, Le Pichon JA dissenting).
[207] *ML v YJ* (2010) 13 HKCFAR 794 (Ribeiro PJ, Litton and Sir Anthony Mason NPJJ, Chan and Bokhary PJJ dissenting).

Section 61A of the MCO provides that the MCO regime does not apply to divorces in Mainland China obtained by means of judicial or other proceedings on or after 15 February 2022. Rather, the MJMFCO (discussed in section VI.E below) applies. Divorce decrees obtained in the Mainland China before that date may be recognised under the MCO regime.

The recognition of foreign decrees of nullity and presumption of death are not regulated by any statute in Hong Kong.[208] There is no reported case law in Hong Kong in relation to the recognition of these foreign decrees. However, it might be expected that the Hong Kong courts are not bound to accept a foreign decree of presumption of death as conclusive, as the manner in which death may be proved is a question of procedure, governed by the *lex fori*.

C. Orders and Judgments on Matters Relating to the Status of the Child

Recognition of children legitimated under foreign law is possible under section 8 of the Legitimacy Ordinance (Cap 184). That section states:

> Where the parents of an illegitimate person marry or have married one another, whether before or after the commencement of this Ordinance, and the father of the illegitimate person was or is, at the time of the marriage, domiciled in or had a substantial connexion with a place outside Hong Kong, by the law of which the illegitimate person became legitimated by virtue of such subsequent marriage, that person, if living, shall in Hong Kong be recognised as having been so legitimated from the commencement of this Ordinance or from the date of the marriage, whichever last happens, notwithstanding that his father was not at the time of the birth of such person domiciled in or did not have a substantial connexion with a place in which legitimation by subsequent marriage was permitted by law.

Moreover, the Hong Kong court will recognise a status of legitimacy or legitimation conferred by foreign law after the birth of a child if the foreign law in question is the law of the domicile of the child at any time after birth.

In relation to general foreign adoptions (those which fall outside the Hague Adoption Convention), section 17 of the Adoption Ordinance (Cap 290) (AO) provides for a set of rather complicated rules:

> (1) Where a person has been adopted, whether before or after the coming into operation of this section, in any place outside Hong Kong according to the law of that place, and the adoption is one to which this section applies, then for the purposes of this Ordinance and all other Hong Kong enactments, the adoption shall have the same effect as an adoption order validly made in accordance with the provisions of this Ordinance, and shall have no other effect.
>
> (2) Subsection (1) shall apply to an adoption in any place outside Hong Kong (other than a Convention adoption), if –

[208] In England, foreign decrees of nullity are recognised under Part II of the Family Law Act 1986. In Scotland, foreign decrees of presumption of death are sufficient evidence of the facts so declared if the person was domiciled or habitually resident in the foreign country on the date on which he was last known to be alive, under s 10 of the Presumption of Death (Scotland) Act 1977.

(a) the adoption is legally valid according to the law of that place; and
(b) in consequence of the adoption, the adoptive parents or any adoptive parent had, or, if the adopted person had been a young child, would have had, immediately following the adoption, according to the law of that place, a right superior to that of any birth parent of the adopted person in respect of the custody of the person; and
(c) either –
   (i) the adoption order was made by an order of any Court whatsoever of a Commonwealth country or of the United States of America or of any State or territory of the United States of America; or
   (ii) in consequence of the adoption, the adoptive parents or any adoptive parent had immediately following the adoption, according to the law of that place, a right superior to or equal with that of any birth parent in respect of any property of the adopted person which was capable of passing to the parents or any parent of the person in the event of the person dying intestate without other next of kin and domiciled in the place where the adoption was made and a national of the State which had jurisdiction in respect of that place,

but not otherwise.

(3) Nothing in this section shall restrict or alter the effect of any other adoption made in any place outside Hong Kong.

For this provision, it should be noted that there is no requirement of indirect jurisdiction for recognition of adoption under foreign law; in other words, the Hong Kong court does not examine whether there are any factors connected with the exercise of the foreign jurisdiction. It is also not clear what section 17(3) leads to; there is a dearth of case law in Hong Kong as to conflicting adoptions under different laws. However, it is suggested that the provision indicates a generous approach as to the recognition of foreign adoptions, subject only to public policy.

In relation to Hague Adoption Convention adoptions, a Convention adoption certificate issued by the competent authority in the place where the adoption was made is for all purposes prima facie evidence of the facts stated on it.[209] Subject to certain provisos, a Convention adoption has the same effect as any other valid adoption order,[210] and must have no other effect.[211]

It is possible for a person to apply to the court for a declaration that a Convention adoption shall not be recognised. The grounds for such an application are either that the Convention adoption should not be recognised on public policy grounds[212] or that the Convention adoption was not a full adoption, the relevant consents have not been given and the application would be more favourable to the adopted person.[213]

The 1996 HCCH Convention on Jurisdiction, Applicable Law, Recognition, Enforcement and Co-operation in Respect of Parental Responsibility and Measures for the Protection of Children (the Hague Child Protection Convention) does not have effect in Hong Kong.

[209] AO, s 20F.
[210] ibid s 20G(2).
[211] ibid s 20F(2).
[212] ibid s 20H. See also eg *Re Valentine's Settlement* [1965] Ch 831; *Bouton v Labiche* (1994) 33 NSWLR 225.
[213] ibid s 20G.

D. Orders and Judgments Relating to Maintenance and Ancillary Rights

It is trite that the recognition of a foreign decree of divorce, legal separation or nullity does not mean that the consequent foreign orders and judgments of ancillary relief will be similarly or automatically recognised. For instance, any foreign orders with a proprietary effect are likely to be subject to the *lex situs* rule of recognition, where the *situs* of the affected property should be within the territorial jurisdiction of the foreign court at the relevant time.

While the 2007 HCCH Convention on the International Recovery of Child Support and Other Forms of Family Maintenance (the Hague Child Support Convention) does not have effect in Hong Kong, there are various ways in which foreign orders and judgments relating to maintenance and ancillary rights may be enforced.

Foreign judgments providing for a lump sum payment and/or other final orders can be enforced under common law or (if applicable) under the FJREO. Such recognition is subject to the same requirements and exceptions as any other monetary judgments.[214]

Foreign orders for maintenance may be enforced if they have fallen into arrears, following the usual enforcement procedures.[215] Moreover, Hong Kong has reciprocal arrangements, under the Maintenance Orders (Reciprocal Enforcement) Ordinance (Cap 188) (MOREO), for facilitating the recovery of maintenance by enforcing non-Hong Kong maintenance orders between reciprocating countries.[216] This regime is based on the 1973 HCCH Convention on the Recognition and Enforcement of Decisions Relating to Maintenance Obligations (the Hague Maintenance Convention), to which the UK (but not the PRC) is a party, and it does not apply to China, except Macao. The machineries of judicial communication, evidential cooperation and enforcement under the MOREO are relatively comprehensive. However, the number of reciprocating countries for maintenance orders are relatively limited, which diminishes the practical importance of the MOREO.[217]

Mainland maintenance-related orders are enforced under the MJMFCO, discussed in section VI.E below.

E. Mainland Judgments in Matrimonial and Family Cases (Reciprocal Recognition and Enforcement) Ordinance (Cap 639)

With the increasing mobility of persons between Mainland China and Hong Kong since the handover, the recognition and harmonisation of matrimonial and family matters

[214] See ss III and IV.A above.

[215] *Beatty v Beatty* [1924] 1 KB 807.

[216] For the definition of 'maintenance order' for these purposes, see MOREO, s 2(1).

[217] See the Maintenance Orders (Reciprocal Enforcement) (Designation of Reciprocating Countries) Order (Cap 188B). The reciprocating jurisdictions for all maintenance orders are: (1) the UK; (2) Bermuda; (3) the Canadian Provinces of Manitoba, Saskatchewan and Ontario; and (4) the Isle of Man. The reciprocating jurisdictions for maintenance orders other than affiliation orders (orders adjudging, finding or declaring a person to be the father of a child, whether or not it also provides for the maintenance of the child) are: (1) Commonwealth of Australia and its territories; (2) the Canadian Province of British Columbia; (3) Brunei; (4) Malaysia; (5) New Zealand; (6) Singapore; (7) the Solomon Islands; (8) South Africa; and (9) Sri Lanka.

between the borders have become an important issue in Hong Kong private international law. The Court of Appeal case of *Lai v Ling* highlighted the lack of mutual arrangement between the Mainland and Hong Kong, and in the context of that case, in relation to a child wrongfully removed by a parent to the Mainland.[218] The court observed with dissatisfaction the then lack of means of directly enforcing Hong Kong custody orders in Mainland China.[219] Reciprocal arrangements, even when subsequently made into law, did not have retrospective effect and could not benefit the petitioner in that case.[220] Subsequently, an Arrangement on Reciprocal Recognition and Enforcement of Civil Judgments in Matrimonial and Family Cases by the Courts of the Mainland and of the Hong Kong Special Administrative Region was made between the Supreme People's Court of the People's Republic of China and the Government of the Hong Kong Special Administrative Region and signed on 20 June 2017. The details of the Arrangement are discussed in chapter twenty-five, section I.F. Reflecting the terms of the Arrangement, the MJMFCO commenced operation on 15 February 2022.

The MJMFCO provides for the reciprocal recognition and enforcement of specified orders and judgments between Hong Kong and the Mainland. The MJMFCO applies to:

1. 'Specified Orders in Mainland Judgments' provided in Schedule 2. These include a variety of care-related orders, status-related orders and maintenance-related orders.
2. Hong Kong judgments resulting from 'Matrimonial or Family Cases in Hong Kong' specified in Schedule 3.

These orders and other judgments given in respect of matrimonial or family cases are excluded from the MJCCMREO.[221]

The requirements for registration are provided in section 8 of the MJMFCO. Guidance for making applications under the MJMFCO is provided in Practice Direction SL10.5. Once these requirements are satisfied, a registration order is made to register the specified order. When registered, a care-related order or a maintenance-related order may be enforced in Hong Kong as if it were an order made by the registering court (assumed to have the requisite jurisdiction) on the day of registration of the order.[222] A status-related order is recognised as valid after the expiry of the period for an application to set aside the registration order, or (if there is an application to set aside) after the application has been finally disposed of.[223]

If a specified order in a Mainland judgment is registered in accordance with a registration order, a party to the judgment (other than the party who applied for the registration) may, within the period specified under section 14 of the MJMFCO, apply to the registering court to set aside the registration of the specified order. Section 16 of the MJMFCO sets out the grounds on which registration *must* be set aside; in other words, the court has no discretion. These grounds are in close correspondence with section 22 of the MJCCMREO

[218] *Lai v Ling* [2017] 5 HKLRD 629.
[219] ibid [67]–[68] and [88]–[91].
[220] ibid [89].
[221] See MJMFCO, ss 5(1)(a) and 6.
[222] ibid s 19.
[223] ibid s 24.

(see section IV.D above) and are not repeated here.[224] An addition in the family context is section 16(2) of the MJMFCO, which provides that, when considering whether the recognition or enforcement of the order is manifestly contrary to the public policy of Hong Kong, the registering court must take into account the best interests of the person if a specified order involves a person under 18 years old.

[224] The list in the MJMFCO does not provide for Hong Kong or foreign arbitral awards with *res judicata* effect.

PART V

Arbitration

24

International Commercial Arbitration in Hong Kong

Hong Kong is a vibrant international arbitration hub, not just for the Asia Pacific, but globally. This chapter focuses on private international law issues that arise in international arbitrations. The issues include the effectiveness of arbitration agreements, an arbitral tribunal's jurisdiction, interim measures, and the recognition and enforcement of arbitral awards. Readers are invited to consult other texts for arbitration law and practice in Hong Kong.[1]

Arbitration in Hong Kong is regulated by the Arbitration Ordinance (Cap 609) (AO). The AO reflects, with some modifications, the United Nations Commission on International Trade Law (UNCITRAL) Model Law on International Commercial Arbitration (1985), with amendments as adopted in 2006. The AO came into effect on 1 June 2011, which repealed the old Arbitration Ordinance (Cap 341). All arbitrations in Hong Kong commenced on or after 1 June 2011 are subject to the new regime.[2]

The AO establishes a unitary arbitration law, so that international and domestic arbitration are subject to the same regime. However, for domestic arbitration, parties may opt in to certain provisions in sections 99–102 and Schedule 2 of the AO.[3] As a book on private international law, the domestic arbitration regime will not be discussed here.

The AO's object is to 'facilitate the fair and speedy resolution of disputes by arbitration without unnecessary expense'.[4] In doing so, the AO is based on the principle that, as much as possible, deference should be given to party autonomy (that is, the parties' agreement on how their dispute should be resolved).[5] Thus, court intervention in the arbitration of a dispute should be kept to a minimum, and then only to the extent provided in the AO.[6]

[1] See, eg Geoffrey Ma and Denis Brock (gen eds), *Arbitration in Hong Kong: A Practical Guide*, 5th edn (Sweet & Maxwell, 2021); Samuel Wong, CK Kwong and Wilson Lui, *Hong Kong Arbitration Judgments and Commentaries: Applications of the UNCITRAL Model Law and the Provisions of the Hong Kong Arbitration Ordinance (Cap 609)* (Hong Kong Institute of Arbitrators, 2023); Samuel Wong and Wilson Lui, *Hong Kong Arbitration Ordinance (Cap 609): A Guide and Commentary*, 2nd edn (Authors, 2024).

[2] AO, s 5(1). The AO also has limited application for arbitrations outside Hong Kong: AO, s 5(2). Recent statutory reforms in the Hong Kong arbitration context include third party funding (AO, Pt 10A) and outcome-related fee structure agreements for arbitration (AO, Pt 10B). Both Parts are also applicable to non-Hong Kong arbitrations: AO, ss 98N and 98ZI.

[3] Under this Schedule 2 regime, there is a wider scope of involvement by the courts. Schedule 2, ss 1, 2 and 3 deal with issues of sole arbitrator, consolidation of arbitrations and preliminary question of law respectively. Sections 4 and 7 deal with grounds of serious irregularity. Sections 5 and 6 deal with appealing and appealing for leave, respectively, against an arbitral award on a question of law.

[4] AO, s 3(1).

[5] ibid s 3(2)(a).

[6] ibid s 3(2)(b).

I. Arbitrability

Arbitrability refers to whether the subject matter can suitably be determined within a private consensual process. Matters with a public interest element (for example, family, taxation, immigration and anti-competition matters) may therefore not be arbitrable.

Common law authorities suggested that whether a subject matter is capable of settlement by arbitration is determined by both the law of the arbitration agreement and the law of the seat.[7] There is a presumption that a dispute which falls within an arbitration clause is arbitrable, unless it is shown that the legislature intended to preclude resort to arbitration for the resolution of the dispute in question or that there is a conflict between arbitration and the public policy considerations arising out of the dispute.[8] That the arbitral tribunal lacks power to grant certain relief which is reserved to the court is insufficient to make a dispute non-arbitrable.[9]

The AO has explicitly dealt with the arbitrability of intellectual property disputes in Part 11A (sections 103A–103J), which came into effect on 1 January 2018.[10] Prior to the introduction of Part 11A, it was unclear whether disputes involving intellectual property rights (IPRs) were arbitrable under Hong Kong law. Arbitration of IPRs raises public policy issue. An IPR is granted by the state and can be enforced against the world, not just a person who is party to an arbitration agreement relating to that IPR. There is therefore a public interest in a decision as to whether an IPR is valid or has been infringed. Such questions should arguably be determined in a public hearing by the court. A declaration that an IPR is invalid could, for instance, potentially affect third parties. Many countries therefore limit the arbitrability of IP disputes.[11]

In contrast, Part 11A makes clear that in Hong Kong disputes involving IPRs can be resolved through arbitration, and it is not contrary to Hong Kong public policy to enforce an arbitral award involving IPRs. By way of example, section 103B specifies ten types of IPRs and adds a catch-all provision[12] for good measure. This ensures that no IPR is excluded from the AO. It includes IPRs which are protected by registration in or outside Hong Kong.[13] Section 103C defines a dispute over an IPR as including a dispute over the enforceability, infringement, subsistence, validity, ownership, scope, duration or any other aspect of an IPR, a dispute over a transaction in respect of an IPR and a dispute over any compensation payable for an IPR.

Section 103D(1) sets out the key principle that an IPR dispute is capable of settlement by arbitration as between the parties to a dispute. However, a finding by an arbitral tribunal that a Hong Kong IPR is invalid will not by itself revoke the right. This is in line with AO, sections 73(1) and 103H, which provide that a judgment on an award is only final and

[7] *Anupam Mittal v Westbridge Ventures II Investment Holdings* [2023] 1 SLR 349. Note, however, the basis of that decision was s 11 of the International Arbitration Act 1994 (2020 Rev Ed) (Singapore), providing for arbitrability unless 'contrary to public policy' (whether local or foreign public policy), which has no equivalent provision in Hong Kong.

[8] *Tomolugen Holdings Ltd v Silica Investors Ltd* [2016] 1 SLR 373 [76].

[9] *Falcon Insurance Co (Hong Kong) Ltd v Bing Lee Crane-Lorry Transportation Co Ltd* [2023] 2 HKLRD 1190, [2023] HKCFI 1129.

[10] AO, s 103J came into effect on 19 December 2019, the same date when a new s 129(1) of the Patents Ordinance (Cap 514) came into effect.

[11] Simon Klopschinski and Mary-Rose McGuire (eds), *Research Handbook on Intellectual Property Rights and Arbitration* (Edward Elgar, 2024).

[12] AO, s 103B(1)(k).

[13] ibid s 103B(2).

binding on the parties to the arbitration. The award therefore does not affect registrations in the Registrar of Patents, Trade Marks or Designs. Only the Court of First Instance or the relevant Registrar has the power to revoke the registration of a patent, a trademark or registered design.[14] Similarly, a third party licensee is not bound by an award which is judged to be enforceable in Hong Kong. That result is also obtained by the application of section 103E(2), subject to contrary agreement or the operation of law.

Section 103D(3) adds that the foregoing principle applies even though the IP dispute is only incidental to the main issue in the arbitration.

Section 103D(4) provides that an IP dispute may be resolved by arbitration if a specified entity in Hong Kong or elsewhere is given jurisdiction to deal with the dispute. This clarifies that an arbitral tribunal may decide an IP-related matter even if a court also has jurisdiction over the dispute. Section 103I provides that section 101(2) of the Patents Ordinance (Cap 514) (which provides that the validity of a patent may only be put in issue in specified proceedings) does not prevent the validity of the patent being raised in arbitral proceedings. Section 103J concerns short-term patents and waives the requirements for a patentee to request a substantive examination prior to enforcing a short-term patent.

II. Arbitration Agreements

Arbitration is a consensual process. The arbitral tribunal's power derives from the parties' agreement to submit their dispute to arbitration. The tribunal's authority or jurisdiction to conduct the arbitration rests entirely on the parties' consent expressed in the arbitration agreement. Subject to public policy considerations, the parties are free to agree the governing law, the seat of the arbitration and the procedures thereof.[15] The court essentially gives effect to the parties' agreement.

The AO defines an 'arbitration agreement' in section 19 by reference to Article 7 (Option I) of the Model Law. It is 'an agreement by the parties to submit to arbitration all or certain disputes which have arisen or which may arise between them in respect of a defined legal relationship, whether contractual or not'. The agreement must be in writing. But the requirement of writing may be met by:

(i) an electronic communication if the relevant information in that communication is accessible;
(ii) an exchange of pleadings whereby the existence of the arbitration agreement is admitted; or
(iii) a subsidiary document containing an arbitration clause which is incorporated into a main contract.

Under the common law, the construction of arbitration agreements involves the presumption in favour of arbitrability and the 'one-stop' adjudication approach.[16] In *Fiona Trust & Holding Corp v Privalov*, Lord Hoffmann referred to the construction of an arbitration clause as starting from 'the assumption that the parties, as rational businessmen, are likely

[14] Patents Ordinance (Cap 514), s 91; Trade Marks Ordinance (Cap 559), ss 52 and 53; Registered Designs Ordinance (Cap 522), ss 46–48.
[15] See, eg *Z v A* [2015] 2 HKC 272 [30].
[16] *Houtai Investment Holdings Ltd v Leung Yat Tung* [2021] HKCFI 1504.

to have intended any dispute arising out of the relationship in which they have entered or purported to enter to be decided by the same tribunal'.[17] An arbitration clause should be construed as being in accordance with the presumption that the parties intended any dispute arising out of the relationship into which they had entered or purported to enter to be decided by the same tribunal, unless the language made it clear that certain questions were intended to be excluded from the arbitrator's jurisdiction. Hong Kong courts have generally interpreted arbitration agreements generously.[18]

Section 20 of the AO incorporates Article 8 of the Model Law, which provides for the court's jurisdiction to grant a stay in favour of arbitration.[19] Once there is a valid written agreement to arbitrate, the Hong Kong courts must grant a stay in favour of arbitration.[20] The onus is on the defendant to prove that there is a prima facie case, predicated on cogent (not dubious or fanciful) evidence that an arbitration clause or agreement existed, that the parties are bound by the arbitration agreement[21] and that the matter falls within the scope of the arbitration agreement.[22] If these are shown, the party seeking to resist going to arbitration must then prove that the arbitration agreement is 'null and void, inoperative or incapable of being performed'. The standard of proof in this respect is said to be 'high', denoting 'impossibility, or practical impossibility, or certainly not mere inconvenience or difficulty'.[23]

In determining an application for stay under section 20 of the AO, the Hong Kong court follows the approach in *Tommy CP Sze & Co v Li & Fung (Trading) Ltd*.[24] Four questions are asked as a 'logical and basic approach':

1. Is the relevant clause an agreement to arbitrate the parties' disputed?
2. Is the arbitration agreement null and void, inoperative or incapable of being performed?
3. Is there a genuine dispute or difference between the parties?
4. Is the dispute or difference within the terms or scope of the arbitration agreement?

For the relationships and interactions between arbitration agreements and insolvency and bankruptcy petitions, see chapter 20, section IV.

III. Choice of Law in Arbitration Agreements

The governing law of an arbitration agreement is not an easy question.[25] There is no authoritative statement in Hong Kong on the correct approach to determining such a law.

[17] *Fiona Trust & Holding Corp v Privalov* [2007] UKHL 40, [2007] 4 All ER 951 [13].

[18] See, eg *Houtai Investment Holdings Ltd* (n 16); *Kinli Civil Engineering Ltd v Geotech Engineering Ltd* [2021] 6 HKC 524, [2021] HKCFI 2503.

[19] *Chok Yick Interior Design & Engineering Co Ltd v Fortune World Enterprises Ltd* [2010] 2 HKC 360. In that case, it is also recognised that the court has inherent jurisdiction to order a stay of proceedings in favour of arbitration.

[20] *Rondabosh International Ltd v China Ping An Insurance (Hong Kong) Co Ltd* (unreported, HCA 581/2009, 29 December 2009) [5].

[21] *Pacific Crown Engineering Ltd v Hyundai Engineering & Construction Co Ltd* [2003] 3 HKLRD 440 [16].

[22] See, eg ibid; *PCCW Global Ltd v Interactive Communications Service Ltd* [2007] 1 HKLRD 309.

[23] *Klöckner Pentaplast Gmbh & Co KG v Advance Technology (HK) Co Ltd* [2011] 4 HKLRD 262.

[24] *Tommy CP Sze & Co v Li & Fung (Trading) Ltd* [2003] 1 HKC 418. For the interactions of a stay application with an application to set aside a default judgment, see *Tongcheng Travel Holdings Ltd v OOO Securities (HK) Group Ltd* [2024] HKCFI 2710.

[25] *BNA v BNB* [2020] 1 SLR 456; *Enka Insaat ve Sanayi AS v OOO Insurance Co Chubb* [2020] UKSC 38, [2020] 1 WLR 4117; *Kabab-Ji SAL v Kout Food Group* [2021] UKSC 48, [2022] 2 All ER 911; *UniCredit Bank GmbH v RusChemAlliance LLC* [2024] UKSC 30.

In *China Railway (Hong Kong) Holdings Ltd v Chung Kin Holdings Co Ltd*,[26] the UK Supreme Court's approach in *Enka* was endorsed, and the express choice of Hong Kong law in the main debt agreement is held to be equally applicable to the dispute resolution clause. That would mean the following approach:

1. If an arbitration agreement has an express choice of governing law, the court will give effect to that choice (regardless of whether the agreement would be invalid under that law). Otherwise, if there is an express or implied choice of law for the main contract, then the arbitration agreement will normally be governed by that law.
2. If there is no express choice of law for the arbitration agreement but the main contract has an express choice of governing law, the latter choice should usually be construed as applying to the entire contract, including the arbitration agreement, in the absence of clear indications to the contrary.
3. If there is no express choice in either the main contract or the arbitration agreement, then the court should look at all the circumstances of the case and determine whether there is an implied choice of governing law for the main contract. If there is such an implied choice, then it is a strong indication that the parties also intended to apply that implied choice to the arbitration agreement.
4. If there is no express or implied choice for the arbitration agreement or the main contract, the law of the seat will apply to the arbitration agreement as the law with the closest connection with the agreement.

The UK Law Commission has, however, cast doubt on the correctness of the approach in *Enka*. It accepts that the applicable law should be the law that the parties expressly agree for the arbitration agreement, if there is such an agreement. If, however, there is no such agreement, the Law Commission has proposed that the law of the seat should govern. This would be more consistent with Article V(1)(a) of the New York Convention, which suggests that, when assessing the validity of an arbitration clause in the context of recognition and enforcement, one should first consider 'the law to which the parties have subjected it'; if the parties have not expressed a choice, then one should look at 'the law of the country where the award was made', that is, the law of the seat.[27] It is unclear whether the Hong Kong court will adopt the Law Commission's analysis. However, the Law Commission's analysis is consistent with the practice in other leading arbitral jurisdictions, such as France and Germany.[28]

There have been attempts to invalidate an arbitration agreement based on the alleged law governing the same. In *Klöckner Pentaplast Gmbh & Co KG v Advance Technology (HK) Co Ltd*,[29] the main contract was governed by German law, whereas the dispute was to be seated in Shanghai. It was noted in obiter that the arbitration clause would have been invalid under PRC law (the law of the seat) as it did not identify an arbitration institution in accordance with PRC law. However, the Court of First Instance held that there was an

[26] *China Railway (Hong Kong) Holdings Ltd v Chung Kin Holdings Co Ltd* [2023] HKCFI 132.

[27] This default position of the New York Convention has been implemented in Hong Kong by AO, s 89(2). It is extended to Mainland awards, Macao awards, and other awards generally: AO, ss 86(1), 95(2) and 98D(2).

[28] Bundesgerichtshof (German Federal Court of Justice), I ZR 245/19 (26 November 2020) [48]–[56]; Cour de cassation (French Court of Cassation), decision no 20-20.260 (28 September 2022). The UK Supreme Court found it inappropriate to revisit the issue in light of the potential legislative change: *UniCredit Bank GmbH* (n 25) [28]–[29].

[29] *Klöckner Pentaplast Gmbh & Co KG* (n 23).

implied choice of German law as the *lex arbitri*, and upheld the validity of the arbitration clause based on German law. The court recognised that there would be practical difficulties when the *lex arbitri* differs from the law of the seat. However, the court held that there is no rule that the *lex arbitri* and the law of the seat of arbitration must always coincide, especially when the latter will invalidate the arbitration agreement. The parties must be presumed, in the absence of contrary indication, to have intended that the arbitration agreement was to be governed by a law that validated (rather than invalidated) it. In *Grand Ocean & Williams Co Ltd v 江苏华西村海洋工程服务有限公司*,[30] the Court of First Instance referred to the obiter in *Klöckner* and held that an arbitration clause which referred to a non-existent arbitral tribunal in Mainland China was void and incapable of being performed under PRC law.

IV. Jurisdiction and Choice of Law of the Arbitral Tribunal

An arbitral tribunal may rule on its own jurisdiction, including any objections as to the existence or validity of the arbitration agreement. This concept is known as competence-competence (*Kompetenz-Kompetenz*). This concept has been given effect by section 34 of the AO, incorporating Article 16 of the Model Law. That section further provides for severability of the arbitration agreement: an arbitration clause which forms part of a contract shall be treated as an agreement independent of the other terms of the contract. An arbitration clause is not rendered invalid despite objections to the existence or validity of the contract.

When a court is asked to review an arbitral tribunal's ruling on jurisdiction, the court conducts an independent de novo review. This means that

> the court must independently determine for itself whether or not the parties had consented to the submission of the dispute to the tribunal, and should not be bound or restricted by the tribunal's preliminary decision on its own jurisdiction. The court should not be in a worse position than the arbitrator in its determination of the challenge. Natural justice also requires such independent review, as otherwise the tribunal would be the final judge of its own powers and cause.[31]

But in reviewing the tribunal's decision, the court is confined to the question of jurisdiction only. It should not review the merits of the parties' dispute.[32]

The common objections to the jurisdiction of arbitral tribunal include:

1. The arbitration agreement is invalid, or a party lacks legal authority or capacity to enter into the arbitration agreement.
2. The subject matter of the dispute is not arbitrable.
3. The dispute is outside the scope of the arbitration.
4. A condition precedent to arbitration has not been fulfilled.

[30] *Grand Ocean & Williams Co Ltd v 江苏华西村海洋工程服务有限公司* [2023] 2 HKC 124, [2023] HKCFI 86.
[31] *S Co v B Co* [2014] 6 HKC 421 [35]. See also *R v A* [2023] 6 HKC 189, [2023] HKCFI 2034 [50].
[32] *S Co* (n 31) [38].

It should be noted, however, that the Hong Kong Court of Final Appeal in *C v D* has held that objection 4 will typically go to admissibility, rather than jurisdiction.[33] Thus, an arbitral tribunal's determination as to whether the parties had first attempted to resolve their dispute by negotiation was not one that could subsequently be challenged in court.

The law determining the procedures of the arbitration are based on the place of arbitration, except if parties (unusually) agree otherwise. The place is determined either by express choice of the parties, or, failing such agreement, 'by the arbitral tribunal having regard to the circumstances of the case, including the convenience of the parties'.[34]

The substantive law applicable to the dispute is the law chosen by the parties, or, failing such agreement, by the arbitral tribunal adopting the conflict of laws rules which the tribunal considers applicable.[35]

V. Interim Measures

Under section 35 of the AO, an arbitral tribunal may grant interim measures at the request of a party.[36] An application may be made to a court for leave to enforce an interim measure granted by a tribunal as an order of the court.[37]

Alternatively, since the court enjoys concurrent jurisdiction to grant interim measures on its own under section 45 of the AO, an application may be made directly to the court for an indirect measure. Under section 45(2) of the AO, the court can itself grant interim measures in aid of contemplated or ongoing arbitration proceedings in or outside Hong Kong. It is only necessary to show that the foreign arbitral proceedings are capable of giving rise to an award which may be enforced in Hong Kong under any ordinance or at common law, and that the interim measure is one that the court can grant.[38] However, where an arbitral tribunal has been constituted or the parties have agreed to arbitral rules providing for resort to an emergency arbitrator where a tribunal has not yet been constituted, the court may refuse to grant an interim measure.[39] The court may instead order the applicant to apply to the tribunal or the emergency arbitrator for the interim measure.

A tribunal should be satisfied that the balance of convenience points to the grant of an interim measure. In that connection, it will typically consider the following:[40]

(i) whether the applicant has a good arguable case on the merits; and

[33] *C v D* (2023) 26 HKCFAR 216, [2023] HKCFA 16. In obiter, the court differed (with Gummow NPJ dissenting) as to whether the conceptual distinction between a challenge to an arbitral tribunal's 'jurisdiction' and a challenge to the 'admissibility' of a particular claim should be adopted to resolve the case. See also *T v B* [2022] 1 HKLRD 279, [2021] HKCFI 3645.

[34] AO, s 48, incorporating Art 20 of the Model Law.

[35] AO, s 64, incorporating Art 28 of the Model Law. A tribunal may only decide *ex aequo et bono* or as *amiable compositeur* (applying notions of fairness and equity rather than law) with parties' express authorisation.

[36] AO, s 35, incorporating Art 17 of the Model Law.

[37] AO, s 61. See also *G v N* [2024] HKCFI 721.

[38] AO, s 45(5); *Top Gains Minerals Macao Commercial Offshore Ltd v TL Resources Pte Ltd* [2016] 3 HKC 44; *Compania Sud Americana de Vapores SA v Hin-Pro International Logistics Ltd* (2016) 19 HKCFAR 586.

[39] ibid s 45(4). AO, s 45(4); *Hsin Chong Construction (Asia) Ltd v Henble Ltd* [2005] 3 HKC 27. For the enforcement of emergency relief granted by emergency arbitrators in Hong Kong, see AO, ss 22A and 22B.

[40] ibid s 36, incorporating Art 17A of the Model Law.

(ii) whether the applicant will suffer harm which cannot adequately be compensated by damages if the measure is refused, and that harm significantly outweighs any harm that the other party may suffer if it later turns out that the measure was erroneously granted.

An anti-suit injunction may be granted as an interim measure under section 35 of the AO by the arbitral tribunal, or section 45 of the AO by the court.[41] The purpose would be to hold the parties to their arbitration agreement. The typical situation would be an order that one party be enjoined from bringing or continuing court litigation in breach of an arbitration agreement. Where the parties have agreed to arbitrate their disputes, a party contesting the anti-suit injunction application will have to show strong reason why it should not be held to its agreement.[42]

The court also has power under section 60 of the AO to grant orders on property being the subject of arbitral proceedings which have been or are to be commenced in or outside Hong Kong. Such power is exercised and restricted in a manner similar to section 45 of the AO.[43]

A party might be benefited from the Arrangement Concerning Mutual Assistance in Court-ordered Interim Measures in Aid of Arbitral Proceedings between the Mainland and Hong Kong.[44]

VI. Recognition and Enforcement of Arbitral Awards

It is important to distinguish between an application to set aside an award and an application for the recognition and enforcement of an award. The former is governed by AO, Part 9 (section 81), incorporating Article 34 of the Model Law. It is a process of recourse against the award in the seat of the arbitration. It is a proceeding in the supervisory court, governed by Hong Kong law as the law under which the award was made. It is solely concerned with Hong Kong arbitration law and practice. The latter process, on the other hand, is governed by AO, Part 10, which provides for the recognition and enforcement of Convention awards,[45] Mainland China awards,[46] Macao awards[47] and awards elsewhere.[48]

[41] This jurisdiction is in addition to the High Court Ordinance (Cap 4), s 21L. See ch 9, s VI. An injunction under s 21L of the High Court Ordinance is a general equitable jurisdiction (as opposed to a supervisory or supporting jurisdiction) to enforce the negative promise contained in the arbitration agreement not to bring court proceedings, which is applicable and enforceable regardless of whether any arbitration proceedings are on foot or proposed which require support: *UniCredit Bank GmbH* (n 25) [96]–[112].

[42] *Ever Judger Holding Co Ltd v Kroman Celik Sanayii Anonim Sirketi* [2015] 2 HKLRD 866 [45]. For a general discussion on anti-suit injunctions, see ch 9, s VI.

[43] AO, ss 60(1), 60(4) and 60(6).

[44] The Arrangement (Fa Shi [2019] No 14) is discussed in ch 25, s I.H.

[45] AO, Part 10, Division 2, ss 87–91.

[46] AO, Part 10, Division 3, ss 92–98. This Division gives effect to the Arrangement Concerning the Mutual Enforcement of Arbitral Awards between the Mainland and Hong Kong (Fa Shi [2000] No 3) in 1999 and the Supplemental Arrangement (Fa Shi [2020] No 13) in 2020. See ch 25, ss I.C and I.D.

[47] AO, Part 10, Division 4, ss 98A–98D. This Division came into effect on 19 December 2013, which gives effect to the Arrangement Concerning Reciprocal Recognition and Enforcement of Arbitral Awards between the Hong Kong Special Administrative Region and the Macao Special Administrative Region in 2013. See ch 25, s II.A.

[48] AO, Part 10, Division 1, ss 82–86.

It is a proceeding in the enforcement court, governed by Hong Kong law as the law of the forum of enforcement. That is the subject matter of this section.

Recognition and enforcement of arbitral awards may be effected at common law or through the AO. The summary procedures under the AO offer a 'short cut' for the enforcement of awards as the AO procedure 'dispenses with the full formalities of the action to enforce an award'.[49] In either scenario, the six-year time limit in section 4(1) of the Limitation Ordinance (Cap 347) will apply.[50] The enforcement of an award by an action at common law is helpfully clarified in *Xiamen Xinjingdi Group Co Ltd v Eton Properties Ltd*.[51] Under the common law action, the party is not suing on the underlying arbitration agreement (which may or may not be governed by Hong Kong law), but on the breach of the implied promise to honour the award, which exists as a separate and distinct contractual obligation and supports an independent cause of action.[52] The enforcing court may accordingly grant relief appropriate in the award. If a monetary award is involved, it may simply be a court judgment enforcing the award as a debt. If it is a non-monetary award which has not been complied with, the court may fashion an apt remedy chosen from the full range of remedies available in ordinary common law action. In contrast, the enforcement of an award under statute can only be by way of a 'judgment in terms of the award'.[53] This means the enforcing court is neither entitled nor bound to go behind the award in question, explore the reasoning of the arbitral tribunal or second-guess its intention.[54]

To enforce an arbitral award under statute, the party must comply with requirements in the AO and the Rules of the High Court (Cap 4A), Order 73, rule 10. Under the AO, the parties must produce:[55]

(i) the duly authenticated original award or a duly certified copy of it;
(ii) the original arbitration agreement or a duly certified copy of it; and
(iii) if the award or agreement is not in either of the official languages, a translation of it in either official language certified by an official or sworn translator or by a diplomatic or consular agent.

Provision of security may be ordered by the court in appropriate circumstances, based on (i) the strength of the arguments and (ii) the ease or difficulty of enforcement of the award, and whether it will be rendered more difficult if enforcement is delayed.[56]

[49] *Xiamen Xinjingdi Group Co Ltd v Eton Properties Ltd* [2016] 2 HKLRD 1106 [98]–[99]. For instance, leave to serve out is required to enforce an award under common law, but is not required for an *ex parte* order giving leave to enforce an arbitral award under statute: Rules of the High Court (Cap 4A), Ord 11, r 1(1)(m) (common law); Ord 73, r 10(5) (statute).

[50] *CL v SCG* [2019] 2 HKLRD 144, [2019] HKCFI 398 [10]. See also AO, s 14.

[51] *Xiamen Xinjingdi Group Co Ltd v Eton Properties Ltd* [2016] 2 HKLRD 1106; *Xiamen Xinjingdi Group Co Ltd v Eton Properties Ltd* (2020) 23 HKCFAR 348, [2020] HKCFA 32. Damages are assessed as if the award had been complied with: *Xiamen Xinjingdi Group Co Ltd v Eton Properties Ltd* [2024] HKCFI 1291.

[52] The implied promise is mutual and either party may enforce an award under common law: *Xu Hongbiao v Oasis Investment Group Ltd* [2023] HKCFI 860; *Xu Hongbiao v Oasis Investment Group Ltd* [2024] HKCA 854.

[53] AO, ss 84(2), 87(1)(b), 92(1)(b) and 98A(1)(b).

[54] *Xiamen Xinjingdi Group Co Ltd v Eton Properties Ltd* [2008] 4 HKLRD 972; *Shandong Hongri Chemical Joint Stock Co v Petrochina International (Hong Kong) Ltd* [2011] 2 HKLRD 124 [12].

[55] AO, ss 85, 88, 94 and 98C.

[56] See, eg *Soleh Boneh International Ltd v Government of the Republic of Uganda* [1993] 2 Lloyd's Rep 208; *Guo Shun Kai v Wing Shing Chemical Co Ltd* [2013] 3 HKLRD 484; *Dana Shipping and Trading SA v Sino Channel Asia Ltd*

The grounds for refusing recognition and enforcement of an award are largely similar (but not identical) to the grounds for setting aside an award, although the sources of these grounds are different. For setting aside, the grounds are from section 81(1) of the AO, which incorporates Article 34 of the Model Law; for recognition and enforcement, the grounds are from sections 86, 89, 95 and 98D of the AO, adapting Article V of the 1958 New York Convention.[57] For the enforcement of Convention awards, Mainland awards and Macao awards, the grounds set out in sections 89, 95 and 98D of the AO are exhaustive, expressly stating that enforcement of those awards 'may not be refused except as mentioned' in those sections.[58] Even if one or more of the grounds are made out, the court retains a discretion to enforce an award.[59]

The grounds to set aside an award or refuse recognition and enforcement of an award can be summarised as follows:

(i) incapacity of a party to the arbitration agreement, or invalidity of the arbitration agreement;[60]
(ii) lack of proper notice;[61]
(iii) inability to present one's case;[62]
(iv) award deals with a dispute not within the terms of the submission to arbitration;[63]
(v) composition of the tribunal or the arbitral procedure not in accordance with the parties' agreement;[64]
(vi) subject matter not capable of settlement by arbitration;[65] and
(vii) award in conflict with public policy.[66]

[2017] 1 HKC 281; *AAD v BBF* [2024] 2 HKLRD 297, [2024] HKCFI 698; *中國機床銷售與技術服務有限公司 v Nationsync Electrical and Machinery Equip Corp Ltd* [2024] 4 HKC 227, [2024] HKCFI 958. Regarding security for costs in setting aside applications, see also *SA v BH* [2024] 3 HKLRD 204, [2024] HKCFI 1357.

[57] The Art V grounds, however, form the basis of Art 36 of the Model Law, which deals with recognition and enforcement.

[58] The enforcement of awards elsewhere (AO, Part 10, Division 1) is non-exhaustive as it provides an additional ground that 'if for any other reason the court considers it just' not to enforce the award (AO, s 86(2)(c)). In practice, it is submitted that this ground does not add much: *U v A* (unreported, HCCT 34/2016, 23 February 2017) [66]–[71].

[59] See, eg *G v X* [2024] 1 HKLRD 685, [2023] HKCFI 3316 [30]. The court has a similar residual discretion not to set aside an award (as shown by the word 'may' in Art 34 of the Model Law): see, eg *Brunswick Bowling & Billiards Corp v Shanghai Zhonglu Industrial Co Ltd* [2011] 1 HKLRD 707; *Pacific China Holdings Ltd (in liq) v Grand Pacific Holdings Ltd* [2012] 4 HKLRD 1; *China Property Development (Holdings) Ltd v Mandecly Ltd* (unreported, CACV 92/2015 and CACV 93/2015, 24 May 2016).

[60] Model Law, Art 34(2)(a)(i) and AO, s 81 (for setting aside); New York Convention, Art V(1)(a) and AO, ss 86(1)(a), 86(1)(b), 89(2)(a), 89(2)(b), 95(2)(a), 95(2)(b), 98D(2)(a) and 98D(2)(b) (for recognition and enforcement of awards generally, of Convention awards, of Mainland awards and of Macao awards respectively).

[61] Model Law, Art 34(2)(a)(ii) and AO, s 81; New York Convention, Art V(1)(b) and AO, ss 86(1)(c)(i), 89(2)(c)(i), 95(2)(c)(i) and 98D(2)(c)(i).

[62] Model Law, Art 34(2)(a)(ii) and AO, s 81; New York Convention, Art V(1)(b) and AO, ss 86(1)(c)(ii), 89(2)(c)(ii), 95(2)(c)(ii) and 98D(2)(c)(ii).

[63] Model Law, Art 34(2)(a)(iii) and AO, s 81; New York Convention, Art V(1)(c) and AO, ss 86(1)(d), 89(2)(d), 95(2)(d) and 98D(2)(d).

[64] Model Law, Art 34(2)(a)(iv) and AO, s 81; New York Convention, Art V(1)(d) and AO, ss 86(1)(e), 89(2)(e), 95(2)(e) and 98D(2)(e).

[65] Model Law, Art 34(2)(b)(i) and AO, s 81; New York Convention, Art V(2)(a) and AO, ss 86(2)(a), 89(3)(a), 95(3)(a) and 98D(3)(a).

[66] Model Law, art 34(2)(b)(ii) and AO, s 81; New York Convention, art V(2)(b) and AO, ss 86(2)(b), 89(3)(b), 95(3)(b) and 98D(3)(b).

Each of the grounds are briefly analysed in turn below.

It is also a ground to refuse recognition and enforcement that an award has not yet become binding on the parties or has been set aside or suspended by a competent authority in the seat.[67] It is not fatal for a party to 'sit and wait' for enforcement proceedings. Hong Kong follows the 'choice of remedies' principle where the parties have two independently available options: setting aside the award in the supervisory court (an active remedy), or resisting enforcement without having challenged the award in the supervisory court (a passive remedy).[68] In considering an application for extension of time to resist enforcement of an award out of time, the court is to look at all relevant matters and consider the overall justice of the case, without promoting or demoting the importance of any particular factors.[69]

(i) Incapacity of party or invalidity of arbitration agreement. In *AB v CD*, the court set aside an arbitral award based on this ground.[70] In that case, there was an arbitration agreement between AB Bureau and CD. Following a series of restructuring, an original subsidiary of AB Bureau became a new and separate legal entity known as AB Engineering. It was held that there was no valid arbitration agreement between AB Engineering and CD. In *Arjowiggins HKK2 Ltd v X Co*, the court dismissed an application to set aside a Hong Kong award.[71] The court rejected the argument that the arbitration agreement was invalid under Article 16 of the PRC Arbitration Law for failing to expressly identify the Hong Kong International Arbitration Centre (HKIAC) as the arbitration commission. It held that the party, having fully participated in the arbitration, breached its duty of good faith and was estopped and precluded from raising the complaint. See also *X v Jemmy Chien*.[72]

(ii) Lack of proper notice. In *Sun Tian Gang v Hong Kong & China Gas (Jilin) Ltd*,[73] the court viewed the service of a notice of arbitration as 'an important step in the arbitration', required by natural justice. The court did not consider that the 'deeming provisions' in the Model Law and the UNCITRAL Arbitration Rules could operate to derogate from the principles of natural justice and fairness. The award was set aside. In *G v P*, the court set aside an enforcement order for an award based on lack of proper notice, as the Notice of Arbitration was not sent to the correct email address stated in the Supplemental Agreement.[74] See also *AB v CD*, in which this ground succeeded.[75]

[67] New York Convention, Art V(1)(e) and AO, ss 86(1)(f), 89(2)(f), 95(2)(f) and 98D(2)(f). But see the discussion below regarding deference to the supervisory court's decision to annul an award. Pending the supervisory court's decision, enforcement proceedings may be adjourned and security may be ordered: AO, ss 86(4), 89(5) and 98D(5). Such power is absent in statute for the enforcement of Mainland awards, although it is still possible to apply for an adjournment: *G v X* [2022] 3 HKLRD 297, [2022] HKCFI 1864.

[68] *Astro Nusantara International BV v PT First Media TBK* (2018) 21 HKCFAR 118, [2018] HKCFA 12 [74]–[79]. However, if a party failed to cure an irregularity by invoking a remedy under the arbitration rules but only raised it for the first time in the setting aside proceedings, then the irregularity might be waived in the enforcement proceedings applying Hong Kong law, as the party was in breach of its duty of good faith in the arbitration: *G v X* (n 67) [23].

[69] ibid [62] and [85].

[70] *AB v CD* [2021] HKCFI 327.

[71] *Arjowiggins HKK2 Ltd v X Co* (unreported, HCCT 53/2015, 12 October 2016).

[72] *X v Jemmy Chien* [2020] 5 HKC 177, [2020] HKCFI 286.

[73] *Sun Tian Gang v Hong Kong & China Gas (Jilin) Ltd* [2016] 5 HKLRD 221.

[74] *G v P* [2023] 4 HKLRD 563, [2023] HKCFI 2173.

[75] *AB v CD* (n 70).

(iii) Inability to present one's case. This is a frequently raised ground but attention must be paid to its narrow scope and application. The court must be satisfied that

> a party has been denied due process. For this purpose, the conduct complained of must be serious or even egregious … Ultimately, in considering whether a party was 'unable to present his case', the question is one of fairness in the arbitral process.[76]

There is a distinction between, on the one hand, a party having no opportunity to address a point or his opponent's case and, on the other hand, a party simply failing to take an opportunity which was available. The requirement for the arbitral tribunal is to give to parties a 'reasonable opportunity' to present their case and to deal with the case of their opponent.[77] See also various Hong Kong cases in which this ground succeeded.[78]

(iv) Award deals with dispute not contemplated within the terms of the submission to arbitration. The words 'decisions on matters beyond the scope of the submission to arbitration' should be narrowly construed.[79] In *China Property Development (Holdings) Ltd v Mandecly Ltd*, the arbitral tribunal had ruled on a point against the claimant, which was clearly indicated by the respondent to be inapplicable to the claimant. The court viewed this as an error under this ground.[80]

(v) Composition of the arbitral tribunal or the arbitral procedure was not in accordance with the agreement of the parties. In *China Nanhai Oil Joint Service Corp Shenzhen Branch v Gee Tai Holdings Co Ltd*,[81] the arbitrator was appointed based on the CIETAC Shenzhen list of arbitrators rather than the CIETAC Beijing list. However, the Court held that the award should still be enforced as the party had nonetheless taken part in the arbitration despite the non-conformity in the appointment of arbitrators. For a successful complaint based on an arbitrator's lack of attention in virtual hearings, see *Song Lihua v Lee Chee Hon*.[82]

(vi) Subject matter not capable of settlement by arbitration. See section I above for a discussion on arbitrability. There are no cases in Hong Kong that consider this ground in the contexts of setting aside or recognition and enforcement.

(vii) Award in conflict with public policy. The definition of 'public policy' in the Hong Kong arbitration context is set out in *Hebei Import & Export Corp v Polytek Engineering Co Ltd*,[83] where it was stated that 'the award must be so fundamentally offensive to that jurisdiction's notions of justice that … it cannot reasonably be expected to overlook the objection'.[84] In other words, an award must not be 'contrary to the fundamental conceptions of morality and justice'.[85] In *Sun Tian Gang v Hong Kong & China Gas (Jilin) Ltd*, the court held that the public policy ground was successfully made out, as

[76] *Pang Wai Hak v Hua Yunjian* [2012] 4 HKLRD 113 [29].
[77] *Maeda Kensetsu Kogyo Kabushiki Kaisha v Bauer Hong Kong Ltd* [2019] HKCFI 1006.
[78] *China Property Development (Holdings) Ltd* (n 59); *Sun Tian Gang* (n 73); *P v M* [2018] HKCFI 2280; *P v M* [2019] HKCFI 1864; *A v R1* [2024] HKCFI 1511.
[79] *Grant Thornton International Ltd v JBPB & Co (a partnership)* (unreported, HCCT 13/2012, 5 April 2013).
[80] *China Property Development (Holdings) Ltd* (n 59).
[81] *China Nanhai Oil Joint Service Corp Shenzhen Branch v Gee Tai Holdings Co Ltd* [1995] 2 HKLR 215.
[82] *Song Lihua v Lee Chee Hon* [2023] 5 HKLRD 488, [2023] HKCFI 2540.
[83] *Hebei Import & Export Corp v Polytek Engineering Co Ltd* (1999) 2 HKCFAR 111. See also ch 8, s I.B.
[84] ibid [31].
[85] ibid [99].

Mr Sun was in prison and was therefore unable to present his case to the arbitral tribunal.[86] See also various Hong Kong cases in which this ground was made out.[87]

Turning now to another usually raised complaint of lack of reasons in the award, it was held in *H v L* that:[88]

> … reasons for an arbitral award do not have to be elaborate or lengthy. Awards have to be read and understood in proper context, in particular against the context as to how the relevant issues had been argued before the Tribunal. This is so because arbitration is a private and confidential dispute resolution process, and an award made in an arbitration is intended to be read by the parties only, who would be familiar with the background and how the issues had been argued, and would not be made public to be read and understood by third parties and strangers to the dispute. Arbitral awards are intended and expected to be 'cost effective, and shorn of complexities and technicalities' (*R v F* [2012] 5 HKLRD 278). So long as the reasoning is expressed to enable parties to understand how and why a conclusion is reached on a particular issue, and the award explains the basis on which a material finding is made, that would be sufficient.

In *LY v HW*,[89] it was held that, when reviewing an award based on an allegation of lack of reasons, 'an award should be read in a reasonable and commercial way, without a meticulous legal eye endeavouring to pick holes, inconsistencies and faults, but generously, and only to remedy serious breaches of rules of natural justice which cause injustice'. See also *A v B*, where recognition and enforcement of an award was refused due to a lack of reasons.[90]

Regarding deference to the supervisory court's decision, it appears that a decision by the PRC court with supervisory jurisdiction not to set aside the award should be given due regard, as established in *Gao Haiyan v Keeneye Holdings Ltd*.[91] This was applied to the context of Convention awards in *Construction Co v Guarantor*.[92] However, in *Song Lihua v Lee Chee Hon*, the fact that the supervisory court in the Mainland had not set the award aside and had permitted its enforcement in the Mainland did not prevent the Hong Kong court '[from applying] its own standards and law when deciding whether it would be contrary to the public policy of Hong Kong to enforce the Award'.[93]

There is no judicial or academic consensus as to whether (and in what circumstances) awards annulled at the supervisory court remain capable of recognition and enforcement in other jurisdictions. Article V(1)(e) of the New York Convention provides that recognition and enforcement of an award may be refused if the award has been set aside or suspended by a competent authority of the country in which, or under the law of which, that award was made. However, it does not prohibit the recognition or enforcement of an annulled award if it is possible pursuant to the state's domestic law. Article VII(1) of the New York Convention provides that contracting states can apply more favourable provisions in their domestic laws for the recognition and enforcement of awards. In *Dana*

[86] *Sun Tian Gang* (n 73).

[87] *A v B* [2015] 3 HKLRD 586; *W v AW* [2021] 5 HKC 476, [2021] HKCFI 1707; *Song Lihua* (n 82); *G v N* [2024] 2 HKC 510, [2023] HKCFI 3366; *A v R1* (n 78).

[88] *H v L* [2021] 2 HKLRD 886, [2021] HKCFI 1203 [29].

[89] *LY v HW* [2022] 6 HKC 129, [2022] HKCFI 2267. See also *AI v LG II* [2023] 4 HKC 135, [2023] HKCFI 1183.

[90] *A v B* [2024] 4 HKC 36, [2024] HKCFI 751. See also *AAB v BBA* [2024] 3 HKC 656, [2024] HKCFI 699.

[91] *Gao Haiyan v Keeneye Holdings Ltd* [2012] 1 HKLRD 627 [65]–[69] and [102].

[92] *Construction Co v Guarantor* [2021] HKCFI 2558 [31].

[93] *Song Lihua* (n 82) [53]. See also *Hebei Import & Export Corp* (n 83) 136.

Shipping and Trading SA v Sino Channel Asia Ltd,[94] the Court of First Instance followed *Yukos Capital Sarl v OJSC Oil Co Rosneft*,[95] and held that there is no *ex nihilo nil fit* ('nothing comes of nothing') principle which precludes the enforcement of awards; the court has power to enforce the awards at common law, notwithstanding the decision of the supervisory court to set aside an award. A re-arbitration in the Mainland China limited to procedural defects with no effect on the original award does not bar enforcement of the original award in Hong Kong.[96]

Costs are awarded on an indemnity basis following unsuccessful challenges to an award.[97]

When a party seeks to stay enforcement of a judgment originating from an arbitral award (particularly in circumstances where the debtor seeks to rely on the claims made in a second pending arbitration as an equitable set-off), the principles governing the court's exercise of its power and discretion are set out in *S v G*.[98] The award creditor should not be deprived of the benefits of the judgment unless there is abuse or manifest injustice. There must be 'very special circumstances' to justify a stay of enforcement. In deciding whether special circumstances exist, the nature of the claims, the extent of the identity between the claim in the judgment and the unresolved cross-claim, the strength and size of the cross-claim, the likely delay before the cross-claim can be adjudicated and the extent of prejudice that may be suffered by the judgment creditor or the judgment debtor are all matters to be taken into consideration. The discretion of the court in granting a stay of execution or enforcement should thus only be exercised in exceptional circumstances, where an injustice would otherwise be caused, to prevent abuse, to preserve the dignity of the court or to facilitate the administration of justice.[99]

[94] *Dana Shipping and Trading SA v Sino Channel Asia Ltd* [2016] 4 HKLRD 345 (Convention award under AO, s 89).

[95] *Yukos Capital Sarl v OJSC Oil Co Rosneft* [2014] EWHC 2188 (Comm), [2014] 2 CLC 162.

[96] *G v X* (n 59).

[97] *A v R* [2009] 3 HKLRD 389; *Grand Pacific Holdings Ltd v Pacific China Holdings Ltd (in liq) (No 2)* [2012] 4 HKLRD 569. Following such approach, indemnity costs are also awarded against unsuccessful challenges to arbitration agreements: *Chimbusco International Petroleum (Singapore) Pte Ltd v Fully Best Trading Ltd* [2016] 1 HKLRD 582. See also *CNG v G* [2024] 2 HKLRD 152, [2024] HKCFI 575 [1]–[3]; Wilson Lui, 'Defending the Indemnity Costs Approach to Unsuccessful Arbitral Award Challenges' [2021] *Asian Dispute Review* 129.

[98] *S v G* [2021] 3 HKC 272, [2021] HKCFI 263.

[99] *Credit Lyonnais v SK Global Hong Kong Ltd* [2003] 4 HKC 104 [3]–[8]; *S v G* [2022] HKCA 383. See also *CF v SHK* [2024] 5 HKC 303, [2024] HKCFI 1493.

PART VI

Harmonisation

25

Private International Law Issues and Mutual Legal Assistance between Hong Kong and Other Inter-regional Jurisdictions

This chapter deals with private international law issues at the inter-regional level, that is, between Hong Kong on the one hand and Mainland China, Macao or Taiwan on the other. After the handover on 1 July 1997, Hong Kong became a Special Administrative Region (SAR) of the People's Republic of China (PRC). As a territorial unit of the PRC, international conventions that apply between countries do not apply between Hong Kong and Mainland China. Nor do international conventions apply between Hong Kong and other territorial units of the PRC, such as the Macao SAR.

Inter-regional private international law and mutual legal assistance between Hong Kong and Mainland China is mainly achieved through arrangements between the relevant authorities. According to Articles 80, 82 and 85 of the Basic Law, the Hong Kong courts exercise judicial power independently of Mainland judicial authorities, including the Supreme People's Court. By Article 95 of the Basic Law, Hong Kong 'may … maintain juridical relations with the judicial organs of other parts of the country, and they may render assistance to each other'. This includes the judicial organs of Mainland China. Article 549 of the PRC's Interpretation of the Supreme People's Court on the Application of the Civil Procedure Law provides that where a people's court in the PRC tries a civil lawsuit involving Hong Kong SAR, Macao SAR or Taiwan, it may refer to the special provisions on foreign-related civil procedures.[1] Free of the concerns of sovereignty among states, these arrangements have provided a direct and convenient way of dealing with day-to-day cross-border issues.

These arrangements also show how inter-regional private international law has been developed uniquely in China, in light of the complex landscape of 'one country, two systems, three legal systems and four jurisdictions'. With the current difficulties and impracticalities in implementing uniform substantive laws and uniform regional rules on private international law across the inter-regional jurisdictions in China, the arrangements provided an avenue for the legislation and implementation of private international law rules among each of these jurisdictions with appropriate coordination. Moreover, the application of

[1] Fa Shi [2022] No 11 (effective from 10 April 2022).

international conventions among these jurisdictions facilitates consensus among jurisdictions and contributes to the harmonisation of inter-regional private international law.[2]

I. Mainland China

Currently, Hong Kong and Mainland China have nine arrangements related to private international law as summarised in this section. While the earlier arrangements were implemented by way of Supreme People's Court judicial interpretations, later arrangements were usually implemented by way of Supreme People's Court judicial interpretations and Hong Kong local legislation concurrently. Consequently, there was usually a time gap (usually two to five years) between the signing of the arrangement and its implementation due to the need to prepare and enact the local legislation in Hong Kong.

A. Arrangement for Mutual Service of Judicial Documents in Civil and Commercial Proceedings

The Arrangement was promulgated by a Supreme People's Court judicial interpretation on 29 March 1999 and came into effect on 30 March 1999.[3] It was the first mutual legal assistance arrangement between Hong Kong and Mainland China after Hong Kong's handover in 1997. Its aim was to build a speedy mechanism for service between Hong Kong and Mainland China. Prior to 1997, the 1965 HCCH Convention on the Service Abroad of Judicial and Extrajudicial Documents in Civil or Commercial Matters applied.

The Arrangement facilitates the service between Hong Kong and Mainland China of documents emanating from the Higher People's Courts in the Mainland or the Hong Kong High Court.[4] Exceptionally, the Supreme People's Court of the PRC may make direct requests for service to the High Court of Hong Kong.[5] Service of documents require a written request with a letter of entrustment duly sealed with the official seal of the entrusting court.[6] The letter, together with the judicial documents to be served, should be in Chinese or accompanied by a Chinese translation.[7] The request must contain the name of the entrusting court, the name and description of the person to be served, that person's address and the nature of the proceedings.[8] The entrusted court will conduct

[2] See also Jin Huang et al (eds), *Guoji Sifa Xue* [*Private International Law*] (Higher Education Press, 2023) chs 17–18.

[3] Arrangement for Mutual Service of Judicial Documents in Civil and Commercial Proceedings between the Mainland and Hong Kong Courts, Fa Shi [1999] No 9, www.doj.gov.hk/en/mainland_and_macao/arrangements_with_the_mainland.html. See also Fa [1999] No 42; Several Provisions of the Supreme People's Court on the Issues Concerning the Service of Judicial Documents of Hong Kong- and Macao-related Civil and Commercial Cases, Fa Shi [2009] No 2.

[4] ibid Art 2.

[5] ibid.

[6] ibid Art 3.

[7] ibid.

[8] ibid.

a formality review of the letter of entrustment and may ask for further information.[9] Service is effected pursuant to the law of the entrusted court.[10] The time that the entrusted court takes to effect service should not be more than two months.[11] If service cannot be effected, the entrusted court shall provide a certificate stating the reason for non-service or, if service has been refused, the reason for refusal.[12] If service is effected, a return form will be issued.[13] Service under the Arrangement is effected free of charge unless a special method of service is requested.[14]

The Arrangement was incorporated into the Rules of the High Court (Cap 4A) (RHC) on 30 March 1999. Currently, service from Hong Kong in Mainland China may be sought pursuant to Order 11, rule 5A of the RHC, while service from Mainland China to Hong Kong is based on Order 69, rule 2 of the RHC.[15]

B. Arrangement on Mutual Taking of Evidence in Civil and Commercial Matters

The Arrangement was promulgated by a Supreme People's Court judicial interpretation on 27 February 2017 and came into effect on 1 March 2017.[16] The Arrangement provides for the taking of evidence to be requested by Hong Kong's Chief Secretary for Administration or by a Higher People's Court in Mainland China.[17] The Supreme People's Court may request the taking of evidence in Hong Kong directly.[18] The letter of request and any attached material should be in Chinese or come with a Chinese translation.[19] The letter of request should state the names of the courts involved, the names and contact details of witnesses, particulars of the requested assistance, and any special manner for taking evidence.[20] The taking of evidence will be subject to the law of the requested jurisdiction.[21] Upon receipt, the requested party shall promptly process the request.[22] Processing should be completed, to the extent possible, within six months.[23] A written reply shall be issued to the requesting party on completion of the assistance.[24] The expenses incurred in the taking of evidence are to be borne by the requested party.[25]

[9] ibid.
[10] ibid Art 6. But service in Mainland China by public announcement is currently impossible under the arrangement: *Su Xin v Qian Xiaochun* [2022] 4 HKC 256, [2022] HKDC 156.
[11] ibid Art 4.
[12] ibid Art 5.
[13] ibid.
[14] ibid Art 8.
[15] See ch 9, ss VII and VIII.
[16] Arrangement on Mutual Taking of Evidence in Civil and Commercial Matters between the Courts of the Mainland and the Hong Kong Special Administrative Region, Fa Shi [2017] No 4, www.doj.gov.hk/en/mainland_and_macao/arrangements_with_the_mainland.html. See also Fa [2017] No 117.
[17] ibid Art 2.
[18] ibid.
[19] ibid Art 4.
[20] ibid. On cross-examination requests, see *Bold Shine Investment Ltd v Zheng Deli* [2023] 2 HKC 417, [2023] HKCA 73.
[21] ibid Art 7; *Tenwow International Holdings Ltd (in liq) v PricewaterhouseCoopers* [2024] HKCA 1193.
[22] ibid.
[23] ibid Art 10.
[24] ibid.
[25] ibid Art 9.

C. Arrangement Concerning Mutual Enforcement of Arbitral Awards

The Arrangement was promulgated by a Supreme People's Court judicial interpretation on 24 January 2000 and came into effect on 1 February 2000.[26] This Arrangement is necessary because the 1958 New York Convention ceased to be applicable between Hong Kong and Mainland China when the former became a territorial unit within a single sovereign state. After the handover and prior to the Arrangement, Mainland arbitral awards are not enforceable directly under the statutory regime, but only by action on the basis of the award.[27] The provisions in the Arrangement (and the Supplemental Arrangement discussed in Section I.D below) are currently given effect by Part 10, Division 3 of the Arbitration Ordinance (Cap 609) (AO).

A Mainland award can be enforced by action in the High Court of Hong Kong[28] or in the same manner as a judgment of the High Court with the leave of the Court.[29] A Hong Kong award can be enforced by the Intermediate People's Court of the place where the party against whom the application is filed is domiciled or the place in which the property of that party is situated.[30]

Ad hoc arbitral awards made in Hong Kong and institutional arbitral awards by the Hong Kong branch of a Mainland or foreign arbitration institution are considered Hong Kong awards.[31] An application for enforcement, the arbitral award and the arbitration agreement must be submitted for enforcement in Hong Kong or Mainland China.[32]

D. Supplemental Arrangement Concerning Mutual Enforcement of Arbitral Awards

The Supplemental Arrangement was signed between the Supreme People's Court and the HKSAR Government on 26 November 2020. The Supreme People's Court judicial interpretation was promulgated on the same date.[33] Articles 1 and 4 entered into force on 27 November 2020, while Articles 2 and 3 entered into force on 19 May 2021. It

[26] Arrangement Concerning Mutual Enforcement of Arbitral Awards between the Mainland and the Hong Kong Special Administrative Region, Fa Shi [2000] No 3, www.doj.gov.hk/en/mainland_and_macao/arrangements_with_the_mainland.html.

[27] *Ng Fung Hong Ltd v ABC* [1998] 1 HKLRD 155.

[28] AO, s 92(1)(a).

[29] ibid s 92(1)(b).

[30] Arrangement Concerning Mutual Enforcement of Arbitral Awards (n 26), Art 2.

[31] Notice of the Supreme People's Court on Issues Concerning the Execution of Hong Kong Arbitral Awards in the Mainland, Fa [2009] No 415; *Ennead Architects International LLP v Fuli Nanjing Dichan Kaifa Youxian Gongsi* (2016) Su 01 Ren Gang No 1.

[32] Arrangement Concerning Mutual Enforcement of Arbitral Awards (n 26), Art 3.

[33] Supplemental Arrangement Concerning Mutual Enforcement of Arbitral Awards between the Mainland and the Hong Kong Special Administrative Region, Fa Shi [2020] No 13, www.doj.gov.hk/en/mainland_and_macao/arrangements_with_the_mainland.html.

made three important changes to the Arrangement in 1999. First, the Supplemental Arrangement provides that all awards rendered pursuant to the PRC's Arbitration Law may be enforced. The scope of enforcement is thus extended from awards made by a 'recognised Mainland arbitral authority'.[34] Second, the applications for enforcement of arbitral awards with the courts of the Mainland and of Hong Kong respectively can be made simultaneously, provided that the respondent to the enforcement application is domiciled or has property in both places, and the total amount sought does not exceed the amount awarded.[35] The only restriction is against double recovery by virtue of the enforcement in the courts of Hong Kong and the Mainland.[36] Third, if an award creditor filed an application for preservatory or mandatory measures, the relevant court can impose those measures pursuant to its laws.[37] The Supplemental Arrangement does not prohibit double protection by way of such measures.[38]

E. Arrangement on Reciprocal Recognition and Enforcement of Judgments in Civil and Commercial Matters Pursuant to Choice of Court Agreements between Parties Concerned

The Arrangement was signed between the Supreme People's Court and the HKSAR Government on 14 July 2006. The Supreme People's Court judicial interpretation was promulgated on 3 July 2008 and the Arrangement came into effect on 1 August 2008.[39] The Arrangement is implemented by the Mainland Judgments (Reciprocal Enforcement) Ordinance (Cap 597) (MJREO). Previously, it was necessary to obtain judgments in both Hong Kong and Mainland China separately. However, given the number of cross-border civil and commercial disputes, the Arrangement establishes a simplified, cost-effective and time-efficient procedure for reciprocal recognition and enforcement, thereby fostering inter-regional trade and investment. For a detailed discussion of the statutory provisions in Hong Kong, see chapter twenty-three, section IV.C. The Arrangement and the Ordinance are not retrospective and only apply to choice of court agreements and judgments made after the effective date.

[34] Supplemental Arrangement Concerning Mutual Enforcement of Arbitral Awards (n 33), Art 2, amending Arrangement Concerning Mutual Enforcement of Arbitral Awards (n 26), Art 1. AO, s 97 was repealed as a result.

[35] Supplemental Arrangement Concerning Mutual Enforcement of Arbitral Awards (n 33), Art 3, amending Arrangement Concerning Mutual Enforcement of Arbitral Awards (n 26), Art 2(3). AO, s 93 was repealed as a result.

[36] *Lin Chien Hsiung v Lin Hsiu Fen* [2022] 4 HKC 590, [2022] HKCFI 1270 [17].

[37] Supplemental Arrangement Concerning Mutual Enforcement of Arbitral Awards (n 33), Art 4, amending Arrangement Concerning Mutual Enforcement of Arbitral Awards (n 26), Art 6(2).

[38] *G v X* [2022] HKCFI 829 [38].

[39] Arrangement on Reciprocal Recognition and Enforcement of Judgments in Civil and Commercial Matters by the Courts of the Mainland and of the Hong Kong Special Administrative Region Pursuant to Choice of Court Agreements between Parties Concerned, Fa Shi [2008] No 9, www.doj.gov.hk/en/mainland_and_macao/arrangements_with_the_mainland.html.

F. Arrangement on Reciprocal Recognition and Enforcement of Civil Judgments in Matrimonial and Family Cases

The Arrangement was signed between the Supreme People's Court and the HKSAR Government on 20 June 2017. The Supreme People's Court judicial interpretation was promulgated on 14 February 2022 and the Arrangement came into effect on 15 February 2022.[40] The Arrangement is implemented by the Mainland Judgments in Matrimonial and Family Cases (Reciprocal Recognition and Enforcement) Ordinance (Cap 639) (MJMFCO) in Hong Kong. For a detailed discussion of the statutory provisions in Hong Kong, see chapter twenty-three, section VI.E. The Arrangement and the Ordinance are not retrospective and only apply to orders or judgments made after the effective date.

The Arrangement allows mutual recognition and enforcement of various judgments and orders regarding matrimonial and family issues. The Arrangement gives effect to final judgments of Hong Kong and Mainland Court courts. However, foreign judgments that have been recognised and enforced by the Hong Kong or Mainland courts cannot be enforced through the Arrangement.[41]

The precise matrimonial and family cases to which the Arrangement applies are specified by the Arrangement. For example, a divorce certificate from the Mainland can be enforced through the Hong Kong courts, and an agreement or memorandum for dissolution certified under Part V or VA of the Marriage Reform Ordinance (Cap 178) can be enforced through the Mainland courts.[42] In respect of Mainland cases, the Arrangement covers disputes over the division of property, divorce, property after divorce, the invalidity of a marriage, the annulment of a marriage, matrimonial property agreements, the custody and maintenance of a child, the confirmation of parentage, spousal maintenance, the confirmation of an adoptive relationship, the guardianship of a minor, rights of access and orders for protection.[43] In respect of Hong Kong cases, the Arrangement includes decrees and orders under Parts III and IV of the Matrimonial Causes Ordinance (Cap 179), Part II or IIA of the Matrimonial Proceedings and Property Ordinance (Cap 192), the Guardianship of Minors Ordinance (Cap 13), the Separation and Maintenance Orders Ordinance (Cap 16), the Married Persons Status Ordinance (Cap 182), the Adoption Ordinance (Cap 290), the Parent and Child Ordinance (Cap 429) and the Domestic and Cohabitation Relationships Violence Ordinance (Cap 189).[44]

An application in Mainland China should be filed with an Intermediate People's Court where the parties reside or have property. An application in Hong Kong should be filed with the District Court. If two or more People's Courts have jurisdiction, the court that

[40] Arrangement on Reciprocal Recognition and Enforcement of Civil Judgments in Matrimonial and Family Cases by the Courts of the Mainland and of the Hong Kong Special Administrative Region, Fa Shi [2022] No 4, www.doj.gov.hk/en/mainland_and_macao/arrangements_with_the_mainland.html.

[41] ibid Art 2. See also *Lai v Ling* [2017] 5 HKLRD 629 [68].

[42] ibid Art 1.

[43] ibid Art 3(1); MJMFCO, Sch 2.

[44] ibid Art 3(2); MJMFCO, Sch 3.

accepted the case first will handle the case.[45] The time limits, procedures and manner for making an application are governed by the law of the requested place.[46]

Not all judgments can be enforced under the Arrangement. Article 9 sets out situations when a judgment may not be enforced. Such situations include those in which: (i) the respondent was not lawfully summoned or afforded a reasonable opportunity to make representations and defend themself; (ii) judgment was obtained by fraud; (iii) the requested court has accepted an action on the same dispute; or (iv) the requested court has already rendered a judgment in respect of the same dispute. Further, if a court considers that the judgment violates basic principles of law or public policy, the court can refuse to enforce or recognise the judgment.[47]

The best interests of the minor, if applicable, are always the priority in cases concerned with a minor.[48] This arrangement eases the need to obtain a 'mirror order' from the Mainland courts to the Hong Kong courts that concerns the relocation, care and control arrangements of the child, and a straightforward final order from the Family Court in Hong Kong to allow better protection of the children.[49]

A judgment can be partially or fully enforced.[50] If the applicant has property in the Mainland and Hong Kong, an applicant can seek enforcement in both courts. However, there is to be no double recovery.[51] If the case is subject to appeal in Hong Kong, the Mainland courts can suspend proceedings, and resume if the appeal is dismissed. Similarly, the Hong Kong courts can stay proceedings if the case is undergoing a retrial.[52] A decision to enforce may be appealed in Hong Kong or reviewed in Mainland China.[53] The requested court may impose preservation measures in accordance with its law.[54] There are rules on *res judicata* and issue estoppel in Articles 16 and 17 of the Arrangement.

G. Arrangement on Reciprocal Recognition and Enforcement of Judgments in Civil and Commercial Matters

The Arrangement was signed between the Supreme People's Court and the Hong Kong government on 18 January 2019. The Supreme People's Court's judicial interpretation was promulgated on 26 January 2024 and the Arrangement came into effect on 29 January 2024.[55] The Arrangement is implemented in Hong Kong by the Mainland

[45] ibid Art 4.
[46] ibid Art 7.
[47] ibid Art 9.
[48] ibid.
[49] *CN v LYP* [2023] HKCA 1173.
[50] Arrangement on Reciprocal Recognition and Enforcement of Civil Judgments in Matrimonial and Family Cases (n 40), Art 10.
[51] ibid Art 13.
[52] ibid Art 11.
[53] ibid Art 15.
[54] ibid Art 18.
[55] Arrangement on Reciprocal Recognition and Enforcement of Judgments in Civil and Commercial Matters by the Courts of the Mainland and of the Hong Kong Special Administrative Region, Fa Shi [2024] No 2, www.doj.gov.hk/en/mainland_and_macao/arrangements_with_the_mainland.html.

Judgments in Civil and Commercial Matters (Reciprocal Enforcement) Ordinance (Cap 645) (MJCCMREO). For a detailed discussion of the statutory provisions in Hong Kong, see chapter twenty-three, section IV.D. The Arrangement and the Ordinance are not retrospective and only apply to orders or judgments made after the effective date.

The Arrangement expands the scope of the 2006 Arrangement, and generally facilitates the enforcement of judgments in civil and commercial cases. Examples of judgments that cannot be enforced under the Arrangement are determinations on family matters, succession, administration or the distribution of estates, the infringement of patents, maritime matters, bankruptcy and in connection with arbitral awards.[56] The operation of the Arrangement is no longer constrained by the requirement of exclusive jurisdiction clauses in writing[57] and can be a basis to show that Hong Kong is clearly the appropriate forum.[58] The time limits, procedures and manner for making an application are governed by the law of the requested place.[59]

H. Arrangement Concerning Mutual Assistance in Court-ordered Interim Measures in Aid of Arbitral Proceedings

The Arrangement was signed between the Supreme People's Court and the HKSAR Government on 2 April 2019. The Supreme People's Court judicial interpretation was promulgated on 26 September 2019 and the Arrangement came into effect on 1 October 2019.[60] It covers property preservation, evidence preservation and conduct preservation in connection with cases from Mainland China and injunctions and other interim measures in connection with cases from Hong Kong.[61] A party may, in the course of Hong Kong arbitral proceedings, apply to a relevant Intermediate People's Court for the grant of interim measures.[62] Similarly, a party to arbitral proceedings in Mainland China can apply for the grant of an interim measure by the Court of First Instance of the Hong Kong High Court. This presents a significant commercial advantage for Hong Kong as a seat of arbitration. Prior to the Arrangement, parties which are seeking (i) recognition and enforcement of interim measures granted by foreign courts (including Mainland courts) and/or (ii) interim measures ordered by local courts over an arbitration commenced in foreign jurisdictions (including Mainland China) had to rely on local legislations. While sections 45 and 60 of the AO in Hong Kong provide for similar mechanisms, the laws in Mainland China do not have equivalent counterparts.

[56] ibid Art 3.

[57] *Choi Hon Cheung v Chan Chong Man* [2024] HKCFI 538 [114]–[117].

[58] *Ethiopian Airlines v Jietong Overseas Trade Co Ltd* [2023] HKCFI 1896 [15(6)].

[59] Arrangement on Reciprocal Recognition and Enforcement of Judgments in Civil and Commercial Matters (n 55), Art 10.

[60] Arrangement Concerning Mutual Assistance in Court-ordered Interim Measures in Aid of Arbitral Proceedings by the Courts of the Mainland and of the Hong Kong Special Administrative Region, Fa Shi [2019] No 14, www.doj.gov.hk/en/mainland_and_macao/arrangements_with_the_mainland.html. See also Fa [2019] No 207.

[61] ibid Art 1.

[62] ibid Art 3.

The Arrangement greatly facilitated the recognition and enforcement of court-ordered interim measures across the border. There were 139 applications to the HKIAC within the Arrangement's first five years of operation, with the Mainland courts granting preservation of assets in 91 out of the 96 known decisions, amounting to assets valued at RMB 21.3 billion.[63]

I. Record of Meeting on Mutual Recognition of and Assistance to Bankruptcy (Insolvency) Proceedings

The Record of Meeting was signed between the Supreme People's Court and the HKSAR Government on 14 May 2021.[64] It establishes a framework for cooperation between the Hong Kong courts and the Mainland courts in corporate insolvency and debt restructuring matters. In particular, a Hong Kong liquidator may apply to the Intermediate People's Court in Shanghai, Xiamen or Shenzhen for the recognition of insolvency and debt restructuring proceedings in Hong Kong. Conversely, a bankruptcy administrator in Mainland China may apply to the Court of First Instance of the Hong Kong High Court for the recognition of Mainland bankruptcy proceedings. For a detailed discussion of the cooperation mechanism's operation, see chapter twenty, section III.B.

II. Macao SAR

Currently, Hong Kong and Macao have two arrangements related to private international law as summarised in this section.

A. Arrangement Concerning Reciprocal Recognition and Enforcement of Arbitral Awards

The Arrangement was signed on 7 January 2013.[65] It is implemented in Hong Kong by Part 10, Division 4 (sections 98A–98D) of the AO. It provides for the reciprocal recognition and enforcement of arbitral awards between Hong Kong and Macao. A prerequisite for enforcement under the Arrangement is that it must be shown that enforcement in only one jurisdiction will be insufficient to satisfy the award.[66]

[63] See HKIAC, 'Interim Measures Arrangement', www.hkiac.org/arbitration/arrangement-interim-measures.

[64] Record of Meeting of the Supreme People's Court and the Government of the Hong Kong Special Administrative Region on Mutual Recognition of and Assistance to Bankruptcy (Insolvency) Proceedings between the Courts of the Mainland and of the Hong Kong Special Administrative Region, www.doj.gov.hk/en/mainland_and_macao/arrangements_with_the_mainland.html.

[65] Arrangement Concerning Reciprocal Recognition and Enforcement of Arbitral Awards between the Hong Kong Special Administrative Region and the Macao Special Administrative Region, www.doj.gov.hk/en/mainland_and_macao/arrangements_with_the_macao_sar.html.

[66] ibid Art 3.

B. Arrangement for Mutual Service of Judicial Documents in Civil and Commercial Cases

The Arrangement was signed on 5 December 2017.[67] It was incorporated into Order 11, rule 5A of the RHC on 1 August 2020. Requests are routed between the High Court in Hong Kong and the Court of Final Appeal in Macao. The Court of First Instance in Macao is responsible for executing requests to serve judicial documents in Macao.[68]

III. Taiwan

Hong Kong has not entered into any arrangements with Taiwan on private international law issues. The PRC's Provisions of the Supreme People's Court on Recognition and Enforcement of the Civil Judgments of Courts of the Taiwan Region do not apply to Hong Kong.[69] Common law rules should therefore apply if such issues arise.

In *Chen Li Hung v Ting Lei Miao*, the Hong Kong Court of Final Appeal recognised the judgment of the Taiwanese court. This case concerns the validity of Taiwan's delegation of trustees-in-bankruptcy, and the argument focused on whether a Taiwanese bankruptcy order should be recognised and given effect in Hong Kong, as Taiwan is 'part of and under the de jure sovereignty of [the PRC] but is in de facto albeit unlawful control of a usurper government'.[70] Bokhary PJ held:

> 37. In certain circumstances our courts will give effect to the orders of non-recognized courts. By the expression 'non-recognized courts' I mean to cover courts sitting in foreign states the governments of which our sovereign does not recognize as well as courts sitting in territory under the *de jure* sovereignty of our sovereign but presently under the *de facto* albeit unlawful control of a usurper government. Our courts will give effect to the orders of non-recognized courts where:
>
> (i) the rights covered by those orders are private rights;
> (ii) giving effect to such orders accords with the interests of justice, the dictates of common sense and the needs of law and order; and
> (iii) giving them effect would not be inimical to the sovereign's interests or otherwise contrary to public policy.
>
> That is the principle; and none of it involves recognizing any unrecognised entity. It goes purely and simply to protecting private rights.

It is therefore feasible to enforce judgments and orders of Taiwan courts in Hong Kong. For example, a Taiwanese monetary judgment will be treated by the Hong Kong courts in the same manner as a judgment obtained in a foreign jurisdiction. It was even suggested

[67] Arrangement for Mutual Service of Judicial Documents in Civil and Commercial Cases between the Hong Kong Special Administrative Region and the Macao Special Administrative Region, www.doj.gov.hk/en/mainland_and_macao/arrangements_with_the_macao_sar.html.

[68] ibid Art 3.

[69] Fa Shi [2015] No 13. However, the Hong Kong Court of Appeal suggested that the Provisions expressed an implied mandate to recognise Taiwanese judgments and orders giving effect to private rights: *Cef New Asia Co Ltd v Wong Kwong Yiu* [1999] 3 HKC 1 [13].

[70] *Chen Li Hung v Tin Lei Miao* (2000) 3 HKCFAR 9 [3], [37].

in an early Hong Kong judgment that the PRC Provisions (although not applicable to Hong Kong) impose an implied mandate on the Hong Kong courts to enforce Taiwanese judgments.[71]

In Taiwan, the private international law rules applicable to civil cases involving Hong Kong or Macao are the same as other foreign civil law cases. Article 38 of Taiwan's Act Governing Relations with Hong Kong and Macau states that:

> The Law Governing the Choice of Law in Civil Cases Involving Foreign Elements shall apply *mutatis mutandis* to civil cases involving Hong Kong or Macau. For cases not provided for in the Law Governing the Choice of Law in Civil Cases Involving Foreign Elements, laws of the locality having the most significant contact with said civil cases shall apply.

Article 42(1) of the same Act provides for recognition and enforcement of Hong Kong and Macao judgments:

> In determining the conditions for the validity, jurisdiction, and enforceability of civil judgments made in Hong Kong or Macau, Article 402 of the Code of Civil Procedure and Article 4, Paragraph 1 of the [Compulsory Enforcement Act] shall apply *mutatis mutandis*.

Thus, a Hong Kong judgment may generally be recognised and enforced in Taiwan, except in the following circumstances:

(i) where the Hong Kong courts lack jurisdiction under the laws of Taiwan;[72]
(ii) where the Hong Kong judgment is a default judgment, unless reasonable notice of the proceedings was given to the defaulting party;[73]
(iii) where the performance of the judgment will be contrary to the public policy or morals of Taiwan;[74] or
(iv) where there exists no mutual recognition between Hong Kong and Taiwan.[75] But this ground has been rendered irrelevant as a result of the recognition and enforcement of Taiwan judgments by the Hong Kong courts.[76]

A Taiwanese arbitral award is not a New York Convention award in the eyes of Hong Kong courts. It is recognised and enforced in Hong Kong pursuant to Part 10, Division 1 (sections 84–86) of the AO.[77] A Hong Kong arbitral award is recognised and enforced in Taiwan by applying Articles 37–43 of Taiwan's Arbitration Act.[78]

Mutual judicial assistance between Taiwan and Hong Kong is to be conducted on a reciprocal basis.[79]

[71] *Cef New Asia Co Ltd* (n 69) [5]–[15].
[72] Code of Civil Procedure (Taiwan), Art 402(1).
[73] ibid Art 402(2).
[74] ibid Art 402(3).
[75] ibid Art 402(4).
[76] *Chen Li Hung* (n 70).
[77] See, eg *X v Y* [2021] 2 HKC 68, [2020] HKCFI 2782.
[78] Act Governing Relations with Hong Kong and Macau (Taiwan), Art 42(2).
[79] ibid Art 56.

26

Hong Kong and International Organisations

I. Introduction

The development of private international law in Hong Kong can be attributed to an extent to the active participation of Hong Kong in international organisations. Article 152 of the Basic Law provides that:

> Representatives of the Government of the Hong Kong Special Administrative Region may, as members of delegations of the People's Republic of China, participate in international organizations or conferences in appropriate fields limited to states and affecting the Region, or may attend in such other capacity as may be permitted by the Central People's Government and the international organization or conference concerned, and may express their views, using the name 'Hong Kong, China'.
>
> The Hong Kong Special Administrative Region may, using the name 'Hong Kong, China', participate in international organizations and conferences not limited to states.
>
> The Central People's Government shall take the necessary steps to ensure that the Hong Kong Special Administrative Region shall continue to retain its status in an appropriate capacity in those international organizations of which the People's Republic of China is a member and in which Hong Kong participates in one capacity or another.
>
> The Central People's Government shall, where necessary, facilitate the continued participation of the Hong Kong Special Administrative Region in an appropriate capacity in those international organizations in which Hong Kong is a participant in one capacity or another, but of which the People's Republic of China is not a member.

Article 152 thus refers to international organisations, the membership of which is limited to states and in which the PRC is a member. In these organisations, representatives of Hong Kong may participate as part of China's delegation using the name 'Hong Kong, China'. The Hague Conference on Private International Law (HCCH) is one such international organisation.[1] The World Trade Organization (WTO) is another example. Hong Kong has been a WTO member since 1 January 1995, before China became a member on 11 December 2001.[2]

The Department of Justice attaches great importance to cooperation with international organisations. Department of Justice officers and occasionally Hong Kong lawyers are able to take part in secondment programmes with the HCCH, the United Nations Commission on International Trade Law (UNCITRAL) and the International Institute for the Unification

[1] For a full list of the international organisations of which membership is limited to states and in which Hong Kong participates, see www.cmab.gov.hk/en/issues/external1.htm.

[2] For a full list of such international organisations of which membership is not limited to states and in which Hong Kong participates, see www.cmab.gov.hk/en/issues/external2.htm.

of Private Law (UNIDROIT).[3] This enables the officers and lawyers to enhance their knowledge and experience of international legal matters and thereby strengthen Hong Kong's capacity in foreign-related legal affairs. To foster closer connection with international organisations overseas, the Secretary for Justice often travels abroad to meet with these organisations.[4] The Secretary is a regular attendee and speaker at private international law conferences initiated by the international organisations.[5] The Department of Justice in turn organises conferences and training programmes in Hong Kong with a view to promoting the region as an international law dispute resolution hub.[6] Examples of Hong Kong initiatives include: the biennial UNCITRAL Asia Pacific Judicial Summit, held since 2015; the Investor–State Dispute Settlement (ISDS) Reform Conference, held in 2019; and the annual China–AALCO Exchange and Research Program on International Law.[7] The Department of Justice also hosts working group sessions of international organisations. For instance, the Informal Working Group II (on Common Courts) and Informal Working Group IV (on Declarations with Respect to Judgments Pertaining to Governments) held their meetings in February 2019. These meetings ultimately contributed to the promulgation of the 2019 HCCH Convention on the Recognition and Enforcement of Foreign Judgments in Civil or Commercial Matters.[8]

The Central People's Government, in consultation with the Hong Kong government, has also entered into arrangements for regional offices of international and intergovernmental organisations to be based in Hong Kong.[9] The Central People's Government currently has agreements with the Commission of the European Communities, the Bank for International Settlements, the International Monetary Fund, the International Bank for Reconstruction and Development, the International Finance Corporation, the Hague Conference on Private International Law and the Permanent Court of Arbitration. The Department of Justice and UNIDROIT are currently exploring the possibility of a liaison office in Hong Kong.[10]

[3] Department of Justice, 'Speech by SJ at The Hague Academy of International Law's Advanced Course in Hong Kong – 1st Edition' (11 December 2023), www.doj.gov.hk/en/community_engagement/speeches/20231211_sj1.html.

[4] See, eg Legislative Council Panel on Administration of Justice and Legal Services, 'Updates on Cooperation with International Legal and Dispute Resolution Bodies and Attracting Their Presence or Carrying Out of Activities in Hong Kong: International Bodies and Organisations other than the International Organization for Mediation (IOMed)' (LC Paper No CB(4)334/2024(05), March 2024), www.legco.gov.hk/yr2024/english/panels/ajls/papers/ajls202400325cb4-334-5-e.pdf.

[5] See, eg the DSJ's visit to Europe to meet with the International Institute for the Unification of Private Law, the Hague Conference on Private International Law and the United Nations Commission on International Trade Law: Department of Justice, 'DSJ to Visit Europe' (3 March 2023), www.doj.gov.hk/en/community_engagement/press/pdf/pr20230303e1.pdf; Department of Justice, 'Speech by DSJ at the UNIDROIT Conference on Promoting Cross-Border Investment through Transnational Legal Standards in Rome' (7 March 2023), www.doj.gov.hk/en/community_engagement/speeches/20230307_sj1.html.

[6] James Ding, 'Introduction to the Work of the IDAR Office' (3 May 2019), www.doj.gov.hk/en/community_engagement/speeches/pdf/lo20190503e1.pdf, slides 4–5.

[7] Legislative Council Panel on Administration of Justice and Legal Services (n 4) para 17.

[8] Legislative Council Panel on Administration of Justice and Legal Services, '2019 Policy Initiatives of the Department of Justice' (LC Paper No CB(4)318/19-20(02), February 2020), www.doj.gov.hk/en/legco/pdf/ajls20200224e1.pdf, para 7.

[9] Department of Justice, 'Establishment of Offices or Operation of International Intergovernmental Organisations in Hong Kong', www.doj.gov.hk/en/external/establishment_of_offices_or_operation_of_international_intergovernmental_organisations_in_hong_kong.html.

[10] Legislative Council Panel on Administration of Justice and Legal Services (n 4) para 7.

Sections II and III will focus on Hong Kong's participation in various international organisations with relevance to private international law.

II. The HCCH and its Conventions

Of great importance is the HCCH, an international organisation which was established in 1893 and which acquired legal personality under a statute of 1955. The HCCH works for the progressive unification of the rules of private international law.[11] It has adopted over 40 conventions and one soft law instrument.[12] The HCCH has a Council on General Affairs and Policy, a Council of Diplomatic Representatives and a Permanent Bureau based in the Hague which serves as the HCCH's Secretariat. HCCH member states negotiate and adopt conventions and other instruments. Special Commissions, working groups and experts meet regularly to advise on, draft, review or update HCCH instruments. The main areas of the HCCH's work are: (i) international family and child protection; (ii) transnational litigation and legal cooperation; and (iii) international commercial and financial law.

The HCCH has set up regional offices to promote greater awareness of its work and its conventions and instruments, to assist countries to become members and to provide technical assistance in the implementation and operation of its conventions and instruments. There are currently two HCCH regional offices. There is the Regional Office for Latin America and the Caribbean, set up in Buenos Aires in 2005, and the Regional Office for Asia and the Pacific (ROAP), set up in Hong Kong in 2012. The Hong Kong Department of Justice collaborates with the HCCH on holding an annual Asia-Pacific Week event to enhance ROAP's presence.

Several HCCH Conventions apply to Hong Kong. Hong Kong, as a special administrative region, is not a sovereign state and therefore cannot sign, ratify or accede to conventions. But Article 153 of the Basic Law provides:

> The application to the Hong Kong Special Administrative Region of international agreements to which the People's Republic of China is or becomes a party shall be decided by the Central People's Government, in accordance with the circumstances and needs of the Region, and after seeking the views of the government of the Region.
>
> International agreements to which the People's Republic of China is not a party but which are implemented in Hong Kong may continue to be implemented in the Hong Kong Special Administrative Region. The Central People's Government shall, as necessary, authorize or assist the government of the Region to make appropriate arrangements for the application to the Region of other relevant international agreements.

Some HCCH Conventions apply to Hong Kong as a result of them having been extended to Hong Kong by a UK Order-in-Council. The PRC made declarations to the HCCH that those Conventions would continue to apply in Hong Kong after the handover of Hong Kong on 1 July 1997, even if some of them do not apply in the rest of China. Similarly, some HCCH Conventions continue to apply to Macao by way of a declaration from the PRC after the handover of Macao on 20 December 1999. Currently, the following HCCH Conventions

[11] Statute of the Hague Conference on Private International Law, Art 1.

[12] For the current status chart of signatures, ratifications and accessions to the HCCH Conventions, see https://www.hcch.net/en/instruments/status-charts.

apply to Mainland China, Hong Kong and Macao: (i) Hague Service Convention; (ii) Hague Evidence Convention; (iii) Hague Adoption Convention; and (iv) Hague Apostille Convention. The following HCCH Conventions apply to Hong Kong only: (i) Hague Form of Wills Convention; (ii) Hague Divorce Convention; and (iii) Hague Trusts Convention. The following HCCH Conventions apply to Macao only: (i) Hague Civil Procedure Convention; (ii) Hague Protection of Minors Convention; (iii) Hague Maintenance Convention;[13] and (iv) Hague Child Protection Convention. The Hague Child Abduction Convention applies to Hong Kong and Macao only.

The subsections below briefly describe the HCCH Conventions that apply to Hong Kong.

A. Hague Form of Wills Convention

The 1961 HCCH Convention on the Conflicts of Laws Relating to the Form of Testamentary Dispositions currently has 42 contracting states. The PRC is not a party. The instrument designates the law governing the form of testamentary dispositions. The Convention has been implemented in Hong Kong by sections 24–29 of the Wills Ordinance (Cap 30) in Hong Kong. See chapter seventeen, section VII.A.

B. Hague Apostille Convention

The 1961 HCCH Convention Abolishing the Requirement of Legalisation for Foreign Public Documents facilitates the use of public documents abroad by abolishing traditional requirements of legalisation. It does this by replacing the legalisation process with the issuance of a single apostille by a competent authority in the place where a document originates. The PRC is a party. In 2006, the electronic Apostille Programme (e-APP) was launched by the HCCH. The programme consists of two parts: an e-Register for the verification of apostilles and the e-Apostille for issuance in lieu of paper apostilles. Hong Kong has implemented the former, but not the latter. Apostilles issued on or after 1 September 2014 can be verified online via the judiciary's website.[14] Apostilles issued before that date have to be verified by applying in writing to the Apostille Service Office of the High Court Registry.

C. Hague Service Convention

The 1965 HCCH Convention on the Service Abroad of Judicial and Extrajudicial Documents in Civil or Commercial Matters currently has 79 contracting states. The PRC is a party. It provides channels for the transmission of judicial documents from one contracting state to another for service in the latter. The main channel of transmission is the designated central authority in each contracting state. Statistical data suggests that 75 per cent of service requests are executed within two months. The Convention has been implemented

[13] The Maintenance Orders (Reciprocal Enforcement) Ordinance (Cap 188) (MOREO) in Hong Kong implements the framework of the Hague Maintenance Convention to facilitate the recovery of maintenance by enforcing foreign maintenance orders from a limited number of reciprocating countries. See ch 23, s VI.D.

[14] See https://e-services.judiciary.hk/apoereg/.

by Orders 11 and 69 of the Rules of the High Court (Cap 4A) (RHC). See chapter nine, sections VII and VIII.

D. Hague Divorce Convention

The 1970 HCCH Convention on the Recognition of Divorces and Legal Separations currently has 20 contracting states. It applies to Hong Kong, but the PRC is not a party. The Convention aims to facilitate the recognition in one contracting state of divorces and legal separations obtained in another. It assures divorced and separated spouses that their new status will receive the same recognition abroad as in the country where the divorce or separation is obtained. This has been implemented by Part IX (sections 55–62) of the Matrimonial Causes Ordinance (Cap 179) in Hong Kong. See chapter twenty-three, section VI.B.

E. Hague Evidence Convention

The 1970 HCCH Convention on the Taking of Evidence Abroad in Civil or Commercial Matters currently has 64 contracting states. The PRC is a party. The Convention establishes two modes of cooperation between states parties for the taking of evidence abroad in civil or commercial matters. It provides for the taking of evidence in cross-border circumstances via (i) letters of request and (ii) diplomatic or consular agents and commissioners. Letters of Request are sent by the judicial authority of one state to the central authority of another state. The central authority for Hong Kong is the Chief Secretary for Administration. The Convention has been implemented by section 75 of the Evidence Ordinance (Cap 8) and Order 70 of the RHC. See chapter seven, section III.

F. Hague Child Abduction Convention

The 1980 HCCH Convention on the Civil Aspects of International Child Abduction has 103 contracting states. It applies to Hong Kong and Macao, but the PRC is not a party.[15] It protects children from wrongful removal or retention across international boundaries by providing a procedure for promptly returning a child to his or her habitual residence immediately before abduction. The Convention has been implemented in Hong Kong through the Child Abduction and Custody Ordinance (Cap 512) in Hong Kong. See chapter nineteen, section III.G.

G. Hague Trusts Convention

The 1985 HCCH Convention on the Law Applicable to Trusts and on Their Recognition current has 14 contracting states. It applies to Hong Kong, but the PRC is not a party.

[15] However, it is not possible to effect the Convention between Hong Kong and Macao as the Convention only applies between contracting states.

It specifies the law applicable to trusts and governs the recognition of trusts. This has been implemented by the Recognition of Trusts Ordinance (Cap 76) in Hong Kong. See chapter sixteen, section II.

H. Hague Adoption Convention

The 1993 HCCH Convention on the Protection of Children and Co-operation in Respect of Intercountry Adoption currently has 106 contracting states. The PRC is a party. The Convention protects children and their families against the risks of illegal, irregular, premature or ill-prepared adoptions abroad. It ensures that intercountry adoptions are made in the best interests of a child and with respect for his or her fundamental rights. The Convention has been implemented in Hong Kong by the Adoption Ordinance (Cap 290). See chapter nineteen, section III.E.

I. Hague Choice of Court Convention and Hague Judgments Convention

The PRC has signed, but not yet ratified, the 2005 HCCH Convention on Choice of Court Agreements. When signing the Convention, the PRC did not make any reservation in relation to Hong Kong. Thus, once the PRC ratifies the Convention, it will also come into effect in Hong Kong. The PRC has not yet considered the 2019 HCCH Convention on the Recognition and Enforcement of Foreign Judgments in Civil or Commercial Matters in detail.

As noted in chapter twenty-three, the Mainland Judgments (Reciprocal Enforcement) Ordinance (Cap 597) and the Mainland Judgments in Civil and Commercial Matters (Reciprocal Enforcement) Ordinance (Cap 645) are modelled on the Hague Choice of Court Convention and the 2018 Draft of the Hague Judgments Convention respectively. Thus, the spirit of the two Conventions has been largely implemented across the borders of Mainland China and Hong Kong, despite them not formally being in operation in either jurisdiction.

III. Other International Organisations

Other international organisations whose work touches on private international law are UNCITRAL, UNIDROIT and the United Nations Conference on Trade and Development (UNCTAD). Unlike the HCCH, which seeks to unify or harmonise the rules of private international law, UNCITRAL and UNIDROIT are more ambitious in seeking to unify or harmonise the substantive law of different jurisdictions. China has been a member of UNCITRAL since 1983 and of UNIDROIT since 1986.

One of the most successful UNCITRAL instruments is the 1958 Convention on the Recognition and Enforcement of Foreign Arbitral Awards (the New York Convention). China is a party to the Convention. Hong Kong has specific provisions in Part 10, Division 2 (sections 87–91) of the Arbitration Ordinance (Cap 609) to deal with the recognition and enforcement of foreign arbitral awards. See chapter twenty-four, section VI.

Other UNCITRAL conventions and soft law instruments have also been well received in Hong Kong. The 1980 United Nations Convention for the International Sale of Goods has been adopted in Hong Kong through the Sale of Goods (United Nations Convention) Ordinance (Cap 641), which came into effect on 1 December 2022. See chapter fifteen, section II.J. The UNCITRAL Model Law on International Commercial Arbitration (1985, with amendments in 2006) has been adapted and incorporated in the Arbitration Ordinance (Cap 609). See chapter twenty-four.[16] Hong Kong has not adopted the UNCITRAL Model Law on Cross-Border Insolvency (1997) in its legislation, but has broadly followed its principles. See chapter twenty, sections II.A and III. The government had indicated some willingness to consider domestic legislation on cross-border insolvency based on the Model Law in 2018.[17] When this happens, regard may also be given to the UNCITRAL Model Law on Recognition and Enforcement of Insolvency-Related Judgments (2018).

Another notable instrument of UNCITRAL is the 2018 United Nations Convention on International Settlement Agreements Resulting from Mediation (the Singapore Convention on Mediation), which provides for the recognition and enforcement of international mediation settlement agreements across borders. Articles 3 and 4 provide the principle and method where an international mediation settlement agreement may be enforceable across convention states. Article 5 states the grounds where relief may be refused. Article 7 preserves the parties' rights under local laws and treaties. China signed the Singapore Convention on 7 August 2019, without any reservations made under Article 8. The Convention has not been implemented in China or Hong Kong to date, but is likely to be in the future, given the Hong Kong government's active promotion of mediation as means of resolving dispute, including the setting up of the headquarters of the International Organization for Mediation in Hong Kong in 2025.

UNIDROIT offers a platform for modernising, harmonising and coordinating private law (including commercial law) among states. It principally does this by formulating uniform law instruments, principles and rules on a variety of civil and commercial law matters. Hong Kong and UNIDROIT signed a memorandum of understanding in respect of cooperation on international private law matters, with special regard to international commercial law.[18] It is expected that Hong Kong and UNIDROIT will continue to collaborate on the development and promotion of transnational private law in the Asia-Pacific region through the organisation of conferences and other initiatives.

[16] For a detailed illustration on the adaptation of the UNCITRAL Model Law in Hong Kong, see Samuel Wong, CK Kwong and Wilson Lui, *Hong Kong Arbitration Judgments and Commentaries: Applications of the UNCITRAL Model Law and the Provisions of the Hong Kong Arbitration Ordinance (Cap 609)* (Hong Kong Institute of Arbitrators, 2023); Samuel Wong and Wilson Lui, *Hong Kong Arbitration Ordinance (Cap 609): A Guide and Commentary*, 2nd edn (Authors, 2024).

[17] Standing Committee on Company Law Reform, *The Thirty-fourth Annual Report* (February 2019) para 12, www.fstb.gov.hk/fsb/co_rewrite/eng/pub-press/doc/SCCLR_ar_2017-2018_e.pdf.

[18] UNIDROIT, 'UNIDROIT and Hong Kong Sign Cooperation MOU' (28 June 2022), www.unidroit.org/unidroit-and-hong-kong-sign-cooperation-mou/.

27

The Future of Private International Law in Hong Kong

What is the potential for the development of private international law in Hong Kong?

Hong Kong's private international law rules are not easy to determine and this book has only attempted a concise summary. The rules are derived from an amalgam of the English common law, domestic ordinances and international conventions. Hong Kong being a small jurisdiction, almost every civil or commercial case potentially involves cross-border issues. Its lawyers have therefore developed a body of experience in the handling of cases involving private international law issues, even though the study of conflict of laws is not a mandatory subject in Hong Kong's law schools. Nonetheless, the Hong Kong courts' approach to private international law questions has understandably been conservative. This means that, in the absence of statute, the court will look to English common law for guidance. But what case law will that be? Before the UK joined the EU, its private international law and that of Hong Kong were closely aligned. Thereafter, private international law in the UK increasingly reflected EU regulations and practice. Not being part of the EU, Hong Kong's jurisprudence on private international law did not follow suit. It did not keep abreast of modern codifications of private international law adopted in the EU (such as the Brussels I (Recast) and the Rome I and II Regulations) and, through the EU, in the UK. Instead, common law principles on conflict of laws applied in Hong Kong remained as they were prior to the UK's joining the EU. The return of sovereignty over Hong Kong to the PRC on 1 July 1997 did not change that. The private international law of Hong Kong has been frozen in time, so that the eleventh edition (1987) of *Dicey, Morris and Collins on the Conflict of Laws* (then known as *Dicey and Morris on the Conflict of Laws*) is often regarded by practitioners as more relevant to Hong Kong than the current sixteenth edition (2022).[1]

Throughout this book, a deliberate attempt has been made to stress Hong Kong rather than English cases. The difficulty is that Hong Kong case law, by comparison with English case law, is small. However, the divergence described in the previous paragraph has the consequence that English case law today may not be so relevant to Hong Kong. One cannot turn back the clock. EU regulations have so influenced the development of case law in private international law in the UK[2] that one cannot automatically adopt post-Brexit English case

[1] Lawrence Collins (gen ed), *Dicey and Morris on the Conflict of Laws*, 11th edn (Stevens & Sons Ltd, 1987); Lord Collins of Mapesbury and Jonathan Harris (gen eds), *Dicey, Morris and Collins on the Conflict of Laws*, 16th edn (Sweet & Maxwell, 2022).

[2] For the current English position, see, eg *Dicey, Morris and Collins* (n 1); Adrian Briggs, *Private International Law in English Courts*, 2nd edn (Oxford University Press, 2023); Adrian Briggs, *The Conflict of Laws*, 5th edn (Oxford University Press, 2024).

precedents as guidance for Hong Kong. Analysis of the development of a present-day private international law rule in England will be required to assess whether it is suitable for Hong Kong. But why stop there? Why merely look at English case law now? It is submitted that Hong Kong judges should not confine themselves to English jurisprudence whether before the UK's accession to the EU or post-Brexit. Hong Kong judges should also proactively (i) consider international conventions and soft law instruments with a view to harmonising Hong Kong and modern international practice and (ii) adopt a comparative law perspective especially in relation to civil law jurisdictions. Hong Kong judges should not shy away from delving into normative arguments and justifications for different approaches in private international law before reaching a conclusion on the appropriate rule to apply.

On inter-regional issues, it is evident that the system of private international law between Hong Kong and other parts of the PRC will continue to thrive. Hong Kong practises the common law system, while the rest of the PRC adheres to the civil law system. This suggests that the courts must be sensitive to the ways in which Hong Kong interacts and reacts with Mainland China and Macao. Hong Kong judges should not merely take a narrow common law stance. The courts should be open to influence by civil law approaches, especially as manifested in Mainland China's jurisprudence.

It can be anticipated that in the future more frameworks will be devised between Hong Kong and Mainland China, especially within the Guangdong–Hong Kong–Macao Greater Bay Region of the Pearl River Delta.[3] For example, the Second Agreement Concerning Amendment to the Agreement on Trade in Services of the Mainland and Hong Kong Closer Economic Partnership Arrangement (CEPA) to be implemented on 1 March 2025 allows Hong Kong-invested enterprises registered in the Greater Bay Area to adopt Hong Kong law as the applicable law in contracts and to choose Hong Kong as the seat of arbitration, both of which were previously impossible under PRC law unless the contract has a 'foreign-related' element. These frameworks are to be welcomed as they will facilitate the development of cross-border law and practice in Hong Kong and Mainland China. The frameworks can also serve as templates or models for other jurisdictions (particularly Asian jurisdictions). Even if the inter-regional cooperation frameworks cannot be adopted as a whole, the mechanisms and texts developed, insofar as private international law is concerned, may be instructive to systems of law wishing to cooperate with other systems of a different legal tradition.[4]

A closer examination of common law principles in private international law suggests that they are not significantly different from principles in civil law systems. In other words, the gap between the common law and the civil law can be bridged and Hong Kong can contribute to this convergence. With the greater maturity of private international law as an academic subject and the continuous development of globalisation, the dialogue between the two legal systems (as manifested especially in the work of the Hague Conference on Private International Law) has made it possible for jurisdictions to learn from each other regarding the mechanisms and techniques of private international law. An Asian example is

[3] See, eg Department of Justice, 'The Department of Justice Action Plan on the Construction of Rule of Law in the Guangdong–Hong Kong–Macao Greater Bay Area: Three Interfaces, Two Connects and One GBA' (12 April 2024), www.doj.gov.hk/en/publications/pdf/gba_action_plan_en.pdf.

[4] Wilson Lui, 'Asian Private International Law and Hong Kong' (2024) 12 *Korean Journal of International and Comparative Law* 73.

the departure from the requirement of de facto to de jure or even presumptive reciprocity evidenced by recent court judgments in common law and civil law states and in the Nanning Declaration in 2017 at the 2nd China–ASEAN Justice Forum.[5] Transnational dispute resolution is likely to be buffeted in the near future by the winds of anti-globalism and trade protection.[6] But that does not detract from the importance and frequency of understanding and cooperation among common law and civil law jurisdictions. Through the Hague Conference's Regional Office for the Asia Pacific, Hong Kong is well positioned to play a significant role in this endeavour.

There have been initiatives from jurisdictions to codify private international law rules in comprehensive statutes or codes. China has implemented a law on choice of law in foreign-related civil relationships and supplemented by Supreme People's Court judicial interpretations.[7] South Korea more recently passed a new Private International Law Act in 2022. Switzerland, by its Federal Act on Private International Law (most recently revised on 1 January 2025), is known to have the most complete codification of private international law in the world. The USA is currently preparing the Restatement (Third) of Conflict of Laws. There does not seem to be any impetus in Hong Kong to codify its private international law rules. That will not be an easy task, given the range of subjects and issues that a code will have to cover. Hong Kong probably has more pressing objectives at the level of policy formulation and law reform. On this front, it is likely that for the foreseeable future, Hong Kong will adopt a scattered approach of developing the law in unsystematic fashion through judicial decisions, statutes and the implementation of international conventions. That does not mean Hong Kong should shy away from pushing for reform. We suggest, among the many issues raised in this book, that the double actionability rule is urgently in need of reconsideration, and that might be a first task.

As envisaged in chapter one, the plurality and interactions of Asian legal systems is a multi-dimensional vector space that can generate pragmatic responses to pressing real-world cross-border problems. Private international law in Hong Kong, with its common law origins and interactions with civil law systems such as that of Mainland China, can contribute towards the harmonisation of private international law principles in Asia and elsewhere. But Hong Kong must be bold and grasp the nettle.

[5] https://cicc.court.gov.cn/html/1/219/208/209/800.html. The concept of presumptive reciprocity is applied in China for the recognition and enforcement of a Thai monetary judgment in *Guangxi Nanning China Travel Service Ltd v Orient Thai Airlines Co Ltd* (2023) Gui 71 Xie Wai Ren No 1.

[6] See, eg Sundaresh Menon and Anselmo Reyes (eds), *Transnational Commercial Disputes in an Age of Anti-globalism and Pandemic* (Hart Publishing, 2022).

[7] Law of the People's Republic of China on Choice of Law for Foreign-related Civil Relationships; Interpretation of the Supreme People's Court on Several Issues Concerning Application of the Law of the People's Republic of China on Choice of Law for Foreign-related Civil Relationships (I) (2020 Amendment), Fa Shi [2020] No 18; Interpretation of the Supreme People's Court on Several Issues Concerning Application of the Law of the People's Republic of China on Choice of Law for Foreign-related Civil Relationships (II), Fa Shi [2023] No 12.

GLOSSARY

This glossary includes terms that are of relevance to Hong Kong private international law. For a general glossary of legal terms in Hong Kong, see www.glossary.doj.gov.hk.

Absolute immunity	絕對豁免
Abuse of process	濫用司法程序
Acknowledgment of service	送達認收書
Act of state	國家行為
Actionability	可訴性
Admissibility	可接納性
Ancillary orders	附屬命令
Annulment	宣布無效
Anti-anti-suit injunction	反禁訴令
Anti-arbitration injunction	禁止仲裁令
Anti-enforcement injunction	禁止執行令
Anti-suit injunction	禁訴令
Apostille	文件加簽
Applicable law	適用法律
Appropriate forum	合適法院
Arbitrability	可仲裁性
Arbitral award	仲裁裁決
Arbitration	仲裁
Arbitration clause	仲裁條款
Asymmetric jurisdiction clause	非對稱管轄權條款
Bad faith (*mala fide*)	惡意
Bankruptcy	破產
Burden of proof	舉證責任
Carriage of goods	貨物運輸

Capacity	能力 / 行為能力
Case management power	案件管理權
Cause of action estoppel	已決訴訟因由不得重提
Centre of main interests	主要利益中心
Characterisation	識別
Chattel	實產
Child abduction	擄拐兒童
Choice of court agreement	選用法院協議
Choice of law	法律選擇 / 法律適用
Clearly or distinctly more appropriate	顯然或明顯更合適
Closest and most real connection	最密切聯繫
Civil law	大陸法
Civil matters	民事
Civil and commercial judgments	民商事判決
Comity	禮讓 / 國際禮讓
Commercial matters	商事
Common law	普通法
Concurrent proceedings	同時進行的程序 / 平行訴訟
Conflict of laws	衝突法
Connecting factors	連結因素
Consular immunity	領事豁免
Cross-border insolvency	跨國破產
Curial law	仲裁程序法
Decline jurisdiction	拒絕行使司法管轄權
Default rule (foreign law same as *lex fori*)	外國法與訴訟地法相同假定
dépeçage	分割
Diplomatic immunity	外交豁免
Discretion	酌情權
Domicile	居籍
Domicile of choice	自選居籍

Domicile of dependency	倚附居籍
Domicile of origin	原生居籍
Double actionability rule	雙重可訴規則
Dual domicile rule	雙重居籍規則
Enforcement	執行
Equity	衡平法
Essential validity	要素有效性
Estoppel	不容反悔原則
Exclusive jurisdiction clause	專有司法管轄權條款
Exemption clauses	免責條款
Exercise of jurisdiction	行使司法管轄權
Existence of jurisdiction	存在司法管轄權
Exorbitant jurisdiction	過度管轄權
Expediency / Inexpediency	便利 / 不便
Express choice of law clause	明訂法律選擇條款
Expropriation	徵用 / 沒收
Extraterritorial jurisdiction	域外司法管轄權
Extraterritoriality	治外法權 / 域外法律效力
Final and conclusive	最終及不可推翻的
Floating choice of law clause	浮動法律選擇條款
Foreign arbitral award	外國仲裁裁決
Foreign creditor	外地債權人
Foreign illegality	外地非法行爲
Foreign law	外地法
Foreign judgment	外地判決
Foreign maintenance orders	外地贍養令
Forum	法院 / 訴訟地
forum conveniens	方便審理的法院
forum non conveniens	不便審理的法院 / 不方便法院 / 非便利公堂

Forum shopping	擇地行訴
Fraud	欺詐
Freezing injunction	資產凍結令
Good arguable case	具充分的可爭辯理據
Good faith (*bona fide*)	善意
Habitual residence	慣常居住地
Hague Conference on Private International Law	海牙國際私法會議
Harmonisation	協調
Immovable property	不動產
Immunity	豁免權
Implied choice of law	隱含法律選擇
in personam	對人
in rem	對物
Incidental question	先決問題
Inherent jurisdiction	固有司法管轄權
Injunction	禁制令 / 強制令
Intangible property	無形財產
Interim relief	臨時濟助
Interim-interim relief	過渡性臨時濟助
International	國際
Issue estoppel	已裁決的爭論點不得重提
Judicial assistance	司法協助
Judicial cooperation	司法合作
Jurisdiction	司法管轄權
Jurisdiction clause	司法管轄權條款
Jurisdiction gateway	在司法管轄權範圍外送達的通道
Kompetenz-Kompetenz	仲裁庭自裁管轄權原則
lex arbitri	仲裁地法
lex causae	準據法
lex domicilii	居籍地法

lex fori	訴訟地法 / 法院地法
lex loci actus	行為地法
lex loci celebrationis	婚姻締結地法
lex loci contractus	合同締結地法
lex loci damni	損害地法
lex loci delicti	侵權行為地法
lex loci protectionis	保護地法
lex loci solutionis	合同履行地法
lex mercatoria	商人習慣法
lex situs	物之所在地法
Limitation	時效
Limitation period	時效期
lis alibi pendens	外地待決案件
lis pendens	待決案件
Mandatory rule	強制性規定
Material validity	實質有效性
Mediation	調解
Moçambique rule	*Moçambique* 規則
Modified universalism	修正普遍主義
Movable property	動產
Nationality	國籍
Natural forum	自然法院
Natural justice	自然公義
Non-exclusive jurisdiction clause	非專有司法管轄權條款
Notice of proceedings	法律程序通知書
Oppressive	欺壓的
Ordinary residence	通常居住地
Overriding statute	凌駕性法律
Party autonomy	當事人意思自治
Penal law	刑法

Permanent residence	永久居住地
Presence	出現
Presumption	推定
Presumption of similarity (foreign law and *lex fori*)	外國法與訴訟地法相似推定
Private international law	國際私法
Private law	私法
Procedure	程序
Proper law	準據法
Protective measure	保護措施
Provisional measure	臨時措施
Public international law	國際公法
Public law	公法
Public order	公共秩序
Public policy	公共政策
Reciprocity	互惠原則
Reciprocity (*de facto*)	事實互惠
Reciprocity (*de jure*)	法律互惠
Reciprocity (presumptive)	推定互惠
Recognition	承認
renvoi	反致
res judicata	已判事項
Residence	居住地
Restrictive immunity	限制豁免
Revenue law	稅法
Serious issue to be tried	重要的待審議題
Service	送達
Service of process	送達法律程序文件
Service within jurisdiction	在司法管轄權範圍內送達
Service out of jurisdiction	在司法管轄權範圍外送達
Severability	可分割性

situs	所在地
Spiliada test	*Spiliada* 測試
Stabilisation clauses	穩定條款
Standard of proof	舉證標準
State immunity	國家豁免
Statutory demand	法定要求償債書
Stay of proceedings	擱置法律程序
Submission to jurisdiction	接受法院的司法管轄權
Substance	實質
Taking evidence abroad	從國外取得證據
Tangible property	有形財產
Territorialism	屬地主義
Transmission	轉致
Total (or double) *renvoi*	二重反致
travaux préparatoires	準備工作資料
Universalism	普遍主義
Vexatious	無理纏擾的
Waiver	放棄
Winding up	清盤

BIBLIOGRAPHY

Books

Diggory Bailey and Luke Norbury, *Bennion, Bailey and Norbury on Statutory Interpretation*, 8th edn (LexisNexis, 2022).

Joseph H Beale, *A Treatise on the Conflict of Laws* (Baker, Voorhis & Co, 1935).

Daniel Beard and Catrina Lam (eds), *Competition Litigation in Hong Kong: Practice and Procedure* (Sweet & Maxwell, 2025).

Paul Beaumont and Jayne Holliday (eds), *A Guide to Global Private International Law* (Hart Publishing, 2023).

Annabelle Bennett and Sam Granata, *When Private International Law Meets Intellectual Property Law: A Guide for Judges* (WIPO, 2019).

Nigel Blackaby and Constantine Partasides, *Redfern and Hunter on International Arbitration*, 7th edn (Oxford University Press, 2022).

William Blackstone, *Commentaries on the Laws of England: Book IV: Of Public Wrongs* (Oxford University Press, 2016).

Charles D Booth et al, *Hong Kong Personal Insolvency Manual*, 3rd edn (LexisNexis, 2024).

Michael Bridge et al, *The Law of Personal Property*, 3rd edn (Sweet & Maxwell, 2022).

Adrian Briggs, *Agreements on Jurisdiction and Choice of Law* (Oxford University Press, 2008).

—— *Private International Law in English Courts*, 2nd edn (Oxford University Press, 2023).

—— *The Conflict of Laws*, 5th edn (Oxford University Press, 2024).

Andrew Burrows, *A Restatement of the English Law of Unjust Enrichment* (Oxford University Press, 2012).

Friedrich Carl von Savigny, *Private International Law: A Treatise on the Conflict of Laws and the Limits of their Operation in Respect of Place and Time*, 2nd edn (trans William Guthrie, Stevens & Sons, 1880).

Thomas K Cheng and Kelvin Hiu Fai Kwok, *Hong Kong Competition Law: Comparative and Theoretical Perspectives* (Cambridge University Press, 2021).

Adeline Chong and Man Yip, *Singapore Private International Law: Commercial Issues and Practice* (Oxford University Press, 2023).

Douglas Clark, *Intellectual Property in Hong Kong*, 3rd edn (LexisNexis, 2024).

Lawrence Collins (gen ed), *Dicey and Morris on the Conflict of Laws*, 11th edn (Stevens & Sons, 1987).

—— *Dicey and Morris on the Conflict of Laws*, 12th edn (Sweet & Maxwell, 1993).

—— *Dicey, Morris and Collins on the Conflict of Laws*, 14th edn (Sweet & Maxwell, 2006).

Lord Collins of Mapesbury (gen ed), *Dicey, Morris and Collins on the Conflict of Laws*, 15th edn (Sweet & Maxwell, 2012).

—— and Jonathan Harris (gen eds), *Dicey, Morris and Collins on the Conflict of Laws*, 16th edn (Sweet & Maxwell, 2022).

James Crawford, *Brownlie's Principles of Public International Law*, 9th edn (Oxford University Press, 2019).

Brainerd Currie, *Selected Essays on the Conflict of Laws* (Duke University Press, 1963).

Martin Davies et al, *Nygh's Conflict of Laws in Australia*, 10th edn (LexisNexis, 2020).

Albert Venn Dicey, *A Digest of the Law of England with Reference to the Conflict of Laws* (Stevens & Sons, 1896).

Richard Fentiman, *Foreign Law in English Courts* (Oxford University Press, 1998).

—— *International Commercial Litigation*, 2nd edn (Oxford University Press, 2015).

Joseph Fok et al (gen eds), *Hong Kong Civil Procedure 2025* (Sweet & Maxwell, 2024).

Richard Garnett, *Substance and Procedure in Private International Law* (Oxford University Press, 2012).

Steven Gee, *Commercial Injunctions*, 7th edn (Sweet & Maxwell, 2021).

Alan Gibb, Richard Morris and King Fung Tsang, *An Introduction to the Conflict of Laws in Hong Kong*, 2nd edn (LexisNexis, 2020).

Roy Goode and Ewan McKendrick, *Goode and McKendrick on Commercial Law*, 6th edn (LexisNexis, 2020).

Jonathan Harris, *The Hague Trusts Convention: Scope, Application and Preliminary Issues* (Hart Publishing, 2002).
Nikitas E Hatzimihail, *Preclassical Conflict of Laws* (Cambridge University Press, 2021).
Georg Wilhelm Fredrich Hegel, *Elements of the Philosophy of Right* (1821) (trans HB Nisbet, Cambridge University Press, 1991).
Philippa Hewitt et al (eds), *Family Law and Practice in Hong Kong*, 3rd edn (Sweet & Maxwell, 2018).
Look Chan Ho, *Cross-Border Insolvency: Principles and Practice* (Sweet & Maxwell, 2016).
Keith Hotten and Dennis Ho, *Hotten and Ho: Family Law Practice and Procedure in Hong Kong*, 4th edn (LexisNexis, 2021).
Jin Huang et al (eds), *Guoji Sifa Xue* [Private International Law] (Higher Education Press, 2023).
Thomas John, Rishi Gulati and Ben Köhler (eds), *The Elgar Companion to the Hague Conference on Private International Law* (Edward Elgar, 2020).
Graeme Johnston, *The Conflict of Laws in Hong Kong*, 2nd edn (Sweet & Maxwell, 2012).
Graeme Johnston and Paul Harris, *The Conflict of Laws in Hong Kong*, 3rd edn (Sweet & Maxwell, 2017).
Patrick Keane, *Spencer Brown and Handley: Res Judicata*, 6th edn (LexisNexis, 2024).
Simon Klopschinski and Mary-Rose McGuire (eds), *Research Handbook on Intellectual Property Rights and Arbitration* (Edward Elgar, 2024).
Kim Lewison, *The Interpretation of Contracts*, 8th edn (Sweet & Maxwell, 2023).
Shuangyuan Li and Fuyong Ou (gen eds), *Guoji Sifa* [Private International Law], 6th edn (Peking University Press, 2022).
Stefan Lo, *Company Law in Hong Kong: Insolvency 2023* (Sweet & Maxwell, 2023).
Maurizio Lupoi, *Trusts: A Comparative Study* (Cambridge University Press, 2001).
Geoffrey Ma and Denis Brock (gen eds), *Arbitration in Hong Kong: A Practical Guide*, 5th edn (Sweet & Maxwell, 2021).
Brooke Marshall, *Asymmetric Jurisdiction Clauses* (Oxford University Press, 2023).
Azan Marwah et al (eds), *Hong Kong Family Court Tables 2024–2025* (Authors, 2024).
Paul Matthews, *Trusts: Migration and Change of Proper Law* (Key Haven Publications, 1997).
Sundaresh Menon and Anselmo Reyes (eds), *Transnational Commercial Disputes in an Age of Anti-globalism and Pandemic* (Hart Publishing, 2022).
Alex Mills, *The Confluence of Public and Private International Law: Justice, Pluralism and Subsidiarity in the International Constitutional Ordering of Private Law* (Cambridge University Press, 2009).
Charles Mitchell, Paul Mitchell and Stephen Watterson (eds), *Goff and Jones on Unjust Enrichment*, 10th edn (Sweet & Maxwell, 2022).
Reid Mortensen, Richard Garnett and Mary Keyes, *Private International Law in Australia*, 5th edn (LexisNexis, 2023).
Debbie Ong, *International Issues in Family Law in Singapore* (Academy Publishing, 2015).
George Panagopoulos, *Restitution in Private International Law* (Hart Publishing, 2000).
Charles Proctor, *Mann and Proctor on the Law of Money*, 8th edn (Oxford University Press, 2023).
Thomas Raphael, *The Anti-Suit Injunction*, 2nd edn (Oxford University Press, 2019).
Ingeborg Schwenzer and Ulrich G Schroeter, *Schlechtriem & Schwenzer: Commentary on the UN Convention on the International Sale of Goods (CISG)*, 5th edn (Oxford University Press, 2022).
Philip St J Smart, *Cross-Border Insolvency*, 2nd edn (Butterworths, 1998).
Poomintr Sooksripaisarnkit and Dharmita Prasad (eds), *Blurry Boundaries of Public and Private International Law: Towards Convergence or Divergent Still?* (Springer, 2022).
Robert Stevens, *The Laws of Restitution* (Oxford University Press, 2023).
Joseph Story, *Commentaries on the Conflict of Laws* (Hilliard, Gray & Co, 1834).
Symeon C Symeonides, *Codifying Choice of Law Around the World: An International Comparative Analysis* (Oxford University Press, 2014).
Paul LC Torremans, *Intellectual Property and Private International Law*, 3rd edn (Oxford University Press, 2024).
Lynton Tucker et al (eds), *Lewin on Trusts*, 20th edn (Sweet & Maxwell, 2020).
Graham Virgo, *The Principles of the Law of Restitution*, 4th edn (Oxford University Press, 2024).
John Westlake, *A Treatise on Private International Law or The Conflict of Laws with Principal Reference to its Practice in the English and Other Cognate Systems of Jurisprudence* (W Maxwell, 1858).
Henry Wheaton, *Elements of International Law*, 8th edn (Little, Brown & Co, 1866).
Kenny Wong and Alice Lee, *Intellectual Property Law and Practice in Hong Kong*, 2nd edn (Sweet & Maxwell, 2017).
Samuel Wong and Wilson Lui, *Hong Kong Arbitration Ordinance (Cap 609): A Guide and Commentary*, 2nd edn (Authors, 2024).

Samuel Wong, CK Kwong and Wilson Lui, *Hong Kong Arbitration Judgments and Commentaries: Applications of the UNCITRAL Model Law and the Provisions of the Hong Kong Arbitration Ordinance (Cap 609)* (Hong Kong Institute of Arbitrators, 2023).
Tiong Min Yeo, *Choice of Law for Equitable Doctrines* (Oxford University Press, 2004).
—— *Commercial Conflict of Laws* (Academy Publishing, 2023).

Book Chapters

Andrew Dickinson, 'Cryptocurrencies and the Conflict of Laws' in David Fox and Sarah Green (eds), *Cryptocurrencies in Public and Private Law* (Oxford University Press, 2019) 93–137.
Justin Hogan-Doran and Dominique Hogan-Doran, 'New and Alternative Approaches to Proof of Foreign Law: A Practitioners' Perspective' in Michael Douglas et al (eds), *Commercial Issues in Private International Law: A Common Law Perspective* (Hart Publishing, 2019) 231–56.
Wilson Lui, 'Hong Kong' in Anselmo Reyes, Wilson Lui and Kazuaki Nishioka (eds), *Choice of Law and Recognition in Asian Family Law* (Hart Publishing, 2023) 51–80.
—— 'Hong Kong' in Kazuaki Nishioka (ed), *Treatment of Foreign Law in Asia* (Hart Publishing, 2023) 25–50.
—— and Anselmo Reyes, 'Introduction' in Anselmo Reyes and Wilson Lui (eds), *Direct Jurisdiction: Asian Perspectives* (Hart Publishing, 2021) 1–10.
Ralf Michaels, 'How Asian should Asian Law be?' in Gary Low (ed), *Convergence and Divergence of Private Law in Asia* (Cambridge University Press, 2022) 227–51.
—— 'Private International Law and the Legal Pluriverse' in Roxana Banu, Michael S Green and Ralf Michaels (eds), *Philosophical Foundations of Private International Law* (Oxford University Press, 2024) 258–77.
Maisie Ooi, 'Choice of Law in the Shifting Sands of Securities Trading' in Andrew Dickinson et al (eds), *A Conflict of Laws Companion: Essays in Honour of Adrian Briggs* (Oxford University Press, 2021) 199–224.
Anselmo Reyes, 'Introduction: Towards a System for the Recognition and Enforcement of Judgments' in Anselmo Reyes (ed), *Recognition and Enforcement of Judgments in Civil and Commercial Matters* (Hart Publishing, 2019) 1–30.

Journal Articles

Ardavan Arzandeh, 'Exclusive Jurisdiction Clauses in International Trust Deeds' (2021) 41(4) *Legal Studies* 527–44.
JH Baker, 'Ascertainment of Foreign Law: Certification to and by English Courts Prior to 1861' (1979) 28(1) *ICLQ* 141–51.
Laurette Barnard, 'Choice of Law in Equitable Wrongs: A Comparative Analysis' (1992) 51(3) *CLJ* 474–507.
Charles D Booth, 'Living in Uncertain Times: The Need to Strengthen Hong Kong Transnational Insolvency Law' (1996) 34 *Columbia Journal of Transnational Law* 389–447.
—— and Philip St J Smart, 'The New Avoidance Powers under Hong Kong Insolvency Law: A Move from Territoriality to Extraterritoriality' (2000) 34 *International Lawyer* 255–65.
Robert Chambers, 'Constructive Trusts in Canada (Pt 2)' (2002) 16 *Trust Law International* 2–20.
Adeline Chong, 'Characterisation and Choice of Law for Knowing Receipt' (2023) 72(1) *ICLQ* 147–77.
—— 'The Common Law Choice of Law Rules for Resulting and Constructive Trusts' (2005) 54(4) *ICLQ* 855–83.
—— 'The Public Policy and Mandatory Rules of Third Countries in International Contracts' (2006) 2(1) *Journal of Private International Law* 27–70.
William Day, 'Pleading and Proving Foreign Law' (2022) 81(1) *CLJ* 24–27.
Andrew Dickinson, 'Third-Country Mandatory Rules in the Law Applicable to Contractual Obligations: So Long, Farewell, Auf Wiedersehen, Adieu?' (2007) 3(1) *Journal of Private International Law* 53–88.
Richard Fentiman, 'Laws, Foreign Laws, and Facts' (2006) 59(1) *Current Legal Problems* 391–426.
Ian Fletcher, 'Foreign Law in English Courts: Pleading, Proof and Choice of Law' (1999) 115 *LQR* 518–20.
Richard Garnett, 'Fraud and Foreign Judgments: The Defence that Refuses to Die' (2002) 2 *Journal of International Commercial Law* 161–86.
—— and Ying Khai Liew, 'Trusts Jurisdiction Clauses: An Analysis' *LQR* (forthcoming).

Alan Gibb and King Fung Tsang, 'Conflicting Limitation Periods: A Comparison between Hong Kong and Mainland China' (2021) 5(1) *Cardozo International and Comparative Law Review* 1–39.
Anthony Gray, 'Choice of Law: The Presumption in the Proof of Foreign Law' (2008) 31(1) *UNSW Law Journal* 136–57.
Jonathan Harris (professor), 'Tracing and the Conflict of Laws' (2002) 74 *British Yearbook of International Law* 65–101.
Jonathan Harris (judge), 'Understanding Cross-Border Insolvency in the Hong Kong Context' (2017) 47 *Hong Kong Law Journal* 55–72.
David Hayton, 'The Hague Convention on the Law Applicable to Trusts and on their Recognition' (1987) 36 *ICLQ* 260–82.
—— 'Reflections on The Hague Trusts Convention after 30 Years' (2016) 12 *Journal of Private International Law* 1–25.
ILA Committee on Intellectual Property and Private International Law, 'International Law Association's Guidelines on Intellectual Property and Private International Law' (2021) 12(1) *Journal of Intellectual Property, Information Technology and E-Commerce Law* 1–93.
Hui Jing, 'The Remedial Constructive Trust Approach in the Hong Kong Law of Proprietary Estoppel' (2023) *Conveyancer and Property Lawyer* 30–50.
Ernest G Lorenzen, 'Huber's De Conflictu Legum' (1919) 13 *Illinois Law Review* 199–242.
Wilson Lui, 'Asian Private International Law and Hong Kong' (2024) 12 *Korean Journal of International and Comparative Law* 73–86.
—— 'Defending the Indemnity Costs Approach to Unsuccessful Arbitral Award Challenges' [2021] *Asian Dispute Review* 129–35.
—— 'Researching and Teaching Asian and Hong Kong Private International Law' (2023) 20(2) *Indonesian Journal of International Law* 173–202.
Maurizio Lupoi, 'The Shapeless Trust' (1995) 1(3) *Trusts and Trustees* 15–18.
Peter North, 'Private International Law: Change or Decay?' (2001) 50(3) *ICLQ* 477–508.
—— 'Problems of Codification in a Common Law System' (1982) 46 *The Rabel Journal of Comparative and International Private Law* 490–508.
PJ Millett, 'Restitution and Constructive Trusts' (1998) 114 *LQR* 399–418.
Alex Mills, 'Arbitral Jurisdiction and the Mischievous Presumption of Identity of Foreign Law' (2008) 67(1) *CLJ* 25–27.
George Panagopoulos, 'Substance and Procedure in Private International Law' (2005) 1(1) *Journal of Private International Law* 69–92.
Charles Z Qu, 'Cross Border Assistance as a Restructuring Device for Hong Kong: The Case For its Retention' (2022) 18(3) *Journal of Private International Law* 468–92.
Anselmo Reyes, 'Cross-border Insolvency and Shipping Companies' [2016] *Lloyd's Maritime and Commercial Law Quarterly* 517–28.
—— 'The Application of Hong Kong Equitable Remedies to Contracts Governed by Mainland Law' (2014) 20(4) *Trusts & Trustees* 325–34.
JJ Spigelman, 'Proof of Foreign Law by Reference to the Foreign Court' (2011) 127 *LQR* 208–16.
Robert Stevens, 'Crypto is not Property' (2023) 139 *LQR* 615–28.
King Fung Tsang and Tsz Wai Wong, 'Enforcement of Non-monetary Judgments in Common Law Jurisdictions: Is the Time Ripe?' (2021) 45(2) *Fordham International Law Journal* 379–428.
RW White, 'Equitable Obligation in Private International Law: The Choice of Law' (1986) 11 *Sydney Law Review* 92–113.

Reports

Trevor Hartley and Masato Dogauchi, 'Convention of 30 June 2005 on Choice of Court Agreements: Explanatory Report by Trevor Hartley and Masato Dogauchi' (Intersentia 2013).
Law Commission, 'Digital Assets: Final Report' Law Com No 412 (June 2023).
—— 'Digital Assets as Personal Property: Supplemental Report and Draft Bill' Law Com No 416 (July 2024).

Law Reform Committee of the Singapore Academy of Law, 'Reform of the Choice of Law Rule Relating to Tort' (31 March 2003).
Report of the Foreign Judgments (Reciprocal Enforcement) Committee, Cmd 4213 (1932).
Report on the Convention on the Law Applicable to Contractual Obligations by Mario Giuliano, Professor, University of Milan, and Paul Lagarde, Professor, University of Paris I [1980] OJ C 282 (31 October 1980).
Alfred E von Overbeck, 'Rapport explicatif de M Alfred E von Overbeck' in Hague Conference on Private International Law Permanent Bureau (ed), *Actes et documents de la Treizième session* (Imprimerie Nationale 1978) 328–84.

Online Resources

'Beijing Brings HK into Line on State Immunity' (South China Morning Post, 27 August 2011), www.scmp.com/article/977252/beijing-brings-hk-line-state-immunity.
Department of Justice, 'DSJ to Visit Europe' (3 March 2023), www.doj.gov.hk/en/community_engagement/press/pdf/pr20230303e1.pdf.
—— 'Establishment of Offices or Operation of International Intergovernmental Organisations in Hong Kong', www.doj.gov.hk/en/external/establishment_of_offices_or_operation_of_international_intergovernmental_organisations_in_hong_kong.html.
—— 'Speech by DSJ at UNIDROIT Conference on Promoting Cross-Border Investment through Transnational Legal Standards in Rome' (7 March 2023), www.doj.gov.hk/en/community_engagement/speeches/20230307_sj1.html.
—— 'Speech by SJ at The Hague Academy of International Law's Advanced Course in Hong Kong – 1st Edition' (11 December 2023), www.doj.gov.hk/en/community_engagement/speeches/20231211_sj1.html.
—— 'The Department of Justice Action Plan on the Construction of Rule of Law in the Guangdong–Hong Kong–Macao Greater Bay Area: Three Interfaces, Two Connects and One GBA' (12 April 2024), www.doj.gov.hk/en/publications/pdf/gba_action_plan_en.pdf
James Ding, 'Introduction to the Work of the IDAR Office' (3 May 2019), available online: www.doj.gov.hk/en/community_engagement/speeches/pdf/lo20190503e1.pdf.
HM Courts & Tribunals Service, *The Commercial Court Guide*, revised 11th edn (2023), www.judiciary.uk/wp-content/uploads/2023/06/14.341_JO_Commercial_Court_Guide_FINAL.pdf.
HKIAC, 'Interim Measures Arrangement', www.hkiac.org/arbitration/arrangement-interim-measures.
Legislative Council Panel on Administration of Justice and Legal Services, '2019 Policy Initiatives of the Department of Justice' (LC Paper No CB(4)318/19-20(02), February 2020), www.doj.gov.hk/en/legco/pdf/ajls20200224e1.pdf.
—— 'Updates on Cooperation with International Legal and Dispute Resolution Bodies and Attracting Their Presence or Carrying Out of Activities in Hong Kong: International Bodies and Organisations other than the International Organization for Mediation (IOMed)' (LC Paper No CB(4)334/2024(05), March 2024), www.legco.gov.hk/yr2024/english/panels/ajls/papers/ajls202400325cb4-334-5-e.pdf.
Legislative Council Panel on Financial Affairs, 'Legislative Proposals of the Companies (Corporate Rescue) Bill' (LC Paper No CB(1)48/20-21(03), 22 October 2020), www.legco.gov.hk/yr20-21/english/panels/fa/papers/fa20201102cb1-48-3-e.pdf.
Standing Committee on Company Law Reform, *The Thirty-fourth Annual Report* (February 2019), www.fstb.gov.hk/fsb/co_rewrite/eng/pub-press/doc/SCCLR_ar_2017-2018_e.pdf.
UNIDROIT, 'UNIDROIT and Hong Kong sign Cooperation MOU' (28 June 2022), www.unidroit.org/unidroit-and-hong-kong-sign-cooperation-mou/.
WIPO, 'About IP', www.wipo.int/about-ip/en/.

INDEX